I

MW01592876

RULES OF
EVIDENCE
WITH TRIAL
OBJECTIONS

SEVENTH EDITION
with updated Rules of Evidence
Issued in March 2017

By

CHARLES B. GIBBONS
Member of the Pennsylvania Bar
Buchanan Ingersoll & Rooney
Pittsburgh

Rules of Evidence current with amendments
effective through January 1, 2017.

For Customer Assistance Call 1-800-328-4880

Mat #41928940

ISBN 978-0-314-84478-1

Attorney Mike Manzo

1948–2011

B.S.E. Princeton University
M.B.A. University of Scranton
J.D. University of Virginia

Fellow, American College of Trial Lawyers
Past President, Academy of Trial Lawyers of
Allegheny County
Partner, Buchanan Ingersoll & Rooney

ABOUT THE AUTHOR

Charles B. Gibbons is a litigation partner at uchanan Ingersoll & Rooney, Pittsburgh, ›ennsylvania. A graduate of the Scranton Preparatory School, the University of Scranton and Boston College Law School, he is a Fellow of the American College of Trial Lawyers and a member of the American Law Institute. He served as Chairman of the Pennsylvania Supreme Court Committee on the Rules of Evidence and was a member of the original drafting committee.

PREFACE

The publication of this Seventh Edition of Pennsylvania Rules of Evidence with Trial Objections coincides with action of the Pennsylvania Supreme Court in amending Rules 803(6), 803(8) and 803(10); revising the Comments to Rules 802, 803(7) and 803(9) and adopting Rule 902(13). These changes specify the burden shift to the opponent to show a lack of trustworthiness with respect to business and public records and codify the statutory requirements regarding the proof and absence of public records. The authentication of a certificate of the non-existence of a public record is addressed in Rule 902(13).

Pennsylvania Law With Respect to Evidentiary Objections

In order to preserve an issue for appellate review in the state court system, a party must make a timely and specific objection at the appropriate state of the proceedings before the trial court. *Commonwealth v. Gonzalez*, 112 A.3d 1232 (Pa. Super. 2015) (in order to preserve an issue on appeal, a party must lodge a timely objection); *Shelhamer v. Crane*, 58 A.3d 767 (Pa. Super. 2012); *Jones v. Dept. of Corrections*, 39 A.3d 599 (Pa. Cmwlth. 2012). Failure to object will result in a waiver of the issue. See, e.g., *Commonwealth v. Tucker*, 143 A.3d 955 (Pa. Super. 2016) (failure to make a timely and specific objection before the trial court at the appropriate stage of the proceedings will result in waiver of the issues); *Commonwealth v. Shataan*, 39 A.3d 310 (Pa. Super. 2012); *Commonwealth v. Stokes*, 38 A.3d 846 (Pa. Super. 2011); *Schmidt v. Boardman Co.*, 11 A.3d 924 (2011) (this Court has taken a stricter approach to waiver than many other jurisdictions by abolishing the plain error doctrine; the general requirement that one challenging a civil verdict must raise and preserve challenges at all stages best reconciles with our existing rules and approach to trial and appellate practice); *Commonwealth v. Ali*, 10 A.3d 282 (Pa. 2010) (failure to raise a contemporaneous objection to a prosecutor's comment at trial waives any claim of error arising from that comment); *Commonwealth v. Rivera*, 983 A.2d 1211 (Pa. 2009) (lack of a contemporaneous objection constitutes a waiver of any challenge to the prosecutor's closing remarks); *Commonwealth v. U.S. Mineral Products*, 956 A.2d 967 (Pa. 2008) (same); *Commonwealth v. Montalvo*, 956 A.2d 926 (Pa. 2008) (in order to preserve a claim on appeal, a party must lodge a timely objection at trial); *Commonwealth v. Reaves*, 923 A.2d 1119 (Pa. 2007) (although contemporaneous objections operate to preserve issues for appellate review, they serve an equally important function in obviating appeals by affording the trial court a timely opportunity to correct mistakes and/or to reconsider decisions); *Commonwealth v. Colavita*, 920 A.2d 836 (Pa. Super. 2007) (failure to object to the prosecutor's opening statement prejudiced defendant and constituted ineffective assistance of counsel).

The need for timely objection is also addressed in Pa. R. E. 103, Rulings on Evidence:

(a) Effect of Erroneous Ruling

Error may not be predicated upon a ruling that admits . . . evidence unless

(1) Objection. In case the ruling is one admitting evidence, a timely objection, motion to strike or motion in limine appears of record,

stating the specific ground of objection, if the specific ground was not apparent from the context . . .

See also Pa. R.A.P. 302 "[i]ssues not raised in the lower court are waived and cannot be raised for the first time on appeal"; *Commonwealth v. Williams*, 58 A.3d 796 (Pa. Super. 2012).

It has been written that objections to the admission or exclusion of evidence must be made at the right time, with the right rule and for the right reason.[1]

The purpose of this book is to assist with the right rule and right reason. But timing is everything and that responsibility falls to the trial lawyer who must also bear in mind Chief Justice Castille's teaching that "Lawyers are not obliged to be obstreperous or to make objections just to make them." *Commonwealth v. Daniels*, 104 A.3d 267, 296 (Pa. 2014)

My sincere thanks to our daughter, Attorney Sara Farley Holland of Louisville, Kentucky and my secretary, Phyllis Stock, for their help with this book.

On the cusp of fifty years of marriage, I dedicate this book, with love, to my wife, Patricia Kilduff Gibbons.

CHARLES B. GIBBONS
PITTSBURGH
February 2017

---

[1] Mauet, Trials, Chap. 10, p. 520 (Aspen Publishers, Inc. 2005).

Table of Contents

ARGUMENTATIVE

See: Pa.R.E. 611(a).

Objection

- Objection. The question is argumentative.
- Objection. Counsel is arguing with the witness.

Response

- I have properly phrased my question to elicit evidence from this witness.

Pennsylvania Law

Pa.R.E. 611(a) provides that the court shall exercise reasonable control over the mode of interrogating witnesses. Any question which is actually an argument is improper. *Commonwealth v. Sneed*, 514 Pa. 597, 526 A.2d 749 (1987); *Commonwealth v. Upsher*, 497 Pa. 621, 444 A.2d 90 (1982); *Commonwealth v. Pearlman*, 126 Pa. Super. 461, 191 A. 365 (1937); *Commonwealth v. Wise*, 67 Dauph. 49 (1954). Argumentative questions are those questions which are not intended to elicit new information but which are intended to argue to the jury through the witness, or which call for an argument in answer to an argument contained in the question. Typically, such a question states a conclusion and asks the witness to agree with it, or is asked in a sarcastic tenor: "Do you mean to tell me . . ." or "Doesn't it seem strange that . . ."

See Commonwealth v. Poplawski, 852 A.2d 323, 329 n.5 (Pa. Super. 2004):

> We also note with disapproval that the prosecutor's cross-examination as a whole was marked by an unusually high number of argumentative, sarcastic, and irrelevant questions, loaded with unnecessary editorial commentary on the witness's answers . . . . While we recognize that trials are stressful and adversarial proceedings, we remind the prosecutor

that our Code of Civility states that attorneys should 'treat all participants in the legal process in a civil, professional and courteous manner at all times.' Code of Civility, Rule II(1).

Compare: Fed. R. Evid. 611(a).

Research References

Packel & Poulin, Pennsylvania Evidence § 611-4 (4th ed. 2013)

McCormick, Evidence Chapter § 7 (7th ed. 2013)

ASKED AND ANSWERED

See: Pa.R.E. 611(a).

Objection

- Objection. The question has been asked and answered.
- Objection. The question is repetitive.

Response

- The witness has not answered this question.
- I have not asked this question previously.

Pennsylvania Law

If a question has been asked and answered, the trial court has broad discretion to limit or exclude repetitive questions. Pa.R.E. 611(a); *Commonwealth v. Simmons*, 482 Pa. 496, 394 A.2d 431 (1978); *Commonwealth v. Delligatti*, 371 Pa. Super. 315, 538 A.2d 34 (1988); *Commonwealth v. Stoner*, 284 Pa. Super. 364, 425 A.2d 1145 (1981); *Cockcroft v. Metro. Life Ins. Co.*, 133 Pa. Super. 598, 3 A.2d 184 (1938). Repetition wastes time and places undue emphasis on certain evidence through cumulative testimony. The form of the question does not have to be absolutely identical in order to raise this objection. If a new question calls for an answer which has essentially already been given, the question is objectionable as repetitious. The objection applies not only when an answer has already been given but also when a witness has already testified that he does not know of or remember a matter.

Compare: Fed. R. Evid. 611(a).

Research Reference

McCormick, Evidence Chapter 2 (7th ed. 2013)

ASSUMING FACTS NOT IN EVIDENCE

See: Pa.R.E. 611(a); see also Pa.R.E. 104(b).

Objection

- Objection. The question assumes facts that have not been introduced into evidence.

Response

- The question is proper; I am entitled to test the credibility or memory of the witness. The witness can deny the asserted facts if he disagrees with the assertion.
- Your Honor, I will establish the fact [and its relevancy] in subsequent testimony. I request that the witness assume the fact for purposes of this question.

Pennsylvania Law

A question which assumes the existence of a fact not established by the evidence is improper. Pa.R.E. 611(a); *Commonwealth v. Rivers*, 537 Pa. 394, 644 A.2d 710 (1994); *Commonwealth v. Baez*, 494 Pa. 388, 431 A.2d 909 (1981); *Boring v. Metropolitan Edison Co.*, 435 Pa. 513, 257 A.2d 565 (1969); *In Interest of M.M.*, 439 Pa. Super. 307, 653 A.2d 1271 (1995), *aff'd.*, 547 Pa. 237, 690 A.2d 175 (1997); *cf. Commonwealth v. May*, 887 A.2d 750 (Pa. 2005) (defendant's own admissions formed good faith basis for questions asked of defense psychiatrist). In certain situations, counsel may ask the court to permit the question to stand as asked, upon representation that the assumed fact will be proven later. Such a representation, however, should not be made if it cannot be fulfilled. In *Commonwealth v. Williams*, 270 Pa. Super. 27, 37–38, 410 A.2d 880, 885 (1979), the court said:

'[i]t is unprofessional conduct to ask a question which implies the existence of a factual predicate which the examiner cannot support by evidence.' A.B.A. Standards, The Prosecution Function, § 5.7(d) (Approved Draft, 1971).

Nevertheless, we do not believe this standard in fact imposes upon counsel the affirmative obligation to offer evidence in support of every fact he infers for purposes of cross-examination; rather it establishes a standard of conduct, restraining an examiner from implying a fact he knows he could not support with evidence.

See also Commonwealth v. Adams, 426 Pa. Super. 332, 336, 626 A.2d 1231, 1234, (1993) ("We do not . . . endorse interrogation where there is no evidentiary basis for the question.")

Similarly, Professor Alan M. Dershowitz has written:

The law requires an attorney to have a 'good-faith basis' before asking any question on cross-examination. This important rule is designed to prevent the irresponsible prosecutor or defense attorney from planting a fictitious accusation in the minds of the jurors by the framing of questions. Without this salutary rule, a lawyer could ask all kinds of variations on the "When did you stop beating your wife?" theme . . . . The rule does not require that the cross-examining lawyer must have proof of the assertion underlying the question, but simply that there must be a good-faith basis—a concept difficult to define.

Dershowitz, Reversal of Fortune, pp. 220–221 (Pocket Books, 1990).

Note: Pa.R.E. 104(b) provides that when the relevancy of evidence depends upon the fulfillment of a condition of fact, the court shall admit it upon, or subject to, the introduction of evidence sufficient to support a finding of the fulfillment of the condition.

Compare: Fed. R. Evid. 611(a).

Research Reference

Haydock and Sonsteng, Trial: Advocacy Before

AUTHENTICATION OF DOCUMENTARY AND DEMONSTRATIVE EVIDENCE

See: Pa.R.E. 901, 902, 903.

Objection

- Objection. The exhibit has not been properly authenticated.

Response

- The exhibit was authenticated by the testimony of the witness that:
    - he was present at the scene at the time in question and that the [*photograph*] [*videotape*] fairly and accurately represents the particular condition at the time in question;
    - he saw the author [*compose*] [*sign*] the document;
    - he recognizes and is familiar with this handwriting;
    - he knows this letter came in reply to his own earlier letter.

Pennsylvania Law

The proponent of evidence is generally required to prove its authenticity as a condition precedent to admission. Authentication is accomplished by proving that the evidence offered is what its proponent claims it to be. *In Re F.P.*, 878 A.2d 91 (Pa. Super. 2005). Depending upon the particular evidence involved, the proof can be as simple as testimony by a person with knowledge that a writing, document or photograph is recognized as genuine or accurately represents a particular condition; or proof may be so complex as to require expert testimony to substantiate authenticity. *Commwealth v. Beltz*, 829 A.2d 680 (Pa. Super. 2003) (state troopers properly authenticated photos of wooded area by testifying about personal knowledge of information in photos; defendant's gun properly authenticated by testimony it was confiscated from his home).

Pa.R.E. 901 states that the foundational requirement of authentication or identification "is satisfied by evidence sufficient to support a finding that the matter in question is what its proponent claims." When a party offers evidence contending either expressly or impliedly that the evidence is connected with a person, place, thing or event, the party must provide evidence sufficient to support a finding of the contended connection. *See Commonwealth v. Pollock*, 414 Pa. Super. 66, 606 A.2d 500 (1992); *Commonwealth v. Hudson*, 489 Pa. 620, 414 A.2d 1381 (1980).

In matters of authentication, the trial court serves a gatekeeping function. *See generally* Pa.R.E. 104(a). If the court finds enough support in the record to cause a reasonable person to believe that the evidence is what it purports to be, then Pa.R.E. 901(a) is satisfied, and the weight to be given to the evidence is left to the jury.

A document may be authenticated by direct proof, such as the testimony of a witness who saw the author sign the document; acknowledgment of execution by the signer; admission of authenticity by an adverse party; or proof that the document or its signature is in the purported author's handwriting. *PHH Mortg. Corp. v. Powell*, 100 A.3d 611 (Pa. Super. 2014) (loan documents); *Zuk v. Zuk*, 55 A.3d 102 (Pa. Super. 2012) (maps); *Commonwealth v. Brooks*, 352 Pa. Super. 394, 508 A.2d 316 (1986); *see also*, 42 Pa.C.S.A. § 6111, Handwriting.

A document may also be authenticated by circumstantial evidence. *Commonwealth v. Collins*, 957 A.2d 237 (Pa. 2008) (letters authenticated as defendant's where mailed from prison where he was jailed with his prison I.D. number, name and return address, urging course of conduct to his sole benefit, using his attorney's name and the addressee's nicknames). Certain recurrent patterns of circumstantial evidence have come to be recognized as distinct rules. These include: the ancient documents rule, which exempts documents from other authentication when the document is at least 30 years old, is free from suspicious alterations, and has been in proper custody, Pa.R.E. 803(16); *Louden v. Apollo Gas Co.*, 273 Pa. Super. 549, 417 A.2d 1185 (1980); the reply letter doctrine, which regards as sufficient authentication evidence that a letter came by mail and corresponds in time and contents to a prior letter sent to the purported author, *Eichenhofer v. City of Philadelphia*, 248 Pa. 365, 93 A. 1065 (1915); and Pa.R.E. 803(6) and the Uniform Business Records As Evidence Act, 42 Pa.C.S.A. § 6108, under which a document is authenticated if a witness testifies as to preparation and maintenance of the records. *In re Indyk's Estate*, 488 Pa. 567, 413 A.2d 371 (1979).

The Superior Court has said that e-mail or text messages and similar forms of electronic communication can be properly authenticated within the existing framework of Rule 901. *Commonwealth v. Koch*, 39 A.3d 996 (Pa. Super. 2011), aff'd by an equally divided court, 106 A.3d 705 (Pa. 2014) (authentication of electronic communications, like documents, requires more than mere confirmation that the number or address belonged to a particular person; direct or circumstantial evidence, which tends to corroborate the identity of the sender, is also required); *In Re F.P.*, 878 A.2d 91 (Pa. Super. 2005) (sufficient circumstantial evidence to show series of threatening instant text messages were written by juvenile defendant). *Koch* was affirmed by an evenly divided Pennsylvania Supreme Court at 106 A.3d 705 (Pa. 2014).

Pursuant to Amendments of January 1, 2002, the business records of American companies are now admissible in civil and criminal cases without the need to call a witness if: (1) accompanied by a written declaration by the custodian or other qualified person that the records (a) were made at or near the time of the occurrence at issue or from information transmitted by a person with knowledge, (b) were kept in the ordinary course of business, (c) were created by the business as a regular practice; and (2) the offering party gives notice of intended use to adverse parties and opportunity to inspect the records and the declaration so as to provide a fair opportunity to challenge them. Pa.R.E. 902(11).

The same procedure applies to foreign business records to be used in civil cases. Pa.R.E. 902(12).

Both rules provide that a party intending to offer a record into evidence under these paragraphs must provide written notice of that intention to all adverse parties, and must make the record and declaration available for inspection sufficiently in advance of the offer into evidence to provide an adverse party with a fair opportunity to challenge it.

To lay a proper foundation for computer-generated visual evidence, the proponent must first establish through witness testimony the accuracy of the exhibit's portrayal of the substantive information in question. *Commonwealth v. Serge*, 896 A.2d 1170 (Pa. 2006) (computer-generated animation of murder).

The following decisions illustrate evidence rejected for lack of proper authentication: *J.M. v. Dep't of Public Welfare*, 52 A.3d 552 (Pa.Cmwlth. 2012) (DVD interview of child re alleged sexual abuse); *Commonwealth Financial Systems v. Smith*, 15 A.3d 492 (Pa. Super. 2011) (in a case of first impression, declining to adopt the rule of incorporation and finding credit card records in custody of debt collection agency insufficiently authenticated); *Kopytin v. Ashinger*, 947 A.2d 739 (Pa. Super. 2008) (surveillance tape taken by former employees could not be authenticated by owner of investigative agency who was not present at filming and had no knowledge of its circumstances); *McMenamin v. Tartaglione*, 139 Pa.Cmwlth. 269, 590 A.2d 802 (1991), aff'd 527 Pa. 286, 590 A.2d 753 (1991) (videotape not admitted where authenticating witness had not seen actual event and could not attest that the tape portrayed events accurately); *Harmon v. Commonwealth*, 119 Pa.Cmwlth. 1, 546 A.2d 726 (1988) (report on landfill fire disallowed where the author was not called to authenticate it); *Stotz v. Shields*, 696 A.2d 806 (Pa. Super. 1997) (materials purportedly setting forth Army regulations regarding physical fitness testing but containing no indication they were printed or issued by governmental authority); *Commonwealth v. Harrison*, 290 Pa. Super. 389, 434 A.2d 808 (1981) (anonymous letters rejected; no evidence as to authorship or when and under what circumstances the letters were written; *accord, Hargrove v. Hargrove*, 252 Pa. Super. 120, 381 A.2d 143 (1977)); *Commonwealth v. Dessus*, 262 Pa. Super. 443, 396 A.2d 1254 (1978) (physician's letter excluded when testimony failed to show the mode of the letter's preparation or the authenticity of the signature); *Semet v. Andorra Nurseries, Inc.*, 421 Pa. 484, 219 A.2d 357 (1966) (plaintiff's vague knowledge and recollection made it impossible for him to establish photographs accurately depicted the ladder from which he fell); *Poelcher v. Zink*, 375 Pa. 539, 101 A.2d 628 (1954) (enlarged photostats allegedly showing alterations of a note under seal rejected for lack of evidence on how they were made, the qualifications of the maker and the genuineness of the reproductions).

In a criminal case, the court may exclude business records that otherwise would meet the standards of authentication if they would violate a defendant's right of confrontation. *Commonwealth v. Schoff*, 911 A.2d 147 (Pa. Super. 2006). See *Commonwealth v. McKellick*, 24 A.3d 982 (Pa. Super. 2011) (dead trooper's dashcam videotape of traffic stop was sufficiently authenticated and did not violate confrontation rights).

Compare: Fed. R. Evid. 901–903.

Research References

Packel & Poulin, Pennsylvania Evidence § 901-1 et seq. (4th ed. 2013)

McCormick, Evidence Chapter 22 (7th ed. 2013)

AUTHENTICATION: VOICE-TELEPHONE CONVERSATIONS, TAPE RECORDINGS

See: Pa.R.E. 901(b)(5), (6).

Objection

- Objection. The substance of the alleged phone conversation is inadmissible. There is [no] [insufficient] foundation establishing the identity of the speaker.

Response

- A proper foundation for the testimony has been established. Identity has been established by [voice recognition] [sufficient circumstantial evidence [specify]].

Pennsylvania Law

A telephone conversation between a witness and another person is admissible only when the identity of the person with whom the witness was speaking is satisfactorily established. Pa.R.E. 901(b)(5), (6); *Bonavitacola v. Cluver*, 422 Pa. Super. 556, 619 A.2d 1363 (1993); *Limestone Products & Supply Co. v. Tom Brown, Inc.*, 198 Pa. Super. 375, 181 A.2d 696 (1962).

Proving identity is no different than proving any other fact and may be accomplished by direct or circumstantial evidence. *Commonwealth v. DeRohn*, 444 Pa. 334, 282 A.2d 256 (1971).

The speaker's identity can be authenticated by testimony from a witness that he recognized the speaker's voice. Pa.R.E. 901(b)(5); *In re K.A.T., Jr.*, 69 A.3d 691 (Pa. Super. 2013) (a witness may testify to a person's identity from his voice alone); *Commonwealth v. Serrano*, 61 A.3d 279 (Pa. Super. 2013); *Commonwealth v. Jones*, 954 A.2d 1194 (Pa. Super. 2008); *Commonwealth v. Fromal*, 572 A.2d 711 (Pa. Super. 1990).

When the witness is unable to identify the speaker's voice, identity may be established by circumstantial evidence. *See* Pa.R.E. 901(b)(6); *Chicchi v. Southeastern Pa. Transp. Auth.*, 727 A.2d 604 (Pa.Cmwlth.1999) (speaker related accident details that only one person would be likely to know); *Bonavitacola v. Cluver*, 422 Pa. Super. 556, 619 A.2d 1363 (1993) (decedent's stated intent to make call was part of routine to obtain medical prescriptions; portion of conversation was overheard by witness and certain details were immediately related to witness; subsequent actions corroborated substance of conversation); *Commonwealth v. Sullivan*, 372 Pa. Super. 88, 538 A.2d 1363 (1988) (caller narrated facts that only one person would be likely to know); *Commonwealth v. Stewart*, 304 Pa. Super. 382, 450 A.2d 732 (1982) (evidence showed defendant was near murder scene, aware of phone call and had volunteered to police much of the information supplied in the call, which he had denied making); *Limestone Products & Supply Co. v. Tom Brown, Inc.*, 198 Pa. Super. 375, 181 A.2d 696 (1962) (telephone orders were authenticated by evidence that defendant accepted some orders and cancelled others); *Smithers v. Light*, 305 Pa. 141, 157 A. 489 (1931) (phone call can be authenticated by telephone company records); *Reach v. National Bedding Co.*, 276 Pa. 467, 120 A. 471 (1923) (phone conversation with unidentified person received in evidence where circumstances following conversation indicated that the person who spoke was speaking with authority).

In the absence of voice recognition or trustworthy circumstantial evidence, it is generally not enough that during the course of a conversation a party stated that he or she was a certain person. *Smithers v. Light*, 305 Pa. 141, 157 A. 489 (1931).

The admissibility of circumstantial evidence can vary, depending upon whether the witness is the recipient of the call or whether the witness placed the call. *See, e.g., Commonwealth v. Zimmer-*

man, 391 Pa. Super. 569, 571 A.2d 1062 (1990) (rejecting testimony and records as to defendant's whereabouts where the witness could not establish that specific phone calls were made by defendant (a courier) or that he actually was at the locations asserted in phone calls and recorded in company records.) If, however, a witness calls a listed telephone number of another person/entity and has a conversation with a person who represents himself or herself as the person called, then testimony as to a conversation had with the person answering the telephone is competent evidence, even if the witness does not recognize the voice of the person who answered and is unable to identify the speaker. Pa.R.E. 901(b)(6); *Commonwealth v. Sullivan*, 372 Pa. Super. 88, 538 A.2d 1363 (1988); *Kobierowski v. Commonwealth Mut. Ins. Co.*, 175 Pa. Super. 387, 105 A.2d 179 (1954).

Compare: Fed. R. Evid. 901(b)(5) and (6).

Research References

Packel & Poulin, Pennsylvania Evidence § 901-9 (4th ed. 2013)

McCormick, Evidence Chapter 22 (7th ed. 2013)

BEST EVIDENCE RULE

See: Pa.R.E. 1002.

Objection

- Objection. This evidence is not the best evidence of the written contract between the parties.
- I object to this exhibit on grounds of the best evidence rule. The original writing has not been accounted for.
- Objection. There is no competent excuse for nonproduction of the original.

Response

- Your Honor, we have established a legally sufficient reason for nonproduction.
- The contents of the document are not in issue.
- The contents are merely collateral and, therefore, the best evidence rule does not apply.

Pennsylvania Law

The general rule in Pennsylvania is that when the **contents of a writing, recording or photograph** are directly in issue, the **original writing** must be produced unless the original is unavailable through no fault of the proponent. *In re A Condemnation Proceeding by South Whitehall Twp.*, 822 A.2d 142 (Pa. Cmwlth. 2003) (a document needs only to be produced where the contents of a writing are at issue); *Commonwealth v. Fisher*, 764 A.2d 82 (Pa. Super. 2000); *Commonwealth v. Al Hamilton Contracting Co.*, 665 A.2d 849 (Pa.Cmwlth.1995); *Noble C. Quandel Co. v. Slough Flooring, Inc.*, 384 Pa. Super. 236, 558 A.2d 99 (1989); *Warren v. Mosites Constr. Co.*, 253 Pa. Super. 395, 385 A.2d 397 (1978).

The best evidence rule is controlling only if the terms of the writing must be proved to make a case or provide a defense. *Commonwealth v. Bennett,*

124 A.3d 327 (Pa. Super. 2013) (rule does not address prosecution's decision to present eyewitness testimony rather than surveillance videotape); *Warren v. Mosites Constr. Co.*, supra.

The rationale for the best evidence rule was discussed in *Hamill-Quinlan, Inc. v. Fisher*, 404 Pa. Super. 482, 489, 591 A.2d 309, 313 (1991):

> The rationale for the rule is readily apparent: in light of the added importance that the fact-finder may attach to the written word, it is better to have available the exact words of a writing, to prevent 'the mistransmitting [of] critical facts which accompanies the use of written copies or recollection,' and to prevent fraud.

Rule 1002 must be read in conjunction with Rule 1003 (governing the admissibility of duplicates) and Rule 1004 (permitting use of other evidence to prove the contents of the original).

Pa.R.E. 1003 creates an exception to the best evidence rule in that a duplicate is admissible to the same extent as an original except where there is a genuine question as to the authenticity of the original or where it would be unfair to admit the duplicate in lieu of the original.

Pa.R.E. 1004 also creates an exception to the best evidence rule. Where the document cannot be produced because, for example, it is lost, destroyed or cannot be obtained by legal process, production of the original is excused and other secondary or substitutional evidence of the contents becomes admissible. Pa.R.E. 1004(1); *Commonwealth v. Loughnane*, 128 A.3d 806 (Pa. Super. 2015) (still photograph of vehicle taken from videotape prior to videotape's inadvertent destruction was admissible); *Commonwealth v. Fisher*, 764 A.2d 82 (Pa. Super. 2000) (tape recording of voice mail was admissible duplicate). The trial judge determines whether there is sufficient proof to establish that the original document is unavailable. *Commonwealth v. Cessna*, 371 Pa. Super. 89, 537 A.2d 834 (1988).

When it has been established that the original document is unavailable through no fault of the proponent, the proponent may introduce a copy of the original as secondary evidence of its contents. Pa.R.E.1004; *Olson & French, Inc. v. Commonwealth*, 399 Pa. 266, 160 A.2d 401 (1960). If no copies are available, a witness who has seen the original document may testify as to its contents. *In re Greggerson's Estate*, 344 Pa. 498, 25 A.2d 711 (1942).

Although the rule is generally invoked with respect to documents, it also includes recordings and photographs. *Commonwealth v. Janda*, 14 A.3d 147 (Pa. Super. 2011) (best evidence rule did not require introduction of digital camera's memory card; printed photographs were sufficient); *Commonwealth v. Dent*, 837 A.2d 571 (Pa. Super. 2003). *Compare Commonwealth v. Lewis*, 424 Pa. Super. 531, 623 A.2d 355 (1993) (remanded for new trial where police testimony concerning alleged retail theft was based solely on officer's subsequent review of surveillance videotape and unavailability of tape was never satisfactorily explained) *with Commonwealth v. Steward*, 762 A.2d 721 (Pa. Super. 2000) (where guard had actually viewed theft on video monitor, his testimony was admissible despite fact that videotape was no longer available).

Where original records are voluminous, the trial court may admit a summary, provided the original records are available for inspection by the opposing party and the preparer of the summary is available for cross examination. Pa.R.E. 1006; *Department of Transp. v. Anjo Constr. Co.*, 666 A.2d 753 (Pa.Cmwlth.1995); *Scaife Co. v. Rockwell-Standard Corp.*, 446 Pa. 280, 285 A.2d 451 (1971); *Royal Pioneer Paper Box Mfg. Co. v. Louis Dejonge & Co.*, 179 Pa. Super. 155, 115 A.2d 837 (1955); *Keller v. Porta*, 172 Pa. Super. 651, 94 A.2d 140 (1953).

Pursuant to Pa.R.E. 901(b)(7), 902 and 1005,

as well as by statute, copies of an official record or of a document authorized to be recorded and filed and actually recorded or filed may be treated as original writings or may be equally as admissible as the original writing. *See* 42 Pa.C.S.A. § 6106 (public records); 42 Pa.C.S.A. § 6109 (Uniform Photographic Copies of Business and Public Records as Evidence Act).

Where an object has been inscribed, the decision to require production of the object itself as the best evidence is a matter of the trial court's discretion. *Commonwealth v. Byers*, 320 Pa. Super. 223, 467 A.2d 9 (1983) (addressed mail and prescription vials with label); *see also United States v. Duffy*, 454 F.2d 809 (5th Cir.1972) (shirt with laundry markings).

Where the terms of a writing were not closely related to a controlling issue or where there did not appear to be a substantial dispute about the terms of the writing, courts have held that the terms were not material or were only collateral and the best evidence rule was not applicable. This is now codified at Pa.R.E. 1004(4). *See Commonwealth v. Dent*, 837 A.2d 571 (Pa. Super. 2003) (under best evidence rule, if Commonwealth does not need to prove the contents of a writing or recording to prove the elements of offense charged, then prosecutor is not required to introduce the original writing or recording); *Commonwealth v. Townsend*, 747 A.2d 376 (Pa. Super. 2000) (detective could testify to contents of defendant's written confession; contents of confession were not an element of the crime but simply part of evidence Commonwealth chose to present); *Noble C. Quandel Co. v. Slough Flooring, Inc.*, 384 Pa. Super. 236, 558 A.2d 99 (1989) (damages testimony without use of business records); *Commonwealth v. Reicherter*, 317 Pa. Super. 256, 463 A.2d 1183 (1983) (oral testimony about existence of search warrant); *Durkin v. Equine Clinics*, 313 Pa. Super. 75, 459 A.2d 417 (1983) (in negligence action, introduction of transcript of tape-recorded interview rather than original recording not violation of best evidence rule since contents of interview were collateral to central issue of whether or not defendant was negligent); *Ragnar Benson, Inc. v. Bethel Mart Assoc.*, 308 Pa. Super. 405, 454 A.2d 599 (1982) (oral testimony regarding damages without attesting to authenticity of bills); *Warren v. Mosites Constr. Co.*, 253 Pa. Super. 395, 385 A.2d 397 (1978) (oral testimony that conduct met standards of PennDOT's Blue Book); *Mars v. Meadville Tel. Co.*, 344 Pa. 29, 23 A.2d 856 (1942); *Perry v. Ryback*, 302 Pa. 559, 153 A. 770 (1931) (testimony about earnings without record books).

Occasionally the rule is incorrectly cited; for example, in a situation where several people know something, to require a party to call that person who knows it "best." There is no such evidentiary principle. *Commonwealth v. Farrar*, 271 Pa. Super. 434, 413 A.2d 1094 (1979). Moreover, merely because the existence of a fact is capable of being proved by documentary evidence does not prohibit a witness from testifying about the fact, nor does it necessitate production of the document where the contents of the document are not at issue. *Commonwealth v. Bennett*, supra (rule does not address decision to present eyewitness testimony rather than surveillance videotape); *Nelson v. State Bd. of Veterinary Medicine*, 938 A.2d 1163 (Pa.Cmwlth. 2007) (written documents are not preferable to oral statements; there is no such evidentiary principle); *Commonwealth v. Slider*, 229 Pa. Super. 93, 323 A.2d 376 (1974).

Compare: Fed. R. Evid. 1002.

Research References

Packel & Poulin, Pennsylvania Evidence, § 1002-1 et seq. (4th ed. 2013)

McCormick, Evidence Chapter 23 (7th ed. 2013)

BEYOND THE SCOPE

See: Pa.R.E. 611(b).

Objection

- Objection. This is beyond the scope of direct examination. This matter was not mentioned in direct testimony; counsel must call this witness in his own case if he wishes to go into this evidence.
- This is not within the scope of proper redirect examination. It is not responsive to anything covered in the cross-examination.

[**NOTE**: *With expert witnesses, demand an offer of proof. If the offer contains facts and opinions beyond the fair scope of the expert's report, request the testimony be excluded. See Experts, Beyond the Fair Scope of Pretrial Discovery*].

Response

- The question is proper:
- it is addressed to the [*inference*] [*deduction*] [*conclusion*] which the witness sought to create in his direct testimony;
- credibility is always in issue;
- I am entitled to show the [*bias*] [*interest*] of the witness;
- I am entitled to test [*memory*] [*perception*].

Pennsylvania Law

Pennsylvania does not subscribe to the notion of wide open cross-examination, i.e., that the cross-examiner is always free to ask about any subject relevant to any issue in the case. *Commonwealth v. Lobel*, 294 Pa. Super. 550, 440 A.2d 602 (1982).

Instead, Pa.R.E. 611(b) draws a clear distinction between the scope of cross-examination of (1) a witness, and (2) a party.

Cross-examination of an adverse witness is generally limited to matters testified to on direct examination and matters affecting credibility. Pa.R.E. 611(b); *Commonwealth v. Ogrod*, 576 Pa. 412, 839 A.2d 294 (2003); *Woodland v. Philadelphia Transp. Co.*, 428 Pa. 379, 238 A.2d 593 (1968); *Commonwealth v. Kimbrough*, 872 A.2d 1244 (Pa. Super. 2005); *Commonwealth v. Katsafanas*, 318 Pa. Super. 143, 464 A.2d 1270 (1983). This is broadly defined as testimony which explains or destroys the effect of the direct testimony, including inferences, deductions or conclusions which may be drawn from the challenged testimony. *See, e.g., Commonwealth v. Robinson*, 583 Pa. 358, 877 A.2d 433 (2005); *Commonwealth v. Begley*, 566 Pa. 239, 780 A.2d 605 (2001); *Commonwealth v. Nunn*, 947 A.2d 756 (Pa. Super. 2008); *McManamon v. Washko*, 906 A.2d 1259 (Pa. Super. 2006) (right of cross-examination includes the right to examine the witness on any facts tending to refute inferences or deductions arising from matters the witness testified to on direct examination); *Boucher v. Pennsylvania Hosp.*, 831 A.2d 623 (Pa. Super. 2003) (in general, every circumstance relating to direct testimony is proper subject for cross-examination including matters which might qualify or diminish impact of direct examination); *Cacurak v. St. Francis Medical Center*, 823 A.2d 159 (Pa. Super. 2003) (reversible error to preclude cross-examination about subsequent bar fights and police altercation where plaintiff's case portrayed him as meek individual who exercised extreme caution after back operation); *Collins v. Cooper*, 746 A.2d 615 (Pa. Super. 2000). Questions which test perception or memory or which show bias or interest are also proper. *See Yacoub v. Lehigh Valley Medical*, 805 A.2d 579 (Pa. Super. 2002) (expert can be cross-examined as to any facts that tend to show partiality including prior work for party's attorney); *Kearns by Kearns v. DeHaas*, 377 Pa. Super. 200, 546 A.2d 1226 (1988); *Commonwealth v. Cessna*, 371 Pa. Super. 89, 537 A.2d 834 (1988).

This rule limiting the scope of cross-examination to the scope of the direct examination does not apply where a party to the action offers himself as a witness. Pa.R.E. 611(b). A party in a civil case may be cross-examined freely as to any matter relevant to the case. Pa.R.E. 611(b); *Geelen v. Pennsylvania R.R. Co.*, 400 Pa. 240, 161 A.2d 595 (1960); *Jess v. McMurray*, 394 Pa. 526, 147 A.2d 420 (1959).

The scope of cross-examination of a defendant in a criminal case is one of great latitude. *Commonwealth v. Charleston*, 16 A.3d 505 (Pa. Super. 2011). The scope of permissible cross-examination will depend on the testimony of the defendant and what, in the discretion of the trial court, becomes relevant by virtue of that testimony. *Commonwealth v. Marinelli*, 910 A.2d 672 (2006).

In all instances, however, a trial court may properly refuse to permit cross-examination which is likely to confuse or mislead the jury or waste time on collateral matters that are unrelated to the issues at trial. Pa.R.E. 611(a); *Downey v. Weston*, 451 Pa. 259, 301 A.2d 635 (1973); *Commonwealth v. Saunders*, 946 A.2d 776 (Pa. Super. 2008) (witness may not be contradicted on collateral matters); *Commonwealth v. Guilford*, 861 A.2d 365 (Pa. Super. 2004) (although defendant is permitted to question motive of a witness to testify or fabricate and is permitted to examine as to interest or bias, questions about witness' drug use at a time other than the time about which the witness is testifying are not permitted); *Commonwealth v. Marchand*, 452 Pa. Super. 625, 682 A.2d 841 (1996); *Commonwealth v. Bright*, 279 Pa. Super. 1, 420 A.2d 714 (1980) (a collateral matter is one which has no relationship to the case at trial).

A defendant may not introduce his defense by way of cross-examination of witnesses. *Woodland v. Philadelphia Transp. Co.*, 428 Pa. 379, 238 A.2d 593 (1968); *Rothermel v. McLaughlin*, 292 Pa. Super. 422, 437 A.2d 746

(1981). For example, where a defendant has been called by the plaintiff as an adverse witness, it is improper for defense counsel to attempt to examine him at that stage as to matters designed to introduce his main defense. *Kline v. Kachmar*, 360 Pa. 396, 61 A.2d 825 (1948).

As to redirect and subsequent examinations of any witness, the practice is uniform that examination is limited to answering only such matter as was drawn out in the immediately preceding examination of the adversary. *Catina v. Maree*, 498 Pa. 443, 447 A.2d 228 (1982).

Direct testimony of an expert witness at trial cannot exceed the scope of testimony in discovery proceedings. Pa.R.Civ.P. 4003.5. The purpose of requiring a party to disclose, at his adversary's discovery request, "the substance of the facts and opinions to which the expert is expected to testify" is to avoid unfair and prejudicial surprise by enabling the adversary to prepare a response. *Wilkes-Barre Iron & Wire Works, Inc. v. Pargas of Wilkes-Barre, Inc.*, 348 Pa. Super. 285, 502 A.2d 210 (1985). Expert testimony which exceeds the scope of discovery and causes unfair and prejudicial surprise will be excluded. *Estate of Hannis, by Hannis v. Ashland State Gen. Hosp.*, 123 Pa.Cmwlth. 390, 554 A.2d 574 (1989). For a trial court to admit testimony beyond the scope of the expert's report is abuse of discretion and reversible error. *DiBuono v. A. Barletta & Sons, Inc.*, 127 Pa.Cmwlth. 1, 560 A.2d 893 (1989).

The scope of cross-examination involving a medical expert includes reports or records which have not been admitted into evidence but which tend to refute that expert's assertion. *Jacobs v. Chatwani*, 922 A.2d 950 (Pa. Super. 2007). An expert witness may be cross-examined on the contents of a publication upon which he or she has relied in forming an opinion and also with respect to any other publication which the expert acknowledges to be a standard work in the field.

Compare: Fed. R. Evid. 611(b).

Research References

Packel & Poulin, Pennsylvania Evidence § 611-3 (4th ed. 2013)

McCormick, Evidence Chapter 4 (7th ed. 2013)

CHAIN OF CUSTODY

See: Pa.R.E. 901.

Objection

- Objection. The exhibit has not been properly authenticated. There is insufficient evidence to demonstrate the identity of this object [*and/or its condition*] is unimpaired.

Response

- A proper foundation for admission has been established. We have met our burden of demonstrating that there has been no [*alteration/ substitution/change of condition*]. Any alleged gap in the chain of custody since the time of the incident goes to the weight of the ·evidence, not its admissibility.

Pennsylvania Law

Real evidence consists of the actual objects involved in a particular event, e.g., the murder weapon, the seized drugs, the defective product. The "chain of custody" rule comes from the principle that real evidence must be authenticated prior to its admission into evidence. Pa.R.E. 901; *Koller Concrete, Inc. v. Tube City IMS, LLC*, 115 A.3d 312 (Pa. Super. 2015) and *UGI Utilities v. Unemployment Comp. Bd.*, 851 A.2d 240 (Pa. Cmwlth. 2004) (discussing concept and collecting cases). The purpose of this threshold requirement is to establish that the item to be introduced is what it purports to be. The ultimate question is whether the authentication testimony is sufficiently complete so as to persuade the court that it is improbable that the original item has been exchanged with another or altered in any material aspect. See *In re D.Y.*, 34 A.3d 177 (Pa. Super. 2011) (chain of custody refers to the manner in which evidence was maintained from the time it was collected to its submission at trial).

The admission of real evidence is a matter committed to the court's discretion. *Commonwealth v. Ford*, 451 Pa. 81, 301 A.2d 856 (1973); *Commonwealth v. Zook*, 532 Pa. 79, 615 A.2d 1 (1992). While the offering party bears the burden of demonstrating some reasonable connection between the proffered exhibit and the true evidence, *Commonwealth v. Pedano*, 266 Pa. Super. 461, 405 A.2d 525 (1979), it need not establish the sanctity of its exhibit beyond a moral certainty. *Commonwealth v. Cugnini*, 307 Pa. Super. 113, 452 A.2d 1064 (1982). The offering party need not produce every individual who came into contact with an item of evidence, nor must it eliminate every hypothetical possibility of tampering. *Commonwealth v. Feliciano*, 67 A.3d 19 (Pa. Super. 2013) (there is no rule requiring the prosecution to produce as witnesses all persons who were in a position to come in contact with the article sought to be introduced in evidence); *Webb v. Commission (PennDOT)*, 934 A.2d 178 (Pa.Cmwlth. 2007) (every person who comes into contact with evidence need not testify personally); *Commonwealth v. Rick*, 244 Pa. Super. 33, 366 A.2d 302 (1976). A complete chain of custody is not required so long as the evidence, direct and circumstantial, establishes a reasonable inference that the identity and condition of the exhibit has remained the same from the time it was first obtained until the time of trial. *Commonwealth v. Hudson*, 489 Pa. 620, 414 A.2d 1381 (1980); *Commonwealth v. Schwartz*, 419 Pa. Super. 251, 615 A.2d 350 (1992). Any gaps in testimony regarding the chain of custody go to the weight to be given the testimony, not to its admissibility. *Commonwealth v. Bolden*, 486 Pa. 383, 406 A.2d 333 (1979) (discrepancy between description of victim's body in police and medical examiner's reports goes only to weight of evidence); *Commonwealth v. Witmayer*, 144 A.3d 939 (Pa. Super. 2016) (physical evidence may be properly admitted despite gaps in testimony regarding custody); *Brunson v. Commonwealth, Unemployment Comp. Bd.*, 131 Pa.Cmwlth. 462, 570 A.2d 1096 (1990) (toxicologist did not need to participate in physical transfer of urine sample to be able to testify to its contents); *Lackawanna Refuse Removal, Inc. v. Commonwealth, Department of Envt'l Res.*, 65 Pa.Cmwlth. 372, 442 A.2d 423 (1982) (chemist could testify to contents of leachate samples even though person who recorded that legal seals were intact at delivery could not be identified); *See Commonwealth v. Hess*, 446 Pa. Super. 222, 666 A.2d 705 (1995) (blood test should have been excluded because of discrepancy in number of vials transported by police to forensic scientist).

See also Commonwealth v. Yohe, 79 A.3d 520 (Pa. Super. 2013) (toxicologist was supervisor of laboratory in which tests were performed and supervised technicians who performed tests on defendant's blood samples, was involved in reviewing all raw data, evaluating results, wrote and signed report and was competent to testify to the truth of report's statements); *Commonwealth v. Barton-Martin*, 5 A.3d 363 (Pa. Super. 2010) (where analyst who prepared lab report did not testify at trial, admission of blood-alcohol test results violated defendant's rights under Confrontation Clause.

In *Bullcoming v. New Mexico*, 564 U.S. 647 (2011) a DUI case involving a blood sample analyzed for alcohol, the United States Supreme Court said the Confrontation Clause does not permit the prosecution to introduce a laboratory report through the testimony of an analyst who did not sign the certification or perform or observe the performance of the test reported in the certification.

In *Melendez-Diaz v. Massachusetts*, 552 U.S. 1256 (2008), the trial court had admitted into evidence state laboratory affidavits with forensic analysis results showing material seized from defendant was cocaine. The United States Supreme Court said that the laboratory reports fell within the core class of testimonial statements since they had been created for the sole purpose of providing evidence against a defendant. Acknowledging that the Confrontation Clause may make prosecution of criminals more burdensome, the Court held that crime laboratory reports may not be used against defendants at trial unless the analysts responsible for creating them give testimony and subject themselves to cross-examination.

In *Commonwealth v. Borovichka*, 18 A.3d 1242 (Pa. Super. 2011), a State Police analyst authenticated his report and the laboratory procedures involved but could not recall specifically testing defendant's blood. The report was read into evidence as recorded recollection. The court said that the *Crawford / Melendez-Diaz* holdings were not implicated because during trial, defendant was able to cross-examine the analyst as well as the hospital phlebotomist who drew his blood. *Commonwealth v. Borovichka*, 18 A.3d 1242, at 1253, n.7 (Pa. Super. 2011).

Pennsylvania Rule of Criminal Procedure 574 provides a mechanism for the admission of a forensic laboratory report supported by a certification. This Rule provides a defendant an opportunity to exercise the right of confrontation and to object to the report on hearsay grounds. Following pre-trial notice by the prosecution, and in the absence of a demand by defendant for declarant's live testimony, the Rule permits the admission of a properly certified forensic laboratory report and the accompanying certification at trial. *See* Pa. R. Crim. P. 574.

Compare: Fed. R. Evid. 901.

Research References

Packel & Poulin, Pennsylvania Evidence § 901-2 (4th ed. 2013)

McCormick, Evidence Chapter 22 (7th ed. 2013)

CHARACTER EVIDENCE

See: Pa.R.E. 404, 405

Objection

- Objection. The character or reputation of [*plaintiff*] [*defendant*] is not at issue here. The evidence sought by the question is irrelevant and inadmissible.

Response

- Good character or reputation is directly at issue; it is an element of the [*claim*] [*defense*] and is, therefore, a material fact and has been attacked by my opponent.

Pennsylvania Law

Civil Cases

As a general rule, evidence of a person's character may not be admitted to show that a person acted in conformity with that character on a particular occasion. Pa.R.E. 404(a). There are, however, exceptions.

In civil actions, evidence of character or reputation is inadmissible unless directly at issue or involved in the nature of the proceedings, and even then, evidence of good character is not admissible unless and until it is attacked by evidence to the contrary. *Greenberg v. Aetna Insurance Co.*, 427 Pa. 494, 235 A.2d 582 (1967); *accord, Hepps v. Philadelphia Newspapers, Inc.*, 506 Pa. 304, 312, n. 1, 485 A.2d 374, 379, n. 1 (1984), *rev'd on other grounds* 475 U.S. 767, 106 S.Ct. 1558, 89 L.Ed.2d 783 (1986); *Butler v. Flo-Ron Vending Co.*, 383 Pa. Super. 633, 557 A.2d 730 (1989). To be "at issue" within the meaning of this rule, character must be of particular importance, i.e., an element of a claim or defense, and, therefore, a material fact in the case.

The limitations that have been developed over the years on the use of reputation evidence are based on the concern, born of experience, that it often distorts the fact-finding process by precluding dispassionate justice. *Michelson v. United States*, 335 U.S. 469, 69 S.Ct. 213, 93 L.Ed. 168 (1948). Character evidence, while typically being of relatively slight value, usually is laden with the dangerous baggage of prejudice, distraction, time consumption and surprise. *McCormick, Evidence* § 186.

In *Greenberg* and *Butler*, the court condemned admission of evidence of a good military record where the party's character had not been attacked.

Similarly, the general rule is that a person's character trait is not relevant to prove that at the time in question the person acted in accordance with that trait. See, Pa.R.E. 404(a); *Jamison v. Ardes*, 408 Pa. 188, 194, 182 A.2d 497, 499 (1962). In *Jamison*, a traffic accident case, the court said: "Evidence of general reputation of a person for carelessness is inadmissible to prove negligence on a particular occasion, since a person may have a very bad reputation and yet have discharged his duties properly on that occasion."

Pa.R.E. 405(b)(1) provides that in a civil action where character is an element of a claim or defense, character may be proved either by reputation evidence or by specific instances of conduct. Libel, slander and other actions to obtain compensation for harm to reputation are classic examples of actions in which character is said to be at issue. *Hepps v. Philadelphia Newspapers, Inc.*, 506 Pa. 304, 485 A.2d 374 (1984). Where self-defense or aggression is at issue in a civil action for assault and battery, evidence of plaintiff's bad reputation for violence is admissible. Pa.R.E. 404(a)(2)(iii); *Stumpf v. Nye*, 950 A.2d 1032 (Pa. Super. 2008); *Bell v. City of Philadelphia*, 341 Pa. Super. 534, 491 A.2d 1386 (1985). Other examples include actions against an employer for negligent employment of an unfit person, *Dempsey v. Walso Bureau, Inc.*, 431 Pa. 562, 246 A.2d 418 (1968), and disputes over child custody, *Commonwealth ex rel. Grimes v. Grimes*, 281 Pa. Super. 484, 422 A.2d 572 (1980).

Criminal Cases

In a criminal case, evidence of a pertinent trait of character of the accused is admissible when offered by the accused, or by the prosecution to rebut the same. *Commonwealth v. Buterbaugh*, 91 A.3d 1247 (Pa. Super. 2014); *Commonwealth v. Kouma*, 53 A.3d 760 (Pa. Super. 2012); Pa. R.E. 404(a)(1). The term 'pertinent' should be interpreted narrowly to refer to a character trait that is relevant to the crime charged against the accused. *Commonwealth v. Reyes-Rodriguez*, 111 A.3d 775 (Pa. Super. 2015). Evidence relating to specific instances of a victim's prior conduct must also be probative of the victim's conduct during the alleged criminal episode on which the current charges are based. *Commonwealth v. Christine*, 125 A.3d 394, 400 (Pa. 2015) (upholding admission of evidence of prior bad acts to prove character or reputation of the victim at the time of the crime in question, but adding ". . . we do not endorse the [Superior Court's] claim that a subsequent conviction can *never* be probative and admissible); *Commonwealth v. Minich*, 4 A.3d 1063 (Pa. Super. 2010) (where rape of minors was charged, defendant could not use evidence of child victim lying in school about wholly unrelated matters since that is not a "pertinent trait" with respect to the alleged sexual offense; if intended as a challenge to credibility, such evidence still could not be used per Rule 608 forbidding impeachment by specific instances of the witness' conduct); *Commonwealth v. Sasse*, 921 A.2d 1229 (Pa. Super. 2007) (ex-wife's character traits for drug and alcohol abuse, sexual promiscuity and depression had no relationship to defendant's allegedly fearful state of mind at time of shooting and were not admissible).

The principle is also illustrated in *Commonwealth v. Charleston*, 16 A.3d 505, 529 (Pa. Super. 2011), where defendant testified he acted in self-defense, had an aversion to guns and dumped his firearm in a sewer to protect neighborhood children. The appeals court said evidence of his tattoos "By any means necessary," "Fuck it" and "Shit happens" was admissible because it undermined testimony of selfless character with an unavoidable message of a selfish nature.

A defendant claiming self-defense may introduce evidence of the victim's violent character to show the defendant reasonably believed his life was in danger. *Commonwealth v. Busanet*, 54 A.3d 35 (Pa. 2012); *Commonwealth v. Dillon*, 598 A.2d 963 (Pa. 1991). The requirement of reasonable belief encompasses two aspects, one subjective and one objective. First, the defendant must have acted out of an honest, bona fide belief that he was in imminent danger, which involves consideration of the defendant's subjective state of mind. Second, the defendant's belief that he needed to defend himself with deadly force, if it existed, must be reasonable in light of the facts as they appeared to the defendant, a consideration that involves an objective analysis. *Commonwealth v. Mouzon*, 53 A.3d 738 (Pa. 2012).

Compare: Fed. R. Evid. 404, 405.

Research References

Packel & Poulin, Pennsylvania Evidence §§ 404-1 et seq., 405-1 (4th ed. 2013)

McCormick, Evidence Chapter 17 (7th ed. 2013)

CHARACTER WITNESS

See Pa.R.E. 405

Objection

To a question—Objection (or, I object). The question is improper because:

- It seeks to elicit the witness' personal opinion about the defendant's character/reputation;
- The character traits asked about are irrelevant to the nature of the crime;
- The real purpose of this cross-examination is not to impeach this character witness but to blacken the defendant in the eyes of the jury;
- It asks about community knowledge of prior arrests which is not permitted.

To an answer—Objection:

- The witness is incompetent to testify since there has been no foundation to establish that this witness is familiar with defendant's reputation in the community;
- The witness is giving her own personal opinion, which is not allowed under state rules.

Response

The question/answer is proper:

- The question does not solicit her personal opinion, but rather, her knowledge of how defendant was viewed among his friends and acquaintances;
- The character traits in question directly bear on the nature of the crime charged;
- The witness is entitled to give negative proof of good reputation. We have shown that she moved in the same circles as defendant and would have heard adverse comment had there been any. *Commonwealth v. Gaines*, 167 Pa. Super. 485, 75 A.2d 617 (1950);
- The cross-examination is proper; I am entitled to test her standard of what constitutes good repute by asking about community knowledge of other conduct.

Pennsylvania Law

A criminal defendant is always entitled to introduce evidence of good character as an element of defense. *Commonwealth v. Cleary*, 135 Pa. 64, 19 A. 1017 (1890); *Commonwealth v. Sandusky*, 77 A.3d 663 (Pa. Super. 2013); *In re R.D.*, 44 A.3d 657 (Pa. Super. 2012) (evidence of good character is substantive and positive evidence and is a factor which may engender reasonable doubt or produce a conclusion of innocence). Character testimony alone can be grounds for acquittal. *Commonwealth v. Neely*, 561 A.2d 1 (Pa. 1989); *Commonwealth v. Hoover*, 16 A.3d 1148 (Pa. Super. 2011) (defendant who presents character evidence is entitled to a jury instruction that evidence of good character may create a reasonable doubt thus requiring a verdict of not guilty). *See Commonwealth v. Kim*, 888 A.2d 847 (Pa. Super. 2005) (while character evidence is admissible to prove defendant did not commit the charged crime, it is inadmissible where issue is whether defendant had a specific intent to kill or did not have the intent due to diminished capacity).

The rationale for the admission of character testimony in a criminal case is that an accused may not be able to produce any other evidence to exculpate himself from the charge he faces except his own oath and evidence of good character. *Commonwealth v. Weiss*, 530 Pa. 1, 606 A.2d 439 (1992) (failure to call available character witnesses constituted ineffective assistance of counsel); *Commonwealth v. Hull*, 982 A.2d 1020 (Pa. Super. 2009) (same); *Commonwealth v. Luther*, 317 Pa. Super. 41, 463 A.2d 1073 (1983). Reputation evidence is an exception to the hearsay rule under Pa.R.E. 803(21).

In order to be qualified to testify as to the reputation of a criminal defendant, a character witness must first demonstrate that she is familiar with that person's reputation in the community or neighborhood. *Commonwealth v. Keaton*, 45 A.3d 1050 (Pa. 2012) (character evidence is not the opinion of one person or even a handful of persons but must represent the consensus of the community); *Commonwealth v. Johnson*, 27 A.3d 244 (Pa. Super. 2011) (in child sex offense case, proper behavior around other family children was not proper character evidence for general reputation for chastity in the community); *Commonwealth v. Presbury*, 329 Pa. Super. 179, 478 A.2d 21 (1984). Unlike the federal rules, Pennsylvania does not permit proof of character by personal opinion evidence. *Commonwealth v. Lauro*, 819 A.2d 100 (Pa. Super. 2003) (witnesses' personal knowledge of defendant inadmissible).

Community or neighborhood is not limited to the immediate vicinity of the defendant's residence; in a modern, mobile and impersonal society, community may also include the workplace and other locations of social interaction. *See United States v. Mandel*, 591 F.2d 1347 (4th Cir.1979).

What a character witness reports about a defendant's reputation in the community is obviously hearsay and, therefore, the form of this testimony is strictly prescribed. The testimony must speak only to the defendant's reputation in the community; the witness must not refer to specific acts or to rumor. *Commonwealth v. Boone*, 467 Pa. 168, 354 A.2d 898 (1975). Although permitted under the Federal Rules of Evidence, **Pennsylvania does not allow a reputation witness to express her personal opinion about the defendant's character**. Pa.R.E. 405; *Commonwealth v. Wilson*, 543 Pa. 429, 672 A.2d 293 (1996) (personal opinion irrelevant); *Commonwealth v. Boring*, 453 Pa. Super. 600, 684 A.2d 561 (1996); *Kinniry v. Abington School Dist.*, 673 A.2d 429 (Pa.Cmwlth. 1996). Character evidence must also be relevant to the crime charged, e.g., a reputation for peacefulness where the crime charged is one of violence. *See Commonwealth v. Fletcher*, 580 Pa. 403, 861

A.2d 898 (2004).

A character witness, like any other witness, can be subjected to cross-examination and impeachment, although the scope of cross-examination has long been a troublesome area for the courts. *Commonwealth v. Scott*, 496 Pa. 188, 436 A.2d 607 (1981); *Commonwealth v. Adams*, 426 Pa. Super. 332, 626 A.2d 1231 (1993).

A distinction is drawn between cases where cross-examination seeks merely to prove specific acts of misconduct and those where the purpose of the examination is to test the accuracy of the testimony by showing either that the character witness is not familiar with defendant's reputation or that her standard of what constitutes good repute is unsound. *Commonwealth v. Becker*, 326 Pa. 105, 191 A. 351 (1937). Evidence of the former is inadmissible. Questions about specific acts may be allowed provided the purpose of the cross-examination is not to show the defendant committed an act or crime for which he is not now accused, but only to test the character witness' knowledge or the standard by which she measures reputation. *Commonwealth v. Treiber*, 121 A.3d 435 (Pa. 2015); *Commonwealth v. Puksar*, 951 A.2d 267 (Pa. 2008) (while character witnesses may not be impeached with specific acts of misconduct, a character witness may be cross-examined regarding his or her knowledge of particular acts of misconduct to test the accuracy of the testimony); *Commonwealth v. Hall*, 867 A.2d 619 (Pa. Super. 2005); *Commonwealth v. Hammond*, 308 Pa. Super. 139, 454 A.2d 60 (1982). Cross-examination may include questions regarding the defendant's prior convictions for crimes involving the relevant character trait. *Commonwealth v. Judd*, 897 A.2d 1224 (Pa. Super. 2006) (if defendant presented evidence to show he was a non-violent person, the Commonwealth would be allowed to present evidence of his more recent prior convictions; impeachment of character witness is allowed through inquiry into specific acts relevant to the character trait in question); *Commonwealth v. Nellom*, 388 Pa. Super. 314, 565 A.2d 770 (1989). **In criminal cases, however, a character witness cannot be cross-examined about community knowledge of a defendant's prior arrests or other criminal misconduct which have not resulted in conviction.** Rule 405(a); *Commonwealth v. Morgan*, 559 Pa. 248, 739 A.2d 1033 (1999) (Commonwealth is not permitted to cross-examine defense character witnesses about allegations of defendant's prior criminal misconduct which had never resulted in an arrest); *Commonwealth v. Scott*, 496 Pa. 188, 436 A.2d 607 (1981) (defendant's proposed character witnesses could not be cross-examined about defendant's prior arrests, neither of which had led to a conviction; mere arrest is equally consistent with guilt and innocence); *Commonwealth v. Kuder*, 62 A.3d 1038 (Pa. Super. 2013) (Commonwealth may not cross-examine a character witness about a defendant's unchanged criminal allegations or arrests that did not lead to convictions).

The following cases are instructive: *Commonwealth v. Kouma*, 53 A.3d 760 (Pa. Super. 2012) (if character witnesses testified to reputation as law-abiding, they could be cross-examined where defendant's illegal alien status which calls into question knowledge of person, law-abiding trait and standard by which they measure reputation); *Commonwealth v. Hoover*, 16 A.3d 1148 (Pa. Super. 2011) (character witnesses could not be questioned about defendant's participation in Accelerated Rehabilitative Disposition program; ARD is not a conviction for impeachment purposes); *Stumpf v. Nye*, 950 A.2d 1032 (Pa. Super. 2008) (in a civil action for assault and battery where self-defense or aggression is in issue, evidence of plaintiff's bad reputation for violence is admissible but not by character witnesses who will only testify to specific instances of conduct); *Commonwealth v. Lauro*, 819 A.2d 100 (Pa. Super. 2003); *Commonwealth v.*

Luther, 317 Pa. Super. 41, 463 A.2d 1073 (1983) (in a rape case, evidence of the character of the defendant is limited to testimony of general reputation in the community with regard to such traits as non-violence, peacefulness, quietness, good moral character, chastity and a disposition to observe good order); *Commonwealth v. King*, 287 Pa. Super. 105, 429 A.2d 1121 (1981) (questions about rape defendant fathering child by another woman permitted to combat character evidence of good conduct around women); *Commonwealth v. Butts*, 204 Pa. Super. 302, 204 A.2d 481 (1964) (cross-examination in vehicular homicide case showing that character witness was a drinking buddy of the accused permissible to show witness' standard of what constitutes good repute for sobriety was unsound).

Compare: Fed. R. Evid. 405.

Research References

Packel & Poulin, Pennsylvania Evidence § 405-1 (4th ed. 2013)

McCormick, Evidence Chapter 17 (7th ed. 2013)

CLOSING ARGUMENT

See: Pa.R.Civ.P. 225; Pa.R.Crim.P. 604.

Objection

- Your Honor, I must object. Counsel is: [*stating her own personal belief about a witness's credibility*] [*misstating the law*] [*stating the law in a manner calculated to confuse the jury*] [*mischaracterizing the evidence*] [*engaging in comment which is inappropriate, inflammatory and prejudicial*]. I request an immediate cautionary instruction. [*I hereby move for a mistrial*].

Response

- Your Honor, my comments are fair deductions and legitimate inferences from the evidence presented and are well within the boundaries of proper advocacy. [*I have stated the law correctly*] [*I have stated the facts accurately and the record will reflect that*].

Pennsylvania Law

The function of a closing argument is to provide counsel the opportunity to marshal the evidence and to present it, along with permissible inferences arising therefrom, to the jury in the best possible light on behalf of his client and to attempt to explain away the evidence which is unfavorable. *Commonwealth v. Bricker*, 525 Pa. 362, 581 A.2d 147 (1990); *Commonwealth v. Zettlemoyer*, 500 Pa. 16, 454 A.2d 937 (1982) (prosecution and defense alike are afforded wide latitude and may employ oratorical flair in arguing to jury). The length of closing arguments and other details are left to the discretion of the trial court. *Commonwealth v. Hutchinson*, 25 A.3d 277 (Pa. 2011) (court "generally limited" counsel to thirty minutes); *Commonwealth v. Brown*, 544 Pa. 406, 676 A.2d 1178 (1996); *Commonwealth v. Garcia*, 443 Pa.

Super. 414, 661 A.2d 1388 (1995) (no abuse of discretion by imposing twenty minute time limit on defendant's closing); *Commonwealth v. Wesley*, 860 A.2d 585 (Pa. Super. 2004) (defendant allowed only one closing argument although represented by two different attorneys on two different sets of charges).

During final argument, counsel may describe and discuss: all facts and opinions which are a part of the record; inferences reasonably derived from the evidence at trial, *Commonwealth v. Arrington*, 86 A.3d 831 (Pa. 2014); *Commonwealth v. Smith*, 580 Pa. 392, 861 A.2d 892 (2004); how the law applies to the facts to support the verdict sought and how the evidence supports the legal theories; anecdotes, analogies and metaphors involving common life experiences. The closing argument is the last opportunity the attorney has to explain the specific result the attorney wants and to convince the jury the facts and the law support a verdict in favor of the client. Haydock and Sonsteng, Trial: Advocacy Before Judges, Jurors And Arbitrators Chapter 11 (4th ed. 2011). The right to present a summation is clearly a component of the right to representation by counsel. *Commonwealth v. Stokes*, 532 Pa. 242, 615 A.2d 704 (1992). Counsel must be afforded reasonable latitude in presenting a case to a jury, and must be allowed to present his or her arguments with logical force and vigor. *Commonwealth v. Johnson*, 139 A.3d 1257 (Pa. 2016); *Commonwealth v. Staton*, 120 A.3d 277 (Pa. 2015); *Commonwealth v. Laird*, 119 A.3d 972 (Pa. 2015); *Commonwealth v. Chamberlain*, 30 A.3d 381 (Pa. 2011); *Commonwealth v. Travaglia*, 541 Pa. 108, 661 A.2d 352 (1995).

However, trial counsel are not permitted to: misstate the evidence or mislead the jury as to the inference it may draw, *Commonwealth v. Ali*, 10 A.3d 282 (Pa. 2010); misstate the law or state it in a manner calculated to confuse the jury, *Commonwealth v. Hardcastle*, 519 Pa. 236, 546 A.2d 1101 (1988); comment on the credibility of witnesses by stating a personal opinion about a witness's credibility, *Commonwealth v. Weiss*, 565 Pa. 504, 776 A.2d 958 (2001); *Commonwealth v. Koehler*, 558 Pa. 334, 737 A.2d 225 (1999); *Commonwealth v. Helsel*, 53 A.3d 906 (Pa. Super. 2012); refer to facts which were not in evidence, *Coffey v. Minwax Co., Inc.*, 764 A.2d 616 (Pa. Super. 2000); *Commonwealth v. Green*, 417 Pa. Super. 119, 611 A.2d 1294 (1992); comment on a criminal defendant's failure to testify on his own behalf, *Griffin v. California*, 380 U.S. 609, 85 S.Ct. 1229, 14 L.Ed.2d 106 (1965); *Commonwealth v. Wright*, 961 A.2d 119 (Pa.2008); *Commonwealth v. Clark*, 551 Pa. 258, 710 A.2d 31 (1998); make remarks that are not justified by the testimony and which are, or may be, unfairly prejudicial to the accused. *Commonwealth v. Chmiel*, 889 A.2d 501 (Pa.2005). Comments will be deemed unfairly prejudicial where their unavoidable effect is to create in the jury such bias and hostility toward a party that they could not weigh the evidence objectively and render a true verdict. *Commonwealth v. Burno*, 94 A.3d 956 (Pa. 2014); *Commonwealth v. Ligons*, 971 A.2d 1125 (Pa. 2009); *Commonwealth v. Abu-Jamal*, 553 Pa. 485, 504 n. 9, 720 A.2d 79, 88 n.9 (1998); *Commonwealth v. Bronshtein*, 547 Pa. 460, 691 A.2d 907 (1997). As long as a prosecutor does not assert his personal opinion, he may, within reasonable limits, comment on the credibility of a witness. *Commonwealth v. Tedford*, 960 A.2d 1 (Pa. 2008); *Commonwealth v. May*, 898 A.2d 559 (Pa. 2006); *Commonwealth v. Williams*, 581 Pa. 57, 863 A.2d 505 (2004); *Commonwealth v. Jones*, 571 Pa. 112, 811 A.2d 994 (2002); *Commonwealth v. Riggle*, 119 A.3d 1058 (Pa. Super. 2015). This is especially true when the credibility of the witness has been previously attacked by the defense. *Commonwealth v. Drummond*, 775 A.2d 849 (Pa. Super. 2001). A prosecutor should not offer his personal opinion as to the guilt of the accused. *Commonwealth v. DeJesus*, 580 Pa. 303, 860 A.2d 102 (2004). It is improper prosecutorial conduct to argue that the jury must believe government agents are lying in order to find defendant not guilty. *Commonwealth v. Rivera*, 939 A.2d 355 (Pa. Super. 2007) (to indicate that if jury does not find defendant guilty, it is calling police "liars" is to inject issue in case beyond issue of guilt or innocence and is calculated to inflame and prejudice jury against defendant). A remark by a prosecutor, otherwise improper, may be appropriate if it is in fair response to the argument and comment of defense counsel. *Commonwealth v. Sanchez*, 82 A.3d 943 (Pa. 2013); *Commonwealth v. Elliott*, 80 A.3d 415 (Pa. 2013); *Commonwealth v. Trivigno*, 561 Pa. 232, 750 A.2d 243 (2000); *Commonwealth v. Manley*, 985 A.2d 256 (Pa. Super. 2009).

While courts traditionally have been tolerant of oratorical flair during argument, *Commonwealth v. Busanet*, 54 A.3d 35 (Pa. 2012) (calling defense "smoke and mirrors" did not inflame jury and prevent a fair verdict); *Commonwealth v. Thomas*, 54 A.3d 332 (Pa. 2012); *Commonwealth v. Philistin*, 53 A.3d 1 (Pa. 2012); *Commonwealth v. Keaton*, 556 Pa. 442, 729 A.2d 529 (1999), during the penalty phase of a criminal trial, references to the Bible or any other religious writing in support of, or in opposition to the death penalty are reversible error *per se* and may subject the attorney to disciplinary action, *Commonwealth v. Cooper*, 941 A.2d 655 (Pa.2007) (reliance on Bible or other religious writing encourages jury to substitute religious precepts for the law of the Commonwealth, only the latter of which jury is required to follow); *Commonwealth v. Brown*, 567 Pa. 272, 786 A.2d 961 (2001); *Commonwealth v. Chambers*, 528 Pa. 558, 599 A.2d 630 (1991); *Commonwealth v. Daniels*, 531 Pa. 210, 612 A.2d 395 (1992); *see also Commonwealth v. Morales*, 549 Pa. 400, 701 A.2d 516 (1997). *See also Commonwealth v. Natividad*, 938 A.2d 310 (Pa. 2007) (declining to extend *Chambers per se* rule to guilt phase closing arguments;

reference to religion at guilt phase does not mandate automatic reversal). In many cases, a cautionary instruction may be adequate to cure the error. *Commonwealth v. DeJesus*, 567 Pa. 415, 787 A.2d 394 (2001); *Commonwealth v. Hawkins*, 567 Pa. 310, 787 A.2d 292 (2001); *Commonwealth v. Caldwell*, 117 A.3d 763 (Pa. Super. 2015). However, in order to cure the error, the cautionary instruction should usually be given promptly and should deal with the specific issue raised by the objection.

The United States Supreme Court has said that an improper closing argument may constitute constitutional error where the prosecutor's comments "so infected the trial with unfairness as to make the resulting conviction a denial of due process." *Donnelly v. DeChristoforo*, 416 U.S. 637, 643, 94 S.Ct. 1868, 1871, 40 L.Ed.2d 431 (1974); *Commonwealth v. Montalvo*, 986 A.2d 84 (Pa.2009).

The Pennsylvania Supreme Court has held that the matter of a mistrial because of a line of argument pursued by counsel in addressing a jury is largely within the discretion of the trial court. *Commonwealth v. Zook*, 532 Pa. 79, 615 A.2d 1 (1992); *Ferguson v. Morton*, 84 A.3d 715 (Pa. Super. 2013). But it is also well settled that not every intemperate remark by an attorney requires a mistrial. *Commonwealth v. Lopez*, 57 A.3d 74 (Pa. Super. 2012); *Dillow v. Myers*, 916 A.2d 698 (Pa. Super. 2007). Whether a court abuses its discretion by refusing to declare a mistrial because of improper remarks of counsel must be determined by the circumstances under which the statement was made, *Commonwealth v. Page*, 965 A.2d 1212 (Pa. Super. 2009), and the precautions taken by the court and counsel to prevent its having a prejudicial effect. *Rivera v. Philadelphia Theological Seminary*, 398 Pa. Super. 264, 580 A.2d 1341 (1990). See also *Commonwealth v. Jaynes*, 135 A.3d 606 (Pa. Super. 2016) (request for mistrial adequately preserved even though defense counsel waited until end of prosecutor's closing to move for mistrial).

In criminal cases, greater latitude in presenting argument is afforded during the penalty phase since the presumption of innocence no longer applies. *Commonwealth v. Poplawski*, 130 A.3d 697 (Pa. 2015); *Commonwealth v. Spotz*, 18 A.3d 244 (Pa. Super. 2011); *Commonealth v. Smith*, 995 A.2d 1143 (Pa. 2010); *Commonwealth v. Gwynn*, 943 A.2d 940 (Pa.2008); *Commonwealth v. Romero*, 938 A.2d 362 (Pa.2007); *Commonwealth v. Williams*, 896 A.2d 523 (Pa. 2006); *Commonwealth v. Hughes*, 581 Pa. 274, 865 A.2d 761 (2004); *Commonwealth v. Eichinger*, 108 A.3d 821 (Pa. 2014) (in closing argument at penalty phase of murder trial, prosecutor may rebut mitigation evidence, urge jury to view such evidence with disfavor and show no mercy).

Illustrative cases: *Commonwealth v. Patton*, 985 A.2d 1283 (Pa. 2009) (urging jury to tell defendant he can't get away with murder is not an improper "send a message" statement); *Commonwealth v. Smith*, 985 A.2d 886 (Pa.2009) (prosecutor may argue that jury should not attach any substantial weight to mitigating circumstances presented by defense); *Commonwealth v. Uderra*, 580 Pa. 492, 862 A.2d 74 (2004) (court does not countenance prosecutors telling members of capital sentencing jury that they are not responsible for the penalty verdict); *Commonwealth v. DeJesus*, 567 Pa. 415, 787 A.2d 394 (2001) (in penalty phase of capital trial, argument that jury "send a message" with its verdict is *per se* prejudicial); *Bennett v. Sakel*, 555 Pa. 560, 725 A.2d 1195 (1999) (new trial ordered in personal injury case where defendant's attorney improperly asked jury to draw adverse inference concerning plaintiff's failure to call certain witnesses where those witnesses were equally available to both sides); *Commonwealth v. Hall*, 549 Pa. 269, 701 A.2d 190 (1997) (condemning arguments exhorting jury to "send a message"); *Deeds v. University of Pa. Medical Center*, 110 A.3d

1009 (Pa. Super. 2015) (reversed; clear violation of collateral source rule for defense closing to suggest that plaintiff's medical costs were being covered by Medicaid and the Affordable Care Act and that she did not require and could not properly seek any additional compensation); *Nelson v. Airco Welders Supply*, 107 A.3d 146 (Pa. Super. 2014) (new trial on damages based upon plaintiff's counsel improperly suggesting to jury a formula for calculating non-economic damages; counsel may not suggest an amount for damages incapable of measurement by a mathematical standard (collecting cases)); *Mirabel v. Morales*, 57 A.3d 144 (Pa. Super. 2012) (where plaintiff injected race, ethnicity and defendant's wealth into closing, a new trial was warranted); *Commonwealth v. Culver*, 51 A.3d 866 (Pa. Super. 2012) (prosecutor's yelling, engaging in menacing behavior and putting his finger in face of defendant and defense counsel unfairly prejudiced defendant); *Commonwealth v. Judy*, 978 A.2d 1015 (Pa. Super. 2009) (a prosecutor cannot intrude upon exclusive function of jury to evaluate credibility of witnesses by broadly characterizing witness testimony as a "big lie" but assertion that witness lied does not warrant new trial when statement is a fair inference from irrefutable evidence rather than a broad characterization); *Commonwealth v. Holley*, 945 A.2d 241 (Pa. Super. 2008) (while prosecutor cannot offer his views as to a defense strategy, he can fairly respond to attacks on a witness's credibility); *Commonwealth v. Brown*, 911 A.2d 576 (Pa. Super. 2006) (characterizing killing as "execution" was neither inaccurate nor particularly prejudicial); *Schweikert v. St. Luke's Hosp.*, 886 A.2d 265 (Pa. Super. 2005) (where all witnesses agreed defendant doctor had saved plaintiff's life in emergency situation, counsel's analogy that defendant was like a fireman who rescued woman in burning building and then got sued for damaging a door in the process was proper in context); *Commonwealth v. Carter*, 855 A.2d 885 (Pa. Super. 2004) (comparing defense to octopus clouding water with ink was oratorical flair not impermissible disparagement and ridicule); *Commonwealth v. Poplawski*, 852 A.2d 323 (Pa. Super. 2004) (new trial ordered where prosecutor asked jury to "send a message" re outsiders bringing guns into the community); *Commonwealth v. Walter*, 849 A.2d 265 (Pa. Super. 2004) (murder conviction reversed; defendant prejudiced by inadmissible evidence and reference to it in closing argument); *Commonwealth v. Rivera*, 828 A.2d 1094 (Pa. Super. 2003) (prosecution may not comment on defendant's decision to remain silent following his arrest).

Compare: Fed.R.Crim.P. 29.1.

Research Reference

Haydock and Sonsteng, Trial: Advocacy Before Judges, Jurors and Arbitrators Chapter 11 (4th ed. 2011)

COMPETENCE TO TESTIFY

See: Pa.R.E. 601.

Objection

- Objection. The witness is incompetent to testify because he:
  - — [*lacked any reasonable ability to perceive the matter*]
  - — [*lacks any reasonable ability to remember the matter*]
  - — [*is incapable of expressing himself so as to be understood by the judge / jury either directly or through an interpreter*]
  - — [*is incapable of understanding the duty of a witness to tell the truth*].

Response

- The witness is presumed competent. There has been no showing of inability regarding perception, recollection, communication or appreciation of the oath.

Pennsylvania Law

Unless expressly excluded by some statute or rule of law, the competency of a witness is presumed and the burden of demonstrating incompetency falls on the objecting party. Pa.R.E. 601; *Commonwealth v. Walter*, 93 A.3d 442 (Pa. 2014); *Commonwealth v. Koehler*, 558 Pa. 334, 737 A.2d 225 (1999); *Commonwealth v. Boich*, 982 A.2d 102 (Pa. Super. 2009); *Commonwealth v. Judd*, 897 A.2d 1224 (Pa. Super. 2006); *see* also 42 Pa.C.S.A. §§ 5911, 5921.

To be testimonially competent, a witness must have the ability to: (1) perceive the event with a substantial degree of accuracy; (2) remember it; (3) communicate about it intelligently; and (4) be mindful of his duty to tell the truth under oath.

Commonwealth v. Counterman, 553 Pa. 370, 719 A.2d 284 (1998); *Commonwealth v. Goldblum*, 498 Pa. 455, 447 A.2d 234 (1982). See also *Wayne Knorr, Inc. v. Dept. of Transp.*, 973 A.2d 1061 (Pa.Cmwlth. 2009) (construction company owner was sufficiently knowledgeable of project and its problems to be a competent witness; any shortcomings went to weight, not competency).

The trial court does not have the duty to order any investigation into a witness' competency unless the court has some doubt after observing the witness. *Commonwealth v. Henkel*, 938 A.2d 433 (Pa. Super. 2007).

When a witness is at least 14 years old, he or she is entitled to the same presumption of competence as an adult witness. *Commonwealth v. McLaurin*, 45 A.3d 1131 (Pa. Super. 2012).

The general rule of presumed competency does not apply when the witness is a child under the age of fourteen or suffers from some mental disability. When a proposed witness is under fourteen years of age, there must be a searching judicial inquiry as to mental capacity. *Commonwealth v. Harvey*, 571 Pa. 533, 812 A.2d 1190 (2002); *Commonwealth v. D.J.A.*, 800 A.2d 965 (Pa. Super. 2002). This inquiry will probe the capacity to communicate, observe and remember as well as an awareness of the duty to speak the truth, in proportion to the witness' chronological immaturity. *Commonwealth v. Dowling*, 584 Pa. 396, 883 A.2d 570 (2005); *Commonwealth v. Shearer*, 584 Pa. 134, 882 A.2d 462 (2005); *Commonwealth v. Delbridge*, 578 Pa. 641, 855 A.2d 27 (2003) (*Delbridge I*); *Rosche v. McCoy*, 397 Pa. 615, 156 A.2d 307 (1959); *Commonwealth v. McMaster*, 446 Pa. Super. 261, 666 A.2d 724 (1995) (collecting cases).

The Pennsylvania Supreme Court has said that in evaluating a child's competency, the trial court must be satisfied the witness has:

(1)   the capacity to observe or perceive the occurrence with a substantial degree of accuracy;

(2)   the ability to remember the event which was observed or perceived;

(3)   the ability to understand questions and to communicate intelligent answers about the occurrence; and

(4)   a consciousness of the duty to speak the truth.

Delbridge I, 578 Pa. 641, 855 A.2d 27 (2003); *Commonwealth v. Harvey*, 571 Pa. 533, 812 A.2d 1190 (2002); *Rosche v. McCoy*, 397 Pa. 615, 156 A.2d 307 (1959); *Commonwealth v. Hunzer*, 868 A.2d 498 (Pa. Super. 2005).

In cases involving allegations of sexual abuse inflicted upon children of tender years, the existence of taint (i.e., implantation of false memories or distortion of actual memories through improper and suggestive interview techniques) is a threshold question to determining competency. *Delbridge I*, 578 Pa. 641, 855 A.2d 27 (2003), and *Commonwealth v. Delbridge*, 580 Pa. 68, 859 A.2d 1254 (2004) (*Delbridge II*); *Commonwealth v. Page*, 59 A.3d 1118 (Pa. Super. 2013); *Commonwealth v. Davis*, 939 A.2d 905 (Pa. Super. 2007). Taint inquiry is not limited only to cases of sexual abuse. *Commonwealth v. Moore*, 980 A.2d 647 (Pa. Super. 2009) (*Delbridge I* indicated procedure for taint hearings was applicable to all child witnesses); *Commonwealth v. Judd*, 897 A.2d 1224 (Pa. Super. 2006) (party alleging taint must produce some evidence of taint as well as showing taint by clear and convincing evidence).

In *Commonwealth v. Washington*, 554 Pa. 559, 722 A.2d 643 (1998), the Pennsylvania Supreme Court created a *per se* rule requiring the trial judge to conduct child witness competency hearings outside the presence of the jury.

A child need not be deemed competent to testify as a witness in order for the trial court to admit the child's out-of-court statements into evidence pursuant to the Tender Years Hearsay Act, 42 Pa.C.S.A. § 5985.1. *Commonwealth v. Walter*, 93

A.3d at 453.

Incompetency of an adult witness is not presumed merely because the witness is mentally ill, insane or mentally retarded. *See Commonwealth v. Counterman*, 553 Pa. 370, 719 A.2d 284 (1998); *Commonwealth v. Garcia*, 478 Pa. 406, 387 A.2d 46 (1978) (schizophrenic allowed to testify); *accord*, *Commonwealth v. Ware*, 459 Pa. 334, 329 A.2d 258 (1974) (testimony received from inmates of hospital for criminally insane). Where the court is presented with credible evidence that a proposed adult witness has or might have a mental disability, there must be an inquiry to determine testimonial capacity. *Cheng v. SEPTA*, 981 A.2d 371 (Pa.Cmwlth. 2009) (no error to exclude testimony of witness with cerebral palsy where record showed testimony was unreliable, self-conflicting and contradictory). The factors the court shall consider are the same relied on to determine the competency of a child witness. *Commonwealth v. Anderson*, 381 Pa. Super. 1, 552 A.2d 1064 (1988).

A witness is not incompetent per se because he was drunk or under the influence of alcohol or drugs at the time he observed the events about which he is to testify. Intoxication or addiction ordinarily goes to the weight of the testimony, and not to competence to testify. *See Commonwealth v. Small*, 559 Pa. 423, 741 A.2d 666 (1999) (testimony about long-term drug and alcohol abuse inadmissible); *Commonwealth v. Fisher*, 545 Pa. 233, 681 A.2d 130 (1996) (while a witness may be questioned about drug or alcohol use at the time of the events about which he is testifying, questions about witness' drug use at other irrelevant times are not permitted); *Commonwealth v. Drew*, 500 Pa. 585, 459 A.2d 318 (1983); *Commonwealth v. Yost*, 478 Pa. 327, 386 A.2d 956 (1978); *Commonwealth v. Boich*, 982 A.2d 102 (Pa. Super. 2009).

Where a party seeks to introduce the testimony of a witness who has previously been hypnotized, that party is required to: (1) advise the court of the existence of the hypnosis; (2) show that the testimony to be presented was established and existed prior to the hypnosis; and (3) demonstrate that the hypnotist was trained in the process and was neutral. In turn, the court must instruct the jury that the witness had been hypnotized and that they should receive the testimony with caution. *Commonwealth v. Robinson*, 581 Pa. 154, 864 A.2d 460 (2004); *Commonwealth v. Smoyer*, 505 Pa. 83, 476 A.2d 1304 (1984). *See Commonwealth v. Nazarovitch*, 496 Pa. 97, 436 A.2d 170 (1981) (hypnotically refreshed testimony is incompetent when the witness had no present recollection of the facts prior to undergoing hypnosis.); *Commonwealth v. DiNicola*, 348 Pa. Super. 405, 502 A.2d 606 (1985) (pre-hypnosis recollection must be proven by clear and convincing evidence; methods approved include signed statements and tape recordings made prior to hypnosis).

However, there is a constitutional limit on these decisions. In *Rock v. Arkansas*, 483 U.S. 44, 107 S.Ct. 2704, 97 L.Ed.2d 37 (1987), the United States Supreme Court held that a defendant in a criminal case has a constitutional right to testify in his or her own behalf and that a per se rule that prohibited hypnotically refreshed testimony violated that right; the reliability of that testimony must be examined on a case-by-case basis. The Court stated that it was expressing no opinion concerning the testimony of witnesses other than a defendant in a criminal case. *Rock v. Arkansas*, 483 U.S. 44, 58, n.15, 107 S.Ct. 2704, 2712, n. 15, 97 L.Ed.2d 37 (1987).

Originally, 42 Pa.C.S.A. § 5912 made those convicted of perjury or subornation of perjury in a Pennsylvania court incompetent to testify in criminal cases, except in a proceeding to punish or prevent injury or violence to the convicted person's person or property. Under 42 Pa.C.S.A. § 5922, the same disqualification applies in civil cases. Later,

42 Pa.C.S.A. § 5912 was amended by the Act of April 22, 1993, P.L. 2, No. 2, so that those convicted of perjury or subornation of perjury are now fully competent to testify in criminal cases; the disqualification in civil cases persists.

Compare: Fed. R. Evid. 601.

Research References

Packel & Poulin, Pennsylvania Evidence §§ 601-1–601-8 (4th ed. 2013)

McCormick, Evidence Chapter 7 (7th ed. 2013)

COMPOUND QUESTION

See: Pa.R.E. 611(a).

Objection

- Objection. Compound question
- Objection. Counsel is asking two questions at the same time.

Response

- I withdraw the question and will ask separate questions.

Pennsylvania Law

Pa.R.E. 611(a) provides that the court shall exercise reasonable control over the mode of interrogating witnesses. A multiple or compound question presents two or more questions within a single question. It is objectionable because the answer will usually be ambiguous. An example of a compound question is, "Did you go to the Red Sox game that afternoon and the Boston College-North Carolina game that evening?" If only one of the two facts in the compound question is true, neither a "yes" nor a "no" answer will be accurate. Answers to multiple or compound questions, which sometimes seem straightforward and understandable in the courtroom, can become extremely confusing when reviewing the record.

Compare: Fed. R. Evid. 611(a).

Research Reference

Haydock and Sonsteng, Trial: Advocacy Before Judges, Jurors and Arbitrators Chapter 5, § 5.7 (4th ed. 2011)

CONTINUING OBJECTION

See: Pa.R.E. 103(a)(1).

Form

- I object to all of the testimony concerning this witness's identification of Exhibit 5 on grounds that [*here state specific grounds*].

- Your Honor, may the record show my continuing objection to all testimony concerning this witness's identification of Exhibit 5 on grounds that [*here state specific grounds*].

Pennsylvania Law

Where an objection has been overruled and the trial court clearly indicates that its ruling will apply to all questions on the same matter, the objecting attorney should consider making a "continuing" objection to every subsequent question and answer on the same subject. *Cominsky v. Donovan*, 846 A.2d 1256 (Pa. Super. 2004) (it is not required that counsel disrupt trial with repeated objections when trial court has rejected earlier challenges to testimony); *Dietrich v. J.I. Case Co.*, 390 Pa. Super. 475, 568 A.2d 1272 (1990) (objection made when jury charge was first given did not have to be repeated on recharge); *Matsko v. Harley Davidson Motor Co.*, 325 Pa. Super. 452, 473 A.2d 155, 159 (1984) ("once an objection has been properly made, counsel is not obliged to repeatedly voice objections . . ."). A continuing objection eliminates the need for the attorney to object repeatedly after each question or answer, which may annoy the judge and/or jury. On this latter point, see, e.g. *Vito v. Vito*, 380 Pa. Super. 258, 551 A.2d 573 (1988).

However, because Pennsylvania law requires a timely and specific objection at the proper stage in the questioning of a witness, Pa.R.E. 103(a)(1); *Commonwealth v. U.S. Mineral Products*, 956 A.2d 967 (Pa. 2008); *Commonwealth v. Montalvo*, 956

A.2d 926 (Pa. 2008); *Commonwealth v. Reaves*, 923 A.2d 1119 (Pa. 2007); *McManamon v. Washko*, 906 A.2d 1259 (Pa. Super. 2006), reliance on only a general request "for a continuing objection" or a general objection "to this entire line of questioning" may be insufficient to preserve all grounds of objection for appeal. The lawyer must initially define the scope of the continuing objection as precisely as possible, and must be alert to any additional grounds for objection that arise during subsequent testimony. If another ground becomes apparent during the line of questioning, that ground must also be stated to create an adequate record for appeal.

In the absence of state appellate decisions, federal law can be instructive. *See, e.g., United States v. Gomez-Norena*, 908 F.2d 497 (9th Cir.1990) (specific objection protects record to extent of grounds specified and no further); *United States v. Ladd*, 885 F.2d 954 (1st Cir.1989) (party may argue violation of Rule 403 on appeal because it posited continuing objection on basis of that particular rule); *United States v. Verrusio*, 803 F.2d 885 (7th Cir.1986) (continuing objection on hearsay grounds would preserve appeal of admission of subsequent hearsay statements); *United States v. Marshall*, 762 F.2d 419, 425 (5th Cir.1985) (overruling of timely specific objection amounted to continuing objection, thereby preserving right of appeal for "subsequent evidence admitted within the scope of the ruling") (*citing* 21 Wright & Graham, Federal Practice and Procedure § 5037 at 191–92 (1977); *United States v. Gillette*, 189 F.2d 449 (2d Cir.1951) (party may not rely on continuing objection lodged on one evidentiary ground to argue different ground on appeal)).

Research References

Packel & Poulin, Pennsylvania Evidence § 103-2 (4th ed. 2013)

McCormick, Evidence § 52 (7th ed. 2013)

Haydock and Sonsteng, Trial: Advocacy Before Judges, Jurors and Arbitrators Chapter 5, § 5.3 (4th ed. 2011)

CUMULATIVE

See: Pa.R.E. 403, 611(a).

Objection

- Objection. This evidence is cumulative. The matter has been covered by [*e.g., three other witnesses/six other exhibits*].

Response

- The evidence will add important details to the evidence already admitted.
- It is not improperly cumulative because corroborative evidence from additional sources is needed to buttress the facts being proved.

Pennsylvania Law

Cumulative evidence is repetitious evidence, *Commonwealth v. Bruner*, 388 Pa. Super. 82, 564 A.2d 1277 (1989), and may properly be excluded by the trial court. *Commonwealth v. Bridges*, 563 Pa. 1, 757 A.2d 859 (2000); *Commonwealth v. Flamer*, 53 A.3d 82 (Pa. Super. 2012) (cumulative evidence is additional evidence of the same character as existing evidence and that supports a fact established by the existing evidence). Whether to exclude repetitive testimony is a matter within the discretion of the trial court. Pa.R.E. 403; *Commonwealth v. Smith*, 548 Pa. 65, 694 A.2d 1086 (1997); *Commonwealth v. Africa*, 524 Pa. 118, 569 A.2d 920 (1990); *Whitaker v. Frankford Hosp.*, 984 A.2d 512 (Pa. Super. 2009); *Commonwealth v. Leighow*, 413 Pa. Super. 372, 605 A.2d 405 (1992); *Leaphart v. Whiting Corp.*, 387 Pa. Super. 253, 564 A.2d 165 (1989). Cf. *Commonwealth v. Hicks*, 91 A.3d 47 (Pa. 2014) (pre-trial ruling that testimony of specific witnesses was cumulative was reversible error; the balancing test of Rule 403 is a trial-oriented rule and such evaluation generally should be deterred until there is a sufficient trial record). If the evidence is important, however, more witnesses or exhibits may relate to some facts without being cumulative. But when many witnesses testify to the same event or when many nearly identical exhibits are offered, they serve no useful purpose and are therefore cumulative. *Baker v. Morjon, Inc.*, 393 Pa. Super. 409, 574 A.2d 676 (1990); *Commonwealth v. Bruner*, 388 Pa. Super. 82, 564 A.2d 1277 (1989).

Cases illustrating the foregoing principles include: *Commonwealth v. Watkins*, 108 A.3d 692 (Pa. 2014) (the fact that medical examiner testified to the nature of the victim's injuries and cause of death does not make photographs of the victim duplicative); *Commonwealth v. Walsh*, 36 A.3d 613 (Pa. Super. 2012) (limiting the number of witnesses whose testimony is similar or cumulative); *Commonwealth v. Robinson*, 834 A.2d 1160 (Pa. Super. 2003) (where deaf mute defendant testified he did not understand police instructions at sobriety checkpoint, proposed testimony by sign language expert that instructions were not understood was properly excluded as cumulative); *Commonwealth v. Conde*, 822 A.2d 45 (Pa. Super. 2003) (trial court entitled to limit scope of cross-examination to prevent cumulative testimony); *Oxford Presbyterian Church v. Weil-McLain Co., Inc.*, 815 A.2d 1094 (Pa. Super. 2003) (fireman's testimony about church fire not cumulative of expert; former had unique perspective of firefighter while expert focused on discrediting church's explanation about source of fire).

Compare: Fed. R. Evid. 403 and 611(a).

Research References

Packel & Poulin, Pennsylvania Evidence § 403-1 (4th ed. 2013)

McCormick, Evidence § 185 (7th ed. 2013)

CURATIVE (CAUTIONARY) INSTRUCTIONS

See: Pa.R.E. 611(a).

Form

- I move to strike the [*statement*] [*answer*] of this witness on grounds [*state specific reason*]. I further ask the Court to instruct the jury to disregard this testimony and to caution them not to consider it for any purpose in this case.

Pennsylvania Law

During the trial, the judge will give curative instructions (also referred to as cautionary instructions) to the jury after an inappropriate event has occurred, after some inadmissible evidence has been improperly referred to, or after trial misconduct. While such instructions can be given on the judge's own initiative, counsel bears the primary responsibility for insuring that error is cured in the manner most advantageous to his client. *See, e.g., Commonwealth v. Kemp*, 562 Pa. 154, 753 A.2d 1278 (2000) (counsel requested instruction be given at end of trial, rather than immediately, so that further attention would not be drawn to objectionable testimony). A curative instruction to the jury, explaining that inadmissible evidence cannot be considered in reaching its verdict, may be used in connection with or independent of a motion to strike.

It has been repeatedly held that a mistrial is not necessary where cautionary instructions are adequate to overcome prejudice. *Commonwealth v. Cash*, 137 A.3d 1262 (Pa. 2016); *Commonwealth v. Bryant*, 67 A.3d 716 (Pa. 2013); *Commonwealth v. Dennis*, 552 Pa. 331, 715 A.2d 404 (1998); *Commonwealth v. Lawson*, 519 Pa. 175, 546 A.2d 589 (1988); *Commonwealth v. Anderson*, 501 Pa. 275, 461 A.2d 208 (1983); *Commonwealth v. Brooker*, 103 A.3d 325 (Pa. Super. 2014); *Commonwealth v.*

Fletcher, 41 A.3d 892 (Pa. Super. 2012).

Prompt curative instructions have been found effective in numerous kinds of occurrences, including: emotional outbursts in the courtroom, *Commonwealth v. Philistin*, 565 Pa. 455, 774 A.2d 741 (2001); *Commonwealth v. Melendez-Rodriguez*, 856 A.2d 1278 (Pa. Super. 2004); reference to unrelated prior criminal activity, *Commonwealth v. Nichols*, 485 Pa. 1, 400 A.2d 1281 (1979); *Commonwealth v. McEachin*, 371 Pa. Super. 188, 537 A.2d 883 (1988); reference to inadmissible evidence, *Mt. Olivet Tabernacle Church v. Edwin L. Wiegand Div.*, 781 A.2d 1263 (Pa. Super. 2001), appeal granted 568 Pa. 739, 798 A.2d 1290 (2002), and order aff'd 571 Pa. 60, 811 A.2d 565 (2002); reference to accused's silence while in police custody, *Commonwealth v. Pearson*, 454 Pa. Super. 313, 685 A.2d 551 (1996); prosecutorial misconduct, *Commonwealth v. Brown*, 925 A.2d 147 (Pa. 2007); *Commonwealth v. Green*, 525 Pa. 424, 581 A.2d 544 (1990); *Commonwealth v. Rivera*, 939 A.2d 355 (Pa. Super. 2007); overly emotional closing argument, *Commonwealth v. Jones*, 530 Pa. 591, 610 A.2d 931 (1992); unfair comment on facts not offered into evidence, *Commonwealth v. Zook*, 532 Pa. 79, 615 A.2d 1 (1992); and counsel's expression of personal opinion about facts in dispute and witness credibility, *Commonwealth v. Young*, 524 Pa. 373, 572 A.2d 1217 (1990).

Pennsylvania courts have long recognized that evidence of prior criminal acts has the potential for misunderstanding on the part of the jury. *Commonwealth v. Richter*, 711 A.2d 464 (Pa. 1998); *Commonwealth v. Chapman*, 763 A.2d 895, 899 (n.4 (Pa. Super. 2000). As a result, such evidence must be accompanied by a cautionary instruction which fully and carefully explains to the jury the limited purpose for which that evidence has been admitted. *Commonwealth v. Claypool*, 495 A.2d 176 (Pa. 1985); *Commonwealth v. Page*, 965 A.2d 1212 (Pa. Super. 2009).

In *Commonwealth v. Aaron*, 419 Pa. Super. 470, 615 A.2d 735 (1992), the trial court issued a strong cautionary instruction to the jury to disregard a witness' statement concerning the victim's veracity. There the jury was told:

> You took the oath as jurors that you would follow my instructions and follow the law, and sometimes, it's very hard to disregard something that you may have heard or picked up. If I tell you to disregard it, you must disregard it. This witness, with all due respect to her and her profession, used the word—the child testified or stated something truthfully. She's unable to do that and you should not consider that under any circumstances . . . . It is not to be considered by you in any way, shape or form that that statement was made to her in a truthful fashion. There are limitations and we would very strictly instruct you to do that. I can't caution you enough. Everyone is entitled to a fair trial and if you disregard that instruction, you are not giving the defendant a fair trial . . . . Again, please follow those instructions. I know it's difficult, but you must do that.

Commonwealth v. Aaron, 419 Pa. Super. 470, 479–480, 615 A.2d 735, 739–740 (1992).

Failure to request a cautionary instruction will constitute a waiver, *Tagnani v. Lew*, 493 Pa. 371, 426 A.2d 595 (1981); *Commonwealth v. Strunk*, 953 A.2d 577 (Pa. Super. 2008); *Commonwealth v. Schoff*, 911 A.2d 147 (Pa. Super. 2006) (failure to request a cautionary instruction upon the introduction of evidence constitutes a waiver of a claim of trial error in failing to issue a cautionary instruction), as will refusal to accept a cautionary instruction in cases where the cautionary instruction would be an adequate cure. *Commonwealth v. Young*, 578 Pa. 71, 74 849 A.2d 1152, 1154 n.2 (Pa. 2004); *Commonwealth v. Kingsley*, 480 Pa. 560, 391 A.2d 1027 (1978); *Commonwealth v. Miller*, 333 Pa. Super. 58, 481 A.2d 1221 (1984). Where error cannot be cured by a cautionary instruction, the court should grant a mistrial if there is a timely request. *Commonwealth v. Brown*, 134 A.3d 1097 (Pa.

Super. 2016); *Maya v. Johnson and Johnson*, 97 A.3d 1203 (Pa. Super. 2014). For cases in which curative instructions could not or did not remedy the harm, *see Commonwealth v. Balodis*, 560 Pa. 567, 747 A.2d 341 (2000) (cautionary instructions could not cure impact of improper expert testimony describing general characteristics of child victims of sexual abuse); *Deeds v. University of Pa. Medical Center*, 110 A.3d 1009, 1014 (Pa. Super. 2015) (in her highly improper closing, defense counsel suggested plaintiff's medical needs were being met by insurance, making a damages award unnecessary; "[t]he ink was in the milk; we cannot now extract it through magic or chemistry."); *Commonwealth v. Brown*, 853 A.2d 1029, 1037 (Pa. Super. 2004) (use of defendant's name in prosecutor's closing argument in context of discussing evidence from non-testifying defendant's confession that implicated defendant in shooting violated confrontation rights and could not be cured by cautionary instruction; "No cautionary instruction could adequately serve to unring the bell that was so clearly sounded in this case.").

Compare: Fed. R. Evid. 611(a).

Research References

Packel & Poulin, Pennsylvania Evidence § 123 (4th ed. 2013)

McCormick, Evidence, § 4 (7th ed. 2013)

DEAD MAN'S ACT

See: Pa.R.E. 601(a).

Objection

- Objection. The Dead Man's Act, 42 Pa.C.S.A. § 5930, prohibits this testimony.

Response

- The witness does not have an interest adverse to the decedent and, therefore, is not incompetent to testify; or
- The Act does not prohibit written evidence; or
- The Act was waived by [*pretrial discovery*] [*offering decedent's deposition testimony into evidence*] [*calling the adverse party as on cross-examination*] [*cross-examination about matters occurring during decedent's lifetime*].

Pennsylvania Law

Pa.R.E. 601(a) provides that every person is competent to be a witness except as otherwise provided by statute. The Dead Man's Act disqualifies surviving parties to a transaction or event who have an interest adverse to the decedent from testifying as to matters which occurred *prior* to the decedent's death. *In re Matthews' Estate*, 431 Pa. 616, 246 A.2d 412 (1968); *ELK Mountain Ski Resort v. WCAB*, 114 A.3d 27 (Pa.Cmwlth. 2015). 42 Pa.C.S.A. § 5930 provides in part:

> . . . in any civil action or proceeding, where any party to a thing or contract in action is dead . . . and his right thereto or therein has passed . . . to a party on the record who represents his interest in the subject in controversy, neither any surviving or remaining party to such thing or contract, nor any other person whose interest shall be adverse to the said right of such deceased . . . shall be a competent witness to any matter occurring before the death of said party . . .

The Dead Man's Act is an exception to the general rule of evidence in Pennsylvania that: "no interest or policy of law . . . shall make any person incompetent as a witness." 42 Pa.C.S.A. § 5921. The purpose of the Act is to prevent the injustice that may result from permitting a surviving party to a transaction or occurrence to give testimony favorable to himself and adverse to the decedent, which the decedent's representative would be in no position to refute by reason of the decedent's death. *Schroeder v. Jaquiss*, 861 A.2d 885 (Pa. 2004); *In re Estate of Hall*, 517 Pa. 115, 535 A.2d 47 (1987); *In re Fiedler*, 132 A.3d 1010 (Pa. Super. 2016); *In re Estate of Snyder*, 13 A.3d 509 (2011); *In re Estate of Petro*, 694 A.2d 627 (Pa. Super. 1997).

Under the Dead Man's Act, three conditions must exist before the surviving party or witness is disqualified: (1) the deceased must have had an actual right or interest in the matter at issue, i.e. an interest in the immediate result of the suit; (2) the interest of the witness—not simply the testimony—must be adverse; and (3) a right of the deceased must have passed to a party of record who represents the deceased's interest. *In re Hendrickson's Estate*, 388 Pa. 39, 130 A.2d 143 (1957); *Punxsutawney Mun. Airport Auth. v. Lellock*, 745 A.2d 666 (Pa. Super. 2000); *Olson v. North American Indus. Supply, Inc.*, 441 Pa. Super. 598, 658 A.2d 358 (1995); *Larkin v. Metz*, 398 Pa. Super. 235, 580 A.2d 1150 (1990). An adverse interest exists when the witness will either gain or lose as the direct legal operation and effect of the judgment. *In re Estate of Gelb*, 425 Pa. 117, 228 A.2d 367 (1967); *Gibbs v. Herman*, 714 A.2d 432 (Pa. Super. 1998).

The Dead Man's Act applies only to oral testimony. Written evidence offered by an adverse surviving party is not rendered incompetent by the Act and is admissible. *In re Estate of Rider*, 487 Pa. 373, 409 A.2d 397 (1979); *Rauenzahn v. Sigman*, 376 Pa. 26, 101 A.2d 688 (1954); *Larkin v. Metz*, 398 Pa. Super. 235, 580 A.2d 1150 (1990).

The protection of the Dead Man's Act is waived and the adverse party becomes competent to testify when the decedent's personal representative:

1. Conducts pretrial discovery against the adverse party by deposition, interrogatories or document production. *Anderson v. Hughes*, 417 Pa. 87, 208 A.2d 789 (1965); *Perlis v. Kuhns*, 202 Pa. Super. 80, 195 A.2d 156 (1963); *Moss v. Klebanoff*, 44 Pa. D. & C.2d 142 (1967).

2. Offers the decedent's deposition into evidence. *Rosche v. McCoy*, 397 Pa. 615, 156 A.2d 307 (1959).

3. Calls the adverse party as on cross-examination. 42 Pa.C.S.A. § 5932.

4. Cross-examines the survivor about matters occurring during the decedent's lifetime where the survivor had testified in his own behalf only as to matters occurring since the death of the decedent. *Estate of Kofsky*, 487 Pa. 473, 409 A.2d 1358 (1979).

Where discovery proceedings were commenced against the adverse party prior to decedent's death, the Act is also waived even though this evidence is not used at trial. *Schroeder v. Jaquiss*, 861 A.2d 885 (Pa. 2004); *Brown v. Saladoff*, 209 Pa. Super. 263, 228 A.2d 205 (1967). The devisavit vel non exception to the Act provides that witnesses are competent to testify in disputes arising over the passage of property through will or intestacy, although their testimony might otherwise be rendered incompetent through operation of the general rule. *In re Estate of McClain*, 481 Pa. 435, 392 A.2d 1371 (1978); *In re Estate of Janosky*, 827 A.2d 512 (Pa. Super. 2003); *In re Estate of Gadiparthi*, 158 Pa. Cmwlth. 537, 632 A.2d 942 (1993). The exception applies to disputes involving the transfer of a decedent's estate both by operation of law or by will and renders competent all witnesses claiming decedent's property by reason of his death. *In re Estate of Gadiparthi*, 158 Pa. Cmwlth. 537, 632 A.2d 942 (1993).

Research References

Packel & Poulin, Pennsylvania Evidence § 601-7

(4th ed. 2013)

McCormick, Evidence § 65 (7th ed. 2013)

DISCOVERY RULES: FAILURE TO COMPLY (CIVIL CASES)

See: Pa.R.Civ.P. 4019.

Objection

- Objection. [*Plaintiff*] [*Defendant*] failed to disclose the existence of this [*evidence*] [*witness*] during pretrial discovery despite our formal requests for disclosure. I respectfully request the [*evidence be excluded*] [*witness be precluded from testifying*].

Response

- There is no prejudice, surprise or bad faith [*citing specifics*]. If the court is persuaded [*plaintiff*] [*defendant*] is entitled to some additional time to meet this evidence, then I would respectfully request that a continuance be granted with trial to resume in two days.

Pennsylvania Law

Pa.R.Civ.P. 4019 permits the court to impose sanctions for failure to comply with pretrial discovery rules. Section 4019(c)(2) authorizes the court to issue:

> an order refusing to allow the disobedient party to support or oppose designated claims or defenses, or prohibiting him from introducing in evidence designated documents, things or testimony, or from introducing evidence of physical or mental condition[.]

Rule 4019 envisions a procedure by which the court, when confronted with a failure or refusal to provide discovery, will exercise judicial discretion to formulate an appropriate sanction order. This requires the court to select a punishment which "fits the crime." *Hein v. Hein*, 717 A.2d 1053 (Pa. Super. 1998); *Brunetti v. Southeastern Pennsylvania Transp. Auth.*, 329 Pa. Super. 477, 478 A.2d 889 (1984).

Since dismissal is the most severe sanction, it should be imposed only in extreme circumstances, and a trial court is required to balance the equities carefully and dismiss only where the violation of the discovery rules is willful and the opposing party has been prejudiced. *Calderaio v. Ross*, 395 Pa. 196, 150 A.2d 110 (1959) (courts highly disfavor dismissal of an action as a sanction for discovery violations absent the most extreme of circumstances); *Pride Contracting Inc. v. Biehn Constr., Inc.*, 553 A.2d 82 (Pa. Super. 1989); *Jetson Direct Mail Services, Inc. v. Department of Labor*, 782 A.2d 631 (Pa.Cmwlth.2001). The following factors are to be weighed: the nature and severity of the discovery violation; the defaulting party's willfulness or bad faith; prejudice to the opposing party; the ability to cure prejudice; and the importance of the precluded evidence in light of the failure to comply. *King v. Pittsburgh Water & Sewer Authority*, 139 A.3d 336 (Pa.Cmwlth. 2016); *Rohm and Haas Co. v. Lin*, 992 A.2d 132 (Pa. Super. 2010); *Cove Centre, Inc. v. Westhafer Const., Inc.*, 965 A.2d 259 (Pa. Super. 2009); *Estate of Ghaner v. Bindi*, 779 A.2d 585 (Pa. Super. 2001); *Grandelli v. Methodist Hosp.*, 777 A.2d 1138 (Pa. Super. 2001).

Cases upholding particular sanctions at trial suggest the importance of demonstrating prejudice, unfair surprise or bad faith. *See Smith v. SEPTA*, 913 A.2d 338 (Pa.Cmwlth. 2006) (excluding expert testimony for failure to comply with disclosure requirements of Pa.R.C.P. 4003.5); *Philadelphia Contributionship Ins. Co. v. Shapiro*, 798 A.2d 781 (Pa. Super. 2002) (dismissal appropriate where plaintiff's dilatory conduct during sixteen-month period prejudiced defendant's ability to defend against claims); *Bindschusz v. Phillips*, 771 A.2d 803 (Pa. Super. 2001) (excluding undisclosed surveillance film); *Crance v. Sohanic*, 344 Pa. Super. 526, 496 A.2d 1230 (1985) (document produced on first day of trial properly excluded given deliberate or careless failure to produce during discovery); *Breslin by Breslin v. Ridarelli*, 308 Pa. Super. 179, 454 A.2d 80 (1982) (witness who failed to appear for deposition not permitted to testify at trial); *Stern v. Vic Snyder, Inc.*, 325 Pa. Super. 423, 473 A.2d 139 (1984) (defendant estopped from introducing financial information which had been shielded from discovery by protective order); *Jewelcor Jewelers and Distributors, Inc. v. Corr*, 373 Pa. Super. 536, 542 A.2d 72 (1988) (testimony of expert witness excluded where first notice was given during trial, three days before he was scheduled to testify).

Where a sanction is disproportionate in terms of the offense and its impact, it will not be upheld. *See, e.g., Philadelphia v. FOP Lodge 5 (Breary)*, 985 A.2d 1259 (Pa. 2009) (arbitrator's discovery sanction precluding City from presenting its case-in-chief violated City's procedural due process rights); *Griffin v. Tedesco*, 355 Pa. Super. 475, 513 A.2d 1020 (1986) (error to preclude damages evidence where there was no prior order compelling production of documents related to damages); *Brunetti v. Southeastern Pennsylvania Transp. Auth.*, 329 Pa. Super. 477, 478 A.2d 889 (1984) (sanction which prohibited plaintiff from presenting testimony on issue of damages is inappropriate when defendant sought and failed to receive discovery information related solely to liability); *Tri-State Asphalt Corp. v. Dept. of Transp.*, 875 A.2d 1199 (Pa. Cmwlth. 2005) (dismissal by Bd. of Claims manifestly unreasonable without hearing or order compelling interrogatory answers).

A party's belief that a court's discovery orders are wrong does not justify or excuse its violation of those orders. Such defiance is a direct affront to the authority of the trial court and to the integrity of the judicial system and rule of law. *See, 6 Standard Pa. Practice 2d*, 34:85 p. 441, citing *Luszczynski v. Bradley*, 729 A.2d 83 (Pa. Super. 1999).

Compare: Fed. R. Civ. P. 37.

Research References

Packel & Poulin, Pennsylvania Evidence § 437-1 (4th ed. 2013)

Gibbons, *Pennsylvania Discovery Practice* Chapter 15, Sanctions

Gibbons, Kraut & Edgar, West's Pennsylvania Forms and Commentary—Civil Procedure Chapter 47, Sanctions.

DISCOVERY RULES: FAILURE TO COMPLY (CRIMINAL CASES)

See: Pa.R.Crim.P. 573.

Objection

- Objection. The [*Commonwealth / Defendant*] failed to disclose the existence of this evidence during pre-trial discovery despite our request for any such evidence.

Response

- This evidence was not material to the issue of guilt or innocence and its relevance could not reasonably have been anticipated.

Pennsylvania Law

Rule 573 of the Pennsylvania Rules of Criminal Procedure details the discovery materials to which a defendant is entitled, both as a matter of right and at the discretion of the court. Rule 573(B)(1) provides in pertinent part:

(1) Mandatory. In all court cases, on request by the defendant, and subject to any protective order which the Commonwealth might obtain under this rule, the Commonwealth shall disclose to the defendant's attorney all of the following requested items or information, provided they are material to the instant case. The Commonwealth shall, when applicable, permit the defendant's attorney to inspect and copy or photograph such items.

    (a) Any evidence favorable to the accused that is material either to guilt or to punishment, and which is within the possession or control of the attorney for the Commonwealth;

    (b) any written confession or inculpatory statement, or the substance of any oral confession or inculpatory statement, and the identity of the person to whom the confession or inculpatory statement was made, that is in the possession or control of the attorney for the Commonwealth;

(c)   the defendant's prior criminal record;

(d)   the circumstances and results of any identification of the defendant by voice, photograph, or in-person identification;

(e)   results or reports of scientific tests, expert opinions, and written or recorded reports of polygraph examinations or other physical or mental examinations of the defendant, that are within the possession or control of the attorney for the Commonwealth;

(f)   any tangible objects, including documents, photographs, fingerprints, or other tangible evidence;

(g)   the transcripts and recordings of any electronic surveillance, and the authority by which the said transcripts and recordings were obtained.

The purpose of the criminal discovery rules is to permit the parties in a criminal matter to be prepared for trial. Trial by ambush is contrary to the spirit and letter of those rules. *Commonwealth v. Moose*, 529 Pa. 218, 602 A.2d 1265 (1992). Under Rule 573 B(1), the Commonwealth is required to disclose to defense counsel all items which have been requested by a defendant provided they are material to the case. *Commonwealth v. Hudgens*, 400 Pa. Super. 79, 582 A.2d 1352 (1990). A similar obligation is imposed on defendants. Rule 573(C). See, *e.g., Commonwealth v. Pagan*, 950 A.2d 270 (Pa. 2008); *Commonwealth v. Poindexter*, 435 Pa. Super. 509, 646 A.2d 1211 (1994) (affirming trial court's refusal to grant request for an alibi charge where defendant failed to provide prosecution with adequate notice of intention to pursue an alibi defense, as required by rule.)

As the Comment to Rule 573 notes, in *Brady v. Maryland*, 373 U.S. 83, 83 S.Ct. 1194, 10 L.Ed.2d 215 (1963), the Supreme Court held that due process requires disclosure by the prosecution of evidence favorable to the accused that is material to guilt or punishment. However, this duty is a constitutional requirement and does not constitute a form of pretrial discovery. *United States v. Maniktala*, 934 F.2d 25, 28 (2d Cir.1991) (*citing United States v. Starusko*, 729 F.2d 256, 262 (3d Cir.1984)); *United States v. Beasley*, 576 F.2d 626, 630 (5th Cir.1978) (*"Brady* is not a discovery rule but a rule of fairness and minimum prosecutorial obligation."); *Commonwealth v. Williams*, 86 A.3d 771 (Pa. 2014) (Brady did not create a constitutional right to broad discovery in a criminal case; the duty to disclose under Brady encompasses only exculpatory evidence, it is not a general rule of discovery); *Commonwealth v. Johnson*, 572 Pa. 283, 815 A.2d 563 (2002) (*Brady's* focus is whether prosecutor's failure to disclose material exculpatory evidence deprived defendant of fair trial.)

The basic *Brady* rules are outlined here for the convenience of bench and bar.

Under *Brady*, the prosecution has a constitutional obligation to disclose exculpatory evidence to a criminal defendant if it is "material" either to guilt or to punishment. *Brady*, 373 U.S. at 87, 83 S.Ct. at 1197; *Commonwealth v. Hutchinson*, 25 A.3d 277 (Pa. 2011); *Commonwealth v. Smith*, 985 A.2d 886 (Pa. 2009); *Commonwealth v. Cam Ly*, 980 A.2d 61 (Pa. 2009). This obligation extends to evidence that could be used to impeach a government witness, *Giglio v. United States*, 405 U.S. 150, 92 S.Ct. 763, 31 L.Ed.2d 104 (1992) (extending Brady rule to embrace certain impeaching evidence, including that which might demonstrate witness bias); *United States v. Bagley*, 473 U.S. 667, 676, 105 S.Ct. 3375, 3380, 87 L.Ed.2d 481 (1985); *Commonwealth v. Spotz*, 47 A.3d 63 (Pa. 2012); *Commonwealth v. Strong*, 563 Pa. 455, 761 A.2d 1167 (2000), and to evidence that was not requested by the defense. *Bagley*, supra; *Commonwealth v. Counterman*, 553 Pa. 370, 719 A.2d 284 (1998) (for purposes of evaluating a claim under *Brady*, there is no distinction between evidence that exculpates and evidence that impeaches.) Evidence is material if "there is a reasonable probability that, had the evidence been disclosed to the defense, the result of the proceeding would have been different. *Commonwealth v. Abdul-Salaam*, 42 A.3d 983 (Pa. 2012); *Commonwealth v. Small*, 980 A.2d 549 (Pa. 2009). A 'reasonable probability' is a probability sufficient to undermine confidence in the outcome." *Bagley*, 473 U.S. at 682, 105 S.Ct. at 3383; *see also Kyles v. Whitley*, 514 U.S. 419, 434, 115 S.Ct. 1555, 1565, 131 L.Ed.2d 490 (1995); *Commonwealth v. Dennis*, 17 A.3d 297 (Pa. 2011); *Commonwealth v. Paddy*, 15 A.3d 431 (Pa. 2011); *Commonwealth v. Ferguson*, 866 A.2d 403 (Pa. Super. 2004). The final determination of materiality is based on the "supposed evidence considered collectively, not item by item." *Kyles*, 514 U.S. at 436–437, 115 S.Ct. at 1567. The prosecution's *Brady* obligation extends to exculpatory evidence in the files of police agencies of the same government bringing the prosecution. *Commonwealth v. Watkins*, 108 A.3d 692 (Pa. 2014) (Commonwealth prosecutors are not responsible to secure and disclose information had by federal authorities); *Commonwealth v. Weiss*, 81 A.3d 767 (Pa. 2013); *Commonwealth v. Miller*, 987 A.2d 638 (Pa. 2009) (no *Brady* violation where unproduced report with impeachment value was in the possession of an agency not involved in defendant's prosecution); *Commonwealth v. Gibson*, 951 A.2d 1110 (Pa. 2008); *Commonwealth v. Lambert*, 584 Pa. 461, 884 A.2d 848 (2005).

Any implication, promise or understanding that the government would extend leniency in exchange for a witness' testimony is relevant to the witness' credibility. Thus the Commonwealth may commit a *Brady* violation by withholding evidence of such a promise or understanding. *Giglio v. United States*, supra; *Commonwealth v. Kinard*, 95 A.3d 279 (Pa. Super. 2014).

For a defendant to establish a *Brady* violation, he must show that: (1) the evidence was suppressed by the State, either willfully or inadvertently; (2) the evidence at issue (whether exculpatory or impeaching) is favorable to the defendant; and (3) the evidence was material, meaning that prejudice must have ensued. *Strickler v. Greene*, 527 U.S. 263, 119 S.Ct. 1936, 144 L.Ed.2d 286 (1999); *Commonwealth v. Blakeney*, 108 A.3d 739 (Pa. 2014); *Commonwealth v. Daniels*, 104 A.3d 267 (Pa. 2014); *Commonwealth v. Tharp*, 101 A.3d 736 (Pa. 2014); *Commonwealth v. Koehler*, 36 A.3d 121 (Pa. 2012); *Commonwealth v. Lesko*, 15 A.3d 345 (Pa. 2011); *Commonwealth v. Lambert*, supra (evidence sought under *Brady* must be material and admissible); *accord, Commonwealth v. Dennis*, 950 A.2d 945 (Pa. 2008); *Commonwealth v. Robinson*, 581 Pa. 154, 864 A.2d 460 (2004); *Commonwealth v. Bryant*, 579 Pa. 119, 855 A.2d 726 (2004). "The mere possibility that an item of undisclosed information might have helped the defense, or might have affected the outcome of the trial, does not establish materiality in the constitutional sense." *United States v. Agurs*, 427 U.S. 97, 109–110, 96 S.Ct. 2392, 2400–2401, 49 L.Ed.2d 342 (1976); *In Re Lokuta*, 11 A.3d 427 (Pa. 2011); *Commonwealth v. Bond*, 985 A.2d 810 (Pa. 2009); *Commonwealth v. Tedford*, 960 A.2d 1 (Pa. 2008).

Brady does not grant a criminal defendant unfettered access to the Commonwealth's files. *See Commonwealth v. Edmiston*, 578 Pa. 284, 851 A.2d 883, 887 n.3 (2004) (defendant has no general right under the Constitution or *Brady* to search Commonwealth files); *Commonwealth v. Williams*, 557 Pa. 207, 732 A.2d 1167 (1999) (the Commonwealth is, in the first instance, the judge of what information must be disclosed; defense counsel has no constitutional right to conduct his own search of state's files to argue relevance); *Commonwealth v. Feese*, 79 A.3d 1101 (Pa. Super. 2013).

No *Brady* violation occurs where the parties

had equal access to the information or if the defendant knew or could have uncovered such evidence with reasonable diligence. *Commonwealth v. Treiber*, 121 A.3d 435 (Pa. 2015); *Commonwealth v. Chamberlain*, 30 A.3d 381 (Pa. 2011); *Commonwealth v. Smith*, 17 A.3d 873 (Pa. 2011); *Commonwealth v. Sattazahn*, 952 A.2d 640 (Pa. 2008).

When a party has failed to comply with Rule 573, the trial court has broad discretion in choosing an appropriate remedy. *Commonwealth v. Causey*, 833 A.2d 165 (Pa. Super. 2003). In this regard, Rule 573(E) states:

> If at any time during the course of the proceedings it is brought to the attention of the court that a party has failed to comply with this rule, the court may order such party to permit discovery or inspection, may grant a continuance, *or may prohibit such party from introducing evidence not disclosed*, other than testimony of the defendant, or it may enter such other order as it deems just under the circumstances.

See Commonwealth v. Deans, 530 Pa. 514, 610 A.2d 32 (1992) (where Commonwealth lost alleged forged lottery ticket before defense had opportunity to examine it, Due Process Clause prohibits Commonwealth from introducing expert testimony concerning lost ticket); *Commonwealth v. Wade*, 867 A.2d 547 (Pa. Super. 2005) (Commonwealth could not use evidence excluded from case-in-chief due to discovery violation in rebuttal case); *Commonwealth v. Galloway*, 302 Pa. Super. 145, 448 A.2d 568 (1982) (exclusion of evidence may be modified if defendant not prejudiced); *Commonwealth v. Smith*, 410 Pa. Super. 384, 599 A.2d 1350 (1991) (court abused discretion by suppressing DNA test results rather than granting continuance where Commonwealth received the results shortly before trial and promptly disclosed them to defense); *Commonwealth v. Crossley*, 439 Pa. Super. 342, 653 A.2d 1288 (1995) (suppression of witness testimony not warranted by late production of statement; continuance would be sufficient); *Commonwealth v. Simmons*, 541 Pa. 211, 662 A.2d 621 (1995) (no prejudice by delay in producing evidence); *Commonwealth v. Brown*, 544 Pa. 406, 676 A.2d 1178 (1996) (continuance during trial was appropriate remedy where Commonwealth did not disclose identity of eyewitness earlier because of protective order it had obtained); *Commonwealth v. Counterman*, 553 Pa. 370, 719 A.2d 284 (1998) (mistrial is required only when discovery violation is of such a nature as to deprive defendant of fair trial).

The remedy of dismissal is appropriate only in extreme circumstances. *Commonwealth v. Burke*, 566 Pa. 402, 781 A.2d 1136 (2001) (in absence of deliberate bad faith overreaching intended to provoke defendant into seeking mistrial or to deprive defendant of fair trial, proper remedy should be less severe than dismissal); *Commonwealth v. Hemingway*, 13 A.3d 491 (Pa. Super. 2011); *Commonwealth v. Smith*, 955 A.2d 391 (Pa. Super. 2008) (continuance rather than dismissal of charges against defendant would have been appropriate remedy). If the Commonwealth intentionally suppresses potentially exculpatory evidence with the intent to prejudice the accused and thereby denies him a fair trial, retrial is barred under the Double Jeopardy Clause of the Pennsylvania Constitution. *Commonwealth v. Smith*, 532 Pa. 177, 615 A.2d 321 (1992). In *Smith*, the suppressed evidence was discovered after conviction and the relief granted was dismissal rather than a new trial. The Superior Court has given *Smith* a narrow reading. *See, e.g., Commonwealth v. Moose*, 424 Pa. Super. 579, 623 A.2d 831 (1993); *Commonwealth v. Rightley*, 421 Pa. Super. 270, 617 A.2d 1289 (1992); *Commonwealth v. Santiago*, 439 Pa. Super. 447, 654 A.2d 1062 (1994). *But see Commonwealth v. Martorano*, 559 Pa. 533, 741 A.2d 1221 (1999).

Compare: Fed. R. Crim. P. 16.

Research References

Packel & Poulin, Pennsylvania Evidence § 437-3 (4th ed. 2013)

Gibbons, *Pennsylvania Discovery Practice* Chapter 20, Pretrial Discovery and Inspection in Criminal Cases.

EVIDENCE EXCLUDED BY STATUTE: ACCIDENT REPORTS AND INVESTIGATIONS

Objection

- Objection. The Vehicle Code, 75 Pa.C.S.A. § 3747(f), § 3751(b) or § 3754(b) excludes this evidence.

Response

- The evidence is admissible. We are entitled to prove constructive notice of a defective or dangerous condition by evidence of similar accidents occurring at substantially the same place and under similar circumstances. The [reports] [investigations] pertain to those prior accidents and not to the accident in question.

Pennsylvania Law

Certain provisions of the Vehicle Code (75 Pa.C.S.A. § 101 et seq.) make accident reports and investigations unavailable for subsequent use as evidence in civil and/or criminal proceedings. The rationale has been explained as follows:

> The object of the Pennsylvania Vehicle Code is to effect a safe and efficient system of motor vehicle transportation in the Commonwealth. To that end it is necessary that the Department of Transportation have an unbiased, honest and accurate body of information regarding motor vehicle accidents. The confidentiality provisions . . . were enacted to avoid the chilling effect which the subsequent use of accident information compiled would have on full and frank disclosure.

Mayfield v. PennDOT, 23 Pa. D. & C.3d 79, 81–82 (1982).

75 Pa.C.S.A. § 3747 requires the driver of a vehicle that is in an accident involving injury, death or serious damage, which a police officer does not investigate, to file an accident report with the

Department of Transportation. Subsection (f) contains the following limitations on the use of reports as evidence:

(f) *Use of reports as evidence.*—No accident reports forwarded under the provisions of this section shall be used as evidence in any trial, civil or criminal, arising out of an accident except that the department shall furnish upon demand of any party to the trial or upon demand of any court, a certificate showing that a specified accident report has or has not been made to the department in compliance with the law and, if the report has been made, the date, time and location of the accident, the names and addresses of the drivers and the owners of the vehicles involved. The reports may be used as evidence when necessary to prosecute charges filed in connection with a violation of section 3748 (relating to false reports).

75 Pa.C.S.A. § 3751 governs accident reports prepared by a local police department. Subsection (b) requires the local police department upon request to furnish copies of its report to any person involved in the accident, their attorney, insurer and to governmental bodies. It also provides that "The copy of the report shall not be admissible as evidence in any action for damages or criminal proceedings arising out of a motor vehicle accident."

It has been held that 75 Pa.C.S.A. § 3751 precludes admission of police reports only in actions arising out of the particular accident about which the report was prepared. *Phillips v. Lock*, 86 A.3d 906 (Pa. Super. 2014) (report prepared by officer who is not a witness to the accident is inadmissible hearsay); *Rox Coal Co. v. WCAB (Snizaski)*, 570 Pa. 60, 807 A.2d 906 (Pa. 2002) (nor should a party be able to get such a report into evidence in an indirect manner); *Ariondo v. Munsey*, 122 Pa.Cmwlth. 475, 553 A.2d 94 (1989) (allowing policeman to testify about similar accidents based on police reports prepared from prior accidents).

75 Pa.C.S.A. § 3754 allows PennDOT to conduct in-depth accident investigations for the

purpose of determining the causes of traffic accidents and factors which may help prevent similar types of accidents. Subsection (b) bars the use of the investigations as evidence:

(b) *Confidentiality of reports.*—Information, records and reports associated with in-depth accident investigations shall not be admissible as evidence in any legal action or other proceeding, nor shall officers or employees or the agencies charged with the procurement or custody of in-depth accident investigation records and reports be required to give evidence pertaining to anything contained in such in-depth accident investigation records or reports in any legal action or other proceeding.

In *Com., Dept. of Transp. v. Taylor*, 576 Pa. 622, 841 A.2d 108 (Pa. 2004), a vehicular homicide case, the Pennsylvania Supreme Court said that § 3754(b) was an absolute privilege, that such information is neither discoverable nor admissible in any proceeding and that the privilege did not violate constitutional due process.

In light of *Taylor*, 576 Pa. 622, 841 A.2d 108 (Pa. 2004), query the continuing vitality of *Commonwealth v. Hall*, 744 A.2d 1287 (Pa. Super. 2000) (vehicular homicide case denying motion to quash defense request for PennDOT records containing local police investigation of accident scene; local records not protected by § 3754(b)).

Compare: Federal Highway Safety Act, 23 U.S.C.A. § 409.

Research Reference

Packel & Poulin, Pennsylvania Evidence § 533 (4th ed. 2013).

EVIDENCE EXCLUDED BY STATUTE: MENTAL HEALTH RECORDS

Objection

- Objection. The Mental Health Procedures Act, 50 P.S. § 7111, excludes this evidence.

Response

- There is no response since the privilege is absolute *except* for use in involuntary and voluntary mental health commitment proceedings where the privilege does not apply.

Pennsylvania Law

In *Zane v. Friends Hospital*, 836 A.2d 25 (Pa. 2003), the Supreme Court said the expectation of confidentiality in mental health records is essential to effective mental health treatment. No psychiatric records may be revealed without the express written consent of the patient, except under limited circumstances. The Mental Health Procedures Act (MHPA), 50 P.S. § 7111 states:

All documents concerning persons in treatment shall be kept confidential and, without the person's written consent, may not be released or their contents disclosed to anyone except:

(1) those engaged in providing treatment for the person;

(2) the county administrator pursuant to § 110;

(3) a court in the course of legal proceedings authorized by this Act; and

(4) pursuant to Federal Rules, statutes and regulations governing disclosure of patient information where treatment is undertaken in a federal agency.

In no event, however, shall privileged communications, whether written or oral, be disclosed to anyone without such written consent. This shall not restrict the collection and analysis of clinical or statistical data by the county administrator or the facility so long as the use and dissemination of such data does not identify individual patients. Nothing herein shall be construed to conflict with Section 8 of the Act of April 14, 1972 (P.L. 221, No. 63), known as the "Pennsylvania Drug and Alcohol Abuse Control Act."

The Act establishes rights and procedures for all involuntary treatment of mentally ill persons, whether inpatient or outpatient, and for all voluntary inpatient treatment of mentally ill persons. 50 P.S. § 7103; *Gormley v. Edgar*, 995 A.2d 1197 (Pa. Super. 2010) (Act did not apply where treatment was voluntary and provided on an outpatient basis); *T.M. v. Elwyn, Inc.*, 950 A.2d 1050 (Pa. Super. 2008).

The Mental Health Procedures Act is to be strictly construed, *Christy Ex rel Christy v. Wordsworth-At-Shawnee*, 749 A.2d 557 (Pa. Cmwlth.2000), and is equally applicable in a child custody dispute as it is in a civil matter. *Gates v. Gates*, 967 A.2d 1024 (Pa. Super. 2009). A patient's mental health records may be used by a court only when the legal proceedings are within the framework of the MHPA, such as, involuntary and voluntary mental health commitment proceedings. *See Commonwealth v. Emmil*, 866 A.2d 420 (2005) (statutory exception allows State Police, by court order, to obtain information in connection with illegal possession of firearms); *Commonwealth v. Moyer*, 407 Pa. Super. 336, 595 A.2d 1177 (1991) (ordering a new trial in sexual assault case where defendant's mental health records were used as evidence against him); *See also, Leonard v. Latrobe Area Hosp.*, 379 Pa. Super. 243, 549 A.2d 997 (1988); *Kakas v. Commonwealth, Dept. of Pub. Welfare*, 65 Pa.Cmwlth. 550, 442 A.2d 1243 (1982) (barring pretrial discovery of mental health records); *Hahnemann Univ. Hosp. v. Edgar*, 74 F.3d 456 (3d Cir.1996) (MHPA prohibited disclosure of two patients' mental health records to third patient whom they allegedly had raped). *But see,*

Commonwealth v. Sanchez, 416 Pa. Super. 160, 610 A.2d 1020 (1992) (permitting use of psychiatric records at trial where no timely objection was made; Judge Johnson's dissent, however, states the better view).

The statutory protections may be waived if one places his mental health at issue. *Kraus v. Taylor*, 710 A.2d 1142 (Pa. Super. 1998); *Rost v. State Board of Psychology*, 659 A.2d 626 (Pa.Cmwlth. 1995). See *Octave ex rel. Octave v. Walker*, 37 A.3d 604 (Pa.Cmwlth. 2011) (plaintiff waived MHPA confidentiality by filing personal injury suit; police report said injuries occurred in an attempted suicide and mental health information was relevant to defense). The Commonwealth does not put a child's mental health at issue by requesting that a child be allowed to testify by closed-circuit television pursuant to 42 Pa.C.S.A. § 5985. *Commonwealth v. Williams*, 84 A.3d 680 (Pa. 2014).

50 P.S. § 7111 is suspended by Pennsylvania Rules of Disciplinary Enforcement, Rule 601 to the extent that it is inconsistent with the disciplinary rules. *See, e.g.*, Rule 301 requiring a formerly admitted attorney, placed on inactive status by reason of incompetency, to supply the names of his psychologist/psychiatrist together with such records as may be requested by court appointed medical experts when seeking reinstatement.

Research Reference

Packel & Poulin, Pennsylvania Evidence § 540 (4th ed. 2013)

EVIDENCE EXCLUDED BY STATUTE: OCCUPANT PROTECTION ACT (SEAT BELT LAW)

Objection

- Objection. The seat belt law, 75 Pa.C.S.A. § 4581, excludes this evidence.

Response

- The question is proper; our defense is the misuse of safety belts which is not excluded by the statute.

Pennsylvania Law

The Occupant Protection Act, 75 Pa.C.S.A. § 4581, requires that children under the age of four and front seat occupants wear safety belt/child re-straint systems. However, evidence that occupants were not wearing seat belts is inadmissible. *Gaudio v. Ford Motor Company*, 976 A.2d 524 (Pa. Super. 2009) (evidence of non-use of seat belts strictly prohibited in civil actions tried in Pennsylvania courts for any purpose); *Pulliam v. Fannie*, 850 A.2d 636 (Pa. Super. 2004) (there is no ambiguity in the statute which sets forth an absolute prohibi-tion against introduction of such evidence); *Grim v. Betz*, 539 A.2d 1365 (1988) (failure to use seat belts cannot be considered as contributory negligence and is not admissible as evidence in any civil ac-tion); *Russo v. Mazda Motor Corp.*, 1992 WL 210232 (E.D. Pa. August 17, 1992) (allowing defendant to introduce evidence of existence of seat belt system falls but a half step short of allowing defendant to introduce evidence of decedent's failure to use the seat belt system). The statute applies to both front and rear seat passengers. *Nicola v. Nicola*, 449 Pa. Super. 293, 673 A.2d 950 (1996).

75 Pa.C.S.A. § 4581 (a)(2)(e) and (f) provide:

(e) **Civil actions.**—In no event shall a violation or alleged violation of this subchapter be used as evidence in a trial of any civil action; nor shall any jury in a civil action be instructed that any conduct did constitute or could be interpreted by them to constitute a violation of this subchapter; nor shall failure to use a child passenger restraint system, child booster seat or safety seat belt system be considered as contributory negligence **nor shall failure to use such a system be admissible as evidence in the trial of any civil action**; nor shall this subchapter impose any legal obligation upon or impute any civil liability whatsoever to an owner, employer, manufacturer, dealer or person engaged in the business of renting or leasing vehicles to the public to equip a vehicle with a child passenger restraint system or child booster seat or to have such child passenger restraint system or child booster seat available whenever their vehicle may be used to transport a child.

(f) **Criminal proceedings.**—The requirements of this subchapter or evidence of a violation of this subchapter are not admissible as evidence in a criminal proceeding except in a proceeding for a violation of this subchapter. No criminal proceeding for the crime of homicide by vehicle shall be brought on the basis of noncompliance with this subchapter.

(Emphasis added.)

A constitutional challenge to this exclusion of evidence has been rejected. *Gaudio*, 976 A.2d at 538 n.6; *Dranzo v. Winterhalter*, 395 Pa. Super. 578, 577 A.2d 1349 (1990); *Carrasquilla v. Mazda Motor Corp.*, 166 F.Supp.2d 181 (M.D.Pa. 2001). Where a party was attempting to show misuse of a seat belt, the exclusionary rule has been held not to apply. *Oliver v. Metrick*, 1 Pa. D. & C.4th 628 (1988); *see also Commonwealth v. Shoup*, 423 Pa. Super. 12, 620 A.2d 15 (1993) (in prosecution for vehicular homicide and DUI, evidence that decedent failed to wear seat belt properly excluded because not relevant to establish cause of accident).

EVIDENCE EXCLUDED BY STATUTE: PEER REVIEW PROTECTION ACT

Objection

- Objection. The Peer Review Protection Act, 63 P.S. § 425.1, excludes this evidence.

Response

- The question is proper. The information was generated in the course of the hospital's routine care of patients and is outside the scope of the Peer Review Act.

Pennsylvania Law

The Peer Review Protection Act, 63 P.S. § 425.1, et seq., provides a limited privilege for the work of peer review committees in the medical field. The Act is to be strictly construed. It protects statements and documents provided exclusively to peer review committees. *Young v. Western Pennsylvania Hospital*, 722 A.2d 153 (Pa. Super. 1998); *Treible v. Lehigh Valley Hospital Inc.*, 75 Pa. D.&C. 4th 22 (Lehigh Cty. 2005); *Sanderson v. Frank S. Bryan, M.D., Ltd.*, 361 Pa. Super. 491, 522 A.2d 1138 (1987) (Act precludes medical malpractice plaintiff from discovering peer review information related to his own and other patients' cases).

The Act provides in relevant part:

The proceedings and records of a review committee shall be held in confidence and shall not be subject to discovery or introduction into evidence in any civil action against a professional health care provider arising out of the matters which are the subject of evaluation and review by such committee and no person who was in attendance at a meeting of such committee shall be permitted or required to testify in any such civil action as to any evidence or other matters produced or presented during the proceedings of such committee or as to any findings, recommendations, evaluations, opinions or other actions of such committee or any members thereof: Provided, however, That information, documents or records otherwise available from original sources are not to be construed as immune from discovery or use in any such civil action merely because they were presented during proceedings of such committee, nor should any person who testifies before such committee or who is a member of such committee be prevented from testifying as to matters within his knowledge, but the said witness cannot be asked about his testimony before such a committee or opinions formed by him as a result of said committee hearings.

63 P.S. § 425.4.

The legislative purpose of the Act was to encourage doctors, nurses and other medical care providers to frankly and confidentially inform hospital committees concerning the performance of medical professionals and hospital personnel in connection with their health care duties. *Cooper v. Delaware Valley Med. Ctr.*, 539 Pa. 620, 654 A.2d 547 (1995); *Venosh v. Henzes*, 121 A.3d 1016 (Pa. Super. 2015) (Blue Cross which sells health insurance does not provide health care services and its quality of care review process did not institute peer review); *Yocabet v. UPMC Presbyterian*, 119 A.3d 1012 (Pa. Super. 2015) (review of kidney transplant by Pa. Dept. of Health on behalf of federal government was not peer review because not conducted by a health care provider); *Piroli v. Lodico*, 909 A.2d 846 (Pa. Super. 2006) (presence of billing manager during peer review activity conducted by ambulatory care facility did not render documents related to peer review of physician discoverable). Courts have also repeatedly refused access to credentialing documents. *Dodson v. DeLeo*, 872 A.2d 1237 (Pa. Super. 2005) (documents used in determination of staff privileges are exactly the type of documents legislature intended to protect); *Troescher v. Grody*, 869 A.2d 1014 (Pa. Super. 2005) (same); *Young v. Western Pennsylvania Hosp.*, 722 A.2d 153 (Pa. Super. 1998) (Act recognizes medical profession itself is in the best position to police its own activities; granting, limiting or revoking staff privileges is one of the strongest tools the medical profession uses to police itself); *Scrima v. UPMC Mercy*, 161 PLJ 568 (Alleg. Co. Ct. Cmn Pls 2013) (case law now gives less weight to when the reports were created and by whom and more weight to the reason or purpose of their creation).

A party claiming a privilege not to disclose information has the burden of proving those facts necessary to sustain the claim of privilege. *Joe v. Prison Health Services, Inc.*, 782 A.2d 24 (Pa.Cmwlth. 2001).

The protection afforded peer review organizations is not absolute. *Hayes v. Mercy Health Corp.*, 559 Pa. 21, 739 A.2d 114 (1999) (confidentiality provision does not apply to internal hospital proceeding in which doctor challenges his own peer review process). Section 4 of the Act provides: "that information, documents or records otherwise available from original sources are not to be construed as immune from discovery or use in any . . . civil action merely because they were presented during proceedings of any such committee." 63 P.S. § 425.4. *See Cooper*, 539 Pa. at 631–632, 654 A.2d at 552–553 (Act offers no shelter to peer review participants who make false or malicious statements about doctor); *Atkins v. Pottstown Memorial Medical Center*, 430 Pa. Super. 279, 634 A.2d 258 (1993) (incident report made after patient slipped and fell in hospital bathroom not protected).

In *Hanzsek v. McDonough*, 44 Pa. D. & C.3d 639 (1987), the court interpreted the Act to mean that a document prepared solely for purposes of peer review is not discoverable. Where a document is prepared solely in connection with recording the events of the treatment of a patient, that document is an "original source," which is discoverable. *Adriansen v. Marworth*, 2 Pa. D. & C.5th 205 (Lacka Cty. 2007). But where a document prepared in the ordinary course of the hospital's routine care of patients is also reviewed for peer review purposes, it remains discoverable. The key inquiry with respect to obtaining and using or withholding a challenged document is the purpose of its preparation and its uses. *Congdon v. Lancaster Gen. Hosp.*, 8 Pa. D. & C.4th 596 (1990).

See also Medical Care and Reduction of Error (MCARE) Act, 40 P.S. § 1303.311(a) which protects from discovery "documents, materials or information . . . which arise out of matters reviewed by the patient safety committee pursuant to section 310(b) of the governing board of a medical facility . . . ."

Research Reference

Packel & Poulin, Pennsylvania Evidence § 543 (4th ed. 2013)

EXPERT WITNESS: ADMISSIBILITY OF NOVEL SCIENTIFIC EVIDENCE—*FRYE*

See: Pa.R.E. 702.

Objection

- Your Honor, I object to this witness's testimony because she has failed to establish that the methodology employed is generally accepted in the relevant scientific/technical community.

Response

- We have established that the methodology employed is generally accepted in the relevant scientific/technical community.

Pennsylvania Law

The *Frye* rule is a limitation on the admissibility of expert witness testimony that derives from the federal appeals decision in *Frye v. United States*, 293 F. 1013 (1923). The *Frye* rule was adopted by *Commonwealth v. Topa*, 471 Pa. 223, 369 A.2d 1277 (1977) and reaffirmed by *Grady v. Frito-Lay, Inc.*, 576 Pa. 546, 839 A.2d 1038 (2003).

The holding of *Frye* reiterated in *Grady*, is that novel scientific evidence is admissible if the **methodology** that underlies the evidence has general acceptance in the relevant scientific community. *Commonwealth v. Safka*, 141 A.3d 1239 (Pa. 2016); *Commonwealth v. Chmiel*, 30 A.3d 1111 (Pa. 2011); *Commonwealth v. Coon*, 26 A.3d 1159 (Pa. Super. 2011) (*Frye* requires that, before novel scientific evidence is admissible, the theories and methods of that evidence must have gained general acceptance in the relevant scientific community). The purpose of the *Frye* test is to help the court determine when a scientific principle or discovery crosses the line between the experimental and demonstrable stages. *Commonwealth v. Puksar*, 951 A.2d 267 (Pa. 2008).

Thus, the court's inquiry into whether a particular scientific process is "generally accepted" is an effort to ensure that the result of the scientific process, i.e., the proffered evidence, stems from scientific research which has been conducted in a fashion that is generally recognized as being sound. *Cummins v. Rosa*, 846 A.2d 148 (Pa. Super. 2004).

However, the conclusions reached by the expert witness from generally accepted principles and methodologies need not also be generally accepted. *Commonwealth v. Harrell*, 65 A.3d 420 (Pa. Super. 2013); *Grady*, 839 A.2d at 1045; *Trach v. Fellin*, 817 A.2d 1102 (Pa. Super. 2003).

Because *Frye* is an exclusionary rule of evidence, it must be construed narrowly so as not to impede admissibility of evidence that will aid the trier of fact in the search for truth. *Id.* at 1104.

A number of courts have noted that a *Frye* analysis is not triggered every time science enters the courtroom; it only applies when the expert seeks to introduce **novel scientific evidence**. *See, e.g., Commonwealth v. Puksar*, 951 A.2d 267 (Pa. 2008) (nothing novel about the methodology of forensic pathologist using physical evidence found at crime scene to opine on cause of death); *Commonwealth v. Foley*, 38 A.3d 882 (Pa. Super. 2012) (DNA analysis done with proprietary software was not novel science); *Folger Ex Rel. Folger v. Dugan*, 876 A.2d 1049 (Pa. Super. 2005); *Haney v. Pagnanelli*, 830 A.2d 978 (Pa. Super. 2003).

The following cases are instructive: *Commonwealth v. Freeman*, 128 A.3d 1231 (Pa. Super. 2015) (a *Frye* hearing is warranted when a trial judge has articulable grounds to believe that an expert witness has not applied accepted scientific methodology in a conventional fashion in reaching his or her conclusions); *Grady v. Frito-Lay, Inc.*, 576 Pa. 546, 839 A.2d 1038 (2003) (testimony did not satisfy *Frye* where plaintiff did not show means used by expert to evaluate characteristics of tortilla chips was generally accepted by scientists who evaluate food safety); *Commonwealth v. Topa*, 471 Pa. 223, 369 A.2d 1277 (1977) (*Frye* precluded expert testimony concerning sound spectrograph and voiceprint analysis); *Betz v. Pneumo Abex LLC*, 998 A.2d 962 (Pa. Super. 2010) (expert testimony which relied on methodology that included extrapolation to form opinion regarding causation between asbestos exposure and mesothelioma admissible under *Frye*); *Folger Ex Rel. Folger v. Dugan*, 876 A.2d 1049 (Pa. Super. 2005) (expert testimony about test results of polymerase chain reaction ("PCR") test did not require a *Frye* hearing; plaintiffs were not challenging the methodology of PCR testing but the accuracy of the test results); *Carroll v. Avallone*, 869 A.2d 522 (Pa. Super. 2005) (*Frye* challenge to toxicology screens and tests by hospital and medical examiner was not a challenge to novel methods but a challenge to the way in which common methods were executed; challenge was properly rejected); *Cummins v. Rosa*, 846 A.2d 148 (Pa. Super. 2004) (*Frye* motion denied because it did not challenge methodology used by defense experts but their conclusions as to cause of injury); *Commonwealth v. Dengler*, 843 A.2d 1241 (Pa. Super. 2004) (expert psychologist's opinion testimony re whether convicted sex offender met statutory criteria for classification as sexually violent predator was not novel scientific evidence and did not require a *Frye* hearing to determine admissibility); *Tucker v. Community Medical Center*, 833 A.2d 217 (Pa. Super. 2003) (testimony about use of Foley catheter and whether plaintiff suffered from pre-existing medical condition making him susceptible to injury was not novel scientific evidence); *M.C.M. v. MHMC of Pa. State University*, 834 A.2d 1155 (Pa. Super. 2003) (expert testimony regarding the number of hospitals that used test for newborn screening was not novel scientific evidence); *Cassell v. Lancaster Mennonite Conference*, 834 A.2d 1185 (Pa. Super. 2003) (*Frye* standard does not require the optimal methodology, just an accepted one);

Reading Radio, Inc. v. Fink, 833 A.2d 199 (Pa. Super. 2003) (testimony regarding radio station's decrease in value was not novel scientific evidence); *Trach v. Fellin*, 817 A.2d 1102 (Pa. Super. 2003) (extrapolation which was methodology used by expert on causation to deduce that plaintiff's glaucoma was result of massive overdose of drug was generally accepted in scientific community and, thus, sufficiently reliable under *Frye*); *Commonwealth v. Passarelli*, 789 A.2d 708 (Pa. Super. 2001) (shaken baby syndrome evidence is opinion but not science and is not subject to *Frye*); *Perez-Rocha v. Com., Bureau of Pro.*, 933 A.2d 1102 (Pa.Cmwlth. 2007) (ethylglucuronide (EtG) testing has gained acceptance as a tool for monitoring presence of alcohol in the system).

Despite the fact that approach used in *Daubert v. Merrell Dow Pharmaceuticals, Inc.*, 509 U.S. 579 (1993) has not been adopted, certain aspects of a typical *Daubert* analysis, such as evaluation of epidemiological data, reliance on animal studies or anecdotal reports and peer review can be relevant in determining whether the methodology at issue has been "generally accepted" for purposes of *Frye*. *See Blum v. Merrell Dow Pharmaceuticals, Inc.*, 564 Pa. 3, 764 A.2d 1 (2000). *See also, Engstrom v. Bayer Corp.*, 855 A.2d 52 (Pa. Super. 2004) (*Frye* is more restrictive than *Daubert*; any information which would satisfy *Frye* would, *a priori*, satisfy *Daubert*).

An expert's self-serving assertion that his conclusions were derived by generally accepted scientific methods is not conclusive. Corroborative evidence may, therefore, be required.

See also Pa.R.C.P. 207.1, Motion to Exclude Expert Testimony Which Relies Upon Novel Scientific Evidence.

Compare: Fed. R. Evid. 702.

Research References

Packel & Poulin, Pennsylvania Evidence §§ 702-

1–702-7 (4th ed. 2013)

McCormick, Evidence Chapter 3, §§ 12–13 (7th ed. 2013)

EXPERT WITNESS: ASSESSING THE CREDIBILITY OF OTHER WITNESSES

See: Pa.R.E. 702.

Objection

- Your Honor, this testimony is improper because the witness will intrude on the jury's function of deciding credibility.

Response

- The matter is sufficiently complex to permit expert testimony.
- The matter is not within the ordinary knowledge and experience of the jury.
- The testimony is relevant and will help the jury understand the (*specify*) issue.

Departing from prior case law, the Pennsylvania Supreme Court holds that the admission of expert testimony regarding eyewitness identification is no longer per se impermissible. Admissibility of such expert testimony is left to the discretion of the trial court. *Commonwealth v. Walker*, 92 A.3d 766 (Pa. 2014). The Court said in light of the magnitude of scientific understanding of eyewitness identification and marked developments in case law during the last thirty years, it is no longer advisable to bar the use of expert testimony to aid a jury in understanding eyewitness identification. *Id*. at 791.

Declining to define precise parameters, the *Walker* Court said the use of such testimony should generally be limited to certain cases where such evidence is relevant and the Commonwealth's case is solely or primarily dependent upon eyewitness testimony. *Id*. at 787.

Defendant must make an on-the-record detailed proffer to the court, including an explanation of precisely how the expert's testimony is relevant to the eyewitness identifications under consideration and how it will assist the jury in its evaluation. *Id.* at 792. *See, Commonwealth v. Selenski*, 117 A.3d 1283 (Pa. Super. 2015) (remanded for trial court to review proffer).

The Court has also upheld the constitutionality of 42 Pa. C.S. § 5920 which, in criminal cases, allows expert testimony regarding victims' responses to sexual violence. *Commonwealth v. Olivo*, 127 A.3d 769 (Pa. 2015); *Accord, Commonwealth v. Carter*, 111 A.3d 1221 (Pa. Super. 2015). However, the statute also provides that the witness's opinion regarding the credibility of any other witness, including the victim, is not admissible. 42 Pa. C.S. § 5920(b)(3).

In *Commonwealth v. Alicia*, 92 A.3d 753 (Pa. 2014), the Court precluded the use of expert testimony on the phenomenon of false confessions, saying it invaded the province of the jury and citing past decisions forbidding expert testimony on the credibility of witnesses. *Id.* At 761. *Accord, Commonwealth v. Pugh*, 101 A.3d 820 (Pa. Super. 2014). *See also, Amato v. Bell & Gossett*, 116 A.3d 607 (Pa. Super. 2015) (excluding testimony by defense expert intended to refute plaintiff's identification of asbestos-containing material he allegedly used forty years earlier; expert testimony unnecessary, jury could assess reliability of witness's memory).

In his *Alicia* dissent, Chief Justice Saylor said the "blanket exclusion of relevant evidence based upon unanalyzed assumptions about juror capabilities, even as those assumptions are challenged by demonstrations of wrongful convictions and developing behavioral science, is no longer satisfactory in my view." 92 A.3d at 766.

Compare: Fed. R. Evidence 702.

Research References

Packel & Poulin, Pennsylvania Evidence § 702-3

(4th ed. 2013)

McCormick, Evidence, Chapter 3, § 13 (7th ed. 2013)

EXPERT WITNESS: BEYOND THE FAIR SCOPE OF PRETRIAL DISCOVERY

See: Pa.R.Civ.P. 4003.5(c).

Objection

- [*To a question*] Objection. The question delves into an area beyond the fair scope of this expert's pretrial report. Any testimony on this point would involve both unfair surprise and prejudice because [*specify*].

- [*To an answer*] Objection, this testimony is beyond the fair scope of any matter disclosed by this expert in pretrial discovery. I move the answer be stricken and the jury be instructed not to consider it for any purpose.

Response

- My opponent did not seek any discovery in this area. Rule 4003.5(c) provides that an expert is not prevented from testifying as to facts or opinions on matters on which he has not been interrogated during discovery proceedings.

- There is neither surprise nor prejudice. My opponent anticipated this testimony and his own expert [*gave*] [*is prepared to give*] a rebuttal position.

Pennsylvania Law

The Pennsylvania Rules of Civil Procedure favor liberal discovery of expert opinions and disfavor unfair and prejudicial surprise. When expert testimony is involved, it is crucial that surprise be prevented since the attorney usually will not have the requisite knowledge of the subject with which to effectively rebut unexpected testimony. *Sindler v. Goldman*, 309 Pa. Super. 7, 454 A.2d 1054 (1982). Pa.R.Civ.P. 4003.5(a)(1)(b) states in pertinent part:

A party may through interrogatories require . . . the

other party to have each expert so identified by him to state the substance of the facts and opinions to which the expert is expected to testify and a summary of the grounds for each opinion.

To prevent incomplete or "fudging" of reports which would fail to reveal fully the facts and opinions of the expert or his grounds therefore, Rule 4003.5(c) provides that an expert's direct testimony at trial may not be inconsistent with or go beyond the fair scope of his testimony as set forth in his deposition, answers to interrogatories, separate report or supplements. The primary purpose of the Rule is to avoid unfair surprise to an adversary concerning the facts and substance of an expert's proposed testimony. *Expressway v. Bucks County Bd. of Assess.*, 921 A.2d 70 (Pa.Cmwlth. 2007). The "fair scope rule" is not, however, a trap for the unwary, requiring that every word an expert witness utters be traceable to his pre-trial report. *Andaloro v. Armstrong World Industries*, 799 A.2d 71 (Pa. Super. 2002). In deciding whether an expert's trial testimony is within the fair scope of his report, the accent is on the word "fair". The question to be answered is whether, under the particular facts and circumstances of the case, the discrepancy between the expert's pre-trial report and his trial testimony is of a nature which would prevent the adversary from making a meaningful response, or which would mislead the adversary as to the nature of the appropriate response. *Commonwealth v. Poplawski*, 130 A.3d 697 (Pa. 2015) (even where an expert's testimony arguably went beyond the scope of his or her report, the defendant still bears the burden of proving he suffered prejudice from the admission of the testimony); *Whitaker v. Frankford Hosp.*, 984 A.2d 512 (Pa. Super. 2009); *Bainhauer v. Lehigh Valley Hosp.*, 834 A.2d 1146 (Pa. Super. 2003); *Feden v. Consolidated Rail Corp.*, 746 A.2d 1158 (Pa. Super. 2000); *see Foflygen v. Allegheny Gen. Hosp.*, 723 A.2d 705 (Pa. Super. 1999) (what constitutes surprise and prejudice depends upon the pre-trial particulars of each case).

If the discrepancy between the expert's pretrial report and his trial testimony is of a nature which would prevent the adversary from preparing a meaningful response or which would mislead the adversary as to the nature of the appropriate response, then there has been unfair surprise and prejudice to the opposing party. *Brodowski v. Ryave*, 885 A.2d 1045 (Pa. Super. 2005) (what defendant physician should have known about patient and what inquiries he should have made prior to admitting her to psychiatric unit was not covered in plaintiff's expert reports and testimony was properly precluded at trial); *Stalsitz v. Allentown Hosp.*, 814 A.2d 766 (Pa. Super. 2002); *Tiburzio-Kelly v. Montgomery*, 452 Pa. Super. 158, 681 A.2d 757 (1996); *Chanthavong v. Tran*, 452 Pa. Super. 378, 682 A.2d 334 (1996); *see, Schweikert v. St. Luke's Hosp.*, 886 A.2d 265 (2005) (expert report's very general assertion of unacceptable practice was not sufficient notice to permit introduction of new theory in expert's trial deposition); *Woodard v. Chatterjee*, 827 A.2d 433 (Pa. Super. 2003) (defendant prejudiced by lack of notice that plaintiff's only expert would testify about findings of other physicians not referred to in expert's own report); *Oxford Presbyterian Church v. Weil-McLain, Co., Inc.*, 815 A.2d 1094 (Pa. Super. 2003) (expert properly allowed to "flesh out" his reports with mathematical calculations and sketches); *Mansour v. Linganna*, 787 A.2d 443 (Pa. Super. 2001) (no surprise in testimony by plaintiff's expert re necessity for and cost of Oxycontin where defendant knew from other discovery that plaintiff was on pain medication); *Greer v. Bryant*, 423 Pa. Super. 608, 621 A.2d 999 (1993) (where report stated that patient should not have been sent home from hospital, it was a fair corollary to opinion for expert to testify that interns should have overruled treating physician if he requested that patient be sent home); *Dible v.*

Vagley, 417 Pa. Super. 302, 612 A.2d 493 (1992) (expert's obvious disapproval of particular medical technique was easily anticipated from his report); *Freeman v. Maple Point, Inc.*, 393 Pa. Super. 427, 574 A.2d 684 (1990) (error in admitting expert testimony where expert's report was produced on the first day of trial and opponent was misled as to amount of damages sought); *Walsh v. Kubiak*, 443 Pa. Super. 284, 661 A.2d 416 (1995) (expert precluded from testifying about medical necessity of surgery where report only covered issue of whether operation was negligently performed); *DiBuono v. A. Barletta & Sons, Inc.*, 127 Pa.Cmwlth. 1, 560 A.2d 893 (1989) (defendant unfairly surprised by expert testimony about possibility of fatal consequences of injury when pretrial report only dealt with actual injury and resulting work disability); *Wilkes-Barre Iron & Wire Works, Inc. v. Pargas of Wilkes-Barre, Inc.*, 348 Pa. Super. 285, 502 A.2d 210 (1985) (defendant unfairly surprised by testimony injecting new definition of product defect not discussed in expert's pretrial report).

An expert's opinion in rebuttal to trial testimony need not be addressed in the expert's report. *Allegheny Ludlum Corp. v. Mun. Auth.*, 659 A.2d 20 (Pa.Cmwlth.1995); *Earlin v. Cravetz*, 264 Pa. Super. 294, 399 A.2d 783 (1979). Where an expert's testimony is fair rebuttal to the other party's expert testimony, it cannot be seen as unfairly surprising or prejudicial. *Duttry v. Patterson*, 741 A.2d 199 (Pa. Super. 1999), rev'd on other grounds 565 Pa. 130, 771 A.2d 1255 (2001). Pennsylvania law does not require a defense expert in a medical malpractice case to state his or her opinion to the same degree of medical certainty applied to the plaintiff, who bears the burden of proof at trial. *Jacobs v. Chatwani*, 922 A.2d 950 (Pa. Super. 2007) (where doctor used terms "supports" and "strongly supports" in his reports, opinion was stated to sufficient degree of certainty for rebuttal purposes).

Where an expert opinion was not acquired or

developed with an eye toward litigation, Rule 4003.5 is inapplicable. *Miller v. Brass Rail Tavern, Inc.*, 541 Pa. 474, 664 A.2d 525 (1995); *Katz v. St. Mary Hosp.*, 816 A.2d 1125 (Pa. Super. 2003) (defendant doctor did not acquire his medical opinions in preparation for trial but long before action commenced).

Criminal Proceedings

Unlike civil cases, there are no specific procedural rules governing expert reports in criminal cases aside from Pa. R. Crim. P. 573 which relates to discovery. The rule requires the Commonwealth to turn over the results of expert opinions in its possession or control.

Although there are no rules of procedure in criminal cases precisely governing expert reports, neither the Commonwealth nor a defendant has caret blanche to allow an expert to testify beyond the information contained in his or her report. To hold otherwise would eviscerate the requirement that reports be disclosed. *Commonwealth v. Roles*, 116 A.3d 122 (Pa. Super. 2015) (state trooper testified beyond the scope of his report).

Pursuant to Pa. R. Crim. P. 573(E), the court has a variety of options at its disposal where a discovery violation exists ranging from a continuance to prohibiting introduction of the evidence. *Commonwealth v. Hemmingway*, 13 A.3d 491 (Pa. Super. 2011).

A discovery violation and testimony exceeding the scope of the expert's report do not automatically command a new trial. Defendant still must establish that the introduction of the expert testimony caused him prejudice to a degree that it affected his trial strategy or likely affected the outcome of the proceedings. *Commonwealth v. Hood*, 872 A.2d 175 (Pa. Super. 2005); *Commonwealth v. Causey*, 833 A.2d 165 (Pa. Super. 2003); *see also*

Commonwealth v. Henry, 706 A.2d 313 (Pa. 1997).
  Compare: Fed. R. Civ. P. 26(4).

Research Reference

  Gibbons, Pennsylvania Discovery Practice (1996)

EXPERT WITNESS: COMPETENCE TO TESTIFY

See: Pa.R.E. 702.

Objection

- Your Honor, I request an offer of proof as to the witness' testimony as well as the right to conduct voir dire.

- In light of the offer and my voir dire, I object to any testimony by this witness since his opinion is beyond the area of expertise in which he is qualified.

Response

- As a foundation for this testimony, I have established that the witness has sufficient [*skill*] [*knowledge*] [*experience*] [*training*] in the field of [*specify*] to qualify as an expert witness. I, therefore, ask for the court's ruling that he is recognized as an expert and permitted to testify to his opinions.

Pennsylvania Law

When a witness is offered as an expert, the first question is whether the subject on which the expert will express an opinion is so distinctly related to some science, profession, business or occupation as to be beyond the knowledge or experience of the average layman. *Commonwealth v. Lopez*, 578 Pa. 545, 854 A.2d 465 (2004); *Mohney v. American General Life Ins. Co.*, 116 A.3d 1123 (Pa. Super. 2015) (error to exclude expert testimony on issue of standards for training claims adjustors in the insurance industry; matter sufficiently complex to permit expert testimony). If the subject is of this type, the next question is whether the witness has sufficient skill, knowledge or experience in that field or calling that his opinion will probably aid the trier of fact in his search for the truth. *Commonwealth v. Passarelli*, 789 A.2d 708 (Pa. Super. 2001); *Daniel v. Wyeth Pharmaceuticals, Inc.*,

15 A.3d 909 (Pa. Super. 2011) (although not a medical doctor, expert witness with doctorate in pharmacology competent to testify whether hormone drug manufacturer's warnings to prescribing physicians were adequate); *Commonwealth v. Jennings*, 958 A.2d 536 (Pa. Super. 2008) (sexual assault nurse examiner qualified to testify as expert as to cause of injuries to victim of alleged sexual assault).

To qualify as an expert, a witness must have sufficient skill, knowledge or experience in the field in question that his opinion will assist the trier of fact to understand the evidence or to determine a fact in issue. *Callahan v. National R.R. Passenger Corp.*, 979 A.2d 866 (Pa. Super. 2009); *Commonwealth v. Jarowecki*, 923 A.2d 425 (Pa. Super. 2007); *Hooker v. State Farm Fire and Cas. Co.*, 880 A.2d 70 (Pa.Cmwlth. 2005). Where a witness possesses neither experience nor education in the subject matter under investigation, he is incompetent to testify as an expert. *Green v. Pennsylvania Hospital*, 123 A.3d 310 (Pa. 2015) (nurse expert witness not qualified to offer causation testimony with respect to physicians; proffered testimony was based on intertwined course of conduct by nurses and doctors and thus, had potential to confuse jury); *Steele v. Shepperd*, 411 Pa. 481, 192 A.2d 397 (1963); *Browne v. Commonwealth*, 843 A.2d 429 (Pa.Cmwlth. 2004) (investigating police officer who did not witness accident may not render opinion as to causation unless officer has been qualified as expert); *Dierolf v. Slade*, 399 Pa. Super. 9, 581 A.2d 649 (1990). Whether a witness is qualified to testify as an expert is within the discretion of the trial court. *Montgomery v. South Philadelphia Med. Group, Inc.*, 441 Pa. Super. 146, 656 A.2d 1385 (1995); *Lira v. Albert Einstein Med. Ctr.*, 384 Pa. Super. 503, 559 A.2d 550 (1989).

The Pennsylvania standard of qualification for an expert witness is a liberal one. *Commonwealth v. Toritto*, 67 A.3d 29 (Pa. Super. 2013). If a witness has any reasonable pretension to specialized knowledge on the subject under investigation, he may testify, and the weight to be given to his testimony is for the jury. *Commonwealth v. Gonzalez*, 519 Pa. 116, 546 A.2d 26 (1988); *Wells Fargo Bank v. Dauphin Cty. Gen. Auth.*, 19 A.3d 14 (Pa.Cmwlth. 2011); *Commonwealth v. Page*, 59 A.3d 1118 (Pa. Super. 2013); *Commonwealth v. Saunders*, 946 A.2d 776 (Pa. Super. 2008). To meet the standard, it is not necessary for the witness to possess all the knowledge in his or her special field of activity. *Novitski v. Rusak*, 941 A.2d 43 (Pa. Super. 2008).

Although the witness must demonstrate some special knowledge or skill, there is no requirement that a witness acquire expertise as a result of formal schooling; expertise acquired by practical experience is sufficient. *See, e.g.*, *Miller v. The Brass Rail Tavern, Inc.*, 541 Pa. 474, 664 A.2d 525 (1995) (coroner, who was not a doctor, can render expert opinion on time of death, based on fifteen years experience as coroner and twenty-seven years as licensed mortician); *Commonwealth v. Ramos*, 920 A.2d 1253 (Pa. Super. 2007) (former state trooper experienced in firearms could give opinion on whether BB gun was deadly weapon); *Commonwealth v. Doyen*, 848 A.2d 1007 (Pa. Super. 2004) (state trooper could testify as expert on subject of coded language used by drug dealers); *In re Estate of Presutti*, 783 A.2d 803 (Pa. Super. 2001) (handwriting expert); *Commonwealth v. Balog*, 448 Pa. Super. 480, 672 A.2d 319 (1996) (SPCA agent qualified to testify about cock fighting); *Smith v. Penbridge Assocs., Inc.*, 440 Pa. Super. 410, 655 A.2d 1015 (1995) (witnesses qualified as experts in emu breeding despite only a few years' experience since industry was new); *Commonwealth v. Long*, 425 Pa. Super. 170, 624 A.2d 200 (1993) (swimming coach qualified to opine on human physiology of swimming, drowning and how boat wakes would affect a swimmer); *Rutter v. Northeastern Beaver*

County Sch. Dist., 496 Pa. 590, 437 A.2d 1198 (1981) (former high school football coach qualified to testify as to customs and safety standards utilized in high school football); *Reardon v. Meehan*, 424 Pa. 460, 227 A.2d 667 (1967) (experienced carpet installer competent to testify in trip/fall case regarding characteristics of fiber rugs); *Hughes v. Emerald Mines Corp.*, 303 Pa. Super. 426, 450 A.2d 1 (1982) (individual who had a plumbing and well repair business competent to render opinion that mining operations were the cause of well pollution).

Pennsylvania is not a "let-it-all-in" state (*see* Huber, Galileo's Revenge, Basic Books, 1991) and the courts draw a distinction between matters which can be addressed by an expert with general qualifications and matters requiring expert testimony of a specialist. *Compare Whistler Sportswear, Inc. v. Rullo*, 289 Pa. Super. 230, 433 A.2d 40 (1981) (civil engineer qualified to testify on roof collapse even though his area of expertise was not roof design; subject in question was not roof design *per se* but knowledge of engineering principles of stress and resiliency) *with Palmer v. Lapp*, 392 Pa. Super. 21, 572 A.2d 12 (1990) (antique automobile appraiser unqualified to give expert testimony on value of antique horse-drawn carriages) *and McDaniel v. Merck, Sharp & Dohme*, 367 Pa. Super. 600, 533 A.2d 436 (1987) (medical doctor with pharmacology expertise in anesthetics not qualified to testify about antibiotics). Other illustrative cases include: *Tucker v. Bensalem Tp. School Dist.*, 987 A.2d 198 (Pa.Cmwlth. 2009) (architect not competent to opine on maintenance of parking lot; moreover, ice and snow removal involved matter of common knowledge); *A.J.B. v. M.P.B.*, 945 A.2d 744 (Pa. Super. 2008) (individual with Ph.D. in mass media not qualified to testify re effect of prolonged use of pornography); *Goldstein v. Phillip Morris, Inc.*, 854 A.2d 585 (Pa. Super. 2004) and *Viguers v. Phillip Morris USA, Inc.*, 837 A.2d 534 (Pa. Super. 2003) (medical doctor not competent to give opinion on defective design of cigarettes because he had no experience in design and manufacture of cigarettes); *Kovalev v. Sowell*, 839 A.2d 359 (Pa. Super. 2003) (excluding testimony by individual with training and experience in general internal medicine but no training or experience in medical subspecialties dealing with spinal injuries); *Yacoub v. Lehigh Valley Medical*, 805 A.2d 579 (Pa. Super. 2002) (neurosurgeon not competent to testify about internal medicine or special care unit nursing).

Before and after passage of the MCARE Act, experts in one area of medicine have been ruled qualified to address other areas of specialization where the specialties overlap in practice, or where the specialist has experience in another related medical field. *Commonwealth v. Page*, 59 A.3d 1118 (Pa. Super. 2013) (pediatrician who also directed hospital unit that evaluated child abuse qualified to supplement autopsy findings re sexual abuse inflected on dead child); *Rettger v. UPMC Shadyside*, 991 A.2d 915 (Pa. Super. 2010) (neurosurgeon who interacted with hospital nurses competent to opine on conduct of neurosurgical nurse); *Hyrcza v. West Penn Allegheny Health*, 978 A.2d 961 (Pa. Super. 2009) (board-certified psychiatrist/neurologist with broad experience re multiple sclerosis competent to testify re standard of care applicable to board-certified psychiatrist treating post-op patient with MS); *Gartland v. Rosenthal*, 850 A.2d 671 (Pa. Super. 2004) (neurologist qualified re standard of care for radiologist reading CT scan of brain where issue was failure to report possibility of tumor and recommend MRI); *B.K. ex rel. S.K. v. Chambersburg Hosp.*, 834 A.2d 1178 (Pa. Super. 2003); *Rittenhouse v. Hanks*, 777 A.2d 1113 (Pa. Super. 2001); *Bindschusz v. Phillips*, 771 A.2d 803 (Pa. Super. 2001); *see Fogg v. Paoli Memorial Hosp.*, 455 Pa. Super. 81, 686 A.2d 1355 (1996) (psychiatrist with expertise in emergency medicine); *Chanthavong v. Tran*, 452 Pa. Super. 378, 682 A.2d 334 (1996) (new trial ordered where experienced general practitioner with substantial personal injury practice and knowledge and use of CAT scans was precluded from testifying as expert on spinal injury); *Kearns v. Clark*, 343 Pa. Super. 30, 493 A.2d 1358 (1985) (urologist qualified to testify against surgeon regarding performance of hysterectomy where urologist was familiar with and had assisted in performance of other hysterectomies); *Pratt v. Stein*, 298 Pa. Super. 92, 444 A.2d 674 (1982) (professor of pharmacology qualified to testify to post-operative care given by orthopedic surgeon with respect to drug administered to patient); *Ragan v. Steen*, 229 Pa. Super. 515, 331 A.2d 724 (1974) (surgeon permitted to testify against radiologist where surgeon was knowledgeable through experience with x-ray treatments). See also *Freed v. Geisinger Medical Center*, 971 A.2d 1202 (Pa. 2009) (registered nurse competent to give expert testimony regarding standard of case in action claiming nursing staff failed to meet nursing standard of care with regard to treatment and prevention of bed sores).

Typically, a plaintiff must present an expert witness who will testify to a reasonable degree of medical certainly that the actions of the physician deviated from good and acceptable medical standards. *K.H. Ex Rel. H.S. v. Kumar*, 122 A.3d 1080 (Pa. Super. 2015). A very narrow exception to the requirement of expert testimony in medical malpractice actions applies where the matter is so simple or the lack of skill or care so obvious as to be within the range of experience and comprehension of even non-professional persons, also conceptualized as the doctrine *"res ipsa loquitur"*. *Sokolsky v. Eidelman*, 93 A.3d 858 (Pa. super. 2014).

Medical Care and Reduction of Error (MCARE) Act.

The MCARE Act, 40 P.S. § 1303.512, et seq., establishes criteria for the qualification of an expert witness in a medical professional liability action against a physician. *Vicari v. Spiegel*, 989 A.2d 1277 (Pa. 2010) (discussing MCARE standards for admissibility of medical expert testimony in medical malpractice action). The Act reflects the Legislature's preference for the testimony of expert witnesses who share the relevant area of expertise with the defendant physician. *Herbert v. Parkview Hosp.*, 854 A.2d 1285 (Pa. Super. 2004). The Act expressly raises the standard for qualifying an expert witness in a medical professional liability action from that which existed at common law. *Freed v. Geisinger Medical Center*, 971 A.2d 1202 (Pa. 2009).

The first requirement is that the testifying expert must possess a physician's license to practice medicine. 40 P.S. § 1303.512(b)(1); *Weiner v. Fisher*, 871 A.2d 1283 (Pa. Super. 2005) (unambiguous meaning of this language is the expert must possess license at the time he testifies); *Bethea v. Philadelphia AFL-CIO Hospital Association*, 871 A.2d 223 (Pa. Super. 2005) (expert who did not possess valid medical license **at the time of trial** not qualified under MCARE Act to testify).

A second requirement is that the testifying expert be engaged in or retired within the previous five years from active clinical practice or teaching. 40 P.S. § 1303.512(b)(2); *Weiner*, 871 A.2d 1283 (Pa. Super. 2005) (the statutory verb is present tense referring to the time of giving testimony.)

The statute mandates that the expert be substantially familiar with the applicable standard of care for the specific care at issue as of the time of the alleged breach of the standard of care. 40 P.S. § 1303.512 (c)(1); *Weiner*, 871 A.2d 1283 (Pa. Super. 2005) (relevant time of consideration is when the alleged breach of the standard of care took place).

The expert must practice in the same subspecialty as the defendant physician or in a subspecialty which has a substantially similar standard of care for the specific care at issue. 40 P.S. § 1303.512 (c)(2); *Wexler v. Hecht*, 928 A.2d 973 (Pa. 2007) (podiatrist who was expert in general field of foot surgery lacked training and experience necessary to opine about standard of care relevant to orthopedic surgeon); *Price v. Catanzariti*, 138 A.3d 8 (Pa. Super. 2016) (in suit against podiatric surgeon, patient not required to meet MCARE standard re expert testimony since podiatrist is not a physician under the Act; common law standard applies).

The trial court, however, may waive same board or same specialty requirements if the proposed expert has sufficient training, experience and knowledge to testify as a result of active involvement in a field of medicine "related" to the subspecialty of the defendant physician. 40 P.S. § 1303.512 (e); *Vicari v. Spiegel*, 989 A.2d 1277 (Pa. 2010) (defining the term "related" and holding oncologist was qualified to testify as expert against otolaryngologist and radiation oncologist); *Renna v. Schadt*, 64 A.3d 658 (Pa. Super. 2013) (board-certified oncologist familiar with biopsy procedures qualified to give expert testimony the standard of care for surgeon who chose fine-needle aspiration as biopsy method for diagnosing breast cancer); *Smith v. Paoli Memorial Hosp.*, 885 A.2d 1012 (Pa. Super. 2005) (expertise of general surgeon and oncologist overlapped with expertise of gastroenterologist with respect to standard of care when presented with a patient with obscure GI bleeding); *Campbell v. Attanasio*, 862 A.2d 1282 (Pa. Super. 2004) (error to prohibit psychiatrist from testifying against specialist in internal medicine; issue was defendant's use of certain sedative which expert also used in his practice); *Herbert v. Parkview Hosp.*, 854 A.2d 1285 (Pa. Super. 2004) (internist qualified to testify against nephrologist; real issue was internal medicine in failing to discover and address patient's airway blockage). *Cf. Gbur v. Golio*, 963 A.2d 443 (Pa. 2009).

Expert testimony is incompetent if it lacks an adequate basis in fact. *City of Philadelphia v. W.C.A.B. (Kriebel)*, 29 A.3d 762 (Pa. 2011) (opinion not competent because based on a series of assumptions that lacked a factual predicate); *McEwing v. Lititz Mut. Ins. Co.*, 77 A.3d 639, 650 (Pa. Super. 2013); *Gillingham v. Consol Energy, Inc.*, 51 A.3d 841 (Pa. Super. 2012); *Helpin v. Trustees of Univ. of Pa.*, 969 A.2d 601 (Pa. Super. 2009); *Kelly v. Thackray Crane Rental, Inc.*, 874 A.2d 649 (Pa. Super. 2005) (expert who misconstrued facts and thus used erroneous standard of care not competent to testify); *Jones v. Wilt*, 871 A.2d 210 (Pa. Super. 2005) (regardless of his skill and experience, expert may not express opinion upon facts which are not warranted in the record); *Viener v. Jacobs*, 834 A.2d 546 (Pa. Super. 2003) (expert based calculations on assumption that there were three investors in corporation when, in fact, there were four); *Morrison v. W.C.A.B. (Rothman Institute)*, 15 A.3d 93, 99 n.7 (Pa.Cmwlth. 2011); *Community Empowerment v. W.C.A.B. (Porch)*, 962 A.2d 1 (Pa.Cmwlth. 2008) (medical opinion not competent if based on inaccurate or false information). The expert is allowed to assume the truth of testimony already in evidence. *Blicha v. Jacks*, 864 A.2d 1214 (Pa. Super. 2004) (defense expert entitled to use facts developed by defendant as predicate for opinion even though plaintiff vigorously contested accuracy of those facts); *Hussey v. May Dept. Stores, Inc.*, 357 A.2d 635 (1976). While an expert's opinion need not be based on an absolute certainty, an opinion based on mere possibilities is not competent evidence. *Childers v. Power Line Equip. Rentals*, 452 Pa. Super. 94, 681 A.2d 201 (1996); *see* Expert Witness: Requisite Degree of Certainty. This means that expert testimony cannot be based solely upon conjecture or surmise. An expert must do more than guess. His or her assumptions must be based upon such facts as the jury would be warranted in finding from the evidence. *Houston v. Canon Bowl, Inc.*,

443 Pa. 383, 278 A.2d 908 (1971).

Expert testimony is not admissible where the issue involves a matter of common knowledge. *Commonwealth v. Minerd*, 753 A.2d 225 (Pa. 2000). In a termination of parental rights case, the court is not required to use expert testimony when evaluating a parental bond. *In re I.E.P.*, 87 A.3d 340 (Pa. Super. 2014) (testimony of social worker and case worker was sufficient).

Compare: Fed. R. Evid. 702.

Research References

Packel & Poulin, Pennsylvania Evidence § 702-5 (4th ed. 2013)

McCormick, Evidence Chapter 3, § 13 (7th ed. 2013)

EXPERT WITNESS: REQUISITE DEGREE OF CERTAINTY

See: Pa.R.E. 702.

Objection

- Your Honor, I object and move to strike the testimony of this witness because his opinion has not been rendered to a reasonable degree of professional certainty.

Response

- The witness is not required to use "magic words" in order for the opinion to be admissible. Taken as a whole, the testimony expresses a reasonable certainty and absolute certainty is not required.

Pennsylvania Law

With regard to expert testimony, the Pennsylvania Supreme Court has held that "[n]o matter how skilled or experienced the witness may be, he will not be permitted to guess or to state a judgment based on mere conjecture." *Collins v. Hand*, 431 Pa. 378, 246 A.2d 404 (1968); *Commonwealth v. Fuentes*, 991 A.2d 935 (Pa. Super. 2010) (expert's opinion rendered to reasonable degree of professional certainty is itself evidence); *Winschel v. Jain*, 925 A.2d 782 (Pa. Super. 2007) (mere speculation does not constitute evidence and was properly excluded).

An expert is generally required to give an opinion "to a reasonable degree of [professional] certainty." *Stimmler v. Chestnut Hill Hosp.*, 981 A.2d 145 (Pa. 2009); *McMahon v. Young*, 442 Pa. 484, 276 A.2d 534 (1971); *Wiggins v. Synthes (U.S.A.)*, 29 A.3d 9 (Pa. Super. 2011); *Betz v. Erie Ins. Exchange*, 957 A.2d 1244 (Pa. Super. 2008) (purpose of standard is to avoid speculation under rubric of "expert opinion"); *Kovach v. Central Trucking, Inc.*, 808 A.2d 958 (Pa. Super. 2002). It is

116

not required that these "magic words" be used, *Commonwealth v. Miller*, 987 A.2d 638 (Pa. 2009); *Commonwealth v. Spotz*, 562 Pa. 498, 756 A.2d 1139 (2000); *Truax v. Roulhac*, 126 A.3d 991 (Pa. Super. 2015); *Klein v. Aronchick*, 85 A.3d 487 (Pa. Super. 2014), and the opinion will be held sufficiently certain if review of the testimony, in its entirety, reveals reasonable certainty. *See, e.g., Commonwealth v. Davido*, 582 Pa. 52, 868 A.2d 431 (2005) (the expert has to testify that in his professional opinion the result in question came from the cause alleged; a less direct expression of opinion falls below the required standard of proof and does not constitute legally competent evidence); *Commonwealth v. Edmiston*, 535 Pa. 210, 221–222, 634 A.2d 1078, 1084 (1993) (expert's use of terms such as "consistent with" and "appears to me" does not render testimony impermissibly uncertain where overall opinion was prefaced as being given with a reasonable degree of professional certainty); *Catlin v. Hamburg*, 56 A.3d 914 (Pa. Super. 2012) (expert need not testify with absolute certainty or rule out all possible causes of a condition as long as in its entirety it expresses reasonable certainty); *Helpin v. Trustees of Univ. of Pa.*, 969 A.2d 601 (Pa. Super. 2009) (while opinion need not be based on absolute certainty, an opinion based on mere possibilities is not competent evidence).

Other linguistic formulations open an opinion to attack that it lacks the requisite certainty. However, an opinion that the alleged cause was "the most probable cause" is sufficient to meet this standard of certainty. *See, e.g., Al Hamilton Contracting Co. v. Department of Envt'l Res.*, 659 A.2d 31 (Pa.Cmwlth.1995); *Argust v. Dick Mackey Gen. Contracting Co.*, 390 Pa. Super. 183, 568 A.2d 255 (1990).

Conversely, an opinion may be excluded as lacking in requisite certainty if it is couched in terms such as "possible," "could have," "could very properly account for," or "very highly probable."

Griffin v. Univ. of Pgh. Med. Center-Braddock Hospital, 950 A.2d 996 (Pa. Super. 2008) (opinion couched as 51% probability of negligence versus 49% probability of non-negligence does not equate to a reasonable degree of certainty); *Corrado v. Thomas Jefferson Univ. Hosp.*, 790 A.2d 1022 (Pa. Super. 2001) ("more likely than not" opinion insufficient); *Cohen v. Albert Einstein Med. Ctr.*, 405 Pa. Super. 392, 398–399, 592 A.2d 720, 723 (1991); *Eaddy v. Hamaty*, 694 A.2d 639, 642 (Pa. Super. 1997) ("in all likelihood" "may have hastened the onset" is insufficient). But see *Mitzelfelt v. Kamrin*, 526 Pa. 54, 584 A.2d 888 (1990) ("could have" sufficient in medical malpractice case).

In *Kravinsky v. Glover*, 263 Pa. Super. 8, 21–22, 396 A.2d 1349, 1356 (1979), the court summarized additional principles applicable to the degree of certainty required of experts:

(i)   An expert need not testify with absolute certainty or rule out all possible alternative causes.

(ii)   Expert testimony is admissible when, taken in its entirety, it expresses reasonable certainty that the event was a substantial factor in bringing about the harm.

(iii)   That an expert may, at some point during his testimony, qualify the assertion does not necessarily render the opinion inadmissibly speculative.

The fact that an expert states his opinion in the first person does not render an opinion fatally subjective; if in its full context the opinion states a general standard of care, it will be admitted. *Joyce v. Boulevard Physical Therapy & Rehab.*, 694 A.2d 648 (Pa. Super. 1997).

In certain instances, the degree of certainty required will depend on which party has the burden of proof. For example, a plaintiff expert, who holds the burden of proof on causation, would be required to testify to a reasonable degree of scientific certainty that toxin X caused the harm, whereas the defense expert may be permitted to testify that it "was a distinct possibility" that the harm was caused by a different factor. *See Neal by Neal v.*

Lu, 365 Pa. Super. 464, 530 A.2d 103 (1987) (reasonable medical certainty not required because defendant did not have burden of proof on causation).

In other instances, the *res ipsa loquitur* doctrine can "supplement" an expert opinion. In *Hightower-Warren v. Silk*, 548 Pa. 459, 698 A.2d 52 (1997), the expert testified to the three prongs of the *res ipsa loquitur* test:

(a)   The event is of the kind which ordinarily does not occur in the absence of negligence;

(b)   Other responsible causes, including conduct of the plaintiffs and third persons, are sufficiently eliminated by the evidence; and

(c)   The indicated negligence is within the scope of the defendant's duty to the plaintiff.

Id., 548 Pa. at 464, 698 A.2d at 54 (1997). The *Hightower* court held that expert testimony as to these elements was sufficient, despite the fact that there was no conclusive expert testimony that negligence had caused the injury at issue. Cf. *Sokolsky v. Eidelman*, 93 A.3d 858 (Pa. Super. 2014) (a very narrow exception to the requirement of expert testimony in medical malpractice actions applies where the matter is so simple or the lack of skill or care so obvious as to be within the range of experience and comprehension of even non-professional persons, also conceptualized as the doctrine of "*res ipsa loquitur*").

The opinion of an expert offered by a party who does not bear the burden of proof on an issue need not be as certain as those of the experts of the party who bears the burden of proof. *Shiner v. Ralston*, 64 A.3d 1 (Pa. Super. 2013); *Jacobs v. Chatwani*, 922 A.2d 950 (Pa. Super. 2007); *Neal by Neal v. Lu*, 530 A.2d 103 (Pa. Super. 1987) (no error allowing defense expert to testify as to "possible" other causes of plaintiff's problems).

In criminal cases, it is not necessary that a prosecution expert testify that his conclusions are stated beyond a reasonable doubt. *Commonwealth v. Stallworth*, 566 Pa. 349, 781 A.2d 110 (2001); *Commonwealth v. Hetzel*, 822 A.2d 747 (Pa. Super. 2003). Whether an expert's testimony is persuasive beyond a reasonable doubt is a matter for the jury's consideration.

Compare: Fed. R. Evid. 702.

Research Reference

Packel & Poulin, Pennsylvania Evidence § 702-6 (4th ed. 2013)

EXPERT WITNESS: TESTIMONY BASED IN PART ON HEARSAY

See: Pa.R.E. 703.

Objection

- Objection, hearsay. I move to strike this testimony since the witness has merely summarized the findings and conclusions of others.

Response

- The objection is not well-founded. The witness has used a variety of sources, along with her own professional experience, to arrive at her own opinion. We have established as foundation for this opinion that the data was of the type reasonably relied on by experts in the particular field. Her testimony is admissible expert testimony under Pa.R.E. 703 and not hearsay evidence.

Pennsylvania Law

The general rule in Pennsylvania is that an expert witness must base his or her testimony on facts of record. *Harley-Davidson Motor Co. v. Springettsburg*, 124 A.3d 270 (Pa. 2015); *Commonwealth v. Paskings*, 447 Pa. 350, 290 A.2d 82 (1972); *Glencannon Homes Ass'n. v. North Strabane*, 116 A.3d 706 (Pa. Cmwlth. 2015); *Harris v. Facilities Management Corp.*, 106 A.3d 183 (Pa. Cmwlth. 2014). But where the common law restricted the expert to testimony based on personal observation or examination, Pennsylvania courts today permit experts to give their opinions based, in part, upon reports, facts and data of others, which are not in evidence but upon which experts customarily rely in the practice of their profession. *Commonwealth v. Fletcher*, 986 A.2d 759 (Pa. 2009) (the law permits experts to render opinions based on factual findings made by others); *Commonwealth v. Vandivner*, 962 A.2d 1170 (Pa. 2009) (pathologist may offer opinions premised in part on information received from another coroner); *Brown v. Trinidad,* 111 A.3d 765 (Pa. Super. 2015) (same); *Commonwealth v. Bruce,* 916 A.2d 657 (Pa. Super. 2007) (although pathologist did not personally perform all of the various tests, he had sufficient involvement in autopsy to testify as expert; no violation of constitutional right to confrontation); *In re D.Y.,* 34 A.3d 177 (Pa. Super. 2011) (hearsay is admissible because the expert's reliance on the material provides its own indication of the material's trustworthiness); *Boucher v. Pennsylvania Hosp.,* 831 A.2d 623 (Pa. Super. 2003). This exception to the rule against hearsay was adopted in *Commonwealth v. Thomas,* 444 Pa. 436, 282 A.2d 693 (1971) and has been applied consistently since then. *See Gunn v. Grossman,* 748 A.2d 1235 (Pa. Super. 2000) and *Sheely v. Beard,* 696 A.2d 214 (Pa. Super. 1997) (testifying physician utilized reports, opinions and diagnoses of other experts as partial support and aid in arriving at and explaining the basis of her own opinion); *Commonwealth v. Bowser,* 425 Pa. Super. 24, 624 A.2d 125 (1993) (accident reconstruction expert could properly utilize inadmissible hearsay in rendering her opinion). Pa.R.E. 703 codifies prior case law.

The rationale for the exception is practical necessity and common sense. An expert's opinion may be based on years of professional experience, schooling and knowledge, not all of which can be presented on a first-hand basis in court. Moreover, the expert is assumed to have the ability to evaluate the trustworthiness of the data upon which he or she relies, both because the expert has demonstrated expert qualifications and because the expert regularly relies on and uses similar data in the practice of his or her profession. *Primavera v. Celotex Corp.,* 415 Pa. Super. 41, 608 A.2d 515 (1992). Thus, when the expert witness has consulted numerous sources and uses that information, together with his or her own professional knowledge and experience to arrive at an opinion, that opinion is regarded as evidence in its own right and not as hearsay in disguise. *Commonwealth v. Daniels*, 480 Pa. 340, 390 A.2d 172 (1978).

While most often applied to the testimony of medical experts (*see, e.g., Commonwealth v. Thomas*, 444 Pa. 436, 282 A.2d 693 (1971); *Commonwealth v. Daniels*, 480 Pa. 340, 390 A.2d 172 (1978); *Detterline v. D'Ambrosio's Dodge, Inc.*, 763 A.2d 935 (Pa. Super. 2000); *Collins v. Cooper*, 746 A.2d 615 (Pa. Super. 2000); *Cohen v. Albert Einstein Med. Ctr.*, 405 Pa. Super. 392, 592 A.2d 720 (1991)), the exception is not limited to the medical profession. *See Milan v. Commonwealth, Dep't of Transp.*, 153 Pa.Cmwlth. 276, 620 A.2d 721 (1993) (in forming opinion, accident reconstruction engineer permitted to use police accident report which was not in evidence, as well as driver's statement and deposition, which had been redacted); *In re Glosser Bros., Inc.*, 382 Pa. Super. 177, 555 A.2d 129 (1989) (stock valuation expert allowed to base opinion in part on appraisal of certain assets by independent appraisal company); *Bolus v. United Penn Bank*, 363 Pa. Super. 247, 525 A.2d 1215 (1987) (expert accountant may rely on tax returns and financial statements in computing lost profits); *Maravich v. Aetna Life and Cas. Co.*, 350 Pa. Super. 392, 504 A.2d 896 (1986) (fire marshal giving expert testimony may rely on information supplied by firemen under his supervision); *Steinhauer v. Wilson*, 336 Pa. Super. 155, 485 A.2d 477 (1984) (construction expert may base cost estimates on figures provided by various contractors). A medical expert may also base his opinion on reports of others which are not in medicine but customarily relied upon in practicing medicine, including the observations of lay persons. *Commonwealth v. Hernandez*, 420 Pa. Super. 1, 615 A.2d 1337 (1992).

However, an expert will not be permitted simply to repeat another's opinion or data without bringing to bear on it his own expertise and judgment. *Commonwealth v. Towles*, 106 A.3d 591 (Pa. 2014) (toxicologist's report based on defendant's statements re consumption of alcohol and drugs on night of murder properly excluded; evidence rules do not provide mechanism for criminal defendant to decline to testify and use an expert witness to introduce his story into the record); *Papach v. Mercy Suburban Hosp.*, 887 A.2d 233 (Pa. Super. 2005) (where ambulance report was clearly inadmissible hearsay, contents should not have come into evidence under guise of information relied upon by experts); *In Re DeFacto Cond. And Taking of Lands*, 972 A.2d 576 (Pa.Cmwlth. 2009) (similar); *Primavera v. Celotex Corp.*, 415 Pa. Super. 41, 608 A.2d 515 (1992); *Luzerne Cty. Flood Protect. Auth. v. Reilly*, 825 A.2d 779 (Pa.Cmwlth. 2003) (real estate appraiser correctly precluded from repeating opinions solicited from attorneys as to legal marketability of title; without legal training he was not able to bring to bear his own expertise to evaluate the legal opinions he sought to relate). This type of expert has been referred to as the "summary" or "conduit" expert, who serves to introduce the contents of extrajudicial statements or writings. *McCormick*, Evidence, § 15. *See, e.g., In Re T.C.*, 984 A.2d 549 (Pa. Super. 2009) (although child welfare expert used agency case file and was updated by case worker, she was not a conduit since her opinions and conclusions were her own); *Dierolf v. Slade*, 399 Pa. Super. 9, 581 A.2d 649 (1990) (doctor's testimony was not his own opinion but that of a colleague, and as such, was inadmissible hearsay). In such a situation, the non-testifying expert is not on the witness stand and truly is unavailable for cross-examination. *See, e.g., Commonwealth v. Rounds*, 518 Pa. 204, 542 A.2d 997 (1988); *Spotts v. Reidell*, 345 Pa. Super. 37, 497 A.2d 630 (1985).

The appeals courts repeatedly have held that an expert witness cannot bolster his credibility by reading into the record the report of a non-testifying expert who has not been subjected to cross-examination. *See Woodard v. Chatterjee*, 827 A.2d 433 (Pa. Super. 2003) (testifying physician merely parroted findings and impressions of non-testifying doctors); *Cacurak v. St. Francis Medical Center*, 823 A.2d 159 (Pa. Super. 2003) (expert witness improperly bolstered his own credibility by reading into record non-testifying doctor's report corroborating witness's own opinion); *Allen v. Kaplan*, 439 Pa. Super. 263, 653 A.2d 1249 (1995) (same); *Oxford Presbyterian Church v. Weil McLain Company, Inc.*, 815 A.2d 1094 (Pa. Super. 2003) (expert cannot read opinions of non-testifying experts into record and say he agrees with them). See also *Klein v. Aronchick*, 85 A.3d 487 (Pa. Super. 2014) (improper bolstering by expert's comments about medical articles in the New England Journal to increase the credibility of his own opinion in the minds of the jurors).

Compare: Fed. R. Evid. 703.

Research References

Packel & Poulin, Pennsylvania Evidence § 703-1 (4th ed. 2013)

McCormick, Evidence § 15 (7th ed. 2013)

EXPERT WITNESS: ULTIMATE ISSUE

See: Pa.R.E. 704.

Objection

- Objection [and move to strike]. Giving an opinion [would not be helpful to the jury], [is unfairly prejudicial], [is improper for this witness] because [specify].

Response

- The [*question/answer*] goes to the ultimate issue in this case and is proper under Rule 704 because [*specify*].

Pennsylvania Law

Pa.R.E. 704 provides that otherwise admissible opinion testimony is not objectionable merely because it reaches an ultimate issue to be decided by the factfinder. This removes the court from the task of determining whether or not an opinion goes to the ultimate issue and eliminates those objections asserting that the testimony "invades the province of the jury" or embraces an "ultimate issue." *See Lewis v. Mellor*, 259 Pa. Super. 509, 393 A.2d 941 (1978); McCormick, Evidence § 12 (5th ed. 1999).

However, opinion testimony must still be "otherwise admissible." The principal effect of Pa.R.E. 704 is to shift the inquiry to whether the opinion is admissible under the standards of Pa.R.E. 701, 702 and 403. Therefore, testimony going to an ultimate issue may be objectionable for any of a number of reasons: because a lay witness is not capable of rendering such an opinion; the opinion is beyond the realm of an expert witness's expertise; the factfinder would not be helped by hearing the opinion; or the probative value of the opinion is outweighed by the danger that it would be unfairly prejudicial, confuse the issues or mislead the jury.

Because admissibility of opinions relating to ultimate issues is highly case-specific, the following decisions simply serve to illustrate application of the rule.

Admitted: *Commonwealth v. Huggins*, 68 A.3d 962 (Pa. Super. 2013) (detective allowed to testify as both a lay and expert witness on matters that embrace the ultimate issue to be decided by fact-finder; trial court was diligent in issuing multiple cautionary instructions and directed prosecution to delineate for jury when testimony was expert and when factual); *Bey v. Sacks*, 789 A.2d 232 (Pa. Super. 2001) (no error to allow expert in dental malpractice action to testify whether risk of nerve root irritation was material risk of tooth extraction and whether risk was not fully explained to plaintiff before procedure); *In Interest of Paul S.*, 380 Pa. Super. 476, 552 A.2d 288 (1988) (CYS caseworker permitted to express her opinion concerning custody and placement of dependant child); *Swartz v. Gen. Elec. Co.*, 327 Pa. Super. 58, 474 A.2d 1172 (1984) (expert should have been permitted to testify that plaintiffs' electrical range was defective at time of sale); *Lewis v. Mellor*, 259 Pa. Super. 509, 393 A.2d 941 (1978) (eyewitness properly allowed to testify that only with luck and skill could defendant driver have avoided accident).

Excluded: *Nertavich v. PPL Elec. Utilities*, 100 A.3d 221 (Pa. Super. 2014) (expert for employee of independent contractor improperly testified land-owner had duty to monitor worker safety at site; existence of duty was a question of law for court to decide); *Houdeshell Ex Rel. Bordas v. Rice*, 939 A.2d 981 (Pa. Super. 2007) (expert testimony whether homeowner should have replaced plate glass in door with safety glass properly excluded; issue was fully capable of being resolved by jury of lay persons); *Browne v. Commonwealth*, 843 A.2d 429 (Pa.Cmwlth. 2004) (whether a party has violated local ordinance is question of law and legal opinion testimony is not admissible); *Kozak v. Struth*, 515 Pa. 554, 531 A.2d 420 (1987) (testimony by defense expert that swimming pool accident was entirely caused by victim's poor judgment); *Commonwealth v. Barnhart*, 722 A.2d 1093 (Pa. Super. 1998) (expert opinion testimony by accountant that defendant could not have understood how to commit crime of theft by deception); *Childers v. Power Line Equip. Rentals, Inc.*, 452 Pa. Super. 94, 681 A.2d 201 (1996) (expert in strict products liability case not permitted to testify operator's station of digger-derrick truck was "safe," although he was permitted to say it was not defective and was in a good, efficient location); *Christiansen v. Silfies*, 446 Pa. Super. 464, 667 A.2d 396 (1995) (accident reconstruction expert precluded from testifying re applicable standards of care of commercial truck drivers operating in hazardous conditions; such matters were beyond his expertise).

The Pennsylvania Supreme Court has consistently held that expert psychiatric testimony is admissible to negate the specific intent to kill which is essential to first-degree murder. *See Commonwealth v. Vandivner*, 962 A.2d 1170 (Pa. 2009) (diminished capacity is an extremely limited defense that can only be established by psychiatric testimony regarding mental disorders affecting cognitive functions of brain necessary to formulate specific intent; testimony that does not go to specific intent and premeditation is irrelevant); *Commonwealth v. Legg*, 551 Pa. 437, 711 A.2d 438 (1998); *Commonwealth v. Terry*, 513 Pa. 381, 521 A.2d 398 (1987); *Commonwealth v. Ventura*, 975 A.2d 1128 (Pa. Super. 2009). The federal rule (704(b)) prohibits such testimony.

Compare: Fed. R. Evid. 704.

Research References

Packel & Poulin, Pennsylvania Evidence § 704-1

(4th ed. 2013)

McCormick, Evidence Chapter 3, § 12 (7th ed. 2013)

HABIT/ROUTINE PRACTICE

See: Pa.R.E. 406.

Objection

- Objection. Counsel has not established that the conduct qualifies as admissible evidence of habit/routine practice under Pa.R.E. 406.

Response

- The evidence is admissible because we have established a sufficient pattern of consistent behavior to support the inference of habit/routine practice [*provide specifics*].

Pennsylvania Law

Pa.R.E. 404 embodies the principle that evidence of a person's character *usually* is not admissible for the purpose of proving that the person acted in conformity with his character on a particular occasion. This general rule of exclusion, applicable to both civil and criminal proceedings, is based upon the assumption that such evidence is of slight probative value yet very prejudicial.

Pa.R.E. 406, however, recognizes the relevance of a person's habit or the routine practice of an organization to prove that conduct on a particular occasion was in conformity with the habit or practice.

Pa.R.E. 406 provides:

Evidence of the habit of a person or of the routine practice of an organization, whether corroborated or not and regardless of the presence of eyewitnesses, is relevant to prove that the conduct of the person or organization on a particular occasion was in conformity with the habit or routine practice.

Like the federal rule, Pa.R.E. 406 does not set forth the ways habit or routine practice may be proven, but leaves this for case-by-case determination. Comment to Rule 406; *see, e.g.,*

Baldridge v. Matthews, 378 Pa. 566, 570, 106 A.2d 809, 811 (1954) (organization's routine business practice may be established by introducing a knowledgeable witness' testimony that the routine practice existed); *accord Beaver Valley Alloy Foundry v. Therma-Fab*, 814 A.2d 217 (Pa. Super. 2002).

Habit

A habit is the person's regular practice of meeting a particular kind of situation with a specific type of conduct, such as the habit of going down a particular stairway two stairs at a time, patronizing a particular pub after each day's work or driving an automobile without using a seat belt. McCormick, Evidence § 195 (7th ed. 2013).

Habit testimony may be admitted only if a sufficient pattern of repeated responses is established so that the conduct of the person may be considered a habit. *See Commonwealth v. Rivers*, 537 Pa. 394, 644 A.2d 710 (1994) (daughter properly allowed to testify about mother's habit of keeping large sums of cash hidden in her home). Evidence that a person had on one or more occasions acted in a particular manner is alone insufficient to establish a regular practice of meeting a particular kind of situation with a specific kind of conduct. *Liles v. Balmer*, 389 Pa. Super. 451, 567 A.2d 691 (1989) (evidence of some occasions when dog was unrestrained and chased vehicles does not establish dog habitually was allowed to run free to chase passing vehicles).

Routine Practice

To obtain a Rule 406 inference of the routine practice of a business, a party must show that the practice was performed with invariable regularity. *Beaver Valley Alloy Foundry v. Therma-Fab*, 814 A.2d 217 (Pa. Super. 2002) (collecting cases). Evidence of actions on only a few occasions is not enough. *See, e.g.*, *Christie v. Open Pantry Food Marts Inc. of Delaware Valley*, 237 Pa. Super. 243, 352 A.2d 165 (1975) (evidence of routine custom of mailing admissible to prove check in question was mailed).

"Courts are inclined to leniency" when it comes to evidence of routine business practice. 2 Jack Weinstein & Margaret Berger, Weinstein's Evidence, ¶ 406 [03] at 406–17 (1992). This is because routine business practices are often relied upon by other businesses and because routine business practices are derived from concerted planning activities driven by economic concerns about efficiency, which are, of necessity, more regimented than individual conduct. 2 Jack Weinstein & Margaret Berger, Weinstein's Evidence, ¶ 406 [03] at 406–17 (1992).

Evidence of habit or routine practice is admissible in the absence of corroboration and is to be weighed and considered by the trier of fact in the same manner as any other type of direct or circumstantial evidence. *Beaver Valley Alloy Foundry v. Therma-Fab*, 814 A.2d 217 (Pa. Super. 2002) (no error admitting company officer's testimony as to routine practice without corroborating testimony citing specific examples of conduct).

Illustrations

Admitted: *In re Estate of Ciaffoni*, 498 Pa. 267, 446 A.2d 225 (1982) (error in will context to exclude evidence of forty other probated wills drafted by same scrivener to show elements of common style were absent from decedent's will); *Baldridge v. Matthews*, 378 Pa. 566, 570, 106 A.2d 809, 811 (1954) (testimony by clerk as to hotel's invariable policy of requiring advance payment for guests without luggage); *Mun. Authority of Midland v. Ohioville Mun.*, 108 A.3d 132 (Pa. Cmwlth. 2015) (trial court permitted to use authority's routine practice of billing at month's end for water used that month in order to interpret supply contract between local government units); *Commonwealth v. A.W. Robl Transport*, 747 A.2d 400 (Pa. Super. 2000) (photos admissible to show company's routine practice of shipping bulk waste under documents which described load as "mixed paper"); *Frey v. Harley Davidson Motor Co., Inc.*, 734 A.2d 1 (Pa. Super. 1999) (testimony by dealership representative that motorcycle dealer "in most instances" would disconnect jumper cables properly admitted as evidence of regular habit or business practice).

Excluded: *Jamison v. Ardes*, 408 Pa. 188, 182 A.2d 497 (1962) (error to permit testimony in pedestrian death case that policeman often warned decedent to stay off road; evidence of similar but disconnected acts of negligence inadmissible to prove negligence on particular occasion because person may have acted properly on that occasion); *Wyatt v. Russell*, 308 Pa. 366, 162 A. 256 (1932) (precluding questions re how fast plaintiff drove car on other trips; negligence on former occasions not admissible to prove later negligence).

Compare: Fed. R. Evid. 406.

Research References

Packel & Poulin, Pennsylvania Evidence § 406-1 (4th ed. 2013)

McCormick, Evidence § 195 (7th ed. 2013)

HEARSAY: AUTHOR'S NOTE
CONFRONTATION-CRIMINAL CASES

Crawford v. Washington 541 U.S. 36 (2004)

Author's Note

The Confrontation Clause of the Sixth Amendment provides that "[i]n all criminal prosecutions, the accused shall enjoy the right . . . to be confronted with the witnesses against him." U.S. Const. amend. VI. "The central concern of the Confrontation Clause is to ensure the reliability of the evidence against a criminal defendant by subjecting it to rigorous testing in the context of an adversary proceeding before the trier of fact." *Lilly v. Virginia*, 527 U.S. 116, 124, 119 S.Ct. 1887, 144 L.Ed.2d 117 (1999) (quoting *Maryland v. Craig*, 497 U.S. 836, 845, 110 S.Ct. 3157, 111 L.Ed.2d 666 (1990). *See also Davis v. Alaska*, 415 U.S. 308, 315, 94 S.Ct. 1105, 39 L.Ed.2d 347 (1974) (a primary interest secured by the Confrontation Clause is the right of cross-examination).

The Sixth Amendment protection has been incorporated into the Fourteenth Amendment and is thus applicable to state court prosecutions. *Pointer v. Texas*, 380 U.S. 400, 85 S.Ct. 1065, 13 L.Ed.2d 923 (1965).

Prior to *Crawford v. Washington*, 541 U.S. 36, 124 S.Ct. 1354, 158, L.Ed.2d 177 (2004), the admissibility of out-of-court statements under the Confrontation Clause was governed by *Ohio v. Roberts*, 448 U.S. 56 (1980). According to *Roberts*, an unavailable witness's out-of-court statement could be admitted against the accused if the statement had adequate indicia of reliability. *Roberts*, 448 U.S. at 66. A statement was considered to have sufficient indicia of reliability if it either fell within a "firmly rooted hearsay exception" or bore "particularized guarantees of trustworthiness." *Ohio v. Roberts*, 448 U.S. 56 (1980). *Crawford*, however, dramatically alters the interplay between the Confrontation Clause and the law of hearsay.

Crawford involved a tape-recorded statement given by defendant's wife to police describing the stabbing with which defendant was charged. Pursuant to the state marital privilege, the wife did not testify at trial, so defendant had no opportunity to cross-examine her. The wife's statement was admitted at trial over objection because the trial court determined that the statement had "particularized guarantees of trustworthiness." *Roberts*, 448 U.S. at 66.

The *Crawford* Court held that the Confrontation Clause bars the state from introducing out-of-court statements which are *testimonial* in nature, unless the declarant is unavailable as a witness and the defendant had a prior opportunity to cross-examine the declarant. The Court categorically rejected, as inconsistent with the Constitution, hearsay exceptions for statements deemed otherwise "reliable" despite the absence of prior cross-examination:

> [D]ispensing with confrontation because testimony is obviously reliable is akin to dispensing with a jury because a defendant is obviously guilty. This is not what the Sixth Amendment proscribes.

Crawford, 541 U.S. at 62.

The Supreme Court, in *Crawford*, "changed the legal landscape for determining whether the admission of . . . hearsay statements violates the accused's right[s]" under the Confrontation Clause. *Horton v. Allen*, 370 F.3d 75, 83 (1st Cir. 2004). The Second Circuit has observed that "*Crawford* departs from prior Confrontation Clause jurisprudence by establishing a *per se* bar on the admission of out-of-court testimonial statements made by unavailable declarants where there was no prior opportunity for cross-examination." *U.S. v. McClain*, 377 F.3d 219, 221 (2d Cir. 2004).

The *Crawford* Court reaffirmed the importance of the confrontation right and drew a distinction between testimonial and nontestimonial statements for Confrontation Clause purposes: "Where testimonial statements are involved, we do not think the Framers meant to leave the Sixth Amendment's protection to the vagaries of the rules of evidence, much less to amorphous notions of 'reliability.'" *Crawford*, 541 U.S. at 61. The Court overruled *Roberts* as to "testimonial evidence," holding that the Sixth Amendment demands what the common law required: unavailability and prior opportunity for cross-examination. *Crawford*, 541 U.S. at 68. While the Court declined to "spell out a comprehensive definition of 'testimonial,'" it stated that the term "applies at a minimum to prior testimony at a preliminary hearing, before a grand jury, or at a former trial; and to police interrogations. These are the modern practices with closest kinship to the abuses against which Confrontation Clause was directed." *Crawford*, 541 U.S. at 68. The Court found that the wife's tape-recorded statement taken by the police was "testimonial under any definition," *Crawford*, 541 U.S. at 61, and reversed defendant's conviction, *Crawford*, 541 U.S. at 69.

Without endorsing one specific definition, *Crawford* referenced three different "formulations of this core class of 'testimonial' statements": (1) "*ex parte* in-court testimony or its functional equivalent-that is, material such as affidavits, custodial examinations, prior testimony that the defendant was unable to cross-examine, or similar pretrial statements that declarants would reasonably expect to be used prosecutorially," *Crawford*, 541 U.S. at 51 (quoting Br. for Pet'r 23); (2) "extrajudicial statements . . . contained in formalized testimonial materials, such as affidavits, depositions, prior testimony or confessions," *Crawford*, 541 U.S. at 51–52 (quoting *White v. Illinois*, 502 U.S. 346, 365 (1992) (Thomas, J., concurring)); and (3) "statements that were made under circumstances which would lead an objective witness reasonably to believe that the statement would be available for use at a later trial," *Crawford*, 541 U.S. at 51–52 (quoting Br. for Nat'l Assoc. of Criminal Def. Lawyers et al. as Amici Curiae 3). These three definitions, the Court found, "all share a common nucleus and then define the Clause's coverage at various levels of abstraction around it." *Crawford*, 541 U.S. at 51–52

Admission of non-testimonial hearsay is still governed by *Roberts. See Crawford, 541 U.S. at 68* ("Where nontestimonial hearsay is at issue, it is wholly consistent with the Framer's design to afford the states flexibility in their development of hearsay law-as does *Roberts*, and as would an approach that exempted such statements from Confrontation Clause scrutiny altogether.") *Accord U.S. v. Scheurer*, 62 M.J. 100, 106 (2005) ("We agree with the conclusion of every published appellate court decision that has considered this issue since *Crawford*: the *Ohio v. Roberts* requirement for particularized guarantees of trustworthiness continues to govern confrontation analysis for nontestimonial statements.")

Thus, in criminal cases, the fundamental question with respect to the admissibility of hearsay evidence is whether the out-of-court statements are testimonial or nontestimonial, the former governed by *Crawford* as to confrontation analysis and the latter, by *Roberts*.

"Where testimonial statements are at issue, the only indicium of reliability sufficient to satisfy constitutional demands is the one the Constitution actually prescribes: confrontation." *Crawford*, 541 U.S. at 68–69. Under *Roberts*, a nontestimonial hearsay statement contains "adequate indicia of reliability" if it falls within a "firmly rooted hearsay exception" or if it bears "particularized guarantees of trustworthiness." 448 U.S. at 66. In determining whether a certain statement contains a "particularized guarantee of trustworthiness" sufficient to allow its admission without violating a defendant's Confrontation Clause rights, the court should "consider the totality of those circumstances that surround the making of the statement and that render the declarant particularly worthy of belief." *U.S. v. Dhinsa*, 243 F.3d 635, 655 (2d Cir. 2001) (quoting *Idaho v. Wright*, 497 U.S. 805, 819 (1990)).

Subsequent Developments

In *Davis v. Washington* and *Hammon v. Indiana*, 547 U.S. 813 (2006), both domestic violence cases, the Court explained that "[s]tatements are nontestimonial when made in the course of police interrogation under circumstances objectively indicating that the [interrogation's] primary purpose . . . is to enable police assistance to meet an ongoing emergency," but they "are testimonial when the circumstances objectively indicate that there is no such ongoing emergency and that the [interrogation's] primary purpose is to establish or prove past events potentially relevant to later criminal prosecution." 547 U.S. at 822. See *Michigan v. Bryant*, 562 U.S. 344 (2011) (clarifying *Davis's* "primary purpose" determination).

In *Melendez-Diaz v. Massachusetts*, 129 S.Ct. 2527, 174 L. Ed. 2d 314 (2009), the trial court had admitted into evidence state laboratory affidavits with forensic analysis results showing material seized from defendant was cocaine. The United States Supreme Court said that the laboratory reports fell within the core class of testimonial statements since they had been created for the sole purpose of providing evidence against a defendant. Acknowledging that the Confrontation Clause may make prosecution of criminals more burdensome, the Court held that crime laboratory reports may not be used against defendants at trial unless the analysts responsible for creating them give testimony and subject themselves to cross-examination.

Accord *Commonwealth v. Barton-Martin*, 5 A.3d 363 (Pa. Super. 2010) (where analyst who prepared lab report did not testify at trial, admission of blood-alcohol test results violated defendant's rights under Confrontation Clause).

In *Bullcoming v. New Mexico*, 564 U.S. 647 (2011), a DUI case involving a blood sample analyzed for alcohol, the Supreme Court said the Confrontation Clause does not permit the prosecution to introduce a laboratory report through testimony of an analyst who did not sign the certification or perform or observe the performance of the test reported in the certification. The laboratory report is testimonial in nature created for the very purpose of criminal prosecution.

Pennsylvania Rule of Criminal Procedure 574 provides a mechanism for the admission of a forensic laboratory report supported by a certification. This Rule provides a defendant an opportunity to exercise the right of confrontation and to object to the report on hearsay grounds. Following pre-trial notice by the prosecution, and in the absence of a demand by defendant for declarant's live testimony, the Rule permits the admission of a properly certified forensic laboratory report and the accompanying certification at trial. *See* Pa. R. Crim. P. 574.

Since *Crawford*, various courts have wrestled with the definition of *"testimonial"* statements. *See, e.g.*, *U.S. v. Eagle*, 515 F.3d 794 (8th Cir. 2008) (statements made to forensic interviewer are testimonial); *U.S. v. Moon*, 512 F.3d 359, 362 (7th Cir. 2008) (instruments' readouts are not "statements"; a machine is not a "witness against" anyone); *U.S. v. Jordan*, 509 F.3d 191 (4th Cir. 2007) (statements made by defendant's alleged coconspirator to friend prior to her suicide in which she admitted her involvement in murder were nontestimonial); *U.S. v. Ellis*, 460 F.3d 920 (7th Cir. 2006) (Confrontation Clause does not forbid use of raw data produced by scientific instruments, though interpretation of data may be testimonial); *U.S. v. Brown*, 441 F.3d 1330 (11th Cir. 2006) (excited utterance "you didn't kill that lady" said during private phone conversation between declarant mother and her son while mother was seated in her dining room with only family members present was nontestimonial); *U.S. v. Hagege*, 437 F.3d 943 (9th Cir. 2006) (business records fall outside the core class of "testimonial evidence" and thus are not subject to the absolute requirement of confrontation established in *Crawford*); *U.S. v. Gilbertson*, 435 F.3d 790 (7th Cir. 2006) (in prosecution for knowingly altering odometers of motor vehicles, odometer statements from state certified certificates of title were not testimonial; not made by respective declarants with an eye toward criminal prosecution); *U.S. v. Hansen*, 434 F.3d 92 (1st Cir. 2006) (challenged statements were nontestimonial because they were either co-conspirator statements made during the course of and in furtherance of the conspiracy or casual remarks which the declarant would not reasonably expect to be available for use at a later trial); *U.S. v. Peneaux*, 432 F.3d 882 (8th Cr. 2005) (where statements are made to a physician seeking to give medical aid in the form of diagnosis or treatment, they are presumptively nontestimonial); *U.S. v. Hinton*, 423 F.3d 355 (3d Cir. 2005) (declarant's identification of assailant to police officers while riding in police cruiser in pursuit of suspect was testimonial and, thus, inadmissible; statements made during earlier 911 call, under the circumstances, were nontestimonial); *U.S. v. Pugh*, 405 F.3d 390, 399 (6th Cir. 2005) (declarant's identification of defendant was testimonial because given during police interrogation, made to government officer and because "any reasonable person would assume that a statement that positively identified possible suspects in a picture of the crime scene would be used against those suspects in either investigating or prosecuting the offense"); *U.S. v. Hendricks*, 395 F.3d 173 (3d Cir.

2005) (wiretap recordings are not testimonial for purposes of *Crawford*); *U.S. v. Rodriguez-Marrero*, 390 F.3d 1 (1st Cir. 2004) (signed confession presented under oath to prosecutor is testimonial hearsay); *U.S. v. Cromer*, 389 F.3d 662 (6th Cir. 2004) (statement made knowingly to authorities that describes criminal activity is almost always testimonial; confidential informer's statement to police implicating defendant in criminal activity constituted testimonial hearsay); *Parle v. Runnels*, 387 F.3d 1030 (9th Cir. 2004) (murder victim's diary was admissible evidence; diary not testimonial because not created under circumstances which would lead an objective witness reasonably to believe that it would be available for use at a later trial); *U.S. v. Saget*, 377 F.3d 223 (2d Cir. 2004) (statements to confidential informant, whose true identity was unknown to declarant, did not constitute "testimony" under *Crawford*); *U.S. v. Bruno*, 383 F.3d 65 (2d Cir. 2004) (plea allocution transcript and grand jury testimony of unavailable witnesses constituted testimonial hearsay); *Horton v. Allen*, 370 F.3d 75 (1st Cir. 2004) (statements made in private conversation were within state of mind exception, nontestimonial in nature, and outside *Crawford's* scope; *Roberts* applies to determine admissibility); *U.S. v. Reyes*, 362 F.3d 536 (8th Cir. 2004) (*Crawford* does not apply to co-conspirator statements because they are nontestimonial).

Pennsylvania Cases

In order to determine if a document or statement created out-of-court is testimonial in nature, the Pennsylvania Supreme Court looks at the primary purpose of the document or statement. *Commonwealth v. Yohe*, 79 A.3d 520 (Pa. 2013) (toxicology report determining amount of alcohol in blood was testimonial.) A document or statement is testimonial if its primary purpose is to establish or prove past events potentially relevant to later crim-

141

inal prosecution. *Id.* A document or statement has such a primary purpose if it is created or given under circumstances which would lead an objective witness reasonably to believe that the document or statement would be available for use at a later trial. *Id.*; *Commonwealth v. Allshouse*, 985 A.2d 847 (Pa.2009) (child's statements to caseworker about sexual abuse were nontestimonial per *Crawford* and *Davis* analysis and admissible under Tender Years doctrine); *Commonwealth v. Dyarman*, 73 A.3d 565 (Pa. 2013) (calibration logs of BAC testing device are not testimonial in nature; logs simply attest approved device was used); *Commonwealth v. Brown*, 139 A.3d 208 (2016) (autopsy report was testimonial and its admission without testimony of doctor who performed it violated defendant's right of confrontation); *Commonwealth v. Rosser*, 135 A.3d 1077 (Pa. Super. 2016) (right of confrontation does not permit fishing expeditions; defendant cannot cross-examine witness on a subject for which defendant cannot provide a factual foundation); *Commonwealth v. Williams*, 103 A.3d 354 (Pa. Super. 2014) (statements to 911 to obtain police and medial help were nontestimonial); *Commonwealth v. McKellick*, 24 A.3d 982 (Pa. Super. 2011) (use of dashcam videotape of traffic stop did not violate defendant's confrontation rights); *Commonwealth v. Borovichka*, 18 A.3d 1242 (Pa. Super. 2011) (lab analyst who tested blood a year earlier but had no recall of this particular defendant allowed to testify from his notes); *Commonwealth v. Abrue*, 11 A.3d 484 (Pa. Super. 2010) (police officer's out-of-court statements to a second officer about what had occurred in fight with defendant before second officer arrived at the scene were testimonial and inadmissible); *Commonwealth v. Mollett*, 5 A.3d 291 (Pa. Super. 2010) (witnesses who testify as to lack of memory are not considered unavailable for cross-examination for purposes of Confrontation Clause); *Commonwealth v. Gray*, 867 A.2d 560, 577 (Pa. Super. 2005) (excited utterances made to police at crime scene were not testimonial because declarant was not subject to police interrogation and volunteered information in effort to remedy "perceived emergency," not to create a record against another for use in a future prosecution").

Admission of a child witness's testimony via videotape to limit emotional trauma per the Videotape Statute, 42 Pa.C.S.A. § 5984.1 does not violate confrontation rights where the testimony is taken under oath; the defendant can observe and hear the testimony; cross examination is permitted and the defense has adequate opportunity to communicate during the testimony in order to mount a proper defense. *Commonwealth v. Geiger*, 944 A.2d 85 (Pa. Super. 2008).

The Supreme Court has said that the right to confrontation is a *trial* right. *Pennsylvania v. Ritchie*, 480 U.S. 39, 52, 107 S.Ct. 989, 999, 94 L.Ed.2d 40 (1987). It is well established at sentencing that a trial court may use reliable hearsay, *U.S. v. Zlatogur*, 271 F.3d 1025 (11th Cir. 2001) and that the right to confrontation does not apply. *U.S. v. Kirby*, 418 F.3d 621 (6th Cir. 2005). Accordingly, a number of circuits have recognized that *Crawford* does not apply to sentencing proceedings. *U.S. v. Smith*, 253 Fed. Appx. 818 (11th Cir. 2007); *U.S. v. Cantellaro*, 430 F.3d 1142 (11th Cir. 2005); *U.S. v. Monteiro*, 417 F.3d 208 (1st Cir. 2005); *U.S. v. Martinex*, 413 F.3d 239 (2d Cir. 2005). See *Commonwealth v. Wantz*, 84 A.3d 324 (Pa. Super. 2014) (confrontation clause rights do not apply to post-conviction proceedings).

Commonwealth v. Wholaver, 989 A.2d 883 (Pa. 2010) acknowledged instances where the often limited scope of a preliminary hearing will not provide the right of confrontation mandated by *Crawford*. Here, however, the preliminary hearing testimony of defendant's subsequently murdered daughter was admissible at trial because there had been fulsome cross-examination at the hearing as to bias, veracity, inconsistency and outside influence conducted by the same trial counsel.

Research References

Goode and Wellborn, Courtroom Handbook on Federal Evidence Chapter 5, Rule 802 (annual ed.)

Graham, Handbook of Federal Evidence § 802.2 (6th ed. 2006)

HEARSAY: GENERALLY

See: Pa.R.E. 801(c), 802.

Objection

- [*To a question*] Objection. The question calls for a hearsay answer.
- [*To an answer*] Objection, hearsay. I move the answer be stricken and the jury be instructed not to consider it for any purpose.

Response

- The statement is not being offered for the truth of the matter asserted but is only offered:

   [*as circumstantial proof of the speaker's state of mind (e.g., malice, hatred, premeditation, knowledge or notice)*]

   [*to show the effect the statement had on the listener (or reader)*]

   [*to impeach the witness with his or her own prior inconsistent statement*]

   [*because the statement is an operative fact or verbal act offered for its legal significance (e.g., words of an offer or acceptance creating a contract, or defamatory words spoken to establish slander)*]

Pennsylvania Law

Hearsay is an out-of-court statement offered to prove the truth of the matter asserted in the statement. Pa.R.E. 801(c); *Commonwealth v. Busanet*, 54 A.3d 35 (Pa. 2012); *Commonwealth v. Begley*, 566 Pa. 239, 780 A.2d 605 (2001); *Commonwealth v. Mosley*, 114 A.3d 1072 (Pa. Super. 2015); *Commonwealth v. Washington*, 63 A.3d 797 (Pa. Super. 2013); *Harris v. Toys "R" Us-Penn, Inc.*, 880 A.2d 1270 (Pa. Super. 2005); *Porter Tp. Initiative v. East Stroudsburg Area School Dist.*, 44 A.3d 1201 (Pa.Cmwlth. 2012); *Jerry v. Dept. of Corrections*, 990 A.2d 112 (Pa.Cmwlth. 2010).

An out-of-court statement is any statement (oral or written) except one made by a witness while testifying at trial. Pa.R.E. 801(c). Thus, face to face communications, telephone conversations, letters, records and reports are all out-of-court statements unless they are made while testifying.

An out-of-court statement is offered to prove the truth of the matter asserted if the proponent is offering it for the purpose of proving the facts communicated in the statement. *Commonwealth v. Koch*, 39 A.3d 996 (Pa. Super. 2011) (text messages which could not be authenticated were hearsay because their evidentiary value depended entirely on the truth of their contents); Pa.R.E. 801(c).

The hearsay rule "is premised on the theory that out-of-court statements are subject to particular hazards. The declarant might be lying; he might have misperceived the events which he relates; he might have faulty memory; his words might be misunderstood or taken out of context by the listener. And the ways in which these dangers are minimized for in-court statements—the oath, the witness' awareness of the gravity of the proceedings, the jury's ability to observe the witness' demeanor, and, most importantly, the right of the opponent to cross-examine—are generally absent for things said out of court." *Williamson v. United States*, 512 U.S. 594, 598, 114 S.Ct. 2431, 2434, 129 L.Ed.2d 476 (1994); *Heddings v. Steele*, 514 Pa. 569, 526 A.2d 349 (1987) (hearsay lacks guarantees of trustworthiness fundamental to the Anglo-American system of jurisprudence); *accord Commonwealth v. Thomas*, 908 A.2d 351 (Pa. Super. 2006). As Justice Musmanno said: ". . . nothing is more adamantly established in our trial procedure than that no one may testify to what somebody else told him. He may only relate what is within the sphere of his own memory brought to him by the couriers of his own senses." *Johnson v. Peoples Cab Co.*, 386 Pa. 513, 514–515, 126 A.2d 720, 721 (1956).

Because hearsay is regarded as unreliable, "[i]t is well settled in our law that hearsay evidence is inadmissible unless it qualifies under one of the recognized exceptions to that rule." *Commonwealth v. Smith*, 523 Pa. 577, 591, 568 A.2d 600, 607 (1989). In order for hearsay testimony to be properly admitted in evidence, the proponent of such testimony must point to some exception to the hearsay rule. *Commonwealth v. Kriner*, 915 A.2d 653 (Pa. Super. 2007). Otherwise, the testimony will be excluded based on the traditional notion that a party should not be deprived of the guaranty of truthfulness provided by the oath of the declarant and the opportunity to cross-examine the declarant in order to test the accuracy of the observations upon which the testimony is based. *Carney v. Pennsylvania R.R. Co.*, 428 Pa. 489, 240 A.2d 71 (1968).

Where a defendant seeks at trial to introduce through another his own statements made at the time of arrest to support his version of the facts, such testimony is clearly offensive to the hearsay rule. *Commonwealth v. Murphy*, 425 A.2d 352 (Pa. 1981); *Commonwealth v. Benson*, 10 A.3d 1268 (Pa. Super. 2010).

As a general rule, the Pennsylvania Rules of Evidence are not applicable to hearings conducted before Commonwealth agencies. 2 Pa.C.S. § 505 or local agencies, 2 Pa.C.S. § 554. Nonetheless, hearsay evidence, properly objected to, is not competent evidence to support a determination of an agency. *Sule v. Philadelphia Parking Authority*, 26 A.3d 1240 (Pa.Cmwlth. 2011). But, hearsay evidence admitted without objection in an administrative hearing will be given its natural probative effect and may support a finding but only if competent evidence of record corroborates it. *Ray v. Civil Service Com'n of Darby*, 131 A.3d 1012 (Pa. Cmwlth.

2016); *Bell Beverage v. Unemployment Compensation*, 49 A.3d 49 (Pa.Cmwlth. 2012); *Walker v. Unemployment Compensation Board of Review*, 367 A.2d 366 (Pa. Cmwlth. 1976). But a finding based solely on hearsay will not stand. *Six L's Packing v. W.C.A.B. (Williamson)*, 2 A.3d 1268 (Pa.Cmwlth. 2010).

Learned Treatise

Pennsylvania did not adopt the Learned Treatise exception. Pa. R.E. 803(18). Learned writings which are offered to prove the truth of their contents are hearsay and may not properly be admitted into evidence. *Aldridge v. Edmunds*, 750 A.2d 292 (Pa. 2000). Subject to appropriate restraint by the trial court, Pennsylvania courts do permit limited identification of textual materials on direct examination of an expert to permit that witness to fairly explain the basis for his reasoning. *Klein v. Aronchick*, 85 A.3d 487 (Pa. Super. 2014) (improper for expert to testify at length regarding specific details of articles in the New England Journal of Medicine). The same rationale applies to cross-examination.

Criminal Cases—*Crawford v. Washington*

Until recently, the constitutional admissibility of hearsay statements in criminal cases was determined according to the two-prong test of *Ohio v. Roberts*, 448 U.S. 56, 100 S.Ct. 2531, 65 L.Ed.2d 597 (1980). Under this test, a court could admit statements made by a declarant if the prosecution showed that: (1) the declarant was unavailable, and (2) the statements were reliable, either because they fell within a "firmly rooted" hearsay exception or because they bore "particularized guarantees of trustworthiness." *Ohio v. Roberts*, 448 U.S. 56, 66, 100 S.Ct. 2531, 65 L.Ed.2d 597 (1980). Later, the Court refined the *Roberts* test, dispensing with the need to show unavailability when the declarant's statements fell within a firmly rooted exception. *See White v. Illinois*, 502 U.S. 346, 112 S.Ct. 736, 116 L.Ed.2d 848 (1992).

In *Crawford v. Washington*, 541 U.S. 36, 124 S.Ct. 1354, 158 L.Ed.2d 177 (2004) (discussed at page 134, *supra*), the Court held that in criminal cases, the Confrontation Clause forbids the admission of "testimonial" statements of a witness who did not appear at trial unless that witness was unavailable to testify and the defendant had had a prior opportunity for cross-examination. As the Third Circuit explained, "The lynchpin of the *Crawford* decision . . . is its distinction between testimonial and nontestimonial hearsay; simply put, the rule announced in *Crawford* applies only to the former category of statements." *United States v. Hendricks*, 395 F.3d 173, 179 (3d Cir. 2005).

The admissibility of "nontestimonial" hearsay for purposes of the Confrontation clause continues to be governed by the standards set forth in *Ohio v. Roberts*, 448 U.S. 56, 66, 100 S.Ct. 2531, 65 L.Ed.2d 597 (1980). Thus, the fundamental question in criminal cases with respect to the admissibility of hearsay evidence is, what confrontation analysis applies—*Crawford* or *Ohio v. Roberts*?

Non-Hearsay

A statement that is not offered for its truth is not hearsay. *Castellani v. Scranton Times, L.P.*, 124 A.3d 1229 (Pa. 2015); *Commonwealth v. Kuder*, 62 A.3d 1038 (Pa. Super. 2013). When a witness testifies that someone said something to him and the purpose is not to show that what was said was true but only that the statement was made, the testimony is not hearsay. *Commonwealth v. Busanet*, 54 A.3d 35 (Pa. 2012) (statement admitted only to show defendant heard it and that it served as his motive); *Am. Future Sys., Inc. v. Better Bus. Bureau*, 872 A.2d 1202 (Pa. Super. 2005); *Commonwealth v.*

Stocker, 424 Pa. Super. 189, 622 A.2d 333 (1993). Evidence of many out-of-court assertions is not hearsay, either because the utterance is not an assertion, or because it is not offered to prove its truth. *Zuk v. Zuk*, 55 A.3d 102 (Pa. Super. 2012). Out-of-court utterances that are not assertions typically can include greetings, pleasantries, expressions of gratitude, questions, offers, instructions, warnings, demands, exclamations, expressions of emotion, etc. *See Alwine v. Sugar Creek Rest, Inc.*, 883 A.2d 605 (Pa. Super. 2005) and *Eagle v. Unemployment Comp. Bd. of Review*, 659 A.2d 60 (Pa.Cmwlth.1995) (instructions); *Kierski v. Township of Robinson*, 810 A.2d 196 (Pa. Cmwlth. 2002) (permitting Township officials to testify to citizen complaints to show knowledge). But see *Commonwealth v. Parker*, 104 A.3d 17 (Pa. Super. 2014) (agreeing with other jurisdictions that have held a question can be hearsay if it contains an implied assertion offered for the truth of the matter; this approach ensures that the substance of an utterance, not its grammatical form controls whether the utterance is admissible).

An out-of-court statement which is not offered for its truth but to explain the witness' course of conduct is not hearsay. *Commonwealth v. Rega*, 933 A.2d 997 (Pa. 2007) (conduct of investigating officer); *accord Commonwealth v. Carson*, 913 A.2d 220 (Pa. 2006), *Commonwealth v. Trinidad*, 96 A.3d 1031 (Pa. Super. 2014); *Commonwealth v. Estepp*, 17 A.3d 939 (Pa. Super. 2011); *Commonwealth v. Hardy*, 918 A.2d 766 (Pa. Super. 2007); *Jerry v. Dept. of Corrections*, 990 A.2d 112 (Pa.Cmwlth. 2010).

Compare: Fed. R. Evid. 801(c), 802.

Research References

Packel & Poulin, Pennsylvania Evidence §§ 801-1–802-1 (4th ed. 2013)

McCormick, Evidence Chapter 24 (7th ed. 2013)

HEARSAY: INDIRECT OR CONCEALED HEARSAY

See: Pa.R.E. 802.

Objection

- Objection. The question seeks to elicit hearsay indirectly by allowing the jury to infer what was said to this witness.

Response

- The evidence is not offered to prove the truth of the matter asserted and, therefore, is not hearsay. It is being offered [*to prove the state of mind of this witness*] [*to explain a course of conduct*] and is admissible for that purpose.

Pennsylvania Law

Testimony which does not directly offer the words of a statement but which indirectly reveals the content of the statement is, in effect, a statement and, therefore, hearsay. McCormick calls such testimony "indirect hearsay"; Professor Irving Younger terms it "concealed hearsay."

As McCormick observes:

> If the purpose of testimony is to use an out-of-court statement to prove the truth of facts stated, the hearsay objection cannot be eliminated by eliciting the content of the statement in an indirect form. Thus, when offered as proof of the facts asserted, testimony regarding "information received" by the witness and the results of investigations made by other persons are properly classed as hearsay.

McCormick, Evidence § 249 (7th ed. 2013) (footnotes omitted).

The following cases illustrate the problem.

In *Commonwealth v. Farris*, 251 Pa. Super. 277, 280, 380 A.2d 486, 487 (1977), the prosecution carefully avoided asking a police officer to give the substance of a conversation with an out-of-court witness but simply asked, "As a result of talking with Gary Moore (an alleged co-conspirator), what did you do?" The answer was, "I arrested Emanuel Farris." The clear implication of this testimony was that Moore had identified Farris as a co-conspirator and this testimony was, therefore, treated as an inadmissible hearsay statement. Accord *Commonwealth v. Thomas*, 396 Pa. Super. 92, 578 A.2d 422 (1990) (improper oblique narrative hearsay was elicited where careful questioning by prosecutor led policeman to testify that, as a result of his interview with absent witness, he proceeded to arrest defendant; jury could readily conclude absent witness had identified defendant as perpetrator); *see also Commonwealth v. Parks*, 273 Pa. Super. 506, 417 A.2d 1163 (1979). Concealed hearsay was impermissibly present in *Commonwealth v. Rush*, 529 Pa. 498, 605 A.2d 792 (1992) where an assault victim's testimony indicated that prior to the attack her assailant had described his unusual hobby of making picture frames out of cigarette boxes. At trial, a detective testified over objection that he had gone to defendant's home and asked his mother if she had any picture frames made by her son and that in response, she produced a picture frame—made out of cigarette boxes. The mother was never called to testify. Thus, her implied statement that defendant had made the picture frame was not subject to cross-examination and was hearsay.

Where the potential prejudicial impact is minimal, certain out-of-court statements offered to explain a course of police conduct are admissible. *Commonwealth v. Rega*, 933 A.2d 997 (Pa. 2007); *Commonwealth v. Carson*, 913 A.2d 220 (Pa. 2006); *Commonwealth v. Bishop*, 936 A.2d 1136 (Pa. Super. 2007); *Commonwealth v. Hardy*, 918 A.2d 766 (Pa. Super. 2007); *Commonwealth v. Dargan*, 897 A.2d 496 (Pa. Super. 2006). *Accord Commonwealth v. Collazo*, 440 Pa. Super. 13, 654

152

A.2d 1174 (1995) (allowing police testimony that informant gave agreed-upon signal of consummated drug deal to explain why police moved in to arrest defendant). The rationale is that such statements do not constitute hearsay because they are not offered for the truth of the matters asserted, but merely to show the information upon which the police acted. *Commonwealth v. Douglas*, 558 Pa. 412, 737 A.2d 1188 (1999); *Commonwealth v. Jones*, 540 Pa. 442, 658 A.2d 746 (1995); *Commonwealth v. Yates*, 531 Pa. 373, 613 A.2d 542 (1992); *Commonwealth v. Phillips*, 879 A.2d 1260 (Pa. Super. 2005). However, the Pennsylvania Supreme Court has indicated that the police conduct rule should not be utilized as a pretext to nullify an accused's right to cross-examine and confront the witnesses against him. *Commonwealth v. Palsa*, 521 Pa. 113, 555 A.2d 808 (1989); *Commonwealth v. Dent*, 837 A.2d 571 (Pa. Super. 2003) (collecting cases); *Commonwealth v. Drummond*, 775 A.2d 849 (Pa. Super. 2001). The right of confrontation, which has been held to include the right to cross-examine accusing witnesses, is violated when an out-of-court statement of a third person implicating the accused is introduced at trial. *Bruton v. United States*, 391 U.S. 123, 88 S.Ct. 1620, 20 L.Ed.2d 476 (1968), *appeal after remand* 416 F.2d 310 (8th Cir.1969), *cert. denied*, 397 U.S. 1014, 90 S.Ct. 1248, 25 L.Ed.2d 428 (1970).

In *Crawford v. Washington*, 541 U.S. 36 (2004) (discussed at page 134, *supra*), a criminal case involving a Confrontation Clause challenge, the United States Supreme Court held that if a hearsay statement was "testimonial" in nature, it could not be introduced at trial, in the absence of the declarant, unless the defendant had a previous opportunity to cross-examine the declarant.

Opposing counsel should be alert to the potential for indirect or concealed hearsay when the examiner instructs the witness, "Don't tell me what your conversation was [with the out-of-court declarant]; just tell me what you did as a result of that conversation."

Compare: Fed. R. Evid. 802.

Research References

Packel & Poulin, Pennsylvania Evidence § 801-1 (4th ed. 2013)

McCormick, Evidence §§ 249–250 (7th ed. 2013)

Irving Younger, Hearsay: A Practical Guide Through the Thicket, § 1.4 at 16–18 (Prentice Hall 1988)

HEARSAY: MULTIPLE HEARSAY

See: Pa.R.E. 805.

Objection

- [*To a question*] Objection. The question calls for multiple hearsay.
- [*To a proposed exhibit*] Objection. The document is/ contains multiple hearsay.
- [*To an answer*] Objection, multiple hearsay. I move the answer be stricken and the jury be instructed not to consider it for any purpose.

Response

- The evidence is admissible; both out-of-court statements qualify as hearsay exceptions [*specify*].

Pennsylvania Law

Pa.R.E. 805 makes hearsay within hearsay admissible only if each of the statements involved falls within an exception to the hearsay rule. Pa.R.E. 805 provides:

> Hearsay included within hearsay is not excluded under the hearsay rule if each part of the combined statements conforms with an exception to the hearsay rule provided in these rules.

When a witness' testimony presents double hearsay, the reliability and trustworthiness of each declarant must be independently established. This requirement is satisfied when each statement comes within an exception to the hearsay rule. *Commonwealth v. May*, 898 A.2d 559 (Pa. 2006); *Alessandro v. W.C.A.B. (Precision Metal)*, 972 A.2d 1245 (Pa.Cmwlth. 2009); *see Keystone Dedicated Logistics v. JGB Ent.*, 77 A.3d 1 (Pa. Super. 2013) (testimony based on hearsay is hearsay); *Semieraro v. Commonwealth Utility Equip. Corp.*, 518 Pa. 454, 544 A.2d 46 (1988) (inadmissible double hearsay for witness to attempt to relate statements by third party about opinions and conclusions of non-testifying experts); *Commonwealth v. Gezovich*, 7 A.3d 300 (Pa. Super. 2010) (police report is double hearsay unless statement made to police and police statement itself are both subject to hearsay exceptions); *Kemp v. Qualls*, 326 Pa. Super. 319, 473 A.2d 1369 (1984) (excluding witness' testimony recounting both sides of alleged phone conversation between decedent and his doctor); *Guthrie v. W.C.A.B. (Travelers' Club)*, 854 A.2d 653 (Pa.Cmwlth. 2004) (excluding witness' testimony re both sides of phone call). While the rule contains no limit on the levels of hearsay, it has been observed that "experience suggests an inverse relationship between the reliability of a statement and the number of hearsay layers it contains."[1] *See, e.g., Commonwealth v. Peay*, 806 A.2d 22 (Pa.Super 2002) (no error to exclude evidence that defense witnesses had heard from third parties that fourth parties had murdered victim).

For cases in which each level was found to fall within a hearsay exception, *see, e.g., Commonwealth v. Chmiel*, 558 Pa. 478, 738 A.2d 406 (1999) (deceased attorney's statements were former testimony containing admissions by party defendant); *Commonwealth v. Galloway*, 302 Pa. Super. 145, 448 A.2d 568 (1982) (where victim told nurse that defendant said he was going to kill her, the statement as between victim and defendant was admissible as an admission; statement as between victim and nurse qualified as an excited utterance).

The fact that one level of a multi-level statement qualifies as a non-hearsay admission or comes within an exception does not excuse other levels from meeting the Pa.R.E. 805 requirement that every level must satisfy the hearsay rule. *Commonwealth v. Laich*, 566 Pa. 19, 777 A.2d 1057

---

[1]*United States v. Fernandez*, 892 F.2d 976 (11th Cir. 1989).

(Pa. 2001) (witness' testimony that victim told her defendant had said he would kill victim not admissible; defendant's statement to victim admissible as admission but victim's statement not admissible under any exception).

Double or multiple hearsay is frequently encountered where the witness purports to have overheard a phone call, *Guthrie*, 854 A.2d 653 (Pa.Cmwlth. 2004), as well as with respect to the contents of business records and other documents. *Commonwealth v. Sanchez*, 416 Pa. Super. 160, 610 A.2d 1020 (1992) (medical records containing statements by defendant held admissible; medical records admissible as business records and defendant's statements admissible as admissions or statements made for purposes of medical diagnosis); *Hreha v. Benscoter*, 381 Pa. Super. 556, 554 A.2d 525 (1989) (portion of hospital record containing patient's extrajudicial statement was incompetent hearsay evidence where statement did not come within any exception to the hearsay rule); *accord, Commonwealth v. Zimmerman*, 391 Pa. Super. 569, 571 A.2d 1062 (1990); *Wilkerson v. Allied Van Lines, Inc.*, 360 Pa. Super. 523, 521 A.2d 25 (1987).

Where the source of the information and the recorder of that information are not the same person, a business record contains hearsay upon hearsay. If both the source and recorder of the information were acting in the regular course of the organization's business, the double hearsay problem may be excused by the business records exception. Pa.R.E. 803(6).

If the document is not a business record, other exceptions to the hearsay rule must be satisfied before its contents can be admitted.

In criminal cases, *see Crawford v. Washington*, 541 U.S. 36, 124 S.Ct. 1354 (2004), involving a Confrontation Clause challenge, where the United States Supreme Court held that if a hearsay statement was "testimonial" in nature, it could not be introduced at trial, in the absence of the declarant, unless the defendant had a previous opportunity to cross-examine the declarant. *Crawford* is discussed at page 134, *supra.*

Compare: Fed. R. Evid. 805.

Research References

Packel & Poulin, Pennsylvania Evidence § 805-1 (4th ed. 2013)

McCormick, Evidence § 324.1 (7th ed. 2013)

HEARSAY EXCEPTION: ADMISSION—PARTY'S OWN STATEMENT

See: Pa.R.E. 803(25)(A).

Objection

- *[To a question]* Objection. The question calls for a hearsay answer.
- *[To an answer]* Objection, hearsay. I move the answer be stricken and the jury be instructed not to consider it for any purpose.

Response

- Admissions by a party opponent are admissible as an exception to the rule of hearsay exclusion.

Pennsylvania Law

Unlike the Federal Rules of Evidence which do not treat admissions as hearsay, Pa.R.E. 803(25)(A) continues to follow the common law view, treating admissions as an exception to the hearsay rule. *See Beardsley v. Weaver*, 402 Pa. 130, 166 A.2d 529 (1961).

In order for a statement to be admitted as an admission, it must have been made by a party opponent. Perhaps because it is self-evident, a good definition of admission by a party-opponent is hard to find in the cases. Therefore, several are offered, as gleaned from the treatises:

1. Out-of-court statements made by an opposing party and out-of-court conduct of that party may be admitted as evidence against that party.[1]
2. Any relevant statement made by a party is evidence against himself.[2]
3. Admissions are the words or acts of a party-

---

[1]Haydock & Sonsteng, Trial § 4.6 p. 120.

[2]Phipson on Evidence, Chap. 24, p. 619.

opponent that are offered as evidence against the party.[3]

4. Anything the other side ever said or did will be admissible so long as it has something to do with the case.[4]

The rationale for the admission of a party's out-of-court statement is not that it is especially reliable, but because the right to confront the evidence is not lost; i.e., the party is present to take the stand and explain or contradict his former statements. *Commonwealth v. Edwards*, 903 A.2d 1139 (Pa. 2006); *Commonwealth v. Chmiel*, 558 Pa. 478, 738 A.2d 406 (1999); *DeFrancesco v. Western Pennsylvania Water Co.*, 329 Pa. Super. 508, 478 A.2d 1295 (1984).

Admissions will frequently be used to discredit or directly impeach the testimony of the opposing party but there is no requirement they do so. A party is entitled to prove any material fact by his opponent's declaration, even though such fact is not inconsistent with the opponent's case. An admission by a party-opponent qualifies for exception to the hearsay rule whether it is an assertion of fact or opinion, and whether or not the declarant had personal knowledge of the matter asserted. *Salvitti v. Throppe*, 343 Pa. 642, 23 A.2d 445 (1942).

Statements in many different forms have been admitted as a party's admission. These include: oral statements, *Bascelli v. Randy, Inc.*, 339 Pa. Super. 254, 488 A.2d 1110 (1985); *Commonwealth v. Galloway*, 302 Pa. Super. 145, 448 A.2d 568 (1982); confessions, *Commonwealth v. Darden*, 311 Pa. Super. 170, 457 A.2d 549 (1983); extrajudicial statements made by a defendant containing no

---

[3]McCormick on Evidence, § 254, p. 140; *Six L's Packing v. W.C.A.B. (Williamson)*, 2 A.3d 1268, 1216, n.7 (Pa. Cmwlth. 2010).

[4]Younger, Hearsay: A Practical Guide Through the Thicket, § 3.2, p. 75.

admission of guilt, *Commonwealth v. Weiss*, 81 A.3d 767 (Pa. 2013); *Commonwealth v. Tervalon*, 463 Pa. 581, 345 A.2d 671 (1975); a party's testimony in another proceeding, *Commonwealth v. Ferguson*, 358 Pa. Super. 98, 516 A.2d 1200 (1986); a guilty plea, *Stidham v. Millvale Sportsmen's Club*, 421 Pa. Super. 548, 618 A.2d 945 (1992); letters, *Commonwealth v. Barnes*, 871 A.2d 812 (Pa. Super. 2005); *Wyke v. Ward*, 81 Pa.Cmwlth. 392, 474 A.2d 375 (1984); statements by a party's attorney, *Commonwealth v. Johnson*, 961 A.2d 877 (Pa. Super. 2008); a written appraisal, *Kremer v. Janet Fleisher Gallery, Inc.*, 320 Pa. Super. 384, 467 A.2d 377 (1983). Silence can also be construed as an admission, but only when the circumstances are such that one ought to speak and does not. *L. Washington & Assoc. v. Unemployment Comp.*, 662 A.2d 1148 (Pa.Cmwlth.1995); *see also Commonwealth v. Coccioletti*, 493 Pa. 103, 425 A.2d 387 (1981); *Levin v. Van Horn*, 412 Pa. 322, 194 A.2d 419 (1963).

In a criminal proceeding, a defendant's voluntary pretrial admissions or confessions which comply with constitutional safeguards are admissible as substantive evidence under the admission exception, regardless of whether the defendant testifies. *Commonwealth v. Watkins*, 557 Pa. 194, 843 A.2d 1203 (2003); *Commonwealth v. Page*, 59 A.3d 1118 (Pa. Super. 2013) (volunteered or spontaneous utterances by an individual are admissible without the administration of Miranda warnings); *Commonwealth v. Fisher*, 564 Pa. 505, 769 A.2d 1116 (2001) (where defendant volunteered statements, they constituted gratuitous utterances unsolicited by the government and were admissible); *Commonwealth v. Gibson*, 553 Pa. 648, 720 A.2d 473 (1998) (voluntary statements not responsive to any queries are admissible); *Commonwealth v. King*, 554 Pa. 331, 721 A.2d 763 (1998) (similar); *Commonwealth v. Baez*, 554 Pa. 66, 720 A.2d 711 (1998); *Commonwealth v. Page*, 965 A.2d 1212 (Pa.

Super. 2009) (defendant not in custody for *Miranda* purposes at time of police interview during which inculpatory statements were made); *Commonwealth v. Davis*, 861 A.2d 310 (Pa. Super. 2004) (spontaneous statements, not the product of police conduct, are admissible even when suspect has not received *Miranda* warnings); *Commonwealth v. Briggs*, 12 A.3d 291 (Pa. 2011); *In Re D.H.*, 863 A.2d 562 (Pa. Super. 2004) (a statement spontaneously volunteered is admissible notwithstanding prior assertion of constitutional rights).

A party's plea of guilty to a crime is an admission, and may be offered in evidence by a party-opponent. *Cromley v. Gardner*, 253 Pa. Super. 467, 385 A.2d 433 (1978) (DUI guilty plea offered by plaintiff in wrongful death action as admission that defendant was driving while drunk). However, a plea of guilty that is later withdrawn, a plea of nolo contendere, or assertions made in connection with plea discussions, may not be admissible for public policy reasons. *See* Pa.R.E. 410(a)(2), *Commonwealth v. Moser*, 999 A.2d 602 (Pa. Super. 2010). 42 Pa.C.S. § 6142 provides that a plea of guilty or nolo contendere to a summary offense under the Pennsylvania Motor Vehicle Code is not admissible in a civil case arising out of the same incident.

In multi-party proceedings, the admission of one party may be inadmissible hearsay as to another party. Depending upon particular circumstances, the trial court may admit the statement accompanied by a limiting instruction or exclude it entirely, where a limiting instruction would be useless and substantial prejudice would occur. *See, McShain v. Indem. Ins. Co. of North America*, 338 Pa. 113, 12 A.2d 59 (1940); *Havasy v. Resnick*, 415 Pa. Super. 480, 609 A.2d 1326 (1992); *Durkin v. Equine Clinics, Inc.*, 376 Pa. Super. 557, 546 A.2d 665 (1988); *Adams v. Mackleer*, 239 Pa. Super. 244, 361 A.2d 439 (1976). *See also Rettger v. UPMC Shadyside*, 991 A.2d 915 (Pa. Super. 2010) (where defendant hospital did not join or cross-claim against defendant doctor, hospital could not use doctor's hearsay statements as opposing party admissions).

An admission (other than a "judicial admission," discussed on page 326) may be denied, explained, contradicted, or otherwise attacked by the party against whom it is offered, just like any other item of evidence introduced against the party.

It is black letter law that the testimony of one who is merely called as a witness for a party but who does not stand in privity with him may not be considered an admission by the party. *Jewelcor Jewelers and Distribs., Inc. v. Corr*, 373 Pa. Super. 536, 542 A.2d 72 (1988).

Compare: Fed. R. Evid. 801(d)(2).

Research References

Packel & Poulin, Pennsylvania Evidence § 803(25)(A)-1 (4th ed. 2013)

Binder, Hearsay Handbook Chapter 35 (4th ed. 2001)

McCormick, Evidence Chapter 25 (7th ed. 2013)

HEARSAY EXCEPTION: ADMISSION BY AGENT

See: Pa.R.E. 803(25)(D).

Objection

- [*To a question*] Objection. The question calls for a hearsay answer.
- [*To an answer*] Objection, hearsay. I move the answer be stricken and the jury be instructed not to consider it for any purpose.

Response

- The statement qualifies as an admission by a party opponent. It was made by [*plaintiffs/defendant's*] agent concerning a matter within the scope of [*agency/employment*] and was made during the existence of that relationship.

Pennsylvania Law

Pa.R.E. 803(25)(D) provides that a statement is not hearsay if it "is offered against a party and is . . . a statement by the party's agent or servant concerning a matter within the scope of the agency or employment, made during the existence of that relationship." Such statements are presumably reliable in the absence of cross-examination because an agent "who speaks on any matter within the scope of his agency or employment during the existence of that relationship, is unlikely to make statements damaging to his principal or employer unless those statements are true."[1]

In order for a statement to be admissible under Pa.R.E. 803(25)(D), the offering party must make a threefold showing that: (1) an employment relationship existed between the declarant and the

---

[1]*Nekolny v. Painter*, 653 F.2d 1164, 1172 (7th Cir. 1981).

party, (2) the statement was made during the agency or employment relationship, and (3) the statement concerned a matter within the declarant's scope of employment. *Harris v. Toys "R" US-Penn, Inc.*, 880 A.2d 1270 (Pa. Super. 2005) (statement inadmissible where identification of alleged declarant was incomplete and confusing; in considering admissibility of evidence, trial court may properly consider credibility); *Sehl v. Vista Linen Rental Serv. Inc.*, 763 A.2d 858 (Pa. Super. 2000) (to be admissible, the statement must concern matters within the scope of declarant's employment, not just made during employment); *Biddle v. Com., Dept. of Transp.*, 817 A.2d 1213 (Pa.Cmwlth. 2003) (plaintiff's testimony that unidentified speaker was PennDOT superintendent who admitted state had notice of road defect properly excluded; could not be established statements concerned matter within scope of unidentified person's responsibilities). Cf. *Millcreek Schl. Dist. v. Erie Bd. of Asmt.*, 140 A.3d 737 (Pa.Cmwlth. 2016) (expert testimony in one case does not serve as a party admission in another and different proceeding).

Although the rule does not define the term "agent," federal courts have held that the corresponding federal rule (Rule 801(d)(2)(D)) is intended to describe the traditional master-servant relationship as understood by common law agency doctrine.[2]

The existence of agency at the time of the statements and the scope of the employment are preliminary matters for the trial court under Pa.R.E.

---

[2]*City of Tuscaloosa v. Harcros Chemicals, Inc.*, 158 F.3d 548, 557 n. 9 (11th Cir.1998) (at common law, senior officers of corporation normally are agents and servants of corporation); *American Eagle Ins. Co. v. Thompson*, 85 F.3d 327 (8th Cir.1996); *Lippay v. Christos*, 996 F.2d 1490 (3d Cir.1993); *Boren v. Sable*, 887 F.2d 1032, 1038 (10th Cir.1989).

104(a).

In determining the agency or employment relationship and its scope, the court must consider the contents of the statement but must also find other supporting evidence independent of the proffered statement. Pa.R.E. 803(25)(D); *Sehl v. Vista Linen Rental Serv., Inc.*, 763 A.2d 858 (Pa. Super. 2000) (plaintiffs failed to show statements by unidentified speaker concerned matter within scope of his responsibilities); *Borough of Grove City v. UCBR*, 928 A.2d 371 (Pa.Cmwlth. 2007) (similar).

This rule (unlike 803(25)(C)) does not require that the agent have the authority to speak for the employer in order to admit the agent's statement into evidence, but only that the statement concern a matter within the scope of agency or employment and be made during the existence of that relationship. *Sehl v. Vista Linen Rental Serv. Inc.*, 763 A.2d 858 (Pa. Super. 2000) (tort case where successor liability was in issue, no error to exclude testimony that delivery man said Vista was told to change its name to DCL because it was being taken over; knowledge of merger or acquisition not within declarant's scope of authority).

This exception to the hearsay rule is new to Pennsylvania law, although it is consistent with the overwhelming majority of American jurisdictions.

The personal knowledge rule (Pa.R.E. 602) is not applicable to admissions. *See Salvitti v. Throppe*, 343 Pa. 642, 23 A.2d 445 (1942).

An admission (other than a "judicial admission," discussed on page 326) may be denied, explained, contradicted, or otherwise attacked by the party against whom it is offered, just like any other item of evidence introduced against a party.

Former Employees

Since a former employee is no longer an agent

of the corporation, a statement made after employment has ceased is not an admission attributable to the organization.

Deposition Testimony

See Pa.R.Civ.P. 4020 which provides:

> The deposition of a party or of anyone who at the time of taking the deposition was an officer, director, or managing agent of a party, or a person designated under Rule 4004(a)(2) or 4007.1(e) to testify on behalf of a public or private corporation, partnership or association or governmental agency which is a party, may be used by an adverse party for any purpose.

Criminal Cases—Crawford v. Washington

In *Crawford v. Washington*, 541 U.S. 36, 124 S.Ct. 1354, 158 L.Ed.2d 177 (2004) (discussed at page 134, *supra*), the Court held that in criminal cases, the Confrontation Clause forbids the admission of "testimonial" statements of a witness who did not appear at trial unless that witness was unavailable to testify and the defendant had had a prior opportunity for cross-examination. But in *United States v. Lafferty*, 387 F.Supp.2d 500 (2005) the court indicated admissions appear to be one area where a testimonial statement can be admitted against a defendant without the right to cross-examination. Inherent in Justice Scalia's analysis in the *Crawford* opinion was the right of confrontation exists as to accusations of third parties implicating a criminal defendant, not a criminal defendant implicating herself. *United States v. Lafferty*, 387 F.Supp.2d 500, 511 (2005). See also 4 Weinstein & Berger, Weinstein's Federal Evidence § 802.05 [3][d] (2d ed. 2005) (noting that "a party cannot seriously claim that his or her own statement should be excluded because it was not made under oath or subject to cross-examination").

Compare: Fed. R. Evid. 801(d)(2)(D).

Research References

Packel & Poulin, Pennsylvania Evidence § 803(25)(D)-1 (4th ed. 2013)

McCormick, Evidence Chapter 25 (7th ed. 2013)

HEARSAY EXCEPTION: ADMISSION— PERSONS AUTHORIZED TO SPEAK

See Pa.R.E. 803(25)(C)

Objection

- [*To a question*] Objection. The question calls for hearsay.
- [*To an answer*] Objection, hearsay. I move that the answer be stricken and the jury be instructed not to consider it for any purpose.

Response

- The statement is admissible since I have already established the authority of the declarant to speak for [*plaintiff/defendant*] in such matters.

Pennsylvania Law

Pa.R.E. 803(25)(C) provides an exception to the hearsay rule for statements used against a party which were made by another person "authorized by the party to make a statement concerning the subject."

In order for a statement to be admissible, the proponent must first establish that the declarant is, in fact, the agent of the party opponent, and that the scope of the agency included the right to make a statement. *Brady v. Commonwealth, Unemployment Comp. Bd. of Review*, 115 Pa.Cmwlth. 221, 539 A.2d 936 (1988). The declarant's authority can be expressed or implied.

In determining whether the declarant was authorized to speak, the court must consider the contents of the statement but must also find other independent evidence of authorization. Pa.R.E. 803(25).

Like all admissions, there is no requirement that the speaker have personal knowledge, *Salvitti v. Throppe*, 343 Pa. 642, 23 A.2d 445 (1942), and the statement may be phrased in the form of an opinion.

For illustrations of the rule, see: *Berkebile v. Brantly Helicopter Corp.*, 462 Pa. 83, 337 A.2d 893 (1975) (memo from chief test pilot to president of defendant corporation admissible as substantive evidence); *Northern Health Facilities v. Unemployment Comp. Bd. of Review*, 663 A.2d 276 (Pa.Cmwlth. 1995) (statement made during press conference by employer's public relations spokesperson authorized and admissible); *Rum Seller, Inc. v. Commonwealth of Pa. Liquor Control Bd.*, 78 Pa.Cmwlth. 414, 467 A.2d 916 (1983) (admissions by sole company officer who stands in position of authority are competent and binding); *Adams v. Mackleer*, 239 Pa. Super. 244, 361 A.2d 439 (1976) (personal injury action where mother's note about condition of bicycle ridden by seventeen year old son should not have been admitted; mother was not son's authorized agent and was not empowered to make admissions on his behalf). See also *Commonwealth v. Johnson*, 961 A.2d 877 (Pa. Super. 2008) (statement by party's attorney during closing argument).

A pleading prepared by an attorney is an admission by one presumptively authorized to speak for his principal. *See* Judicial Admissions. When a pleading is amended or withdrawn, the superseded portion ceases to be a conclusive judicial admission. But it still remains as a statement once seriously made by an authorized agent, and as such, is competent evidence of the facts stated, though controvertible like any other admission made by a party or his agent. If the agent made the admission without adequate information, that goes to weight not admissibility.

Criminal Cases—*Crawford v. Washington*

In *Crawford v. Washington*, 541 U.S. 36, 124 S.Ct. 1354, 158 L.Ed.2d 177 (2004) (discussed at page 134, *supra*), the Court held that in criminal cases, the Confrontation Clause forbids the admission of "testimonial" statements of a witness who did not appear at trial unless that witness was unavailable to testify and the defendant had had a prior opportunity for cross-examination. But in *United States v. Lafferty*, 387 F.Supp.2d 500 (2005) the court indicated admissions appear to be one area where a testimonial statement can be admitted against a defendant without the right to cross-examination. Inherent in Justice Scalia's analysis in the *Crawford* opinion was the right of confrontation exists as to accusations of third parties implicating a criminal defendant, not a criminal defendant implicating herself. *United States v. Lafferty*, 387 F.Supp.2d 500, 511 (2005).

Compare: Fed.R.Evid. 801(d)(2)(C).

Research References

Packel & Poulin, Pennsylvania Evidence § 803(25)(C)-1 (4th ed. 2013)

Binder, Hearsay Handbook Chapter 35 (4th ed. 2001)

McCormick, Evidence Chapter 25 (7th ed. 2013)

HEARSAY EXCEPTION: ADMISSION BY CO-CONSPIRATOR

See: Pa. R.E. 803(25)(E).

Objection

- *[To a question]* Objection. The question calls for hearsay.

- *[To an answer]* Objection, hearsay. I move that the answer be stricken and the jury be instructed not to consider it for any purpose.

Response

- The statement is the admission of a co-conspirator. As foundation, I have established that: (i) a conspiracy did, in fact, exist; (ii) the declarant and the defendant were members of the conspiracy; and (iii) the statement was made during the course of and in furtherance of the conspiracy.

Pennsylvania Law

The rationale for the co-conspirator exception is based on principles of agency. During the course of a conspiracy, each conspirator is considered the agent of the other and, thus, a statement by one is an admission by all. *Commonwealth v. Johnson*, 576 Pa. 23, 838 A.2d 663 (2003). If the statement is made in furtherance of and during the continuance of the common purpose of the conspiracy, it is admissible against all. *Commonwealth v. Timer*, 415 Pa. Super. 376, 609 A.2d 572 (1992); *Commonwealth v. Scarborough*, 313 Pa. Super. 521, 460 A.2d 310 (1983). When a person joins an existing conspiracy, he is deemed to have adopted all prior assertions of the conspirators made during the course of and in furtherance of the conspiracy. *See United States v. U.S. Gypsum Co.*, 333 U.S. 364, 68 S.Ct. 525, 92 L.Ed. 746 (1948); *United States v. Goldberg*, 105 F.3d 770 (1st Cir.1997).

The admissibility of co-conspirators' statements under Pa.R.E. 803(25)(E) is determined by the trial court pursuant to Pa.R.E. 104(a) which permits consideration of any non-privileged evidence, regardless of its admissibility.

To admit statements under this rule, the proponent must establish by a preponderance of the evidence that: (1) there was a conspiracy; (2) its members included the declarant and the party against whom the statement is now being offered; and (3) the statement was made both (a) during the course of, and (b) in furtherance of the conspiracy. *Bourjaily v. United States*, 483 U.S. 171, 107 S.Ct. 2775, 97 L.Ed.2d 144 (1987); *Commonwealth v. Fox*, 422 Pa. Super. 224, 619 A.2d 327 (1993); *Commonwealth v. Cherpes*, 360 Pa. Super. 246, 520 A.2d 439 (1987).

While the trial court may consider the hearsay statement itself to determine the existence of a conspiracy, *Bourjaily*, 483 U.S. at 181, 107 S.Ct. at 2781, there must be some independent corroborating evidence of the defendant's participation in the conspiracy. *Commonwealth v. Dreibelbis*, 493 Pa. 466, 426 A.2d 1111 (1981).

The trial court can admit such statements "upon only slight evidence of the conspiracy." *Commonwealth v. Kersten*, 333 Pa. Super. 343, 350, 482 A.2d 600, 603 (1984). The proponent need not prove conspiracy beyond a reasonable doubt; proof by a fair preponderance of the evidence will suffice. *Commonwealth v. Stocker*, 424 Pa. Super. 189, 622 A.2d 333 (1993); *Commonwealth v. Basile*, 312 Pa. Super. 206, 458 A.2d 587 (1983). Moreover, for purposes of this rule, the conspiracy may be inferentially established by showing the relation, conduct or circumstances of the parties. *Commonwealth v. Chester*, 526 Pa. 578, 587 A.2d 1367 (1991); *Commonwealth v. Jones*, 874 A.2d 108 (Pa. Super. 2005). A co-conspirator's statement is only inadmissible where it is the sole evidence of the conspiracy. *Commonwealth v. Feliciano*, 67

A.3d 19 (Pa. Super. 2013).

The exception applies in both criminal and civil cases. *Marshall v. Faddis*, 199 Pa. 397, 49 A. 225 (1901); *Wagner v. Aulenbach*, 170 Pa. 495, 32 A. 1087 (1895). It also applies even where no party has been formally charged with conspiracy. *Commonwealth v. Dreibelbis*, 493 Pa. 466, 426 A.2d 1111 (1981). Moreover, the conspiracy between the declarant and the defendant need not be identical to any conspiracy that is specifically charged in the indictment. *United States v. Gigante*, 166 F.3d 75 (2d Cir.1999); *United States v. Narviz-Guerra*, 148 F.3d 530 (5th Cir.1998).

"In Furtherance" Requirement

The requirement that the words spoken be "in furtherance of the conspiracy" implies that the statements must, in some way, have been designed to promote or facilitate achievement of the goals of the ongoing conspiracy. By contrast, conversations that represent "mere idle chatter" or which are just narratives of past conduct are not in furtherance of the conspiracy, regardless of whether an individual co-conspirator was implicated in the conversation. *See* Ohlbaum on the Pennsylvania Rules of Evidence § 803.25[14][d] (2004–2005 ed.).

Duration

Hearsay statements made after a conspiracy has terminated are not admissible. But the duration of a conspiracy depends upon the facts of a particular case, i.e., it depends upon the scope of the agreement entered into by its members. In *Commonwealth v. Pass*, 468 Pa. 36, 360 A.2d 167 (1976), the Pennsylvania Supreme Court addressed the issue of the duration of a conspiracy and adopted the following language from *United States v. Hickey*, 360 F.2d 127, 141 (7th Cir.1966), *cert. denied*, 385 U.S. 928, 87 S.Ct. 284, 17 L.Ed.2d 210

(1966):

> The duration of a conspiracy depends upon the facts of the particular case, that is, it depends upon the scope of the agreement entered into by its members. Generally, the conspiracy ends when its principal objective is accomplished because no agreement to retain secrecy after the achievement of the unlawful end can be shown or implied by mere 'acts of covering up.' . . . But the fact that the 'central objective' of the conspiracy has been nominally attained does not preclude the continuance of the conspiracy. Where there is evidence that the conspirators originally agreed to take certain steps after the principal objective of the conspiracy was reached, or evidence from which such an agreement may reasonably be inferred, the conspiracy may be found to continue. *Atkins v. United States*, 307 F.2d 937, 940 (9th Cir.1962); cf., *United States v. Allegretti*, 340 F.2d 254, 256 (7th Cir.1964), cert. denied, 381 U.S. 911, 85 S.Ct. 1531, 14 L.Ed.2d 433 (1965) . . . . The crucial factor is the necessity for some showing that the later activities were part of the original plan.

Commonwealth v. Pass, 468 Pa. at 45–46, 360 A.2d at 171; *accord*, *Commonwealth v. Gribble*, 580 Pa. 647, 863 A.2d 455 (2004); *Commonwealth v. Cull*, 540 Pa. 161, 656 A.2d 476 (1995); *Commonwealth v. Mayhue*, 536 Pa. 271, 639 A.2d 421 (1994) (assertion made by a conspirator in attempt to conceal a completed crime may be admitted against co-conspirators when concealment of the crime was an integral part of the common design to which the conspirators agreed).

In *Crawford v. Washington*, 541 U.S. 36, 124 S.Ct. 1354, 158 L.Ed.2d 177 (2004) (discussed at page 134, *supra*), a criminal case involving a Confrontation Clause challenge, the United States Supreme Court held that if a hearsay statement was "testimonial" in nature, it could not be introduced at trial, in the absence of the declarant, unless the defendant had a previous opportunity to cross-examine the declarant. However, the Court also described statements in furtherance of a con-

175

spiracy as "by their nature . . . not testimonial." *Crawford v. Washington*, 541 U.S. 36, 56, 124 S.Ct. 1354, 158 L.Ed.2d 177 (2004). *See United States v. Hendricks*, 395 F.3d 173 (3d Cir. 2005) (*Crawford* did not apply to co-conspirator statements at issue because they were nontestimonial). For a Pennsylvania case applying the *Crawford* analysis to coconspirator statements and finding them admissible, *see Commonwealth v. Holton*, 906 A.2d 1246 (Pa. Super. 2006).

Compare: Fed. R. Evid. 801(d)(2)(E).

Research References

Packel & Poulin, Pennsylvania Evidence § 803(25)(E)-1 (4th ed. 2013)

Binder, Hearsay Handbook Chapter 35 (4th ed. 2001)

McCormick, Evidence § 259 (7th ed. 2013)

HEARSAY EXCEPTION: ADOPTIVE ADMISSION

See: Pa.R.E. 803(25)(B).

Objection

- [*To a question*] Objection. The question calls for a hearsay answer.
- [*To an answer*] Objection, hearsay. I move that the answer be stricken and the jury be instructed not to consider it for any purpose.

Response

- The statement/document is an adoptive admission. The evidence establishes that plaintiff/defendant heard, understood and acquiesced in the statement [*specify*] and manifested adoption by [*specify*].

Pennsylvania Law

Under Pa.R.E. 803(25)(B), evidence is not hearsay if it "is offered against a party and is . . . a statement of which the party has manifested an adoption or belief in its truth."

An adoptive admission is dependent upon a showing by the proponent of the evidence that the party-opponent heard, understood and acquiesced in the statement. *Rox Coal Co. v. W.C.A.B. (Snizaski)*, 570 Pa. 60, 807 A.2d 906 (2002) (offering police accident report into evidence solely to establish time of accident was not an adoption of the truth of its substantive statements; report remained inadmissible hearsay).

Adoption, which may be express or implied (tacit), can be manifested by any appropriate means, such as language, conduct or silence. *Commonwealth v. Holloway*, 559 Pa. 258, 739 A.2d 1039 (1999) (where detective testified defendant gave statement to police, had it read back verbatim and acknowledged "it's what I said but I'm not go-

177

ing to sign it," statement admissible as adoptive admission); *Commonwealth v. Cheeks*, 429 Pa. 89, 239 A.2d 793 (1968) (defendant expressly adopted co-defendants' written statements when he was shown statements and said they were correct); *Commonwealth v. Scarborough*, 313 Pa. Super. 521, 460 A.2d 310 (1983) (implied adoption where defendant did not reply to co-defendant's statements about participation in murder).

Failure to contest an assertion is considered evidence of acquiescence only if it would have been natural under the circumstances to object to the assertion in question. *Levin v. Van Horn*, 412 Pa. 322, 194 A.2d 419 (1963) (silence is considered an admission only when the circumstances are such that one ought to speak and does not); *Burton v. Horn & Hardart Baking Co.*, 371 Pa. 60, 88 A.2d 873 (1952) (no error to exclude evidence of store manager's silence in face of customer's complaint; maxim "silence gives consent" is not an invariable rule of evidence and manager may have been motivated by desire to avoid dispute); *L. Washington & Assoc., Inc. v. Unemployment Comp. Bd. Of Review*, 662 A.2d 1148 (Pa.Cmwlth.1995) (employer's testimony that when confronted, employee did not deny sleeping on the job was admission and substantive evidence that claimant was sleeping on the job); *Commonwealth v. O'Kicki*, 408 Pa. Super. 518, 597 A.2d 152 (1991) (defendant Judge's silence when told that a person said he had paid the judge for a job could be considered by jury to be a tacit admission); *Commonwealth v. Faraci*, 319 Pa. Super. 416, 466 A.2d 228 (1983) (testimony re co-conspirator's statements and defendant's silent approval thereof qualified as tacit admissions).

An important limitation on implied admissions is that this rule is not applicable in criminal cases where the defendant is in police custody or in the presence of police officers. To treat silence as an admission under such circumstances would be inconsistent with the defendant's Fifth Amendment right to remain silent. *Commonwealth v. Dravecz*, 424 Pa. 582, 227 A.2d 904 (1967); *Commonwealth ex rel. Shadd v. Myers*, 423 Pa. 82, 223 A.2d 296 (1966); *Commonwealth v. Kitchen*, 730 A.2d 513 (Pa. Super. 1999).

In *Crawford v. Washington*, 541 U.S. 36, 124 S.Ct. 1354, 158 L.Ed.2d 177 (2004) (discussed at page 134, *supra*), the Court held that in criminal cases, the Confrontation Clause forbids the admission of "testimonial" statements of a witness who did not appear at trial unless that witness was unavailable to testify and the defendant had had a prior opportunity for cross-examination. In *United States v. Lafferty*, 387 F.Supp. 2d 500 (2005), a case involving statements made in a joint interview where Defendant had waived her Fifth Amendment rights, the court said an adoptive admission "appears to be one area where a testimonial statement can be admitted against a Defendant without the right to cross-examination." Inherent in Justice Scalia's analysis in the *Crawford* opinion was that the right of confrontation exists as to accusations of third parties implicating a criminal defendant, not a criminal defendant implicating herself.

Compare: Fed. R. Evid. 801(d)(2)(B).

Research References

Packel & Poulin, Pennsylvania Evidence § 803(25)(B)-1 (4th ed. 2013)

Binder, Hearsay Handbook Chapter 35 (4th ed. 2001)

McCormick, Evidence Chapter 25 (7th ed. 2013)

HEARSAY EXCEPTION: ANCIENT DOCUMENTS

See: Pa.R.E. 803(16).

Objection

- I object to the introduction of this document and any testimony about its contents. There has been no foundation to authenticate it and its contents constitute inadmissible hearsay.

Response

- The document is admissible under the ancient documents exception to the hearsay rule. As foundation, I have established that the document is at least 30 years old, is free from any suspicious alteration and has been in proper custody.

Pennsylvania Law

The ancient documents rule, now codified at Pa.R.E. 803(16), exempts documents from the general rule requiring authentication by the testimony of subscribing witnesses when the document is at least 30 years old, is free from suspicious alterations, and has been in proper custody. *Commonwealth v. Brooks*, 352 Pa. Super. 394, 508 A.2d 316 (1986); *Louden v. Apollo Gas Co.*, 273 Pa. Super. 549, 417 A.2d 1185 (1980). The rule creates a presumption that a document meeting the foregoing conditions is self-authenticating. Otherwise, the antiquity of the document itself would create great difficulty or impossibility of actual authentication.

The rule has been applied to a variety of documents, including a memorandum of agreement (*Louden v. Apollo Gas Co.*, 273 Pa. Super. 549, 417 A.2d 1185 (1980)), business records (*Jones v. Scranton Coal Co.*, 274 Pa. 312, 118 A. 219 (1922)), corporate minutes (*Commonwealth ex rel. Ferguson v. Ball*, 277 Pa. 301, 121 A. 191 (1923)), receipts

(*McReynolds v. Lougenberger*, 75 Pa. 13 (1874)) and surveys (*Mineral R.R. and Mining Co. v. Auten*, 188 Pa. 568, 41 A. 327 (1898)). Excluded was a document purporting to be an oil and gas agreement bearing a 1948 date but with no other indicia of reliability or chain of custody. *Lesnick v. Chartiers Natural Gas Co.*, 889 A.2d 1282 (Pa. Super. 2005).

In *Commonwealth ex rel. Ferguson v. Ball*, 277 Pa. 301, 121 A. 191 (1923), the court said that in some cases, proof of proper custody may not be required where the authenticity of the document is clearly established by its appearance.

Compare: Fed. R. Evid. 803(16) [document need only be 20 years old], 901(b)(8).

Research References

Packel & Poulin, Pennsylvania Evidence § 803(16)-1 (4th ed. 2013)

Binder, Hearsay Handbook Chapter 24 (4th ed. 2001)

McCormick, Evidence § 323 (7th ed. 2013)

HEARSAY EXCEPTION: ASSERTIONS AS TO BOUNDARIES OF LAND

See: Pa.R.E. 803(20).

Objection

- [*To a question*] Objection. The question calls for a hearsay answer.
- [*To a document*] Objection. The document constitutes inadmissible hearsay.
- [*To an answer*] I move the answer be stricken and the jury be instructed not to consider it for any purpose.

Response

- The [*question*] [*document*] is proper. The evidence is admissible as one of the recognized exceptions to the hearsay rule in boundary disputes.

Pennsylvania Law

Since land survives and people (and sometimes, documents) do not, Pennsylvania recognizes a number of alternative proofs as exceptions to the hearsay rule in boundary disputes. In *Hostetter v. Commonwealth*, 367 Pa. 603, 606, 80 A.2d 719, 720 (1951), the court said:

> When a right or title is of ancient origin or where the transaction under investigation is so remote as to be incapable of direct proof by living witnesses or by the ordinary documentary evidence, the law, of necessity, relaxes the rules of evidence and requires less evidence to substantiate the fact in controversy. For example, ancient maps, records, surveys, ancient town plots, historical books which have been generally treated as authentic, reports made by disinterested parties apparently conversant with the facts and now dead, have been held admissible as furnishing evidence of remote transactions. Maps, surveys, monuments, pedigree and even reputation evidence have been held to be admissible to establish boundaries. Moreover, boundaries may be established

by circumstantial as well as by direct evidence. (citations omitted)

See Hallman v. Turns, 334 Pa. Super. 184, 482 A.2d 1284 (1984) (declarations of a deceased owner with respect to boundaries are competent evidence).

As *Hostetter* noted, one of the recognized exceptions to the hearsay exclusionary rule pertains to declarations by a surveyor. This exception holds that declarations of a deceased surveyor regarding a line surveyed are admissible in boundary disputes. Authenticated field notes of a deceased surveyor are also admissible as declarations contemporaneous with the work done on the ground. *Niles v. Fall Creek Hunting Club, Inc.*, 376 Pa. Super. 260, 545 A.2d 926 (1988). However, the deceased surveyor exception applies only to observations and notes made by the surveyor which relate to his surveying duties; it does not extend to collateral matters. The declarant must have been on the land at the time the declaration was made and engaged at the time in pointing out the boundaries of the land. In *Niles*, a surveyor's statements and letter to the effect that other parties consented to and agreed with his survey were collateral, not part of his duties and, hence, inadmissible hearsay.

In *School Dist. of Donegal Twp. v. Crosby*, 178 Pa. Super. 30, 112 A.2d 645 (1955), the court noted that while reputation was admissible to prove boundaries, it was not admissible to prove title to property.

Compare: Fed. R. Evid. 803(20).

Research References

Packel & Poulin, Pennsylvania Evidence § 803(20)-1 (4th ed. 2013)

Binder, Hearsay Handbook Chapter 29 (4th ed. 2001)

McCormick, Evidence § 322 (7th ed. 2013)

HEARSAY EXCEPTION: BUSINESS RECORDS

See: Pa.R.E. 803(6).

Objection

- Objection. The records have not been properly authenticated pursuant to Pa.R.E. 803(6). Therefore, the contents are inadmissible hearsay since they are offered to prove the truth of the matters asserted in them.

Response

- The evidence is admissible under the business records exception to the hearsay rule. As foundation, I have established:
  1. That the record was made at or near the time of the event or transaction described;
  2. That the record was made [*by a person with knowledge of the event or transaction described*] [*from information transmitted to the preparer by a person with knowledge*];
  3. That the record was made in the course of a regularly conducted business activity;
  4. That it was a part of that regularly conducted business activity to make and keep that record; and,
  5. That the witness [*is able to identify the document from actual knowledge of its preparation*] [*is the business custodian of the record*] [*is a qualified witness because (specify)*].

Pennsylvania Law

The purpose of the business records exception codified at Pa.R.E. 803(6) is to permit the introduction of records that are inherently reliable. *Commonwealth v. Sanchez*, 416 Pa. Super. 160, 610

A.2d 1020 (1992); *see also* Uniform Business Records as Evidence Act, 42 Pa.C.S.A. § 6108; *First Ward Republican Club v. Commonwealth*, 11 A.3d 38 (Pa.Cmwlth. 2010) (in context of this case, police incident reports not properly qualified and thus inadmissible under Uniform Act as either business or official records).

To satisfy the requirements of the Rule, a business record must be made at or near the time of the events reflected in the records. A determination as to whether the recording of the event is sufficiently contemporaneous with the event is left to the broad discretion of the trial court. *In re Estate of Indyk*, 488 Pa. 567, 413 A.2d 371 (1979); see *Commonwealth v. Morocco*, 375 Pa. Super. 367, 544 A.2d 965 (1988); *Thomas v. Allegheny & Eastern Coal Co.*, 309 Pa. Super. 333, 455 A.2d 637 (1982).

The records must also be kept in the course of a regularly conducted business, and it must be the regular practice of the business to keep records of the type offered into evidence. *Papach v. Mercy Suburban Hosp.*, 887 A.2d 233 (Pa. Super. 2005) (all persons contributing information to the business record must be acting in the course and scope of their duties); *Centennial Station Condominium v. Schaefer*, 800 A.2d 379 (Pa.Cmwlth.2002) (records of contractors' estimates to complete work were not the business records of condominium association and were inadmissible hearsay in suit against developer).

These requirements must be established by testimony of the current custodian or other qualified witness or by certification that complies with Rules 902(11), 902(12) or statute permitting certification.[1] The authenticating witness need not be the person who actually made the entries in

---

[1]The 2001 amendment allowing certification is intended to save the time and expense which would otherwise be spent on foundation witnesses when there is

question nor the custodian of the record at the time the entries were made. A witness called for the purpose of qualifying a business record need not have any personal knowledge of the facts which are reported in the particular records. *Commonwealth v. Graver*, 461 Pa. 131, 334 A.2d 667 (1975). The witness need only possess adequate knowledge of the regularity of the record keeping process to qualify the records under the Rule. *Keystone Dedicated Logistics v. JGB Ent.*, 77 A.3d 1 (Pa. Super. 2013) (reversed-plaintiff could not simply rely on the fact that certain documents were produced during discovery and plaintiff's officer could not verify the authenticity and trustworthiness of invoices made between two other businesses; discovery of documents and proof of their reliability at trial are two different matters); *Commonwealth v. McEnany*, 732 A.2d 1263 (Pa. Super. 1999) (admitting cell phone records; company's computer program designer testified to accuracy of records maintained in computer language and subsequently translated into English); *Commonwealth v. Sullivan*, 372 Pa. Super. 88, 538 A.2d 1363 (1988). The exception was meant to allow for the situation where large departments recording business transactions make it virtually impossible to identify each person at each phase of the recording process. *Campbell v. Royal Indem. Co. of New York*, 256 Pa. Super. 312, 389 A.2d 1139 (1978).

It is essential that no lack of trustworthiness appear in the source of information or the method or circumstances of preparation. The factors to be weighed in evaluating the trustworthiness of business records include whether there was either motive or opportunity to prepare an inaccurate record; the period of delay prior to preparation of the record; the nature of the information recorded; the

---

no real question as to the authenticity of records.

systematic checking; whether there was regularity and continuity in maintaining the records; and whether the business relied on them. *Papach v. Mercy Suburban Hosp.*, 887 A.2d 233 (Pa. Super. 2005) (if any person in the process is not acting in the regular course of business, then an essential link in the trustworthiness chain fails); *Commonwealth v. Zimmerman*, 391 Pa. Super. 569, 571 A.2d 1062 (1990); *Ganster v. Western Pennsylvania Water Co.*, 349 Pa. Super. 561, 504 A.2d 186 (1985).

Business records are considered by the part, not the whole, for purposes of this exception to the hearsay rule. One entry may be excepted to the hearsay rule, and another may not, though both are contained in the same document. *Birt v. First-energy Corp.*, 891 A.2d 1281 (Pa. Super. 2006) (characterizing a document as a business record is insufficient to justify its admission because a business record which includes multiple levels of hearsay is admissible only if each level falls within a recognized exception to the hearsay rule).

As the Pennsylvania Rules of Evidence were originally promulgated in 1998, the scope of the business records exception was not limited to private business entities; government records were also included. *Paey Associates v. Penn. Liquor Control Bd.*, 78 A.3d 1187 (Pa. Cmwlth. 2013) (police incident reports); *Hill v. Department of Corrections*, 64 A.3d 1159 (Pa. Cmwlth. 2013) (invoices from division of DOC for standard issue prison items); *Commonwealth v. Jasper*, 531 Pa. 1, 610 A.2d 949 (1992) (FBI records); *Ariondo v. Munsey*, 122 Pa.Cmwlth. 475, 553 A.2d 94 (1989) (police accident reports); *Siler v. Harrisburg*, 54 Pa.Cmwlth. 303, 422 A.2d 704 (1980) (city disciplinary record). With the 2017 adoption of the Public Records hearsay exception, Rule 803(8), case law involving government records will develop under that new Rule.

The Rule should not be overread. There is no

hearsay exception if the subject matter of the entry is extraneous to the purpose of the business. *See Commonwealth v. Harris*, 351 Pa. 325, 41 A.2d 688 (1945). Pa.R.E. 803(6) does not make relevant that which is irrelevant nor does it make all business and professional records competent regardless of by whom, in what manner and for what purpose they were compiled. *See, e.g., Ganster v. Western Pennsylvania Water Co.*, 349 Pa. Super. 561, 504 A.2d 186 (1985) (business report containing expert opinion excluded where author was not identified or available for cross-examination); *accord, Thomas v. Allegheny & Eastern Coal Co.*, 309 Pa. Super. 333, 455 A.2d 637 (1982); *Mapp v. Dube*, 330 Pa. Super. 284, 479 A.2d 553 (1984) (building inspector's letter about site of fatal fire excluded where there was no testimony as to mode of preparation of letter or writer's sources of information).

In *Crawford v. Washington*, 541 U.S. 36 (2004) (discussed at page 134, *supra*), a criminal case involving a Confrontation Clause challenge, the United States Supreme Court held that if a hearsay statement was "testimonial" in nature, it could not be introduced at trial, in the absence of the declarant, unless the defendant had a previous opportunity to cross-examine the declarant. However, the Court also described business records as "by their nature . . . not testimonial." *Crawford v. Washington*, 541 U.S. 36, 56 (2004). But one commentator has cautioned that "[s]ome business records may concern matters that are understood at the time they were made to be destined for litigation or may be clearly accusatory." Mosteller, *Crawford v. Washington*: Encouraging and Ensuring the Confrontation of Witnesses, 39 U.Rich.L. Rev. 511, 548 (2005). In *Melendez-Diaz v. Massachusetts*, 129 S.Ct. 2527, 174 L. Ed. 2d 314 (2009), the trial court had admitted into evidence state laboratory affidavits with forensic analysis results showing material seized from defendant was cocaine. The Court reiterated that documents kept in the ordinary course of business usually may be admitted at trial despite their hearsay status but said that is not the case if the regularly conducted business activity is the production of evidence for use at trial. 129 S.Ct. at 2538. The United States Supreme Court said that the laboratory reports fell within the core class of testimonial statements since they had been created for the sole purpose of providing evidence against a defendant. Acknowledging that the Confrontation Clause may make prosecution of criminals more burdensome, the Court held that crime laboratory reports may not be used against defendants at trial unless the analysts responsible for creating them give testimony and subject themselves to cross-examination.

Pennsylvania Rule of Criminal Procedure 574 provides a mechanism for the admission of a forensic laboratory report supported by a certification. This Rule provides a defendant an opportunity to exercise the right of confrontation and to object to the report on hearsay grounds. Following pre-trial notice by the prosecution, and in the absence of a demand by defendant for declarant's live testimony, the Rule permits the admission of a properly certified forensic laboratory report and the accompanying certification at trial. *See* Pa. R. Crim. P. 574.

Pa.R.E. 1003 allows the use of accurately reproduced copies of original records. *See also* 42 Pa.C.S.A. § 6109, the Uniform Photographic Copies of Business and Public Records as Evidence Act; *Commonwealth v. Jasper*, 531 Pa. 1, 610 A.2d 949 (1992).

Compare: Fed. R. Evid. 803(6).

Research References

Packel & Poulin, Pennsylvania Evidence § 803(6)-1 (4th ed. 2013)

Binder, Hearsay Handbook Chapter 16 (4th ed. 2001)

McCormick, Evidence Chapter 29 (7th ed. 2013)

HEARSAY EXCEPTION: BUSINESS RECORDS/HOSPITAL RECORDS

See: Pa.R.E. 803(6).

Objection

- Objection. The documents contain inadmissible hearsay in the form of medical [*opinion*] [*diagnosis*] [*conclusion*].

Response

- The records are offered for the legitimate and limited purpose of establishing the fact of hospitalization and the treatment given and not to show medical opinion.

Pennsylvania Law

Hospital records are admissible under the business records exception to the hearsay rule to show the *facts* of hospitalization, treatment prescribed, symptoms found, and/or the existence of some readily ascertainable substance or chemical within the body. *Williams v. McClain*, 520 A.2d 1374 (Pa. 1987); *Commonwealth v. Xiong*, 630 A.2d 446 (Pa. Super. 1993). When a record is offered merely to prove these facts, generally there are no doubts concerning the record's reliability and accuracy. *Braun v. Target Corp.*, 983 A.2d 752 (Pa. Super. 2009). However, medical opinions, diagnoses and conclusions contained in hospital records are inadmissible. *Commonwealth v. Garcia*, 478 Pa. 406, 387 A.2d 46 (1978); *Commonwealth v. DiGiacomo*, 463 Pa. 449, 345 A.2d 605 (1975); *Phillips v. Gerhart*, 801 A.2d 568 (Pa. Super. 2002) (medical opinion contained in hospital record is not admissible unless doctor who prepared report is available for in-court cross-examination regarding accuracy, reliability, and veracity of opinion). Medical diagnosis or opinion entails a "conclusion concerning a condition not visible but reflected circumstantially by the existence of other visible and known symptoms." *Paxos v. Jarka Corp.*, 314 Pa. 148, 153–54, 171 A. 468, 471 (1934).

In *Folger Ex Rel. Folger v. Dugan*, 876 A.2d 1049 (Pa. Super. 2005), the Court admitted the line between fact and opinion has been difficult to discern, saying:

> In general, when the record reveals what is or is not present in the patient, or that a test occurred, the record reflects facts. On the other hand, when the record reflects what the presence or absence of something means, the record more likely reflects a medical diagnosis or opinion. *Folger Ex Rel. Folger v. Dugan*, 876 A.2d 1049, 1056 (Pa. Super. 2005).

Pa.R.E. 803(6) sets forth the requirements which must be met prior to admission of a business record, including a hospital record, into evidence:

> (b) A . . . record . . . made at or near the time by, or from information transmitted by, a person with knowledge, if kept in the course of a regularly conducted business activity, and if it was the regular practice of that business activity to make the . . . record . . . .

A witness called for the purpose of qualifying a hospital record (often, the medical records librarian) need not have any personal knowledge of the facts which are reported in the particular record. *Commonwealth v. Kravontka*, 384 Pa. Super. 346, 558 A.2d 865 (1989).

Where authenticity is not in issue, the 2001 amendment dispenses with any need for custodian testimony in favor of certification that complies with Rules 902(11), 902(12) or statute permitting certification.

The business records exception was recognized in the following cases to admit facts from hospital records to prove the event of hospitalization, treatment prescribed, symptoms given or the existence of some readily ascertained substance or chemical within the body: *Commonwealth v. Mobley*, 450 Pa. 431, 301 A.2d 622 (1973) (record of hospitalization at certain times for certain wounds); *Folger*, 876 A.2d 1049, 1056 (Pa. Super. 2005) (PCR test result indicating presence of herpes DNA in spinal fluid is a fact); *Commonwealth v. Xiong*, 630 A.2d 446 (Pa. Super. 1993) (notation on physician's report that victim had "no hymen" was factual assertion); *Commonwealth v. Nieves*, 582 A.2d 341 (Pa. Super. 1990) (finding standard gonorrhea tests sufficiently similar to spermatozoa and blood alcohol tests to warrant admission of test results under business record exception); *Commonwealth v. Green*, 251 Pa. Super. 318, 380 A.2d 798 (1977) (hospital record showing rape victim exhibited excoriations (scratches) of elbow and forehead); *Commonwealth v. Campbell*, 244 Pa. Super. 505, 368 A.2d 1299 (1976) (presence of sperm in rape victim); *accord Commonwealth v. Kravontka*, 384 Pa. Super. 346, 558 A.2d 865 (1989) (blood-alcohol test). *See also Commonwealth v. Serge*, 837 A.2d 1255, 1265 (Pa. Super. 2003) (citing with approval *Commonwealth v. Ellis*, 608 A.2d 1090 (Pa. Super. 1992) for the proposition that notwithstanding regulations regarding medical record confidentiality, information in medical records is admissible in criminal proceedings where necessary for the administration of justice).

The rationale for excluding *medical opinion* in hospital records is that such evidence is expert testimony and is not admissible unless the doctor who prepared the report is available for in-court cross-examination regarding the accuracy, reliability, and veracity of his or her opinion. *Commonwealth v. Seville*, 266 Pa. Super. 587, 405 A.2d 1262 (1979). Medical opinions and conclusions are often the subject of conflicting judgment among qualified physicians and hence should be subject to "the severest of examinations to test [their] strength." *Paxos*, 314 Pa. at 154, 171 A. at 471 (1934).

The rule excluding opinions, diagnoses and conclusions is illustrated in the following cases: *Commonwealth v. DiGiacomo*, 463 Pa. 449, 345 A.2d 605 (1975) (hospital records showing diagnosis of patient's injuries inadmissible); *Commonwealth v. McCloud*, 457 Pa. 310, 322 A.2d 653 (1974) (hospital record showing cause of death held inadmissible as opinion evidence); *Walsh v. Kubiak*, 443 Pa. Super. 284, 661 A.2d 416 (1995) (record containing opinions expressed by consulting physician was inadmissible hearsay); *Morris v. Moss*, 290 Pa. Super. 587, 435 A.2d 184 (1981) (admission of hospital record showing patient as conscious held error; determination not a routine finding of fact but an application of scientific principles); *Commonwealth v. McNaughton*, 252 Pa. Super. 302, 381 A.2d 929 (1977) (medical record showing appellant was in possession of morphine inadmissible since conclusion that drug was morphine was expert opinion and required author's presence in court); *see also Liles v. Balmer*, 389 Pa. Super. 451, 567 A.2d 691 (1989) (hospital admission and discharge records containing plaintiff's version of accident did not satisfy requirement of trustworthiness). *See also Papach v. Mercy Suburban Hosp.*, 887 A.2d 233 (Pa. Super. 2005) (EMS report was inadmissible hearsay; bystanders' statements not made in course and scope of employment.

Note: A document such as a medical record may contain more than one hearsay statement. This multiple form of hearsay is called "hearsay within hearsay." Where a business record contains multiple levels of hearsay, it is admissible only if each level falls within a recognized exception to the hearsay rule. *See* Pa.R.E. 805; *Birt v. Firstenergy Corp.*, 891 A.2d 1281 (Pa. Super. 2006); *Hreha v. Benscoter*, 381 Pa. Super. 556, 554 A.2d 525 (1989) (portion of hospital record containing patient's extrajudicial statement was incompetent hearsay evidence where statement did not come within any exception to the hearsay rule).

Crawford v. Washington—Criminal Cases

The impact of *Crawford v. Washington*, 541 U.S. 36, 124 S.Ct. 1354, 158 L.Ed.2d 177 (2004) on the law of hearsay in criminal cases is discussed at page 134. In *Crawford*, the Supreme Court said in dicta that business records are "by their nature . . . not testimonial and not subject to the requirements of the Confrontation Clause," 541 U.S. at 51, 56, 124 S.Ct. 1354; *see also* 541 U.S. at 51, 76, 124 S.Ct. 1354 (Rehnquist, C.J., concurring in judgment) (noting that "the Court's analysis of 'testimony' excludes some hearsay exceptions, such as business records and official records"). Some courts have said that the mere fact a person creating a business record (or other similar record) knows the record might be used for criminal prosecution does not by itself make that record testimonial. *See U.S. v. De La Cruz*, 514 F.3d 121 (1st Cir. 2008) (autopsy report made in ordinary course of business by medical examiner excluded from reach of Crawford); *U.S. v. Ellis*, 460 F.3d 920 (7th Cir. 2006) (medical records establishing methamphetamine in defendant's system were nontestimonial business records; admission did not violate right to confrontation; records were created as a result of government investigation but were made by professionals recording observations made in the ordinary course of business). But one commentator has cautioned that "[s]ome business records may concern matters that are understood at the time they were made to be destined for litigation or may be clearly accusatory." Mosteller, *Crawford v. Washington*: Encouraging and Ensuring the Confrontation of Witnesses, 39 U.Rich.L.Rev. 511, 548 (2005). In *Melendez-Diaz v. Massachusetts*, 129 S.Ct. 2527, 174 L. Ed. 2d 314 (2009), the trial court had admitted into evidence state laboratory affidavits with forensic analysis results showing material seized from the defendant was cocaine. The Court reiterated that documents kept in the ordinary course of business usually may be admitted at trial despite their hearsay status but said that is not the case if the regularly conducted business activity is the production of evidence for use at trial. 129 S.Ct. at 2538. The United States Supreme Court said that the laboratory reports fell within the core class of testimonial statements since they had been created for the sole purpose of providing evidence against a defendant. Acknowledging that the Confrontation Clause may make prosecution of criminals more burdensome, the Court held that crime laboratory reports may not be used against defendants at trial unless the analysts responsible for creating them give testimony and subject themselves to cross-examination. *Accord Commonwealth v. Barton-Martin*, 5 A.3d 363 (Pa. Super. 2010) (where analyst who prepared lab report did not testify at trial, admission of blood-alcohol test results violated defendant's rights under Confrontation Clause).

Compare: Fed. R. Evid. 803(6) (which unlike Pennsylvania permits reports containing opinions and diagnoses).

Research References

Packel & Poulin, Pennsylvania Evidence § 803(6)-1 (4th ed. 2013)

Binder, Hearsay Handbook Chapter 16 (6th ed. 2006)

McCormick, Evidence Chapter 29 (7th ed. 2013)

HEARSAY EXCEPTION: CHILD SEXUAL ABUSE VICTIM (TENDER YEARS EXCEPTION)

See: 42 Pa.C.S.A. § 5985.1.

Objection

- [*To a question*] Objection. The question calls for a hearsay answer. No notice was given that this evidence would be offered and it has not been determined to be reliable.

- [*To an answer*] Objection, hearsay. I move the answer be stricken and the jury be instructed not to consider it for any purpose.

Response

- The statement is admissible under the tender years exception to the hearsay rule. Notice was given; relevance and reliability were determined in an *in camera* proceeding.

Pennsylvania Law

The Tender Years Hearsay Act creates an exception to the hearsay rule in recognition of the fragile nature of the victims of childhood sexual abuse. *Commonwealth v. Barnett*, 50 A.3d 176 (Pa. Super. 2012). A child need not be deemed competent to testify as a witness in order for the trial court to admit the child's out-of-court statements into evidence pursuant to the Act. *Commonwealth v. Walter*, 93 A.3d 442 (Pa. 2014) (a child's competency to testify as a witness under Rule 601 is a distinct issue from the admissibility of a child's out-of-court statements under the Tender Years Act).

42 Pa.C.S.A. § 5985.1 provides in relevant part:

(a)   General Rule. An out-of-court statement made by a child victim or witness, who at the time the statement was made was 12 years of age or younger, describing any of the offenses enumerated in 18 Pa.C.S. Chs. 25 (relating to criminal homicide), 27 (relating to assault), 29 (relating to kidnapping), 31 (relating to sexual offenses), 35 (relating to burglary and other criminal intrusion) and 37 (relating to robbery), not otherwise admissible by statute or rule of evidence, is admissible in evidence in any criminal or civil proceeding if:

(1) The court finds, in an in camera hearing, that the evidence is relevant and that the time, content and circumstances of the statement provide sufficient indicia or reliability; and

(2) The child either:

    (i)   testifies at the proceeding; or

    (ii) is unavailable as a witness.

(a.1)   Emotional Distress. In order to make a finding under subsection (a)(2)(ii) that the child is unavailable as a witness, the court must determine, based on evidence presented to it, that testimony by the child as a witness will result in the child suffering serious emotional distress that would substantially impair the child's ability to reasonably communicate. In making this determination, the court may do all of the following:

(1) observe and question the child, either inside or outside the courtroom.

(2) Hear testimony of a parent or custodian or any other person, such as a person who has dealt with the child in a medical or therapeutic setting.

(a.2)   Counsel and Confrontation. If the court hears testimony in connection with making a finding under subsection (a)(2)(ii), all of the following apply:

(1) Except as provided in paragraph (2), the defendant, the attorney for the defendant and the attorney for the Commonwealth or, in the case of a civil proceeding, the attorney for the plaintiff has the right to be present.

(2) If the court observes or questions the

child, the court shall not permit the
defendant to be present.

(b)   Notice Required. A statement otherwise admissible under subsection (a) shall not be received into evidence unless the proponent of the statement notifies the adverse party of the proponent's intention to offer the statement and the particulars of the statement sufficiently in advance of the proceeding at which the proponent intends to offer the statement into evidence to provide the adverse party with a fair opportunity to prepare to meet the statement.

Provided proper notice is given, hearsay statements of a child sexual abuse victim are admissible in civil and criminal proceedings if the statements are determined to be relevant and possess the requisite indicia of reliability. *Commonwealth v. Walter*, supra (criminal prosecution for sexual offenses committed against minor); *Fidler v. Cunningham-Small*, 871 A.2d 231 (Pa. Super. 2005) (child custody proceeding). The child may be deemed unavailable due to incompetence by reason of age or because the court has determined the child would be harmed by the trauma of testifying. The definition of unavailability for purposes of the Act is unlike standard definitions for the term in the context of hearsay. The law requires the trial court to determine that, based on evidence presented to it, the giving of testimony by the child would cause the child to suffer "serious emotional distress" such that it would "substantially impair the child's ability to reasonably communicate." 42 Pa. C.S.A. § 5985.1(a.l). In making this finding, the trial court has the option of observing and questioning the child. It may also rely on testimony from others connected to the child, such as a parent, guardian, or a person who has dealt with the child in a medical or therapeutic setting. *Commonwealth v. Kriner*, 915 A.2d 653 (Pa. Super. 2007) (child victim who died in traffic accident before trial was not unavailable within meaning of statute; because of her death the prerequisites to a finding of unavailability could not be made); *Commonwealth v. Lyons*, 833 A.2d 245 (Pa. Super. 2003) (trial court not required to question child directly but could rely on testimony of doctor who provided therapeutic treatment). When the victim testifies, there is no need for a finding of emotional distress. *Commonwealth v. G.D.M., Sr.*, 926 A.2d 984 (Pa. Super. 2007).

Where the child testifies at trial, prior statements of the child are admissible substantively or to corroborate the child's testimony.

The tender years exception allows for the admission of a child's out-of-court statement due to the fragile nature of young victims of sexual abuse. *Commonwealth v. Charlton*, 902 A.2d 554 (Pa. Super. 2006); *Commonwealth v. Fink*, 791 A.2d 1235 (Pa. Super. 2002). Any statement admitted under 42 Pa. C.S. § 5985.1 must possess sufficient indicia of reliability, as determined from the time, content and circumstances of its making. 42 Pa. C.S.A. § 5985.1(a)(1); *Commonwealth v. Walter*, supra.

Because the court must first determine whether a statement has sufficient indicia of reliability, it has been held that 42 Pa.C.S. § 5985.1 does not violate the confrontation clauses of the Sixth Amendment to the United States Constitution or Article 1 § 9 of the Pennsylvania Constitution. *Commonwealth v. Hanawalt*, 419 Pa. Super. 411, 615 A.2d 432 (1992); *see In re A.D.*, 771 A.2d 45 (Pa. Super. 2001) (no requirement that child victim statement be audio or video recorded).

The guidelines for determining whether such hearsay statements possess the requisite indicia of reliability to be admissible are enunciated in *Idaho v. Wright*, 497 U.S. 805, 110 S.Ct. 3139, 111 L.Ed.2d 638 (1990). They include, but are not limited to: (1) the spontaneity and consistent repetition of the statements; (2) the mental state of the declarant; (3) the use of terminology unexpected of a child of similar age; and (4) the lack of motive to fabricate. *Commonwealth v. Walter*, supra; *Commonwealth v. Delbridge*, 771 A.2d 1 (Pa. Super. 2001); *Commonwealth v. Hanawalt*, 419 Pa. Super. 411, 615 A.2d 432 (1992). *See Commonwealth v. Bishop*, 936 A.2d 1136 (Pa. Super. 2007) (statements made by minor victim to mother, father and investigating officer properly admitted).

For cases which subject the Tender Years Act to the requirements of *Crawford v. Washington*, 541 U.S. 36, 124 S.Ct. 1354 (2004) (discussed at page 134, *supra*) *see Commonwealth v. Allshouse*, 985 A.2d 847 (Pa. 2009) (child's statement to caseworker was nontestimonial and thus, admissible) and *Commonwealth v. Kemmerer*, 33 A.3d 39 (Pa. Super. 2011) (no Crawford violation where defense had ample opportunity to confront and cross-examine child victim at pretrial TYHA hearing and at trial after child testified via closed circuit television); accord, *Commonwealth v. Charlton*, 902 A.2d 554 (Pa. Super. 2006). In *Crawford*, the United States Supreme Court partially overruled *Ohio v. Roberts*, 448 U.S. 56 (1980) and adopted a new test for determining whether hearsay testimony will violate the defendant's constitutional right of confrontation. The Court ruled that "testimonial" statements by a witness not present at trial may only be admitted if the witness: (1) is unavailable, and (2) was previously subject to cross-examination about the statement. As the Third Circuit explained, "The lynchpin of the *Crawford* decision . . . is its distinction between testimonial and nontestimonial hearsay; simply put, the rule announced in *Crawford* applies only to the former category of statements." *United States v. Hendricks*, 395 F.3d 173, 179 (3d Cir. 2005).

The admissibility of "nontestimonial" hearsay for purposes of the Confrontation Clause apparently continues to be governed by the standards set forth in *Ohio v. Roberts*, 448 U.S. 56 (1980), i.e., hearsay can be admitted at trial only when: (1) the evidence falls within a firmly rooted hearsay exception, or (2) the statements contain particularized guarantees of trustworthiness such that adversarial testing of the statements would add little to the statements' reliability. *Allshouse*, 985 A.2d at 855. Thus, the fundamental question in criminal cases with respect to the admissibility of hearsay evidence is, what confrontation analysis applies— *Crawford* or *Ohio v. Roberts*? *See Commonwealth v. Cesar*, 911 A.2d 978 (Pa. Super. 2006) (where the child testified at trial, dictates of *Crawford* not violated); *Huckabee v. Adams*, 2005 WL 3470670 (E.D. Cal.) (child's videotaped statement describing indecent acts admissible under *Crawford* where child testified at trial and was available for cross-examination).

Terming the Tender Years statute "a special accommodation" to the prosecution that "poses unique challenges" for the defense, the court in *Commonwealth v. Crossley*, 711 A.2d 1025 (Pa. Super. 1998) held that the Commonwealth's failure to comply with the statutory notice provisions mandated exclusion of the evidence without any requirement for defendant to show prejudice. The court said that the Act's explicit notice requirement mandates more than mere compliance with discovery requests. *Commonwealth v. Crossley*, 711 A.2d 1025 (Pa. Super. 1998). *See Commonwealth v. Hunzer*, 868 A.2d 498 (Pa. Super. 2005) (Act merely requires notice contain "the particulars of the statement, not an exact word-for-word recitation).

See 42 Pa.C.S. § 5986 which governs the use of child victim hearsay in dependency proceedings but is also followed in administrative hearings in expungement requests. *A.Y. v. Dep't Pub. Welfare*, 641 A.2d 1148 (Pa. 1994); *J.M. v. Dep't Pub. Welfare*, 52 A.3d 552 (Pa. Cmwlth. 2012); *R.A. v. Dep't Pub. Welfare*, 82 A.3d 370 (Pa. 2013).

Research References

Packel & Poulin, Pennsylvania Evidence § 824

(4th ed. 2013)

McCormick, Evidence § 253 (7th ed. 2013)

HEARSAY EXCEPTION: DYING DECLARATION

See: Pa.R.E. 804(b)(2).

Objection

- *[To a question]* Objection. The question calls for a hearsay answer.
- *[To an answer]* Objection, hearsay. I move the answer be stricken and the jury be instructed not to consider it for any purpose.

Response

- The statement is within the dying declaration exception to the hearsay rule. As foundation, I have already established that when the declarant made the statement to this witness: (1) declarant believed his death was imminent; (2) the statement was based on personal knowledge; and (3) the statement addresses what declarant believed to be the cause or circumstances of his imminent death. I have also met the requirement of showing the declarant is unavailable within the definition of Pa.R.E. 804(a).

Pennsylvania Law

In any civil or criminal proceeding, the statement of a person about the cause or circumstances of what he believes to be his impending death qualifies as a dying declaration if the following conditions are met: (1) declarant believed his death was imminent (whether, in fact, it occurred or not); (2) the statement was based on personal knowledge; and (3) the statement concerns the cause or circumstances of what declarant believed to be his imminent death. Pa.R.E. 804(b)(2). The offering party must also demonstrate by a preponderance of the evidence that the declarant is unavailable under the definition provided in Pa.R.E. 804(a).

In other words, the admissibility of such evidence depends initially upon the state of the declarant's mind. *Commonwealth v. Knable*, 369 Pa. 171, 85 A.2d 114 (1952). The required sense of imminent death may be shown by the victim's own statements, *Commonwealth v. Priest*, 18 A.3d 1235 (Pa. Super. 2011); *Commonwealth v. Logan*, 361 Pa. 186, 63 A.2d 28 (1949), or may be inferred from the existing circumstances, including the nature of the wound and the state of the declarant's illness. *Commonwealth v. Chamberlain*, 557 Pa. 34, 731 A.2d 593 (1999) (inferred from gunshot wounds to head and chest that victim believed she was going to die); *Commonwealth v. Smith*, 454 Pa. 515, 314 A.2d 224 (1973) (sense of imminent death inferred where victim was 66 year-old doctor with multiple stab wounds who expressed repeated concern about his loss of blood and said "he did not think he would make it"); *see Commonwealth v. Levanduski*, 907 A.2d 3 (Pa. Super. 2006) (victim's letter inadmissible; did not contain any suggestion that death was imminent).

The dying declaration must concern the cause of death or the circumstances surrounding its occurrence. *Commonwealth v. Perry*, 364 Pa. 537, 73 A.2d 425 (1950). A dying declaration need not be inculpatory; exculpatory statements have been admitted under this exception. *Commonwealth v. Plubell*, 367 Pa. 452, 80 A.2d 825 (1951). The fact that the victim lingers for some period of time is not a disqualification. *Commonwealth v. Smith*, 454 Pa. 515, 314 A.2d 224 (1973); *Commonwealth v. Priest*, 18 A.3d 1235 (Pa. Super. 2011) (statements qualified as dying declaration notwithstanding lapse of six hours between victim's statements and his actual death).

The rationale for this exception has often been stated to rest on the religious belief that knowledge of impending death deters falsehood, *Commonwealth v. Riggins*, 478 Pa. 222, 386 A.2d 520 (1978); *Commonwealth v. Douglas*, 461 Pa. 749, 337 A.2d 860 (1975), as well as the necessity for the testimony of the deceased declarant. *Commonwealth v. Brown*, 388 Pa. 613, 131 A.2d 367 (1957).

Whether the facts and circumstances of a case warrant the admission of a statement as a dying declaration is decided by the trial judge. *Commonwealth v. Miller*, 987 A.2d 638 (Pa. 2009). The credibility, interpretation and weight to be given a dying declaration are matters exclusively for the jury. *Commonwealth v. Riggins*, 478 Pa. 222, 386 A.2d 520 (1978).

In *Crawford v. Washington*, 541 U.S. 36, 124 S.Ct. 1354, 158 L.Ed.2d 177 (2004) (discussed at page 134, *supra*), a criminal case involving a Confrontation Clause challenge, the United States Supreme Court held that if a hearsay statement was "testimonial" in nature, it could not be introduced at trial, in the absence of the declarant, unless the defendant had a previous opportunity to cross-examine the declarant. The Court also wrote: "We need not decide in this case whether the Sixth Amendment incorporates an exception for testimonial dying declarations. If this exception must be accepted on historical grounds, it is *sui generis."* *Crawford v. Washington*, 541 U.S. 36, 56 n.6, 124 S.Ct. 1354, 158 L.Ed.2d 177 (2004). *See Michigan v. Bryant*, 562 U.S. 344 (2011) ("were the issue properly tendered here, I would take up the question whether the exception for dying declarations survives our recent Confrontation Clause decisions." (Ginsburg, J. dissenting); *Commonwealth v. Williams*, 103 A.3d 354 (Pa. Super. 2014) (it is unclear whether the rule survives after *Crawford* and its progeny). One commentator has suggested "[w]hen a statement is accusatory and intended to be conveyed beyond those who would be expected to keep it confidential—to government agents, private agencies that perform government functions, and strangers at arms length from the witness—it should be considered testimonial." Mosteller, *Crawford v. Washington*: Encouraging and Ensuring the Confrontation of Witnesses, 39

U.Rich. L.Rev. 511, 542 (2005); *see also United States v. Jordan*, 2005 WL 513501 (D.Colo.) (dying declaration inadmissible under *Crawford*; statements to investigators could not be tested by cross-examination).

Compare: Fed. R. Evid. 804(b)(2).

Research References

Packel & Poulin, Pennsylvania Evidence § 804(b)(2)-1 (4th ed. 2013)

Binder, Hearsay Handbook Chapter 34 (4th ed. 2001)

McCormick, Evidence Chapter 32 (7th ed. 2013)

HEARSAY EXCEPTION: EXCITED UTTERANCE
See: Pa.R.E. 803(2).

Objection

- *[To a question]* Objection. The question calls for a hearsay answer.
- *[To an answer]* Objection, hearsay. I move the answer be stricken and the jury be instructed not to consider it for any purpose.

Response

- The statement is admissible as an excited utterance. I have established that the statement relates to a startling event or condition; that it was made under the stress and excitement of the event and that the declarant *[witnessed]* *[participated in]* the event.

Pennsylvania Law

Pa.R.E.803(2) provides an exception to the hearsay rule for any "statement relating to a startling event or condition made while the declarant was under the stress of excitement caused by the event or condition."

The rationale for the excited utterance exception is that such statements are given under circumstances which eliminate the possibility of fabrication or coaching. *Idaho v. Wright*, 497 U.S. 805, 110 S.Ct. 3139, 111 L.Ed.2d 638 (1990); *Commonwealth v. Murray*, 83 A.3d 137 (Pa. 2013); *Commonwealth v. Counterman*, 553 Pa. 370, 719 A.2d 284 (1998); *Commonwealth v. Colon*, 102 A.3d 1033 (Pa. Super. 2014) (statement must be spontaneous, excited or impulsive rather than product of reflection and deliberation); *Commonwealth v. Carmody*, 799 A.2d 143 (Pa. Super. 2002) (victim's oral statements to police about beating qualified under this exception; her written statement of events did not).

In one sense, this exception operates more narrowly than the exception for a present sense impression, because it requires an event or condition that is *startling*. However, it is broader in scope than Pa.R.E. 803(1) because an excited utterance: (1) need not describe or explain the startling event or condition; it need only *relate* to it, and (2) need not be made contemporaneously therewith, or immediately thereafter. It is sufficient if the stress of excitement created by the startling event or condition persists as a substantial factor in provoking the utterance. *Commonwealth v. Stephens*, 74 A.3d 1034 (Pa. Super. 2013).

The prerequisite to an excited utterance is a startling event or condition. The startling event or condition is usually something dramatic, like an accident or a crime. *Commonwealth v. Mitchell*, 135 A.3d 1097 (Pa. Super. 2016). But it need not be, so long as it has an exciting effect on the declarant.

To qualify under the excited utterance exception to the hearsay rule, the statement must be:

> a spontaneous declaration by a person whose mind has been suddenly made subject to an overpowering emotion caused by some unexpected and shocking occurrence, which that person had just participated in or closely witnessed, and made in reference to some phase of that occurrence which he perceived, and this declaration must be made so near the occurrence both in time and place as to exclude the likelihood of its having emanated in whole or in part from his reflective faculties.

Commonwealth v. Boczkowski, 577 Pa. 421, 846 A.2d 75, 95 (2004) (quoting *Commonwealth v. Stallworth*, 566 Pa. 349, 781 A.2d 110, 119–20 (2001)); *Commonwealth v. Luster*, 71 A.3d 1029 (Pa. Super. 2013); *Commonwealth v. Bibbs*, 970 A.2d 440 (Pa. Super. 2009).

The basis for the admission of the utterance is its spontaneity; thus all utterances which do not display the mandated instinctive naturalness must be excluded for fear that the words will emanate in whole or in part from the declarant's reflective faculties. The declaration must be spoken under conditions which insure that it is not the result of premeditation, consideration or design, and it cannot be in the form of a narration, or attempted explanation of past events. *Cody v. S.K.F. Indus., Inc.*, 447 Pa. 558, 291 A.2d 772 (1972); *see also Commonwealth v. Levanduski*, 907 A.2d 3 (Pa. Super. 2006) (exception did not apply to a recounting of past events); *Commonwealth v. Sanford*, 397 Pa. Super. 581, 580 A.2d 784 (1990); *Reichman v. Wallach*, 306 Pa. Super. 177, 452 A.2d 501 (1982).

The excited utterance exception includes statements made in response to questioning as well as those made shortly after the event. *Commonwealth v. Sherwood*, 982 A.2d 483 (Pa. 2009); *Commonwealth v. Lester*, 554 Pa. 644, 722 A.2d 997 (1998); *Commonwealth v. Crosby*, 791 A.2d 366 (Pa. Super. 2002). What is required is a "sufficient confluence of time and events to vest special reliability in the statement." *Commonwealth v. Coleman*, 458 Pa. 112, 326 A.2d 387, 390 (1974).

The declaration usually is, but need not be, strictly contemporaneous with the existing cause, nor is there a definite and fixed time limit. *Commonwealth v. Pronkoskie*, 477 Pa. 132, 383 A.2d 858 (1978); *Commonwealth v. Manley*, 985 A.2d 256 (Pa. Super. 2009); *Boykin v. Brown*, 868 A.2d 1264 (Pa. Super. 2005). Rather, each case must be judged on its own facts, and a lapse of time of several hours has not negated a statement as an excited utterance. *See Commonwealth v. Douglas*, 558 Pa. 412, 737 A.2d 1188 (1999) (eleven minutes); *Commonwealth v. Cheeks*, 423 Pa. 67, 223 A.2d 291 (1966) (forty-five minutes); *Commonwealth v. Dugan*, 252 Pa. Super. 377, 381 A.2d 967 (1977) (two and one-half to three hours). *But see Commonwealth v. Wholaver*, 989 A.2d 883 (Pa. 2010) (five to ten minutes was sufficient time for defendant to have engaged in reflective thought re statements about murder scene); *Croyle v. Smith*, 918 A.2d 142 (Pa. Super. 2007) (exception did not apply where ten minutes after speaking to accident participants, witness gave narrative statement in response to police questions); *Commonwealth v. Vining*, 744 A.2d 310 (Pa. Super. 1999) (statements made ten to twelve hours after event and in response to persistent questioning inadmissible). The crucial question, regardless of the time lapse, is whether at the time the statement is made the nervous excitement continues to dominate while the reflective processes remain in abeyance. *Commonwealth v. Gore*, 262 Pa. Super. 540, 396 A.2d 1302 (1978).

In determining admissibility, the courts have considered: (1) whether the declarant, in fact, witnessed the startling event, *Carney v. Pennsylvania R.R. Co.*, 428 Pa. 489, 240 A.2d 71 (1968); (2) the elapsed time between the startling event and the declaration, *Commonwealth v. Pronkoskie*, 477 Pa. 132, 383 A.2d 858 (1978) and, (3) whether the declarant spoke to others before making the statement, or had the opportunity to do so, *Hammel v. Christian*, 416 Pa. Super. 78, 610 A.2d 979 (1992). None of these factors, except the requirement that the declarant had witnessed the startling event, is in itself dispositive. Rather, the factors are to be considered with all the surrounding circumstances to determine whether a statement is an excited utterance. *Commonwealth v. Blackwell*, 343 Pa. Super. 201, 494 A.2d 426 (1985).

In Pennsylvania, there must be independent evidence to corroborate the occurrence of the startling event; an excited utterance alone cannot be used to prove that an exciting event did, in fact, happen. *Commonwealth v. Barnes*, 310 Pa. Super. 480, 456 A.2d 1037 (1983). In the federal courts the existence of a startling event or condition may be inferred from the excited utterance alone, or in combination with surrounding circumstances.

United States v. Brown, 254 F.3d 454 (3d Cir.2001). *See* McCormick, Evidence § 272 at 206 (5th ed. 2001).

Where the declarant is unidentified, the proponent may have difficulty establishing the requirements of spontaneity and personal knowledge. *See Harris v. Toys "R" US-Penn, Inc.*, 880 A.2d 1270 (Pa. Super. 2005) (no showing that unidentified declarant showed any emotion or that he participated in or closely witnessed plaintiff's accident); *Williamson v. Philadelphia Transp. Co.*, 244 Pa. Super. 492, 368 A.2d 1292 (1976) (utterance excluded where it was not clear that bystanders had actually seen auto accident); *Miller v. Keating*, 754 F.2d 507 (3d Cir.1985) (evidence did not establish unidentified declarant saw accident or was excited when he allegedly spoke). If the declarant cannot be identified, there is also the possibility that the declarant never existed. That, however, is really an issue of credibility to be decided by the court or other factfinder. *But see Commonwealth v. Hood*, 872 A.2d 175 (Pa. Super. 2005) and *Commonwealth v. Upshur*, 764 A.2d 69 (Pa. Super. 2000) (proponent must offer independent corroborating evidence that unidentified declarant actually viewed the event). The *Upshur* dissent, declining to find such requirement, states the better view.

Crawford v. Washington, 541 U.S. 36, 124 S.Ct. 1354, 158 L.Ed.2d 177 (2004) (discussed at page 134 *supra*), is a criminal case involving a Confrontation Clause challenge, where the United States Supreme Court held that if a hearsay statement was "testimonial" in nature, it could not be introduced at trial, in the absence of the declarant, unless the defendant had a previous opportunity to cross-examine the declarant. Justice Scalia did say that "[a]n accuser who makes a formal statement to government officers bears testimony in a sense that a person who makes a casual remark to an acquaintance does not." *Crawford v. Washington*, 541 U.S. 36, 51, 124 S.Ct. 1354, 158 L.Ed.2d 177 (2004).

The Sixth Circuit has said that in the wake of *Crawford*, even if statements qualify as excited utterances, there remains the further question of whether the statements are "testimonial" and, thus, inadmissible. *United States v. Hadley*, 431 F.3d 484 (6th Cir. 2005). The Pennsylvania Supreme Court said: "*Crawford* did not abolish the excited utterance exception to the hearsay rule when the declarant is unavailable." *Commonwealth v. Jones*, 912 A.2d 268, 283 (Pa. 2006).

In *Commonwealth v. Gray*, 867 A.2d 560, 577 (Pa. Super. 2005), excited utterances made to police at a crime scene were not testimonial because declarant was not subject to police interrogation and volunteered information in an effort to remedy a "perceived emergency, not to create a record for use in a future prosecution." *See Commonwealth v. Williams*, 103 A.3d 354 (Pa. Super. 2014) and *Commonwealth v. Rolan*, 964 A.2d 398 (Pa. Super. 2008) (under the circumstances, statements made during 911 call were nontestimonial); *see also Commonwealth v. Keys*, 814 A.2d 1256 (Pa. Super. 2003) (victim's statements did not qualify as excited utterance and admission of this hearsay denied the accused the right of confronting and cross-examining the sole eyewitness against him). The First Circuit has rejected any categorical rule that would classify excited utterances as either testimonial or non-testimonial. Instead, the court concluded that "the excited utterance and testimonial hearsay inquiries are separate but related." *United States v. Brito*, 427 F.3d 53, 63 (1st Cir. 2005).

Compare: Fed. R. Evid. 803(2).

Research References

Packel & Poulin, Pennsylvania Evidence § 803(2)-1 (4th ed. 2013)

Binder, Hearsay Handbook Chapter 9 (4th ed. 2001)

McCormick, Evidence § 272 (7th ed. 2013)

HEARSAY EXCEPTION: FORFEITURE BY WRONGDOING

See: Pa.R.E. 804(b)(6).

Objection

- [*To a question*] Objection. The question calls for hearsay.

- [*To an answer*] Objection, hearsay. I move the answer be stricken and the jury be instructed not to consider it for any purpose.

Response

- The evidence has already established that the absence of the declarant was wrongfully procured; any hearsay objection has been forfeited.

- We intend to prove that the absence of the declarant was wrongfully procured. I ask the court to allow this testimony subject to our fulfilling that condition.

Commentary

As a codification of the long-standing doctrine of waiver by misconduct,[1] Pa.R.E. 804(b)(6) provides that a party forfeits the right to object to the

---

[1]Because evidentiary rules cannot abrogate constitutional rights, it should be noted that the United States Supreme Court has held repeatedly that a defendant's intentional misconduct can effect a waiver of Confrontation Clause rights under the Sixth Amendment. *See, e.g., Crawford v. Washington*, 541 U.S. 36, 62, 124 S.Ct. 1354 (2004) (forfeiture by wrongdoing extinguishes confrontation claims on essentially equitable grounds); *Taylor v. United States*, 414 U.S. 17, 94 S.Ct. 194, 38 L.Ed.2d 174 (1973); *Illinois v. Allen*, 397 U.S. 337, 90 S.Ct. 1057, 25 L.Ed.2d 353 (1970). A well-established corollary is that the right of confrontation is forfeited with respect to any witness or potential witness whose absence a defendant wrongfully procures. *Reynolds v. United States,* 98 U.S. (8 Otto) 145, 25 L.Ed. 244 (1878); *United States v. Houlihan*,

introduction of hearsay if the party wrongfully causes the declarant to be unavailable to testify at trial.

The exception is new to Pennsylvania evidence law and is only discussed in a few cases, *Commonwealth v. Wholaver*, 989 A.2d 883, 900 n.12 (Pa. 2010) (defendant forfeits his confrontation right by wrongdoing only where the wrongful act was committed for the very purpose of preventing the witness' trial testimony); *Commonwealth v. Laich*, 566 Pa. 19, 28 n. 4, 777 A.2d 1057, 1062 n. 4 (2001) (victim's out-of-court statement not admissible under forfeiture exception when defendant murdered her not to prevent testimony but because of personal animosity); *Commonwealth v. Paddy*, 569 Pa. 47, 800 A.2d 294, 310 n.10 (2002); *Commonwealth v. King*, 959 A.2d 405 (Pa. Super. 2008) (Rule 804(b)(6) does not limit subject matter of declarant's statements that can be offered to prove defendant murdered declarant); *Commonwealth v. Levanduski*, 907 A.2d 3 (Pa. Super. 2006) (victim's letter was hearsay where no evidence suggested defendant and her lover murdered victim to procure his unavailability); *Commonwealth v. Santiago*, 822 A.2d 716 (Pa. Super. 2003). Accordingly, federal case law can provide interim guidance.[2] *See Laich*, dissenting opinion of Castille, J.

The rule applies to all parties including the government. The wrongdoing that procures the unavailability of the declarant as a witness need not consist of a criminal act. *See* Advisory Committee's Note to Fed. R. Evid. 804(b)(6); *see also United*

---

92 F.3d 1271 (1st Cir.1996); *United States v. Mastrangelo*, 693 F.2d 269 (2d Cir.1982); *United States v. Carlson*, 547 F.2d 1346 (8th Cir.1976).

[2]Decisions of the federal courts are not binding on Pennsylvania courts but are persuasive authority. *Efford v. Jockey Club*, 796 A.2d 370 (Pa. Super. 2002).

States v. Ochoa, 229 F.3d 631, 639 n. 3 (7th Cir. 2000).

Whether a party has engaged in conduct justifying forfeiture is determined by the preponderance of the evidence standard contained in Rule 104(a). *See Davis v. Washington*, 547 U.S. 813, 833 (2006) (while not taking a position on the standard necessary to demonstrate that a defendant has procured the unavailability of a witness and forfeited Confrontation Clause rights against that witness, the Supreme Court stated that "federal courts . . . have generally held the Government to the preponderance-of-the-evidence standard."). Prior to finding defendant waived his confrontation rights with respect to out-of-court statements by an actual or potential witness admitted pursuant to Fed. R. Evid. 804(b)(6), the court must hold an evidentiary hearing outside the presence of the jury in which the government has the burden of proving by a preponderance of the evidence that: (1) the defendant (or party against whom the out-of-court statement is offered) was involved in, or responsible for, procuring the unavailability of the declarant through knowledge, complicity, planning or in any other way, and (2) the defendant (or other party) acted with the intent of procuring declarant's unavailability. The government need not show defendant's sole motivation was to procure declarant's absence. It need only show defendant was motivated in part by a desire to silence the witness. *United States v. Dhinsa*, 243 F.3d 635 (2d Cir. 2001), *and United States v. Cherry*, 217 F.3d 811 (10th Cir.2000) (judge must hold evidentiary hearing outside the presence of jury).

In *Giles v. California*, 554 U.S. 353, 128 S.Ct. 2678 (2008), the Supreme Court held that unconfronted testimony is not admissible without a showing that by his conduct, defendant intended to and did prevent declarant from testifying. *See also U.S. v. Lentz*, 524 F.3d 501, 528–29 (4th Cir. 2008) (statements that defendant made to kidnapping victim, who related statements to third parties, were admissible upon trial court's determination, by preponderance of evidence, that defendant engaged in wrongdoing that was intended, at least in part, to procure victim's unavailability as witness); *U.S. v. Gray*, 405 F.3d 227, 242 (4th Cir. 2005) (in applying Rule 804(b)(6) "we have held that a defendant need only intend 'in part' to procure the defendant's unavailability").

A number of circuits have held that Rule 804(b)(6) allows the admission of hearsay against a defendant by virtue of his having acquiesced in the acts taken to procure the declarant's unavailability. *Johnson*, 495 F.3d at 971 (forfeiture by wrongdoing doctrine applies when a defendant aids and abets murder of a potential witness against another person); *U.S. v. Rivera*, 412 F.3d 562 (4th Cir. 2005) (rejecting argument that defendant has to personally commit wrongful act which caused declarant's unavailability; Rule 804(b)(6) allows hearsay statements to be admitted against "a party who has engaged or acquiesced in" wrongdoing intended to procure unavailability of declarant); *U.S. v. Thompson*, 286 F.3d 950, 963–64 (7th Cir. 2002) (imputing co-conspirators actions to defendant for purposes of Rule 804(b)(6)); *U.S. v. Cherry*, 217 F.3d 811 (10th Cir. 2000) (same); *U.S. v. Mastrangelo*, 693 F.2d 269, 273–74 (2d Cir. 1982) (bare knowledge of plot to kill victim and failure to give warning to appropriate authorities sufficient to constitute waiver); *Olson v. Green*, 668 F.2d 421, 429 (8th Cir. 1982) (noting that someone acting on defendant's behalf to procure unavailability of witness can operate to waive defendant's hearsay objection). *See also U.S. v. Stewart*, 485 F.3d 666, 671 (2d Cir. 2007) (government was not required to show by direct evidence defendant's involvement in conspiracy to secure absence of witness via murder; defendant's participation with requisite knowledge and criminal intent may be established through circumstantial evidence).

Compare: Fed. R. Evid. 804(b)(6).

Research References

Packel & Poulin, Pennsylvania Evidence § 804(b)(6)-1 (4th ed. 2013)

Binder, Hearsay Handbook Chapter 42 (4th ed. 2001)

Goode and Wellborn, Courtroom Handbook on Federal Evidence Chapter 5, Rule 804 (annual ed.)

Graham, Handbook of Federal Evidence § 804.6 (6th ed. 2006)

McCormick, Evidence § 253 (7th ed. 2013)

HEARSAY EXCEPTION: FORMER TESTIMONY

See: Pa.R.E. 804(b)(1).

Objection

- Objection, hearsay. The use of former testimony of the witness is inadmissible here because:
  - [*plaintiff/defendant had no opportunity and/or similar motive to develop this testimony at the prior proceeding (explain)*]
  - [*the prior proceeding did not involve the same subject matter/criminal issue*]
  - [*the witness has not been shown to be unavailable (specify)*]

Response

- The former testimony is admissible because:
  - [*plaintiff/defendant was present and had a right to develop the testimony but chose not to*]
  - [*the testimony was developed by a prior party in a civil case who qualifies as plaintiff's/defendant's predecessor in interest*]
  - [*unavailability has been established pursuant to Rule 804(a) (specify details)*]

Pennsylvania Law

In order for former testimony to be admissible under Pa.R.E. 804(b)(1): (i) the declarant must be unavailable; (ii) the testimony must have been taken at a hearing or deposition in the same or another proceeding, and (iii) the party against whom the testimony is now offered must have had (or, in a civil action, its predecessor in interest must have had) an opportunity and similar motive to develop the testimony by direct, cross or redirect examination. *Commonwealth v. Wholaver*, 989 A.2d

883 (Pa. 2010); *Commonwealth v. McGrogan*, 523 Pa. 614, 568 A.2d 924 (1990); *Commonwealth v. Chestnut*, 511 Pa. 169, 512 A.2d 603 (1986); *Sutch v. Roxborough Memorial Hosp.*, 142 A.3d 38 (Pa. Super. 2016); *Commonwealth v. Buford*, 101 A.3d 1182 (Pa. Super. 2014) (prior testimony does not offend the right of confrontation provided defendant had counsel and a full opportunity to cross-examine that witness at the prior proceeding); *Commonwealth v. Leak*, 22 A.3d 1036 (Pa. Super. 2011); *Beaumont v. ETL Servs., Inc.*, 761 A.2d 166 (Pa. Super. 2000). The exception is predicated on the indicia of reliability normally afforded by adequate cross-examination. *Commonwealth v. Bazemore*, 531 Pa. 582, 614 A.2d 684 (1992).

Predecessor In Interest—Civil Action

Although the rule does not define "predecessor in interest," the Superior Court has indicated that privity or a common property interest is not required. *See Beaumont v. ETL Servs., Inc.*, 761 A.2d at 175 (deceased plaintiff's testimony in prior federal action against crane manufacturer admissible in subsequent state action against seller of crane; manufacturer "would have had as great an incentive to vigorously cross-examine [plaintiff] during the taking of his deposition as current defendants would have . . ."); *see also Gosha v. City of Philadelphia*, 30 Pa. D. & C.3d 190 (Pa.C.P. Phila.Cty. 1982), aff'd *Commonwealth v. Gosha*, 84 Pa.Cmwlth. 466, 479 A.2d 85 (1984) (party has been constructively represented at the taking of a deposition if the party in the previous action had the incentive to vigorously protect the same interests that the parties to the current action would want to protect).

It should be noted that, while the rule has some flexibility in civil actions, when trial testimony is offered against a criminal defendant, the defendant must have been a party to the prior proceeding with

221

the opportunity for cross-examination. *Commonwealth v. Smith*, 436 Pa. Super. 277, 647 A.2d 907 (1994); *see* McCormick, Evidence § 303.

Opportunity and Similar Motive To Develop The Testimony

In order for testimony from a prior hearing or deposition to be admissible, the party against whom it is offered must have had a full and fair opportunity and similar motive to cross-examine that testimony. *Commonwealth v. Ramtahal*, 33 A.3d 602 (Pa. 2011) (grand jury testimony inadmissible where defendant's use of 5th Amendment precluded Commonwealth's cross-examination); *Commonwealth v. Wholaver*, 989 A.2d 883 (Pa. 2010); *Bugosh v. Allen Refractories Co.*, 932 A.2d 901 (Pa. Super. 2007). *See Commonwealth v. Bazemore*, 531 Pa. 582, 614 A.2d 684 (1992) (prior testimony of prosecution witness at preliminary hearing inadmissible where Commonwealth had not disclosed vital impeachment evidence); *Beaumont v. ETL Servs., Inc.*, 761 A.2d 166 (Pa. Super. 2000) (admitting deposition testimony from prior proceeding); *Commonwealth v. Smith*, 436 Pa. Super. 277, 647 A.2d 907 (1994) (prior testimony of sole eyewitness inadmissible; state failed to disclose prior criminal history and pending criminal charges); *cf. Commonwealth v. Fink*, 791 A.2d 1235 (Pa. Super. 2002) (no error admitting prior testimony; although defendant did not have vital impeachment evidence at preliminary hearing, defendant did not take advantage of trial court's offer to cure by providing opportunity to call victim for cross-examination re prior inconsistent statements).

The fact that a party changes counsel or that tactical decisions are made with respect to the extent of questioning does not negate the existence of opportunity and similar motive to develop the testimony. *See, e.g., Commonwealth v. Douglas*, 558

Pa. 412, 737 A.2d 1188 (1999) (prior testimony admissible; defendant did not avail himself of opportunity at preliminary hearing to cross-examine as fully as possible); *Commonwealth v. Thompson*, 538 Pa. 297, 648 A.2d 315 (1994) (same); *see also Hendrix v. Raybestos-Manhattan, Inc.*, 776 F.2d 1492, 1506 (11th Cir.1985) ("As a general rule, a party's decision to limit cross-examination in a discovery deposition is a strategic choice and does not preclude his adversary's use of the deposition at a subsequent proceeding").

Unavailability

The definition of witness "unavailability" is provided in Pa.R.E. 804(a) and includes, but is not limited to: assertion of privilege; refusal to testify; loss of memory; death, infirmity, physical or mental illness; or inability to compel attendance by process (subpoena) or other reasonable means. *See Commonwealth v. Nelson*, 438 Pa. Super. 325, 652 A.2d 396 (1995); *Commonwealth v. Smith*, 436 Pa. Super. 277, 647 A.2d 907 (1994) (refusal to testify); *Commonwealth v. Sandutch*, 498 Pa. 536, 449 A.2d 566 (1982); *Commonwealth v. Yabor*, 376 Pa. Super. 356, 546 A.2d 67 (1988) (privilege against self-incrimination); *Beaumont*, 761 A.2d 166 (Pa. Super. 2000) (death); *Commonwealth v. Stasko*, 471 Pa. 373, 370 A.2d 350 (1977); *Shields v. Larry Constr. Co.*, 370 Pa. 582, 88 A.2d 764 (1952) (physical illness or disability, which must be proved by affirmative evidence); *Commonwealth v. Graves*, 484 Pa. 29, 398 A.2d 644 (1979); *Commonwealth v. Bibbs*, 970 A.2d 440 (Pa. Super. 2009); *Commonwealth v. Fink*, 791 A.2d 1235 (Pa. Super. 2002) (complete or partial loss of memory). When loss of memory is asserted, the witness must take the stand to testify as to the extent of his or her present memory and be available for cross-examination by the opposing party. *Commonwealth v. Hook*, 364 Pa. Super. 447, 528 A.2d 241 (1987).

Pa.R.E. 804(a)(5) provides that in both civil and criminal cases, a declarant is unavailable if his presence cannot be secured by process or other reasonable means. The proponent has the burden of demonstrating unavailability and mere absence of the declarant is insufficient. *Commonwealth v. Blair*, 460 Pa. 31, 331 A.2d 213 (1975); *Hall v. Owens Corning Fiberglass Corp.*, 779 A.2d 1167 (Pa. Super. 2001) (proponent of deposition at trial must demonstrate unavailability of witness or the exercise of due diligence in attempting to locate witness). The trial court has the discretion to determine the sufficiency of proof of unavailability. *Commonwealth v. Wayne*, 553 Pa. 614, 720 A.2d 456 (1998); *Katz v. Montague*, 181 Pa. Super. 476, 124 A.2d 506 (1956). *See, e.g.*, *Consolidated Rail Corp. v. Delaware River Port Auth.*, 880 A.2d 628 (Pa. Super. 2005) (declarant not unavailable per Rule 804 solely by virtue of participation in witness protection program); *Commonwealth v. Lebo*, 795 A.2d 987 (Pa. Super. 2002) (although witness was in South Carolina boot camp program, lack of evidence to show Commonwealth did anything to procure witness' attendance precluded finding of unavailability); *Commonwealth v. Douglas*, 558 Pa. 412, 737 A.2d 1188 (1999) (police made good faith effort to find witness at apartment, at mother's apartment, in bars he frequented and at girlfriend's as well as contacting family, friends and neighbors); *Vattimo v. Eaborn Truck Serv., Inc.*, 777 A.2d 1163 (Pa. Super. 2001) (no error excluding deposition testimony; witness was not a party and there was no showing that he could not be subpoenaed or was otherwise unavailable); *Corl v. Kacmar*, 391 Pa. Super. 376, 571 A.2d 417 (1990) (unavailability not shown by a few unsuccessful phone calls to witness three days before trial), *accord Commonwealth v. Walloe*, 472 Pa. 473, 372 A.2d 788 (1977); *Commonwealth v. Connors*, 311 Pa. Super. 553, 458 A.2d 190 (1983); *Commonwealth v. Blair*, 460 Pa. 31, 331 A.2d 213 (1975) (witness "not found" and former testimony could be used when subpoena went unserved, phone calls were not answered and search of home verified absence); *Commonwealth v. Griffin*, 243 Pa. Super. 115, 364 A.2d 477 (1976) (good faith effort made where witness had moved and authorities unsuccessfully sought to compel her presence by legal proceedings in California); *Del Vitto v. Schiavo*, 370 Pa. 299, 87 A.2d 913 (1952) (plaintiff's multiple and varied efforts to locate soldier witness sufficient to support finding of unavailability).

Because of the constitutional preference for "face-to-face accusation," *Ohio v. Roberts*, 448 U.S. 56, 65, 100 S.Ct. 2531, 2538, 65 L.Ed.2d 597 (1980), a witness in a criminal case cannot be found unavailable unless the prosecution has made reasonable good faith efforts to locate and present the witness, 448 U.S. at 74, 100 S.Ct. at 2543. "Good faith" and "reasonableness" are factual matters to be determined on a case-by-case basis. The central constitutional inquiry is whether or not the government's actions were reasonable given all the circumstances of a particular case. *Roberts*, 448 U.S. at 74, 100 S.Ct. at 2543; *see, e.g.*, *Commonwealth v. Cruz-Centeno*, 447 Pa. Super. 98, 668 A.2d 536 (1995) (preliminary hearing testimony of murder eyewitness admissible; bench warrant issued and numerous efforts made to locate witness by prosecuting attorney, police and victim's family).

Crawford v. Washington

In *Crawford v. Washington*, 541 U.S. 36, 124 S.Ct. 1354, 158 L.Ed.2d 177 (2004) (discussed at page 134, *supra*), a criminal case involving a Confrontation Clause challenge, the United States Supreme Court held that if a hearsay statement was "testimonial" in nature, it could not be introduced at trial in the absence of the declarant, unless the defendant had a previous opportunity to cross-examine the declarant. *See United States v.*

Avants, 367 F.3d 433 (5th Cir. 2004) (the qualities that made deceased witness' preliminary hearing testimony admissible under Rule 804(b)(1) satisfy *Crawford's* Confrontation Clause test: unavailability and prior opportunity for cross-examination). In resolving the issue of admissibility under Rule 804(b)(1), federal courts have also said that the opportunity for cross-examination is generally satisfied when the defense is given a full and fair opportunity to probe and expose the infirmities of testimony through cross-examination, thereby calling to the attention of the factfinder the reasons for giving scant weight to the witness' testimony. *Delaware v. Fensterer*, 474 U.S. 15, 106 S.Ct. 292, 88 L.Ed.2d 15 (1985); *United States v. Salim*, 855 F.2d 944 (2d Cir. 1988). *See Commonwealth v. McCrae*, 574 Pa. 594, 832 A.2d 1026 (2003) (introduction of unavailable witness' prior recorded testimony from preliminary hearing is admissible at trial and will not offend the right of confrontation provided defendant had counsel and full opportunity to cross-examine witness at hearing; collecting cases).

Commonwealth v. Wholaver, 989 A.2d 883 (Pa. 2010), acknowledged instances where the often limited scope of a preliminary hearing will not provide the right of confrontation mandated by *Crawford*. Here, however, the preliminary hearing testimony of defendant's subsequently murdered daughter was admissible at trial because there had been fulsome cross-examination at the hearing as to bias, veracity, inconsistency and outside influence conducted by the same trial counsel.

Forfeiture

A party cannot interfere with the testimonial process and profit by his wrongdoing. If a witness is absent or refuses to testify because of the actions of the proponent of a statement, the witness is not unavailable and his statement cannot be used.

226

Pa.R.E. 804(a); *Baysmore v. Brownstein*, 771 A.2d 54 (Pa. Super. 2001) (defendant was not deemed unavailable and use of his deposition testimony was not allowed when he left country on vacation having had adequate notice of trial date). Conversely, if a witness has given a prior statement or testimony but then is silenced by a party for the purpose of excluding his testimony entirely, then the prior testimony is admissible.

See Hearsay Exception, Forfeiture By Wrongdoing.

Statutes—Rules of Procedure

In addition to the rules of evidence, there are two statutes permitting use of former testimony: 42 Pa.C.S.A. § 5917 (criminal cases—*see Commonwealth v. Rolan*, 964 A.2d 398 (Pa. Super. 2008)) and 42 Pa.C.S.A. § 5934 (civil cases). Preservation of testimony in criminal cases is governed by Pa.R.Crim.P. 500 and 501. In civil cases, use at trial of deposition testimony is addressed by Pa.R.Civ.P. 4020 and 4017 (medical witness, expert witness). Note: Rule 4020(a)(2) allows an adverse party to use the deposition of a party opponent (including corporate officers, directors, managing agent or corporate designee) at trial for any purpose with no need to show unavailability. *El v. Murzyn*, 831 A.2d 724 (Pa. Super. 2003).

Compare: Fed. R. Evid. 804(b)(1).

Research References

Packel & Poulin, Pennsylvania Evidence § 804(b)(1)-1 (4th ed. 2013)

Binder, Hearsay Handbook Chapter 33 (4th ed. 2001)

McCormick, Evidence Chapter 31 (7th ed. 2013)

HEARSAY EXCEPTION: MARKET REPORTS, COMMERCIAL PUBLICATIONS

See: Pa.R.E. 803(17).

Objection

- [*To a question*] Objection. The question calls for a hearsay answer.
- *To a document*] Objection. The document is inadmissible hearsay.
- [*To an answer*] Objection, hearsay. I move the answer be stricken and the jury be instructed not to consider it for any purpose.

Response

- Market quotations are made admissible when the price or value of goods traded in any established commodity market is in issue, Pa.R.E. 803(17). The document in question is a(n) [*official publication*] [*trade journal*] [*newspaper*] [*periodical of general circulation*].

Pennsylvania Law

Pa.R.E. 803(17) excepts from the hearsay rule market quotations, tabulations, lists, directories or other published compilations generally used and relied upon by the public or by persons in particular occupations. A publication may be qualified for this exception by the testimony of a knowledgeable witness. Alternatively, its qualification for the exception may be judicially noticed by the trial judge under Pa.R.E. 201.

The Uniform Commercial Code also creates an exception to the hearsay rule in UCC cases for market quotations of goods regularly bought and sold in any established commodity market. 13 P.S. § 2724, Admissibility of Market Quotations, provides:

Whenever the prevailing price or value of any goods

regularly bought and sold in any established commodity market is in issue, reports in official publications or trade journals or newspapers or periodicals of general circulation published as the reports of such market shall be admissible in evidence. The circumstances of the preparation of such a report may be shown to affect its weight but not its admissibility.

Other jurisdictions have held that blue books and red books for automobiles are not admissible under § 2-724 since cars are not sold on the commodity market. *See Jones v. Morgan*, 58 Mich.App. 455, 228 N.W.2d 419 (1975); *Rowe Auto and Trailer Sales, Inc. v. King*, 257 Ark. 484, 517 S.W.2d 946 (1975). Use of such documents concerning the value of automobiles has not been directly presented in Pennsylvania although use of the red book value of collateral was disapproved in *Savoy v. Beneficial Consumer Discount Co.*, 503 Pa. 74, 468 A.2d 465 (1983), under the particular facts of an Article 9 case. In *U.S. v. Masferrer*, 514 F.3d 1158 (11th Cir. 2008), historical financial data derived from computerized records of Bloomberg Financial Service fell within this exception where such information was universally relied upon by individuals and institutions involved in financial markets.

Compare: Fed. R. Evid. 803 (17).

Research References

Packel & Poulin, Pennsylvania Evidence § 803(17)-1 (4th ed. 2013)

Binder, Hearsay Handbook Chapter 25 (4th ed. 2001)

McCormick, Evidence § 321 (7th ed. 2013)

HEARSAY EXCEPTION: OFFICIAL RECORDS OF PENNSYLVANIA

See: Pa.R.E. 803(6), 803(8), 803(10), 42 Pa.C.S.A. § 6103, et seq.; see also Pa.R.E. 901(b)(7), 902 and 1005, 75 Pa. C.S.A. § 6328.

Objection

- Objection. The records have not been properly authenticated pursuant to Pa.R.E. 803(6) or 803(8). Therefore, the contents are inadmissible hearsay since they are offered to prove the truth of the matters asserted in them.

Response

- A proper foundation has been established in that we are offering copies attested to by the custodian with a certificate under seal that the officer has custody of said records. Additionally, the documents also qualify under the business records exception to the hearsay rule.

Pennsylvania Law

The biggest regularly conducted business activity is that of government: federal, state and local. Governmental records were included within the business records exception originally codified at Pa.R.E. 803(6) and are now addressed by the new Public Records Exception, Rule 803(8), effective January, 2017.

Several statutes also address the admissibility of governmental records. 42 Pa.C.S.A. § 6103 permits proof of an official record kept by a government department within this Commonwealth by: (i) an official publication; or (ii) a copy attested by its custodian or his deputy and accompanied by a certificate under seal that the officer has custody of said record.

42 Pa.C.S.A. § 6103 provides:

(a)   *General Rule.*—An official record kept within this Commonwealth by any court, magisterial district justice or other government unit, or an entry therein, when admissible for any purpose, may be evidenced by an official publication thereof or by a copy attested by the officer having the legal custody of the record, or by that officer's deputy, and accompanied by a certificate that the officer has the custody. The certificate may be made by any public officer having a seal of office and having official duties with respect to the government unit in which the record is kept, authenticated by the seal of his office, or if there is no such officer, by:

    (1) The Department of State, in the case of any Commonwealth agency.

    (2) The Clerk of the court of common pleas of the judicial district embracing any county in which the government unit has jurisdiction, in the case of any government unit other than a Commonwealth agency.

(b)   *Lack of record.*—A written statement that after an examination of the records of the government unit no record or entry of a specified tenor is found to exist in the records designated by the statement, authenticated as provided in subsection (a), is admissible as evidence that the records contain no such record or entry.

The exception to the hearsay rule is set forth in 42 Pa.C.S.A. § 6104:

(a)   *General rule.*—A copy of a record of governmental action or inaction authenticated as provided in section 6103 (relating to proof of official records) shall be admissible as evidence that the governmental action or inaction disclosed therein was in fact taken or omitted.

(b)   *Existence of facts.*—A copy of a record authenticated as provided in section 6103 disclosing the existence or nonexistence of facts which have been recorded pursuant to official duty or would have been so recorded had the facts existed, shall be admissible as evidence of the existence or nonexistence of such facts, unless the sources of information or other circumstances indicate lack of trustworthiness.

Although the Pennsylvania Rules of Evidence did not originally contain a rule corresponding to the federal public rules exception to the hearsay rule found at F.R.E. 803(8), an equivalent rule was embodied by these statutes regarding the authentication and admissibility of official records. *D'Alessandro v. Pennsylvania State Police*, 937 A.2d 404 (Pa. 2007). These statutes also provide a means for satisfying the authentication requirement, and, thus, to dispense with the need for the custodian of records to appear in court at least in civil cases. *See* discussion of *Crawford v. Washington*, 541 U.S. 36, 124, S.Ct. 1354, 158 L.Ed.2d 177 (2004). *See also* Pa.R.E. 902 (self-authentication of public documents).

The policy behind this hearsay exception is to avoid the inconvenience to and disruption of public affairs that would result if public officials were required to appear in court to authenticate records prepared in the normal course of official duties. *See Commonwealth v. Long*, 395 Pa. Super. 495, 577 A.2d 899 (1990). For a document to be admissible, it is necessary that the evidence show that it was prepared pursuant to an official duty. *Commonwealth v. Slider*, 229 Pa. Super. 93, 323 A.2d 376 (1974). However, the official duty need not arise from an express statute or regulation but may arise from the oral or casual directions of a superior or from functions necessarily inherent in the office. *Commonwealth v. Sabb*, 269 Pa. Super. 206, 409 A.2d 437 (1979); *see Githens, Rexsamer & Co. v. Wildstein*, 428 Pa. 201, 236 A.2d 792 (1968) (fire investigation report by Philadelphia Department of Licenses and Inspections was hearsay which did not qualify under official records exception since fire investigation was not part of that department's duties and responsibilities).

Where records are otherwise properly certified,

use of official's facsimile signature is acceptable. *Commonwealth Dep't of Transp. v. Faust*, 28 Pa. D. & C.3d 218 (C.P. Berks County, 1984). Pa.R.E. 1005 and the Uniform Photographic Copies of Business and Public Records as Evidence Act, 42 Pa.C.S.A. § 6109, permit the use at trial of photographic copies of official records.

Pa.R.E. 901(b)(7) indicates that public records and reports may be authenticated in the same manner as other writings. Additionally, public records and reports may be self-authenticating as provided in Pa.R.E. 902.

The following cases are instructive: *Paey Associates v. Penn. Liquor Control Bd.*, 78 A.3d 1187 (Pa.Cmwlth. 2013) (in license revocation proceeding, because police did not attest to the official copies of the proffered incident reports, and did not certify they had custody of the original reports, the reports were inadmissible under Sections 6103 and 6104 of the Judicial Code and trial court erred by admitting them); *Commonwealth v. Schoff*, 911 A.2d 147 (Pa. Super. 2006) (records from the Department of Social Services concerning child-abuse investigation admissible under business records exception to hearsay rule); *Commonwealth v. Brody*, 25 Pa. D. & C.3d 338 (C.P. Mercer County, 1982) (highway map used by State Police to time speed from airplane rejected for lack of certification); *Commonwealth v. Corradino*, 403 Pa. Super. 251, 588 A.2d 936 (1991) (National Crime Information Center records were not official records of government unit but did qualify as business records of State Police); *Commonwealth v. Visconto*, 301 Pa. Super. 543, 448 A.2d 41 (1982) (properly certified records of the Bureau of Unemployment Compensation); *Commonwealth v. Sabb*, 269 Pa. Super. 206, 409 A.2d 437 (1979) (police height/weight measurements of suspect were properly authenticated); *Commonwealth v. Hartman*, 15 Pa. D. & C.3d 627 (C.P. Berks County, 1980) (illustrating lack of official record under § 6103(b) by letters under seal stating defendant accused of illegal possession of weapon did not have city-issued gun permit); *accord Commonwealth v. Kaufman*, 307 Pa. Super. 63, 452 A.2d 1039 (1982) (certifying no record found that defendant had license to possess or distribute controlled substance); *Haas v. Kasnot*, 371 Pa. 580, 92 A.2d 171 (1952) (records of U.S. Weather Bureau are admissible as official records).

75 Pa. C.S.A. § 6328 provides for the admissibility of electronically transmitted PennDOT records in court proceedings when offered by an authorized user. The statute defines authorized users as, among others, state and local police and district attorneys. *Commonwealth v. Carr*, 887 A.2d 782 (Pa. Super. 2005).

Crawford v. Washington—Criminal Cases

The impact of *Crawford v. Washington*, 541 U.S. 36, 124, S.Ct. 1354, 158 L.Ed.2d 177 (2004) on the law of hearsay in criminal cases is discussed at page 134. In *Crawford*, the Supreme Court said in dicta that business records, which are analogous to public records, are "by their nature . . . not testimonial" and not subject to the requirements of the *Confrontation Clause*, 541 U.S. at 51, 56, 124 S.Ct. 1354; *see also* 541 U.S. at 76, 124 S.Ct. 1354 (Rehnquist, C. J., concurring in judgment) (noting that "the Court's analysis of 'testimony' excludes at least some hearsay exceptions, such as business records and official records"). *See U.S. v. De La Cruz*, 514 F.3d 121 (1st Cir. 2008) (autopsy reports are nontestimonial under *Crawford*); *U.S. v. Valdez-Maltos*, 443 F.3d 910 (5th Cir. 2006) (warrants of deportation do not constitute testimonial hearsay under *Crawford*).

One commentator has cautioned that "[s]ome business records may concern matters that are understood at the time they were made to be destined for litigation or may be clearly accusatory."

Mosteller, *Crawford v. Washington*: Encouraging and Ensuring the Confrontation of Witnesses, 39 U.Rich.L.Rev. 511, 548 (2005). In *Melendez-Diaz v. Massachusetts*, 552 U.S. 1256 (2008), the trial court had admitted into evidence state laboratory affidavits with forensic analysis results showing material seized from defendant was cocaine. The Court reiterated that documents kept in the ordinary course of business usually may be admitted at trial despite their hearsay status but said that is not the case if the regularly conducted business activity is the production of evidence for use at trial. 129 S.Ct. at 2538. The United States Supreme Court said that the laboratory reports fell within the core class of testimonial statements since they had been created for the sole purpose of providing evidence against a defendant. Acknowledging that the Confrontation Clause may make prosecution of criminals more burdensome, the Court held that crime laboratory reports may not be used against defendants at trial unless the analysts responsible for creating them give testimony and subject themselves to cross-examination.

Pennsylvania Rule of Criminal Procedure 574 now provides a mechanism for the admission of a forensic laboratory report supported by a certification. This Rule provides a defendant an opportunity to exercise the right of confrontation and to object to the report on hearsay grounds. Following pre-trial notice by the prosecution, and in the absence of a demand by defendant for declarant's live testimony, the Rule permits the admission of a properly certified forensic laboratory report and the accompanying certification at trial. *See* Pa. R. Crim. P. 574.

Compare: Fed. R. Evid. 803(8), 901(b)(7), 902, 1005.

Research References

Packel & Poulin, Pennsylvania Evidence

§ 803(8)-1 (4th ed. 2013)

McCormick, Evidence Chapter 30 (7th ed. 2013)

HEARSAY EXCEPTION: OFFICIAL RECORDS OF OTHER STATES AND FOREIGN COUNTRIES

See: 42 Pa.C.S.A. § 5328; see also Pa.R.E. 803(6), 901(b)(7) and 902.

Objection

- Objection. The records have not been properly authenticated pursuant to 42 Pa.C.S.A. § 5328. Therefore, the contents are inadmissible hearsay since they are being offered to prove the truth of the matters asserted in them.

Response

[There is no response if the requirements of Section 5328 have not been established since the statute is strictly construed]

Pennsylvania Law

When a party seeks to use the official records of another state or foreign country at trial, *strict compliance* with the provisions of 42 Pa.C.S.A. § 5328 is required to provide the necessary authentication.

Patterned after the Uniform Interstate and International Procedure Act, 42 Pa. C.S.A. § 5328 relevantly provides:

(a) **Domestic record.**—An official record kept with the United States, or any state, district, commonwealth, territory, insular possession thereof, or the Panama Canal Zone, the Trust Territory of the Pacific Islands, or an entry therein, when admissible for any purpose, may be evidenced by an official publication thereof or by a copy attested by the officer having the legal custody of the record, or by his deputy, and accompanied by a certificate that the officer has the custody. The certificate may be made by a judge of a court of record having jurisdiction in the government unit in which the record is kept, authenticated by the seal of the court, or by any public officer having seal of office and having official duties in the governmental unit in which the record is kept, authenticated by the seal of his office.

(b) **Foreign record**.—A foreign official record, or an entry therein, when admissible for any purpose, may be evidenced by an official publication or copy thereof, attested by a person authorized to make the attestation, and accompanied by a final certification as to the genuineness of the signature and official position:

(1) of the attesting person; or

(2) of any foreign official whose certificate of genuineness of signature and official position either:

(i) relates to the attestation; or

(ii) is in a chain of certificates of genuineness of signature and official position relating to the attestation.

A final certification may be made by a secretary of embassy or legation, consul general, consul, vice consul, or consular agent of the United States, or a diplomatic or consular official of the foreign country assigned or accredited to the United States. If reasonable opportunity has been given to all parties to investigate the authenticity and accuracy of the documents, the tribunal may, for good cause shown, admit an attested copy without final certification or permit the foreign official record to be evidenced by an attested summary with or without a final certification.

The effect of these provisions is to provide a means for satisfying the authentication requirement now contained in Pa.R.E. 901, and, in effect, to dispense with the need for the custodian of the records to appear in court. Pa.R.E. 902(1)–(4) permits various kinds of domestic and foreign public documents to be self-authenticating. *See In re*

Estate of Rosen, 819 A.2d 585 (Pa. Super. 2003) (documents and records presented by foreign citizens claiming to be relatives of intestate decedent were admissible; evidence complied with procedural statutes concerning acts of foreign notaries and proof of official foreign records and genealogist testified to the procedure she followed in obtaining documents).

Where the proper certification required by the Pennsylvania Rules of Evidence or by statute is absent, such records will be deemed inadmissible hearsay. *See Shapiro v. State Board of Accountancy*, 856 A.2d 864 (Pa.Cmwlth. 2004) (official records of accountants' disciplinary proceedings by the SEC were inadmissible hearsay in proceedings before state board; SEC records were not certified as required nor did a records custodian appear to testify to authenticity).

42 Pa.C.S.A. §§ 6103 and 6109 regarding official Pennsylvania records do not apply to the records of other states and foreign countries. *Rhoads v. Commonwealth*, 620 A.2d 659 (Pa.Cmwlth. 1993). The mere fact that documents from another state have been forwarded here and kept with Pennsylvania records does not validate the out-of-state documents independently of the requirements of Pa.R.E. 901(b)(7), 902 or Section 5328. *See Naglich v. Commonwealth, State Bd. of Motor Vehicle Mfrs., Dealers and Salesmen*, 86 Pa.Cmwlth. 478, 485 A.2d 851 (1984).

Crawford v. Washington—Criminal Cases

The impact of *Crawford v. Washington*, 541 U.S. 36, 124, S.Ct. 1354, 158 L.Ed.2d 177 (2004) on the law of hearsay in criminal cases is discussed at page 134. In *Crawford*, the Supreme Court said in dicta that business records, which are analogous to public records, are "by their nature . . . not testimonial" and not subject to the requirements of the Confrontation Clause, 541 U.S. at 51, 56, 124

S.Ct. 1354; *see also* 541 U.S. at 76, 124 S.Ct. 1354 (Rehnquist, C. J., concurring in judgment) (noting that "the Court's analysis of 'testimony' excludes at least some hearsay exceptions, such as business records and official records"). *See U.S. v. De La Cruz*, 514 F.3d 121 (1st Cir. 2008) (autopsy reports are nontestimonial under *Crawford*); *U.S. v. Valdez-Maltos*, 443 F.3d 910 (5th Cir. 2006) (warrants of deportation do not constitute testimonial hearsay under *Crawford*).

One commentator has cautioned that "[s]ome business records may concern matters that are understood at the time they were made to be destined for litigation or may be clearly accusatory." Mosteller, *Crawford v. Washington*: Encouraging and Ensuring the Confrontation of Witnesses, 39 U.Rich.L.Rev. 511, 548 (2005). In *Melendez-Diaz v. Massachusetts*, 129 S.Ct. 2527, 174 L. Ed. 2d 314 (2009), the trial court had admitted into evidence state laboratory affidavits with forensic analysis results showing material seized from defendant was cocaine. The Court reiterated that documents kept in the ordinary course of business usually may be admitted at trial despite their hearsay status but said that is not the case if the regularly conducted business activity is the production of evidence for use at trial. 129 S.Ct. at 2538. The United States Supreme Court said that the laboratory reports fell within the core class of testimonial statements since they had been created for the sole purpose of providing evidence against a defendant. Acknowledging that the Confrontation Clause may make prosecution of criminals more burdensome, the Court held that crime laboratory reports may not be used against defendants at trial unless the analysts responsible for creating them give testimony and subject themselves to cross-examination.

Compare: Fed. R. Evid. 803(8), 901(b)(7) and 902.

Research References

Packel & Poulin, Pennsylvania Evidence § 803(8)-1 (4th ed. 2013)

McCormick, Evidence Chapter 30 (7th ed. 2013)

HEARSAY EXCEPTION: PERSONAL OR FAMILY HISTORY

See: Pa.R.E. 803(11), (12), (13), (19); Pa.R.E. 804(b)(4).

Objection

- *[To a question]* Objection. The question calls for hearsay.

- *[To a document]* Objection. The document is inadmissible hearsay.

- *[To an answer]* Objection, hearsay. I move the answer be stricken and the jury be instructed not to consider it for any purpose.

Response

The evidence is admissible:

- *[as a record of a religious society / municipality pursuant to Rule 803(11) or (12)]*

- *[as a family record or artifact under Rule 803(13)]*

- *[as a statement of reputation among family members or associates within the community concerning personal or family history under Rule 803(19)]*

- *[under Rule 804(b)(4), as a statement by a family member or intimate associate concerning a fact of family history. As a foundation, I have established that declarant is unavailable [specify] as well as his / her status as [a family member] [one who was intimately associated with the family]].*

Pennsylvania Law

One of the oldest exceptions to the hearsay rule is the "pedigree" exception which encompasses statements concerning family history, such as the date and place of birth and death of members of the family and facts about marriage, descent and relationship. Such facts are considered inherently trustworthy in light of "the 'natural effusions' . . . of those who talk over family affairs when no special reason for bias or passion exists." *Commonwealth v. Collins*, 957 A.2d 237, 270 (Pa. 2008), citing 5 Wigmore On Evidence at § 1482.

Facts concerning family history may be proven in three different ways:

1. By documents and artifacts including records of religious organizations, marriage and baptismal certificates, notations in family Bibles, genealogies, charts, engravings on rings, urns, crypts, tombstones and inscriptions on family portraits. Pa.R.E. 803(11), (12), (13); *see In re Garrett's Estate*, 371 Pa. 284, 89 A.2d 531 (1952); *Clark v. Pennsylvania State Police*, 760 A.2d 1202 (Pa.Cmwlth.2000) (baptismal certificates are admissible to prove the fact and date of baptism but not individual's birth date).

2. By evidence of reputation (i) among members of a person's family, (ii) among associates, or (iii) in the community. Pa.R.E. 803(19).

3. Where the declarant is unavailable as a witness, by declarant's statements about either his own history or about the history of another person. When the statements concern the history of another person, trustworthiness must first be established by proof that declarant was related to or intimately associated with the other person or family and that the statements were made before the controversy arose (i.e., *ante litem motam*). Pa.R.E. 804(b)(4).

When proof consists of a public record, such as a civil marriage or birth certificate, a properly authenticated document is sufficient evidence. The rules of evidence are augmented by statute in that 42 Pa.C.S.A. § 6110 also makes the records of religious societies within the Commonwealth admissible evidence of any marriage, birth or burial.

Whereas the exceptions contained in Pa.R.E. 803(11), (12) and (13) are directed to documents and artifacts, Pa.R.E. 803(19) permits the use of reputation evidence to prove personal or family history. This includes testimony by a witness about his or her own history or the history of another person. *In Re Estate of Rosen*, 819 A.2d 585 (Pa. Super. 2003).

A witness who gives reputational testimony pursuant to Pa.R.E. 803(19) concerning another person's history must first demonstrate that he knows of the person and is truly familiar with the family, associates or community in which the reputation has been formed and that the basis of the reputation is likely to be reliable. Pa.R.E. 804(b)(4) does not require that the witness who testifies in court be related to or an intimate associate of the person whose pedigree is under consideration, only that the declarant whose statements are given in evidence was so related. *In re McClain's Estate*, 481 Pa. 435, 392 A.2d 1371 (1978). Pa.R.E. 804(b)(4)(A) clearly states that the declarant need not have personal knowledge when speaking of his or her own pedigree. Pa.R.E. 804(b)(4)(B) is silent on whether the declarant must have personal knowledge of the personal or family history of another person.[1] A person's reputed nickname is not a "fact of personal or family history" that is similar to one's birth, adoption, marriage, divorce, death, legitimacy, or relationship. *Commonwealth v. Collins*, 957 A.2d at 270.

The rationale for requiring that the declarant

---

[1] In his treatise on the federal rules, Professor Graham writes:

With respect to . . . statements concerning another person, the requirement of personal knowledge is satisfied if the unavailable declarant is shown to be a member of the family and thus in a position to be familiar with the matter, or so intimately associated with the other family member as to be likely to have accurate information upon the matter addressed. Rule 804(b)(4)(B). Moreover, as provided in Rule 602, evidence of personal knowledge may consist of the statement of the declarant himself.

Graham, Handbook of Federal Evidence § 804.4 (8th ed. 2016).

244

be related to or an intimate associate of the family about which he/she spoke is that statements by unrelated persons do not have the same likelihood of accuracy as statements by family members or intimate associates of the family.

See Crawford v. Washington, 541 U.S. 36, 124 S.Ct. 1354, 158 L.Ed.2d 177 (2004) (discussed at page 134, *supra*), a criminal case involving a Confrontation Clause challenge, where the United States Supreme Court held that if a hearsay statement was "testimonial" in nature, it could not be introduced at trial, in the absence of the declarant, unless the defendant had a previous opportunity to cross-examine the declarant. *See also United States v. Gonzalez-Marichal*, 317 F.Supp.2d 1200 (S.D. Calif. 2004) (in prosecution for transporting illegal aliens, unavailable material witness's statements concerning her citizenship, personal and family history excluded by *Crawford*).

Compare: Fed. R. Evid. 803(11), (12), (13), (19); Fed. R. Evid. 804(b)(4).

Research References

Packel & Poulin, Pennsylvania Evidence §§ 803(11)-1, 803(12)-1, 803(13)-1, 803(19)-1, 804(b)(4)-1 (4th ed. 2013)

Binder, Hearsay Handbook Chapters 19, 20, 21, 27, 37 (4th ed. 2001)

McCormick, Evidence § 322 (7th ed. 2013)

HEARSAY EXCEPTION: PRESENT SENSE IMPRESSION

See: Pa.R.E. 803(1).

Objection

- [*To a question*] Objection. The question calls for hearsay.
- [*To an answer*] Objection, hearsay. I move that the answer be stricken and the jury be instructed not to consider it for any purpose.

Response

- The statement is admissible under Rule 803(1) as a present sense impression. I have established that the statement concerns [*an event*] [*a condition*] which the declarant was witnessing at the time she made the statement to this witness.

Pennsylvania Law

A statement of present sense impression describes or explains an event or condition while the declarant was perceiving the event or condition, or immediately thereafter. *Bell Beverage v. Unemployment Compensation*, 49 A.3d 49 (Pa. Cmwlth. 2012); Pa.R.E. 803(1). To qualify under the present sense impression exception to the hearsay rule, an out-of-court statement must be nearly contemporaneous with the incident described and made with little chance for reflection. *Bugosh v. Allen Refractories Co.*, 932 A.2d 901 (Pa. Super. 2007); *Harris v. Toys "R" Us-Penn Inc.*, 880 A.2d 1270 (Pa. Super. 2005); *Commonwealth v. Gray*, 867 A.2d 560 (Pa. Super. 2005). The declarant must also have personal knowledge of what he or she describes. *Commonwealth v. Chamberlain*, 557 Pa. 34, 731 A.2d 593 (1999) (murder victim's telephone statement to witness that ex-husband had just shot her and her boyfriend admissible as present sense impression); *Commonwealth v. Peterkin*, 511 Pa.

299, 513 A.2d 373 (1986) (statements that defendant was locking door and getting into car admissible because they were contemporaneous verbalizations of victim's present observation of then occurring events); *Commonwealth v. Cunningham*, 805 A.2d 566 (Pa. Super. 2002) (911 transcript of cell phone calls from roofers who were witnessing robbery admissible as present sense impression).

Under this exception, a startling event or accident is not required. *Commonwealth v. Harper*, 419 Pa. Super. 1, 614 A.2d 1180 (1992) (admitting declarant's statement to policeman that a sock which she observed on victim's bed belonged to her own boyfriend).

The underlying rationale of the present sense impression exception is that substantial contemporaneity of event and statement minimizes unreliability due to defective recollection or conscious fabrication. *Commonwealth v. Stephens*, 74 A.3d 1034 (Pa. Super. 2013) (statements denying sexual assault made in recorded phone call not admissible; statements not made while contemporaneously perceiving event and there was ample opportunity to fabricate); *Commonwealth v. Levanduski*, 907 A.2d 3 (Pa. Super. 2006) (victim's letter suggesting wife and her lover might kill him did not qualify under this exception; because time of writing was unknown, there may have been opportunity to misstate facts and the writing did not occur at or immediately after perceiving facts recounted); Comment to Pa.R.E. 803(1). There is no *per se* rule indicating what time interval is too long under Pa.R.E. 803(1).

A common use of this exception has been to permit a witness to testify about assertions that a declarant made immediately after participating in a telephone conversation concerning what was said on the phone. *See, e.g., Chamberlain*, 557 Pa. 34, 731 A.2d 593 (1999); *Peterkin*, 511 Pa. 299, 513 A.2d 373 (1986); *Commonwealth v. Coleman*, 458

Pa. 112, 326 A.2d 387 (1974); *Cunningham*, 805 A.2d 566 (Pa. Super. 2002); *Commonwealth v. Harris*, 442 Pa. Super. 6, 658 A.2d 392 (1995).

Unidentified Declarant

Nothing in the language of Pa.R.E. 803(1) requires that the declarant be identified. An unidentified declarant, however, can present two possible problems: (1) the declarant did not exist and the statement was invented by the witness, or (2) the declarant did not have personal knowledge of the event. *See Commonwealth v. Hood*, 872 A.2d 175 (Pa. Super. 2005) (Rule 803(1) restricts exception to statements made while declarant is perceiving event; corroborative proof that declarant actually viewed event is required).

The possibility that the declarant never existed is not a hearsay problem but rather an issue of credibility to be decided by the fact finder. But where the declarant did not have personal knowledge of the event, any statement purporting to describe the event is inadmissible.

See Crawford v. Washington, 541 U.S. 36 (2004) (discussed at page 134, *supra*), a criminal case involving a confrontation Clause challenge, where the United States Supreme Court held that if a hearsay statement was "testimonial" in nature, it could not be introduced at trial, in the absence of the declarant, unless the defendant had a previous opportunity to cross-examine the declarant. But Justice Scalia did say that "[a]n accuser who makes a formal statement to government officers bears testimony in a sense that a person who makes a casual remark to an acquaintance does not." *Crawford v. Washington*, 541 U.S. 36, 51 (2004).

Compare: Fed. R. Evid. 803(1)

Research References

Packel & Poulin, Pennsylvania Evidence

§ 803(1)-1 (4th ed. 2013)

Binder, Hearsay Handbook Chapter 8 (4th ed. 2001)

McCormick, Evidence § 271 (7th ed. 2013)

HEARSAY EXCEPTION: PRIOR INCONSISTENT STATEMENTS

See: Pa.R.E. 803.1(1).

Objection

- *[To a question]* Objection. The question calls for a hearsay answer.
- *[To a document]* Objection. The document is inadmissible hearsay.
- *[To an answer]* Objection, hearsay. I move the answer be stricken and the jury be instructed not to consider it for any purpose.

Response

The statement is admissible as substantive evidence under Pa.R.E. 803.1(1). It is a prior inconsistent statement by the witness and was *[given under oath subject to the penalty of perjury at a formal proceeding]* or *[is a writing signed and adopted by the witness]* or *[is a verbatim contemporaneous recording of an oral statement]*.

Pennsylvania Law

Prior to codification of the Rules of Evidence, Pennsylvania had abandoned the traditional view that a witness' prior inconsistent statements are not admissible as substantive evidence. *Commonwealth v. Brady*, 510 Pa. 123, 507 A.2d 66 (1986) (recorded statement of witness to murder, inconsistent with her trial testimony, was hearsay exception properly admitted as substantive evidence).

Under certain circumstances defined in Pa.R.E. 803.1(1), a prior inconsistent statement of a declarant, who testifies at trial or other proceeding and is available for cross-examination, may be used as substantive evidence to prove the truth of the matters asserted. *Commonwealth v. Pitner*, 928 A.2d

1104 (Pa. Super. 2007).

As the *Brady* court stated:

> The availability of cross-examination at trial . . . assures a meaningful opportunity for the trier of fact to observe the declarant who has been called upon and sworn as a witness and questioned as to the discrepancy between the prior statement and the direct testimony. The trier of fact may bring to bear his or her sensory observations, experience, common sense and logic upon the witness to assess credibility and to determine the truth and accuracy of both the out-of-court declarations and the in-court testimony.

Commonwealth v. Brady, 510 Pa. 123, 129, 507 A.2d 66, 69 (1986).

To qualify for use as substantive evidence under Pa.R.E. 803.1(1), the prior inconsistent statement must have been: (1) given under oath at a formal legal proceeding; or (2) reduced to a writing signed and adopted by the witness; or (3) recorded verbatim contemporaneously with the making of the statement. *Commonwealth v. Collins*, 957 A.2d 237 (Pa. 2008); *Commonwealth v. Lively*, 530 Pa. 464, 610 A.2d 7 (1992); *Commonwealth v. Bibbs*, 970 A.2d 440 (Pa. Super. 2009) (collecting cases and discussing development of the rule); *Commonwealth v. Henkel*, 938 A.2d 433 (Pa. Super. 2007). In *Commonwealth v. Halsted*, 542 Pa. 318, 329–330, 666 A.2d 655, 661 (1995), the Pennsylvania Supreme Court said that "a verbatim contemporaneous recording of an oral statement" qualifies for exception to the hearsay rule only if it is an audiotape or videotape recording. It cannot be a police officer's handwritten notes.

As a foundation, the witness must first be confronted with his inconsistent statement in order to provide the jury with the opportunity to observe the witness' demeanor and hear his testimony and explanation regarding the discrepancy. *Commonwealth v. Romero*, 555 Pa. 4, 722 A.2d 1014 (1999); *Commonwealth v. Burgos*, 530 Pa. 473, 610

A.2d 11 (1992). Where the witness denies making the inconsistent statement or otherwise equivocates, the inconsistent statement may then be introduced through other witnesses. *Commonwealth v. Peay*, 806 A.2d 22 (2002) (after witness recanted, detective allowed to testify to contents of prior statement to police).

There is no requirement that a witness, at the time of trial, again adopt his or her prior statement as being truthful in order for the statement to be admissible under *Commonwealth v. Lively*, 530 Pa. 464, 610 A.2d 7 (1992). *Commonwealth v. Presbury*, 445 Pa. Super. 362, 665 A.2d 825 (1995). As long as the witness previously had adopted the statement, later recantation or modification does not affect admissibility but goes only to weight.

Once the witness' statement is admitted as substantive evidence, it is up to the factfinder to accept or reject the prior statement contradicting the subsequent testimony. *Plair v. Commonwealth, Pennsylvania Bd. of Prob. and Parole*, 104 Pa.Cmwlth. 297, 521 A.2d 989 (1987).

In *Crawford v. Washington*, 541 U.S. 36, 124 S.Ct. 1354, 158 L.Ed.2d 177 (2004) (discussed at page 134, *supra*), a criminal case involving a Confrontation Clause challenge, the United States Supreme Court held that if a hearsay statement was "testimonial" in nature, it could not be introduced at trial in the absence of the declarant, unless the defendant had a previous opportunity to cross-examine the declarant. However, the Court also said that "when the declarant appears for cross-examination at trial, the Confrontation Clause places no constraint at all on the use of his prior testimonial statements." *Crawford v. Washington*, 541 U.S. 36, 59 n.9, 124 S.Ct. 1354, 158 L.Ed.2d 177 (2004). *See United States v. Hadley*, 431 F.3d 484 (6th Cir. 2005) (use of wife's prior inconsistent statement posed no Confrontation Clause concerns in light of defendant's decision to call wife as witness).

Illustrative cases include: *Commonwealth v. Brown*, 52 A.3d 1139 (Pa. 2012) (convictions resting only on prior inconsistent statements do not deprive defendant of due process as long as these statements taken as a whole established every element of the offense charged beyond a reasonable doubt); *Commonwealth v. Romero*, 555 Pa. 4, 722 A.2d 1014 (1999) (prior statement not admissible where witness refused to testify about defendant's involvement in crime or to answer questions about portion of prior statement that related to defendant; witness was not subject to cross-examination as required by *Brady*); *O'Donnell v. Westinghouse Elec. Corp.*, 515 Pa. 307, 528 A.2d 576 (1987) (prior inconsistent deposition testimony may be used as substantive evidence in civil trial); *Mickel v. Pennsylvania Bd. of Prob. and Parole*, 810 A.2d 728 (Pa.Cmwlth.2002) (despite fact that witness recanted and said she had lied, written, notarized statement given to parole officer admissible as substantive evidence); *Commonwealth v. Buford*, 101 A.3d 1182 (Pa. Super. 2014) (the Commonwealth may not be deprived of its ability to present inculpatory evidence at trial merely because defendant, despite having the opportunity to do so, did not cross-examine the witness at the preliminary hearing stage as extensively as he might have done at trial); *Petrina v. Allied Glove Corp.*, 46 A.3d 795 (Pa. Super. 2012) (a corporation's answers to interrogatories are a writing signed and adopted and encompassed by Rule 803.1(1) governing admissibility of prior inconsistent statements); *Commonwealth v. Stays*, 70 A.3d 1256 (Pa. Super. 2013) (not imperative that defendant actually cross-examine witness so long as he had adequate opportunity to do so with full knowledge of inconsistent statements); *Rissi v. Cappella*, 918 A.2d 131 (Pa. Super. 2007) (statement not admissible because it was never signed or adopted by witness and he denied any knowledge of it); *Commonwealth v. Carmody*, 799 A.2d 143 (Pa. Super. 2002) (victim's written statement given to police did not qualify as excited utterance but was admissible as prior inconsistent statement when victim recanted); *Commonwealth v. Baez*, 759 A.2d 936 (Pa. Super. 2000) (court properly admitted written statement signed and adopted by witness who, at trial, denied making statements); *Commonwealth v. Carter*, 443 Pa. Super. 231, 661 A.2d 390 (1995) (where declarant is not present in court and available for cross-examination, his prior inconsistent statement does not qualify as admissible substantive evidence under *Brady* rule); *Commonwealth v. Jones*, 434 Pa. Super. 469, 644 A.2d 177 (1994) (prior inconsistent statement given twelve days after events under reliable circumstances admissible as substantive evidence); *Durkin v. Equine Clinics, Inc.*, 376 Pa. Super. 557, 546 A.2d 665 (1988) (upholding exclusion of prior inconsistent statement since it was riddled with double hearsay and, therefore, not "otherwise admissible" under *Brady*).

An out-of-court statement made by a witness, inconsistent with the witness's testimony at trial but which does not meet the requirements of Pa.R.E. 803.1(1), may be offered simply to impeach the witness's credibility. *Commonwealth v. Henkel*, 938 A.2d 433 (Pa. Super. 2007); *Croyle v. Smith*, 918 A.2d 142 (Pa. Super. 2007) (insurance investigator's summary of a witness's statement could not be used for impeachment unless witness adopted summary as his/her own); *McManamon v. Washko*, 906 A.2d 1259 (Pa. Super. 2006) (a party may impeach the incredibility of an adverse witness by introducing evidence that the witness has made one or more statements inconsistent with his trial testimony). In such event, it is not hearsay, since it is not offered to prove its truth. It is, instead, circumstantial evidence from which the trier of fact may infer that the witness lied, or is mistaken, confused, or generally unreliable. Its admissibility is governed by principles of relevance, not hearsay.

See Pa.R.E. 613 and *Commonwealth v. Charleston*, 16 A.3d 505 (Pa. Super. 2011) (where turncoat witness denied making certain statements about defendant's stated intentions, murder victim's mother permitted to testify statements were made to her for the purpose of impeaching turncoat witness).

Mere dissimilarities or omissions in prior statements do not suffice as impeaching evidence. The dissimilarities or omissions must be substantial enough to cast doubt on a witness's testimony to be admissible as prior inconsistent statements. *Commonwealth v. Luster*, 71 A.3d 1029 (Pa. Super. 2013).

A summary of a witness's statement cannot be used for impeachment purposes absent adoption of the statement by the witness as his own. The rationale for this rule is that it would be unfair to allow a witness to be impeached on a police officer's interpretation of what was said rather than the witness's verbatim words. *McManamon*, 906 A.2d at 1268.

Compare: Fed. R. Evid. 801(d)(1)(A).

Research References

Packel & Poulin, Pennsylvania Evidence § 803. 1(1)-1 (4th ed. 2013)

McCormick, Evidence § 251 (7th ed. 2013)

HEARSAY EXCEPTION: PUBLIC RECORDS AND REPORTS
See: Pa. R.E. 803(8), 803(10)

Objection:

- *[To a question]* Objection. The question calls for hearsay.

- *[To an answer]* Objection, hearsay. I move that the evidence be stricken and the jury be instructed not to consider if to any purpose.

Response

- The evidence is admissible under the public records exception to the hearsay rule. As foundation, I have established that the record sets forth [*the activities of a public office or agency*], [*matters observed in the course of official duties*], and my opponent has no evidence to indicate a lack of trustworthiness.

Commentary

Under the new public records exception, effective January 1, 2017, records, reports, statements or data compilations, in any form, of public offices or agencies which set forth:

(A)   the activities of the office or agency;

(B)   matters observed in the course of official duties;

(C)   may be admitted unless the sources of information or other circumstances indicate lack of trustworthiness. Rule 803(8).

The justification for the exception is the assumption that a public official will perform his duty properly and the unlikelihood that he will remember details independently of the record. Admitting records under the 803(8) exception is a practical necessity that must be afforded to government officers who, in the course of their duties, have made thousands of similar written hearsay statements concerning events within their jurisdiction.

The Rule is also intended to avoid the inconvenience to and disruption of public affairs that would result if public officials were required to appear in court to authenticate records prepared in the normal course of official duties. *See Commonwealth v. Long*, 395 Pa. Super. 495, 577 A.2d 899 (1990). For a document to be admissible, it is necessary that the evidence show that it was prepared pursuant to an official duty. *Commonwealth v. Slider, 229 Pa. Super., 93*, 323 A.2d 376 (1974). However, the official duty need not arise from an express statute or regulation but may arise from the oral or casual directions of a superior or from functions necessarily inherent in the office. *Commonwealth v. Sabb*, 269 Pa. Super. 206, 409 A.2d 437 (1979); *See Githens, Rexsamer & Co. v. Wildstein*, 428 Pa. 201, 236 A.2d 792 (1968) (fire investigation report by Philadelphia Department of Licenses and Inspections was hearsay which did not qualify under official records exception since fire investigation was not part of that department's duties and responsibilities).

In *D'Alessandro v. Pennsylvania State Police*, 937 A.2d 404 (Pa. 2007), the Supreme Court held that there is a presumption of trustworthiness of public records or reports, thus placing the burden of proof on the opposing party to establish lack of trustworthiness, as is the case for records of regularly conducted activity.

In *Crawford v. Washington*, 541 U.S. 36 (2004) (discussed at page 134, *supra*), a criminal case involving a Confrontation Clause challenge, the United States Supreme Court held that if a hearsay statement was "testimonial" in nature, it could not be introduced at trial, in the absence of the declarant, unless the defendant had a previous opportunity to cross-examine the declarant. However, the Court also described business records as "by their nature . . . not testimonial." *Crawford v. Washington*, 541 U.S. 36, 56 (2004). But one commentator has cautioned that "[s]ome business records may concern matters that are understood at the time they were made to be destined for litigation or may be clearly accusatory." Mosteller, *Crawford v. Washington*: Encouraging and Ensuring the Confrontation of Witnesses, 39 U.Rich.L. Rev. 511, 548 (2005). In *Melendez-Diaz v. Massachusetts*, 129 S.Ct. 2527, 174 L. Ed. 2d 314 (2009), the trial court had admitted into evidence state laboratory affidavits with forensic analysis results showing material seized from defendant was cocaine. The Court reiterated that documents kept in the ordinary course of business usually may be admitted at trial despite their hearsay status but said that is not the case if the regularly conducted business activity is the production of evidence for use at trial. 129 S.Ct. at 2538. The United States Supreme Court said that the laboratory reports fell within the core class of testimonial statements since they had been created for the sole purpose of providing evidence against a defendant. Acknowledging that the Confrontation Clause may make prosecution of criminals more burdensome, the Court held that crime laboratory reports may not be used against defendants at trial unless the analysts responsible for creating them give testimony and subject themselves to cross-examination.

Pennsylvania Rule of Criminal Procedure 574 now provides a mechanism for the admission of a forensic laboratory report supported by a certification. The Rule also provides a defendant an opportunity to exercise the right of confrontation and to object to the report on hearsay grounds. Following pre-trial notice by the prosecution, and in the absence of a demand by defendant for declarant's live testimony, Rule 574 permits the admission of a properly certified forensic laboratory report and the accompanying certification at trial.

For authentication of public records, see Rule 901(b)(7), 902(1)-(4), (11-13), and 42 Pa. C.S. § 5328 (domestic records outside the Commonwealth and foreign records), § 6103 (authentication of official records). Rule 803(10) and 42 Pa. C.S.A. §§ 5328(d),

6103(b) and 6104(b) all provide that absence of a record is admissible. Absence of a record is circumstantial evidence of the nonexistence of a fact that would have been recorded in the normal course of governmental activity.

Compare: Fed. R.E. 803(8), 803(10)

Research References

Packel & Poulin, Pennsylvania Evidence §§ 803(8)-1, 803(10)-1 (4th ed. 2013)

McCormick, Evidence Chapter 30 (7th ed. 2013)

HEARSAY EXCEPTION: RECORDED RECOLLECTION

See: Pa.R.E. 803.1(3).

Objection

- Objection. The document is hearsay and a proper foundation cannot be established. It has not been shown that this witness, after reviewing the document, lacks sufficient memory. Moreover, there has been no proof that the witness made the record at a time when the matter was still fresh in her memory and that it accurately reflects her knowledge.

Response

- I have established that the contents of this writing are admissible under Rule 803.1 (3). As foundation, I have demonstrated:
  - (1) the record pertains to a matter about which the witness once had personal knowledge;
  - (2) the witness now has an insufficient recollection about the matter to testify fully and accurately;
  - (3) the record was made [or adopted] by the witness when the matter was fresh in the witness's memory; and
  - (4) the witness has vouched for the accuracy of the written record.

Pennsylvania Law

If a witness cannot testify from unaided or refreshed memory, Pa.R.E. 803.1(3) allows a memorandum or record of an event to be read into evidence where: (1) the witness once had personal knowledge about the matters in the document; (2) the witness now has insufficient recollection to testify fully and accurately; (3) the record was made or adopted by the witness at a time when the matter was fresh in his memory and reflected his knowledge; and (4) the witness has vouched for the accuracy of the written record. Pa.R.E. 803.1(3); *Commonwealth v. Young*, 561 Pa. 34, 748 A.2d 166 (1999) (*Young 1*); *Commonwealth v. Cargo*, 498 Pa. 5, 444 A.2d 639 (1982); *Commonwealth v. Shaw*, 494 Pa. 364, 431 A.2d 897 (1981); *Commonwealth v. Cooley*, 484 Pa. 14, 398 A.2d 637 (1979); *Miller v. Borough of Exeter*, 366 Pa. 336, 77 A.2d 395 (1951); *Croyle v. Smith*, 918 A.2d 142 (Pa. Super. 2007) (exception only applies where witness lacks a present recollection of the event).

Before a document may be admitted as a recording of a witness's recollection of a past event, the witness himself must have had an opportunity to review the document. If, after reviewing the document, the witness testifies that while his memory has not been refreshed, the record is accurate; then the document may be admitted into evidence. *Commonwealth v. Kendig*, 215 Pa. Super. 139, 257 A.2d 354 (1969). The contents of the memorandum may not be disclosed to the jury until after the witness has reviewed it, indicated whether his recollection is refreshed and vouched for the document's accuracy. *Commonwealth v. Kendig*, 215 Pa. Super. 139, 257 A.2d 354 (1969).

A showing that the witness lacks all recollection of the event or condition described is not required; it is enough that the witness lacks sufficient recollection to testify fully and completely. *Nationwide Mut. Ins. Co. v. Hassinger*, 473 A.2d 171 (Pa. Super. 1984) (preliminary hearing testimony admissible after witness repeatedly testified he was "not positive" or "not sure" and agreed he had no present recollection of event).

It is not necessary that the statement be prepared or written by the witness if he reviewed and adopted the document while the event was fresh in his memory. *Commonwealth v. Cooley*, 484 Pa. 14, 398 A.2d 637 (1979).

Pa.R.E. 803.1(3) does not have specific constraints on the timing of the preparation and adoption of the memorandum or record. Whether the document was prepared sufficiently close to the time of the event may depend upon a variety of factors, including: the nature of the event; the nature of the relationship between the witness and the recorder; and, whether the witness inspected the statement of the recorder. *Compare*, *Nationwide Mut. Ins. Co. v. Hassinger*, 473 A.2d 171 (Pa. Super. 1984) (six days after event deemed admissible), *and Commonwealth v. Young*, 561 Pa. 34, 748 A.2d 166 (1999) (statement given two years after murder but described events likely to be remembered) *with Heller v. Commonwealth, Unempl. Comp. Bd. of Review*, 58 Pa.Cmwlth. 194, 427 A.2d 737 (1981) (three months later too remote).

Compare: Fed. R. Evid. 803(5). Under the federal rule, the statement may be read into evidence but may not be received as an exhibit unless offered by an adverse party. In Pennsylvania, the document may be read to the jury and either party may offer the statement as an exhibit. Pa.R.E. 803.1(3) grants the trial judge discretion to show the statement to the jury in exceptional circumstances, even when not offered by an adverse party.

Crawford v. Washington—Criminal Cases

In *Crawford v. Washington*, 541 U.S. 36, 124 S.Ct. 1354, 158 L.Ed.2d 177 (2004) (discussed at page 134, *supra*), a criminal case involving a Confrontation Clause challenge, the United States Supreme Court held that if a hearsay statement was "testimonial" in nature, it could not be introduced at trial in the absence of the declarant, unless the defendant had a previous opportunity to cross-examine the declarant.

In *Commonwealth v. Borovichka*, 18 A.3d 1242 (Pa. Super. 2011), *Crawford* was discussed in dicta. There a State Police analyst authenticated his report on blood alcohol level and the laboratory procedures involved, but could not recall specifically testing defendant's blood. The appeals court upheld reading the report into evidence. The court said the *Crawford* / *Melendez-Diaz* holdings were not implicated because during trial, defendant was able to cross-examine the analyst as well as the hospital phlebotomist who drew his blood. 18 A.3d at 1253 n.7.

For whatever additional guidance may be provided, counsel can also consult a few decisions in other states. In *State v. Gorman*, 854 A.2d 1164 (Me. 2004), where defendant's mother claimed no memory of her grand jury testimony about her son's murder confession, the Supreme Judicial Court held there was no Confrontation Clause violation admitting such testimony as recorded recollection. The Maine court cited to *Crawford* (when declarant appears for cross-examination at trial, Confrontation Clause places no constraints at all on use of his prior testimonial statements); *United States v. Owens*, 484 U.S. 554, 108 S.Ct. 838, 98 L.Ed.2d 951 (1988) (even when a witness has no present memory of a prior out-of-court statement, the right of confrontation is satisfied if the accused has the opportunity to cross-examine the witness at trial), and *California v. Green*, 399 U.S. 149, 90 S.Ct. 1930, 26 L.Ed.2d 489 (19770) (upholding admission of witness' preliminary hearing testimony since truth-seeking purpose of Confrontation Clause is satisfied if declarant is present and testifying at trial). *See Clark v. State*, 808 N.E.2d 1183 (Ind. 2004) and *Government of the Virgin Islands v. George*, 2004 WL 3546285. *But see* Ruebner & Scahill, *Crawford v. Washington*, the Confrontation Clause, and Hearsay: A New Paradigm for Illinois Evidence Law, 36 Loy. U. Chi. L.J. 703, 778 (2005):

> The presence of the declarant at trial as a witness will likely not cure Confrontation Clause problems. One essential condition for the admissibility under this exception is that the witness has no present rec-

ollection of the event recorded. This foundational requirement negates a constitutional condition for the admissibility of an out-of-court statement and will deny the accused a sufficient opportunity to cross-examine the witness concerning the out-of-court statement in violation of the Confrontation Clause and *Crawford*.

Research References

Packel & Poulin, Pennsylvania Evidence § 803. 1(3)-1 (4th ed. 2013)

Binder, Hearsay Handbook Chapter 15 (4th ed. 2001)

McCormick, Evidence §§ 279–283 (7th ed. 2013)

HEARSAY EXCEPTION: STATEMENT AGAINST INTEREST

See: Pa.R.E. 804(b)(3).

Objection

- [*To a question*] Objection. The question calls for hearsay. The evidence cannot qualify as a statement against interest since it has not been shown that:
  - [*the statement was against the declarant's pecuniary / penal interest*]
  - [*the declarant had any personal knowledge of these facts and is unavailable to testify*]
  - [*the declarant was exposed to any criminal liability*]
  - [*the statement has any guarantees of trustworthiness (specify)*]
  - [*the statement is testimonial under* Crawford v. Washington *and there was no prior opportunity for cross-examination*]
- [*To an answer*] Objection, hearsay. I move the answer be stricken and the jury be instructed not to consider it for any purpose.

Response

- The evidence is admissible as a statement against [*pecuniary*] [*proprietary*] interest. As foundation, I have established that declarant: (i) knew the statement was contrary to his interest; (ii) had personal knowledge of the facts; and (iii) is unavailable to testify.
- The evidence qualifies as a statement against penal interest: the declarant is unavailable to testify at trial; the statement was against declarant's penal interest; and corroborating circumstances bolster the statement's trustworthiness [*specify*].

Pennsylvania Law

An oral or written statement of fact which a

person knew to be against his own pecuniary, proprietary or penal interest when made is excepted from the hearsay rule, provided that the declarant had personal knowledge of the fact and is now unavailable to testify as a witness. *Commonwealth v. Brown*, 52 A.3d 1139 (Pa. 2012); Pa.R.E. 804(b)(3).

Statements against interest by an unavailable declarant are admissible as a hearsay exception because their trustworthiness is safeguarded by the improbability that a declarant would fabricate a statement that is contrary to his own interest. *See Williamson v. United States*, 512 U.S. 594, 599, 114 S.Ct. 2431, 2434–2435, 129 L.Ed.2d 476 (1994) (exception is "founded on the commonsense notion that reasonable people, even reasonable people who are not especially honest, tend not to make self-inculpatory statements unless they believe them to be true"); *Commonwealth v. Colon*, 461 Pa. 577, 337 A.2d 554 (1975).

The proponent of the evidence bears the burden of showing that the declarant is unavailable. *Commonwealth v. Spotz*, 18 A.3d 244 (Pa. Super. 2011). Unavailability based on Fifth Amendment privilege satisfies the rule. Pa.R.E. 804(a)(1); *Commonwealth v. Statum*, 769 A.2d 476 (Pa. Super. 2001).

An assertion against interest, though excepted from the hearsay rule, may be excluded if it appears that declarant lacked personal knowledge of the facts related.

Pecuniary or Proprietary Interest

In a civil context, the exception is illustrated in such cases as *Rudisill v. Cordes*, 333 Pa. 544, 5 A.2d 217 (1939) (decedent's declaration that a fatal accident was not defendant's fault) and *Taylor v. Gould*, 57 Pa. 152 (1868) (receipts showing contested payments had, in fact, been made). *See Movie Distribs. Liquidating Trust v. Reliance Ins. Co.*,

407 Pa. Super. 588, 595 A.2d 1302 (1991) (statements tending to subject declarant to criminal liability admissible in civil cases). The Pennsylvania Supreme Court has expressly declined to extend the exception to include statements against social interest, i.e., facts which would make one the object of hatred, ridicule, or disgrace in the community. *Heddings v. Steele*, 514 Pa. 569, 526 A.2d 349 (1987) (excluding statements regarding an incestuous relationship).

Crawford v. Washington

In *Crawford v. Washington*, 541 U.S. 36 (2004) (discussed at page 134, *supra*), the United States Supreme Court held that in criminal cases, the Confrontation Clause forbids the admission of "testimonial" statements of a witness who did not appear at trial unless that witness was unavailable to testify and the defendant had had a prior opportunity for cross-examination. As the Third Circuit explained, "The lynchpin of the *Crawford* decision . . . is its distinction between testimonial and nontestimonial hearsay; simply put, the rule announced in *Crawford* applies only to the former category of statements." *United States v. Hendricks*, 395 F.3d 173, 179 (3d Cir. 2005).

The admissibility of nontestimonial hearsay for purposes of the Confrontation Clause continues to be governed by the standards set forth in *Ohio v. Roberts*, 448 U.S. 56 (1980). There the Court held that hearsay statements could be admitted at trial only when: (1) "the evidence falls within a firmly rooted hearsay exception," or (2) they contained "particularized guarantees of trustworthiness" such that adversarial testing of the statements would add little to the statements' reliability. *Ohio v. Roberts*, 448 U.S. 56, 66 (1980).

Thus, the fundamental question in criminal cases with respect to the admissibility of hearsay evidence is what confrontation analysis applies—

Crawford or *Ohio v. Roberts*? For post-*Crawford* federal decisions involving statements against interest, *see, e.g.*, *United States v. Scheurer*, 62 M.J. 100 (2005) (statements by defendant's wife to co-worker implicating both her husband and herself in drug offenses did not violate the Confrontation Clause); *United States v. Franklin*, 415 F.3d 537 (6th Cir. 2005) (declarant's statements against penal interest to friend and confidant were not testimonial within meaning of *Crawford* rule); *United States v. Saget*, 377 F.3d 223 (2d Cir. 2004) (co-conspirator's statements to confidential informer were sufficiently self-inculpatory to be admissible in defendant's prosecution for firearms trafficking); *United States v. Manfre*, 368 F.3d 832 (8th Cir. 2004) (deceased co-conspirator's statements to girlfriend about arson admissible; comments were made to loved ones or acquaintances and were not the kind of memorialized, judicial-process-created evidence of which *Crawford* speaks; *United States v. Savoca*, 335 F.Supp.2d 385 (S.D.N.Y. 2004) (inculpatory statements made to girlfriend admissible).

Penal Interest

A defendant offering hearsay evidence under Pa.R.E. 804(b)(3) to exculpate himself must show: (1) an unavailable declarant; (2) from the perspective of the average, reasonable person, the statement must have been truly adverse to the declarant's penal interest, considering when it was made; and (3) sufficient corroboration to indicate the trustworthiness of the statement. *Commonwealth v. Williams*, 537 Pa. 1, 640 A.2d 1251 (1994); *Commonwealth v. Statum*, 769 A.2d 476 (Pa. Super. 2001).

This exception does not apply where the out-of-court statement does not expose the declarant to any increased criminal liability. *Commonwealth v. Collins*, 957 A.2d 237 (Pa. 2008). This is because of the "inherent unreliability of a confession exculpating possible accomplices at no cost to the declarant." *Commonwealth v. Colon*, 846 A.2d 747 (Pa. Super. 2004) (declarant's statement to police that he acted alone in killing was properly excluded since statement admitted no additional crime and subjected declarant to no additional punishment); *accord*, *Commonwealth v. Ayala*, 277 Pa. Super. 363, 419 A.2d 1187 (1980); *Commonwealth v. Cristina*, 481 Pa. 44, 391 A.2d 1307 (1978) (accomplice's exculpatory letter did not qualify as admission against penal interest where its trustworthiness could not be demonstrated).

A statement tending to expose the unavailable declarant to criminal liability which is offered to exculpate the accused is not admissible unless corroborating circumstances clearly indicate the trustworthiness of the statement. Pa.R.E. 804(b)(3); *Commonwealth v. Yarris*, 557 Pa. 12, 731 A.2d 581 (1999) (corroboration lacking where witness admitted her memory was not good, said she could not tell if people were high or drunk, could not recall declarant's words in confessing to murder for which defendant had been convicted and provided no explanation of how and why declaration came to be made); *Commonwealth v. Statum*, 769 A.2d 476 (Pa. Super. 2001) (error to exclude statement made under circumstances lending credibility; without any personal benefit and aware of possibility of prosecution, declarant admitted her role in drug transaction in front of attorney, his staff members and her own mother). The purpose of the corroboration requirement is to protect against the possibility that a statement would be fabricated to exculpate the accused. *See United States v. Brainard*, 690 F.2d 1117, 1124 (4th Cir.1982) (rule requires not a determination that declarant is credible but a finding that the circumstances clearly indicate that statement was not fabricated; it is the statement rather than the declarant which must be trustworthy).

Statements That Inculpate The Accused

Although Pa.R.E. 804(b)(3) also applies to statements offered to inculpate an accused, Pennsylvania courts have thus far excluded such statements. *Commonwealth v. Robins*, 571 Pa. 248, 812 A.2d 514 (2002); *Commonwealth v. Young*, 561 Pa. 34, 748 A.2d 166 (1999) (Young II); *Commonwealth v. Colon*, 846 A.2d 747 (Pa. Super. 2004); *Commonwealth v. Robinson*, 298 Pa. Super. 447, 444 A.2d 1260 (1982).

In *Lilly v. Virginia*, 527 U.S. 116, 135 (1999), a four-Justice plurality indicated that accomplices' confessions that inculpate a criminal defendant are not within a firmly rooted exception to the hearsay rule as that concept has been defined in Confrontation Clause jurisprudence. Rather, such statements are "presumptively unreliable." *Lilly v. Virginia*, 527 U.S. 116, 131 (1999). Thus, in cases where *Crawford* does not apply, courts will scrutinize such statements to determine whether they bear sufficient particularized guarantees of trustworthiness to overcome this presumption of unreliability. *United States v. Scheurer*, 62 M.J. 100 (2005). Such guarantees must be shown by the circumstances of the statements themselves and cannot be proven by other evidence produced at trial. *Lilly*, 527 U.S. at 137–138; *Idaho v. Wright*, 497 U.S. 805, 820 (1990) (guarantees of trustworthiness must "be drawn from the totality of circumstances that surround the making of the statement and that render the declarant particularly worthy of belief"); *United States v. Castelan*, 219 F.3d 690 (7th Cir. 2000) (guarantees must be inherent in the circumstances of the testimony itself; the fact that other evidence corroborates the testimony in question does not suffice); *Commonwealth v. Robins*, 571 Pa. 248, 812 A.2d 514 (2002) (rejecting as untrustworthy statements of non-testifying alleged accomplice made to cellmate and during sting operation tying defendant to burglary; statements made one year after crime and in settings where declarant may have been trying to enhance his image before other criminals); *Commonwealth v. Young*, 561 Pa. 34, 748 A.2d 166 (1999) (*Young II*) (using *Lilly* analysis to find reversible error in admitting co-defendants' statements implicating defendant while limiting their own involvement). A very strong presumption of unreliability attaches to non-self-inculpatory statements of co-conspirators made while in police custody. *Lilly*, 527 U.S. at 137, 119 S.Ct. at 1900.

Corroboration of the trustworthiness of the inculpatory or exculpatory out-of-court statement should focus on the circumstances of the making of the statement and the motivation of the declarant. *Commonwealth v. Cascardo*, 981 A.2d 245 (Pa. Super. 2009). The use of hindsight or "bootstrapping" based upon independent evidence is proscribed. *Commonwealth v. Robins*, 571 Pa. 248, 812 A.2d 514, 525–526 (2002) ("Although the United States Supreme Court has declined to endorse any specific enumeration of factors to be considered, courts have evaluated: the circumstances under which the statements were uttered, including the custodial/non-custodial aspect of the setting and the identity of the listener; the contents of the statement, including whether the statements minimize the responsibility of the declarant or spread or shift the blame; other possible motivations of the declarant, including improper motive such as to lie, curry favor, or distort the truth; the nature and degree of the 'against interest' aspect of the statements, including the extent to which the declarant apprehends that the making of the statement is likely to actually subject him to criminal liability; the circumstances or events that prompted the statements, including whether they were made with the encouragement or at the request of a listener; the timing of the statement in relation to events described; the declarant's relationship to the defendant; and any other factors bearing upon the reliability of the statement at issue"). The confession of a defendant's relative or close friend's confession should be closely scrutinized for motive to fabricate the confession. *Commonwealth v. Padillas*, 997 A.2d 356 (Pa. Super. 2010) (collecting cases).

The Pa.R.E. 804(b)(3) corroborating circumstances requirement is applicable to civil cases.

Compare: Fed. R. Evid. 804(b)(3).

References

Packel & Poulin, Pennsylvania Evidence § 804(b)(3)-1 (4th ed. 2013)

Binder, Hearsay Handbook Chapter 36 (4th ed. 2001)

McCormick, Evidence Chapter 33 (7th ed. 2013)

HEARSAY EXCEPTION: STATEMENTS FOR PURPOSES OF MEDICAL DIAGNOSIS OR TREATMENT

See: Pa.R.E. 803(4).

Objection

- [*To a question*] Objection. The question calls for hearsay.
- [*To an answer*] Objection, hearsay. I move that the answer be stricken and the jury be instructed not to consider it for any purpose.

Response

- The statement is admissible as a hearsay exception under Pa.R.E. 803(4) because I have established it was made to this witness for the purpose of medical diagnosis and treatment.

Pennsylvania Law

Pa.R.E. 803(4) excepts from the hearsay rule "[a] statement made for purposes of medical treatment, or medical diagnosis in contemplation of treatment, and describing medical history, or past or present symptoms, pain, or sensations, or the inception or general character of the cause or external source thereof, insofar as reasonably pertinent to treatment, or diagnosis in contemplation of treatment." *Turner v. Valley Housing Development Corp.*, 972 A.2d 531 (Pa. Super. 2009).

A statement comes within this exception when two requirements are met: (1) the declarant must make the statement for the purpose of receiving medical treatment; and (2) the statement must be of the type reasonably pertinent to a physician for purposes of diagnosis or treatment. *Commonwealth v. Belknap*, 105 A.3d 7 (Pa. Super. 2014); *Commonwealth v. Smith*, 545 Pa. 487, 681 A.2d 1288 (1996); *Commonwealth v. Fink*, 791 A.2d 1235 (Pa. Super. 2002); *Estate of Swift v. Northeastern*

Hosp., 456 Pa. Super. 330, 690 A.2d 719 (1997).

The rationale for the exception is that a person seeking medical assistance has a strong, self-interested motivation to give the doctor truthful information. *See* Pa.R.E. 803(4) (Official Comment 1998); *see also White v. Illinois*, 502 U.S. 346, 356, 112 S.Ct. 736, 743, 116 L.Ed.2d 848 (1992) ("a statement made in the course of procuring medical services, where the declarant knows that a false statement may cause misdiagnosis or mistreatment, carries special guarantees of credibility").

The assertion need not be made by the patient. It may be made by someone on the patient's behalf, such as a parent concerning its child, or a policeman concerning an unconscious victim of an accident or crime. *See, e.g., United States v. Yazzie*, 59 F.3d 807 (9th Cir.1995) (plain language of Rule does not limit its application to patient-declarants; in most instances, statements to doctor by parent of injured child could easily qualify as statement for purpose of obtaining proper medical diagnosis); *Commonwealth v. Belknap*, supra (statements made by unconscious defendant's unidentified friends that he may have overdosed on heroin); *King v. Stefenelli*, 862 A.2d 666 (Pa. Super. 2004) (statements by prior treating physician).

The assertion need not be made to a doctor. For example, it may be made to a nurse, ambulance attendant or hospital-admitting clerk. *Commonwealth v. Smith*, 545 Pa. 487, 681 A.2d 1288 (1996) (statements to nurse); *Commonwealth v. Belknap*, supra (statements made to police officer); *Commonwealth v. Williams*, 103 A.3d 354 (Pa. Super. 2014) (paramedic). It is the purpose of the assertion, i.e., to aid in medical treatment or diagnosis leading to treatment, and not the identity of its immediate recipient, that qualifies the statement for exception to the hearsay rule. *Commonwealth v. Blackwell*, 343 Pa. Super. 201, 494 A.2d 426 (1985).

A declarant's statement to a physician that assigns fault or identifies the person responsible for the declarant's injuries is generally inadmissible under Pa.R.E. 803(4) because fault and identity are usually unnecessary either for accurate diagnosis or effective treatment. *Commonwealth v. Smith*, 545 Pa. 487, 681 A.2d 1288 (1996) (prosecution for aggravated assault; reversible error to permit nurse to testify that child said defendant placed her in scalding water); *Commonwealth v. Vining*, 744 A.2d 310 (Pa. Super. 1999). *But see Commonwealth v. Sanford*, 397 Pa. Super. 581, 580 A.2d 784 (1990) (suggesting in context of describing her condition, child's statements to doctor identifying her assailant might be relevant given the possibility of sexually transmitted disease).

The principal difference between the state and federal rules is that in Pennsylvania, statements are admissible only if made for purposes of treatment. Pa.R.E. 803(4) (Official Comment 1998); *Commonwealth v. Fink*, 791 A.2d 1235 (Pa. Super. 2002). Under the federal rule, an examining physician may testify to statements made for the purpose of medical diagnosis to the same extent as the treating physician, even though the only purpose of the examination was to enable the doctor to testify. *United States v. Iron Shell*, 633 F.2d 77 (8th Cir. 1980). However, federal criminal cases are now controlled by *Crawford v. Washington*, 541 U.S. 36, 124 S.Ct. 1354 (2004) discussed at page 134, *supra*) a criminal case involving a Confrontation Clause challenge where the United States Supreme Court held that if a hearsay statement was "testimonial" in nature, it could not be introduced at trial, in the absence of the declarant, unless the defendant had a previous opportunity to cross-examine the declarant. Thus, statements to examining physicians (often used in child sex abuse cases) may now be problematic. *See* Mosteller, *Crawford v. Washington*: Encouraging and Ensuring the Confrontation of Witnesses, 39 U.Rich. L.Rev. 511

(2005).

Compare: Fed. R. Evid. 803(4).

Research References

Packel & Poulin, Pennsylvania Evidence § 803(4)-1 (4th ed. 2013)

Binder, Hearsay Handbook Chapter 13 (4th ed. 2001)

McCormick, Evidence Chapter 27 (7th ed. 2013)

HEARSAY EXCEPTION: STATEMENTS IN DOCUMENTS AFFECTING AN INTEREST IN PROPERTY

See: Pa.R.E. 803(15).

Objection

- I object to the introduction of this document and any testimony about its contents. It is inadmissible hearsay.

Response

- The evidence is admissible under Rule 803(15) which creates an exception for statements in a document affecting an interest in property. As a foundation, I have established (*specify*).

Pennsylvania Law

Pa.R.E. 803(15) creates an exception to the rule against hearsay for:

> A statement contained in a document, other than a will, purporting to establish or affect an interest in property if the matter stated was relevant to the purpose of the document, unless dealings with the property since the document was made have been inconsistent with the truth of the statement of the purport of the document.

The requirements for admissibility under Pa.R.E. 803(15) are that the document has been authenticated and is trustworthy, that it affects an interest in property, and that the dealings with the property since the document was made have been consistent with the truth of the statement.

Pa.R.E. 803(15) is not applicable to wills. In *Estate of Kostick*, 514 Pa. 591, 526 A.2d 746 (1987), the Pennsylvania Supreme Court held that testator's statement in his will that his wife had deserted him was not admissible to prove that she had deserted him. *See* Comment to Pa.R.E. 803(15).

Compare: Fed. R. Evid. 803(15).

Research References

Packel & Poulin, Pennsylvania Evidence § 803(15)-1 (4th ed. 2013)

Binder, Hearsay Handbook Chapter 23 (4th ed. 2001)

McCormick, Evidence § 323 (7th ed. 2013)

HEARSAY EXCEPTION: THEN EXISTING MENTAL, EMOTIONAL CONDITION (STATE OF MIND)

See: Pa.R.E. 803(3).

Objection

- *[To a question]* Objection. The question calls for hearsay.
- *[To an answer]* Objection, hearsay. I move that the answer be stricken and the jury be instructed not to consider it for any purpose.

Response

- The statement comes within Rule 803(3), the state of mind exception to the hearsay rule. As foundation, I have established that the declarant made the statement to this witness contemporaneously with the event in question and that the statement referred to declarant's *[then existing state of mind]* *[intent]* *[motive]* *[emotion]*.

Pennsylvania Law

Pa.R.E. 803(3) creates a hearsay exception for a statement of the declarant's "then existing state of mind, emotion, sensation or physical condition (such as intent, plan, motive, design, mental feeling, pain and bodily health)."[1] The rationale for admissibility is: (1) the necessity which is said to arise from the fact that subjective state of mind, intent, motive or feeling is often impossible to prove in the absence of such statements; and (2) reliability created by the spontaneous nature of such statements. *Schmalz v. Manufacturers & Traders Trust*, 67 A.3d 800 (Pa. Super. 2013); *Commonwealth v. Hess*, 378 Pa. Super. 221, 548 A.2d 582 (1988).

The exception does not include a statement of

---

[1]*See* Hearsay Exception: Then Existing Physical Condition.

memory or belief to prove the fact remembered or believed unless it relates to the execution, revocation, identification or terms of the declarant's will. *Commonwealth v. Levanduski*, 907 A.2d 3 (Pa. Super. 2006); Pa.R.E. 803(3).

For a statement to be admissible, it must have been contemporaneous with the state of mind sought to be proved and the declarant must not have had an opportunity to reflect and possibly fabricate or misrepresent his thoughts. McCormick, Evidence § 274 (7th ed. 2013).

The exception applies only to a statement describing a state of mind expressed by the declarant. Such statements, however, cannot be used to prove the cause of that state of mind. *See e.g.*, *United States v. Emmert*, 829 F.2d 805, 810 (9th Cir.1987) ("If the reservation in the text of the rule is to have any effect, it must be understood to narrowly limit those admissible statements to declarations of condition—'I'm scared'—and not belief—'I'm scared because [someone] threatened me.' ") (quoting *United States v. Cohen*, 631 F.2d 1223, 1225 (5th Cir.1980)).

In *Crawford v. Washington*, 541 U.S. 36, 124 S.Ct. 1354, 158 L.Ed.2d 177 (2004) (discussed at page 134, *supra*), a criminal case involving a Confrontation Clause challenge, the United States Supreme Court held that if a hearsay statement was "testimonial" in nature, it could not be introduced at trial in the absence of the declarant, unless the defendant had a previous opportunity to cross-examine the declarant. But Justice Scalia did say that "[a]n accuser who makes a formal statement to government officers bears testimony in a sense that a person who makes a casual remark to an acquaintance does not." *Crawford v. Washington*, 541 U.S. 36, 51, 124 S.Ct. 1354, 158 L.Ed.2d 177 (2004).

Statements of Memory and Belief Excluded

Statements of memory and belief are expressly

excluded from the ambit of the exception. Almost any statement used to describe events that a speaker has experienced in the past can be characterized as a "memory," which is a presently-existing state of mind when it is conveyed. If such statements were admissible under Pa.R.E. 803(3) to prove the facts remembered, parties could offer hearsay to establish almost any past fact, a result that would mark the virtual destruction of the hearsay rule.

The exclusion of statements of memory or belief grew out of Justice Cardozo's opinion in *Shepard v. United States*, 290 U.S. 96, 54 S.Ct. 22, 78 L.Ed. 196 (1933), where the Supreme Court refused to admit, under the state of mind exception, a statement by defendant's wife that "Dr. Shepard has poisoned me." The court said that, "[t]he testimony now questioned faced backward and not forward . . . What is even more important, it spoke to a past act, and even more than that, to an act by someone not the speaker." 290 U.S. at 104, 54 S.Ct. at 25.

Credibility

Since credibility is a matter for the jury, the fact that a statement is self-serving is not a basis for exclusion. Federal cases are instructive. *United States v. Cardascia*, 951 F.2d 474 (2d Cir.1991) (self-serving nature of statement is considered when the jury weighs evidence at conclusion of trial); *United States v. DiMaria*, 727 F.2d 265 (2d Cir.1984) (although prosecution argued defendant's statement was classic false exculpatory statement, if it fell within Rule 803(3), its truth or falsity was for jury to determine); *United States v. Dellinger*, 472 F.2d 340 (7th Cir.1972) (exclusion of declarations of party on grounds they are self-serving, even though otherwise free from objection under the hearsay rule and exceptions, detracts from relevant information which should be available to jury).

Relevance

The declarant's state of mind must be relevant to the case. *Commonwealth v. Begley*, 566 Pa. 239, 780 A.2d 605 (2001) (victim's statement that she was going to get a job from defendant provided circumstantial proof she met with him, affording opportunity to kidnap and murder her); *Commonwealth v. Parker*, 104 A.3d 17 (Pa. Super. 2014) (murder victim's assertions to his grandmother relevant to show defendant had a motive to kill victim); *Commonwealth v. Luster*, 71 A.3d 1029 (Pa. Super. 2013) (victim's statements showed defendant's malice towards her which debunked various defenses). Accord *Commonwealth v. Kunkle*, 79 A.3d 1173 (Pa. Super. 2013).

Contemporaneous Statements as to State of Mind or Emotion

Evidence of a declarant's out-of-court assertion of his or her then existing state of mind or emotional feeling was recognized as a hearsay exception in the following illustrative cases: *Commonwealth v. Killen*, 545 Pa. 127, 680 A.2d 851 (1996) (sexual banter was proper state of mind evidence inconsistent with having just been sexually assaulted); *Commonwealth v. Ilgenfritz*, 466 Pa. 345, 353 A.2d 387 (1976) (error to exclude victim's statement that she intended to see doctor because she fell, injuring her head; rebutted Commonwealth's evidence that if decedent had suffered blows other than from defendant, she would have sought medical assistance); *Commonwealth v. Parker*, 104 A.3d 17 (Pa. Super. 2014) (statements of then existing state of mind by homicide victim are admissible when they are relevant to show proof of malice or motive).

For cases where the exception was held not to apply, see: *Commonwealth v. Johnson*, 107 A.3d 52 (Pa. 2014); *Commonwealth v. Moore*, 937 A.2d 1062

(Pa. 2007); *Commonwealth v. Laich*, 566 Pa. 19, 777 A.2d 1057 (2001) (error to admit victim's statement that if defendant ever caught her with another man, he would kill them both; defense was crimes were committed in heat of passion and victim's state of mind regarding her relationship with defendant was irrelevant); *Commonwealth v. Thornton*, 494 Pa. 260, 431 A.2d 248 (1981) (similar); *Commonwealth v. Hess*, 378 Pa. Super. 221, 548 A.2d 582 (1988) (excluding defendant's statement to witness that police beat confession out of him; statement made three weeks after alleged beating).

Conduct of Declarant and Others

As Justice Saylor noted, concurring and dissenting in *Commonwealth v. Stallworth*, 566 Pa. 349, 781 A.2d 110, 126–130 (2001), a series of Pennsylvania cases blur the distinction between Rule 803(3), state of mind hearsay exception (statements offered for their truth) and what have been termed non-hearsay statements offered to show the declarant's state of mind, and not for the truth of the matter asserted. *See* extensive discussion in *Commonwealth v. Moore*, supra (victim's statements to family and friends re bullying by defendant not admissible; victim's state of mind was not relevant and real purpose of using this evidence was to establish prior events).

A deceased victim's out of court statements evincing an intent to meet the defendant shortly before the killing are admissible pursuant to the state of mind exception because such an intent provides circumstantial proof that the victim acted in accordance with his or her stated intent, and thereby provided the defendant with an opportunity to commit the crime in question. *Commonwealth v. Begley*, 566 Pa. 239, 780 A.2d 605 (2001); *Commonwealth v. Collins*, 550 Pa. 46, 703 A.2d 418 (1997); *Commonwealth v. Lowenberg*, 481 Pa. 244,

392 A.2d 1274 (1978); *Commonwealth v. Cascardo*, 981 A.2d 245 (Pa. Super. 2009).

The Pennsylvania Supreme Court has also admitted a victim's out-of court statement, if the statement was relevant in establishing the victim's state of mind regarding his or her relationship with the defendant, under the state of mind exception to the hearsay rule to establish the presence of ill-will, malice or motive for the killing. *Commonwealth v. Fletcher*, 561 Pa. 266, 750 A.2d 261 (2000); *Commonwealth v. Puksar*, 559 Pa. 358, 740 A.2d 219 (1999); *Commonwealth v. Chandler*, 554 Pa. 401, 721 A.2d 1040 (1998); *Commonwealth v. Collins*, 550 Pa. 46, 703 A.2d 418 (1997).

Pennsylvania courts have admitted into evidence, as non-hearsay, out-of court statements made by the victim to show the victim's state of mind regarding the relationship between him or her and the defendant and the malice and/or ill-will the victim perceived, and inferentially the defendant's intent or motive. The Court has stated that the statements are not offered to prove the truth of the matter asserted, but rather are offered solely to show the victim's state of mind. *Commonwealth v. Stallworth*, 566 Pa. 349, 781 A.2d 110 (2001); *see also In re Adoption of R.K.Y.*, 72 A.3d 669 (Pa. Super. 2013); *Commonwealth v. Randall*, 758 A.2d 669 (Pa. Super. 2000).

In his dissenting opinion in *Commonwealth v. Stallworth*, Justice Saylor criticized the Pennsylvania Supreme Court's use of a victim's out-of-court statements to establish the presence of ill-will, malice or motive for a killing. First, Justice Saylor argued that a victim's statements regarding his or her perceived relationship with the defendant are probative of the defendant's intent and motive only if it is assumed that the statements are true, i.e., that the defendant did in fact threaten the victim with harm in the past. Thus, the statement cannot be both relevant and non-hearsay. If the victim's statements are in any way relevant, they have to be offered for their truth. Second, Justice Saylor argued that if the victim's state of mind is not directly at issue in the case, but rather the victim's out-of court statements are offered to prove the defendant's state of mind, then the statements do not fall within the state of mind exception. The victim's out-of court statements are not probative of the defendant's intent and motive.

The Pennsylvania Supreme Court has decided cases consistent with Justice Saylor's critique and held that statements by a victim evincing the victim's state of mind regarding his or her relationship with the defendant were inadmissible and could not be used to prove the defendant's ill-will, malice or motive. *See Commonwealth v. Moore*, 937 A.2d 1062 (Pa. 2007); *Commonwealth v. Laich*, 566 Pa. 19, 777 A.2d 1057 (2001); and *Commonwealth v. Thornton*, 494 Pa. 260, 431 A.2d 248 (1981).

Justice Saylor is undoubtedly correct in arguing that a victim's statements regarding his or her perceived relationship with the defendant are probative of the defendant's intent and motive only if it is assumed that the statements are true. Thus, the rationale used by the court in *Commonwealth v. Stallworth* for admitting into evidence the victim's out-of court statements is unpersuasive. However, it is not clear whether Justice Saylor's argument that a victim's out-of court statements regarding his or her relationship with the defendant should not be admitted under the state of mind exception as circumstantial evidence to establish the presence of ill-will, malice or motive on the part of the defendant will establish a bright line and mark the end of such holdings. The statements are admitted not to directly establish the state of mind of the defendant, but to establish the state of mind of the victim thereby inferentially providing the motive or intent of the defendant. This application of the exception applies reasoning similar to the situation in which the victim's out-of court statements are admitted to evince an intent to meet the defendant thereby inferentially providing the defendant with an opportunity to commit the crime.

Statements may be inadmissible if they were made at a time so remote from the incident to which they purportedly pertain that their probative value is *de minimis*. *Commonwealth v. England*, 474 Pa. 1, 375 A.2d 1292 (1977); *Commonwealth v. Hess*, 378 Pa. Super. 221, 548 A.2d 582 (1988).

Compare: Fed. R.Evid. 803(3).

Research References

Packel & Poulin, Pennsylvania Evidence § 803(3)-1 (4th ed. 2013)

Binder, Hearsay Handbook Chapter 11 (4th ed. 2001)

McCormick, Evidence §§ 273–276 (7th ed. 2013)

HEARSAY EXCEPTION: THEN EXISTING PHYSICAL CONDITION

See: Pa.R.E. 803(3).

Objection

- [*To a question*] Objection. The question calls for a hearsay answer.
- [*To an answer*] Objection, hearsay. I move the answer be stricken and the jury be instructed not to consider it for any purpose.

Response

- The statement is admissible as an exception to the hearsay rule under Pa.R.E. 803(3) since it was a declaration as to then existing physical condition. I have established as foundation that the declarant made the statement to this witness contemporaneously with the event in question and that at that time, the statement referred to the declarant's then existing physical condition.

Pennsylvania Law

A declaration as to then existing physical condition is one of the hearsay exceptions that was formerly considered under the "*res gestae*" label but now is codified at Pa.R.E. 803(3). *See Commonwealth v. Pronkoskie*, 477 Pa. 132, 383 A.2d 858 (1978). As with the other "res gestae" exceptions, such statements (typically expressing pain or bodily harm) are considered trustworthy because of their spontaneous nature.

While the exception was firmly recognized prior to codification, case law is sparse. In *Commonwealth v. Blackwell*, 343 Pa. Super. 201, 494 A.2d 426 (1985), the court treated statements to a hospital nurse by a kidnap victim who subsequently suffered a fatal heart attack as statements of then existing physical condition. However, the court did not seem to draw any distinction between this hearsay exception and the separate exception for declarations made to a physician for the purpose of receiving medical diagnosis or treatment now codified at Pa.R.E. 803(4). In *Hreha v. Benscoter*, 381 Pa. Super. 556, 554 A.2d 525 (1989), the court recognized the exception but found the statement in issue (patient could not find nurse to empty his bedpan) did not qualify since it did not relate to a then existing physical condition.

This exception does not include statements of past physical conditions.

As with the analogous federal rule, Fed. R. Evid. 803(3), there is no requirement that statements of present physical condition be made to a physician. They can be made to members of the family, friends or other persons.

Pa.R.E. 803(4) differs from Pa.R.E. 803(3) in that Rule 803(4) is applicable to statements "describing medical history, or past or present symptoms, pain or sensations, or the inception or the general character of the cause or external source thereof." Rule 803(3) is limited to statements of "then existing" physical condition.

Criminal Cases—*Crawford v. Washington*

In *Crawford v. Washington*, 541 U.S. 36, 124 S.Ct. 1354, 158 L.Ed.2d 177 (2004) (discussed at page 134, *supra*), the Court held that in criminal cases, the Confrontation Clause forbids the admission of "testimonial" statements of a witness who did not appear at trial unless that witness was unavailable to testify and the defendant had had a prior opportunity for cross-examination. But Justice Scalia did say that "[a]n accuser who makes a formal statement to government officers bears testimony in a sense that a person who makes a casual remark to an acquaintance does not." *Crawford v. Washington*, 541 U.S. 36, 51, 124 S.Ct. 1354, 158 L.Ed.2d 177 (2004).

Compare: Fed. R. Evid. 803(3).

Research References

Packel & Poulin, Pennsylvania Evidence § 803(3)-1 (4th ed. 2013)

Binder, Hearsay Handbook Chapter 12 (4th ed. 2001)

McCormick, Evidence § 273 (7th ed. 2013)

HEARSAY EXCEPTION: VITAL STATISTICS

See: Pa.R.E. 803(6).

Objection

- I object to the introduction of this document and any testimony about its contents. There has been no foundation to authenticate it and its contents constitute inadmissible hearsay.

Response

- The document qualifies under the business records exception to the hearsay rule.

Pennsylvania Law

Records of vital statistics are business records and entries therein may be excepted to the hearsay rule pursuant to Pa.R.E. 803(6).

The Vital Statistics Law of 1953, 35 Pa. §§ 450.101–450.1003, provides for a statewide system of gathering and recording information with regard to births, deaths, marriages, and related matters. 35 P.S. § 450.810 provides:

> Any record or duly certified copy of a record or part thereof which is (1) filed with the department in accordance with the provisions of this act and the regulations of the Advisory Health Board and which (2) is not a "delayed" record filed under section seven hundred two of this act[1] or a record "corrected" under section seven hundred three of this act[2] shall constitute prima facie evidence of its contents, except that in any proceeding in which paternity is controverted and which affects the interests of an alleged father or his successors in interest no record or part thereof shall constitute prima facie evidence of paternity unless the alleged father is the husband of the mother of the child.

The vital statistic record may be authenticated

---

[1]Section 450.702 of this Title.

[2]Section 450.703 of this Title.

in the same manner as other official records. *See* Pa.R.E. 901, 902 and 1005.

In the context of the Vital Statistics Law, the term "prima facie evidence" means that the vital statistic record is admissible. However, evidence contained in the record may be explained, contradicted, rebutted, or even excluded under certain circumstances. *Compare Johnson v. Valvoline Oil Co.*, 131 Pa. Super. 266, 200 A. 224 (1938), *with Pittsburgh Nat. Bank v. Mutual Life Ins. Co. of N.Y.*, 273 Pa. Super. 592, 417 A.2d 1206 (1980), *affirmed* 493 Pa. 96, 425 A.2d 383 (1981).

There is some conflict on whether death certificates are admissible regarding the cause of death, as distinguished from merely the date and fact of death. The weight of authority in Pennsylvania, however, is that a properly authenticated death certificate is generally admissible as proof, albeit not conclusive, of both the fact and the cause of death. *Hauck v. Workmen's Comp. Appeal Bd.*, 47 Pa.Cmwlth. 554, 408 A.2d 585 (1979) (error not to admit death certificate listing cause and other significant conditions in the absence of any indication of untrustworthiness). If, however, there is some reason to suspect the trustworthiness of facts asserted in the certificate or the competency of its author, the certificate is not competent evidence of the facts in question. *See Pittsburgh Nat. Bank v. Mutual Life Ins. Co. of N.Y.*, 273 Pa. Super. 592, 417 A.2d 1206 (1980) (death certificate received for limited purposes but not to establish that death was accidental where attesting doctor was not the pathologist who performed autopsy but the coroner who had no personal knowledge of the circumstances of death).

Compare: Fed. R. Evid. 803(9).

Research References

Packel & Poulin, Pennsylvania Evidence

§ 803(9)-1 (4th ed. 2013)

McCormick, Evidence § 297 (7th ed. 2013)

HYPOTHETICAL QUESTION

Objection

- Objection. The witness is being asked to assume facts, which have never been established. An expert witness is not permitted to base his opinion on facts which are not warranted by the record.

Response

- A proper factual foundation has been established. To the extent the witness has been asked to assume the truth of certain facts not yet of record, they will be proved by subsequent witnesses.

Pennsylvania Law

In Pennsylvania practice, the hypothetical question remains a viable and accepted method of allowing the expert witness to render an opinion based on facts not known to him personally. *See* Comment to Pa.R.E. 705; *Ranieli v. Mut. Life Ins. Co. of America*, 271 Pa. Super. 261, 413 A.2d 396 (1979). While the expert must base his testimony on evidence that is part of the record, he may also base his answer on assumed facts, which later become part of the record. *Commonwealth v. Montalvo*, 986 A.2d 84 (Pa. 2009) (expert may respond to a hypothetical with an opinion so long as the operative set of facts is eventually supported by competent evidence); *Commonwealth v. Galvin*, 985 A.2d 783 (Pa. 2009) (use of hypothetical questions is proper when there is evidence of record supporting the hypothetical); *Commonwealth v. Rollins*, 738 A.2d 435 (1999); *Commonwealth v. LaCava*, 666 A.2d 221 (Pa. 1995); *Commonwealth v. Petrovich*, 648 A.2d 771 (Pa. 1994). The facts which are assumed to be true for purposes of a hypothetical question must be put into evidence by witnesses other than the expert himself. *Houston v. Canon Bowl, Inc.*, 443 Pa. 383, 278 A.2d 908 (1971); *Viener v. Jacobs*, 834 A.2d 546 (Pa. Super. 2003). "[T]he opinion of the expert does not constitute proof of the existence of facts necessary to support the opinion." *Collins v. Hand*, 431 Pa. 378, 390, 246 A.2d 398, 404 (1968).

A hypothetical question need not be based upon evidence conclusively proven; the rule is rather that the evidence must "tend to establish" the assumptions. *Whistler Sportswear, Inc. v. Rullo*, 289 Pa. Super. 230, 433 A.2d 40 (1981). Likewise, a hypothetical question need not be based on every fact of record. To the extent that opposing counsel believes that relevant facts have been omitted, he is free on cross-examination to pose his own hypothetical question which includes those facts. *Commonwealth v. Roberts*, 496 Pa. 428, 437 A.2d 948 (1981); *Battistone v. Benedetti*, 385 Pa. 163, 122 A.2d 536 (1956); *O'Malley v. Peerless Petroleum, Inc.*, 283 Pa. Super. 272, 423 A.2d 1251 (1980).

Although federal practice permits expert testimony without prior disclosure of the underlying facts and data (Fed. R. Evid. 705), Pennsylvania specifically rejects this approach. *Kozak v. Struth*, 515 Pa. 554, 531 A.2d 420 (1987). Disclosure is required so that the jury will know which facts the expert relied on in forming his or her opinion. The jury will then be able to evaluate the opinion based on whether or not it finds the assumed facts to be true. *Kelly v. Martino*, 375 Pa. 244, 99 A.2d 901 (1953).

Where an expert attempts to express an opinion based on guess or conjecture or on facts not introduced at trial, the testimony is properly subject to a motion to strike and will be excluded. *See Laubach v. Haigh*, 433 Pa. 487, 252 A.2d 682 (1969); *Collins v. Hand*, 431 Pa. 378, 246 A.2d 398 (1968); *Gombar v. Commonwealth, Dep't of Transp.*, 678 A.2d 843 (Pa.Cmwlth.1996); *Commonwealth v. Pilosky*, 239 Pa. Super. 233, 362 A.2d 253 (1976).

While Pennsylvania courts apparently have not addressed the issue, several federal courts have condemned guilt-assuming hypothetical questions asked of character witnesses who have testified about a defendant's good reputation in criminal cases. Such a question might typically be phrased: "If you knew the defendant had sold cocaine to an undercover agent, would your opinion as to his integrity and honesty change at all?" Several circuits have held such hypothetical questions strike at the very heart of the presumption of innocence and have no place in a criminal trial. *United States v. Candelaria-Gonzalez*, 547 F.2d 291 (5th Cir.1977); *see also United States v. Wilson*, 983 F.2d 221 (11th Cir.1993); *United States v. Oshatz*, 912 F.2d 534 (2d Cir.1990); *United States v. Williams*, 738 F.2d 172 (7th Cir.1984).

Compare: Fed. R. Evid. 705.

Research References

Packel & Poulin, Pennsylvania Evidence § 705-1 (4th ed. 2013)

McCormick, Evidence § 14 (7th ed. 2013)

IMPEACHMENT: BIAS, INTEREST, MOTIVE

See: Pa.R.E. 607, 611(b).

Objection

- Objection. The question has no relevance to or bearing on the witness' testimony or credibility. It is nothing more than an attempt to [*smear the witness*] [*place unfairly prejudicial evidence before the jury*].

Response

- The line of inquiry is proper. I am entitled to impeach the witness by showing that his direct testimony was colored by [*bias*] [*prejudice*] [*interest*] [*corrupt motive*].

Pennsylvania Law

The exposure of a witness' motivation in testifying is a proper and important function of the constitutionally protected night of cross-examination. Although cross-examination ordinarily is limited to matters brought out on direct examination, an exception exists where the cross-examiner seeks to impeach the witness by showing bias, prejudice, interest, corrupt/ulterior motive or defects in his ability to observe, remember or recount the matter about which he has testified. Pa.R.E. 607, 611(b); *Commonwealth v. Bridges*, 563 Pa. 1, 757 A.2d 859 (2000) (a witness may be cross-examined as to any matter tending to show interest or bias of that witness so jury can properly evaluate witness' credibility); *Commonwealth v. Cox*, 556 Pa. 368, 728 A.2d 923 (1999) (defense has right to cross-examine Commonwealth witnesses for bias stemming from existence of open criminal charges which is highly important if guilt depends upon the credibility of witness in question or where there are conflicting versions of the evidence); *Commonwealth v. Thomas*, 783 A.2d 328 (Pa.

Super. 2001) (cross-examination may be used to test a witness' story, to impeach credibility or to establish motive for lying); *Fisher v. North Hills Passavant Hosp.*, 781 A.2d 1232 (Pa. Super. 2001) (where there were conflicting versions of facts in medical malpractice action and credibility of staff nurse was pivotal, trial court committed reversible error by restricting plaintiff's cross-examination of nurse's potential bias); *see also Pennsylvania v. Ritchie*, 480 U.S. 39, 51–52, 107 S.Ct. 989, 998, 94 L.Ed.2d 40 (1987) (the right to cross-examination includes the opportunity to show that a witness is biased, or that the testimony is exaggerated or unbelievable); *Delaware v. Van Arsdall*, 475 U.S. 673, 678–79, 106 S.Ct. 1431, 1434–1435, 89 L.Ed.2d 674 (1986) (exploring possible bias is a proper and important function of right of cross-examination).

Bias has been defined as "the relationship between a party and a witness which might lead the witness to slant, unconsciously or otherwise, his testimony in favor of or against a party." *United States v. Abel*, 469 U.S. 45, 52, 105 S.Ct. 465, 469, 83 L.Ed.2d 450 (1984); accord *Commonwealth v. Murray*, 83 A.3d 137 (Pa. 2013).

Bias is not limited to personal animosity against a party or pecuniary gain. Courts have found bias in a wide variety of situations, including familial or sexual relationships, friendships, common organizational memberships and situations in which the witness has a litigation claim against another party or witness. *See, e.g., Commonwealth v. Hayward*, 437 Pa. 215, 263 A.2d 330 (1970) (district attorney properly permitted to impeach credibility of girlfriend witness and establish her interest in outcome of trial by showing she was pregnant by defendant); *Commonwealth v. Brewington*, 740 A.2d 247 (Pa. Super. 1999) (gang membership).

Whenever a prosecution witness may be biased, for example, because of outstanding criminal charges or a non-final criminal disposition, a defendant must be permitted to cross-examine as to actual or possible favorable treatment by the prosecuting authority. *Commonwealth v. Evans*, 511 Pa. 214, 512 A.2d 626 (1986); *Commonwealth v. Hyland*, 875 A.2d 1175 (Pa. Super. 2005); *Commonwealth v. Causey*, 833 A.2d 165 (Pa. Super. 2003).

Cross-examination as to bias, interest or corrupt motive may incidentally expose otherwise inadmissible facts to the jury. This alone is not a basis for excluding impeachment evidence. *Commonwealth v. Cheatham*, 429 Pa. 198, 239 A.2d 293, (1968); *Lenahan v. Pittston Coal Mining Co.*, 221 Pa. 626, 70 A. 884 (1908); *see also United States v. Abel*, 469 U.S. at 56, 105 S.Ct. at 470 ("[T]here is no rule of evidence which provides that testimony admissible for one purpose and inadmissible for another purpose is thereby rendered inadmissible; quite the contrary is the case."). This is not to say that all evidence of a collateral nature offered to attack the credibility of a witness is admissible. The trial court has discretion to limit or exclude collateral evidence where its prejudicial impact outweighs its impeachment value. Pa.R.E. 403; *Ely v. Susquehanna Aquacultores, Inc.*, 130 A.3d 6 (Pa. Super. 2015); *Klein v. Aronchick*, 85 A.3d 487 (Pa. Super. 2014) (plaintiff's history of bulimia, or lack thereof, has nothing to do with the issues before the court); *Valentine v. Acme Markets, Inc.*, 455 Pa. Super. 256, 687 A.2d 1157 (1997); *Commonwealth v. Childress*, 452 Pa. Super. 37, 680 A.2d 1184 (1996); *Commonwealth v. Williams*, 344 Pa. Super. 493, 496 A.2d 1213 (1985); *see Commonwealth v. Petrillo*, 341 Pa. 209, 19 A.2d 288 (1941) (no witness can be contradicted on everything he testifies to in order to test his credibility; the pivotal issues in a trial cannot be side-tracked for the determination of whether or not a witness lied in making a statement about something which has no relationship to the case on trial).

Impeachment may not be used merely as a pretext to place prejudicial evidence before the fact-finder. *Commonwealth v. Green*, 290 Pa. Super. 76, 434 A.2d 137 (1981). Impeaching evidence may also be disallowed because it is not relevant to the witness' credibility or because it is based on speculation. *Mohn v. Hahnemann Med. Coll. and Hosp. of Philadelphia*, 357 Pa. Super. 173, 515 A.2d 920 (1986) (expert's total yearly income irrelevant).

In criminal cases, the accused is constitutionally entitled to explore a witness' motivation in testifying against him. *Commonwealth v. Laird*, 988 A.2d 618, 630 (Pa. 2010); *Commonwealth v. Rosser*, 135 A.3d 1077 (Pa. Super. 2016); *Commonwealth v. Saunders*, 946 A.2d 776 (Pa. Super. 2008) (a defendant's right of confrontation includes the right to cross-examine witnesses about possible motives to testify). The Confrontation Clause of the Sixth Amendment to the United States Constitution guarantees the reliability of "evidence against a criminal defendant by subjecting it to rigorous testing in the context of an adversary proceeding before the trier of fact." *Maryland v. Craig*, 497 U.S. 836, 845, 110 S.Ct. 3157, 3163, 111 L.Ed.2d 666 (1990); *U.S. v. Smith*, 308 F.3d 726, 738 (7th Cir. 2002) ("limitations on cross-examination rise to the level of a Sixth Amendment violation when they prevent the exposure of a witness' bias and motivation to lie."). Cross-examination of a witness testifying against the accused allows the jury to observe the witness' demeanor so they may assess her credibility and evaluate the truth of her testimony. *California v. Green*, 399 U.S. 149, 158, 90 S.Ct. 1930, 1935, 26 L.Ed.2d 489 (1970). A defendant's right of confrontation is violated when he is prohibited from pursuing areas of cross-examination that may undermine the credibility of the witness. *Olden v. Kentucky*, 488 U.S. 227, 233, 109 S.Ct. 480, 484, 102 L.Ed.2d 513 (1988). However, the Confrontation Clause is satisfied "when the defense is given a full and fair opportunity to probe and expose . . . infirmities through cross-examination, thereby calling to the attention of the fact finder the reasons for giving scant weight to the witness' testimony." *Delaware v. Fensterer*, 474 U.S. 15, 22, 106 S.Ct. 292, 295–296, 88 L.Ed.2d 15 (1985). The United States Supreme Court has also said that the Confrontation Clause only "guarantees an *opportunity* for effective cross-examination, not cross-examination that is effective in whatever way, and to whatever extent, the defense might wish." 474 U.S. at 20, 106 S.Ct. at 294–295 (emphasis in original).

The following cases are instructive: *Polett v. Poblic Communications, Inc.*, 126 A.3d 895 (Pa. 2015) (tolling agreements are not indicative of the nature and degree of a signatory's potential bias without full explication of circumstances which led to agreement; have slight probative value was outweighed by potential for causing jury confusion and delay to trial); *Commonwealth v. Rizzuto*, 566 Pa. 40, 777 A.2d 1069 (2001) (alcohol or drug use relevant if witness was under influence at time of events about which testimony is offered but use of alcohol or drugs at irrelevant times may not be used for impeachment); *Commonwealth v. Butler*, 529 Pa. 7, 601 A.2d 268 (1991) (defendant who had filed a civil suit against a prosecution witness should have been permitted to cross-examine the witness regarding bias arising from the civil claim); *accord Commonwealth v. Birch*, 532 Pa. 563, 616 A.2d 977 (1992); *Commonwealth v. Borders*, 522 Pa. 161, 560 A.2d 758 (1989) (pending juvenile charges admissible to show motive or bias); *Commonwealth v. Abu-Jamal*, 521 Pa. 188, 555 A.2d 846 (1989) (character witness is not exempt from examination to show bias or motive); *Commonwealth v. Thompson*, 559 Pa. 229, 739 A.2d 1023 (1999); *Commonwealth v. Evans*, 511 Pa. 214, 512 A.2d 626 (1986) (whenever prosecution witness may be biased in favor of the prosecution because of outstanding criminal charges or because of any non-final criminal disposition against him within the same jurisdiction, that possible bias, unfairness, must be made known to the jury); *Commonwealth v. Cheatham*, 429 Pa. 198, 239 A.2d 293, (1968) (error to exclude impeachment evidence of homosexual relationship to establish bias of witness); *Commonwealth v. Rivera*, 816 A.2d 282 (Pa. Super. 2003) (impeachment by prior inconsistent statements); *Zamsky v. Pub. Parking Auth. of Pittsburgh*, 378 Pa. 38, 105 A.2d 335 (1954); *Grutski v. Kline*, 352 Pa. 401, 43 A.2d 142 (1945) (proper to inquire of expert witness the fee he is being paid to testify); *Commonwealth v. Buksa*, 440 Pa. Super. 305, 655 A.2d 576 (1995) (error to deny cross-examination re probation (collecting cases)). *But see Mohn v. Hahnemann Med. Coll. and Hosp. of Philadelphia*, 357 Pa. Super. 173, 515 A.2d 920 (1986) (permissible bounds of impeachment exceeded by questions about defense expert's total income); *Smith v. Celotex Corp.*, 387 Pa. Super. 340, 564 A.2d 209 (1989); *Douglass v. Licciardi Constr. Co., Inc.*, 386 Pa. Super. 292, 562 A.2d 913 (1989) (cross-examination as to whether expert had been employed by party or his attorney on previous occasions held proper); *Downey v. Weston*, 451 Pa. 259, 301 A.2d 635 (1973); *Tiburzio-Kelly v. Montgomery*, 452 Pa. Super. 158, 681 A.2d 757 (Pa. Super. 1996) (evidence of friendship or ongoing relationship between expert witnesses and attorneys is information which jury is entitled to know about). *See generally Cooper v. Schoffstall*, 905 A.2d 482 (Pa. 2006) (addressing obtaining additional information to support charge of potential favoritism of non-party expert witness).

Pa.R.E. 607(a) abolishes completely the common law rule that prohibited a party from impeaching a witness called by that party.

Compare: Fed. R. Evid. 607, 611(b).

Research References

Packel & Poulin, Pennsylvania Evidence § 607-3

(4th ed. 2013)

McCormick, Evidence § 39 (7th ed. 2013)

IMPEACHMENT: GENERAL REPUTATION FOR TRUTHFULNESS

See: Pa.R.E. 608

Objection

- Objection. This witness lacks the necessary knowledge to testify about general reputation for truthfulness.
- Objection. The question calls for the witness' own opinion and is therefore prohibited.

Response

- A proper foundation has been established. I have shown that he knows the other witness and his general reputation for truthfulness in the community. He has not been asked to state, nor will he give his own opinion; his testimony will be limited to the community opinion of the individual in question.

Pennsylvania Law

Pa.R.E. 608 codifies the long established rule limiting the type of evidence admissible to challenge a witness's credibility to evidence of the witness's general reputation for truthfulness or untruthfulness. *Commonwealth v. Minich*, 4 A.3d 1063 (Pa. Super. 2010). This is because the reputation of any witness for truthfulness or untruthfulness is always in issue and his or her credibility may be impeached by evidence of bad reputation for truth or veracity. Pa.R.E. 608; *Commonwealth v. Gaddy*, 468 Pa. 303, 362 A.2d 217 (1976); *Commonwealth v. Fowler*, 434 Pa. Super. 148, 642 A.2d 517 (1994). Subsection (b)(1) of this rule specifically prohibits a witness from supporting or attacking another witness's credibility with instances of specific conduct. *Commonwealth v. Patterson*, 91 A.3d 55, 68 (Pa. 2014); *Commonwealth v. W.H.M., Jr.*, 932 A.2d 155 (Pa. Super. 2007).

Questioning, however, is limited to general reputation in the community for truthfulness and may not include bad reputation in any other respect. The courts will not allow a party to blacken the reputation of a witness by introducing evidence that does not clearly bear on the witness' reputation for truth. *See, e.g., Downey v. Weston*, 451 Pa. 259, 301 A.2d 635 (1973) (no error to exclude evidence of breach of medical ethics because it did not bear directly on the witness' character for truth (collecting cases)).

On direct examination, the impeaching witness cannot be asked questions or give answers regarding specific acts, as distinguished from what he or she has heard in the neighborhood. *In Interest of Lawrence J.*, 310 Pa. Super. 351, 456 A.2d 647 (1983). An individual's own opinion as to a witness' "character for truthfulness" is never admissible. *Commonwealth v. Wilson*, 543 Pa. 429, 672 A.2d 293 (1996); *Commonwealth v. Lauro*, 819 A.2d 100 (Pa. Super. 2003); *Commonwealth v. Boring*, 453 Pa. Super. 600, 684 A.2d 561 (1996); *Kinniry v. Abington Sch. Dist.*, 673 A.2d 429 (Pa.Cmwlth. 1996).

The proper procedure on direct examination is to ask the impeaching witness whether he is acquainted with the other witness and with his general reputation for truthfulness and honesty in the community and if so, what that reputation is. The evidence must relate to the reputation of the witness at or about the time he is called to testify and in the neighborhood in which he lives. *Commonwealth v. Stilley*, 455 Pa. Super. 543, 689 A.2d 242 (1997).

The trial court may permit the cross-examination of a character witness with specific instances of conduct showing the truthfulness or untruthfulness of the person about whose character he or she testified. Pa.R.E. 608(b)(2).

If a witness is impeached by proof of bad reputation for truthfulness, only then may evidence be admitted to prove good reputation for truth and veracity. *Commonwealth v. Gwynn*, 555 Pa. 86, 723 A.2d 143 (1998); *Commonwealth v. Fisher*, 764 A.2d 82 (Pa. Super. 2000). Bolstering evidence, however, is not admissible unless the character of the witness has been attacked. *Commonwealth v. Schwenk*, 777 A.2d 1149 (Pa. Super. 2001).

Not all forms of impeachment constitute an attack on a witness' character for truthfulness. Impeachment by contradiction, bias, prejudice, interest, perception or memory do not challenge a witness' truthfulness. *Commonwealth v. Fulton*, 574 Pa. 282, 830 A.2d 567 (2003); *Commonwealth v. Fisher*, 764 A.2d 82 (Pa. Super. 2000) (vigorous cross-examination attempting to establish that victim's version of events was more credible than defendant's did not attack defendant's reputation for truthfulness; bolstering evidence properly excluded); *Commonwealth v. Boyd*, 448 Pa. Super. 589, 592, 672 A.2d 810, 812 (1996) ("It is within the ordinary capacity of a jury to assess whether a particular witness is lying, and resolving questions of a witness' credibility is a function reserved exclusively for the jury. Allowing a defendant to offer bolstering evidence of his or her good reputation for truth or veracity whenever the defendant's testimony contradicts the testimony of the Commonwealth's witnesses would infringe on the credibility determining function of the jury.").

Compare: Fed. R. Evid. 608.

Research References

Packel & Poulin, Pennsylvania Evidence §§ 608-1–608-3 (4th ed. 2013)

McCormick, Evidence §§ 41, 47–48 (7th ed. 2013)

IMPEACHMENT: PRIOR CONVICTIONS (CRIMEN FALSI)

See: Pa.R.E. 609; see also Rule 608.

Objection

- Objection. May we approach the bench to discuss my objection? [*At side bar*]—The question seeks disclosure of a conviction for a crime which did not involve dishonesty or false statement; or, the conviction is more than ten years old and the attempt to introduce it is purely an effort to smear the witness.

Response

- The crime did involve [*dishonesty*] [*false statement*] and impeachment is permitted by Pa.R.E. 609.
- The ten-year period is computed not by the original confinement but by the witness' reconfinement for parole violation, *Commonwealth v. Jackson*, 385 Pa. Super. 401, 561 A.2d 335 (1989).
- Measured by the *Bighum* factors, the evidence is admissible [*specify*].

Pennsylvania Law

Evidence regarding the character and conduct of a witness is relevant only as it relates to the character for truthfulness or untruthfulness of the witness. *Commonwealth v. Sasse*, 921 A.2d 1229 (Pa. Super. 2007); Pa.R.E. 609.

Evidence of prior convictions is *per se* admissible for the purpose of impeaching the credibility of any witness **if, but only if, the conviction was for an offense involving dishonesty or false statement (crimen falsi)**, and the date of conviction or the last day of confinement is less than ten years old. Pa.R.E. 609; *Commonwealth v. Patterson*, 91 A.3d 55 (Pa. 2014). Probation does not qualify as confinement under Rule 609. *Commonwealth v. Treadwell*, 911 A.2d 987 (Pa. Super. 2006). If the conviction involves a period greater than ten years, the proponent must give sufficient advance written notice of intent to use to provide the adverse party with fair opportunity to contest. Pa.R.E. 609(b). The trial judge will then determine whether the value of the evidence substantially outweighs its prejudicial effect. Pa.R.E. 609(b); *Commonwealth v. Hoover*, 107 A.3d 723 (Pa. 2014); *Commonwealth v. Randall*, 515 Pa. 410, 528 A.2d 1326 (1987); accord, *Commonwealth v. Williams*, 524 Pa. 404, 573 A.2d 536 (1990). The same rules apply to the impeachment of witnesses in civil actions. *Russell v. Hubicz*, 425 Pa. Super. 120, 624 A.2d 175 (1993).

Evidence of proof of prior convictions to impeach witness veracity is a subset of character evidence generally. The underlying rationale for allowing impeachment by showing prior convictions is that a person who has demonstrated his contempt for social constraints by committing crimes of dishonesty or false statement is less reluctant to lie under oath than persons who have not been convicted of committing crimes those types of crimes. *Carlson Mining Co. v. Titan Coal Co., Inc.*, 343 Pa. Super. 364, 368, 494 A.2d 1127, 1129 (1985).

In deciding whether a particular offense is *crimen falsi*, the court must consider both the elemental aspects of that offense and the conduct of the defendant which forms the basis of the anticipated impeachment. *Commonwealth v. Coleman*, 664 A.2d 1381 (Pa. Super. 1995). Courts employ a two-step procedure to determine whether a crime is *crimen falsi*. *Commonwealth v. Cascardo*, 981 A.2d 245 (Pa. Super. 2009). First, it examines the essential elements of the offense to determine if the crime is inherently *crimen falsi*—whether dishonesty or false statement are a necessary prerequisite to commission of the crime. Second, if the crime is not inherently *crimen falsi*, the court inspects the underlying facts that led to conviction to determine if dishonesty or false statement facilitated the commission of the crime. *Commonwealth v. Davis*, 17

A.3d 390 (Pa. Super. 2011). The burden of proof is on the party offering the conviction during cross-examination. *Commonwealth v. Boyd*, 344 A.2d 864 (Pa. 1975); *Commonwealth v. Davis*, 17 A.3d 390 (Pa. Super. 2011) (criminal mischief and defiant trespass could not be used to impeach since there was no showing of dishonesty or false statement in the commission of those acts).

Pennsylvania courts have indicated that armed robbery (*Commonwealth v. May*, 898 A.2d 559 (Pa. 2006)), insurance fraud (*Birt v. Firstenergy Corp.*, 891 A.2d 1281 (Pa. Super. 2006)), writing improper prescriptions for controlled substances (*Allen v. Kaplan*, 439 Pa. Super. 263, 653 A.2d 1249 (1995)), burglary (*Commonwealth v. Nenninger*, 359 Pa. Super. 444, 519 A.2d 433 (1986)), larceny (*Commonwealth v. Kahley*, 467 Pa. 272, 356 A.2d 745 (1976)), theft (*Commonwealth v. Vickers*, 260 Pa. Super. 479, 394 A.2d 1027 (1978)), retail theft (*Commonwealth v. Gordon*, 355 Pa. Super. 25, 512 A.2d 1191 (1986)), unauthorized use of a credit card (*Commonwealth v. Weiss*, 530 Pa. 1, 606 A.2d 439 (1992)), unauthorized use of a motor vehicle (*Commonwealth v. Johnson*, 340 Pa. Super. 26, 489 A.2d 821 (1985)), receiving stolen property (*Commonwealth v. Kaster*, 300 Pa. Super. 174, 446 A.2d 286 (1982)), bribery (*Harmon v. Commonwealth*, 119 Pa.Cmwlth. 1, 546 A.2d 726 (1988)), tax evasion (*Commonwealth v. Vitale*, 445 Pa. Super. 43, 664 A.2d 999 (1995)) and perjury (*Commonwealth v. Haag*, 522 Pa. 388, 562 A.2d 289 (1989)) are crimes involving dishonesty or false statement.

Conversely, statutory rape, aggravated assault, disorderly conduct, resisting arrest, fornication, pandering, prostitution, corrupting the morals of a minor, deviate sexual intercourse, assault with intent to kill and murder do not constitute crimes of dishonesty and false statement. Packel & Poulin, Pennsylvania Evidence § 609-1 (4th ed. 2013). *Commonwealth v. Davis*, 17 A.3d 390 (Pa. Super.

2011) (defiant trespass not inherently crimin falsi); *Commonwealth v. Hyland*, 875 A.2d 1175 (Pa. Super. 2005) (DUI, leaving scene of accident not *crimen falsi*); *Commonwealth v. Dale*, 836 A.2d 150 (Pa. Super. 2003) (sex crimes, prison escape are not *crimen falsi*). Simple possession of a controlled substance is not evidence of *crimen falsi*. *Commonwealth v. Causey*, 833 A.2d 165 (Pa. Super. 2003) (drug-related offense did not bear on witness' honesty or truthfulness); *Commonwealth v. Correa*, 423 Pa. Super. 57, 620 A.2d 497 (1993); *see also, Commonwealth v. Nieves*, 560 Pa. 529, 746 A.2d 1102 (2000) (drug trafficking and firearms offenses did not involve dishonesty or false statement); *Commonwealth v. Coleman*, 664 A.2d 1381 (Pa. Super. 1995) (under facts at issue, possession with intent to deliver not *crimen falsi*).

In *Commonwealth v. Vitale*, 445 Pa. Super. 43, 664 A.2d 999 (1995), the court said that even if a crime would not be in and of itself *crimen falsi*, it would be considered as such if it was committed in part through the use of false written or oral statements.

An arrest without conviction can never be the basis of impeachment, *Commonwealth v. Chmiel*, 889 A.2d 501 (Pa. 2005); *Commonwealth v. Jackson*, 475 Pa. 604, 381 A.2d 438 (1977), nor can admission into the Accelerated Rehabilitative Disposition (ARD) program. *Commonwealth v. Hoover*, 16 A.3d 1148 (Pa. Super. 2011); *Commonwealth v. Krall*, 290 Pa. Super. 1, 434 A.2d 99 (1981). *But see Commonwealth v. Bowser*, 425 Pa. Super. 24, 624 A.2d 125 (1993). However, summary convictions of crimes involving dishonesty can be used to impeach a witness' credibility. *Commonwealth v. Howard*, 823 A.2d 911 (Pa. Super. 2003).

When a conviction more than ten years old is sought to be admitted, the courts continue to employ the balancing test of *Commonwealth v. Randall*, 515 Pa. 410, 528 A.2d 1326 (1987);

Commonwealth v. Bighum, 452 Pa. 554, 307 A.2d 255 (1973) and *Commonwealth v. Roots*, 482 Pa. 33, 393 A.2d 364 (1978). The factors to be considered are: (1) the degree to which the commission of the prior offense reflects upon the veracity of the defendant-witness; (2) the likelihood, in view of the nature and extent of the prior record, that it would have a greater tendency to smear the character of the defendant and suggest a propensity to commit the crime for which he stands charged, rather than provide a legitimate reason for discrediting him as an untruthful person; (3) the age and circumstances of the defendant; (4) the strength of the prosecution's case and the prosecution's need to resort to this evidence as compared with the availability to the defense of other witnesses through which its version of the events surrounding the incident can be presented; and (5) the existence of alternative means of attacking the defendant's credibility. *Commonwealth v. Hoover*, supra; *Commonwealth v. Palo*, 24 A.3d 1050 (Pa. Super. 2011); *Commonwealth v. Cascardo*, 981 A.2d 245 (Pa. Super. 2009); *Commonwealth v. Harris*, 884 A.2d 920 (Pa. Super. 2005); *Commonwealth v. McEnany*, 732 A.2d 1263 (Pa. Super. 1999) (where murder prosecution was based solely on circumstantial evidence and defendant presented an alibi defense, his credibility was a critical issue and a *crimen falsi* conviction beyond the ten-year limit could be used to impeach).

A criminal defendant may not be impeached by prior convictions of a *crimen falsi* nature on cross-examination unless (1) the defendant has introduced evidence of his good character, or (2) has testified against a co-defendant charged with the same offense. 42 Pa.C.S.A. § 5918; *Commonwealth v. Pursell*, 555 Pa. 233, 724 A.2d 293 (1999); *Commonwealth v. Stokes*, 532 Pa. 242, 615 A.2d 704 (1992). However, the statute does not prohibit offering evidence of prior convictions in rebuttal after the defendant has testified. *Commonwealth v. Bighum*, 452 Pa. 554, 307 A.2d

255 (1973). The statute affects only the timing and method of impeaching a defendant; it does not bar the impeachment entirely.

In a criminal case only, evidence of an adjudication of delinquency for an offense under the Juvenile Act, 42 Pa.C.S. § 6301 et seq., may be used to impeach the credibility of a witness if conviction of the offense would be admissible to attack the credibility of an adult. Pa.R.E. 609(e); *see Commonwealth v. Rivera*, 983 A.2d 1211 (Pa. 2009) (juvenile adjudications for theft admissible); *Commonwealth v. McKeever*, 455 Pa. Super. 604, 689 A.2d 272 (1997) (juvenile adjudications for robbery, theft and attempted theft admissible).

Compare: Fed. R. Evid. 609.

Research References

Packel & Poulin, Pennsylvania Evidence §§ 609-1–609-4 (4th ed. 2013)

McCormick, Evidence § 42 (7th ed. 2013)

IMPROPER REBUTTAL

See: Pa.R.E. 611(a).

Objection

- Objection. This is improper rebuttal evidence. [This evidence should have been part of plaintiff's case in chief] [This evidence is cumulative and does not rebut any defense testimony or respond to any new matter].

Response

- This evidence is admissible as a matter of right; it directly impeaches my opponent's witnesses.

Pennsylvania Law

Recognizing the necessity for an orderly presentation of evidence, the general rule in Pennsylvania is that the plaintiff must prove during his case in chief all essential elements of his action as to which he has the burden of proof, and that he may not, as a matter of right, introduce evidence in rebuttal which is properly part of his case in chief. *Downey v. Weston*, 451 Pa. 259, 301 A.2d 635 (1973); *Murphy v. City of Philadelphia*, 420 Pa. 490, 218 A.2d 323 (1966).

The trial court has discretion to admit or exclude as rebuttal evidence that which is properly part of the case in chief. *Flowers v. Green*, 420 Pa. 481, 218 A.2d 219 (1966); *Commonwealth v. United States Mineral Products Co.*, 809 A.2d 1000 (Pa. Cmwlth.2002); *Pittsburgh-Des Moines Steel Co., Inc. v. McLaughlin*, 77 Pa.Cmwlth. 565, 466 A.2d 1092 (1983). However, where the evidence proposed impeaches the testimony of the opponent's witnesses, it is admissible as a matter of right. *American Future Systems, Inc. v. BBB*, 872 A.2d 1202 (Pa. Super. 2005); *Harsh v. Petroll*, 840 A.2d 404 (Pa.Cmwlth. 2003) (proper to admit rebuttal testimony which discredited defense expert.)

The following cases are instructive: *Commonwealth v. Hitcho*, 123 A.3d 731 (Pa. 2015) and *Commonwealth v. Ballard*, 80 A.3d 380 (Pa. 2013) (The appropriate scope of rebuttal evidence is defined by the evidence that it is intended to rebut); *Commonwealth v. Weiss*, 565 Pa. 504, 776 A.2d 958 (2001) (witness' testimony properly admitted since it directly rebutted assertions made by defendant during cross-examination); *Commonwealth v. Miles*, 846 A.2d 132 (Pa. Super. 2004) (it is not proper to submit on rebuttal, evidence which does not, in fact, rebut the opponent's evidence); *Ratti v. Wheeling Pittsburgh Steel Corp.*, 758 A.2d 695 (Pa. Super. 2000) (same); *Mishkin v. Redevelopment Auth. of City of Lancaster*, 6 Pa.Cmwlth. 97, 293 A.2d 135 (1972) (proposed rebuttal evidence excluded where it did not impeach defense witnesses or respond to any new matter but was properly part of case-in-chief); *Kline v. Behrendt*, 396 Pa. Super. 302, 578 A.2d 526 (1990) (rebuttal not intended as vehicle to repeat prior testimony so as to have the last word); *Klyman v. Southeastern Pa. Transp. Auth.*, 331 Pa. Super. 172, 480 A.2d 299 (1984) (where party failed to provide discovery as to expert witness per Pa. R.C.P. 4003.5, he cannot do an "end run" by calling expert as rebuttal witness); *Estate of Hannis v. Ashland State Gen. Hosp.*, 123 Pa.Cmwlth. 390, 554 A.2d 574 (1989) (proposed rebuttal cumulative of direct testimony and did not impeach defense witness); *Remy v. Michael D's Carpet Outlets*, 391 Pa. Super. 436, 571 A.2d 446 (1990) (although somewhat repetitive of prior testimony, rebuttal was properly received to discredit opposing expert); *Commonwealth v. Smith*, 548 Pa. 65, 694 A.2d 1086 (1997) (a party may produce evidence to rebut testimony which he himself elicited from his opponent's witness on cross-examination).

See also Commonwealth v. Bond, 985 A.2d 810 (Pa. 2009) (where penalty phase witness testified defendant expressed regret for murder for purposes of establishing his character under the catch-all mitigator, it was proper rebuttal for the Commonwealth to introduce comments defendant made during trial indicating total lack of remorse).

Compare: Fed. R. Evid. 611(a).

Research References

Packel & Poulin, Pennsylvania Evidence § 611-2 (4th ed. 2013)

McCormick, Evidence § 4 (7th ed. 2013)

INSURANCE (COLLATERAL SOURCE RULE)[1]

See: Pa.R.E. 411

Objection

- Objection. [*request sidebar*] This evidence is irrelevant and highly prejudicial. I move for a mistrial.

Response

- [*The question is proper / the answer is admissible*] because the purpose is to show [*bias or prejudice of the witness*] [*agency*] [*ownership or control*] [*other, specify*].
- The collateral source rule does not apply; there is a substantive legal issue regarding coverage and I am entitled to develop it.

Pennsylvania Law

Rule 411 provides that evidence of liability insurance is not admissible to prove negligence or other wrongdoing.

It has long been the rule in Pennsylvania that evidence of insurance is irrelevant and prejudicial and can justify the grant of a mistrial. *Paxton Nat'l Ins. Co. v. Brickajlik*, 513 Pa. 627, 522 A.2d 531 (1987). In a personal injury action, evidence which

---

[1] The collateral source rule provides that payments from a collateral source shall not diminish the damages otherwise recoverable from the wrongdoer. *Johnson v. Beane*, 541 Pa. 449, 664 A.2d 96 (1995). The rule was intended to avoid precluding a claimant from obtaining redress for his or her injury merely because coverage for the injury was provided by some collateral source, e.g., insurance. *Beechwoods Flying Serv., Inc. v. Al Hamilton Contracting Corp.*, 504 Pa. 618, 476 A.2d 350 (1984); *see also id.* 504 Pa. at 624–624, 476 A.2d at 353, (the rule is "intended to prevent a wrongdoer from taking advantage of the fortuitous existence of a collateral remedy").

informs the jury that a defendant is insured against liability is inadmissible. *Zauflik v. Pennsbury School Dist.*, 104 A.3d 1096 (Pa. 2014); *Price v. Yellow Cab Co.*, 443 Pa. 56, 278 A.2d 161 (1971). The general prohibition is equally applicable to plaintiff's insurance matters. *Price v. Guy*, 558 Pa. 42, 735 A.2d 668 (1999) (court committed reversible error by telling jury that plaintiffs elected limited tort option resulting in lower premiums).

Prejudice is said to arise in one of several ways: (1) in a close liability case, the jury might assume defendant's loss will be covered anyway; (2) the jury might assume that an insured defendant was probably careless; or (3) the jury might assume that a defendant with no insurance had every reason to be careful. *See Trimble v. Merloe*, 413 Pa. 408, 197 A.2d 457 (1964) (calculated introduction of liability insurance as a means of informing jury that defendant would not be personally responsible for paying verdict).

A plaintiff is forbidden to show that he has no insurance or workmen's compensation to cover the loss he has suffered, *Hileman v. Pittsburgh & Lake Erie R.R. Co.*, 546 Pa. 433, 685 A.2d 994 (1996), or that defendant is insured. *Flenke v. Huntington*, 111 A.3d 1197 (Pa. Super. 2015). Likewise, Pennsylvania courts do not permit a defendant to offer evidence that the plaintiff has been compensated by a third party (collateral source—i.e. workman's compensation, pension benefits, continued salary payments) in order to reduce the damages payable to the plaintiff. *Boudwin v. Yellow Cab Co.*, 410 Pa. 31, 33, 188 A.2d 259 (1963) ("[A] tortfeasor may not ride to immunity from his wrong on the back of workers' compensation paid by someone else."); *Lobalzo v. Varoli*, 409 Pa. 15, 185 A.2d 557 (1962); *Palandro v. Bollinger*, 409 Pa. 296, 186 A.2d 11 (1962); *Deeds v. University of Pa. Medical Center*, 110 A.3d 1009 (Pa. Super. 2015) (reversed where cross-examination and closing argument suggested plaintiff's medical costs were covered by Medicaid and the Affordable Care Act); *Nigra v. Walsh*, 797 A.2d 353 (Pa. Super. 2002); *Boscia v. Massaro*, 365 Pa. Super. 271, 529 A.2d 504 (1987). The rationale is that it is unfair for the wrongdoer to receive the benefit of payments made by a collateral source or for the jury to assume that plaintiff is seeking a double recovery. *Palandro v. Bollinger*, 409 Pa. 296, 186 A.2d 11 (1962); *Lengle v. North Lebanon Twp.*, 274 Pa. 51, 117 A. 403 (1922); *Trump v. Capek*, 267 Pa. Super. 355, 406 A.2d 1079 (1979); *Kagarise v. Shover*, 218 Pa. Super. 287, 275 A.2d 855 (1971). Cf. *Simmons v. Cobb*, 906 A.2d 582 (Pa. Super. 2006) (plaintiff should have been allowed to show he was receiving social security disability benefits to buttress claim that accident left him disabled; collateral source rule applies to defense offers of evidence, not to those made by plaintiff—a questionable holding).

Pa.R.E. 411 contemplates that evidence of insurance may be admissible on issues other than liability. The existence of insurance may be shown in connection with matters such as agency, ownership or control, or bias or prejudice of a witness. *Gallagher v. PLCB*, 584 Pa. 362, 883 A.2d 550 (2005) (where identity of employer was contested, evidence of payment of workers' compensation premiums was relevant in determining which defendant was employer); *O'Donnell v. Bachelor*, 429 Pa. 498, 240 A.2d 484 (1968) (where a damaging statement had been obtained, plaintiff should have been permitted to identify the witness as defendant's insurance company investigator); *Fidelity Nat. Title v. Suburban West*, 852 A.2d 318 (Pa. Super. 2004) (evidence of title search company's errors and omissions insurance properly admitted to rebut its defense of limited liability). Where the issue is whether a particular loss was already covered by no-fault insurance, the collateral source rule is not applicable. *Finely v. Lohr*, 45 Pa. D. & C.2d 62 (C.P.1968).

Pennsylvania courts have held that inadvertent reference to insurance does not automatically necessitate a new trial. As Justice Musmanno noted, "we have never said that the mention of insurance, *per se*, like dynamite with a live fuse, will blow up a case." *O'Donnell v. Bachelor*, 240 A.2d at 487 (1968). The aggrieved party must be able to demonstrate prejudice. *See, e.g. Tuttle v. Suznevich*, 394 Pa. 614, 149 A.2d 888 (1958) (innocuous reference to insurance which did not point to any particular person as carrying insurance); *Dolan v. Fissell*, 973 A.2d 1009 (Pa. Super. 2009) (brief inadvertent mention did not render trial unfair); *Carpinet v. Mitchell*, 853 A.2d 366 (Pa. Super. 2004) (no error denying mistrial where question about insurance business referred to defendant's past employment and not to whether she had liability insurance); *Allied Elec. Supply Co. v. Roberts*, 797 A.2d 362 (Pa. Super. 2002) (mention of insurance was brief, inadvertent and not intentionally elicited); *Havasy v. Resnick*, 415 Pa. Super. 480, 609 A.2d 1326 (1992) (passing reference to workmen's compensation did not reasonably infer that plaintiff had sought or received workmen's compensation); *Pushnik v. Winky's Drive-In Rests., Inc.*, 242 Pa. Super. 323, 363 A.2d 1291 (1976) (while there was mention of sending a report to an insurance company, there was no reference to the fact that any of the defendants were insured); *Knapp v. Willys-Ardmore, Inc.*, 174 Pa. Super. 90, 100 A.2d 105 (1953) (passing reference to insurance did not disclose that defendant was insured against the type of claim at issue in case).

Compare: Fed. R. Evid. 411.

Research References

Packel & Poulin, Pennsylvania Evidence § 411-1 (4th ed. 2013)

McCormick, Evidence § 201 (7th ed. 2013)

JUDGE'S QUESTIONS/CONDUCT

See: Pa.R.E. 614.

Objection

- [*Request sidebar*] I object to the court's question. Your Honor, that question goes well beyond seeking clarification; [*it is cross-examination of the witness*], [*you are improperly questioning the witness' credibility*], [*the jury will fairly interpret your (questions/conduct) as indicating a distinct bias against my client*].

Response

- [*Although the court will defend itself, opposing counsel, if asked, should be prepared to argue the correctness of the court's questions*].

Pennsylvania Law

While a trial judge should normally leave questioning of witnesses to counsel, justice may require that a trial judge ask questions when absurd, ambiguous or frivolous testimony is given or testimony is in need of further clarification. *Commonwealth v. Carson*, 913 A.2d 220 (Pa. 2006); *Merrell v. Chartiers Valley School Dist.*, 51 A.3d 286 (Pa. Cmwlth. 2012); *Jordan v. Jackson*, 876 A.2d 443 (Pa. Super. 2005); *Commonwealth v. Manuel*, 844 A.2d 1 (Pa. Super. 2004) (questioning from bench should not show bias or feeling nor be unduly protracted); *Mansour v. Linganna*, 787 A.2d 443 (Pa. Super. 2001); *Tiburzio-Kelly v. Montgomery*, 452 Pa. Super. 158, 681 A.2d 757 (1996); Pa.R.E. 614 (B).

The judge may also comment on the evidence, bring out facts not yet adduced and maintain the pace of the trial by interrupting or setting time limits on counsel. *See Lakeside v. Oregon*, 435 U.S. 333, 341–342, 98 S.Ct. 1091, 1096, 55 L.Ed.2d 319 (1978) ("[T]he judge is not a mere moderator, but is the governor of the trial for the purpose of assuring its proper conduct and of determining questions of law.") At the same time, judges should avoid any conduct that gives the appearance of favoritism, prejudice, or bias for or against one party. *Commonwealth v. Baumhammers*, 960 A.2d 59 (Pa. 2008); *Commonwealth v. Rega*, 933 A.2d 997 (Pa. 2007); *Harman ex rel. Harman v. Borah*, 562 Pa. 455, 756 A.2d 1116 (2000); *Hileman v. Pittsburgh & Lake Erie R.R. Co.*, 546 Pa. 433, 685 A.2d 994 (1996); *Downey v. Weston*, 451 Pa. 259, 301 A.2d 635 (1973); *Commonwealth v. Hogentogler*, 53 A.3d 866 (Pa. Super. 2012). *See Commonwealth v. Hughes*, 865 A.2d 761 (Pa.2004) (court may refer to evidence or summarize testimony during its charge provided that comments are impartial and do not invade province of jury).

Because trial judges have substantial influence over juries, a judge's discretion to question witnesses is not unlimited. *See Starr v. United States*, 153 U.S. 614, 626, 14 S.Ct. 919, 923, 38 L.Ed. 841 (1894) ("the influence of the trial judge on the jury is necessarily and properly of great weight, and . . . his lightest word or intimation is received with deference and may prove controlling"); *Commonwealth v. Hammer*, 508 Pa. 88, 103, 494 A.2d 1054, 1061 (1985) ("Where the judge oversteps the bounds of propriety in examining witnesses, by exhibiting opinion, bias or prejudice, the jury must be deemed to be inordinately impressed by this evidence of the judge's opinion such that the defendant is deprived of a fair and impartial trial."); *Commonwealth v. Myma*, 278 Pa. 505, 123 A. 486 (1924) (an expression indicative of favor or condemnation is quickly reflected in the jury box). A judge cannot assume the role of advocate for either side. *Commonwealth v. McCoy*, 401 Pa. 100, 162 A.2d 636 (1960) (new trial ordered where judge's questions would make satisfactory reading if the prosecuting attorney were putting the questions).

While a judge can question a witness in an effort to make the testimony clear for the jury, this should not include questions which indicate the judge's belief about a witness' honesty, *See Commonwealth v. Williams*, 468 Pa. 453, 364 A.2d 281 (1976), especially when a criminal defendant testifies on his own behalf.

Pa.R.E. 614(C) requires a party to object to the court's interrogation of a witness "at the time or at the next available opportunity when the jury is not present."[1]

A curative instruction from the trial judge may serve to cure any prejudice resulting from the appearance of judicial bias. *Harman ex rel. Harman v. Borah*, 562 Pa. 455, 756 A.2d 1116 (2000).

In the following cases, the trial judge's questions and/or conduct departed from the required impartiality to such an extent as to deny a fair trial: *Hileman v. Pittsburgh and Lake Erie R.R. Co.*, 546 Pa. 433, 685 A.2d 994 (1996) (reversible error in FELA action where court commented to jury that plaintiff did not receive worker's compensation benefits); *Hammer*, 508 Pa. 88, 103, 494 A.2d 1054, 1061 (1985) (trial court repeatedly interrupted defense counsel during direct examination of defendant and defense witnesses to ask prosecutorial-style questions, failed to rule on defense objections and bolstered Commonwealth's case with comments and questions); *Commonwealth v. Williams*, 468 Pa. 453, 364 A.2d 281 (1976) (judge's questions indicated to jury his disbelief of

---

[1]While counsel generally has an obligation to make a timely objection, the *Hammer* court recognized a limited exception to the waiver doctrine. Where it appears from all the circumstances that a timely objection to judicial misconduct would be meaningless, a party may choose to raise the issue for the first time at post-trial motions to preserve it for appellate review. An objection is not meaningless merely because the judge is likely to overrule it. *Harman ex rel. Harman v. Borah*, 562 Pa. 455, 756 A.2d 1116 (2000).

defendant's testimony); *Taylor v. Urban Redevelopment Auth. of Pittsburgh*, 419 Pa. 430, 214 A.2d 623 (1965) (comments in eminent domain case about public officials and size of claim—which jury might interpret as excessive—were prejudicial error); *McKown v. Demmler Properties, Inc.*, 419 Pa. 475, 214 A.2d 626 (1965) (appearance of bias; trial judge greeted defendant on witness stand, told jury they were old friends who worked together as football referees); *Commonwealth v. McCoy*, 401 Pa. 100, 162 A.2d 636 (1960) (judge conveyed distinct partiality to prosecution by repetitive accusation and sarcasm in his questioning of defendant); *Commonwealth v. Rhodes*, 990 A.2d 732 (Pa. Super. 2009) (sentencing judge relied on impermissible considerations including police reports obtained *ex parte*); *Commonwealth v. McIntosh*, 911 A.2d 513 (Pa. Super. 2006), appeal granted, decision aff'd in part, rev'd in part, 592 Pa. 7, 922 A.2d 873 (2007) (judge depreciated seriousness of crime, disregarded psychological harm to victim in fashioning sentence; remand to another judge for resentencing); *DiMonte v. Neumann Med. Ctr.*, 751 A.2d 205 (Pa. Super. 2000) (numerous instances of distracting conduct indicating judge was indifferent to plaintiff's case); *Commonwealth v. Elmore*, 241 Pa. Super. 470, 362 A.2d 348 (1976) (court's examination was protracted and a clear substitution of its judgment of how case should have been tried); *Cheng v. SEPTA*, 981 A.2d 371 (Pa.Cmwlth. 2009) (trial court erred in refusing short continuance to allow defense expert to appear for testimony).

However, every unwise or irrelevant remark by a judge does not compel granting a new trial. *Downey v. Weston*, 451 Pa. 259, 301 A.2d 635 (1973) (facetious remark better left unsaid but no prejudice); *Commonwealth v. Sullivan*, 820 A.2d 795 (Pa. Super. 2003); *Tiburzio-Kelly v. Montgomery*, 452 Pa. Super. 158, 681 A.2d 757 (Pa. Super. 1996) (judge's questions tended to ensure that jury understood difference between established facts and fallible human predictions).

In a criminal case, where the trial judge approves the use of restraints, it must state on the record, outside the presence of the jury, its reasons for permitting them. *Commonwealth v. Smith*, 985 A.2d 886 (Pa. 2009) (court ordered defendant be shackled based on information received from sheriffs).

Standards for Recusal

If a party questions the impartiality of a judge, the proper recourse is a motion for recusal, requesting that the judge make an independent, self-analysis of the ability to be impartial. If content with that inner examination, the judge must then decide whether his or her continued involvement in the case creates an appearance of impropriety and/or would tend to undermine public confidence in the judiciary.

The Pennsylvania Supreme Court presumes judges of this Commonwealth are "honorable, fair and competent," and, when confronted with a recusal demand, have the ability to determine whether they can rule impartially and without prejudice. *Commonwealth v. Druce*, 848 A.2d 104, 108 (Pa. 2004); *Commonwealth v. Kearney*, 92 A.3d 51 (Pa. Super. 2014); *Commonwealth v. Timchak*, 69 A.3d 765 (Pa. Super. 2013).

The party requesting recusal has the burden of producing evidence establishing bias, prejudice or unfairness which raises a substantial doubt as to the judge's ability to preside impartially. *Commonwealth v. Birdsong*, 24 A.3d 319 (Pa. 2011); *Commonwealth v. Flor*, 998 A.2d 606 (Pa. 2010); *Commonwealth v. White*, 557 Pa. 408, 734 A.2d 374 (1999); *Commonwealth v. Abu-Jamal*, 553 Pa. 485, 720 A.2d 79 (1998); *Commonwealth v. Postie*, 110 A.3d 1034 (Pa. Super. 2015); *Cellucci v. Laurel Homeowners Ass'n*, 142 A.3d 1032 (Pa. Cmwlth.

2016). As a general rule, a motion for recusal is initially directed to and decided by the judge whose impartiality is being challenged. *Commonwealth v. Travaglia*, 541 Pa. 108, 661 A.2d 352 (1995); *Commonwealth v. Brown*, 141 A.3d 491 (Pa. Super. 2016); *Vargo v. Schwartz*, 940 A.2d 459 (Pa. Super. 2007). A party seeking recusal must raise the objection at the earliest possible moment or be time barred. *Commonwealth v. Miller*, 951 A.2d 322 (Pa. 2008). In considering a recusal request, the judge must first make a conscientious determination of his or her ability to act in an impartial manner, free of personal bias or interest in the outcome. The judge must then consider whether his or her continued involvement in the case creates an appearance of impropriety and/or would tend to undermine public confidence in the judiciary. *Goodheart v. Casey*, 523 Pa. 188, 565 A.2d 757 (1989); *Commonwealth v. Stevenson*, 829 A.2d 701 (Pa. Super. 2003). When a judge rules that he or she can hear and dispose of a case fairly and without prejudice, that decision will not be overturned on appeal except for abuse of discretion. *Commonwealth v. Blakeney*, 946 A.2d 645 (Pa. 2008); *In re Bridgeport Fire Litigation*, 5 A.3d 1250 (Pa. Super. 2010); *Commonwealth v. King*, 990 A.2d 1172 (Pa. Super. 2010).

The Supreme Court has said where the appearance of judicial impropriety has been established, no showing of actual prejudice is required. *In Re Lokuta*, 11 A.3d 427 (Pa. 2011); *Joseph v. Scranton Times L.P.*, 987 A.2d 633 (Pa. 2009). See generally *In re Adoption of L.J.B.*, 18 A.3d 1098 (Pa. 2011) (sua sponte removal as an exercise of supervisory power without hearing at trial level).

See also Code of Judicial Conduct Canon 3(C) ("A judge should disqualify himself in a proceeding in which his impartiality might reasonably be questioned").

An order denying a motion for recusal is not a

final appealable order nor an appealable collateral order. *In re Bridgeport Fire Litigation*, 51 A.3d 224 (Pa. Super. 2012).

Compare: Fed. R. Evid. 614.

Research References

Packel & Poulin, Pennsylvania Evidence § 614-2 (4th ed. 2013)

McCormick, Evidence § 8 (7th ed. 2013)

JUDICIAL ADMISSION

Objection

- *[To a question]* Objection. The question is directed to facts judicially admitted by the *[specify source, e.g., complaint, answer, stipulation, answers to requests for admission, or, by counsel's own statement]*. Those judicially admitted facts cannot be contradicted.

- *[To an answer]* Objection, the response contradicts a judicially admitted fact. I move the answer be stricken and the jury be instructed not to consider it for any purpose.

Response

- The potential responses are limited because a judicially admitted fact cannot be contradicted by the party who made the admission. If there are grounds, counsel might argue the fact was not admitted or that the alleged admission was not unequivocal and, therefore, the evidence should be received. Pa.R.C.P. 4014, Request for Admission, subdivision (d) does allow the court to permit withdrawal or amendment of an admission, "when the presentation of the merits of the action will be subserved thereby and the party who obtained the admission fails to satisfy the court that withdrawal or amendment will prejudice him in maintaining his action or defense on the merits." Where appropriate, counsel can argue that a party cannot admit a legal theory or question of law.

Pennsylvania Law

A judicial admission is an express waiver made in court or prior to trial by a party or his attorney, conceding for the purposes of trial, the truth of the admitted fact. *Century Sur. Co. v. Essington Auto Center*, 140 A.3d 46 (Pa. Super. 2016) (collecting cases); *Estate of Sacchetti v. Sachetti*, 128 A.3d 273 (Pa. Super. 2015) (judicial admissions are conclusive in the cause of action in which they are made, and any appeals thereof, and the opposing party need not offer further evidence to prove the fact admitted); *Newman Dev. v. Genuardi's Family Market*, 98 A.3d 645 (Pa. Super. 2014) (judicial admissions are conclusive, whereas evidentiary admissions may always be contradicted or explained); *Cogley v. Duncan*, 32 A.3d 1288 (Pa. Super. 2011) (judicial admissions are limited to factual matters otherwise requiring evidentiary proof). It has the effect of a confessory pleading in that the admitted fact is deemed to be conclusively established and no evidence need be offered to prove it. A judicial admission cannot be subsequently contradicted by the party who made it. *Rizzo v. Haines*, 520 Pa. 484, 555 A.2d 58 (1989); *Wills v. Kane*, 2 Grant 60, 63 (Pa. 1853) ("When a man alleges a fact in a court of justice, for his advantage, he shall not be allowed to contradict it afterwards. It is against good morals to permit such double dealing in the administration of justice."); *Sherrill v. W.C.A.B. (School District of Philadelphia)*, 154 Pa.Cmwlth. 492, 624 A.2d 240 (1993); *John B. Conomos, Inc. v. Sun Co., Inc.*, 831 A.2d 696 (Pa. Super. 2003); *Nasim v. Shamrock Welding Supply Co.*, 387 Pa. Super. 225, 563 A.2d 1266 (1989); *Jewelcor Jewelers & Distribs., Inc. v. Corr*, 373 Pa. Super. 536, 542 A.2d 72 (1988). For an averment to qualify as a judicial admission, it must be a clear and unequivocal admission of fact. *Jones v. Constantino*, 429 Pa. Super. 73, 631 A.2d 1289 (1993) (no admission where evidence could be reasonably construed to admit of more than one meaning).

As one treatise has said: "Judicial admissions are not evidence at all but rather have the effect of withdrawing a fact from contention." Graham, Handbook of Federal Evidence, § 801.26.

Judicial admissions may arise from: a party's statement in his pleadings, *Tops Apparel Mfg. Co. v. Rothman*, 430 Pa. 583, 244 A.2d 436 (1968); *Steinhouse v. Herman Miller, Inc.*, 443 Pa. Super. 395, 661 A.2d 1379 (1995); *Nasim v. Shamrock Welding*

Supply Co., 387 Pa. Super. 225, 563 A.2d 1266 (1989)); failure to file a responsive pleading, *Milan v. Commonwealth, Dept. of Transp.*, 153 Pa.Cmwlth. 276, 620 A.2d 721 (1993); a response or failure to respond to a request for admission, Pa.R.Civ.P. 4014(d); answers to interrogatories, *Wilkerson v. Allied Van Lines, Inc.*, 360 Pa. Super. 523, 521 A.2d 25 (1987); a stipulation of facts, *Phillips v. Schoenberger*, 369 Pa. Super. 52, 534 A.2d 1075 (1987); *Commonwealth v. Lemanski*, 365 Pa. Super. 332, 529 A.2d 1085 (1987); *Park v. Greater Delaware Valley Savings & Loan Ass'n*, 362 Pa. Super. 54, 523 A.2d 771 (1987); a statement of fact made at trial by the party's attorney, *Lower Mount Bethel Tp. v. North River Co.*, 41 A.3d 156 (Pa. Cmwlth. 2012); concession in trial brief and oral representation to the court, *City of Philadelphia v. F.A. Realty*, 95 A.3d 377 (Pa. Cmwlth. 2014); *In re Petition to Contest Gen. Election*, 695 A.2d 476 (Pa.Cmwlth. 1997). *See also Glick v. White Motor Co.*, 458 F.2d 1287, 1291 (3d Cir.1972), "The scope of judicial admissions is restricted to matters of fact which otherwise would require evidentiary proof, and does not include counsel's statement of his conception of the legal theory of a case."

The court is bound by judicially admitted facts, *Park v. Greater Delaware Valley Savings & Loan Assoc.*, 362 Pa. Super. 54, 523 A.2d 771 (1987), but not by the pleader's conclusions of law. *Newman Dev. v. Genuardi's Family Market*, supra (a party cannot admit a legal theory or question of law); *In Re Paxson Trust I*, 893 A.2d 99, 113 n.10 (Pa. Super. 2006); *Silco Vending Co. v. Quinn*, 461 A.2d 1324 (Pa. Super. 1983). A judicial admission is binding only in the litigation in which it is made. In any other suit, it operates merely as an evidentiary admission. *Dale Mfg. Co. v. Bressi*, 491 Pa. 493, 421 A.2d 653 (1980); *Light v. Miller*, 303 Pa. Super. 527, 450 A.2d 51 (1982).

The rationale for treating judicial admissions as conclusive is that they expedite the trial of cases by eliminating the need for proof of facts that are not disputed. *Durkin v. Equine Clinics, Inc.*, 376 Pa. Super. 557, 546 A.2d 665 (1988). Statements made by a party while testifying at trial or in deposition do not serve the same procedural purpose and, therefore, are not treated as judicial admissions. Such statements may be contradicted or explained. *Thomas v. Hutchinson*, 442 Pa. 118, 275 A.2d 23 (1971) (deposition); *Szawlinsky v. Campbell*, 402 Pa. 651, 168 A.2d 581 (1961) (testimony).

Pa.R.Civ.P. 1020(c) specifically permits alternative pleading. Accordingly, judicial admissions should not be applied to undermine the right to allege inconsistent facts in alternative pleadings. When a pleading is amended or withdrawn, the superceded portion ceases to be considered as a binding judicial admission. It does, however, continue in force and effect as an evidentiary admission which may be controverted or explained by the party who made it.

In *General Equipment Manufacturers v. Westfield Insurance Co.*, 430 Pa. Super. 526, 635 A.2d 173 (1993), it was held that an averment in a party's pleading was not admissible when offered by a party-opponent who had denied the averment in a responsive pleading. Apparently, the two conflicting judicial admissions cancelled each other out.

Compare: *Medcom Holding Co. v. Baxter Travenol Labs.*, 106 F.3d 1388 (7th Cir.1997) (binding judicial admissions are any deliberate, clear and unequivocal statement, either written or oral, made in the course of judicial proceedings).

Research References

Packel & Poulin, Pennsylvania Evidence § 127 (4th ed. 2013)

McCormick, Evidence Chapter 25 (7th ed. 2013)

JUDICIAL NOTICE

See: Pa.R.E. 201.

Form

- I request that the court take judicial notice of the fact that [*specify*].

Response

- Objection. The fact in question is not the subject of common knowledge nor is it verifiable with certainty. Therefore, it is not the proper subject of judicial notice.

Pennsylvania Law

Certain facts are beyond any serious dispute because they are of such common knowledge or accurate determination that evidence of their existence is unnecessary. The doctrine of judicial notice is intended to avoid the necessity for the formal introduction of evidence in certain cases when there is no real need for it. *Commonwealth v. Brown*, 839 A.2d 433 (Pa. Super. 2003); *Interest of D.S.*, 424 Pa. Super. 350, 622 A.2d 954 (1993). A court may take judicial notice at any stage of a proceeding. *Drake Mfg. Co., Inc. v. Polyflow, Inc.*, 109 A.3d 250 (Pa. Super. 2015); *Commonwealth v. Semenza*, 127 A.3d 1 (Pa. Super. 2015) (appeals court would take judicial notice that 2010 census showed population in old Forge, Pa. was 96.9% Caucasian).

The fact to be noticed must be one not subject to reasonable dispute in that it is either (1) generally well known within the territorial jurisdiction of the trial court, or (2) capable of accurate and ready determination by resort to sources whose accuracy cannot reasonably be questioned. *Commonwealth v. Casper*, 481 Pa. 143, 392 A.2d 287 (1978); *HYK Const. Co., Inc. v. Smithfield Tp.*, 8 A.3d 1009 (Pa. Cmwlth. 2010); *Kinley v. Bierly*,

876 A.2d 419 (Pa. Super. 2005).

If the fact to be noticed is not generally known, the court may take notice if the existence of the fact can be ascertained by resort to sources whose accuracy cannot reasonably be questioned. Such sources include historical works, science and art books, language and medical journals, dictionaries, calendars, encyclopedias, commercial lists, maps, charts, statutes and legislative reports. *See, e.g., Niedermayer v. Commonwealth, D.O.T.*, 797 A.2d 409 (Pa.Cmwlth.2002), limited by *Slaughter v. Commonwealth, Dept. of Transp., Bureau of Licensing*, 819 A.2d 1209 (Pa.Cmwlth.2003) (judge's age and dates of service appearing in Pennsylvania Manual).

Pennsylvania courts have applied the doctrine of judicial notice to (1) adjudicative facts, (2) legislative facts, and (3) Pennsylvania and foreign law. The scope of Pa.R.E. 201 is confined to adjudicative facts which are facts about the events, persons and places involved in the lawsuit. Legislative facts, on the other hand, are used exclusively by the judge when he is developing law and policy. They are used not to discover the facts to which the law will be applied, but rather to discover and develop the law itself. *Urey v. Zoning Hearing Bd. Of Hermitage*, 806 A.2d 502 (Pa.Cmwlth.2002); *In Interest of D.S.*, 424 Pa. Super. 350, 622 A.2d 954 (1993).

The party wishing the court to take judicial notice must supply the information to the court and request that it be admitted into evidence. *U.S. Bank, N.A. v. Pautenis*, 118 A.3d 386 (Pa. Super. 2015) (notice refused where no information was supplied to permit to conclusion that the "fact" was subject to judicial notice). The court may also take judicial notice of certain facts on its own motion. When the doctrine is invoked, the opposing party must be accorded the due process right to disprove the fact sought to be noticed if he believes it disputable. *Appeal of Albert*, 372 Pa. 13, 92 A.2d

663 (1952); *Wells v. Pittsburgh Bd. of Pub. Ed.*, 31 Pa.Cmwlth. 1, 374 A.2d 1009 (1977); *see Floors, Inc. v. Altig*, 963 A.2d 912 (Pa. Super. 2009) and *Commonwealth v. Covert*, 322 Pa. Super. 192, 469 A.2d 248 (1983) (judicial notice should not serve to deny the opposing party the chance to disprove the fact sought to be judicially noticed). If the evidence derived from judicial notice remains unrebutted, it may support a finding of fact.

Prior to the Rules of Evidence, the taking of judicial notice was discretionary. Pa.R.E. 201(d) now provides that judicial notice by the court of adjudicative facts is mandatory "if requested by a party and supplied with the necessary information."

A court may judicially notice an indisputable fact even though it establishes an element of a crime. *See, e.g. Commonwealth v. Bigelow*, 250 Pa. Super. 330, 333 n. 2, 378 A.2d 961, 963 n. 2 (1977), *aff'd*, 484 Pa. 476, 399 A.2d 392 (1979) (court could have taken judicial notice that Philadelphia is a city of the first class in prosecution for carrying a firearm on a public street in a city of the first class); *Commonwealth v. Morgan*, 265 Pa. Super. 225, 401 A.2d 1182 (1979) (dicta) (in determining whether an element of possessing an instrument of crime existed, court may take judicial notice that a gun is commonly used for criminal purposes).

The following cases illustrate the historical application of the doctrine:

Adjudicative Facts: (1) historical facts, if sufficiently notorious: *Wiley v. Pennsylvania Bd. of Prob. & Parole*, 801 A.2d 644 (Pa.Cmwlth.2002) (terrorist attack on Sept. 11, 2001); *Fatemi v. Fatemi*, 371 Pa. Super. 101, 537 A.2d 840 (1988) (civil unrest in Iran and open warfare with Iraq); *Appeal of Albert*, 372 Pa. 13, 92 A.2d 663 (1952) (the Communist Party advocates the violent overthrow of the government); *Alko Exp. Lines v. Pennsylvania Pub. Util. Comm'n.*, 152 Pa. Super. 27, 30 A.2d 440 (1943) (economic effects of the Depression); **(2)**

facts capable of accurate determination: *Commonwealth v. Laniewski*, 427 Pa. 455, 235 A.2d 136 (1967) (the California Angels entered the American League in April, 1961); *In re Siemens' Estate*, 346 Pa. 610, 31 A.2d 280 (1943) (the meaning of the abbreviation "Penna. S.P.C.A."); *Commonwealth v. Britton*, 134 A.3d 83 (Pa. Super. 2016) (last day to file notice of appeal); *Meyer v. Law Firm of Malone Middleman*, 95 A.3d 893 (Pa. Super. 2014), rev'd on other grounds, 137 A.3d 1247 (Pa. 2016) (original attorney died in auto accident); **(3) geographical facts:** *Goff v. Armbrecht Motor Truck Sales, Inc.*, 284 Pa. Super. 544, 426 A.2d 628 (1980) (Youngstown, Ohio is approximately ten miles from the Pennsylvania border); **(4) scientific facts:** *Meehan v. Philadelphia Electric Co.*, 424 Pa. 51, 225 A.2d 900 (1967) (electricity is a highly dangerous agent); **(5) public records:** *Commonwealth v. Tau Kappa Epsilon*, 609 A.2d 791, 793 n.2 (Pa. 1992); *In re Estate of Schulz*, 139 A.2d 560 (Pa. 1958); *Krenzel v. SEPTA*, 840 A.2d 450 (Pa. Cmwlth. 2003) (judicial notice can be taken of pleadings and judgments in other proceedings where appropriate); **(6) miscellaneous:** *Miller v. Commonwealth*, 804 A.2d 73 (Pa.Cmwlth.2002) (South Carolina drivers licenses are issued by Department of Motor Vehicles, a part of the South Carolina Department of Public Safety); *Commonwealth v. Weller*, 399 Pa. Super. 168, 581 A.2d 1390 (1990) (lite beer was "malt or brewed beverage" within meaning of statutory prohibition); *Commonwealth v. Allen*, 394 Pa. Super. 127, 575 A.2d 131 (1990) (laboratory staff qualified to take blood samples in DUI case); *Keirs by Keirs v. Weber Nat'l Stores, Inc.*, 352 Pa. Super. 111, 507 A.2d 406 (1986) (a particular coat could be described as an ordinary baseball jacket).

Legislative Facts: *In re Estate of Teaschenko*, 393 Pa. Super. 355, 574 A.2d 649 (1990) ($232 per month in public assistance was not enough money to allow a mother to contribute substantially to child's support); *Moore v. Borough of Ridley Park*, 135 Pa.Cmwlth. 555, 581 A.2d 711 (1990) (fundamental role of police officer is to protect public and to be available to respond to calls for aid); *Petro v. Kennedy Tp. Bd. of Comm'rs.*, 49 Pa.Cmwlth. 305, 411 A.2d 849 (1980) (the people have a compelling interest in imposing strict requirements in the selection of police).

Law: *Commonwealth v. Taylor*, 137 A.3d 611 (Pa. Super. 2016) (prior violations and convictions); *V.S. v. Dept of Public Welfare*, 131 A.3d 523 (Pa.Cmwlth 2015) (public statutes); *Valley Forge Sewer Authority v. Hipwell*, 121 A.3d 1164 (Pa.Cmwlth. 2015) (local ordinances); *In re Dawkins*, 98 A.3d 755 (Pa. Cmwlth. 2014) (election information on Dept of State's website); *Hill v. Dept of Corrections*, 64 A.3d 1159 (Pa. Cmwlth. 2013) (policies and handbooks on DOC website); *Department of Auditor General v. SERS*, 836 A.2d 1053 (Pa. Cmwlth. 2003) (judicial notice of General Assembly's legislative journals); *Cosom v. Marcotte*, 760 A.2d 886 (Pa. Super. 2000), appeal granted, order vacated 570 Pa. 78, 808 A.2d 177 (2002) (FDA rulings with respect to pedicle screws used in spinal operations); *Givnish v. Commonwealth, State Bd. of Funeral Dirs.*, 134 Pa.Cmwlth. 146, 578 A.2d 545 (1990) (regulations of State Board of Funeral Directors); *Jackson v. Southeastern Pennsylvania Transp. Auth.*, 129 Pa.Cmwlth. 596, 566 A.2d 638 (1989) (State Highway Act of 1961 designated street as state highway); *Goldberg v. Friedrich*, 279 Pa. 572, 124 A. 186 (1924) (Child Labor Act of 1915); *see also* 42 Pa.C.S.A. § 5327 (determination of foreign law); 42 Pa.C.S.A. § 6107 (ordinances of municipal corporation *shall be* judicially noticed); *Seitel Data, Ltd. v. Center Tp.*, 92 A.3d 851 (Pa.Cmwlth. 2014); *Commonwealth v. Marcus*, 690 A.2d 842 (Pa. Cmwlth.1997); *Dream Mile Club v. Tobyhanna Tp.*, 150 Pa.Cmwlth. 309, 615 A.2d 931 (1992) (counsel should take the initiative in requesting that the court take judicial notice of an ordinance); 45

Pa.C.S.A. § 506 (the contents of the Pennsylvania Code, the permanent supplement thereto and the Pennsylvania Bulletin).

Judicial notice **was refused** in the following cases because the fact sought to be noticed either was not a matter of common knowledge or was not capable of ready determination: *Kinley v. Bierly*, 876 A.2d 419 (Pa. Super. 2005) (implication that everyone knows stallions are vicious and will bite); *Commonwealth v. Brown*, 839 A.2d 433 (Pa. Super. 2003) (abuse of discretion in sentencing by taking judicial notice of distance determined by Map Quest between school and site of drug deal); *Grover v. Commonwealth, Dep't of Transp.*, 734 A.2d 941 (Pa.Cmwlth.1999) (meaning of PennDOT's work identification number on certification of motorist's DUI conviction); *Overbeck v. Cates*, 700 A.2d 970 (Pa. Super. 1997) (reinflation of tire which has been operated in flat condition can result in injury or death); *In Interest of D.S.*, 424 Pa. Super. 350, 622 A.2d 954 (1993) (whether facility in which assault victim and delinquent resided was "a school" for purposes of criminal statute); *Commonwealth, Dep't of Transp. v. Moss*, 146 Pa.Cmwlth. 330, 605 A.2d 1279 (1992) (medical effects of a migraine headache); *Commonwealth v. Cassidy*, 103 Pa.Cmwlth. 582, 521 A.2d 59 (1987) (side effects of blood pressure medicine combined with alcohol); *Commonwealth v. Casper*, 481 Pa. 143, 392 A.2d 287 (1978) (defendant was a well-known political figure in the community); *Wells v. Pittsburgh Bd. of Pub. Ed.*, 31 Pa.Cmwlth. 1, 374 A.2d 1009 (1977) (impossibility of operating school system during teachers' strike); *Savoy v. Beneficial Consumer Disc. Co.*, 503 Pa. 74, 468 A.2d 465 (1983) (redbook value of automobile in the absence of evidence of its actual condition). See also *V.B. v. J.E.B.*, 55 A.3d 1193 (Pa. Super. 2012) (in child custody case, reversible error to take judicial notice of facts established at a prior proceeding where parties were not the same).

"Official notice" is the administrative agency counterpart to judicial notice. The doctrine authorizes the fact finder to waive proof of facts that cannot seriously be contested. *Ramos v. Pa. Bd. of Probation and Parole*, 954 A.2d 107 (Pa. Cmwlth. 2008); *Falasco v. Pa. Bd. of Probation and Parole*, 521 A.2d 991 (Pa. Cmwlth. 1987) (agency can take official notice of facts obvious and notorious to an expert in the agency's field, facts contained in reports and records in the agency's files as well as facts obvious and notorious to average person). See *Castello v. Unemployment Comp. Bd. of Rev.*, 86 A.3d 294 (Pa.Cmwlth. 2013).

Official notice is a broader doctrine than judicial notice and recognizes the special competence of the administrative agency in its particular field and also recognizes that the agency is a storehouse of information on that field consisting of reports, case files, statistics and other data relevant to its work. *Falasco* (collecting cases).

Compare: Fed. R. Evid. 201.

Research References

Packel & Poulin, Pennsylvania Evidence § 201-1–201-3 (4th ed. 2013)

McCormick, Evidence §§ 328–335 (7th ed. 2013)

JURY INSTRUCTIONS

See: Pa.R.C.P. 227(b); Pa.R.Crim.P. 647(B); see also Pa.R.C.P. 226.

Illustration

[*at sidebar*] I object.

- The instruction misstates the law because [*specify citing controlling legal authority*].
- There is no factual support in the record for the instruction [*specify*].
- The court's instruction will mislead or confuse the jury because [*specify*].
- The [*plaintiff/defendant*] is entitled to the instruction which I submitted on the issue [*specify issue citing controlling legal authority*], and it is error to have omitted it.

Pennsylvania Law

In a civil trial, objections to jury instructions are governed by Rule 227(b) of the Rules of Civil Procedure. The Rule provides:

(b) Unless specially allowed by the court, all exceptions to the charge to the jury shall be taken before the jury retires. On request of any party all such exceptions and arguments thereon shall be made out of hearing of the jury.

The analogue to Rule 227(b) in a criminal trial is Pa.R.Crim.P. 647(B)[1] Applicable to all trials is Pennsylvania Rule of Appellate Procedure 302(b) which states:

A general exception to the charge to the jury will not

---

[1]Rule 647(B) provides:

No portions of the charge nor omissions therefrom may be assigned as error, unless specific objections are made thereto before the jury retires to deliberate. All such objections shall be made beyond the hearing of the jury.

preserve an issue for appeal. Specific exception shall be taken to the language or omission complained of.

By requiring parties *to make a timely and specific objection* before the jury retires, the rules ensure that the trial court is made aware of and given an opportunity to correct any error in the charge, including special interrogatories, before the jury begins its deliberations. *McNeil v. Owens-Corning Fiberglas Corp.*, 545 Pa. 209, 680 A.2d 1145 (1996); *Dilliplaine v. Lehigh Valley Trust Co.*, 457 Pa. 255, 322 A.2d 114 (1974); *Braun v. Wal-Mart Stores, Inc.*, 24 A.3d 875 (Pa. Super. 2011); *Carpinet v. Mitchell*, 853 A.2d 366 (Pa. Super. 2004). Where counsel fails to make a specific objection, the alleged error will be deemed waived and will not be considered by a reviewing court. *Commonwealth v. Diggs*, 949 A.2d 873 (Pa. 2008); *Commonwealth v. Moury*, 992 A.2d 162 (Pa. Super. 2010); *Commonwealth v. Marquez*, 980 A.2d 145 (Pa. Super. 2009); *Commonwealth v. Dorm*, 971 A.2d 1284 (Pa. Super. 2009); *Commonwealth v. Baker*, 963 A.2d 495 (Pa. Super. 2008); *Commonwealth v. Kerrigan*, 920 A.2d 190 (Pa. Super. 2007).

Prudent counsel will make objections at the charging conference and then renew all objections to the instructions at the close of the charge. On both occasions, objections must be made on the record and outside the hearing of the jury. See generally *Chaudhuri v. Capital Area Transit*, 131 A.3d 589 (Pa.Cmwlth. 2016) (failure to object to supplemental charge waived the issue); *Phillips v. Lock*, 86 A.3d 906 (Pa. Super. 2014) (an exception to court's refusal to charge jury as requested is sufficient to preserve the issue for appeal, even of there is no specific objection to the charge at trial).

Some General Rules Applicable To Jury Instructions

When a court instructs a jury, the objective is to explain to the jury how it should approach its task and the factors it should consider in reaching its verdict. *Commonwealth v. Chambers*, 980 A.2d 35 (Pa. 2009).

A trial court has wide discretion in fashioning jury instructions. *Commonwealth v. Bennett*, 57 A.3d 1185 (Pa. 2012); *Commonwealth v. Philistin*, 53 A.3d 1 (Pa. 2012); *Copper ex rel. Cooper v. Lankenau Hosp.*, 51 A.3d 183 (Pa. 2012); *Commonwealth v. Williams*, 980 A.2d 510 (Pa. 2009). The trial court may refuse to give a requested point for charge when the substance of that request has already been given in another general or specific instruction. *Gunn v. Grossman*, 748 A.2d 1235 (Pa. Super. 2000). The court is not bound to use the exact language of a requested charge; it may choose another form of expression so long as it adequately and clearly covers the subject. *Commonwealth v. Carson*, 913 A.2d 220 (Pa. 2006); *Commonwealth v. Johnson*, 572 Pa. 283 (2002); *Commonwealth v. Hawkins*, 567 Pa. 310, 787 A.2d 292 (2001); *Sears Roebuck v. 69th Street Retail Mail*, 126 A.3d 959 (Pa. Super. 2015); *Commonwealth v. Barnett*, 121 A.3d 534 (Pa. Super. 2015); *Commonwealth v. Charleston*, 94 A.3d 1012 (Pa. Super. 2014); *Commonwealth v. Pope*, 14 A.3d 139 (Pa. Super. 2011); *Commonwealth v. Willis*, 990 A.2d 773 (Pa. Super. 2010); *Commonwealth v. Williams*, 959 A.2d 1272 (Pa. Super. 2008). The court may refuse to submit for the jury's consideration a point for charge that is not strictly in accordance with the facts in evidence or the law in the case. *Schneider v. Lindenmuth-Cline Agency, Inc.*, 423 Pa. Super. 73, 620 A.2d 505 (1993). Likewise, the trial court may refuse points for charge that require qualification or modification, as the court is not responsible to mold or restate points that are not accurate as drawn. *Schneider v. Lindenmuth-Cline Agency, Inc.*, 423 Pa. Super. 73, 620 A.2d 505 (1993); *see also Ferrer v. Trustees of University of Pa.*, 573 Pa. 310, 825 A.2d 591 (2002) (argumentative instruction properly refused; jury instructions are not intended to supplement arguments of opposing counsel). The court may refer to portions of the evidence during its charge, but it must remain absolutely impartial and not invade the province of the jury. *Commonwealth v. Hughes*, 581 Pa. 274, 865 A.2d 761 (2004); *Commonwealth v. Pursell*, 555 Pa. 233, 724 A.2d 293 (1999).

When a jury returns on its own motion and indicates confusion, the court has a duty to give such additional instructions as the court may deem necessary to clarify the jury's doubt or confusion. *Chicchi v. Southeastern Pa. Transp. Auth.*, 727 A.2d 604 (Pa.Cmwlth.1999). A reiterative instruction is a critical stage of a criminal trial and counsel have the right to be in attendance. *Commonwealth v. Johnson*, 574 Pa. 5, 828 A.2d 1009 (2003) (exclusion of counsel during reiterative instruction presumptively prejudicial to defendant, requiring new trial.)

A jury charge is erroneous if the charge as a whole is inadequate, unclear, or has a tendency to mislead or confuse the jury rather than clarify a material issue. *Tincher v. Omega Flex, Inc.*, 104 A.3d 328 (Pa. 2014); *Passarello v. Grumbine*, 87 A.3d 285 (Pa. 2014); *Commonwealth v. Conaway*, 105 A.3d 755 (Pa. Super. 2014) (reversible error to instruct jury that prosecution had established an element of the crime); *Drew v. Work*, 95 A.3d 324 (Pa. Super. 2014); *Hyrcza v. West Penn Allegheny Health*, 978 A.2d 961 (Pa. Super. 2009).

The Pennsylvania Suggested Standard Jury Instructions are not controlling and merely reflect the developed state of the law to the date of their publication. *Commonwealth v. Simpson*, 66 A.3d 253 (Pa. 2013); *Maloney v. Valley Medical Facilities, Inc.*, 984 A.2d 478 (Pa. 2009).

Compare: Fed.R.Civ.P. 51; Fed.R.Crim.P. 30.

Research References

Packel & Poulin, Pennsylvania Evidence § 103-1

(4th ed. 2013)

Gibbons, Kraut & Edgar, West's Pennsylvania Forms and Commentary—Civil Procedure, Chapter 58, Jury Instructions

Haydock and Sonsteng's Trial: Advocacy Before Judges, Jurors and Arbitrators Chapter 12 (4th ed. 2011)

LAY WITNESS OPINION

See: Pa.R.E. 701.

Objection

- Objection. The witness is being asked to give an opinion [*that is not based on personal knowledge*], [*that would not be helpful to the jury because (explain)*], [*that can only be given by an expert.*]

Response

- The question does not seek an expert opinion. The witness has firsthand knowledge and his opinion will be helpful because [*explain*].

Pennsylvania Law

Lay opinion testimony is admissible when it is: (a) rationally based on the perception of the witness, (b) helpful to a clear understanding of the witness' testimony or the determination of a fact in issue, and (c) not based on scientific, technical, or other specialized knowledge within the scope of Rule 702. Pa.R.E. 701; *Commonwealth v. Buterbaugh*, 91 A.3d 1247 (Pa. Super. 2014); *Cave v. Wampler Foods, Inc.*, 961 A.2d 864 (Pa. Super. 2008); *Carpenter v. Pleasant*, 759 A.2d 411 (Pa. Cmwlth.2000).

The witness also must meet the "personal knowledge" requirements set forth in Pa.R.E. 602. *McManamon v. Washko*, 906 A.2d 1259, 1276 (Pa. Super. 2006); *Slappo v. J's Development Assocs., Inc.*, 791 A.2d 409 (Pa. Super. 2002).

A lay witness may testify as to an ultimate issue of fact, so long as the testimony is otherwise admissible. Pa.R.E. 704; *Lewis v. Mellor*, 259 Pa. Super. 509, 393 A.2d 941 (1978) (no abuse of discretion admitting motorist's testimony that only with luck and skill could driver of northbound car have found another way to avoid southbound car which had crossed over medial barrier). The lay witness may not, however, testify as to a legal conclusion, such as the correct interpretation of a contract or whether conduct met the reasonable person standard because without legal training such testimony is not helpful. *Commonwealth v. McLean*, 387 Pa. Super. 354, 564 A.2d 216 (1989) (lay opinion on whether parties were in common law marriage excluded).

The Pa.R.E. 701(a) requirement that a lay witness' opinion be rationally based on the perception of the witness simply means that the opinion or inference is based on firsthand knowledge and is one that a normal person would form on the basis of observed facts. *Deeds v. University of Pa. Medical Center*, 110 A.3d 1009 (Pa. Super. 2015) (fact testimony may include opinion or inferences so long as those opinions or inferences are rationally based on the witness's perceptions and helpful to a clear understanding of his or her testimony); *Ratti v. Wheeling Pittsburgh Steel Corp.*, 758 A.2d 695 (Pa. Super. 2000).

The helpfulness requirement (Pa.R.E. 701(b)) is designed to guard against the admission of opinions which merely tell the jury what result to reach. If attempts are made to introduce meaningless assertions which amount to little more than choosing up sides, such evidence should be excluded for lack of helpfulness. *See* Jack B. Weinstein and Margaret A. Berger, Weinstein's Federal Evidence § 701.05 (2d ed. 2000) ("[L]ay testimony generally is not helpful on matters that are essentially a jury question, such as credibility issues").

Lay opinion is appropriate where it is difficult for a witness to explain through factual testimony the combination of circumstances that led him to formulate the opinion. *Commonwealth v. Knight*, 469 Pa. 57, 364 A.2d 902 (1976) (lay opinion permits evidence that constitutes shorthand renditions of total situation or statements of collective facts).

In *Asplundh Mfg. Div. v. Benton Harbor Eng'g.*, 57 F.3d 1190, 1196–98 (3d Cir.1995), the Third Circuit summarized the "prototypical" or "core area" examples of opinions routinely admitted under Fed. R. Evid. 701 as including: appearance of persons and things, identity, the manner of conduct, competency of a person, degrees of light or darkness, sound, size, weight, distance, speed, value of property and other situations in which the differences between fact and opinion blur and it is difficult or cumbersome to elicit an answer from the witness that will not be expressed in the form of an opinion.

Pa.R.E. 701 was amended in 2001 in order to distinguish more precisely between opinions that may be rendered by lay persons and those that may be rendered only by experts. Pa.R.E. 701 provides that scientific, technical or other specialized knowledge may not form the basis for opinions and inferences of lay witnesses. The amendment is intended to eliminate the risk that the reliability requirements for admissibility of scientific, technical or specialized knowledge under Pa.R.E. 702 and the disclosure requirements of Pa.R.Civ.P. 4003.5 and Pa.R.Crim.P. 573 will be evaded by offering an expert as a lay witness under Pa.R.E. 701. Thus, a party cannot use Pa.R.E. 701 as a back door attempt to admit testimony of expert nature under guise of lay opinion and thus strip court of its *"Frye"* gatekeeping functions.

The following cases are instructive. **Lay opinion excluded:** *Gibson v. W.C.A.B. (Armco Stainless)*, 580 Pa. 470, 861 A.2d 938 (2004) (material contained asbestos); *Young v. Commonwealth, Dep't of Transp.*, 560 Pa. 373, 744 A.2d 1276 (2000) (eye witnesses without specialized skill, knowledge or training not competent to testify as to whether warning signs should have been placed over three miles from road construction site); *Slappo*, 791 A.2d

409 (Pa. Super. 2002) (no error to exclude witness from testifying as to value of trees removed from land; no evidence witness had firsthand knowledge); *Ratti*, 758 A.2d 695 (Pa. Super. 2000) (foreman properly excluded from testifying which contractor had obligation to monitor steam line; no showing that witness was involved in drafting or negotiating contract documents or had personal knowledge of their contents); *In re Involuntary Commitment of Barbour*, 733 A.2d 1286 (Pa. Super. 1999) (lay witness testimony that appellant suffered from severe bi-polar disorder). **Lay opinion admitted:** *Commonwealth v. Boczkowski*, 577 Pa. 421, 846 A.2d 75 (2004) (fellow inmate permitted to testify that defendant's demeanor was "serious" when he admitted it was stupid to kill both wives in same manner; demeanor testimony was based on personal observation)**;** *Commonwealth v. Counterman*, 553 Pa. 370, 719 A.2d 284 (1998) (hospital social worker's opinion that defendant did not appear to be grieving over deaths of his children and that wife appeared frightened of defendant); *Commonwealth v. Allison*, 550 Pa. 4, 703 A.2d 16 (1997) (observations concerning apparent physical condition or appearance of another); *Weir by Gasper v. Estate of Ciao,* 521 Pa. 491, 556 A.2d 819 (1989) (opinion as to mental competence of transferor of real estate); *Commonwealth v. Stickle*, 484 Pa. 89, 398 A.2d 957 (1979) (detectives could opine that marks on defendant's arms appeared to be burn marks); *Nelson v. State Bd. of Veterinary Medicine*, 938 A.2d 1163 (Pa.Cmwlth. 2007) (veterinarian's testimony alone was sufficient to prove his net worth); *Hasson v. Com., Dept. of Transp.*, 866 A.2d 1181 (Pa.Cmwlth. 2005) (driver was under influence of alcohol); *Commonwealth v. United States Mineral Products Co.*, 809 A.2d 1000 (Pa.Cmwlth. 2002) (reasons for decision to demolish contaminated government building); *Commonwealth v. Brown*, 134 A.3d 1097 (Pa. Super. 2016) (detective could describe certain events in surveillance video);

In Re Estate of Nalaschi, 90 A.3d 8 (Pa. Super. 2014) (evidence of testamentary capacity can be supplied by lay witnesses as well as experts); *Fisher v. Central Cab Co.*, 945 A.2d 215 (Pa. Super. 2008) (having had adequate opportunity to observe, witness could testify as to speed of approaching car); *Commonwealth v. Smith*, 904 A.2d 30 (Pa. Super. 2006) (veteran policeman could testify defendant was under influence of alcohol and incapable of safe driving); *J.W.S. Delavau v. Eastern America Transport*, 810 A.2d 672 (Pa. Super. 2002) (value of property destroyed by warehouse's leaking roof); *Commonwealth v. Dunne*, 456 Pa. Super. 523, 690 A.2d 1233 (1997) (if sufficient foundation is laid, lay opinion as to whether a person is under influence of narcotics is admissible); *Commonwealth v. Neiswonger*, 338 Pa. Super. 625, 488 A.2d 68 (1985) (state of intoxication); *Atwell v. Beckwith Machinery Co.*, 872 A.2d 1216 (Pa. Super. 2005); *Kremer v. Janet Fleisher Gallery, Inc.*, 320 Pa. Super. 384, 467 A.2d 377 (1983) (owner of personalty traditionally permitted to testify to its value in civil cases).

A lay witness may testify as to certain matters involving health, the apparent physical condition of a person and as to obvious symptoms, but his testimony must be confined to facts within his knowledge, and may not be extended to matters involving the existence or non-existence of a disease, which is only discoverable through the training and experience of a medical expert. *Lebanon Cty. Housing v. Landeck*, 967 A.2d 1009 (Pa. Super. 2009) (lay person should have been permitted to testify about tenant's mental illness for purpose of demonstrating need for reasonable accommodation of a disability under Fair Housing Act); *In Re Mampe*, 932 A.2d 954 (Pa. Super. 2007) (testimony from lay witnesses as to testator's weakened intellect admissible in will contest; testimony limited to behaviors testator exhibited throughout her lifetime); *Commonwealth v. Allison*, 550 Pa. 4, 703 A.2d 16 (1997) (lay witness could not testify regarding "split and open" condition of complainant's hymen); *Cominsky v. Donovan*, 846 A.2d 1256 (Pa. Super. 2004) (error to allow lay testimony that person in persistent vegetative state experienced pain and suffering); *Barbour*, 733 A.2d 1286 (Pa. Super. 1999) (lay person could not testify about existence of bipolar disorder); *Fogg v. Paoli Hospital*, 455 Pa. Super. 81, 686 A.2d 1355 (1996) (allowing testimony that person was moaning, groaning and losing a lot of blood).

Compare: Fed. R. Evid. 701.

Research References

Packel & Poulin, Pennsylvania Evidence § 701-1 (4th ed. 2013)

McCormick, Evidence § 11 (7th ed. 2013)

LEADING QUESTIONS

See: Pa.R.E. 611(c).

Objection

- Objection. Counsel is leading the witness.
- I object to the question as leading.

Response

- Your Honor, I request permission to lead [*because these are only uncontested preliminary matters*] [*given the young age of the witness*] [*because the witness is having difficulty in answering any questions*] [*because of this witness' handicap*] [*because this witness is hostile*].

Pennsylvania Law

A leading question is one which puts the desired answer in the mouth of the witness. *Commonwealth v. Chambers*, 528 Pa. 558, 599 A.2d 630 (1991); *In re Rogan's Estate*, 404 Pa. 205, 171 A.2d 177 (1961); *Commonwealth v. Stultz*, 114 A.3d 865 (Pa. Super. 2015). The problem with leading questions is that the attorney is testifying (telling the story) and the witness is merely affirming the lawyer's testimony, typically by responding by "yes" or "no" answers. *Buckman v. Philadelphia & Reading Ry. Co.*, 227 Pa. 277, 75 A. 1069 (1910); *Commonwealth v. Culver*, 51 A.3d 866 (Pa. Super. 2012) (leading questions can cause undue prejudice because they functionally substitute the attorney's testimony for that of a witness); *Commonwealth v. A.D.B.*, 752 A.2d 438 (Pa.Cmwlth.2000) (although witness said boat was traveling at "moderate" speed, by using improper leading questions prosecutor had witness agree "moderate" meant "sort of fast"); *c.f. Commonwealth v. O'Hannon*, 557 Pa. 256, 732 A.2d 1193 (1999) (attorney's questions and statements are not evidence).

Pa.R.E. 611(c) follows the traditional common

law rule that leading questions ordinarily should be confined to cross-examination and should not be asked on direct examination. However, the trial court has the discretion to allow leading questions, *Commonwealth v. Chmiel*, 777 A.2d 459 (Pa. Super. 2001); *Commonwealth v. Upchurch*, 355 Pa. Super. 425, 513 A.2d 995 (1986), and may allow them in a variety of situations if not prejudicial or if helpful to develop testimony. *Katz v. St. Mary Hosp.*, 816 A.2d 1125 (Pa. Super. 2003); *Fish v. Gosnell*, 316 Pa. Super. 565, 463 A.2d 1042 (1983). Leading questions have been deemed permissible: with child witnesses, *Commonwealth v. Chambers*, 528 Pa. 558, 599 A.2d 630 (1991); *Commonwealth v. Bailey*, 322 Pa. Super. 249, 469 A.2d 604 (1983); where, because of physical or mental limitations, a witness is experiencing difficulty in answering questions, *Commonwealth v. Smolko*, 446 Pa. Super. 156, 666 A.2d 672 (1995); *Commonwealth v. Tavares*, 382 Pa. Super. 317, 555 A.2d 199 (1989); where the witness is hostile, biased or reluctant to testify, *Commonwealth v. Settles*, 442 Pa. 159, 275 A.2d 61 (1971); *Commonwealth v. Bibbs*, 970 A.2d 440 (Pa. Super. 2009) (hostile witness); or where the witness is having emotional difficulties, such as in testifying about sex crimes, *Commonwealth v. Bell*, 328 Pa. Super. 35, 476 A.2d 439 (1984); *Commonwealth v. Guess*, 266 Pa. Super. 359, 404 A.2d 1330 (1979).

A party may call his adversary as a witness, as on cross-examination, and put leading questions to the witness, and draw from the adversary's testimony those facts or admissions which weaken the adversary's case or strengthen the case of the calling party. *Commonwealth v. Fransen*, 42 A.3d 1100 (Pa. Super. 2012). However, a witness, other than a party, is not considered adverse simply because his testimony is adverse to the calling party. As the term is understood in this context, a witness is adverse to the calling party if the witness has an interest in the issue being tried, and his interest would be increased or promoted if the calling party's adversary prevails. If the witness is not a party and has no "legal" interest in the outcome of the proceedings, then the witness is not an adverse witness. Whether a witness' interest is adverse to the calling party is a factual determination within the trial court's discretion. *Commonwealth v. Lambert*, 765 A.2d 306, 360–61 (Pa. Super. 2000) (collecting cases). *See also* Pa.R.E. 611(c); 42 Pa.C.S.A. § 5935 (the statutory right to call witnesses as on cross-examination is confined to civil proceedings). The court may, however, prohibit leading questions when the line of questioning is cross-examination in *form only* and not in fact. An example of such sham cross-examination is the "cross-examination" of a party by his own counsel after being called and questioned by the opponent. *In re Rogan's Estate*, 404 Pa. 205, 171 A.2d 177 (1961) (trial court should not authorize use of leading questions when it is cross-examination in form only).

When the court gives permission to use leading questions to a party who has called a hostile witness, the court should not extend that permission to whom the witness is not hostile or adverse. Examination by these parties should be as if under redirect examination. Pa.R.E. 611(c)(2).

With respect to the use of deposition transcripts, if a party fails to object to the form of a leading question during the deposition, the party waives its ability to raise the objection at trial. Pa.R.Civ.P. 4016 (b). Depositions as trial evidence would quickly lose their value if a party could strategically withhold objection during deposition and later exclude testimony that could have been elicited if objection had been raised promptly. *See Wilson v. A.P. Green Indus., Inc.*, 807 A.2d 922 (Pa. Super. 2002) (where deposition questions were objected to as leading, answers were not admissible and could not serve as basis for surviving summary judgment motion).

Leading questions are a standard technique of impeachment. Pa.R.E. 607 allows the credibility of a witness to be impeached by any party, including the party calling the witness. Rule 607 abolishes the voucher rule (i.e., the traditional view that a party vouched for the credibility of the witnesses it called).

When a witness with an adverse interest is called as for cross-examination, he may thereafter be questioned by the other side as to related matters inquired about during cross-examination. However, when this subsequent examination is designed to introduce a defense, the trial court should not allow it. *Bell v. City of Philadelphia*, 341 Pa. Super. 534, 491 A.2d 1386 (1985).

Compare: Fed. R. Evid. 611(c).

Research References

Packel & Poulin, Pennsylvania Evidence § 611-4 (4th ed. 2013)

McCormick, Evidence Chapter 2 (7th ed. 2013)

LEGAL CONCLUSION

See: Pa.R.E. 701.

Objection

- Objection. The question calls for a legal conclusion which this witness is not competent to render.

Response

- The question is proper. I am using the term [*specify*] only in its established lay meaning and not as a legal term of art.
- I shall rephrase the question.

Pennsylvania Law

Under Pa.R.E. 701, a witness, not testifying as an expert, is limited in testimony in the form of opinions and inferences to those which are based on his perception and helpful to a clear understanding of his testimony or the determination of a fact in issue. When a witness is asked whether conduct was "unlawful" or "willful" or whether the defendants "conspired," terms that demand an understanding of the nature and scope of the law, the trial court may properly conclude that any response would not be helpful to the trier of fact. The witness, unfamiliar with the contours of the law, may erroneously feel that the legal standard is either higher or lower than it really is. In either event, a jury may give too much weight to such a legal conclusion. *Anderson v. Guerrein Sky-Way Amusement Co.*, 346 Pa. 80, 29 A.2d 682 (1943) (improper for witness to be asked whether nurse would disturb "a reasonable person"); *Commonwealth v. Joseph*, 848 A.2d 934 (Pa. Super. 2004) (trial court properly precluded questions to detective which sought to elicit legal conclusions about e-mails allegedly used to entrap defendant); *Commonwealth v. McLean*, 387 Pa. Super. 354, 564 A.2d 216 (1989) (excluding testimony re whether victim's living arrangement was "a common law marriage"); *Commonwealth v. Johnson*, 373 Pa. Super. 312, 541 A.2d 332 (1988) (psychiatrist not qualified to testify whether his definition of mental illness was same as legal definition); *McCrery v. Scioli*, 336 Pa. Super. 455, 485 A.2d 1170 (1984) (trial court correctly sustained objections to questions asking landlord if he had duty to see that tenant operated its business properly).

While no Pennsylvania cases were found, the federal courts have held that where words have an established lay meaning, they can be used in that context rather than as legal terms of art. *United States v. Levine*, 180 F.3d 869, 872 (7th Cir.1999) (no error in allowing prosecutor to ask defendant if he had "forged" signatures on checks; " 'Forgery' was an apt description of the acts Levine performed; that the crime is also called 'forgery' does not close the subject to inquiry"); *United States v. Standard Oil Co.*, 316 F.2d 884 (7th Cir.1963) (trial court erred in not permitting defense witnesses to answer questions as to whether there had been an "agreement", "understanding", "promise", or "commitment" concerning prices; such words have well-established lay meanings and do not demand a conclusion as to the legal implications of conduct). By the same reasoning, the *Levine* court noted:

> Witnesses can't insist that the prosecutor use euphemisms when inquiring into conduct that the indictment labels a crime. A prosecutor may ask an accused thief whether he stuck up the teller and robbed the bank; he may ask an accused drug peddler whether he sold drugs to an undercover agent; he may ask an accused price-fixer whether he joined a cartel; he may ask an accused killer whether he murdered the deceased . . . . all are proper subjects of cross-examination, provided only that the judge makes it clear to the jury that neither the questioner nor the witness defines the elements of the offense.

180 F.3d at 872.

Compare: Fed. R. Evid. 701.

Research Reference

Packel & Poulin, Pennsylvania Evidence § 701-1 (4th ed. 2013)

LIE DETECTOR TESTS

Objection

- [*To a question*] Objection. The question seeks inadmissible evidence.
- [*To an answer*] Objection. I move for a mistrial; or, I move the answer be stricken and request a cautionary instruction.

Response

- The remark was an isolated one and was not so prejudicial as to require a new trial. A curative instruction will remedy any alleged harm.

Pennsylvania Law

Polygraph tests require the examiner to measure and interpret a set of physiological correlates of anxiety in order to offer an opinion about whether the witness was deceptive in answering questions about matters at issue in a trial.

Pennsylvania courts have consistently held that polygraph or lie detector tests are inadmissible in criminal or civil cases because they have not attained acceptance as a reliable means of ascertaining truth or deception. *Commonwealth v. Marinelli*, 547 Pa. 294, 690 A.2d 203 (1997); *Commonwealth v. Chester*, 526 Pa. 578, 587 A.2d 1367 (1991); *Office of Disciplinary Counsel v. Wittmaack*, 513 Pa. 609, 522 A.2d 522 (1987); *Commonwealth v. Miller*, 497 Pa. 257, 439 A.2d 1167 (1982); *Commonwealth v. Pfender*, 280 Pa. Super. 417, 421 A.2d 791 (1980) (prosecutor and defense cannot stipulate admissibility). A reference to polygraph testing is inadmissible for any purpose. *Commonwealth v. Chester*, 526 Pa. 578, 587 A.2d 1367 (1991); *Commonwealth v. Watkins*, 750 A.2d 308 (Pa. Super. 2000). Where the prohibition is violated and the reference reveals the test results or raises inferences concerning the guilt or innocence of a defendant, a conviction will not be permitted to stand. *Commonwealth v. Johnson*, 441 Pa. 237, 272 A.2d 467 (1971); *Commonwealth v. Watkins*, 750 A.2d 308 (Pa. Super. 2000); *see Quigley v. Philadelphia Civil Serv. Comm'n.*, 528 Pa. 195, 596 A.2d 144 (1991) (civil case).

In determining whether a testimonial reference to a polygraph test warrants a mistrial in a criminal case, three factors are generally considered: (1) whether the Commonwealth prompted the reference to the polygraph test; (2) whether the reference suggested the results of the polygraph; and (3) whether the trial court issued prompt and adequate instructions regarding the unreliability and inadmissibility of polygraph tests. *See Commonwealth v. Miller*, 439 A.2d 1167, 1171 (Pa. 1982). After consideration of these three factors, courts must assess the resulting prejudice to the defendant, an evaluation which turns on whether such reference, considered in light of the circumstances of the case, causes an inference to arise as to the defendant's guilt or innocence. *Commonwealth v. Fortenbaugh*, 69 A.3d 191 (Pa. 2013).

A new trial is not required where only a passing reference is made without indicating test results. *Commonwealth v. Elliott*, 80 A.3d 415 (Pa. 2013); *Commonwealth v. Sneeringer*, 447 Pa. Super. 241, 668 A.2d 1167 (1995) (single reference with immediate cautionary instruction); *Butler v. Flo-Ron Vending Co.*, 383 Pa. Super. 633, 557 A.2d 730 (1989); *Commonwealth v. Upchurch*, 355 Pa. Super. 425, 513 A.2d 995 (1986) (remote reference not prompted by any question with no indication of whether test was given).

See also Pa.R.Crim.P. 573 (B)(1)(e), requiring the Commonwealth to disclose to defendant's attorney written or recorded reports of polygraph examinations.

Compare: *United States v. Scheffer*, 523 U.S.

303, 118 S.Ct. 1261, 140 L.Ed.2d 413 (1998). In upholding the *per se* ban on polygraph evidence under the Military Rules of Evidence, the principal opinion noted that "there is simply no consensus that polygraph evidence is reliable." 523 U.S. at 309, 118 S.Ct. at 1264–1265. The four member concurrence agreed: "The continuing good-faith disagreement among experts and courts on the subject of polygraph reliability counsels against our invalidating a *per se* exclusion of polygraph results . . ." 523 U.S. at 318, 118 S.Ct. at 1269. The Supreme Court indicated that trial courts must look to the rule in their own circuit. "Individual jurisdictions . . . may reasonably reach differing conclusions as to whether polygraph evidence should be admitted." 523 U.S. at 312, 118 S.Ct. at 1266. Nonetheless, such evidence continues to be generally disfavored throughout the federal court system. *See, e.g., United States v. Benavidez-Benavidez*, 217 F.3d 720 (9th Cir.2000).

See generally, Commonwealth v. A.R., 80 A.3d 1180 (Pa. 2013) (results of therapeutic polygraph exam in sex offender treatment program were admissible at probation revocation hearing (which is not a trial) under stringent conditions); *In Re S.H.*, 96 A.3d 448 (Pa. Cmwlth. 2014) (ALJ erred in assuming polygraph test results are universally inadmissible evidence; rules of evidence are relaxed in administrative proceedings and these are no fixed rules on admissibility of polygraph tests in such proceedings); *Commonwealth v. Shrawder*, 940 A.2d 436 (Pa. Super. 2007) (therapeutic polygraph testing as a part of sex offender counseling did not violate probationer's privilege against self-incrimination).

Research References

Packel & Poulin, Pennsylvania Evidence § 722 (4th ed. 2013)

McCormick, Evidence § 206 (7th ed. 2013)

LIMITING INSTRUCTIONS

See: Pa.R.E. 105; see also Pa.R.Crim.P. 647(D).

Form

- [*At sidebar*] Your Honor, in light of your ruling that you are going to admit this evidence for a limited purpose, I request that the jury be given the following cautionary instruction:

    1. *Evidence Admissible Against One Party But Not Others.* The testimony of this witness [*summarize substance*] is only admissible against [*name of party*]. You must not consider this evidence in connection with any other party.

    2. *Evidence Admissible On One Claim But Not Others.* The testimony of this witness [*summarize substance*] is only admissible in connection with [*count 1 of the indictment/the claim of negligence*]. You must not consider this evidence in connection with [*any other count of the indictment/any other claim in the case*].

    3. *Evidence Admissible On One Issue But Not Others.* The testimony of this witness is only admissible in connection with one issue in this case, namely [*state issue*]. You must not use this evidence for any other purpose.

Pennsylvania Law

When evidence is admitted for a limited purpose, or against only one party, the judge must instruct the jury as to the proper scope of the evidence if requested to do so. *Blumer v. Ford Motor Co.*, 20 A.3d 1222 (Pa. Super. 2011); Pa.R.E. 105; *see, e.g., Commonwealth v. Travers*, 564 Pa. 362, 768 A.2d 845 (2001) and *Commonwealth v. Akbar*, 91 A.3d 227 (Pa. Super. 2014) (redaction of co-defendant's statement replacing defendant's name with neutral pronoun together with limiting instruction sufficient to protect defendant's 6th Amendment right to confrontation); *Commonwealth v. Holloway*, 429 Pa. 344, 240 A.2d 532 (1968) (one defendant's statement admissible against him as admission but inadmissible hearsay as to co-defendant). Normally, the opponent of the evidence will request a limiting instruction. *Commonwealth v. Serge*, 896 A.2d 1170, 1187 n.12 (2006) ("Though the trial court may, on its own initiative, give a limiting instruction to the jury, the onus is on a party who is entitled to such an instruction to ask for one."). Pa.R.E.105, however, has no restrictions, and a proponent of evidence who is satisfied with limited use and wishes to protect the record against a possible appeal can also make the request. While the rule speaks only of instructions to the jury, on request in a bench trial, the court should rule on how it intends to limit the use of the evidence.

Although Pa.R.E. 105 obligates the trial judge to restrict the evidence to its proper scope, it does not specify the time at which a limiting instruction should be given. The better practice is a specific instruction at the time the evidence is admitted followed by a general instruction at the end of the case reminding the jurors that some evidence may be used only for limited purposes. *Commonwealth v. Housman*, 986 A.2d 822 (Pa. 2009); *Commonwealth v. Spotz*, 563 Pa. 269, 759 A.2d 1280 (2000); *Commonwealth v. Covil*, 474 Pa. 375, 378 A.2d 841 (1977); *Commonwealth v. Enders*, 407 Pa. Super. 201, 595 A.2d 600 (1991); Wright & Graham, Federal Practice and Procedure: Evidence § 5066. *See also* Pa.R.Crim.P. 647(D) (trial judge may give limiting instruction "any time during the trial as the judge deems necessary and appropriate for the jury's guidance in hearing the case"). Failure to request a limiting instruction at the time the evidence is introduced does not bar a party from making a later request at the time of the general charge to the jury. Pa.R.Crim.P. 647(D).

The judge may give a limiting instruction *sua sponte* but generally has no such duty under Pa.R.E. 105 in the absence of a request. Counsel occasionally will choose not to request limiting instructions for strategic reasons; where, for example, it might focus the jury's attention on the damaging evidence. A party who makes it clear he does not want a limiting instruction cannot later complain that the failure to give one was error.

However, Pennsylvania courts have long recognized that evidence of prior criminal acts has the potential for misunderstanding on the part of the jury. *Commonwealth v. Richter*, 711 A.2d 464 (Pa. 1998); *Commonwealth v. Chapman*, 763 A.2d 895, 899 n.4 (Pa. Super. 2000). As a result, such evidence *must be accompanied by a cautionary instruction* which fully and carefully explains to the jury the limited purpose for which that evidence has been admitted. *Commonwealth v. Weiss*, 81 A.3d 767 (Pa. 2013); *Commonwealth v. Claypool*, 495 A.2d 176 (Pa. 1985); *Commonwealth v. Page*, 965 A.2d 1212 (Pa. Super. 2009).

When a party requests a limiting instruction, and asserts a specific ground for the instruction, the party waives all other grounds for the instruction that were not raised. *Blumer v. Ford Motor Co.*, 20 A.3d 1222 (Pa. Super. 2011).

Compare: Fed. R. Evid. 105.

Research References

Packel & Poulin, Pennsylvania Evidence § 105-1 (4th ed. 2013)

McCormick, Evidence § 59 (7th ed. 2013)

MISLEADING QUESTIONS

See: Pa.R.E. 611(a).

Objection

- Objection. The question is misleading because [*it assumes facts not established by the evidence*] [*it assumes facts which are actually in issue*] [*it misstates the evidence*] [*it mischaracterizes the witness's testimony*].

Response

- The question is proper; I am entitled to test the credibility or memory of the witness. The witness can deny the asserted facts if he disagrees with the assertion.

Pennsylvania Law

Pa.R.E. 611(a) provides that the court shall exercise reasonable control over the mode of interrogating witnesses. A question is misleading when it assumes facts not established by the evidence, *Boring v. Metro. Edison Co.*, 435 Pa. 513, 257 A.2d 565 (1969); *Pascone v. Thomas Jefferson Univ.*, 357 Pa. Super. 524, 516 A.2d 384 (1986), or assumes facts which are actually in controversy. *Kirschman v. Pitt Publishing Co.*, 318 Pa. 570, 178 A. 828 (1935). It is also misleading to misstate the evidence or mischaracterize the witness's testimony. Setting verbal traps for a witness is not a legitimate branch of the art of cross-examination. *Di Bona v. Philadelphia Transp. Co.*, 356 Pa. 204, 51 A.2d 768 (1947).

Compare: Fed. R. Evid. 611(a).

Research References

McCormick, Evidence § 7 (7th ed. 2013)

Haydock and Sonsteng, Trial: Advocacy Before Judges, Jurors and Arbitrators Chapter 5, § 5.7

(4th ed. 2011)

MISTRIAL—MOTION

See: Pa.R.Crim.P. 605.

Illustration

- Objection, your Honor. Counsel has referred to evidence that the court previously ruled inadmissible. I now move for a mistrial on grounds that this misconduct is so unfairly prejudicial that my client is denied a fair trial. A curative instruction will not remove from the minds of the jurors what they have heard. This inadmissible and unduly prejudicial information which counsel has presented prevents them from considering the evidence in a fair and impartial manner.

Response

- Nothing in this isolated remark was so prejudicial as to require a new trial. A curative instruction will remedy any alleged harm.

- A new trial is not required unless the unavoidable effect of the evidence would be to prejudice the jury, forming in their minds a fixed bias and hostility such that they cannot weigh the evidence and render a true verdict. *Commonwealth v. Spotz*, 552 Pa. 499, 716 A.2d 580 (1998). That has not happened here.

Pennsylvania Law

Incidents may occur during trial that give rise to a motion for mistrial. Grounds that support a mistrial motion include statements or conduct by counsel, witnesses, jurors, court officials or the judge that:

- — are substantially and unfairly prejudicial;
- — constitute gross misconduct;
- — intentionally violate a court order;
- — deliberately and unfairly attempt to influence the judge or jury;
- — provide false evidence;

- improperly and adversely affect the substantial rights of a party;
- result in substantial irregularities in the trial proceedings; and,
- make a fair trial impossible.

Examples of errors supporting a motion for mistrial include: *Commonwealth v. Santiago*, 456 Pa. 265, 318 A.2d 737 (1974) (comments by prosecution witness to jurors); *Commonwealth v. Stewart*, 449 Pa. 50, 295 A.2d 303 (1972) (victim's father on panel of jurors from which trial jury selected); *Commonwealth v. Robson*, 461 Pa. 615, 337 A.2d 573 (1975) (illness of trial judge); *Commonwealth v. Mehmeti*, 501 Pa. 589, 462 A.2d 657 (1983) (deadlocked jury); *Lengle v. North Lebanon Twp.*, 274 Pa. 51, 117 A. 403 (1922) (impermissible reference to insurance); *Rice v. Hill*, 315 Pa. 166, 172 A. 289 (1934) (improper comments by attorney); *Nelson v. Airco Welders Supply*, 107 A.3d 146 (Pa. Super. 2014) (improperly suggesting that jury should award a specific amount of non-economic damages); *Commonwealth v. Culver*, 51 A.3d 866 (Pa. Super. 2012) (prosecutor's yelling, engaging in menacing behavior and putting his finger in the face of defendant and defense counsel during opening and closing unfairly prejudiced defendant); *Commonwealth v. Ford*, 414 Pa. Super. 470, 607 A.2d 764 (1992), *Commonwealth v. Watson*, 355 Pa. Super. 160, 512 A.2d 1261 (1986) (reference to prior criminal activity).

The grounds for mistrial must be so severe and uncorrectable that a party is denied a fair and impartial trial. *Commonwealth v. Travaglia*, 28 A.3d 868 (Pa. 2011); *Commonwealth v. Laird*, 988 A.2d 618 (Pa. 2010); *Commonwealth v. Wright*, 961 A.2d 119 (Pa. 2008); *Commonwealth v. Powell*, 956 A.2d 406 (Pa. 2008); *Commonwealth v. Tharp*, 830 A.2d 519 (Pa. 2003); *Commonwealth v. Jaynes*, 135 A.3d 606 (Pa. Super. 2016) (court has discretion to grant mistrial whenever prejudicial event may reasonably be said to deprive defendant of fair and impartial trial); *Commonwealth v. Lopez*, 57 A.3d 74 (Pa. Super. 2012); *Commonwealth v. Bedford*, 50 A.3d 707 (Pa. Super. 2012); *Commonwealth v. Ragland*, 991 A.2d 336 (Pa. Super. 2010); *Commonwealth v. Judy*, 978 A.2d 1015 (Pa. Super. 2009); *Commonwealth v. King*, 959 A.2d 405 (Pa. Super. 2008). *See, e.g. Commonwealth v. Martorano*, 559 Pa. 533, 741 A.2d 1221 (1999) (pervasive prosecutorial misconduct, including blatantly disregarding trial court's evidentiary rulings, disparaging the integrity of the court in front of jury and repeatedly alluding to evidence that did not exist); *Poust v. Hylton*, 940 A.2d 380 (Pa. Super. 2007) (defense counsel's violation of pretrial ruling tainted entire trial and compromised plaintiff's ability to receive fair trial); *Commonwealth v. Satzberg*, 358 Pa. Super. 39, 516 A.2d 758, 763 (1986) (references to defendant's alleged drug use for which there was little or no evidence created prejudice "too great to be negated by a curative instruction"). The mere occurrence of misconduct or other event is not sufficient to support the granting of the motion since the adverse affect can ordinarily be reduced by providing the jurors with a curative instruction to disregard the misconduct, *Commonwealth v. Smith*, 131 A.3d 467 (Pa. 2015) (immediate curative instruction dispelled potential prejudice from inference of prior criminality; the law presumes juries follow a court's instruction); *Commonwealth v. Fortenbaugh*, 69 A.3d 191 (Pa. 2013) (not every mention of a polygraph is prejudicial or worthy of a mistrial); *Commonwealth v. Chamberlain*, 30 A.3d 381 (Pa. 2011); *Commonwealth v. Rega*, 933 A.2d 997 (Pa. 2007); *Commonwealth v. Thompson*, 106 A.3d 742 (Pa. Super. 2014) (it is imperative that the trial court's curative instruction be clear and specific and must instruct the jury to disregard the improper evidence); *Commonwealth v. Fletcher*, 41 A.3d 892 (Pa. Super. 2012); *Commonwealth v. Moury*, 992 A.2d 162 (Pa. Super. 2010), or by admonishing the offending person. *Commonwealth v. Begley*, 566 Pa. 239, 780 A.2d 605 (2001) (witness' misleading testimony cured by court's instruction that jury should completely disregard it); *Commonwealth v. Philistin*, 565 Pa. 455, 774 A.2d 741 (2001) (spectators' emotional outburst at verdict cured by thorough instruction prior to penalty hearing); *Commonwealth v. Simpson*, 562 Pa. 255, 754 A.2d 1264 (2000) (allegedly prejudicial statement cured by immediate cautionary instruction); *Bugosh v. Allen Refractories Co.*, 932 A.2d 901 (Pa. Super. 2007) (plaintiff's death during trial did not warrant mistrial where jury was repeatedly cautioned death was imminent and that sympathy could not determine verdict); *Commonwealth v. Tejeda*, 834 A.2d 619 (Pa. Super. 2003) (throwing water cup at jury adequately addressed by immediate instruction and by polling jury as to whether they could still be fair); *Commonwealth v. Boone*, 862 A.2d 639 (Pa. Super. 2004) (reference to post-arrest silence cured by immediate cautionary instruction and another during jury charge).

Pa. R. Crim. P. 605(b) provides:

> When an event prejudicial to the defendant occurs during trial only the defendant may move for a mistrial; the motion shall be made when the event is disclosed. Otherwise, the trial judge may declare a mistrial only for reasons of manifest necessity.

In criminal cases, the circumstances surrounding a mistrial dictate whether the Double Jeopardy Clause bars retrial. If the defendant gives consent, express or implied, to the mistrial, retrial is allowed. If the defendant does not consent, retrial will be permitted only if the mistrial was justified by "manifest necessity." *United States v. Jorn*, 400 U.S. 470, 481, 91 S.Ct. 547, 555, 27 L.Ed.2d 543

(1971).[1]

Where there is manifest necessity for a trial judge to declare a mistrial sua sponte, neither the Fifth Amendment to the United States Constitution, nor Article 1, § 10 of the Pennsylvania Constitution will bar retrial. *Commonwealth v. Orie*, 88 A.3d 983 (Pa. Super. 2014); *Commonwealth v. Walker*, 954 A.2d 1249 (Pa. Super. 2008). However, there is no rigid rule for finding manifest necessity since each case is individual. *Commonwealth v. Young*, 35 A.3d 54 (Pa. Super. 2011); *Commonwealth v. Rivera*, 715 A.2d 1136 (Pa. Super. 1998).

Even if a mistrial is declared at defendant's request, the Pennsylvania Supreme Court has said that the Double Jeopardy Clause of the Pennsylvania Constitution prohibits retrial not only when

---

[1]The United States Supreme Court has repeatedly declined to define "manifest necessity" with rigid precision, explaining, "those words do not describe a standard that can be applied mechanically or without attention to the particular problem confronting the trial judge." *Arizona v. Washington*, 434 U.S. 497, 506, 98 S.Ct. 824, 831, 54 L.Ed.2d 717 (1978). The level of necessity must be of a "high degree" before mistrial may be declared. *Id.* "Under [this] rule, a trial can be discontinued when particular circumstances manifest a necessity for so doing, and when the failure to discontinue would defeat the ends of justice." *Wade v. Hunter*, 336 U.S. 684, 690, 69 S.Ct. 834, 837, 93 L.Ed. 974 (1949). The manifest necessity standard does not require the court to look at the mistrial dilemma from a single point of view. *United States v. Givens*, 88 F.3d 608, 613 (8th Cir.1996). It is a flexible standard which seeks fairness to the defendant, the government and the public interest alike. *Wade*, 336 U.S. at 691, 69 S.Ct. at 837. A court's inability or appearance of inability to proceed impartially and the consequent need for recusal constitute manifest necessity for a mistrial. *Commonwealth v. King*, 990 A.2d 1172 (Pa. Super. 2010). Where such a manifest necessity for a mistrial exists, a retrial is not barred by principles of double jeopardy. *Commonwealth v. Leister*, 712 A.2d 332 (Pa. Super. 1998).

prosecutorial misconduct is intended to provoke the defendant into moving for a mistrial, but also when the conduct of the prosecutor is intentionally undertaken to prejudice the defendant to the point of denial of a fair trial. *Commonwealth v. Martorano*, 559 Pa. at 537–538, 741 A.2d at 1223.

Research Reference

Packel & Poulin, Pennsylvania Evidence § 130 (4th ed. 2013)

MODELS, MAPS, CHARTS AND OTHER VISUAL AIDS

See: Pa.R.E. 611(a), 901.

Objection

- Objection. This [*chart*] [*diagram*] [*map*] is not supported by the evidence; it is inaccurate and misleading.
- Objection. This model is so dissimilar to the actual object that it will only serve to mislead the jury.

Response

- The necessary foundation has been established to show that this visual aid [*is a fair representation*] [*correctly summarizes the testimony*].
- It is accepted practice to use [*models*] [*drawings*] to illustrate testimony and argument; we are not seeking to mark this visual aid as an exhibit and the stricter standard of authentication for exhibits has no application here.

Pennsylvania Law

Use of models, maps, charts, diagrams and other visual aids **simply as illustrations** is a matter largely within the discretion of the trial judge. *Commonwealth v. Parker*, 919 A.2d 943 (Pa. 2007) (court's decision to allow prosecutor to display gun during opening statement was well within its discretion); *Commonwealth v. Persichini*, 444 Pa. Super. 110, 663 A.2d 699 (1995); *Commonwealth v. Pelzer*, 531 Pa. 235, 612 A.2d 407 (1992).

Where a visual aid such as a drawing, chart, diagram or animation is to be admitted **as an exhibit**, it will be admissible if it: (1) is properly authenticated under Rule 901 as a fair and accurate representation of the evidence it purports to portray (or summarizes correctly evidence of record); (2) is relevant under Rules 401 and 402, and (3) has probative value that is not outweighed by the danger of unfair prejudice. *See, e.g.*, Comment to Pa.R.E. 901; *Commonwealth v. Schroth*, 479 Pa. 485, 388 A.2d 1034 (1978); *Pascale v. Hechinger Co. of Pa.*, 627 A.2d 750 (Pa. Super. 1993).

The use of a model as a clarifying illustration without placing the model in evidence has long been recognized as proper. *Geist v. Rapp*, 206 Pa. 411, 55 A. 1063 (1903). The fact that a model differs from the original item does not prevent either its use as an illustration or its admission in evidence where the dissimilarity is clearly explained to the jury or where it does not mislead the jury. *Commonwealth v. Watkins*, 108 A.3d 692 (Pa. 2014) (firearms and ballistics expert allowed to use same type of gun to explain to jury how killings took place; it was made clear to jury that gun was not the actual murder weapon); *Pfister v. Fish*, 51 Erie C.L.J. 44 (1968); *see also McClellan v. Sitkin's Junk Co.*, 430 Pa. 522, 244 A.2d 34 (1968) (permitting the use of small toy model crane and miniature tanks).

Pa.R.Crim.P. 646 states that only **exhibits** may go to the jury. *See Commonwealth v. Strong*, 575 Pa. 433, 836 A.2d 884 (2003).

A computer-generated animation should be deemed admissible as demonstrative evidence if it: (1) is properly authenticated pursuant to Pa.R.E. 901 as a fair and accurate representation of the evidence it purports to portray; (2) is relevant pursuant to Pa.R.E. 401 and 402; and (3) has a probative value that is not outweighed by the danger of unfair prejudice pursuant to Pa.R.E. 403. *Commonwealth v. Serge*, 896 A.2d 1170 (Pa. 2006); *Commonwealth v. Hardy*, 918 A.2d 766 (Pa. Super. 2007) (no error to show computer-generated videotape of Shaken Baby Syndrome; tape was short, non-dramatic computer animation consistent with Commonwealth's theory of the case and helped medical expert explain his testimony). The trial judge must issue limiting instructions to the jury explaining the nature of the specific computer-generated animation. *Serge*, 896 A.2d at 1179.

The following cases are instructive: *Zuk v. Zuk*, 55 A.3d 102 (Pa. Super. 2012) (maps used as aid were not hearsay because they were not entered for truth of matter asserted, but to assist party in describing the property in issue); *Jones v. Spidle*, 446 Pa. 103, 286 A.2d 366 (1971) (rejecting inaccurate diagram); *Phoenix Mut. Life Ins. Co. v. Radcliffe on the Delaware, Inc.*, 439 Pa. 159, 266 A.2d 698 (1970) (paper with damages calculation properly permitted to go to the jury with the admonition that it was not evidence); *Wilson v. Nelson*, 437 Pa. 254, 258 A.2d 657 (1969) (chart barred where claimed wage loss not supported by the evidence); *In re Thirty West Broad Corp.*, 425 Pa. 36, 227 A.2d 827 (1967) (typed memoranda of gross receipts and fair market valuations inaccurate and prejudicial); *Swift v. Dept. of Transp. of Com.*, 937 A.2d 1162 (Pa. Cmwlth. 2007) (expert permitted to use not-to-scale map); *Harsh v. Petroll*, 840 A.2d 404 (Pa. Cmwlth. 2003) (computerized animations of fuel tank mechanism, underside of car and accident sequence all admissible); *Commonwealth, Dept. of General Services v. United States Mineral Products Co.*, 809 A.2d 1000 (Pa.Cmwlth.2002) (barring admission of illustrative exhibits explaining complicated toxicological concepts on grounds of unfair surprise); *Commonwealth v. Serge*, 896 A.2d 1170 (Pa. 2006) (computer-generated animation admissible to illustrate expert opinions as to how fatal shooting occurred); *Commonwealth v. Cullen*, 340 Pa. Super. 233, 489 A.2d 929 (1985) (chart properly used to track complex series of crimes); *Reichman v. Wallach*, 306 Pa. Super. 177, 452 A.2d 501 (1982) (impossible for appeals court to determine prejudice where blackboard damage calculations were not preserved); *Pratt v. Stein*, 298 Pa. Super. 92, 444 A.2d 674 (1982) (chart summarizing hospital records ruled to have probative value in medical malpractice case); *Commonwealth*

v. *Ayala*, 277 Pa. Super. 363, 419 A.2d 1187 (1980) (use of blackboard to chart drug deals aided jury in ferreting out facts of case); *Solomon v. Luria*, 45 Pa. D. & C.2d 291 (C.P. Phila.Cnty, 1967) *aff'd* 213 Pa. Super. 87, 246 A.2d 435 (1968) (damage calculation chart proper where all items are supported by evidence); *Ward v. Davis*, 24 Beaver L.J. 137 (1962) (admitting general diagram of cervical vertebrae as representing a true and correct portion of the human anatomy); *see also* 42 Pa.C.S.A. § 5987, Use of Dolls:

> In any criminal proceeding charging unlawful sexual contact or penetration with or on a child, the court shall permit the use of anatomically correct dolls or mannequins to assist an alleged victim in testifying on direct examination and cross-examination.

See Commonwealth v. Loner, 415 Pa. Super. 580, 609 A.2d 1376 (1992).

Compare: Fed. R. Evid. 611(a).

Research References

Packel & Poulin, Pennsylvania Evidence § 425-4 (4th ed. 2013)

McCormick, Evidence § 214 (7th ed. 2013)

MOTION TO STRIKE

See: Pa.R.E. 103(a)(1).

Illustration

- I move to strike the witness' last statement on two grounds: first, it is inadmissible hearsay; secondly, it was not responsive to the question asked. I also ask the court to instruct the jury to disregard this last answer and caution them not to consider it for any purpose in this case.

Pennsylvania Law

To preserve an issue for appeal, Pa.R.E. 103(a)(1) provides that a party objecting to the admission of evidence must make "a timely objection or motion to strike . . . stating the specific ground of objection . . ." *Commonwealth v. U.S. Mineral Products*, 956 A.2d 967 (Pa. 2008); *Commonwealth v. Montalvo*, 956 A.2d 926 (Pa. 2008).

Occasionally the jury will hear inadmissible evidence when counsel did not object to a question because:

1. while the question was proper, the witness' answer was not;
2. the witness answered so quickly, opposing counsel did not have time to object; or,
3. the ground for objection was not apparent at the time the evidence was offered (*e.g.*, where subsequent cross-examination demonstrates that the witness lacked personal knowledge and was relating hearsay).

When this occurs, counsel must move to strike the testimony and request the court to instruct the jury that the answer constitutes no evidence whatsoever and is to be disregarded. *See* Curative Instructions.

In *Jones v. Spidle*, 446 Pa. 103, 107, 286 A.2d 366, 368 (1971), the court established the following approach for motions to strike:

> Where either party to a proceeding discovers at any time that improper testimony has been inadvertently admitted, he may have the error corrected by applying to the court to have the evidence stricken . . . . As a rule, such motion will be allowed only in cases where the ground of the objection was unknown and could not have been known with ordinary diligence at the time the evidence was received.
>
> . . . The matter is within the discretion of the trial judge.

See Appeal of Emerick, 25 Pa. D. & C.3d 343 (C.P. Dauphin County, 1981) (where cross-examination has established that a witness' direct testimony was based on hearsay, it is proper to strike such testimony and disregard it, even though the infirmity is not revealed until during cross-examination).

Compare: Fed.R.Evid. 103(a)(1).

Research References

Packel & Poulin, Pennsylvania Evidence § 103-3 (4th ed. 2013)

McCormick, Evidence § 52 (7th ed. 2013)

NARRATIVE ANSWER

See: Pa.R.E. 611(a).

Objection

- Objection. The question calls for a narrative answer.
- Objection. The witness is giving a narrative answer.

Response

[*Where the testimony involves only preliminary matters which the parties do not contest, counsel should ask the court's permission to allow testimony in narrative form to expedite the trial. Otherwise, counsel should rephrase the question and proceed by specific questions and answers.*]

Pennsylvania Law

Pa.R.E. 611(a) provides that the court shall exercise reasonable control over the mode of interrogating witnesses. An improper narrative question allows the witness to tell a long, uncontrolled story. For example, "In your own words, Ms. Witness, tell the jury everything that happened to you that day." Sometimes a witness will give a narrative response to an otherwise permissible question. A narrative answer may be objected to as being a narrative answer or as being non-responsive. The reason for examining witnesses by specific questions and answers is to provide an orderly means by which objections to improper evidence can be raised and ruled on before the evidence is heard by the jury. Narrative questions or answers allow the witness to interject inadmissible testimony without giving the opposing attorney a reasonable opportunity to object in a timely manner. By requiring the direct examiner to proceed by specific questions and succinct answers, opposing counsel will have a reasonable opportunity to object. See

Commonwealth v. Stollar, 84 A.3d 635 (Pa. 2014) (trial court correctly prohibited defendant from presenting narrative statement to jury in lieu of normal testimony).

Compare: Fed. R. Evid. 611(a).

Research Reference

Haydock and Sonsteng, Trial: Advocacy Before Judges, Jurors and Arbitrators Chapter 5, P. 184 (4th ed. 2011)

NON-RESPONSIVE ANSWER

See: Pa.R.E. 611(a).

Objection

- Objection. The answer was not responsive to the question. I move the answer be stricken and the jury be instructed not to consider it for any purpose. I further request the court to admonish the witness and direct her to answer the questions specifically without volunteering further information.

Response

- The answer was responsive. The witness is entitled to [*explain*] [*qualify*] her answer.

Pennsylvania Law

A non-responsive or volunteered answer occurs when a witness provides information not required by the attorney's question. Any response that extends beyond the specific information required is objectionable. *See Lehigh Valley Trust Co. v. Pennsylvania Turnpike Comm'n*, 401 Pa. 135, 163 A.2d 86 (1960). Some authorities believe that only the examining attorney can make this objection. *See, e.g.*, Mauet, Trials, page 553 (Aspen 2005). In practice, however, many judges will sustain an opposing lawyer's objection if the witness under examination testifies in a non-responsive manner.

Compare: Fed. R. Evid. 611.

Research Reference

Haydock and Sonsteng, Trial: Advocacy Before Judges, Jurors and Arbitrators, Chapter 5 (4th ed. 2011)

NONSUIT (COMPULSORY)—MOTION

See: Pa.R.Civ.P. 230.1.

Form

- *[Defendant's Counsel:]* I move for a compulsory nonsuit in favor of defendant on grounds that *[here state the specific reasons supporting the motion]*.

Response

- *[Plaintiff's Counsel:]* Defendant cannot be granted nonsuit since the necessary elements of the cause of action have been established *[explain]*.

Pennsylvania Law

A motion for compulsory nonsuit allows a defendant to test the sufficiency of a plaintiff's evidence. *Kramer v. Port Auth. of Allegheny Co.*, 876 A.2d 487 (Pa. Cmwlth. 2005); *Billig v. Skvarla*, 853 A.2d 1042 (Pa. Super. 2004); *Rachlin v. Edmison*, 813 A.2d 862 (Pa. Super. 2002).

Pa.R.Civ.P. 230(A)(1) provides that in a case involving only one plaintiff and one defendant, the court upon oral motion of the defendant may enter a nonsuit at the close of the plaintiff's case on liability. A compulsory nonsuit can only be granted in cases where it is clear that a plaintiff has failed to establish a cause of action. *Green v. Pennsylvania Hosp.*, 123 A.3d 310 (Pa. 2015); *Scampone v. Highland Park Care Center, LLC*, 57 A.3d 582 (Pa. 2012); *Neidert v. Charlie*, 143 A.3d 384 (Pa. Super. 2016) (a compulsory nonsuit is valid only in a clear case where the facts and circumstances lead to one conclusion—the absence of liability); *Oliver v. Ball*, 136 A.3d 162 (Pa. Super. 2016); *Staiger v. Holohan*, 100 A.3d 622 (Pa. Super. 2014). The plaintiff must be given the benefit of all favorable evidence along with all reasonable inferences of fact arising from that evidence, with any conflict in the evidence resolved in favor of the plaintiff. *Commonwealth v. Ortho-McNeil-Janssen Pharma.*, 52 A.3d 498 (Pa. Cmwlth. 2012); *Keffer v. Bob Nolan's Auto Service, Inc.*, 59 A.3d 621 (Pa. Super. 2012); *Gillard v. Martin*, 13 A.3d 482 (Pa. Super. 2010).

Prior practice that a nonsuit could not be granted if defendant had introduced any evidence has been abandoned. Rule 230.1(a) now provides that if defendant presents evidence prior to the close of plaintiff's case, the court shall consider, in addition to the plaintiff's evidence, only that defense evidence which is "favorable to the plaintiff."

Rule 230.1(c) continues prior practice that in an action involving more than one plaintiff or defendant, the court may not nonsuit any plaintiff until the close of the case of all plaintiffs. Nonsuit then may be entered in favor of all defendants or any defendant who has moved for nonsuit if all other defendants stipulate on the record that no evidence will be presented that would establish liability of the moving defendant.

The provision for such a stipulation in favor of the moving defendant(s) is a new procedure.

Compare: Fed.R.Civ.P. 50

Research Reference

Gibbons, Kraut & Edgar, West's Pennsylvania Forms and Commentary—Civil Procedure, Chapter 57 Dispositive Motions at Trial

OFFER OF PROOF

See: Pa.R.E. 103(a)(2).

Form

- Your Honor, in light of your ruling sustaining my opponent's objection, may I approach the bench to make an offer of proof. I offer to prove by this [*witness/document*] that [*state evidence which the witness/document will present*]. This proof is offered for the purpose of establishing [*state purpose of evidence*].

Pennsylvania Law

When an objection is sustained and evidence is excluded as a result, the examining attorney *must* make an offer of proof to preserve the error for appellate review. Pa.R.E. 103(a); *Romeo v. Manuel*, 703 A.2d 530 (Pa. Super. 1997); *Watson v. Philadelphia*, 162 Pa.Cmwlth. 340, 638 A.2d 489 (1994).

An offer of proof serves two purposes: (1) it informs the court and opposing counsel of the substance of the excluded evidence, enabling them to take appropriate action; and (2) it provides the appellate court with a record allowing it to determine whether the exclusion was erroneous and whether the offering party was prejudiced by the exclusion.

The offer of proof must be sufficiently detailed to alert the trial judge to the purpose for which the evidence is being offered, *Commonwealth v. Gibson*, 264 Pa. Super. 548, 400 A.2d 221 (1979), and a trial court's exclusion of evidence must be evaluated on appeal by a review of the contents of the offer at the time it was made. *Commonwealth v. Newman*, 382 Pa. Super. 220, 555 A.2d 151 (1989). Counsel must be careful to articulate every purpose for which evidence is admissible. Once an offer of proof is made, specifying the purpose for which evidence is admissible, all other grounds for admission are waived. A party cannot later complain on appeal that the evidence was admissible for still another purpose since those other reasons have not been preserved and are thus waived. *Commonwealth v. Gibson*, 264 Pa. Super. 548, 400 A.2d 221 (1979).

Offers of proof must conform to the rules of evidence and opposing counsel may make other new objections after the offer has been made.

There are several ways to make an offer of proof, each of which occurs *on the record* outside the hearing of the jury. *See* Pa.R.E. 103(c). All these involve an explanation to the judge of the anticipated testimony and the grounds for its admissibility. In making an offer: (1) counsel may narrate the intended testimony for the record; (2) the testimony may be elicited from the witness; (3) the offering attorney may submit a written statement of the proffered testimony; or (4) if the evidence is contained in a document, the document may be incorporated in the record.

The offer of proof provides an opportunity for the judge to reconsider the original ruling. *Commonwealth v. Clair*, 458 Pa. 418, 326 A.2d 272 (1974). Sometimes, after hearing the proposed evidence, the judge understands why it is not objectionable and overrules the objection. The offer of proof also provides an opportunity for the examining lawyer to explain why the evidence is admissible. This argument, coupled with proposed evidence, may convince the judge to admit the evidence, but, in any event, preserves the point on appeal.

A party opposed to the admission of certain evidence may make a request for an offer of proof prior to the testimony of a specific witness, in order to head off the presentation of prejudicial evidence. *See, e.g., Bascelli v. Randy, Inc.*, 339 Pa. Super. 254, 488 A.2d 1110 (1985).

To further clarify that a trial court's ruling on a motion in limine can preserve a claim of error in the admission or exclusion of evidence without a renewed objection or offer of proof at trial, Pa.R.E. 103(a) was subsequently amended to provide:

> Once the court makes a definitive ruling on the record admitting or excluding evidence, either at or before trial, a party need not renew an objection or offer of proof to preserve a claim of error for appeal.

The amendment is intended to govern all evidentiary rulings regardless of when made.

However, the court's ruling must be "definitive," meaning there must be no suggestion that the trial court would reconsider the matter at trial.

Even a definitive ruling extends only to those reasons which a party specifies or the court uses for its ruling. If new facts or circumstances emerge at trial, the party must renew its offer of proof in order to preserve the issue for appeal.

If there is any doubt that the record reflects a definitive ruling, the safest course is to renew the offer of proof on the record at trial.

When an offer of proof contains evidence, part of which is admissible and part of which is not, the court may reject the entire offer, *Purcell v. Metropolitan Life Insurance Co.*, 336 Pa. 588, 10 A.2d 442 (1940), since it is not the duty of the court to separate the good from the bad. *Jones v. Dubuque Fire & Marine Ins. Co.*, 317 Pa. 144, 176 A. 208 (1934); *Cockcroft v. Metro. Life Ins. Co.*, 133 Pa. Super. 598, 3 A.2d 184 (1938).

Compare: Fed. R. Evid. 103(a)(2).

Research Reference

Packel & Poulin, Pennsylvania Evidence § 103-5 (4th ed. 2013)

OPENING THE DOOR—CURATIVE ADMISSIBILITY

Objection

- I object; this evidence is inadmissible.

Response

- My opponent opened the door on this matter and I am permitted to introduce this evidence under the doctrine of curative admissibility.

Pennsylvania Law

The doctrine of curative admissibility typically arises in the following way. One party offers evidence which is inadmissible. Because the adversary fails to object, or because he has no opportunity to do so, or because the judge erroneously overrules his objection, the incompetent evidence comes in. Is the adversary entitled to fight fire with fire, that is, to answer this evidence by testimony in denial or explanation of the facts so proved?

Pennsylvania courts have used a variety of theories to hold that admission of inadmissible evidence does allow the opponent to reply with what would otherwise be inadmissible evidence. *See, e.g., Commonwealth v. DiNicola*, 581 Pa. 550, 866 A.2d 329 (2005) (where defense counsel opened door questioning state trooper, testimony that defendant exercised his right to remain silent was "fair response"); accord, *Commonwealth v. Molina*, 104 A.3d 430 (Pa. 2014); *Commonwealth v. Fischere*, 70 A.3d 1270 (Pa. Super. 2013); *Commonwealth v. Adams*, 39 A.3d 310 (Pa. Super. 2012); *Cacurak v. St. Francis Medical Center*, 823 A.2d 159 (Pa. Super. 2003) (evidence that plaintiff was meek individual who exercised extreme caution after back operation opened door to testimony about subsequent bar fights and police altercation); *Rittenhouse v. Hanks*, 777 A.2d 1113 (Pa. Super. 2001) (in medical malpractice case, no error permitting plaintiff to inquire about standard of care in later (irrelevant) time period because defense opened door by first asking same questions).

In *Western Show Co. Inc. v. Mix*, 315 Pa. 139, 173 A. 183 (1934), it was held that where irrelevant and collateral matter is elicited by one party, the opposite party has the right to contradict it as a matter of fundamental fairness. *See Sweener v. First Baptist Church*, 516 Pa. 534, 533 A.2d 998 (1987); *Jamison v. Ardes*, 408 Pa. 188, 182 A.2d 497 (1962); *Gaudio v. Ford Motor Co.*, 976 A.2d 524 (Pa. Super. 2009); *Leaphart v. Whiting Corp.*, 387 Pa. Super. 253, 564 A.2d 165 (1989); *Shoup v. Mannino*, 188 Pa. Super. 457, 149 A.2d 678 (1959).

In *Commonwealth v. Stakley*, 243 Pa. Super. 426, 365 A.2d 1298 (1976), the court said opening the door with improper evidence results in a waiver. "If defendant delves into what would be objectionable testimony . . . then the Commonwealth can probe further into the objectionable area." 243 Pa. Super. 426, 365 A.2d at 1300; *see Commonwealth v. Lewis*, 885 A.2d 51 (Pa. Super. 2005); *Commonwealth v. Harris*, 884 A.2d 920 (Pa. Super. 2005); *Commonwealth v. Bey*, 294 Pa. Super. 229, 439 A.2d 1175 (1982). The unifying thread of all these cases is that the rule of curative admissibility allows an opponent to introduce similar evidence to combat any prejudice which may ensue from the original inadmissible evidence. *See also Commonwealth v. Murphy*, 540 Pa. 318, 657 A.2d 927 (1995); *Commonwealth v. Walker*, 540 Pa. 80, 656 A.2d 90 (1995); *Commonwealth v. Ford*, 539 Pa. 85, 650 A.2d 433 (1994) (where defendant opens the evidentiary door to his past criminal conduct, the Commonwealth may cross-examine on that point); *Commonwealth v. Fransen*, 42 A.3d 1100 (Pa. Super. 2012) (defense opened the door regarding gun; Commonwealth allowed to follow up "to complete the record"); *Burkholz v. Commonwealth, Dep't. of Transp.*, 667 A.2d 513 (Pa.Cmwlth.1995).

That one party opened the door, however, does not provide the other party with an excuse to introduce whatever irrelevant evidence it wishes. Once a subject is opened up, evidence by the other party must be within the scope of the evidence originally offered. *Gaudio v. Ford Motor Co.*, 976 A.2d 524 (Pa. Super. 2009); *Shoup v. Mannino*, 188 Pa. Super. 457, 149 A.2d 678 (1959).

Certain Pennsylvania rules and cases explicitly recognize "the opened door" albeit triggered by admissible evidence introduced by the opposing party.

A prior consistent statement which might otherwise be inadmissible becomes admissible for rehabilitation purposes under Pa.R.E. 613(c) when consistent with the witness' trial testimony and offered to rebut a charge of recent fabrication, improper influence or motive. *Commonwealth v. Koehler*, 558 Pa. 334, 737 A.2d 225 (1999).

Evidence of the same pertinent bad character trait of the accused may be introduced once a defendant has introduced evidence of a pertinent trait of good character. Pa.R.E. 404(a)(1); *see Michelson v. United States*, 335 U.S. 469, 479, 69 S.Ct. 213, 220, 93 L.Ed. 168 (1948) ("The price a defendant must pay for attempting to prove his good name is to throw open the entire subject which the law has kept closed for his benefit and to make himself vulnerable where the law otherwise shields him."); *Commonwealth v. Pursell*, 555 Pa. 233, 724 A.2d 293 (1999) (by taking the witness stand, defendant opened the door to the Commonwealth to impeach him by prior *crimen falsi* convictions); Pa.R.E. 405(a), *Commonwealth v. Fletcher*, 580 Pa. 403, 861 A.2d 898 (2004) (by presenting reputation evidence as to his character for peacefulness and non-violence, defendant opened the door for Commonwealth to cross-examine his character witness regarding specific instances of conduct probative of character trait in question).

Evidence of a witness' character for truthfulness is admissible only after the witness' character for truthfulness has been attacked by reputation evidence or otherwise. Pa.R.E. 608; *Commonwealth v. Harris*, 785 A.2d 998 (Pa. Super. 2001); *Commonwealth v. Schwenk*, 777 A.2d 1149 (Pa. Super. 2001).

When a defendant testifies at trial that he cooperated with police, the door is open for the Commonwealth to present its own version of interactions with police. *Commonwealth v. Lettau*, 986 A.2d 114 (Pa. 2009) (testimony about defendant's pre-arrest silence permissible to rebut defendant's claim he cooperated with police investigation).

Compare: *United States v. Beason*, 220 F.3d 964 (8th Cir.2000); *United States v. Hanley*, 190 F.3d 1017 (9th Cir.1999), and *Reilly v. Natwest Markets Group, Inc.*, 181 F.3d 253 (2d Cir.1999), applying same rule in federal practice.

Research Reference

Packel & Poulin, Pennsylvania Evidence §§ 125, 126 (4th ed. 2013)

OPENING STATEMENT

See: Pa.R.Civ.P. 225; Pa.R.Crim.P. 604.

Objection

- Objection. It is improper in opening statement for counsel to be [*arguing the case*] [*arguing the law*] [*mentioning inadmissible or unprovable evidence*] [*giving personal opinions*] [*speculating about our case*] [*making disparaging comments*].

Response

- Your Honor, my comments are proper. I am entitled to [*review the facts and opinions which will be introduced as evidence*] [*discuss the theories of the case and issues presented*] [*refer to the legal issues presented*].

Pennsylvania Law

The purpose of an opening statement is to inform the jurors of the nature of the action and the issues and the questions of fact involved, in order to aid their understanding of the evidence to be presented. *Commonwealth v. Nelson*, 311 Pa. Super. 1, 456 A.2d 1383 (1983). *See also Commonwealth v. Montgomery*, 533 Pa. 491, 626 A.2d 109 (1993) (opening statement can be the most critical stage of trial because it is there the jury forms its first and often lasting impression of case). Although the right to present an opening statement in a civil or criminal case is part of a party's constitutional right to be represented by an attorney, there is discretion in the trial court to regulate addresses by counsel. *Speer v. Barry*, 349 Pa. Super. 365, 503 A.2d 409 (1985).

The opening statement is a roadmap, and not a dry-run. It is a chance to outline and describe the case, and not an opportunity to pre-try the matter. *Commonwealth v. Parker*, 919 A.2d 943, 952 (Pa. 2007) (Castille, J. concurring). The opening is not to be used as a subterfuge to present inadmissible or nonexistent evidence to the jury or to circumvent the rules of evidence and professional responsibility. *See, e.g.*, *Commonwealth v. Culver*, 51 A.3d 866 (Pa. Super. 2012) (prosecutor's act of yelling, engaging in menacing behavior and putting his finger in the face of defendant and defense counsel served to deny defendant a fair and impartial trial); *Commonwealth v. Colavita*, 920 A.2d 836 (Pa. Super. 2007) (reversible error where prosecution's opening discussed the negative inference to be drawn from defendant's pre-arrest consultation with attorney).

What Can Be Presented

1. Facts and opinions which will be introduced as evidence. The facts that can be described include direct and circumstantial evidence and reasonable inferences drawn from the evidence. *See Commonwealth v. Arrington*, 86 A.3d 831 (Pa. 2014) (a prosecutor's remarks in opening statements must be fair deductions from the evidence the commonwealth intends to other, which the prosecutor believes, in good faith, will be available and admissible at trial); *Commonwealth v. Montalvo*, 986 A.2d 84 (Pa. 2009) (remarks in prosecutor's opening must be fair deductions from evidence that he in good faith plans to introduce and not mere assertions designed to inflame passions of jury); *Commonwealth v. Robinson*, 583 Pa. 358, 877 A.2d 433 (2005).

2. Case theories and issues.

3. The law. In a jury trial, the judge explains the law to the jury. However, the attorney can concisely refer to the legal issues in the case, the elements that comprise a claim or defense and the burden of proof. *Commonwealth v. Carson*, 913 A.2d 220, 241 (Pa. 2006); *Commonwealth v. Hardy*, 918 A.2d 766 (Pa. Super. 2007).

What Cannot Be Presented

1. Referring to inadmissible or unprovable evidence.

Counsel must not refer to inadmissible evidence or unprovable facts during opening statement. This prohibition extends to evidence excluded by pretrial rulings, or likely to be excluded by the rules of evidence, as well as facts, opinions or inferences that are not supported by the evidence. *Young v. Washington Hosp.*, 761 A.2d 559 (Pa. Super. 2000).

2. Explaining details of the law or giving jury instructions. While making brief references regarding the law in the case is proper, counsel should not give lengthy descriptions of the law or give instructions to the jury.

3. Making argumentative statements. The opening is the opportunity to present the evidence that will be introduced and not to argue the facts, the law or the case.

4. Stating personal beliefs and opinions. The attorney should not give the jurors a personal opinion or belief concerning the evidence or the case. *Arnold v. Zangrilli*, 389 Pa. Super. 103, 566 A.2d 865 (1989); Pa. Rules of Professional Conduct 3.4, "Fairness to Opposing Party and Counsel."

5. Speculating about the other side's case. A prosecutor in a criminal case cannot suggest what the defense will prove because the defense has no obligation to prove anything. (But see *Commonwealth v. Al Hamilton Contracting Co.*, 383 Pa. Super. 429, 557 A.2d 15 (1989), where such comment was held not to be grounds for mistrial.) Speculation about the other side's case in a civil matter is argumentative, does not represent what the evidence will show, and is usually improper.

6. Making disparaging remarks. Counsel may not make remarks during opening statement which disparage opposing counsel, the opposing case, the opposing party, or witnesses. Such conduct is improper, unfairly prejudicial and unethical and may be grounds for mistrial. *Young v. Washington Hospital*, 761 A.2d 559 (Pa. Super. 2000) (new trial ordered where defense counsel strongly intimated during opening that motives of parents of child seriously damaged during birth in filing suit were mercenary and directed toward their own financial gain). However, this does not preclude vigorous

advocacy. *See Commonwealth v. Robinson*, 581 Pa. 154, 864 A.2d 460 (2004) (in triple murder case referring to defendant as "a predator" was appropriate in context of Commonwealth's case).

In *Commonwealth v. Parker*, 919 A.2d 943, 952 (Pa. 2007), the prosecutor displayed a handgun during his opening. The Supreme Court held that the use of tangible evidence during opening is permitted. But the Court cautioned that such evidence must be admissible, used with restraint and not presented in a flamboyant or frightening manner. In *Butler v. Flo-Ron Vending Co.*, 383 Pa. Super. 633, 557 A.2d 730 (1989), the court held that while a trial court may not preclude counsel from making an opening statement to the jury, a twenty-minute time limit was not an abuse of discretion.

Research References

Haydock and Sonsteng, Trial: Advocacy Before Judges, Jurors and Arbitrators Chapter 7 (4th ed. 2011)

OTHER CRIMES, WRONGS OR ACTS

See: Pa.R.E. 404(b).

Objection

- Objection. [*request sidebar*] The question seeks to elicit improper character evidence for the purpose of showing propensity or disposition. The evidence is immaterial to any issue in this case and is highly prejudicial to defendant.

Response

- I am not attempting to cause unfair prejudice to the defendant by showing him to be a person of bad character. Evidence of other crimes is admissible here because [*state specific exception which permits the use of this evidence*]. The probative value of this evidence clearly outweighs any potential for prejudice and a cautionary instruction by the court will ensure that the jury does not misunderstand the purpose for which this evidence is offered.

Pennsylvania Law

Pa.R.E. 404(b) is a rule both of exclusion and inclusion.

As a rule of exclusion, it expresses the traditional principle that other misconduct is inadmissible to show criminal propensity, i.e. that the defendant is a bad person likely to have committed the crime for which he or she is presently charged. *Commonwealth v. Hitcho*, 123 A.3d 731 (Pa. 2015); *Commonwealth v. Weiss*, 81 A.3d 767 (Pa. 2013); *Commonwealth v. Tedford*, 960 A.2d 1 (Pa. 2008) (past conduct or information of other crimes cannot be introduced solely to show defendant is of bad character and has a propensity to commit criminal acts); *Commonwealth v. Rizzuto*, 566 Pa. 40, 777 A.2d 1069 (2001); *Commonwealth v. Bullock*, 948 A.2d 818 (Pa. Super. 2008); *Commonwealth v. Russell*, 938 A.2d 1082 (Pa. Super. 2007).

In *Michelson v. United States*, 335 U.S. 469, 475–476, 69 S.Ct. 213, 218–219, 93 L.Ed. 168 (1948), Justice Jackson wrote:

> The State may not show defendant's prior trouble with the law, specific criminal acts, or ill name among his neighbors, even though such facts might logically be persuasive that he is by propensity a probable perpetrator of the crime. The inquiry is not rejected because character is irrelevant; on the contrary, it is said to weigh too much with the jury and to so over persuade them as to prejudge one with a bad general record and deny him a fair opportunity to defend against a particular charge.

See also Commonwealth v. Spruill, 480 Pa. 601, 391 A.2d 1048 (1978) (evidence of other crimes is probably only equaled by a confession in its prejudicial impact on jury).

As a rule of inclusion, evidence of "other crimes, wrongs or acts" may be admitted under Pa.R.E. 404(b) for purposes other than demonstrating criminal propensity, including but not limited to proving defendant's motive, opportunity, intent, preparation, plan, knowledge, identity or absence of mistake or accident. *Commonwealth v. Dillon*, 925 A.2d 131 (Pa. 2007); *Commonwealth v. Reid*, 571 Pa. 1, 811 A.2d 530 (2002); *Commonwealth v. Mayhue*, 536 Pa. 271, 639 A.2d 421 (1994); *Commonwealth v. Griffin*, 804 A.2d 1 (Pa. Super. 2002); *Commonwealth v. Dargan*, 897 A.2d 496 (Pa. Super. 2006). See *Commonwealth v. Sitler*, 144 A.3d 156 (Pa. Super. 2016) (while the rule gives was to recognized exceptions, the exceptions cannot be stretched in ways that effectively eradicate the rule).

Pa.R.E. 404(b) is not limited to evidence of crimes that have been proven beyond a reasonable doubt in court. It encompasses both prior crimes and prior wrongs and acts, the latter of which by their nature often lack definitive proof. *Commonwealth v. Ardinger*, 839 A.2d 1143 (Pa. Super. 2003) (fact that similar sex crimes committed in Maryland were still awaiting trial did not render them inadmissible); *Commonwealth v. Lockcuff*, 813 A.2d 857 (Pa. Super. 2002). *See also Commonwealth v. Wattley*, 880 A.2d 682 (Pa. Super. 2005) (at least with respect to sex crimes involving the same victim, evidence of *subsequent* bad acts is also admissible).

The rule applies in civil as well as criminal cases. *Hutchison ex rel. Hutchison v. Luddy*, 763 A.2d 826 (Pa. Super. 2000) (other instances of priests' sexual abuse of young boys admissible to establish church's notice).

To be admissible, however, evidence of other crimes and bad acts must pass two related tests: (1) under Pa.R.E. 404(b)(2), the evidence must be relevant for a special purpose, that is, to prove something other than bad character or propensity to commit crimes; and (2) the probative value of the evidence must outweigh risks of prejudice, confusion, or waste of time. *See*, Pa.R.E. 403; *Commonwealth v. Cousar*, 928 A.2d 1025 (Pa. 2007); *Commonwealth v. Seiders*, 531 Pa. 592, 614 A.2d 689 (1992); *Commonwealth v. Billa*, 521 Pa. 168, 555 A.2d 835 (1989); *Commonwealth v. Diehl*, 140 A.3d 34 (Pa. Super. 2016) (enumerating probative value/prejudice balancing test factors). *See also United States v. Morley*, 199 F.3d 129, 133 (3d Cir.1999) where the court issued the following caution:

> [T]here is no alchemistic formula by which 'bad act' evidence that is not relevant for a proper purpose under Rule 404(b) is transformed into admissible evidence. Thus, a proponent's incantation of the proper uses of such evidence under the rule does not magically transform inadmissible evidence into admissible evidence. 'Relevance is not an inherent characteristic,' *Huddleston*, 485 U.S. at 689, 108 S.Ct. at 1501, 'nor are prior bad acts intrinsically relevant to 'motive, opportunity, intent, preparation, plan, knowledge, identity or absence of mistake.' *United States v. Sampson*, 980 F.2d 883, 888 (3d Cir.1992).

Thus, when prior bad act evidence is both relevant and admissible for a proper purpose, 'the proponent must clearly articulate how that evidence fits into a chain of logical inferences, no link of which may be the inference that the defendant has the propensity to commit the crime charged.' *United States v. Himelwright*, 42 F.3d 777, 782; *United States v. Jemal*, 26 F.3d 1267 (3d Cir.1994).

Some of the exceptions recognized by Pa.R.E. 404(b)(2) as legitimate bases for admitting evidence of a defendant's distinct crimes include, but are not limited to:

1. Motive: *Commonwealth v. Romero*, 938 A.2d 362 (Pa. 2007) (testimony of prior bad acts provided the motive for the crime, was probative of intent and gave the background of the planning of the murder); *Commonwealth v. Dowling*, 584 Pa. 396, 883 A.2d 570 (2005) (evidence of earlier attempt to rape and rob victim admissible as motive for defendant to kill her shortly before he was to be tried for these other crimes); *Commonwealth v. Fisher*, 564 Pa. 505, 769 A.2d 1116 (2001) (evidence that victims recently had cheated defendant in drug deal admissible to show defendant killed them in revenge); *Commonwealth v. Spotz*, 562 Pa. 498, 756 A.2d 1139 (2000) (*Spotz II*) (to be admissible to show motive, evidence must be sufficient to show crime currently being considered grew out of or was in some way caused by the prior set of circumstances; here robbery/murder was to avoid capture for earlier robbery/murder); *Commonwealth v. Counterman*, 553 Pa. 370, 719 A.2d 284 (1998) (prior marijuana use relevant to motive because it led to argument with wife, ending in fatal fire); *Commonwealth v. Ross*, 57 A.3d 85 (Pa. Super. 2012) (mere similarities between prior bad acts and crime at issue do not establish motive; there must be firm basis for concluding crime on trial grew out of or was in any way caused by prior set of facts and circumstances; there was no explanation how defendant's prior incidents with women provided motive to kill victim); *Commonwealth v. Constant*, 925 A.2d 810 (Pa. Super. 2007) (evidence regarding defendant's alleged hatred of and prior confronta-

tions with police relevant to motive at the time of shooting policeman);

2. Intent: *Commonwealth v. Towles*, 106 A.3d 591 (Pa. 2014) (evidence that defendant frequently borrowed murder weapon and had fired it from moving auto admissible to prove intend, preparation, knowledge and absence of mistake in murder prosecution); *Commonwealth v. Sherwood*, 982 A.2d 483 (Pa. 2009) (defendant's prior physical assaults of child victim admissible to show intent, lack of mistake, ill-will and malice); *Commonwealth v. Bracey*, 541 Pa. 322, 662 A.2d 1062 (1995); *Commonwealth v. Grzegorzewski*, 945 A.2d 237 (Pa. Super. 2008) (possession of stolen computer admissible to establish defendant's intent in prosecution for unlawful use of computer, identity theft, attempted theft by deception and receiving stolen goods); *Commonwealth v. Jackson*, 900 A.2d 936 (Pa. Super. 2006) (evidence of prior abuse between defendant and homicide victim tending to establish intent is generally admissible); *Commonwealth v. Passmore*, 857 A.2d 697 (Pa. Super. 2004) (same); *Commonwealth v. Aguado*, 760 A.2d 1181 (Pa. Super. 2000) (reversible error to admit prior conviction for drug trafficking; disputed issue here was possession, therefore need to establish intent was nonexistent); *Commonwealth v. Butler*, 729 A.2d 1134 (Pa. Super. 1999) (evidence of other recent and repeated physical abuse admissible to prove intent to kill);

3. Absence of mistake or accident: *Commonwealth v. Boczkowski*, 577 Pa. 421, 846 A.2d 75 (2004) (manner in which both of defendant's wives were killed supported reasonable inference death was not accidental; Commonwealth had burden of proof and did not have to reserve evidence until rebuttal); *Commonwealth v. Donahue*, 519 Pa. 532, 549 A.2d 121 (1988); *Commonwealth v. Tyson*, 119 A.3d 353 (Pa. Super. 2015) (factual similarities between rapes admitted to show absence of mistake or accident).

4. A common scheme, plan or design embracing commission of two or more crimes so related to each other that proof of one naturally tends to prove the others, *Commonwealth v. Arrington*, 86 A.3d 831

(Pa. 2014) (in prosecution for murder of girlfriend, evidence of violence, harassment and intimidation of prior girlfriends established that defendant acted pursuant to a common plan or scheme); *Commonwealth v. Robinson*, 864 A.2d 460 (Pa. 2004); *Commonwealth v. Bronshtein*, 547 Pa. 460, 691 A.2d 907 (1997); *Commonwealth v. Miller*, 541 Pa. 531, 664 A.2d 1310 (1995); *Commonwealth v. Aikens*, 990 A.2d 1181 (Pa. Super. 2010) (in prosecution for corruption of minor, prior sexual abuse admissible under common plan or scheme exception to Rule 404(b)); *Commonwealth v. G.D.M. Sr.*, 926 A.2d 984 (Pa. Super. 2007) (similar); *Commonwealth v. Einhorn*, 911 A.2d 960 (Pa. Super. 2006) (prior assaults of girlfriends helped establish common plan or scheme relevant to victim's murder); *Commonwealth v. O'Brien*, 836 A.2d 966 (Pa. Super. 2003) (admitting evidence of prior sex crimes and collecting cases addressing whether prior crimes are too remote in time to be relevant); *Commonwealth v. Strong*, 825 A.2d 658 (Pa. Super. 2003) (excluding "other acts evidence" where crimes not similar, geographical locations varied and incidents were remote in time); *Commonwealth v. Giusto*, 810 A.2d 123 (Pa. Super. 2002); *Commonwealth v. Davis*, 737 A.2d 792 (Pa. Super. 1999) (pattern of actions committed over time made relevant by stalking statute, 18 Pa. C.S.A. § 2709(b), and sufficient to sustain stalking charge);

The following factors should be considered in establishing similarity: (i) the elapsed time between the crimes; (ii) the geographical proximity of the crime scenes; and (iii) the manner in which the crimes were committed. *Commonwealth v. Clayton*, 483 A.2d 1345 (Pa. 1984); *Commonwealth v. Judd*, 897 A.2d 1224 (Pa. Super. 2006).

5. To establish identity of the person charged with the commission of the crime on trial where there is such a logical connection between the crimes that proof of one will naturally tend to show that the accused is the person who committed the other: *Commonwealth v. Keaton*, 556 Pa. 442, 729 A.2d 529 (1999) (rape/murders involving bondage or strangulation of black female crack cocaine addicts

in abandoned houses in period of less than six months); *Commonwealth v. Hawkins*, 534 Pa. 123, 626 A.2d 550 (1993) (the pattern and characteristics of the crimes must be so unusual and distinctive as to be like a signature); *Commonwealth v. Dozzo*, 991 A.2d 898 (Pa. Super. 2010) (numerous similarities among seven robberies at or near train stations); *Commonwealth v. Weakley*, 972 A.2d 1182 (Pa. Super. 2009) (sufficient commonality between crimes dispels notion they are merely coincidental and permits contrary conclusion they are so logically connected they share a perpetrator); *Commonwealth v. Shamberger*, 788 A.2d 408 (Pa. Super. 2001) (identity established by pattern of movie theatre thefts); *Commonwealth v. Galindes*, 786 A.2d 1004 (Pa. Super. 2001) (in prosecution for attempted burglary, evidence of prior attempts at same residence admissible to show that victim recognized defendant's voice);

6. To impeach the credibility of a defendant who testifies in his trial: *Commonwealth v. Hernandez*, 862 A.2d 647 (Pa. Super. 2004) (admitting evidence of other convictions to impeach defendant's testimony that he never sold drugs)*; Commonwealth v. Novasak*, 414 Pa. Super. 21, 606 A.2d 477 (1992); *see also* 42 Pa. C.S.A. § 5918(1) (examination of defendant as to other offenses);

7. Situations where a defendant's prior criminal history had been used by him to threaten or intimidate the victim: *Commonwealth v. Cook*, 952 A.2d 594 (Pa. 2008) (prior threats relevant to explain why witnesses delayed in telling police about defendant's participation in murder); *Commonwealth v. Claypool*, 508 Pa. 198, 495 A.2d 176 (1985); *Commonwealth v. Dillon*, 863 A.2d 597 (Pa. Super. 2004) (threats against victim's family to explain why she did not make prompt complaint about sexual abuse); and

8. Situations where the distinct crimes were part of a chain or sequence of events which formed the history of the case and were part of its natural development (sometimes called the "complete story" rationale). *Commonwealth v. Hairston*, 84 A.3d 657 (Pa. 2014) (where arson was not changed, evidence that defendant set his house or fire after murder-

ing his family admissible for res gestae purposes to explain history and course of events on the day in question); *Commonwealth v. Johnson*, 42 A.3d 1017 (Pa. 2012) (prior injuries inflicted on murdered child to show nature of relationship between victim and defendant); *Commonwealth v. Flor*, 998 A.2d 606 (Pa. 2010) (off-duty state trooper's testimony explained why he stopped defendant's car—an act that initiated sequence of events that ended in murder of another officer); *Commonwealth v. Reed*, 990 A.2d 1158 (Pa. 2010) (evidence of earlier abuse relevant to subsequent murder); *Commonwealth v. Powell*, 956 A.2d 406 (Pa. 2008) (evidence of other injuries inflicted on child provided insight into relationship characterized by defendant's anger and impatience which supplied motive for killing child); *Commonwealth v. Williams*, 896 A.2d 523 (Pa. 2006) (testimony re bank robberies and drug deals connected defendant either to the murder weapon or the sequence of events leading to the murder); *Commonwealth v. Robinson*, 581 Pa. 154, 864 A.2d 460 (2004) ("other acts" evidence provided jury with complete story of defendant's crime spree during one-year period); *Commonwealth v. Drumheller*, 570 Pa. 117, 808 A.2d 893 (2002) (prior incidents of abuse over three-year period relevant to show sequence and escalating nature of conduct ending with murder of girlfriend); *Commonwealth v. Rizzuto*, 566 Pa. 40, 777 A.2d 1069 (2001) (evidence that defendant had cashed wife's checks without authorization relevant to history of events involving same acts leading to murder of elderly neighbor); *Commonwealth v. Murphy*, 540 Pa. 318, 657 A.2d 927 (1995); *Commonwealth v. Walker*, 540 Pa. 80, 656 A.2d 90 (1995); *Commonwealth v. Lark*, 518 Pa. 290, 543 A.2d 491 (1988); *Commonwealth v. Gonzalez*, 112 A.3d 1232 (Pa. Super. 2015) (evidence of violent physical attacks on victim's mother served to explain why rapes were not promptly reported and to establish complete story surrounding the crimes changed); *Commonwealth v. Flamer*, 53 A.3d 82 (Pa. Super. 2012) (in murder trial, evidence of conspiracy to kill Commonwealth witness admissible to prove history of case; also known as res gestae exception); *Commonwealth v. Lomax*, 8

A.3d 1264 (Pa. Super. 2010) (in prosecution for rape of child, prior sexual misconduct with victim ten months earlier admissible to show conduct was of continuing and escalating nature); *Commonwealth v. Melendez-Rodriguez*, 856 A.2d 1278 (Pa. Super. 2004) (prior acts were part of the proof that defendant intended to terrorize victim). *But see Commonwealth v. Miles*, 846 A.2d 132 (Pa. Super. 2004) (there is no "history of the case" exception in Rule 404(b)(2)).

This list is not exhaustive. *Commonwealth v. Williams*, 936 A.2d 12, 31 (Pa. 2007); *Commonwealth v. Brown*, 52 A.3d 320 (Pa. Super. 2012) (list is non-exclusive); *Commonwealth v. Cascardo*, 981 A.2d 245 (Pa. Super. 2009) (court will recognize additional exceptions to general rule prohibiting evidence of prior crimes). There is, for example, precedent allowing for the introduction of testimony regarding the facts and circumstances of defendant's prior convictions for purposes of proving the application of aggravating circumstances at the penalty phase of a criminal trial. *Commonwealth v. Brown*, 987 A.2d 699 (Pa. 2009).

Admissibility to Rebut a Material Assertion

Prior misconduct may be admissible for the purpose of rebutting a material assertion by the defendant regardless of whether the evidence fits into one of the traditional categories such as motive, intent, or identity. *See, e.g., Commonwealth v. Saxton*, 516 Pa. 196, 532 A.2d 352 (1987); *accord Commonwealth v. Powers*, 395 Pa. Super. 231, 577 A.2d 194 (1990) (other crimes evidence properly introduced to rebut specific false statements/impressions made or created by defense); *Commonwealth v. Days*, 784 A.2d 817 (Pa. Super. 2001) (admission of prior crimes made relevant by defendant's alibi testimony making himself a victim).

It is black letter law that the Commonwealth may impeach a defendant's credibility with reference to prior crimes where the defense opens the door. *Commonwealth v. Hood*, 872 A.2d 175 (Pa. Super. 2005) (evidence of defendant's prior incarceration could be used to show that alibi witness evidence was not truthful); *Commonwealth v. Days*, 784 A.2d 817 (Pa. Super. 2001) (a defendant is not insulated from being discredited about factual accuracy simply because that proof involves other crimes).

Reverse 404(b)

Evidence regarding other crimes is admissible for defensive purposes if it tends, alone or with other evidence, to negate the defendant's guilt of the crime charged against him. Such evidence is sometimes referred to as "reverse 404(b)" evidence. *See, e.g.*, *Commonwealth v. Thompson*, 779 A.2d 1195 (Pa. Super. 2001) (prior and subsequent drug activity of third party admissible to prove that he, and not defendant, was possessor of drugs); *see also United States v. Reed*, 259 F.3d 631 (7th Cir.2001) (acknowledging use of such evidence in appropriate circumstances but finding no error in excluding defendant's proffered evidence that his brother had manufactured methamphetamine on numerous occasions when brother had not been on defendant's property in many months and drug residue collected at time of arrest indicated recent manufacture); *United States v. Walton*, 217 F.3d 443 (7th Cir.2000) (no error precluding defendants charged with ATM theft from offering evidence of another unsolved ATM theft as reverse 404(b) evidence since it neither tended to prove or disprove defendants' involvement in charged offense).

See also Commonwealth v. Palagonia, 868 A.2d 1212 (Pa. Super. 2005) (collecting cases discussing circumstances under which criminal defendants are entitled to offer evidence that some other person committed a similar crime at or around time they are alleged to have committed the crime).

Rule 404(b)(3)

Compliance with Pa.R.E. 404(b)(2) does not itself assure admission of "other crimes" evidence. Pursuant to Pa.R.E. 404(b)(3) such evidence is admissible only if its probative value outweighs the potential for prejudice. *Commonwealth v. Horvath*, 781 A.2d 1243 (Pa. Super. 2001) (in prosecution for reckless endangerment, no error to exclude evidence of summary convictions for, *inter alia*, reckless driving; jury could improperly infer that reckless driving conviction equates with reckless endangerment and convict on that basis).

Notice

Pa.R.E. 404(b)(4) requires the prosecution to provide reasonable notice in advance of trial of its intention to present "other acts" evidence if the accused has requested such notice. The policy behind this requirement is to reduce surprise and promote early resolution on the issue of admissibility. *Commonwealth v. Hicks*, 91 A.3d 47 (Pa. 2014) (purpose is to give defendant reasonable time to prepare an objection). The rule also provides that notice to the defense may be provided during trial if the court excuses pretrial notice on good cause shown. *Commonwealth v. Mawhinney*, 915 A.2d 107 (Pa. Super. 2006). The rule imposes no specific time limits beyond requiring reasonable pretrial notice. What constitutes a reasonable disclosure will depend largely on the circumstances of each case.

Given the potential for misunderstanding on the part of the jury, evidence of **similar prior criminal acts** must be accompanied by a cautionary instruction which carefully explains to the jury the limited purpose for which that evidence has been admitted. *Commonwealth v. Young*, 561 Pa. 34, 748 A.2d 166 (1999) (*Young I*); *Commonwealth v. Page*, 965 A.2d 1212 (Pa. Super. 2009); *Commonwealth v. Henkel*, 938 A.2d 433 (Pa. Super.

2007). Otherwise, cautionary instructions are given, if requested. *See Commonwealth v. Kemp*, 562 Pa. 154, 753 A.2d 1278 (2000) (counsel requested court to wait until end of trial to give instruction in order not to highlight testimony).

Compare: Fed. R. Evid. 404(b).

Research References

Packel & Poulin, Pennsylvania Evidence §§ 404-1–404-11 (4th ed. 2013)

McCormick, Evidence § 190 (7th ed. 2013)

PAROL EVIDENCE RULE

Objection

- Objection. The question seeks to elicit testimony which violates the parol evidence rule.

Response

- The rule does not apply. Extrinsic evidence is admissible: to prove the meaning of ambiguous terms; to show fraud in the execution, accident or mutual mistake; to show by custom and usage the meaning of these terms in this particular industry.

Pennsylvania Law

When a contract is expressed in a writing which is intended to be the complete and final expression of the rights and duties of the parties, parol evidence of prior or contemporaneous oral or written agreements, negotiations or understandings, which varies or contradicts the written contract is not admissible. *Yocca v. Pittsburgh Steelers Sports, Inc.*, 578 Pa. 479, 854 A.2d 425 (2004); *American Bank & Trust Co. of Pennsylvania v. Lied*, 487 Pa. 333, 409 A.2d 377 (1979); *Gianni v. R. Russell & Co.*, 281 Pa. 320, 126 A. 791 (1924); *WMI Group, Inc. v. Fox*, 109 A.3d 740 (Pa. Super. 2015); *Giant Food v. THF Silver Spring Dev.*, 959 A.2d 438 (Pa. Super. 2008); *Ragnar Benson, Inc. v. Authority*, 916 A.2d 1183 (Pa. Super. 2007). The primary purpose for the rule is to preserve the integrity of written contracts by refusing to permit the contracting parties' attempt to change the meaning of the contract through the use of extraneous information. *Commonwealth, Dep't of Transp. v. E-Z Parks*, 153 Pa.Cmwlth. 258, 620 A.2d 712 (1993). Despite its name, the parol evidence rule is not a discretionary rule of evidence but rather an element of substantive contract law. *See Giant Food Stores, Inc. v. Marketplace Communications Corp.*,

717 F.Supp. 1071 (M.D.Pa.1989) (applying Pennsylvania law.) The parol evidence rule does not preclude the admission of evidence to establish whether the parties *intended* the writing to be a complete embodiment of their agreement. *Lenzi v. Hahnemann Univ.*, 445 Pa. Super. 187, 664 A.2d 1375 (1995); *Murray v. University of Pennsylvania Hosp.*, 340 Pa. Super. 401, 490 A.2d 839 (1985).

There are fairly well-defined situations in which parol evidence is admissible and the rule excluding it does not apply:

(1) Ambiguity—where the agreement is ambiguous, parol evidence is admissible to explain the agreement and resolve ambiguities in order to determine the meaning of the parties. *Kripp v. Kripp*, 849 A.2d 1159 (Pa. 2004); *Synthes USA Sales v. Harrison*, 83 A.3d 242 (Pa. Super. 2013); *Adamitis v. Erie Ins. Exchange*, 54 A.3d 371 (Pa. Super. 2012). Ambiguity within a contract may be latent or patent. A patent ambiguity appears on the face of the contract and is a result of defective or obscure language. *Samuel Rappaport Family Partnership v. Meridian Bank*, 441 Pa. Super. 194, 657 A.2d 17 (1995). Although Pennsylvania law provides that parol evidence may not be introduced unless the language of the written agreement is ambiguous on its face, extrinsic facts and circumstances may be proved to show that language apparently clear and unambiguous on its face is, in fact, latently ambiguous. *Baney v. Eoute*, 784 A.2d 132 (Pa. Super. 2001) (easement for use of private road meant existing 20-foot-wide road and not the metes and bounds description that was wider than actual road). It is for the court to decide, as a matter of law, whether contract terms are clear or ambiguous. *Chester Upland Sch. v. Edward J. Meloney*, 901 A.2d 1055 (Pa. Super. 2006).

Whether an ambiguity exists is to be determined by the court as a question of law. *Novak v. Commonwealth, Dep't of Transp.*, 133 Pa.Cmwlth. 220, 575 A.2d 661 (1990). To determine whether a contract is ambiguous, the court must look at the contract as a whole and not at isolated portions of it. *Shepard v. Temple University*, 948 A.2d 852 (Pa. Super. 2008); *Lampenfeld v. Seitz*, 450 Pa. Super. 527, 676 A.2d 684 (1996). A contract will be found to be ambiguous if, and only if, it is reasonably or fairly susceptible of different constructions and is capable of being understood in more senses than one and is obscure in meaning through indefiniteness of expression or has a double meaning. *Insurance Adjus. Bur. v. Allstate*, 905 A.2d 462 (Pa.2006); *Madison Constr. Co. v. Harleysville Mut. Ins. Co.*, 557 Pa. 595, 735 A.2d 100 (1999); *Genaeya Corp. v. Harco Nat. Ins. Co.*, 991 A.2d 342 (Pa. Super. 2010); *Safe Auto Ins. Co. v. Berlin*, 991 A.2d 327 (Pa. Super. 2010). A contract is not ambiguous if the court can determine its meaning without any guide other than a knowledge of the facts on which, from the nature of the language in general, its meaning depends. A contract is not rendered ambiguous by the mere fact that the parties do not agree upon the proper construction. *County of Delaware v. J.P. Mascaro & Sons, Inc.*, 830 A.2d 587 (Pa. Super. 2003); *J.W.S. Delavau, Inc. v. Eastern America Transport & Warehousing, Inc.*, 810 A.2d 672 (Pa. Super. 2002); *Seven Springs Farm, Inc. v. Croker*, 748 A.2d 740 (Pa. Super. 2000), aff'd 569 Pa. 202, 801 A.2d 1212 (2002); *Commonwealth, State Highway and Bridge Auth. v. E. J. Albrecht Co.*, 59 Pa.Cmwlth. 246, 430 A.2d 328 (1981). However, when ambiguity exists in a contract, parol evidence is admissible to explain, clarify or resolve the ambiguity, irrespective of whether the ambiguity is patent (created by the language of the contract) or latent (created by extrinsic or collateral circumstances). *Lenau v. Co-Exprise, Inc.*, 102 A.3d 423 (Pa. Super. 2014); *Vinikoor v. Pedal Pennsylvania, Inc.*, 974 A.2d 1233 (Pa. Cmwlth.2009); *see In Re Wilton*, 921 A.2d 509 (Pa. Super. 2007) (addressing differences between and resolution of patent and latent ambiguity).

(2) Fraud in the execution—the parol evidence rule does not exclude evidence offered to prove fraudulent omission of agreed-upon terms from the final writing. *HCB Contractors v. Liberty Place Hotel Assocs.*, 539 Pa. 395, 652 A.2d 1278 (1995); *Boehm v. Riversource Life Ins. Co.*, 117 A.3d 308 (Pa. Super. 2015); *1726 Cherry St. Partnership v. Bell Atl. Props., Inc.*, 439 Pa. Super. 141, 653 A.2d 663 (1995); *see also Sunquest Info. Sys., Inc. v.*

Dean Witter Reynolds, 40 F.Supp. 2d 644 (W.D.Pa. 1999) (applying Pennsylvania law and collecting cases to show that **fraud in the inducement is not an exception**); *accord Toy v. Metropolitan Life Ins. Co.*, 928 A.2d 186 (Pa.2007); *Heritage Surveyors and Engineers Inc. v. National Penn Bank*, 801 A.2d 1248 (Pa. Super. 2002).

(3) Accident or mutual mistake—parol evidence is admissible to show that a mistake has been made and the contract does not reflect the true agreement of the parties. *Dunn v. Orloff*, 420 Pa. 492, 218 A.2d 314 (1966); *PNC Bank v. Bluestream Technology*, 14 A.3d 831 (Pa. Super. 2010); *Step Plan Services, Inc. v. Koresko*, 12 A.3d 401 (Pa. Super. 2010).

(4) Custom and usage—by custom and usage in particular trades and businesses, certain words acquire a meaning different from their dictionary definition or the meaning as used generally. Parol evidence of custom and usage is admissible to show that, not only ambiguous words, but even ordinary words in common use were included in the written contract to designate a performance other than that which would ordinarily be ascribed to them. *See Daset Mining Corp. v. Industrial Fuels Corp.*, 326 Pa. Super. 14, 473 A.2d 584 (1984) (coal mining terminology); *see also* 13 Pa.C.S.A. § 2202(1) permitting course of dealing or usage of the trade to be considered in interpreting a writing; *Campbell v. Hostetter Farms, Inc.*, 251 Pa. Super. 232, 380 A.2d 463 (1977).

Research Reference

Packel & Poulin, Pennsylvania Evidence § 430 (4th ed. 2013)

PERSONAL KNOWLEDGE

See: Pa.R.E. 602.

Objection

- *[To a question]* Objection. It has not been established that the witness has the personal knowledge to be able to answer that question. Any answer will be purely speculative.

- *[To an answer]* Objection. The answer demonstrates that the witness lacks personal knowledge and that her response was purely speculative. I move the answer be stricken and the jury be instructed not to consider it for any purpose.

Response

- The witness does have firsthand knowledge. To the extent that she has expressed any hesitancy or uncertainty, that goes only to the weight of the evidence and not its admissibility.

Pennsylvania Law

A witness may not testify to any matter unless evidence is introduced which is sufficient to support a finding that the witness has personal knowledge of the matter. Pa.R.E. 602; *Commonwealth v. Smith*, 580 Pa. 392, 861 A.2d 892 (2004); *In re Involuntary Termination of Parental Rights*, 449 Pa. 543, 297 A.2d 117 (1972); *Fauceglia v. Harry*, 409 Pa. 155, 185 A.2d 598 (1962); *Wayne Knorr, Inc. v. Dept. of Transp.*, 973 A.2d 1061 (Pa.Cmwlth. 2009); *Lesher v. Henning*, 302 Pa. Super. 508, 449 A.2d 32 (1982). "Personal knowledge" means a present recollection of an impression derived from the exercise of the witness' own senses. 2 Wigmore, Evidence § 657 at 762 (3d ed. 1940); *see Johnson v. Peoples Cab Co.*, 386 Pa. 513, 514–15 126 A.2d 720, 721 (1956) ("The primary object of a trial in our American courts is to bring to the tribunal, which is passing on the dispute involved, those persons who know of their own knowledge the facts to which they testify."). "Absolute certainty either of observation or of recollection is not required to establish personal knowledge. All that is required is an opportunity to observe and a belief that what is related depicts the perception." Graham, Handbook of Federal Evidence § 602.02 at 28 (5th ed. 2001). Where a witness has observed an occurrence and formed an impression of it, the fact that, at the trial, due to the passage of time and the fading of memory, she is not able to state with positive or absolute certainty exactly what she observed, but only what "I think" or "I vaguely remember" occurred, will not preclude the introduction of the witness' testimony. *Commonwealth v. Stickle*, 484 Pa. 89, 398 A.2d 957 (1979). The extent of a witness' knowledge of matters about which she offers to testify goes to the weight rather than the admissibility of the testimony.

The general rule in this Commonwealth is that an investigating police officer, who was not actually a witness to an accident, is not competent to render an opinion as to the cause of that accident. *Reed v. Hutchinson*, 331 Pa. Super. 404, 480 A.2d 1096 (1984); *see also Brodie v. Philadelphia Transp. Co.*, 415 Pa. 296, 203 A.2d 657 (1964); *Smith v. Clark*, 411 Pa. 142, 190 A.2d 441 (1963); *Lesher v. Henning*, 302 Pa. Super. 508, 449 A.2d 32 (1982). This rule is based on the fact that the officer has no firsthand knowledge of the accident and, thus, his conclusions would be speculative at best. *Reed v. Hutchinson*, 331 Pa. Super. at 410, 480 A.2d at 1099.

Opinion testimony by a lay witness may be admissible only if it is based on first-hand knowledge or observation. Pa.R.E. 701; *Gibson v. W.C.A.B. (Armco Stainless & Alloy Products)*, 580 Pa. 470, 861 A.2d 938 (2004) (actual knowledge and observation by lay witness are essential bases for reception of opinion); *Slappo v. J's Dev. Assocs., Inc.*, 791 A.2d 409, 419 n. 6 (Pa. Super. 2002); *Ratti v. Wheeling Pittsburgh Steel Corp.*, 758 A.2d 695 (Pa. Super.

2000).

The Supreme Court has said that Rule 602 applies to agency proceedings. *Gibson v. WCAB*, 580 Pa. 470, 861 A.2d 938 (2004); *accord, William Penn School Dist. v. Dept. of Ed.*, 902 A.2d 583 (Pa.Cmwlth. 2006).

When opposing counsel believes the witness lacks personal knowledge, she should object pursuant to Pa.R.E. 602 and request voir dire of the witness to establish that the witness is not competent. When lack of personal knowledge is established by cross-examination, a motion to strike the witness' testimony should be made.

Compare: Fed. R. Evid. 602.

Research References

Packel & Poulin, Pennsylvania Evidence § 602-1 (4th ed. 2013)

McCormick, Evidence Chapter 3 (7th ed. 2013)

PHOTOGRAPHS

See: Pa.R.E. 901, 1001–1004, 403.

Objection

- Objection. The photographs violate Rule 901 in that they do not fairly and accurately represent the particular condition at the time of the accident.

- Objection. The photographs will necessarily have an inflammatory and prejudicial impact which cannot be adequately addressed by a cautionary instruction. They should be excluded under Rule 403. Moreover, they are cumulative to the testimonial evidence and cannot be shown to have essential evidentiary value.

Response

- The law does not require that every object depicted in photographs remain unchanged from the time of the accident until the photographs are taken. Where there is a change, it can be specifically pointed out. These photographs are readily capable of being understood by the jury and will assist it in evaluating the facts; or,

- Photographs are not excluded merely because they are horrid or gruesome, *Commonwealth v. Small*, 559 Pa. 423, 741 A.2d 666 (1999). We have limited the photographs to those necessary to illustrate the witness's testimony; their evidentiary value clearly outweighs the likelihood they will inflame the passions of the jurors. A cautionary instruction can be given.

Pennsylvania Law

Demonstrative evidence such as photographs, videotapes and motion pictures must be authenticated by evidence sufficient to support a finding that the evidence fairly and accurately represents that which it purports to depict. *See Commonwealth v. Reid*, 571 Pa. 1, 811 A.2d 530 (2002); *Kopytin v. Aschinger*, 947 A.2d 739 (Pa. Super. 2008) (surveillance tape inadmissible where the person who attempted to authenticate it had no personal knowledge). Admission of photographs is a matter largely within the discretion of the trial judge. *Commonwealth v. Cox*, 546 Pa. 515, 686 A.2d 1279 (1996); *Commonwealth v. Auker*, 545 Pa. 521, 681 A.2d 1305 (1996). As a foundation, in both civil and criminal cases, a photograph can be authenticated by the testimony of the person who took it. It may also be verified by a person with sufficient knowledge to state that it fairly and accurately represents the object or place reproduced as it existed at the time of the event, *Commonwealth v. Loughnane*, 128 A.3d 806, 814 (Pa. Super. 2015), or if there is a difference or change, the difference or change is specifically pointed out and is readily capable of being clearly understood and appreciated by the factfinder. *Tolbert v. Gillette*, 438 Pa. 63, 260 A.2d 463 (1970); *Semet v. Andorra Nurseries, Inc.*, 421 Pa. 484, 219 A.2d 357 (1966); *Taylor v. Borough of Modena*, 370 Pa. 100, 87 A.2d 195 (1952); *Capoferri v. CHOP*, 893 A.2d 133 (Pa. Super. 2006) (where hospital did not have the technology to print and preserve color ultrasound, no error to allow references to color images while using only black and white photos); *Aiello v. Southeastern Pa. Transp. Auth.*, 687 A.2d 399 (Pa.Cmwlth.1996).

In criminal matters, and especially with respect to photographs of a corpse in homicide cases, the court must first determine whether the photograph is inflammatory. *Commonwealth v. Kendricks*, 30 A.3d 499 (Pa. Super. 2011). If it is not, the photograph may be admitted if it has relevance and can assist the jury's understanding of the facts. *Commonwealth v. Wright*, 961 A.2d 119 (Pa. 2008); *Commonwealth v. Robinson*, 864 A.2d 460 (Pa. 2004) (collecting cases); *Commonwealth v. Hetzel*, 822 A.2d 747 (Pa. Super. 2003). If the photograph is inflammatory, the trial court must apply a balancing test of whether or not the photographs are of such essential evidentiary value that the need for their admission clearly outweighs the likelihood of inflaming the minds and passions of the jurors. *Commonwealth v. Ballard*, 80 A.3d 380 (Pa. 2013) (although the court's precautionary measures could not completely sanitize the inflammatory nature of the photographs, such is not the test for admissibility). See *Commonwealth v. Cash*, 137 A.3d 1262 (Pa. 2016) (surveillance video of shooting helped to establish defendant acted with malice); *Commonwealth v. Haney*, 131 A.3d 24 (Pa. 2015) (photos supported prosecution theory that child had been beaten to death and not accidentally injured); *Commonwealth v. Woodard*, 129 A.3d 480 (Pa. 2015) (same); *Commonwealth v. Lyons*, 79 A.3d 1053 (Pa. 2013) (photos were highly relevant to the nature of the attack, the issues of intent, identity and torture as well as to understanding witness testimony); *Commonwealth v. Travaglia*, 28 A.3d 868 (Pa. 2011) (crime scene admissible; photo was in black and white and body was covered with blanket); *Commonwealth v. Spell*, 28 A.3d 1274 (Pa. 2011) (photos corroborated witness testimony about crime); *Commonwealth v. Pruitt*, 951 A.2d 307 (Pa. 2008) (photos of homicide victim are often relevant to intent element of crime of first-degree murder—in some cases the only evidence of defendant's intent); *Commonwealth v. Solano*, 906 A.2d 1180 (Pa. 2006) (photos of victim's bloody clothes relevant to Commonwealth's other forensic evidence); *Commonwealth v. Tharp*, 574 Pa. 202, 830 A.2d 519 (2003) (photos of emaciated child inherently inflammatory but relevant to jury issue of whether defendant starved child to death); *Commonwealth v. Brown*, 567 Pa. 272, 786 A.2d 961 (2001) (photos of child victim of sexual assault and murder admissible at penalty hearing; probative of intent to inflict pain and suffering with exceptional depravity); *Commonwealth v. Begley*, 566 Pa. 239, 780 A.2d 605 (2001) (photo of shotgun wounds in victim's head admissible to prove intent to kill and to support pathologist's testimony that shots were fired at close range); *Commonwealth v. Saranchak*, 544 Pa. 158, 675 A.2d 268 (1996) (victim's photo allowed jury to visualize how defendant murdered his grandmother and to prove intent to kill); *Commonwealth v. Jacobs*, 536 Pa. 402, 639 A.2d 786 (1994) (even where body's condition can be described by medical examiner, such testimony does not obviate admissibility of photographs); *Commonwealth v. Hatcher*, 746 A.2d 1142 (Pa. Super. 2000) (aggravated assault prosecution; photos graphically demonstrating victim's wounds relevant in determining seriousness of wounds); *see also* Pa.R.E. 403.

Trial courts approach the admissibility of photographs and films on a case-by-case basis, with the paramount concerns being relevance and the avoidance of unfair prejudice. Courts have accepted: photographic/videotape reenactment of crime, *Commonwealth v. Spotz*, 562 Pa. 498, 756 A.2d 1139 (2000) (photos), *Commonwealth v. Foster*, 425 Pa. Super. 61, 624 A.2d 144 (1993) (video); day in the life films depicting injuries/disabilities, *Wagner by Wagner v. York Hosp.*, 415 Pa. Super. 1, 608 A.2d 496 (1992); *Reimer v. Delisio*, 296 Pa. Super. 205, 442 A.2d 731 (1982), *aff'd* 501 Pa. 662, 462 A.2d 1308 (1983); surveillance films, *Clemente-Volpe v. W.C.A.B. (Westinghouse Air Brake Division)*, 154 Pa.Cmwlth. 594, 624 A.2d 666 (1993); sound and video recordings of actual events, *Houston v. Canon Bowl, Inc.*, 443 Pa. 383, 278 A.2d 908 (1971); staged or posed photograph, *Vanic v. Ragni*, 435 Pa. 26, 254 A.2d 618 (1969); *Commonwealth v. Sanders*, 339 Pa. Super. 373, 489 A.2d 207 (1985); slides of serious body burns which depicted wounds objectively, rather than sensationally, *Piso v. Weirton Steel Co., Div. of Nat'l Steel Corp.*, 235 Pa. Super. 517, 345 A.2d 728 (1975); photographs taken several months after truck accident where vehicle was largely dismantled but air brake supply line had not been altered, *Woods v. Pleasant Hills Motor Co.*, 454 Pa. 224, 309 A.2d 698 (1973); still photographs taken from videotape, *Commonwealth v. Hindi*, 429 Pa. Super. 169, 631 A.2d 1341 (1993); pictures of murder victim, *Commonwealth v. Malloy*, 856 A.2d 767 (Pa. 2004); *Commonwealth v. Freeman*, 573 Pa. 532, 827 A.2d 385 (2003); *Commonwealth v. Marshall*, 570 Pa. 545, 810 A.2d 1211 (2002) (collecting cases); photos of burglar's car taken by digital camera installed for observing wildlife, *Commonwealth v. Janda*, 14 A.3d 147 (Pa. Super. 2011).

Courts have excluded: macabre color slides of murder victim, some with bone fragments and brain tissue protruding from head wound; insanity defense pled and cause of death not contested; and photographs shed little, if any, light on state of mind, *Commonwealth v. Garrison*, 459 Pa. 664, 331 A.2d 186 (1975); photographs of incinerated body where defendant did not deny burning his wife, *Commonwealth v. Woods*, 454 Pa. 250, 311 A.2d 582 (1973); multiple slides of murder victim, including heart removed from body with no attempt to limit pictures to those reasonably necessary to aid pathologist's testimony, *Commonwealth v. Scaramuzzino*, 455 Pa. 378, 317 A.2d 225 (1974); but see *Commonwealth v. Eichinger*, 915 A.2d 1122 (Pa. 2007) (where jury was empanelled only for penalty phase after stipulated bench trial, court properly deemed autopsy photos more probative than prejudicial in that they informed jury as to nature of defendant's acts; cautionary instruction given); accident scene photographs taken under weather conditions different from event, showing mirror image and distorting the view, *Flynn v. City of Chester*, 429 Pa. 170, 239 A.2d 322 (1968); beyond the fair scope of the expert's report where photos (taken a year later) were not part of the original report, *Betz v. Erie Ins. Exchange*, 957 A.2d 1244 (Pa. Super. 2008); inability to authenticate where witness had no personal knowledge re surveillance tape; *Kopytin v. Aschinger*, 947 A.2d 739 (Pa. Super. 2008); lack of foundation, where photographer testified photographs did not show the injuries he saw, *Commonwealth v. Schwartz*, 419 Pa. Super. 251, 615 A.2d 350 (1992); slow motion and freeze frames from a videotape, *Commonwealth v. Hindi*, 429 Pa. Super. 169, 631 A.2d 1341 (1993); *see also Commonwealth v. Rivers*, 537 Pa. 394, 644 A.2d 710 (1994) (where victim's existence as a life in being was established by witness testimony, introduction of photos taken during her life was error; real purpose was to create sympathy for victim and prejudice against defendant).

Photographs are subject to the best evidence requirement of production of the original. Pa.R.E. 1002. This is usually of no significance since a duplicate is also admissible to the same extent as an original unless: (1) a genuine question is raised as to the authenticity of the original, or (2) under the circumstances it would be unfair to admit the duplicate in lieu of the original. Pa.R.E. 1003.

Videotape evidence is categorized as photographic evidence under Pa.R.E. 1001(2). See *Commonwealth v. McKellick*, 24 A.3d 982 (Pa. Super. 2011) (dash mounted video camera automatically activated by emergency lights of deceased trooper's vehicle sufficiently authenticated by another state policeman who was allowed to narrate tape contents).

The Pennsylvania Supreme Court has said that although the possibility of inflaming the passions of the jury is not to be lightly dismissed, a trial judge can minimize this danger with an appropriate instruction, warning the jury members not to be swayed emotionally by the disturbing images, but to view them only for their evidentiary value. *Commonwealth v. Pruitt*, 951 A.2d at 319. See also *Commonwealth v. Gravelle*, 55 A.3d 753 (Pa. Super. 2012) (limiting the number of photos proffered by prosecution).

Compare: Fed. R. Evid. 901, 1001–1004, 403.

Research References

Packel & Poulin, Pennsylvania Evidence § 425-2 (4th ed. 2013)

McCormick, Evidence § 215 (7th ed. 2013)

POLLING THE JURY

See: Pa.R.Crim.P. 648(G).

Form

- I respectfully request that the court poll the jurors individually.

Pennsylvania Law

Although not a constitutional right, the right to have the jury polled is of ancient origin and basic importance. *Commonwealth v. Downey*, 557 Pa. 154, 732 A.2d 593 (1999). It applies in both civil and criminal cases.

A verdict is not valid and final until the result is announced in open court and no dissent by a juror is registered. *Barefoot v. Penn Cent. Transp. Co.*, 226 Pa. Super. 558, 323 A.2d 271 (1974) (the verdict is not what the jurors agreed to in the jury room, but what they agree to in open court); *see also Drum v. Shaull Equip. and Supply Co.*, 787 A.2d 1050 (Pa. Super. 2001) (requirement that jury verdict be announced openly in court met by foreman announcing jury reached verdict, court reading jury's responses to special interrogatories and jury poll).

A jury poll gives each juror an opportunity, before the verdict is recorded, to declare in open court assent to the verdict which the foreman has returned. This enables the court and the parties to ascertain with certainty that no juror has been coerced or induced to agree to a verdict to which he or she has not fully assented. *Commonwealth v. Chester*, 557 Pa. 358, 733 A.2d 1242 (1999); *Commonwealth v. Rompilla*, 539 Pa. 499, 653 A.2d 626 (1995); *Commonwealth v. Conner*, 445 Pa. 36, 282 A.2d 23 (1971); *Commonwealth v. Martin*, 379 Pa. 587, 109 A.2d 325 (1954).

The right to a jury poll is codified in Rule

648(G) of the Pennsylvania Rules of Criminal Procedure. Denial of a timely request for a poll under Rule 648(G) is reversible error. *Commonwealth v. Downey*, 557 Pa. 154, 732 A.2d 593 (1999) (denial of right to jury poll is so fundamental, there is no need to show prejudice). A poll under Rule 648(G), however, is not required unless requested by a party and is waived if the request is not timely.

Polling the jury is not addressed in the civil rules and thus, in civil cases, appears to be a matter which rests within the sound discretion of the trial court. *In re Dettra's Estate*, 415 Pa. 197, 202 A.2d 827 (1964); *Ebner v. Ewiak*, 335 Pa. Super. 372, 484 A.2d 180 (1984).

When a jury is polled, it is the duty of the court to determine whether their answers clearly indicate the assent of their individual minds to the verdict before the court accepts the verdict. The assent or lack of assent of the individual jurors is not to be determined based solely on the words used by the juror. The demeanor and appearance of the juror as well as all of the surrounding circumstances must be considered. A juror might verbally indicate assent to the verdict while his manner and appearance might indicate the contrary. If the answer of any juror is not clear, or if it is questioned, the juror may be further interrogated before the court determines whether or not to accept the verdict. *Commonwealth ex rel. Ryan v. Banmiller*, 400 Pa. 326, 162 A.2d 354 (1960).

A motion to poll, whether made at the moment the verdict is first announced in court or after it has been affirmed and entered of record, is still timely so long as it is made before the jury has dispersed. *Commonwealth v. Downey*, 557 Pa. 154, 732 A.2d 593 (1999); *Reed v. Kinnik*, 389 Pa. 143, 132 A.2d 208 (1957); *Commonwealth v. Pacini*, 224 Pa. Super. 497, 307 A.2d 346 (1973). A jury may also be polled as to the existence of outside influence but not as to the effect the outside influence may have had on deliberations. *Carter by Carter v. U.S. Steel Corp.*, 529 Pa. 409, 604 A.2d 1010 (1992).

In a criminal case, either party has the right to poll the jury. If the poll reveals no concurrence, the jury will be directed to retire for further deliberations. Pa.R.Crim.P. 648(F); *Commonwealth v. Stafford*, 749 A.2d 489 (Pa. Super. 2000). However, where a juror dissents from a sealed verdict, a new trial must be granted. Pa.R.Crim.P. 1121(c); *Commonwealth v. Watson*, 211 Pa. Super. 394, 236 A.2d 567 (1967).

Note: In civil cases, when a party seeks to challenge a jury verdict on grounds that the jury returned inconsistent answers to interrogatories, a timely and specific objection must be made when the verdict is rendered. *Criswell v. King*, 575 Pa. 34, 834 A.2d 505 (2003); *Philadelphia Police Dept. v. Gray*, 534 Pa. 467, 633 A.2d 1090 (1993). This allows the court to immediately address errors which are subject to correction before the trial ends. Failure to object to a jury's allegedly inconsistent verdict before the jury is dismissed waives that particular issue in any appeal. *Philadelphia Police Dept. v. Gray*, 534 Pa. 467, 633 A.2d 1090 (1993).

Compare: Fed. R. Crim. P. 31(d).

PRETRIAL EXPERIMENTS

See: Pa.R.E. 402, 403.

Objection

- Objection. The [*test/experiment*] was not made under conditions sufficiently similar to those of the actual event and, therefore, is irrelevant, misleading and unfairly prejudicial.

Response

- Similarity has been established. Any differences between the experiment and the event go only to the weight to be given the experimental evidence.

Pennsylvania Law

A party seeking to admit tests or experiments for the purpose of showing how a particular event did or did not occur must first demonstrate a substantial similarity of circumstances and conditions between the test and the event in question. *Commonwealth v. Sero*, 478 Pa. 440, 387 A.2d 63 (1978); *Commonwealth v. Smith*, 808 A.2d 215 (Pa. Super. 2002); *Harsh v. Petroll*, 840 A.2d 404 (Pa.Cmwlth. 2003); *McGrorey v. Obermayer, Rebmann, Maxwell & Hippel*, 14 Pa. D. & C.3d 335 (C.P. Phila.Cnty. 1978), *aff'd* 274 Pa. Super. 646, 423 A.2d 1314 (1979). The problem presented by the use of experiments is the danger of misleading the jury which may attach exaggerated significance to the test results. *Leonard by Meyers v. Nichols Homeshield, Inc.*, 384 Pa. Super. 1, 557 A.2d 743 (1989).

Perfect identity between experimental and actual conditions is neither attainable nor required. But the conditions of the experiment and of the actual occurrence must be sufficiently similar to provide a fair comparison. Once similarity is established, differences, if any, between the experiment and the actual event go only to the weight to be given to the experimental evidence. *Randall v. Warnaco, Inc.*, 677 F.2d 1226 (8th Cir.1982). In the exercise of its discretion, the court should weigh the probative value of the experimental evidence (that is the extent of similarity of experimental conditions with the litigated event) against the dangers of confusing the issues before the jury, unfair prejudice and undue consumption of trial time. Pa.R.E. 403; *McGrorey v. Obermayer, Rebmann, Maxwell & Hippel*, 14 Pa. D. & C.3d 335 (C.P. Phila.Cnty. 1978), *aff'd* 274 Pa. Super. 646, 423 A.2d 1314 (1979).

The courts have found probative value in the following: demonstration showing effect on nails of a wooden board breaking downward, *Pascale v. Hechinger Co. of Pennsylvania.*, 426 Pa. Super. 426, 627 A.2d 750 (1993); test crash films, *Jackson v. Spagnola*, 349 Pa. Super. 471, 503 A.2d 944 (1986); chemical testing of liquor, *In re Clover Bar Inc.*, 203 Pa. Super. 11, 198 A.2d 366 (1964); dynamic experiments on the same year and model car, *McGrorey v. Obermayer, Rebmann, Maxwell & Hippel*, 14 Pa. D. & C.3d 335 (C.P. Phila.Cnty. 1978), *aff'd* 274 Pa. Super. 646, 423 A.2d 1314 (1979). Rejected as dissimilar were experiments on a boiler, *Dougherty v. Edward J. Meloney, Inc.*, 443 Pa. Super. 201, 661 A.2d 375 (1995), window screens, *Leonard by Meyers v. Nichols Homeshield*, 384 Pa. Super. 1, 557 A.2d 743 (1989), and an EEG obtained through laboratory-induced intoxication, *Commonwealth v. Henry*, 524 Pa. 135, 569 A.2d 929 (1990). *See also Harsh v. Petroll*, 840 A.2d 404 (Pa.Cmwlth. 2003) (court properly rejected crash tests which were not substantially similar to actual accident); *Yankowsky v. Katz, Inc.*, 443 Pa. Super. 494, 662 A.2d 665 (1995) (plaintiff not permitted to demonstrate to jury how nightgown caught fire by wearing garment of different size).

The Superior Court has cautioned that because a videotape re-enactment has the potential to make a stronger impact than oral testimony, the trial judge should view the tape *in camera* prior to showing it to the jury, especially where the opposing party claims the tape is overly prejudicial. *Commonwealth v. Impellizzeri*, 443 Pa. Super. 296, 661 A.2d 422 (1995). The Supreme Court has said a trial judge must issue limiting instructions to the jury explaining the nature of the specific computer-generated animation. *Commonwealth v. Serge*, 896 A.2d 1170 (Pa. 2006).

Compare: *Jones v. Ralls*, 187 F.3d 848 (8th Cir. 1999); *Pandit v. Am. Honda Motor Co.*, 82 F.3d 376 (10th Cir.1996); *Four Corners Helicopters, Inc. v. Turbomeca, S.A.*, 979 F.2d 1434 (10th Cir.1992) (experimental evidence is admissible so long as it is relevant and probative; such evidence has probative value if the conditions of the experiment are identical with or similar to the conditions of the transaction in litigation).

Research References

Packel & Poulin, Pennsylvania Evidence § 726 (4th ed. 2013)

McCormick, Evidence § 202 (7th ed. 2013)

PRIOR CONSISTENT STATEMENT

See: Pa.R.E. 613(c).

Objection

- Objection. The question calls for hearsay and has no other purpose except to bolster trial testimony with allegedly prior consistent statements.

Response

- Pennsylvania law does not treat prior consistent statements as hearsay and the question is proper. We are entitled to rebut the charge that the witness' testimony [*was recently fabricated*] [*is the product of a faulty memory*].

Pennsylvania Law

Unlike the Federal Rules of Evidence,[1] Pennsylvania adheres to the common law view and does not treat any prior consistent statement of a witness as substantive evidence. A prior consistent statement is always received for rehabilitation purposes only. *Commonwealth v. Baumhammers*, 960 A.2d 59 (Pa. 2008); *Commonwealth v. Curley*, 910 A.2d 692 (Pa. Super. 2006). The admissibility of a prior consistent statement is governed by principles of relevance, not hearsay. *See* Pa.R.E.

---

[1]Under Fed.R.Evid. 801(d)(1)(B), a prior consistent statement is excluded from the definition of hearsay and may be admitted as substantive evidence if: (1) the witness testifies at trial and is subject to cross-examination; (2) the prior statement is consistent with the witness' trial testimony; (3) the statement is offered to rebut an express or implied charge of recent fabrication or improper influence or motive; and (4) the statement was made before the witness had a motive to fabricate. *Tome v. United States*, 513 U.S. 150, 115 S.Ct. 696, 130 L.Ed.2d 574 (1995) (adding the temporal requirement that the consistent statement must pre-date the motive to falsify).

613(c).

As a general rule, prior statements consistent with the present testimony of a witness are not admissible merely to buttress or corroborate the witness' in-court testimony. *Commonwealth v. Swint*, 488 Pa. 279, 412 A.2d 507 (1980); *Commonwealth v. Swinson*, 426 Pa. Super. 167, 626 A.2d 627 (1993). The primary reasons for excluding evidence of prior consistent statements are the need to avoid unnecessary repetition of cumulative evidence, and the need to prevent the fabrication of evidence. *See Commonwealth v. Willis*, 380 Pa. Super. 555, 552 A.2d 682 (1988).

The principal exception to the general rule of exclusion is that prior consistent statements may be admitted to rehabilitate a witness whose credibility has been attacked with a charge of faulty memory or to rebut accusations or suggestions that an improper motive or influence prompted the witness to fabricate the trial testimony. Pa.R.E. 613(c); *Commonwealth v. Harris*, 578 Pa. 377, 852 A.2d 1168 (2004); *Commonwealth v. Koehler*, 558 Pa. 334, 737 A.2d 225 (1999); *Commonwealth v. Murphy*, 540 Pa. 318, 657 A.2d 927 (1995); *Commonwealth v. Griffin*, 511 Pa. 553, 515 A.2d 865 (1986); *Commonwealth v. Tucker*, 143 A.3d 955 (Pa. Super. 2016) (permissible rehabilitation under Rule 613(c)(1) to use prior consistent statement to rebut conspiracy theory offered by defense); *Commonwealth v. Hunzer*, 868 A.2d 498 (Pa. Super. 2005); *Commonwealth v. Fielder*, 417 Pa. Super. 455, 612 A.2d 1028 (1992); *Havasy v. Resnick*, 415 Pa. Super. 480, 609 A.2d 1326 (1992).

For such testimony properly to be admitted as a prior consistent statement, the opposing party must have the opportunity to cross-examine the declarant about the statement. Pa.R.E. 613(c); *Commonwealth v. Kuder*, 62 A.3d 1038 (Pa. Super. 2013).

It is not necessary that the impeachment be by

direct attack on the witness; it may be implied, inferred or insinuated either by cross-examination, presentation of conflicting evidence, or a combination of the two. *Commonwealth v. Tucker*, supra (in opening statement, defense counsel said motorcycle club members met and fabricated stories about shooting); *Commonwealth v. Willis*, 380 Pa. Super. 555, 552 A.2d 682 (1988). For example, an assertion that the witness is testifying in order to receive lenient treatment is an adequate claim of corrupt motive or influence to permit introduction of prior consistent statements. *Commonwealth v. Mokluk*, 298 Pa. Super. 360, 444 A.2d 1214 (1982); *see Keefer v. Byers*, 398 Pa. 447, 159 A.2d 477 (1960) (questioning "strongly suggested" that testimony was a recent fabrication).

In order for the prior consistent statement to be admissible, it must have been made before its effect in the case could have been foreseen, or before the alleged improper motive or influence existed. Pa.R.E. 613(c)(1); *Commonwealth v. Smith*, 17 A.3d 873 (Pa. 2011) (prior consistent statement admissible only if made before declarant has motive to fabricate); *Commonwealth v. Montalvo*, 986 A.2d 84 (Pa. 2009); *Commonwealth v. Harris*, 578 Pa. 377, 852 A.2d 1168 (2004) (Rule 613 does not require that the prior consistent statement was made before the prior inconsistent statement); *Commonwealth v. Hutchinson*, 521 Pa. 482, 556 A.2d 370 (1989); *Commonwealth v. Gore*, 262 Pa. Super. 540, 396 A.2d 1302 (1978).

In order to support the credibility of the witness, prior consistent statements can be proved through testimony of the person to whom the statements were made. *Commonwealth v. Hutchinson*, 556 A.2d 370 (Pa. 1989); *Commonwealth v. Handfield*, 34 A.3d 187 (Pa. Super. 2011) (prior consistent statement of Commonwealth witness admitted through testimony of another witness); *Commonwealth v. Gore*, 396 A.2d 1302 (Pa. Super. 1978) (prior consistent statement of victim to police officer admitted through officer's testimony after victim testified).

Not every impeachment of a witness will permit rehabilitation by means of prior consistent statements. Rehabilitation is not permissible where the witness is impeached by contradiction or by a showing of the implausibility of his testimony. *Commonwealth v. Carr*, 436 Pa. 124, 259 A.2d 165 (1969). The reason for this limitation is that when there is a contradiction between the testimonies of two witnesses, it cannot help the trier of fact in deciding between them merely to show that one of the witnesses has asserted the same thing previously. "If that were an argument, then the witness who had repeated his story to the greatest number of people would be the most credible." 4 Wigmore on Evidence § 1127 (Chadborn rev. 1972).

Generally, evidence of a prior consistent statement is admissible only in rebuttal. *Commonwealth v. Gaddy*, 468 Pa. 303, 362 A.2d 217 (1976). However, where the defense is centered on attacking a witness's credibility in a way that would permit introduction of a prior consistent statement to rehabilitate, the trial court has discretion to allow anticipatory admission of the prior statement. *Commonwealth v. Cook*, 952 A.2d 594 (Pa. 2008); *Commonwealth v. Wilson*, 580 Pa. 439, 861 A.2d 919 (2004); *Commonwealth v. Counterman*, 553 Pa. 370, 719 A.2d 284 (1998) (trial court had discretion to admit prior consistent statement during Commonwealth's case in chief where there had been extensive cross-examination of prosecution witness as to inconsistent statements coupled with attack on her ability to remember specific details); *Commonwealth v. Smith*, 518 Pa. 15, 540 A.2d 246 (1988) (prosecution allowed to introduce prior consistent statement before cross-examination where defense counsel in opening argument had charged the witness with fabricating the evidence; order of proof is a matter of the trial court's discretion); *Commonwealth v. Tocker*, supra (where defense opening statement claimed witnesses conspired to shape testimony against defendant, prior consistent statement introduced as part of prosecutor's direct examination of witness).

Whether a witness had a motive to fabricate at the time he made the prior consistent statement is a preliminary question under Pa.R.E. 104 to be resolved by the trial court based upon the particular circumstances of an individual case.

Compare: Fed. R. Evid. 801 (d)(1)(B).

Research References

Packel & Poulin, Pennsylvania Evidence § 613-5 (4th ed. 2013)

McCormick, Evidence § 47 (7th ed. 2013)

PRIVILEGE: ACCOUNTANT-CLIENT

See: Pa.R.E. 501.

Objection

- Objection. [*Request sidebar*] The question calls for disclosure of privileged information which the witness obtained pursuant to his engagement as accountant for [*the client (specify)*].

Response

- The objection is not well founded. The CPA Act excludes from the assertion of privilege any information required to be disclosed by the standards of the profession in reporting on the examination of financial statements. Generally accepted accounting principles (GAAP) require disclosure of the information sought here.

Pennsylvania Law

The C.P.A. Law of May 26, 1947, P.L. 318, as amended, 63 Pa. Cons. Stat. § 9.11(a) provides:

Except by permission of the client . . . a certified public accountant . . . shall not be required to, and shall not voluntarily, disclose or divulge information of which he may have become possessed relative to and in connection with any professional services as a certified public accountant . . . . The information derived from or as a result of such professional services shall be deemed confidential and privileged: Provided, however, that nothing herein shall be taken or construed as prohibiting the disclosure of information required to be disclosed by the standards of the profession in reporting on the examination of financial statements . . . .

The accountant-client privilege belongs only to the client. *James Talcott, Inc. v. C.I.T. Corp.*, 14 Pa. D. & C.3d 204 (C.P. Allegheny County, 1980). This privilege—unlike the attorney-client privilege—is statutory only and was not recognized at common law. Traditionally, it has been more narrowly construed than the attorney-client privilege.

Wolfington v. Wolfington Body Co., 47 Pa. D. & C.4th 225 (C.P. Phila. Cnty. 2000); *Greenfield Foundation v. Bankers Sec. Corp.*, 7 Pa. D. & C.3d 535 (C.P. Phila.Cnty, 1978). Moreover, the broad exclusion from privilege of information required to be disclosed by the standards of the profession in reporting on the examination of financial statements (which is a reference to the disclosure requirements mandated by generally accepted accounting principles) in contrast to the absolute privilege afforded the attorney-client relationship demonstrates a legislative intent to provide fewer protections to the accountant-client relationship. *See Orix USA Corp. v. DVI, Inc.*, 37 Pa. D. & C.4th 491 (C.P. Allegheny County, 1997) (there is a crime-fraud exception to 63 P.S. § 9.11(a) that is identical to the crime-fraud exception to the attorney-client privilege; no privilege exists when client utilizes accountant services to commit fraud or crime).

Compare: *Wm. T. Thompson Co. v. Gen. Nutrition Corp.*, 671 F.2d 100 (3d Cir.1982), holding that federal common law does not recognize any confidential accountant-client privilege.

Research References

Packel & Poulin, Pennsylvania Evidence § 531 (4th ed. 2013)

McCormick, Evidence § 76.2 (7th ed. 2013)

PRIVILEGE: ATTORNEY-CLIENT

See: Pa.R.E. 501.

Objection

- Objection. The question calls for disclosure of a privileged communication between the witness and his attorney.

Response

- The evidence is not privileged because *[the communication took place in the presence of a third party] [the privilege has been waived (specify)] [the communication was made with the expectation that it would be revealed to others] [the attorney is rebutting the client's attack on his integrity / professional competence] [the attorney was acting in a nonlegal capacity]*.

Pennsylvania Law

The attorney-client privilege, the oldest of the privileges for confidential communications known to the common law, *Upjohn Co. v. United States*, 449 U.S. 383, 101 S.Ct. 677, 66 L.Ed.2d 584 (1981), rests on the need for the advocate and counselor to know all that relates to the client's reasons for seeking representation if the professional mission is to be carried out. *Trammel v. United States*, 445 U.S. 40, 100 S.Ct. 906, 63 L.Ed.2d 186 (1980); *Commonwealth v. Chmiel*, 558 Pa. 478, 738 A.2d 406 (1999); *Board of Sup'rs of Milford Tp. v. McGogney*, 13 A.3d 569 (Pa.Cmwlth.2011); *Carbis Walker, LLP v. Hill, Barth and King, LLC*, 930 A.2d 573 (Pa. Super. 2007). The privilege (also codified by statute in civil[1] and criminal[2] proceedings) exists to protect not only the giving of professional

---

[1] 42 Pa.C.S. § 5928.

[2] 42 Pa.C.S. § 5916.

advice to those who can act on it but also the giving of information to the lawyer to enable him to give sound and informed advice. *Upjohn*, 449 U.S. at 390–391, 101 S.Ct. at 683. When the privilege applies, it affords confidential communications between lawyer and client absolute protection from disclosure. *See Estate of Kofsky*, 487 Pa. 473, 409 A.2d 1358 (1979) (purpose is to foster confidence between client and advocate that will lead to trusting and open attorney-client dialogue); *Berkeyheiser v. A-Plus Investigations*, 936 A.2d 1117 (Pa. Super. 2007). The privilege applies to communications made by the client to the attorney and by the attorney to the client, *Gillard v. AIG Insurance Co.*, 15 A.3d 44 (Pa.2011); *Custom Designs & Mfg. Co. v. Sherwin-Williams Co.*, 39 A.3d 372 (Pa. Super. 2012); *Slusaw v. Hoffman*, 861 A.2d 269 (Pa. Super. 2004); and survives the client's death, *Swidler & Berlin v. United States*, 524 U.S. 399, 118 S.Ct. 2081, 141 L.Ed.2d 379 (1998).

The shelter afforded by the privilege "only protects disclosure of communications; it does not protect disclosure of the underlying facts by those who communicated with the attorney," *Upjohn*, 449 U.S. at 395, 101 S.Ct. at 685, unless such disclosure would reveal confidential communications. The client cannot be compelled to answer the question, "What did you say or write to the attorney?", but may not refuse to disclose any relevant fact within his knowledge merely because he incorporated such fact into his communication to his attorney. *See, e.g., Gould v. City of Aliquippa*, 750 A.2d 934 (Pa.Cmwlth.2000) (protecting communications between city officials and attorney; noting that facts could be obtained via depositions and interrogatories). The scope of the attorney-client privilege is fact sensitive and must be addressed on a case-by-case basis. *Upjohn*, 449 U.S. at 396–397, 101 S.Ct. at 686; *In re Search Warrant B-21778*, 513 Pa. 429, 521 A.2d 422 (1987).

The client is the holder of the privilege, *Law*

Office of Harris v. PHI. Waterfront, 957 A.2d 1223 (Pa. Super. 2008) and he alone may waive it. *Commonwealth v. McKenna*, 206 Pa. Super. 317, 213 A.2d 223 (1965). A client may be an individual or any kind of entity, including a governmental unit, corporation or unincorporated association. *See, e.g., Commonwealth v. United States Mineral Prods. Co.*, 809 A.2d 1000 (Pa.Cmwlth.2002) (government entity). The privilege does not extend to aiding and abetting a client in fraudulent or criminal activities. *Commonwealth v. Maguigan*, 511 Pa. 112, 511 A.2d 1327 (1986); *Nadler v. Warner*, 321 Pa. 139, 184 A. 3 (1936).

The party invoking the privilege must prove: (1) the asserted holder of the privilege is or sought to become a client; (2) the person to whom the communication was made (a) is a member of the bar of a court, or his subordinate, and (b) in connection with the communication is acting as a lawyer; (3) the communication relates to a fact of which the attorney was informed (a) by his client, (b) without the presence of strangers, (c) for the purpose of securing primarily either (i) an opinion on law or (ii) legal services or (iii) assistance in some legal proceeding, and not (d) for the purpose of committing a crime or tort; and (4) the privilege has been (a) claimed and (b) not waived by the client. *In re Investigating Grand Jury of Philadelphia County*, No. 88-00-3503, 527 Pa. 432, 593 A.2d 402 (1991); *United States v. United Shoe Mach. Corp.*, 89 F.Supp. 357, 358–359 (D.Mass.1950); *Andritz Sprout-Bauer, Inc. v. Beazer East, Inc.*, 174 F.R.D. 609 (M.D.Pa.1997).

Once the party asserting the privilege shows that the privilege is properly invoked, the burden shifts to the party seeking disclosure to show that the disclosure of the information will not violate the privilege. *In re Investigating Grand Jury of Philadelphia County No. 88-00-3503*, 527 Pa. 432, 593 A.2d 402 (1991); *Salsman v. Brown*, 51 A.3d 892 (Pa. Super. 2012).

432

Information that corporate counsel obtains from lower ranking corporate employees will be protected where: (1) corporate management had directed the employees to provide information to corporate counsel; (2) the lower level employees are told that the investigation is highly confidential; (3) the responses are furnished only to counsel, and (4) the information collected by counsel is disseminated only to those in upper management who will play a substantial role in deciding and directing the corporation's response. *Upjohn Co. v. United States*, 449 U.S. 383, 101 S.Ct. 677, 66 L.Ed.2d 584 (1981); *Commonwealth v. Schultz*, 133 A.3d 294 (Pa. Super. 2016) (when the client is a corporation, privilege extends to communications between corporation's attorney and agents or employees authorized to act on corporation's behalf); *Commonwealth v. Curley*, 131 A.3d 994 (Pa. Super. 2016).

Where a business is dissolved and/or has ceased to operate, and has neither a legal successor or some remaining management with authority to handle post-dissolution windup, then there is no longer any client to waive or raise the privilege. Therefore, there is no attorney-client privilege. *Red Vision Sys. v. Nat'l Real Estate Info.*, 108 A.3d 54 (Pa. Super. 2015).

The privilege has several well-established exceptions. A communication between an attorney and his client is not privileged: (1) if it takes place in the presence of a third person or of the adverse party, *In re Beisgen's Estate*, 387 Pa. 425, 128 A.2d 52 (1956); (2) where the attorney's conduct has been challenged by the client, *Commonwealth v. Flor*, 136 A.3d 150 (Pa. 2016) (waiver only as to those aspects of the attorney's conduct being challenged); *Commonwealth v. Chmiel*, 558 Pa. 478, 738 A.2d 406 (1999); *Salsman v. Brown*, 51 A.3d 892 (Pa. Super. 2012); (3) where two or more persons employ the same attorney for the same transaction, communications made to the attorney are not privileged in a subsequent dispute between those parties if the dispute concerns the transaction for which they had joint representation, *Loutzenhiser v. Doddo*, 436 Pa. 512, 260 A.2d 745 (1970); *Southeastern Pennsylvania Transp. Auth. v. Transit Cas. Co.*, 55 F.R.D. 553 (E.D.Pa.1972); (4) where, in context, the client's rights or interest cannot be adversely affected and the administration of justice is advanced, *Cohen v. Jenkintown Cab Co.*, 238 Pa. Super. 456, 357 A.2d 689 (1976).

Where the client reasonably but mistakenly believes that his or her confidential communication was with a licensed attorney, the privilege still applies. *Triffin v. DiSalvo*, 434 Pa. Super. 326, 643 A.2d 118 (1994); *c.f.*, *Joyner v. SEPTA*, 736 A.2d 35 (Pa.Cmwlth.1999) (privilege did not apply to plaintiff's inadvertent voice mail message to opposing counsel).

Where an individual is acting as an agent for one of the parties to the privilege, the privilege is not destroyed. Thus, the presence of certain third parties (such as investigators, experts, litigation assistants) if essential to and in furtherance of the communication, does not waive the privilege. *Commonwealth v. Baumhammers*, 960 A.2d 59 (Pa. 2008); *Commonwealth v. Hetzel*, 822 A.2d 747 (Pa. Super. 2003) (extending privilege to work product of forensic dentist retained by criminal defense counsel); *Commonwealth v. Noll*, 443 Pa. Super. 602, 662 A.2d 1123 (1995) (investigator); *Commonwealth v. Mrozek*, 441 Pa. Super. 425, 657 A.2d 997 (1995) (legal secretary); *Commonwealth v. Hutchinson*, 290 Pa. Super. 254, 434 A.2d 740 (1981).

For authority recognizing the existence of the joint defense/common interest privilege, see *In Re Condemnation By City*, 981 A.2d 391 (Pa.Cmwlth. 2009); *Executive Risk Indemnity, Inc. v. Cigna Corp.*, 81 Pa. D. & C.4th 410 (2006); *Young v. Presbyterian Homes, Inc.*, 50 Pa. D. & C.4th 190 (2001).

Even after formal representation ends, a

lawyer retains a professional relationship with the client and unless it is made clear that there is no confidentiality in the communication, the attorney-client privilege remains. *In re Investigating Grand Jury*, 887 A.2d 257 (Pa. Super. 2005) (prisoner's phone call to attorney he had fired was about his case and, therefore, was privileged).

Compare: Fed. R. Evid. 501.

Research References

Packel & Poulin, Pennsylvania Evidence § 521 (4th ed. 2013)

McCormick, Evidence Chapter 10 (7th ed. 2013)

PRIVILEGE: CLERGY

See: Pa.R.E. 501.

Objection

- Objection. [*Request sidebar*] The question seeks information communicated to a clergyman which is privileged under 42 Pa.C.S.A. § 5943.

Response

- This evidence is not privileged and is admissible because [*the statements made were not in the context of religious counseling*] [*the circumstances in which the statements were made were such that they were not religious, in that nothing spiritual or in the nature of forgiveness was ever discussed*] [*the statements were made in the presence of a third person who was not an agent for one of the parties to the privilege*].

Pennsylvania Law

The clergy privilege protects communications to a member of the clergy, in his or her spiritual or professional capacity, by persons who seek spiritual counseling and who reasonably expect that their words will be kept in confidence. *Commonwealth v. Stewart*, 547 Pa. 277, 690 A.2d 195 (1997); *Hutchison v. Luddy*, 414 Pa. Super. 138, 606 A.2d 905 (1992); *Commonwealth v. Musolino*, 320 Pa. Super. 425, 467 A.2d 605 (1983); *Commonwealth v. Shallenberger*, 38 Pa. D. & C.3d 201 (1985); *LeGore v. LeGore*, 31 Pa. D. & C.2d 107 (1963).

42 Pa.C.S.A. § 5943 provides:

Confidential communications to clergymen. No clergyman, priest, rabbi or minister of the gospel of any regularly established church or religious organization, except clergymen or ministers, who are self-ordained or who are members of religious organizations in which members other than the leader thereof are deemed clergymen or ministers, who while in the course of his duties has acquired information from any person secretly and in confidence shall be compelled, or allowed without consent of such person, to disclose that information in any legal proceeding, trial or investigation before any government unit.

The privilege does not prohibit all testimony by members of the clergy. Rather, the privilege is limited to information told in confidence to them in their role as confessor or counselor. *Commonwealth v. Stewart*, 547 Pa. 277, 690 A.2d 195 (1997); *Commonwealth v. Patterson*, 392 Pa. Super. 331, 572 A.2d 1258 (1990). The trial court will look at the circumstances to determine whether a person's statements were made in secrecy and confidence to a clergyman in the course and context of his religious duties. Statements made to ministers in their respective roles as court-appointed counselor and as auxiliary parole supervisor did not qualify for the privilege, *Commonwealth v. Patterson*, 392 Pa. Super. 331, 572 A.2d 1258 (1990); *Fahlfeder v. Commonwealth, Pennsylvania Bd. of Probation and Parole*, 80 Pa.Cmwlth. 86, 470 A.2d 1130 (1984), nor did a statement by a decedent to her priest that she had no will, *In re McGrogan's Will*, 26 Pa. D. & C.2d 37 (Orphan's Ct. Chester County, 1962). The privilege does not protect information regarding the manner in which a religious institution conducts its affairs or information acquired by a church as a result of independent investigations not involving confidential communications between priest and penitent. *Commonwealth v. Stewart*, 547 Pa. 277, 690 A.2d 195 (1997); *Hutchison v. Luddy*, 414 Pa. Super. 138, 606 A.2d 905 (1992).

Compare: Fed. R. Evid. 501. Although the question of who may assert the privilege has rarely arisen, at least one federal court has held that the privilege may only be waived by the clergyman, thus safeguarding a clergyman's status as a secure repository for the confessant's confidences. *Eckmann v. Board of Educ. Hawthorn Sch. Dist.*, 106 F.R.D.

70 (E.D.Mo.1985); *see also In re Grand Jury Investigation*, 918 F.2d 374, 385 n. 15 (3d Cir.1990) (acknowledging authority for proposition that privilege can be asserted by clergyperson on behalf of communicant).

Research References

Packel & Poulin, Pennsylvania Evidence § 532 (4th ed. 2013)

McCormick, Evidence § 76.2 (7th ed. 2013)

PRIVILEGE: CONFIDENTIAL INFORMER

See: Pa.R.E. 501.

Objection

- I object on grounds of privilege. The question seeks [*the identity of*] [*information which will lead to the identity of*] the Commonwealth's informant.

Response

- Your Honor, we believe the informant was the only eyewitness to the event and since we are asserting a defense of mistaken identity, the right to call or cross-examine him is vital to the defense.

Pennsylvania Law

What is usually referred to as the informer's privilege is, in reality, the government's privilege to refuse to disclose the identity of persons who furnish information concerning crimes to law enforcement officers. *Commonwealth v. Watson*, 69 A.3d 605 (Pa. Super. 2013) (collecting cases). The purpose of the privilege is the furtherance and protection of the public interest in effective law enforcement. The privilege recognizes the obligation of citizens to communicate their knowledge of the commission of crimes to law enforcement officials and, by preserving their anonymity and, hence, their safety, encourages them to perform that obligation. *Roviaro v. United States*, 353 U.S. 53, 77 S.Ct. 623, 1 L.Ed.2d 639 (1957).

Under Pennsylvania case law and Pa.R.Crim.P. 573, the privilege with respect to the disclosure of confidential informants is a qualified privilege. This privilege allows the Commonwealth to withhold the identity of an informer, and limits the prosecution's duty to make available to the defense the names and whereabouts of all material witnesses. *Commonwealth v. Carter*, 427 Pa. 53, 233 A.2d 284 (1967); *Commonwealth v. Delligatti*, 371 Pa. Super.

315, 538 A.2d 34 (1988); *cf. Com. Ex Rel. Dist. Attorney of Blair County*, 823 A.2d 147 (2003) (civil case; court may issue injunctive relief in form of protective order to prevent disclosure of confidential informant). In order to obtain an informer's identity, the defense must do more than merely assert that such a disclosure might be helpful to the defense. *Commonwealth v. Herron*, 475 Pa. 461, 380 A.2d 1228 (1977); *Commonwealth v. Fleck*, 324 Pa. Super. 227, 471 A.2d 547 (1984). Although the defendant cannot be expected to predict exactly what the informant would say if called as a witness, he must at least suggest a reasonable possibility that the informant could give testimony that would tend to exonerate the defendant, so that it would be unfair to withhold it. *Commonwealth v. Roebuck*, 545 Pa. 471, 681 A.2d 1279 (1996); *Commonwealth v. Jordan*, 125 A.3d 55 (Pa. Super. 2015); *Commonwealth v. Washington*, 63 A.3d 797 (Pa. Super. 2013).

Where the confidential informer is not a witness to the incident at issue, the defendant must show that the Commonwealth's disclosure of the identity of the informant is: (1) material to his defense; (2) reasonable; and (3) in the interests of justice. *Commonwealth v. Washington*, 63 A.3d 797 (Pa. Super. 2013); *Commonwealth v. Baker*, 946 A.2d 691 (Pa. Super. 2008); *Commonwealth v. King*, 932 A.2d 948 (Pa. Super. 2007). Once such a showing is made by the defendant, it is within the discretion of the trial court to determine whether the circumstances require production of the informant. *Commonwealth v. Bonasorte*, 337 Pa. Super. 332, 486 A.2d 1361 (1984).

The fundamental concern is one of fairness. There is no fixed rule with respect to disclosure. *Commonwealth v. Marsh*, 997 A.2d 318 (Pa. 2010) (whether disclosure should be made depends on the particular circumstances of each case). The public interest in non-disclosure of an informer's identity in the particular circumstances of a given case must

440

be balanced against the individual's right to prepare his defense. *Commonwealth v. Moscardelli*, 774 A.2d 754 (Pa. Super. 2001); *Commonwealth v. Speaks*, 351 Pa. Super. 149, 505 A.2d 310 (1986). Consideration is given to the crime charged, the possible defenses and the possible significance of the informer's testimony. *See, e.g. Commonwealth v. Bing*, 551 Pa. 659, 713 A.2d 56 (1998) (balance initially weighted toward Commonwealth to preserve effective law enforcement but tips in favor of disclosure where guilt is found solely on police testimony from a single observation and testimony from a disinterested source, such as the informant, is available); *Commonwealth v. Heater*, 899 A.2d 1126 (Pa. Super. 2006).

Disclosure of the informer's identity has been ordered to support a defense of mistaken identity, *Commonwealth v. Carter*, 427 Pa. 53, 233 A.2d 284 (1967); entrapment, *Commonwealth v. Washington*, 463 Pa. 206, 344 A.2d 496 (1975); and where informant had information concerning alternative suspect, *Commonwealth v. Redmond*, 577 A.2d 547 (Pa. Super. 1990), but refused where positive identification was supplied by other persons independent of the informant, *Commonwealth v. Garvin*, 448 Pa. 258, 293 A.2d 33 (1972). *See also*, *Commonwealth v. Ross*, 623 A.2d 827 (Pa. Super. 1993) (where defendant knew informer and was in the same position as the Commonwealth to subpoena him, trial court properly denied request to compel disclosure); *Commonwealth v. Hritz*, 444 Pa. Super. 264, 663 A.2d 775 (1995) (defendant presented speculative allegations and record was devoid of foundation to suggest that informant's identity might have been helpful to entrapment defense).

Confidential Surveillance Sites

When the Commonwealth asserts that a surveillance location is confidential, the defendant bears the initial burden of demonstrating that disclosure is necessary to conduct his defense. The Commonwealth must then explain why confidentiality must be preserved. The trial court must then balance the *Roviaro* factors to determine whether the state's interest outweighs the defendant's need for information as it relates to his ability to adequately defend against the pending criminal charges. *Commonwealth v. Rodriquez*, 543 Pa. 651, 674 A.2d 225 (1996) (identity of site protected; there was sufficient other information available for defense counsel to conduct effective cross-examination); *Commonwealth v. Clark*, 746 A.2d 1128 (Pa. Super. 2000) (same); *Commonwealth v. Nobles*, 941 A.2d 50 (Pa. Super. 2008) (request denied; to reveal which rooftop officer was on when he witnessed drug deal could endanger person who gave access and officers using same location in future investigations).

Compare: Fed. R. Evid. 501. The federal courts have consistently held both that a defendant has no absolute constitutional right to the disclosure of an informant's identity, *United States v. Bowser*, 941 F.2d 1019 (10th Cir.1991), and that the government has no absolute right to withhold the informant's identity. *United States v. Mendoza-Salgado*, 964 F.2d 993 (10th Cir.1992).

The privilege is also available in civil cases. *Matter of Search of 1638 E. 2nd St., Tulsa, Okl.*, 993 F.2d 773 (10th Cir.1993); *Hoffman v. Reali*, 973 F.2d 980 (1st Cir.1992); *Holman v. Cayce*, 873 F.2d 944 (6th Cir.1989); *Dole v. Local 1942, IBEW, AFL-CIO*, 870 F.2d 368 (7th Cir.1989). See also *Stein v. Plymouth Tp.*, 994 A.2d 1179 (Pa. Cmwlth. 2010) (Right to Know Law did not require Township to reveal name of person who complained about property owner's misuse of his properties). In civil cases, the privilege is arguably stronger and more difficult to overcome because not all constitutional guarantees which inure to criminal defendants are similarly available to civil litigants. *Dole*, 870 F.2d at 372.

Research References

Packel & Poulin, Pennsylvania Evidence §§ 535, 535-1 (4th ed. 2013)

McCormick, Evidence § 111 (7th ed. 2013)

PRIVILEGE: DELIBERATIVE PROCESS

See: Pa.R.E. 501.

Objection

- [*At sidebar*] The court earlier ruled that the deliberative process privilege applies in this case. This question now seeks to elicit privileged information.

Response

- The privilege does not apply to factual information and that is all the question asks for.

Pennsylvania Law

Drawing upon a well-developed body of federal law, a plurality of the Pennsylvania Supreme Court recognized a deliberative process privilege in *Commonwealth ex rel. Unified Judicial System v. Vartan*, 557 Pa. 390, 733 A.2d 1258 (1999) (privilege protected deliberations by Supreme Court justices about lease of proposed new court building). *See also In re Interbranch Commission on Juvenile Justice*, 988 A.2d 1269, 1278 (Pa. 2010) (no basis to permit disclosure of matters protected by the deliberative process privilege); *LaValle v. Office of Gen. Counsel*, 564 Pa. 482, 769 A.2d 449 (2001) (applying deliberative process analysis to Right To Know Act claim; state senators denied access to audit commissioned by executive branch for purpose of settling lawsuit); *Ario v. Deloitte & Touche LLP*, 934 A.2d 1290 (Pa.Cmwlth. 2007) (communications between office of General Counsel and Insurance Commissioner re failing insurance company protected by deliberative process privilege); *Leber v. Stretton*, 928 A.2d 262 (Pa. Super. 2007) (deliberative process of judicial officer may not be inquired into); *see Tribune-Review Pub. Co. v. DCED*, 859 A.2d 1261, 1269 (Pa. 2004) (while not necessary to decision, referring to privilege with approval). *But see Rae v. Pa. Funeral Directors*, 925 A.2d 197, 205 (Pa.Cmwlth. 2007), vacated, 602 Pa. 65, 977 A.2d 1121 (2009) (". . . there is no clear common law deliberative process privilege protecting the executive branch.").

The *Vartan* Court said that the " 'deliberative process privilege' permits the government to withhold documents containing confidential deliberations of law or policymaking, reflecting opinions, recommendations, or advice." *Commonwealth ex rel. Unified Judicial System v. Vartan*, 557 Pa. 390, 402, 733 A.2d 1258, 1265 (1999) (citing *Redland Soccer Club, Inc. v. Department of the Army of the United States*, 55 F.3d 827, 853 (3d Cir. 1995)). The privilege protects the decision-making processes of judges and administrators since questioning a judge or a decision maker about the process by which a decision had been reached would undermine judicial or administrative process. *Commonwealth ex rel. Unified Judicial System v. Vartan*, 557 Pa. 390, 733 A.2d 1258 (1999) (citing *United States v. Morgan*, 313 U.S. 409, 422, 61 S.Ct. 999, 1004–05, 85 L.Ed.1429 (1941)); *Commonwealth v. Orie*, 88 A.3d 983, 1012 (Pa. Super. 2014) (privilege benefits the public, not the officials who assert the privilege).

In determining whether the privilege applies, a three-prong analysis is employed. The court must determine whether the communications (1) were made before the deliberative process was completed; (2) whether the communications were deliberative in character; and (3) whether the communications were a "direct part of the deliberative process in that it makes recommendation or expresses opinions on legal or policy matters." *Vartan*, 557 Pa. at 400, 733 A.2d at 1264. The privilege does not apply to factual information, so long as the factual information is severable from the advice or underlying confidential deliberations of law or policymaking. *Vartan*; *Koken v. One Beacon Insurance Company, C.G.U.*, 911 A.2d 1021, 1029 (Pa.Cmwlth.2006).

To satisfy the first step the party asserting the privilege must show that the information is both pre-decisional and deliberative. The information is "pre-decisional if it reflects matters leading to a final decision of an agency." *Cipolla v. County of Rensselaer*, 2001 WL 1223489, 2001 U.S. Dist. Lexis 16150 (N.D.N.Y. Oct. 10, 2001); accord *Vartan*. The information is deliberative if it reflects the process the agency used to reach the decision. *Cipolla*; *Vartan*.

The privilege has received uneven treatment in the judicial panels of the Commonwealth Court. *Compare, Rae v. PA Funeral Directors*, 925 A.2d 197 (Pa.Cmwlth.2007) (no clear common law deliberative process privilege protecting the executive branch) *with Ario v. Deloitte & Touche LLP*, 934 A.2d 1290 (2007) (Supreme Court recognized privilege in *Vartan*).

A summary of federal law is as follows.

One of the traditional evidentiary privileges available to the government is the common law deliberative process privilege. This qualified privilege protects the consultative functions of government by maintaining the confidentiality of advisory opinions, recommendations and deliberations comprising part of a process by which governmental decisions and policies are formulated. *Dow Jones & Co. v. Dep't of Justice*, 917 F.2d 571, 573 (D.C.Cir. 1990) (privilege "predicated on the recognition that the quality of administrative decisionmaking would be seriously undermined if agencies were forced to operate in a fish bowl"). The privilege attaches to inter-and intra-agency communications that are part of the deliberative process *preceding* the adoption and promulgation of an agency policy. *United States v. Farley*, 11 F.3d 1385 (7th Cir.1993); *F.T.C. v. Warner Communications, Inc.*, 742 F.2d 1156 (9th Cir.1984); *Jordan v. United States Dep't of Justice*, 591 F.2d 753 (D.C.Cir.1978); *Arizona Rehab. Hosp., Inc. v. Shalala*, 185 F.R.D. 263 (D.

Ariz.1998); *United States v. Rozet*, 183 F.R.D. 662 (N.D.Cal.1998).

The three primary purposes of the privilege are: (1) to assure that subordinates within an agency will feel free to provide the decisionmaker with their uninhibited opinions and recommendations without fear of criticism; (2) to protect against premature disclosure of proposed policies before they have been adopted; and (3) to protect against confusing the issues and misleading the public by dissemination of documents suggesting reasons and rationales for a course of action which were not in fact the ultimate reasons for the agency's action. *Coastal States Gas Corp. v. Department of Energy*, 617 F.2d 854, 866 (D.C.Cir.1980).

Only predecisional deliberative communications are protected. *United States v. Fernandez*, 231 F.3d 1240 (9th Cir.2000) (death penalty evaluation form and prosecution memorandum are predecisional and deliberative because designed to help Attorney General decide whether death penalty is appropriate in a given case); *Hopkins v. United States Dep't of Housing & Urban Dev.*, 929 F.2d 81 (2d Cir.1991); *Access Reports v. Department of Justice*, 926 F.2d 1192, 1194 (D.C.Cir.1991); *Conoco Inc. v. United States Dep't of Justice*, 687 F.2d 724 (3d Cir.1982). The privilege does not apply to communications made subsequent to the agency's decision. *Elkem Metals Co. v. United States*, 126 F.Supp.2d 5672 (CIT 2000). Subjective materials that "reflect the personal opinion of the writer, rather than the policy of the agency", are also privileged because they are considered predecisional. *Lee v. F.D.I.C.*, 923 F.Supp. 451, 456 (S.D.N.Y.1996).

The privilege usually does not extend to factual or objective material or to documents that the agency adopts as its position on an issue. *Hopkins*, 929 F.2d at 84; *Arthur Andersen & Co. v. IRS*, 679 F.2d 254 (D.C.Cir.1982); *K.L. v. Edgar*, 964 F.Supp.

1206 (N.D.Ill.1997). However, factual information that reflects or reveals the deliberative processes of an agency is protected by the privilege. *Mapother v. Department of Justice*, 3 F.3d 1533 (D.C.Cir.1993).

The government must bear the initial burden of showing that the privilege applies. *Schreiber v. Society for Sav. Bancorp, Inc.*, 11 F.3d 217 (D.C. Cir.1993). Three procedural requirements must be satisfied: (1) there must be a formal claim of privilege made by the head of the department or his designated subordinate which has control over the matter, after actual consideration by that officer, *United States v. Reynolds*, 345 U.S. 1, 73 S.Ct. 528, 97 L.Ed. 727 (1953); *Landry v. F.D.I.C.*, 204 F.3d 1125 (D.C.Cir.2000) (assertion of privilege by highest official not required; lesser officials may assert privilege); (2) the responsible agency official must provide precise and certain reasons for asserting confidentiality with respect to the information, *United States v. O'Neill*, 619 F.2d 222 (3d Cir.1980); *Mobil Oil Corp. v. Department of Energy*, 520 F.Supp. 414 (N.D.N.Y.1981), and (3) the government information or documents must be identified and described, *Resident Advisory Bd. v. Rizzo*, 97 F.R.D. 749 (E.D.Pa.1983).

Once the government makes a *prima facie* showing of entitlement, the trial court must then balance the competing interests of the parties, including: (1) the relevance of the evidence sought to be protected; (2) the availability of other relevant evidence; (3) the seriousness of the litigation and the issues involved; (4) the government's role in the litigation; and (5) the extent to which disclosure would chill future deliberations within agencies. *First Eastern Corp. v. Mainwaring*, 21 F.3d 465 (D.C.Cir.1994); *Redland Soccer Club v. Department of Army of U.S.*, 55 F.3d 827, 853 (3d Cir. 1995); *see Ferrell v. U.S. Dep't of Housing and Urban Dev.*, 177 F.R.D. 425 (N.D.Ill.1998) (in contempt action against HUD for violation of consent decree, plaintiffs' need for information overcame privilege).

The privilege is not absolute. It "disappears altogether when there is any reason to believe government misconduct occurred." *In re Sealed Case*, 121 F.3d 729, 746 (D.C.Cir.1997). Documents also will not be protected from disclosure if their content reflects an attempt by an agency to establish "secret law" or policies that are not subject to public scrutiny. *Sterling Drug, Inc. v. FTC*, 450 F.2d 698, 708 (D.C.Cir.1971) ("[T]o prevent the development of secret law within the Commission, we must require it to disclose orders and interpretations which it actually applies in cases before it.").

Some courts have severely restricted the use of the privilege by government agencies when those agencies are seeking affirmative judicial relief. These decisions hold that when the government seeks affirmative relief, fundamental fairness requires the government to disclose materials that a private plaintiff would have to reveal. *United States v. Ernstoff*, 183 F.R.D. 148 (D.N.J.1998); *F.D.I.C. v. Hatziyannis*, 180 F.R.D. 292 (D.Md. 1998); *EEOC v. Citizens Bank & Trust Co.*, 117 F.R.D. 366 (D.Md.1987); *see also* Wright & Graham, Federal Practice and Procedure: Evidence § 5690 (1992) (noting that courts have rejected qualified deliberative process privilege when government acts as plaintiff); *In re Subpoena Duces Tecum*, 145 F.3d 1422 (D.C.Cir.), *on rehearing in part* 156 F.3d 1279 (D.C.Cir.1998) (privilege does not apply when cause of action is directed at the agency's subjective motivation; also noting that the privilege has no place in Title VII actions or constitutional claims for discrimination because when the Constitution or a statute makes the nature of governmental deliberations *the* issue, the privilege is a non sequitur).

Even if the privilege is found to apply, a court may still order disclosure if the party seeking the information can demonstrate that its need for disclosure of such material is greater than the government's interest in non-disclosure. *Star-Kist Foods, Inc. v. United States*, 600 F.Supp. 212, 217 (CIT 1984) ("Once the proponent of privilege has complied with the established criteria for asserting privilege, the opposing party must demonstrate clearly and persuasively that the need for disclosure outweighs the harm that could result from disclosure.") (citing *Melamine Chem., Inc. v. United States*, 1 C.I.T. 65, 66 (1980)).

There is no deliberative process privilege for private entities. *Wilstein v. San Tropai Condo. Master Ass'n*, 189 F.R.D. 371 (N.D.Ill.1999) (privilege not available to condominium association sued under federal Fair Housing Act).

Compare: Fed. R. Evid. 501.

Research References

Packel & Poulin, Pennsylvania Evidence § 533 (4th ed. 2013)

McCormick, Evidence § 108 (7th ed. 2013)

Graham, Handbook of Federal Evidence § 509.1 (6th ed. 2006)

Larkin, Federal Testimonial Privileges Chapter 5, § 5.02[2] (2001 ed.)

PRIVILEGE: HUSBAND AND WIFE

See: Pa.R.E. 501.

Objection

- Objection: As the spouse of the [*plaintiff/ defendant*], the witness invokes the privilege not to furnish any testimony against [*his/her wife/ husband*].
- Objection: Privilege, the question calls for disclosure of a confidential communication between husband and wife.

Response

- Any testimonial privilege ended with the parties' divorce/spouse's death.
- The testimony is not privileged because [*the privilege has been waived*] [*the evidence does not touch or concern a confidential communication*] [*there is no confidentiality since a third party was present*].

Pennsylvania Law

Pennsylvania law recognizes two separate and distinct marital privileges: (1) the adverse spousal testimony privilege, and (2) the confidential marital communications privilege. The former allows a spouse called as a witness against his or her spouse in a civil or criminal proceeding to refuse to testify, 42 Pa.C.S.A. §§ 5913 (criminal), 5924 (civil), while the latter protects from disclosure private communications between the spouses in the confidence of the marital relationship. *Commonwealth v. Small*, 980 A.2d 549 (Pa. 2009) (analyzing the differences between the privileges and collecting cases); *Commonwealth v. May*, 540 Pa. 237, 656 A.2d 1335 (1995).

Adverse Spousal Testimony

The adverse spousal testimony privilege permits an individual to refuse to testify in a civil or criminal proceeding against his or her spouse, subject to certain exceptions and waiver.

In civil cases, neither husband nor wife is competent or permitted to testify against the other spouse. 42 Pa.C.S.A. § 5924(a). There are certain statutory exceptions including divorce, support, property division, child custody and protection from abuse proceedings or where otherwise provided by statute. 42 Pa.C.S.A. § 5924(b). *B.K. v. Dep't of Public Welfare*, 36 A.3d 649 (Pa. Cmwlth. 2012) (child abuse exception).

By marked contrast, in criminal cases, the testifying spouse holds the privilege and is free to waive it. 42 Pa.C.S.A. § 5913. *Commonwealth v. Lewis*, 39 A.3d 341 (Pa. Super. 2012). However, there is no testimonial privilege in proceedings for desertion and maintenance or where the criminal charges involve injury to or violence against a spouse or child or where the charge against defendant includes murder, rape or involuntary deviate sexual intercourse. Criminal cases holding such testimony is a matter of judicial discretion have been overruled. *Commonwealth v. Kirkner*, 569 Pa. 499, 805 A.2d 514 (2002) (trial court had no discretion in spousal assault case to determine whether reluctant wife should testify against husband; quashing subpoena for wife's testimony was error). Murder is different from and does not encompass the crime of homicide by vehicle. *Commonwealth v. Bobin*, 916 A.2d 1164 (Pa. Super. 2007).

The testimonial privilege ceases to exist if the parties do not remain married. *Huffman v. Simmons*, 131 Pa. Super. 370, 200 A. 274 (1938). The privilege set forth in 42 Pa. C.S.A. § 5913 applies in situations where the couple has filed for divorce but a divorce decree has not yet been entered. *Commonwealth v. Valle-Velez*, 995 A.2d 1264 (Pa. Super. 2010). The communications protected by § 5913 are not limited to confidential communications. *Commonwealth v. Valle-Velez*, 995 A.2d 1264, 1269 (Pa. Super. 2010); *Bobin*, 916 A.2d 1164 (Pa. Super. 2007). A spouse does not waive this privilege by sharing the nature of the information with third parties. *Valle-Velez*, 995 A.2d 1264, 1269 (Pa. Super. 2010). Even where a witness gives testimony adverse to his or her spouse, he or she is not permitted to disclose confidential communications. *Commonwealth v. Newman*, 534 Pa. 424, 633 A.2d 1069 (1993).

Confidential Marital Communications

In civil and criminal cases, the confidential marital communications privilege bars testimony of private communications between spouses during a valid marriage. 42 Pa.C.S.A. § 5914 (criminal); 42 Pa.C.S.A. § 5923 (civil); *Commonwealth v. May*, 540 Pa. 237, 656 A.2d 1335 (1995); *Commonwealth v. Borris*, 247 Pa. Super. 260, 372 A.2d 451 (1977).

The purpose of the privilege is to foster intimate communication between spouses by assuring that their statements will never be subjected to forced disclosure. *Commonwealth v. Savage*, 695 A.2d 820 (Pa. Super. 1997); *see also United States v. Neal*, 532 F.Supp. 942, 946 (D.Colo.1982) (privilege preserves "some small island of privacy as a refuge for the human spirit"). The privilege does not extend to communications intended to create or further marital disharmony. *Commonwealth v. Spetzer*, 572 Pa. 17, 39, 813 A.2d 707, 721 (2002) (husband's statements about actual and contemplated crimes against wife and children showed contempt for and abuse of marital union and were not privileged). As a policy matter, where there are parallel proceedings and defendant spouse is the alleged perpetrator in current child abuse proceedings and this abuse also forms the bane of criminal proceedings against that defendant spouse, the confidential spousal communication privilege does not apply to the criminal proceeding. *Commonwealth v. Hunter*, 60 A.3d 156 (Pa. Super. 2013); see Child Protective Services Law, 23 Pa.C.S.A. § 6381(c) (confidential communications admissible in proceedings regarding child abuse or the cause of child abuse). However, there is no fraud or crime-fraud exception to the confidential communications privilege. *CAP Glass, Inc. v. Coffman*, 130 A.3d 783 (Pa. Super. 2016) (civil); *Commonwealth v. Davis*, 121 A.3d 551 (Pa. Super. 2015) (criminal).

The privilege may be asserted against the production of evidence when four prerequisites are met: (1) there must have been a communication, *Commonwealth v. Chiappini*, 566 Pa. 507, 782 A.2d 490 (2001) (conduct is communication only if a message or meaning can be attributed to the conduct); (2) there must have been a valid marriage at the time of the communication, *Commonwealth v. Borris*, 247 Pa. Super. 260, 372 A.2d 451 (1977); (3) the communication must have been made in confidence, *Commonwealth v. Dubin*, 399 Pa. Super. 100, 581 A.2d 944 (1990); and (4) the privilege must not have been waived.

While the party asserting the communications privilege bears the burden of establishing that answering the question would require disclosure of words or acts intended as communication to/from the other spouse, and that the communication was made during a valid marriage, the final element of confidentiality is presumed. *Commonwealth v. McBurrows*, 779 A.2d 509, 514 (Pa. Super. 2001); *see also United States v. Byrd*, 750 F.2d 585 (7th Cir.1984) (communications intended to be private are often made without a request for secrecy; the difficult matter of proving the intent to keep the communications confidential is avoided by the presumption).

Although privileged communication between spouses need not only be expressed in words, it must involve more than mere observation by one spouse of the conduct of another; it must involve the attribution of a message or meaning to that conduct. *Commonwealth v. Chiappini*, 566 Pa. 507, 782 A.2d 490 (2001) (former wife could testify in arson prosecution to actions of ex-husband which she had observed); *Commonwealth v. McBurrows*, 779 A.2d 509, 514 (Pa. Super. 2001) (wife's observance of her husband's act of disposing of tool used in beating death of child did not fall within privilege; act did not convey any message induced by confidential nature of marital relationship).

The communications privilege survives termination of the marriage by annulment, divorce or death. *Commonwealth v. Weiss*, 565 Pa. 504, 776 A.2d 958 (2001); *Commonwealth v. Clark*, 347 Pa. Super. 128, 500 A.2d 440 (1985); *see Commonwealth v. Chiappini*, 566 Pa. 507, 782 A.2d 490 (2001) (where marriage has been terminated, statutory privilege does not apply; common law rule must be consulted).

The privilege belongs to both spouses and either may invoke it to avoid interrogation or to prevent the other spouse from testifying about protected communications.

In the absence of contrary indications, the privilege generally does not extend to the ordinary daily exchanges between spouses, such as matters of business or property, *Commonwealth v. Darush*, 279 Pa. Super. 140, 420 A.2d 1071 (1980), *vacated on other grounds*, 501 Pa. 15, 459 A.2d 727 (1983), and in a civil action, will not shield communications or acts in furtherance of a fraudulent transaction. *Kine v. Forman*, 205 Pa. Super. 305, 209 A.2d 1 (1965). Communications made in the presence of a third party are not deemed confidential. *Commonwealth v. Borris*, 247 Pa. Super. 260, 372 A.2d 451 (1977). When communications between spouses have been overheard, intercepted or otherwise obtained by a third party (even if from a spouse), the communications may be offered in evidence by the third party. *Commonwealth v. Mattison*, 82 A.3d 386 (Pa. 2013) (presence of third parties negates confidential nature of communication); *Commonwealth v. G.Y.*, 63 A.3d 259 (Pa. Super. 2013) (communication divulged to third parties does not quality as confidential communication); *Commonwealth v. Dubin*, 399 Pa. Super. 100, 581 A.2d 944 (1990).

Compare: Fed. R. Evid. 501.

Research References

Packel & Poulin, Pennsylvania Evidence §§ 527, 528 (4th ed. 2013)

McCormick, Evidence Chapter 9 (7th ed. 2013)

PRIVILEGE: MEDIATION COMMUNICATIONS AND DOCUMENTS

See: Pa.R.E. 501.

Objection

- Objection. The question calls for disclosure of a privileged mediation communication [and/or document].

Response

- This evidence existed independent of the mediation and is not subject to the privilege.

Pennsylvania Law

Increased use of alternative dispute resolution processes has caused the Pennsylvania legislature to create a new privilege for confidential mediation communications and documents. *See* 42 Pa.C.S.A. § 5949.

The statute establishes a broad general rule that all mediation communications and mediation documents are privileged. Disclosure may not be required or compelled through discovery or any other process and these communications and documents are not admissible as evidence in any action or proceeding, including, but not limited to, a judicial, administrative or arbitration action or proceeding. 42 Pa.C.S.A. § 5949(a).

The accompanying definitions are also very broad. *See* 42 Pa.C.S.A. § 5949(c). "Mediation" is defined as the deliberate and knowing use of a third person by disputing parties to help them reach a resolution of their dispute. The definition further states that mediation begins at the time of the initial contact with a mediator or a mediation program. This definition is seemingly broad enough to include arbitration, facilitation, mini trials, fact finding, conciliation and other alternate dispute resolution processes under the mediation privilege umbrella.

"Mediation communication" is a communication, verbal or nonverbal, oral or written, made by, between or among a party, mediator, mediation program or any other person present to further the mediation process when the communication occurs during a mediation session or outside a session when made to or by the mediator or mediation program. "Mediation document" is written material, including copies, prepared for the purpose of, in the course of or pursuant to mediation. The term includes, but is not limited to, memoranda, notes, files, records and work product of a mediator, mediation program or party.

The privilege is subject to four exceptions. 42 Pa.C.S.A. § 5949(b).

First, a written agreement signed by the parties may be introduced in an action or proceeding to enforce the settlement agreement expressed in the document unless the document by its terms states that it is unenforceable or not intended to be legally binding.

Second, to the extent that the communication or conduct is relevant evidence in a criminal matter, the privilege does not apply to a threat that bodily injury may be inflicted on a person, a threat that damage may be inflicted on real or personal property under the circumstances constituting a felony, or conduct during a mediation session causing direct bodily injury to a person.

Third, the privilege does not apply to fraudulent communication during a mediation that is relevant evidence in an action to enforce or set aside a mediated agreement reached as a result of that fraudulent communication.

Under the fourth exception to the general rule, any document which otherwise exists or existed independent of the mediation and is not otherwise covered by this section, is not subject to the privilege.

Most federal courts have recognized a federal mediation privilege. *Sheldone v. Pa. Turnpike Comm.*, 104 F.Supp.2d 511 (W.D. Pa. 2000). *Gatto v. Verizon Pennsylvania, Inc.*, 2009 WL 3062316 (W.D. Pa.), where a mediator was compelled to testify about mediation proceedings, would seem to be an aberration.

Research Reference

Packel & Poulin, Pennsylvania Evidence § 547 (4th ed. 2013)

PRIVILEGE: NEWS REPORTERS

See: Pa.R.E. 501.

Objection

- Objection. The Shield Law, 42 Pa.C.S.A. § 5942, confers upon the news media an absolute privilege against disclosure of their confidential sources.

Response

- This evidence is not privileged because [*the evidence sought is not intended to and cannot reasonably, lead to the discovery of the identity of a confidential media-informant*] [*the evidence sought is not the product of confidential information*] [*the Shield Law protects only confidential sources of information, not the thought or editorial processes of reporters or news organizations*] [*the privilege has been lost for failure to comply with subsection (b)*].

Pennsylvania Law

42 Pa.C.S.A. § 5942, Confidential Communications to News Reporters, provides:

(a) **General rule.**—No person engaged on, connected with, or employed by any newspaper of general circulation or any press association or any radio or television station, or any magazine of general circulation, for the purpose of gathering, procuring, compiling, editing or publishing news, shall be required to disclose the source of any information procured or obtained by such person, in any legal proceeding, trial or investigation before any government unit.

(b) **Exception.**—The provisions of subsection (a) insofar as they relate to radio or television stations shall not apply unless the radio or television station maintains and keeps open for inspection, for a period of at least one year from the date of the actual broadcast or telecast, an exact recording, transcription, kinescopic film or certified written transcript of the actual broadcast or telecast.

Originally enacted in 1937, the purpose of 42 Pa.C.S.A. § 5942 (commonly known as the Shield Law) is to maintain a free flow of information to members of the media. *In re Taylor*, 412 Pa. 32, 193 A.2d 181 (1963). The privilege was designed to be an absolute one in that it immunizes the media against any legal compulsion directed at requiring disclosure of a confidential source of information. *In re Dauphin County Fourth Investigating Grand Jury*, 19 A.3d 491 (Pa. 2011); *Commonwealth v. Bowden*, 838 A.2d 740 (Pa.2003). While the statute on its face protects only against compelled disclosure of the "source of . . . information," the phrase has been interpreted to encompass not only the identity of a confidential informant, but also includes documents, inanimate objects and all sources of information which even if redacted, might reveal a confidential informant. *Commonwealth v. Bowden*, 838 A.2d 740 (Pa. 2003); *Davis v. Glanton*, 705 A.2d 879 (Pa. Super. 1997) (Shield Law creates absolute privilege which, if applicable to information sought, protects it from disclosure without analysis of plaintiff's need for information). The Shield Law does not have a crime/fraud exception. *Castellani v. Scranton Times, L.P.*, 956 A.2d 937 (Pa. 2008).

Where documentary information does not reveal the identity of a confidential source of information or may be redacted to eliminate the revelation of a confidential source of information, the privilege does not apply and the material is discoverable. Commonwealth v. Bowden, supra; *Hatchard v. Westinghouse Broadcasting Co.*, 516 Pa. 184, 532 A.2d 346 (1987); *DiPaolo v. Times Publishing Co.*, 142 A.3d 837 (Pa. Super. 2016); *Davis v. Glanton*, 705 A.2d 879 (Pa. Super. 1997). This result accommodates the right of a free press recognized in Pa. Const. Art. 1, § 7, as further protected by the Shield Law, while also taking into consideration the fundamental right to protection of reputation contained in Pa. Const. Art 1, § 1.

Photographs of objects not obtained as a result of information from a source are not within the privilege. *Commonwealth v. Ruch*, 28 Pa. D. & C.3d 488 (C.P. Montgomery County, 1984) (refusing to quash a subpoena for news photographs of an automobile accident which were not obtained as a result of a tip, lead, or inside information from a source).

Compare: Fed. R. Evid. 501. The qualified journalist's privilege, established in *Branzburg v. Hayes*, 408 U.S. 665, 92 S.Ct. 2646, 33 L.Ed.2d 626 (1972), allows reporters to decline to disclose information about their sources. Derived from the First Amendment, the privilege recognizes society's interest in protecting the integrity of the news gathering process and in ensuring the free flow of information to the public. It is an interest of "sufficient social importance to justify some incidental sacrifice of sources of facts needed in the administration of justice." *Herbert v. Lando*, 441 U.S. 153, 183, 99 S.Ct. 1635, 1652, 60 L.Ed.2d 115 (1979) (Brennan, J. dissenting).

The privilege is not absolute and will be overcome whenever society's need for the confidential information outweighs the intrusion on the reporter's First Amendment interests. *Ashcraft v. Conoco, Inc.*, 218 F.3d 282 (4th Cir.2000).

After *Branzburg*, courts faced with the journalist's privilege have proceeded on a case-by-case basis, balancing the potential harm to the free flow of information that might result against the asserted need for the requested information. *Cusumano v. Microsoft Corp.*, 162 F.3d 708 (1st Cir.1998); *United States v. Caporale*, 806 F.2d 1487 (11th Cir.1986); *United States v. Criden*, 633 F.2d 346 (3d Cir.1980); *United States v. Cuthbertson*, 630 F.2d 139 (3d Cir.1980) (*Cutherbertson I*); *Miller v. Transamerican Press, Inc.*, 621 F.2d 721 (5th Cir.1980); *Palandjian v. Pahlavi*, 103 F.R.D. 410 (D.D.C.1984); *Continental Cablevision, Inc. v.*

Storer Broadcasting Co., 583 F.Supp. 427 (E.D.Mo. 1984). As a result of this analysis, the courts have fashioned a three-part test, first articulated in *Garland v. Torre*, 259 F.2d 545 (2d Cir.1958), to resolve privilege cases. The reporter's privilege is overridden only if: (1) the information sought is relevant, (2) it cannot be obtained by alternative means, and (3) there is a compelling interest in the information. *See, e.g., In re Petroleum Prods. Antitrust Litig.*, 680 F.2d 5 (2d Cir.1982); *Criden*, 633 F.2d 346 (3d Cir.1980); *Cuthbertson*, 630 F.2d 139 (3d Cir.1980); *Sanders v. Alabama State Bar*, 887 F.Supp. 272 (M.D.Ala.1995); *Continental Cablevision*, 583 F.Supp. 427 (E.D.Mo.1984). *But see In re Grand Jury Proceedings*, 810 F.2d 580 (6th Cir.1987) (rejecting privilege); *United States v. King*, 194 F.R.D. 569, 584 (E.D.Va.2000) ("[A] survey of the decisions in this circuit teaches that our Court of Appeals has recognized that *Branzburg* does not create a reportorial privilege, but that it entitles reporters to protection under certain circumstances.").

The showing that the information sought is relevant and material must be specific. *United States v. Bingham*, 765 F.Supp. 954 (N.D.Ill.1991). "Relevant" means the information goes to the heart of, or is crucial to, the claims made by the requesting party. *Neal v. City of Harvey, Ill.*, 173 F.R.D. 231 (N.D.Ill.1997).

In addition to traditional journalists, the privilege has been extended to: academic investigators, *Cusumano*, 162 F.3d at 708; a documentary film maker, *Silkwood v. Kerr-McGee*, 563 F.2d 433 (10th Cir.1977); the author of a technical publication, *Apicella v. McNeil Lab. Inc.*, 66 F.R.D. 78 (E.D.N. Y.1975); an investigative book author, *Shoen v. Shoen*, 5 F.3d 1289 (9th Cir.1993). *But see In re Madden*, 151 F.3d 125 (3d Cir.1998) (privilege not available to pro wrestling publicist).

The critical question in determining if an individual falls within the protected class is whether the person at the inception of the investigatory process had the intent to disseminate to the public the information obtained through the investigation. *von Bulow by Auersperg v. von Bulow*, 811 F.2d 136 (2d Cir.1987).

Research References

Packel & Poulin, Pennsylvania Evidence § 536 et seq. (4th ed. 2013)

McCormick, Evidence § 76.2 (7th ed. 2013)

PRIVILEGE: PHYSICIAN-PATIENT

See: Pa.R.E. 501.

Objection

- Objection. The question calls for disclosure of a privileged communication between physician and patient.

Response

- The evidence is not privileged and is admissible because [*it does not tend to blacken the patient's character*] [*the information was not acquired as a result of communication by the patient but from the doctor's own examination*] [*this witness is an unrelated third party who overheard the conversation and is thus permitted to testify*].

Pennsylvania Law

Pennsylvania has a limited testimonial privilege statute which promotes the confidentiality of patient-physician communications in civil cases. 42 Pa.C.S.A. § 5929 states:

No physician shall be allowed, in any civil matter, to disclose any information which he acquired in attending the patient in a professional capacity, and which was necessary to enable him to act in that capacity, which shall tend to blacken the character of the patient, without consent of said patient, except in civil matters brought by such patient, for damages on account of personal injuries.

The purpose of the privilege is to foster a confidential relationship between the physician and patient which enables a patient to freely discuss information relating to his illness with his physician, and in turn, allows the physician to render effective treatment. *Grimminger v. Maitra*, 887 A.2d 276 (Pa. Super. 2005); *Miller Oral Surgery, Inc. v. Dinello*, 416 Pa. Super. 310, 611 A.2d 232 (1992).

To be within the scope of the physician-patient

privilege, the testimony of the doctor must:

1. involve information gathered by communication from patient to doctor, and
2. the information must tend to blacken the patient's character.

Both criteria must be met to give rise to the privilege. *Jones v. Faust*, 852 A.2d 1201 (Pa. Super. 2004).

The statute bars only confidential communications from patient to physician; it does not bar a physician's testimony concerning information acquired through his own examination and observation. *In Re June 1979 Allegheny County Investigating Grand Jury*, 490 Pa. 143, 415 A.2d 73 (1980); *Grimminger v. Maitra*, 887 A.2d 276 (Pa. Super. 2005) (statements to patient's employer were based on doctor's own observations and did not violate privilege). Where a physician learns from his own examination (and not from the patient) that she is suffering from syphilis, the information is not privileged. *In re Phillips' Estate*, 295 Pa. 349, 145 A. 437 (1929).

The patient is the holder of the privilege and he alone may waive it. *Commonwealth ex rel. Romanowicz v. Romanowicz*, 213 Pa. Super. 382, 248 A.2d 238 (1968). By filing an action for personal injury, the plaintiff-patient waives the privilege and impliedly consents to disclosure by the physician of relevant matters relating to plaintiff-patient's medical condition. *Aiello v. Southeastern Pennsylvania Transp.*, 687 A.2d 399 (Pa.Cmwlth. 1996); *Moses v. McWilliams*, 379 Pa. Super. 150, 549 A.2d 950 (1988); *see also* Pa. R.C.P. 4003.6. Waiver does not permit opposing counsel to obtain medical information in any way he sees fit. *Pennsylvania State Univ. v. WCAB (Sox)*, 83 A.3d 1081 (Pa.Cmwlth. 2013); *Marek v. Ketyer*, 733 A.2d 1268 (Pa. Super. 1999); Pa.R.C.P. 4003.6. The privilege does not apply in criminal proceedings. *Commonwealth v. Ellis*, 415 Pa. Super. 220, 608

A.2d 1090 (1992).

Testimony concerning a "loathsome disease" would tend to blacken the patient's character. *Evans v. Workmen's Compensation Appeal Board (Julia Ribaudo Home)*, 151 Pa.Cmwlth. 490, 617 A.2d 826 (1992). Thus, the identity of a patient who contracted AIDS from tainted blood is protected. *Stenger v. Lehigh Valley Hosp. Center*, 530 Pa. 426, 609 A.2d 796 (1992); *Agriss v. Roadway Exp., Inc.*, 334 Pa. Super. 295, 483 A.2d 456 (1984) (sexually transmitted disease is loathsome disease which blackens character). However, the fact of psychiatric treatment does not blacken character, although any information is otherwise protected, *In re B*, 482 Pa. 471, 394 A.2d 419 (1978), nor do hospital records which disclose chronic alcoholism, *Soltaniuk v. Metro. Life Ins. Co.*, 133 Pa. Super. 139, 2 A.2d 501 (1938). *But see Kuney v. Benjamin Franklin Clinic*, 751 A.2d 662 (Pa. Super. 2000) (information about treatment of patient for various physical ailments and psychiatric problem protected by privilege).

The privilege applies solely to the physician-patient relationship and does not apply to a school nurse, *Farris v. Pennsbury Sch. Dist.*, 74 Pa. D. & C.2d 786 (C.P. Bucks County, 1975), unless the nurse secured the information in the presence of a physician whom she was assisting. *Gilham v. Gilham*, 177 Pa. Super. 328, 110 A.2d 915 (1955). If a non-essential third party overhears the communication, he may testify to it. *Gilham v. Gilham*, 177 Pa. Super. 328, 110 A.2d 915 (1955). Where there is no expectation of privacy, such as with statements to a company medical director whose normal duty is to report to the employer, the privilege does not bar disclosure to the employer. *Szostek v. Commonwealth, Unemp. Comp. Bd. of Review*, 116 Pa.Cmwlth. 7, 541 A.2d 48 (1988).

Federal Law:

The federal courts have been unanimous in

rejecting a physician-patient privilege. *E.g.*, *Gilbreath v. Guadalupe Hosp. Found.*, 5 F.3d 785 (5th Cir.1993); *Hancock v. Dodson*, 958 F.2d 1367, 1373 (6th Cir.1992) ("the federal courts do not recognize a federal physician-patient privilege"). But these cases all preceded *Jaffee v. Redmond*, 518 U.S. 1, 116 S.Ct. 1923, 135 L.Ed.2d 337 (1996) (recognizing psychotherapist-patient privilege). Although the Court there both distinguished ordinary medical care from psychotherapy and relied on the Advisory Committee's decision to promulgate a psychotherapist-patient privilege in Proposed Rule 504, 518 U.S. at 10, 116 S.Ct. at 1928, its decision may nonetheless prompt a re-evaluation of the status of a physician-patient privilege. One important factor in the *Jaffee* decision was the widespread acceptance of a psychotherapist-patient privilege among the states. Since most states also recognize at least a limited physician-patient privilege, the case can be made for acceptance of such a privilege in federal court.

Research References

Packel & Poulin, Pennsylvania Evidence § 523 (4th ed. 2013)

McCormick, Evidence Chapter 11 (7th ed. 2013)

PRIVILEGE: PSYCHIATRIST-PSYCHOLOGIST

See: Pa.R.E. 501.

Objection

- Objection. [*Request sidebar*] The question seeks information communicated to a [*psychiatrist*] [*psychologist*] which is privileged under 42 Pa. C.S.A. § 5944.

Response

- This evidence is not privileged because [*the statements were made in the presence of a third person who was not an agent for one of the parties to the privilege*] [*there was no confidential relationship nor any confidential communications*] [*the witness has placed her mental condition in issue by (specify)*].

Pennsylvania Law

42 Pa.C.S.A. § 5944 provides:

Confidential communications to psychiatrists or licensed psychologists. No psychiatrist or person who has been licensed under the act of March 23, 1972 (P.L. 136, No. 52), to practice psychology shall be, without the written consent of his client, examined in any civil or criminal matter as to any information acquired in the course of his professional services in behalf of such client. The confidential relations and communications between a psychologist or psychiatrist and his client shall be on the same basis as those provided or prescribed by law between an attorney and client.

The absolute privilege afforded by Section 5944 is rooted in the imperative need for confidence and trust by the client and to encourage full disclosure to the psychologist or psychiatrist. By preventing the latter from making public any information which would result in humiliation, embarrassment or disgrace to the client, the privilege is designed to promote effective treatment and to insulate the client's private thoughts from public disclosure. *Commonwealth v. Dowling*, 883 A.2d 570 (Pa. 2005) (privilege is not outweighed by defendant's right to cross-examine witnesses or his due process rights); accord *Commonwealth v. Henkel*, 90 A.3d 16 (Pa. Super. 2014); *Zane v. Friends Hospital*, 575 Pa. 236, 836 A.2d 25 (2003) (expectation of confidentiality essential to effective mental health treatment); *Gates v. Gates*, 967 A.2d 1024 (Pa. Super. 2009) (same, in context of child custody case); *Commonwealth v. Fewell*, 439 Pa. Super. 541, 654 A.2d 1109 (1995) (privilege codified strong public policy that confidential communication made by patient to psychiatrist should be absolutely protected from disclosure); *Commonwealth v. Kyle*, 367 Pa. Super. 484, 533 A.2d 120 (1987). But see *Commonwealth v. T.J.W.*, 114 A.3d 1098 (Pa. Super. 2015) (notwithstanding cases that refer to the privilege as absolute, often disposition of a claim of privilege involves impartial assessment of competing claims). The privilege shields both testimony and records from discovery, absent the consent of the patient. *Commonwealth v. Smith*, 414 Pa. Super. 208, 606 A.2d 939 (1992).

In order for the privilege to apply, the client must be seeking treatment, counseling or advice for a mental or emotional problem. *M. v. State Bd. of Medicine*, 725 A.2d 1266 (Pa.Cmwlth.1999).

The privilege attaches only to the patient's confidential communications to the therapist. The privilege is not designed to specifically protect the psychotherapist's own opinion, observations, diagnosis, or treatment alternatives particularly when such information finds its way beyond the patient's personal file. *In re S.T.S. Jr.*, 76 A.3d 24 (Pa. Super. 2013); *Commonwealth v. Moody*, 843 A.2d 402 (Pa. Super. 2004); *Commonwealth v. G.P.*, 765 A.2d 363 (Pa. Super. 2000); *Commonwealth v. Simmons*, 719 A.2d 336 (Pa. Super. 1998).

The privilege does not apply in those instances

where there is actual notice or indication due to the circumstances, that the communications will not be kept confidential, as is frequently the case with agency or court-ordered psychiatric or psychological examinations. *M. v. State Bd. of Medicine*, 725 A.2d 1266 (Pa.Cmwlth.1999) (court-ordered examination does not invoke privilege because treatment is not contemplated in conducting the exam); *In Interest of Bender*, 366 Pa. Super. 450, 531 A.2d 504 (1987); *Matter of Adoption of Embick*, 351 Pa. Super. 491, 506 A.2d 455 (1986); *see also Commonwealth v. Szuchon*, 548 Pa. 37, 693 A.2d 959 (1997) (admission of psychiatrist's testimony did not violate Fifth Amendment privilege against self-incrimination where defendant requested psychiatric examination and raised diminished capacity defense); *Commonwealth v. Santiago*, 541 Pa. 188, 662 A.2d 610 (1995) (privilege waived by insanity defense in first trial cannot be reclaimed in new trial); accord, *Commonwealth v. Rosen*, 42 A.3d 988 (Pa. 2012); *Commonwealth v. Goldblum*, 498 Pa. 455, 447 A.2d 234 (1982). Confidential communications between a patient and a therapist not licensed by the state may be protected by a right of privacy even though they are not protected by Section 5944. *Miller v. Roberts*, 38 Pa. D. & C.3d 74 (C.P. Northampton County, 1985).

The Superior Court has held that there are differing standards to be applied in civil and criminal proceedings with respect to the results of a court directed examination. *Commonwealth v. G.P.*, 765 A.2d 363 (Pa. Super. 2000) (defendant's admissions made during course of court-ordered evaluation in connection with CYS hearing could not be used in subsequent criminal prosecution because there was no waiver of constitutional rights).

Allegations of mental injury, severe emotional trauma or psychiatric/psychological conditions may result in a waiver of the privilege. *Gormley v. Edgar*, 995 A.2d 1197 (Pa. Super. 2010) (plaintiff placed mental condition at issue when she alleged suffering from anxiety as result of auto accident). But general averments of shock, mental anguish and humiliation alone do not place mental condition at issue or result in a waiver of privilege. Id. In child custody litigation, father did not waive the psychiatrist privilege by submitting to a court-ordered psychological examination under Pa.R.C.P. 1915.8. *M.M. v. L.M.*, 55 A.3d 1167 (Pa. Super. 2012).

In *Sprague v. Walter*, 441 Pa. Super. 1, 656 A.2d 890 (1995), the court found that any privilege for psychiatric records was waived by failure to assert the privilege in discovery.

Statements of a juvenile made to a mental health professional while in treatment remain privileged and may not be released to the State Sexual Offenders Assessment Board (SAOB) unless the juvenile gives written consent. *In re T.B.*, 75 A.3d 485 (Pa. Super. 2013).

Compare: Fed. R. Evid. 501 and *Jaffee v. Redmond*, 518 U.S. 1, 116 S.Ct. 1923, 135 L.Ed.2d 337 (1996) (communications between patients and their psychotherapists, including licensed clinical social workers, are privileged in federal litigation). *Commonwealth v. Simmons*, 719 A.2d 336 (Pa. Super. 1998), held that the privilege applied to social workers in the limited situation where the social worker works as an agent under the direct supervision of a licensed psychiatrist/psychologist who approves the patient's individual treatment plan and had close contact with the social worker to discuss the patient's progress and goals. Whether licensed clinical social workers are covered did not need to be reached in *In Re L.F.*, 995 A.2d 356 (Pa. Super. 2010).

Research References

Packel & Poulin, Pennsylvania Evidence § 524 (4th ed. 2013)

McCormick, Evidence § 98 (7th ed. 2013)

PRIVILEGE: SCHOOL PERSONNEL-CONFIDENTIAL COMMUNICATIONS

See: Pa.R.E. 501.

Objection

- Objection. [*Request sidebar*] The question seeks information communicated in confidence by a student to her [*guidance counselor*] [*school nurse*] [*psychologist*] [*home and school visitor*] which is privileged under 42 Pa.C.S.A. § 5945.

Response

- This evidence is not privileged and is admissible because [*the statements were made in the presence of a third person who was not an agent for one of the parties to the privilege*] [*the student and / or her parent consented to dissemination and use of the information*] [*the information was not acquired in the course of professional duties*].

Pennsylvania Law

42 Pa.C.S.A. § 5945, Confidential communications to school personnel, provides:

(a)   *General Rule.*—No guidance counselor, school nurse, school psychologist, or home and school visitor in the public schools or in private or parochial schools or other educational institutions providing elementary or secondary education, including any clerical worker of such schools and institutions, who, while in the course of his professional or clerical duties for a guidance counselor, home and school visitor, school nurse or school psychologist, has acquired information from a student in confidence shall be compelled or allowed:

(1)   without the consent of the student, if the student is 18 years of age or over; or

(2)   without the consent of his parent or guardian, if the student is under the age of 18 years;

to disclose such information in any legal proceeding, trial, or investigation before any government unit.

Case law is sparse. It has been held, however, that information disclosed by a student and his parent to an assistant principal was properly received into evidence where nothing in the record indicated the assistant principal was acting as a guidance counselor or that the conversation was confidential. *Appeal of McClellan*, 82 Pa.Cmwlth. 75, 475 A.2d 867 (1984); *Commonwealth v. Mitchell*, 902 A.2d 430 (Pa.2006) (similar).

The Family Educational Rights and Privacy Act (FERPA), 20 U.S.C. § 1231g does not create an evidentiary privilege in Pennsylvania courts. *T.M. v. Elwyn, Inc.*, 950 A.2d 1050 (Pa. Super. 2008) (rejecting argument that FERPA protected school records in lawsuit alleging sexual abuse, battery and negligent hiring.)

Research References

Packel & Poulin, Pennsylvania Evidence § 538 (4th ed. 2013)

McCormick, Evidence § 76.2 (7th ed. 2013)

PRIVILEGE: SELF-INCRIMINATION

See: Pa.R.E. 501.

Objection

● Objection. The question is one that the witness cannot be compelled to answer because of the privilege against self-incrimination, which is hereby invoked.

Response

[Opposing counsel should request a side bar and demand an offer of proof on the validity of the claim of privilege. Where the trial court determines the requested evidence would tend to incriminate the witness, there is no response since the privilege is absolute].

Pennsylvania Law

U.S. Const., amend. V: "No person . . . shall be compelled in any criminal case to be a witness against himself . . . ." Pa. Const. Art. 1, § 9: "In all criminal prosecutions the accused . . . cannot be compelled to give evidence against himself . . . ." The provision in Article I, § 9 against self-incrimination tracks its federal counterpart, *Commonwealth v. Padillas*, 997 A.2d 356 (Pa. Super. 2010).

The Fifth Amendment privilege may be asserted in civil as well as criminal actions. *National Life Ins. Co. v. Hartford Acc. & Indem. Co.*, 615 F.2d 595 (3d Cir.1980). Moreover, the privilege protects a witness as fully as it does one who is a party. Id. Only natural persons may invoke the privilege against self-incrimination; corporations, partnerships, associations may not. *Bellis v. United States*, 417 U.S. 85, 94 S.Ct. 2179, 40 L.Ed.2d 678 (1974). Fifth Amendment rights are personal to the individual and may not be asserted by another. *Hull v. Hannahstown Mut. Ins. Co.*, 451 Pa. Super. 164,

678 A.2d 815 (1996) (error for trial judge to invoke privilege on behalf of witness). *See* 42 Pa.C.S.A. § 5941(a): "Except defendants actually upon trial in a criminal proceeding, any competent witness may be compelled to testify in any matter, civil or criminal; but he may not be compelled to answer any question which, in the opinion of the trial judge, would tend to incriminate him . . . ." The general rule is that waiver of the privilege in one proceeding does not affect the right to invoke it in an independent proceeding. *Commonwealth v. Reid*, 99 A.3d 427 (Pa. 2014).

The Fifth Amendment privilege against self-incrimination not only protects the individual from involuntarily testifying as a witness against himself in a criminal prosecution, but also privileges him not to answer official questions put to him in any other proceeding, civil or criminal, formal or informal, where the answers might incriminate him in future criminal proceedings. *Lefkowitz v. Turley*, 414 U.S. 70, 94 S.Ct. 316, 38 L.Ed.2d 274 (1973); *Commonwealth v. Brown*, 26 A.3d 485 (Pa. Super. 2011) (privilege applicable to decertification hearings on whether to transfer case from criminal to juvenile court); *In Re A.C.*, 991 A.2d 884 (Pa. Super. 2010); *Commonwealth v. Shrawder*, 940 A.2d 436 (Pa. Super. 2007). The privilege extends not only to the disclosure of facts which would in themselves establish guilt, but also to any fact which might constitute an essential link in a chain of evidence by which guilt can be established. *Commonwealth v. Saranchak*, 866 A.2d 292 (2005); *Commonwealth v. Fink*, 990 A.2d 751 (Pa. Super. 2010).

However, introduction of non-testimonial evidence does not implicate the privilege under federal or state law. *See United States v. Patane*, 542 U.S. 630 (2004) (although statement was inadmissible, physical evidence of gun which defendant had disclosed was admissible); *Commonwealth v. Abbas*, 862 A.2d 606 (Pa. Super. 2004) (statement properly excluded as violating *Miranda v. Arizona*, 384 U.S.

436 (1966) but victim's photos which defendant had produced were admissible).

A prosecutor may not comment adversely on a defendant's refusal to testify as to the merits of the charges against him since to do so would compromise both the privilege and the presumption of innocence. *Griffin v. California*, 380 U.S. 609 (1965) (5th Amendment precludes use of defendant's post-arrest silence as substantive evidence of consciousness of guilt); *Doyle v. Ohio*, 426 U.S. 610 (1976) (post-arrest silence cannot be used to impeach testifying defendant); *Commonwealth v. Wesley*, 562 Pa. 7, 753 A.2d 204 (2000); *Commonwealth v. Clark*, 551 Pa. 258, 710 A.2d 31 (1998). Moreover, it is a clear violation of an accused's constitutional right against self-incrimination to make a reference at trial to his post-*Miranda* silence while in police custody. *Commonwealth v. Costa*, 560 Pa. 95, 742 A.2d 1076 (1999); *Commonwealth v. Clark*, 533 Pa. 579, 626 A.2d 154 (1993); *Commonwealth v. Clark*, 802 A.2d 658 (Pa. Super. 2002). However, with respect to pre-arrest silence, the distinction between a testifying and non-testifying defendant is critical. Where the defendant chooses to testify at trial, pre-arrest pre-*Miranda* silence can be used to impeach his credibility. *Jenkins v. Anderson*, 447 U.S. 231 (1980); *Commonwealth v. Lettau*, 986 A.2d 114 (Pa. 2009) (testimony about defendant's pre-arrest silence permissible to rebut his claim he cooperated with police investigation); *Commonwealth v. Spotz*, 870 A.2d 822 (Pa. 2005); *Commonwealth v. Bolus*, 545 Pa. 103, 680 A.2d 839 (1996). *See also Commonwealth v. DiNicola*, 581 Pa. 550, 866 A.2d 329 (2005) (reference to defendant's pre-arrest silence was "fair response" to defense that police investigation was biased and incomplete). But see *Commonwealth v. Molina*, 104 A.3d 430 (Pa. 2014) holds that under the state constitution, use of pre-arrest silence as substantive evidence of guilt violates a non-testifying defendant's constitutional rights. Exceptions such as impeachment of a testifying defendant or fair response to an argument of the defense continue to be recognized.

Although the privilege is liberally construed, *Commonwealth v. Bazemore*, 531 Pa. 582, 614 A.2d 684 (1992), it applies only to evidence that would tend to incriminate the witness. *Commonwealth v. Allen*, 501 Pa. 525, 462 A.2d 624 (1983). The privilege does not extend to consequences of a noncriminal nature. Fear of public disgrace, personal danger or civil liability are not adequate constitutional grounds to successfully invoke the privilege. *Petition of Specter [Appeal of Riccobene]*, 439 Pa. 404, 268 A.2d 104 (1970); *Commonwealth v. Moody*, 843 A.2d 402 (Pa. Super. 2004) (because Megan's Law is non-punitive, it is non-criminal; privilege does not apply to sexually violent predator assessments). Evidence is incriminating if it could be a link in a chain of prosecution. *Commonwealth v. West*, 321 Pa. Super. 329, 468 A.2d 503 (1983).

When an individual is called to testify in a judicial proceeding, he or she is not excused from answering questions merely by declaring that to do so doing would be self-incriminating. It is always for the court to judge if the silence is justified and an illusory claim should be rejected. *Commonwealth v. McGrogan*, 523 Pa. 614, 568 A.2d 924 (1990). For a court properly to overrule a claim of privilege, it must be perfectly clear from a careful consideration of all of the circumstances, that the witness is mistaken in the apprehension of self-incrimination and the answer demanded cannot possibly have such tendency. *Commonwealth v. Saranchak*, 866 A.2d 292 (2005); *Commonwealth v. Carrera*, 424 Pa. 551, 227 A.2d 627 (1967).

A witness cannot refuse to answer any questions by a blanket invocation of the privilege but must claim the constitutional privilege as particular questions are asked. *In re Commonwealth Fin. Corp.*, 288 F.Supp. 786 (E.D.Pa.1968), *affirmed*,

408 F.2d 640 (3d Cir.1969); *United States v. Roundtree*, 420 F.2d 845 (5th Cir.1969); *Commonwealth v. Treat*, 848 A.2d 147 (Pa. Super. 2004); *Commonwealth v. Kirwan*, 847 A.2d 61 (Pa. Super. 2004). *But see, Commonwealth v. Allen*, 501 Pa. 525, 462 A.2d 624 (1983) (holding blanket privilege properly permitted where record suggested witness' complicity in crime); *Commonwealth v. Doolin*, 24 A.3d 998 (Pa. Super. 2011) (same).

The privilege does not offer protection from the compelled production of demonstrative, physical or real evidence such as fingerprints, photographs, measurements, writing or speaking for identification, appearing in court, standing, walking or making a particular gesture. *See Pennsylvania v. Muniz*, 496 U.S. 582 (1990) (field sobriety test); *U.S. v. Dionisio*, 410 U.S. 1, 93 S.Ct. 764, 35 L.Ed.2d 67 (1973) (voice exemplar); *U.S. v. Wade*, 388 U.S. 218, 87 S.Ct. 1926, 18 L.Ed.2d 1149 (1967) (same); *Gilbert v. California*, 388 U.S. 263, 87 S.Ct. 1951, 18 L.Ed.2d 1178 (1967) (handwriting sample); *Schmerber v. California*, 384 U.S. 757, 87 S.Ct. 1951, 18 L.Ed.2d 1178 (1966) (blood sample); *U.S. v. Montgomery*, 100 F.3d 1404 (8th Cir. 1996) (Fifth Amendment does not protect a person from having to try on clothing); *U.S. v. Clark*, 847 F.2d 1467 (10th Cir. 1988) (handwriting sample); *U.S. v. Holloway*, 906 F.Supp. 1437 (D. Kan. 1995) (no violation to extract drugs from defendant's mouth); *Commonwealth v. Pagan*, 950 A.2d 270 (Pa. 2008) (defendant had no right to retain physical evidence taken from the crime scene); *Commonwealth v. Hayes*, 544 Pa. 46, 674 A.2d 677 (1996); *Commonwealth v. Stewart*, 846 A.2d 738 (Pa. Super. 2004) (field sobriety test); *Commonwealth v. Durr*, 32 A.3d 781 (Pa. Super. 2011) (request for identification does not violate privilege); *Commonwealth v. Reed*, 19 A.3d 1163 (Pa. Super. 2011) (same).

Pennsylvania courts have followed the rule of law established in *Baxter v. Palmigiano*, 425 U.S.

308, 96 S.Ct. 1551, 47 L.Ed.2d 810 (1976), that the Fifth Amendment does not forbid adverse inferences against parties in civil actions when they refuse to testify in response to probative evidence offered against them. *In re Griffin*, 456 Pa. Super. 440, 690 A.2d 1192 (1997) (inference that parties had misstated their income in adoption application); *Hughes v. Public Sch. Employes' Ret. Bd.*, 662 A.2d 701 (Pa.Cmwlth.1995); *Moore v. City of Philadelphia*, 131 Pa.Cmwlth. 586, 571 A.2d 518 (1990) (plaintiff permitted to argue to the jury that a negative inference could be implied from the fact that police officers had refused to testify until after statute of limitations had passed for bringing criminal charges); *Kaczorowski v. Gay*, 140 P.L.J. 415 (1992) (in accident case involving underage drinking, adverse inference could be drawn against those defendants who invoked Fifth Amendment privilege as to source of beer). It is well-settled that a witness' unprivileged refusal to testify is plainly contempt. *Commonwealth v. Pirela*, 398 Pa. Super. 76, 580 A.2d 848 (1990).

Where defendant raises the defense of insanity, his Fifth Amendment privilege is not violated by a court-ordered psychiatric examination. However, psychiatric testimony is then limited to the issue of sanity and cannot include incriminating statements made during a compulsory examination on the issue of guilt. *Commonwealth v. Morley*, 545 Pa. 420, 681 A.2d 1254 (1996) (collecting cases); *see also, Commonwealth v. Sartin*, 561 Pa. 522, 751 A.2d 1140 (2000) (where defendant was examined by his own psychiatrist and announced intention to use findings only during penalty phase, privilege did not prevent trial judge from ordering independent examination but results were to be sealed until penalty phase). See also *Commonwealth v. Rosen*, 988 A.2d 146 (Pa. Super. 2009) (defendant's waiver of his right against self-incrimination in first murder trial by admitting to psychiatrists during preparation of insanity defense that he killed his wife continued to apply at second murder trial and could be used by state as direct or impeachment evidence).

Miranda in a Nutshell

Per Supreme Court Justice David Wecht:

It is a fundamental precept enshrined in the United States Constitution that a suspect subject to a custodial interrogation by police must be warned that he has the right to remain silent, that anything he says may be used against him in court, and that he is entitled to the presence of an attorney. *Miranda*, 384 U.S. at 469, 86 S. Ct. 1602. If an individual is not advised of his *Miranda* rights prior to custodial interrogation by law enforcement officials, evidence obtained through the interrogation cannot be used against him, *In re K.Q.M.*, 873 A.2d 752, 755 (Pa. Super. 2005). "[I]n order to trigger the safeguards of *Miranda*, there must be both custody and interrogation. Statements not made in response to custodial interrogation are classified as gratuitous and are not subject to suppression for lack of *Miranda* warnings." *Commonwealth v. Heggins*, 809 A.2d 908, 914 (Pa. Super. 2002).

Commonwealth v. Cruz, 71 A.3d 998, 1003 (Pa. Super. 2013).

The Hit and Run Statute, 75 Pa. C.S.A. §§ 3741–3755 requiring a driver to stop, render aid and disclose identity does not violate self-incrimination. *Commonwealth v. Long*, 831 A.2d 737 (Pa. Super. 2003).

Compare: Fed. R. Evid. 501.

Research References

Packel & Poulin, Pennsylvania Evidence § 549 (4th ed. 2013)

McCormick, Evidence Chapter 13 (7th ed. 2013)

PRIVILEGE: SEXUAL ASSAULT COUNSELOR

See: Pa.R.E. 501.

Objection

- Objection. [*Request sidebar*] The question seeks information which is privileged under 42 Pa.C.S.A. § 5945.1.

Response

[*Opposing counsel should request a side bar and demand an offer of proof on the validity of the claim of privilege. Where the trial court determines the information sought was communicated between a victim of sexual assault and a sexual assault counselor in the course of that relationship and that there has been no written waiver, there is no response since the privilege is absolute*].

Pennsylvania Law

42 Pa.C.S.A. § 5945.1(b) provides:

(1) No sexual assault counselor or an interpreter translating the communication between a sexual assault counselor and a victim may, without the written consent of the victim, disclose the victim's confidential oral or written communications to the counselor nor consent to be examined in any court or criminal proceeding.

(2) No co-participant who is present during counseling may disclose a victim's confidential communication made during the counseling session nor consent to be examined in any civil or criminal proceeding without the written consent of the victim.

Confidential communications are defined as:

All information, oral or written, transmitted between a victim of sexual assault and a sexual assault counselor in the course of their relationship, including, but not limited to, any advice, reports, statistical data, memoranda, working papers, records, or the like, given or made during that relationship, including matters transmitted between the sexual assault counselor and the victim through the use of an interpreter. 42 Pa.C.S.A. § 5945.1(a).

The Pennsylvania Supreme Court has held that the Commonwealth has a significant interest in protecting the confidentiality of communications between victim and counselor and that the privilege codified at 42 Pa.C.S.A. § 5945.1 is intended to be absolute, applying to the production of documents as well as to the testimony of counselors as explicitly stated. *Commonwealth v. Wilson*, 529 Pa. 268, 602 A.2d 1290 (1992); *Commonwealth v. Askew*, 446 Pa. Super. 301, 666 A.2d 1062 (1995); *Commonwealth v. Kunkle*, 424 Pa. Super. 499, 623 A.2d 336 (1993). The statute was intended to remedy what the legislature perceived was a grave injustice committed against those who, because of lesser economic means, were forced to seek counseling from a public center rather than a private therapist (where privilege was previously recognized). Id. Prior inconsistent cases are overruled. *Commonwealth v. Kennedy*, 413 Pa. Super. 95, 604 A.2d 1036 (1992). However, if the Commonwealth has obtained access to information pertaining to the sexual assault counseling which it seeks to shield from the defense, the statutory privilege must yield to the defendant's rights of confrontation and compulsory process. *Commonwealth v. Davis*, 543 Pa. 628, 674 A.2d 214 (1996). The privilege will also yield to the Commonwealth's interest in protecting children from abuse. *Pittsburgh Action Against Rape v. Dep't. of Pub. Welfare*, 120 A.3d 1078 (Pa.Cmwlth. 2015) (testimony otherwise privileged is made admissible by Child Protective Services Law, 23 Pa.C.S.A. § 6381(a), (c), in child abuse expungement proceedings which should not be limited to alleged perpetrator's statements but also include victim's statement of sexual abuse made to counselor); *T.D. v.*

Dep't of Public Welfare, 54 A.3d 437 (Pa. Cmwlth. 2012) (notwithstanding the privilege, mother's admission to sex assault counselor that she had planned to kill her child was admissible).

Research References

Packel & Poulin, Pennsylvania Evidence § 525 (4th ed. 2013)

McCormick, Evidence § 76.2 (7th ed. 2013)

PROMPT COMPLAINT IN SEXUAL ASSAULT CASES—(PRIOR CONSISTENT STATEMENT)

Objection

- Objection. The question calls for a hearsay answer.
- The alleged victim has not testified, so there is no testimony to corroborate with this evidence and the evidence does not meet the test of the excited utterance exception.

Response

- The question is proper; the testimony is clearly admissible as evidence of a prompt complaint.

Pennsylvania Law

In prosecutions for sexual assault, statements of prompt complaint made by the alleged victim to another person which are consistent with the victim's testimony at trial, benefit from a special evidentiary rule making such evidence admissible in the Commonwealth's case-in-chief. Comment to Pa.R.E. 613(c); *Commonwealth v. Fink*, 791 A.2d 1235 (Pa. Super. 2002); *Commonwealth v. Freeman*, 295 Pa. Super. 467, 441 A.2d 1327 (1982). The prompt complaint is not admissible for its truth or as substantive evidence that a sexual assault occurred; it is admissible to bolster the credibility of the complainant.

Although the rule has been extended to a number of sex crimes committed against both sexes, evidence of the alleged victim's "hue and cry" following rape has long been admissible at common law. As one court said: ". . . the testimony of a woman that she was raped is automatically vulnerable to attack by the defendant as recent fabrication in the absence of hue and cry on her part. This justifies a special evidentiary rule permitting introduction of her fresh complaints in the prosecution's case-in-chief." *Commonwealth v. Freeman*,

295 Pa. Super. 467, 441 A.2d 1327 (1982).

It is important to note that the evidence which may be offered is limited to the fact that a complaint was made and only so much of its detail as is necessary to identify the occurrence complained of with the crime charged. *Commonwealth v. Pettiford*, 265 Pa. Super. 466, 402 A.2d 532 (1979); *Commonwealth v. Krick*, 164 Pa. Super. 516, 67 A.2d 746 (1949). Authority is divided on whether the portion of the victim's statement which names the defendant as the assailant is admissible as part of the prompt complaint or is treated as inadmissible hearsay. Compare *Commonwealth v. Freeman*, 295 Pa. Super. 467, 441 A.2d 1327 (1982) (statement of identification not within prompt complaint rule), with *Commonwealth v. Stohr*, 522 A.2d 589 (Pa. Super. 1987) (characterizing discussion in *Freeman* as dictum and holding statement of identification admissible). An all-encompassing statement which does more than identify the complaint and its nature will be excluded. *Commonwealth v. Green*, 487 Pa. 322, 409 A.2d 371 (1979).

If the alleged victim does not testify concerning the sexual assault, there is nothing to corroborate with evidence of prompt complaint and this special evidentiary rule is not invoked. However, prompt complaints may sometimes qualify as excited utterances under Pa.R.E. 803(2) and be admitted as substantive evidence under that exception to the hearsay rule. *See Commonwealth v. Pettiford*, 265 Pa. Super. 466, 402 A.2d 532 (1979).

The determination of whether or not a complaint was prompt is dependent upon the facts of the case. *Commonwealth v. Bryson*, 860 A.2d 1101 (Pa. Super. 2004) (complaint by mentally disabled young woman 30 hours after attack was prompt complaint); *Commonwealth v. Stohr*, 522 A.2d 589 (Pa. Super. 1987) (4-year-old child's statement 24 hours later was permissible as prompt complaint).

Modern Pennsylvania decisions treat statements of prompt complaint as non-hearsay prior consistent statements (the view expressed by Professors Packel and Poulin). *See* Comment to Pa.R.E. 613(c). Since prior consistent statements are not admitted for truth and thus, are not hearsay, the confrontation concerns addressed in *Crawford v. Washington*, 541 U.S. 36, 124 S.Ct. 1354, 158 L.Ed.2d 177 (2004) (discussed at page 134, *supra*) are not applicable.

See also *Commonwealth v. Snoke*, 525 Pa. 295, 580 A.2d 295 (1990) which held that, where the actual occurrence of the sexual assault is challenged, the trial judge is required to charge the jury as to the relevance of a delay in disclosure and the significance of a prompt complaint.

See generally 18 Pa.C.S.A. § 3105, Prompt Complaint which provides:

> Prompt reporting to public authority is not required in a prosecution under this chapter: Provided, however, that nothing in this section shall be construed to prohibit a defendant from introducing evidence of the complainant's failure to promptly report the crime if such evidence would be admissible pursuant to the rules of evidence.

Commonwealth v. Dillon, 925 A.2d 131 (Pa. 2007) ("other acts" evidence of defendant's physical abuse of victim's mother and brother that intimidated victim was admissible in trial for sex offense as substantive evidence in Commonwealth's case-in-chief to explain victim's lack of prompt complaint) (collecting cases); accord *Commonwealth v. Gonzalez*, 112 A.3d 1232 (Pa. Super. 2015).

For a discussion of the prompt complaint instruction found at Section 4.13A of the Pennsylvania Suggested Standard Criminal Jury Instructions, see *Commonwealth v. Sandusky*, 77 A.3d 663 (Pa. Super. 2013).

Research Reference

Packel & Poulin, Pennsylvania Evidence § 613-6

(4th ed. 2013)

RAPE SHIELD LAW

See: 18 Pa.C.S.A. § 3104.

Objection

- Objection. The information sought by this question is absolutely barred by 18 Pa.C.S.A. § 3104; it is not relevant and it is unfairly prejudicial.

Response

- [*Consent*] [*Motive for false accusation*] is an issue; the appropriate motion was filed and a ruling of relevance and admissibility was made.

Pennsylvania Law

The purpose of the Rape Shield Law is to prevent a sexual assault trial from becoming an attack upon the victim's reputation for chastity. *Commonwealth v. Weber*, 549 Pa. 430, 701 A.2d 531 (1997) (precluding evidence of abortion). The fundamental premise is that evidence of a victim's past sexual behavior generally is irrelevant to the credibility of her testimony and that her prior sexual activity with third parties has no bearing on the issue of whether she consented to the sexual violence charged. The statute permits evidence of past sexual conduct to be introduced in only one instance: past sexual conduct with the defendant is admissible where consent of the victim is at issue and the evidence is otherwise admissible. The Rape Shield Law, 18 Pa.C.S.A. § 3104 provides:

(a) General rule—Evidence of specific instances of the alleged victim's past sexual conduct, opinion evidence of the alleged victim's past sexual conduct, and reputation evidence of the alleged victim's past sexual conduct shall not be admissible in prosecutions under this Chapter except evidence of the alleged victim's past sexual conduct with the defendant where consent of the alleged victim is at issue and such evidence is otherwise admissible pursuant to the rules of evidence.

(b) Evidentiary proceedings—A defendant who proposes to offer evidence of the alleged victim's past sexual conduct pursuant to subsection (a) shall file a written motion and offer proof at the time of trial. If, at the time of trial, the court determines that the motion and offer of proof are sufficient on their faces, the court shall order an in camera hearing and shall make findings on the record as to the relevance and admissibility of the proposed evidence pursuant to the standards set forth in subsection (a).

The Rape Shield Law represents a significant departure from the traditional rule that evidence of a rape victim's bad character for chastity was admissible as circumstantial evidence of consent. In fact, as this statute recognizes, such evidence is highly prejudicial and of limited or no probative value. *See Commonwealth v. K.S.F.*, 102 A.3d 480 (Pa. Super. 2014) (rape shield law was enacted to prevent a trial from shifting its focus from the culpability of the accused toward the virtue and chastity of the victim and to exclude irrelevant and abusive inquiries regarding prior sexual conduct of sexual assault complainants).

The statute and subsequent case law have created narrow exceptions to the bar on use of past conduct evidence.

Statutory Exception

The statute allows the trial court to determine whether past conduct evidence is admissible only if the victim and the defendant had past sexual relations and the asserted defense is consent.

Section 3104(b) sets forth a rigorous procedure to determine whether to admit or to exclude the evidence. The process begins with the defendant submitting in writing a specific proffer to the court of exactly what evidence he or she seeks to admit and precisely why it is relevant to the defense.

Commonwealth v. Smith, 410 Pa. Super. 363, 599 A.2d 1340 (1991); *Commonwealth v. Beltz*, 829 A.2d 680 (Pa. Super. 2003) (failure to submit written motion and offer of proof is fatal to claim). This procedure forces the defendant to frame the precise issues involved and prevents fishing expedition intrusions on Rape Shield Law protections. Where the proffer is vague and conjectural, evidence of the victim's past sexual conduct will be excluded and no further inquiry need be entertained. *Commonwealth v. Fernsler*, 715 A.2d 435 (Pa. Super. 1998); *Commonwealth v. Guy*, 454 Pa. Super. 582, 686 A.2d 397 (1996).

Where the proffer is sufficiently specific, the court must then undertake a three-part analysis of the substance of the proffer. In an *in camera* hearing, the court must determine: (1) whether the proffered evidence is relevant to the defense at trial; (2) whether the proffered evidence is cumulative of evidence otherwise admissible at trial; and (3) whether the proffered evidence is more probative than prejudicial. *Commonwealth v. Nieves*, 399 Pa. Super. 277, 582 A.2d 341 (1990).

Judicial Exceptions

In order to accommodate a defendant's constitutional rights to confrontation and cross-examination, Pennsylvania courts have held that in certain limited situations, evidence of prior sexual conduct is admissible even though consent is not an issue. These exceptions include: (1) evidence that negates directly the act of intercourse with which a defendant is charged; (2) evidence demonstrating a witness's bias or evidence that attacks credibility; and (3) evidence tending to directly exculpate the accused by showing that the alleged victim is biased and thus has a motive to lie, fabricate or seek retribution via prosecution. *Commonwealth v. Burns*, 988 A.2d 684 (Pa. Super. 2009); *Commonwealth v. Northrip*, 945 A.2d 198

(Pa. Super. 2008).

Generally speaking, the Rape Shield Law does not prohibit the admission of relevant evidence which may exculpate a defendant of the crime with which he is charged. *Commonwealth v. Ruggiano*, 14 A.3d 844 (Pa. Super. 2010), appeal granted, order vacated, 26 A.3d 473 (Pa. 2011). The statute also must yield to a defendant's constitutional right to challenge the credibility of a witness and present evidence necessary to allow a jury to make a fair determination of the defendant's guilt or innocence. *Commonwealth v. Spiewak*, 533 Pa. 1, 617 A.2d 696 (1992).

Thus where the alleged victim and defendant had consensual intercourse two hours before the rape allegedly occurred, evidence of sexual conduct close enough in time to contradict the charged act of rape and to explain the objective signs of intercourse was admissible. *Commonwealth v. Majorana*, 503 Pa. 602, 470 A.2d 80 (1983). Evidence of other sexual conduct to prove a specific bias against and hostility toward defendant and a motive to seek retribution by false accusation has also been permitted. *Commonwealth v. Black*, 337 Pa. Super. 548, 487 A.2d 396 (1985) (constitutional right to show bias and attack credibility with evidence that victim was having sexual relationship with her brother and wanted her father, the defendant, out of the way); *see also Commonwealth v. Northrip*, 945 A.2d 198 (Pa. Super. 2008); *Commonwealth v. Eck*, 413 Pa. Super. 538, 605 A.2d 1248 (1992).

In *Commonwealth v. Wall*, 413 Pa. Super. 599, 606 A.2d 449 (1992), the court held that evidence of past conduct which logically tends to show that the claim was fabricated must be deemed relevant since such evidence tends to exculpate the defendant of the charges and exculpatory evidence must be admitted to comply with the defendant's constitutional right to confrontation and cross-examination. *See Commonwealth v. Killen*, 545 Pa. 127, 680 A.2d

851 (1996) (sexually provocative statements of victim made to third persons shortly after alleged sexual assault admissible to establish victim's state of mind); *Commonwealth v. Spiewak*, 533 Pa. 1, 617 A.2d 696 (1992) (under facts of case, error to prohibit defendant from introducing evidence that stepdaughter had previously and falsely accused another older man of having sex with her); *Commonwealth v. Jorgenson*, 512 Pa. 601, 517 A.2d 1287 (1986) (evidence of victim's prior sexual conduct admissible to explain presence of seminal acid phosphatase in victim's clothing and internal bruising of her vagina).

Other illustrative cases include: *Commonwealth v. Johnson*, 536 Pa. 153, 638 A.2d 940 (1994), and *Commonwealth v. Schley*, 136 A.3d 511 (Pa. Super. 2016) (Rape Shield Law does not prohibit evidence of false sexual assault allegations since evidence of fabricating such claims does not constitute "past sexual conduct" and does not reflect on victim's reputation for chastity); *Commonwealth v. Durst*, 522 Pa. 2, 559 A.2d 504 (1989) (evidence that others in addition to defendant may have had sexual contact with victim is inadmissible because it does not exonerate defendant); *accord Commonwealth v. Allburn*, 721 A.2d 363 (Pa. Super. 1998); *Commonwealth v. Jones*, 826 A.2d 900 (Pa. Super. 2003) (Rape Shield Law prohibits evidence of specific instances of victim's entire sexual history that occurred prior to trial; prostitution conviction after alleged crime was inadmissible); *Commonwealth v. Fink*, 791 A.2d 1235 (Pa. Super. 2002) (no error to disallow defendant's proffers of other sexual activity by victim where evidence was conjectural, did not exonerate or establish bias, was irrelevant or was waived).

There is no correspondent legislative authority in Pennsylvania for excluding past sexual conduct in civil actions. If evidence of sexual character or conduct in a civil action is otherwise relevant and admissible under the Pennsylvania Rules of Evidence, it is not excludable under 18 Pa.C.S.A. § 3104.

Compare: Fed. R. Evid. 412.

Research References

Packel & Poulin, Pennsylvania Evidence § 412-1 (4th ed. 2013)

McCormick, Evidence §§ 189–193 (7th ed. 2013)

REFRESHING PRESENT RECOLLECTION

See: Pa.R.E. 612.

Technique

[*After demonstrating that the witness needs to review a document (or thing) to revive his recollection, the attorney for the proponent shows the writing (or object) to the witness and asks him to review it silently. Counsel then asks the witness if his memory is refreshed. If so, the document (or object) is put aside and the witness can testify*].

Objection

- Objection. There is no foundation showing that the witness' present memory is inadequate. The witness never testified that he could not recall specific details and, in fact, admitted to having an independent present recollection of events.

Response

- I have established: (1) that the witness' present memory is inadequate; (2) that the writing could refresh the witness' present memory; and (3) after reviewing the writing, the witness has indicated that this writing actually does refresh his present memory.

Pennsylvania Law

It is not uncommon for a witness at trial or deposition to forget information or to recollect information only partially or inaccurately. A witness whose memory is shown to be inadequate or exhausted may use any writing or other aid to refresh or revive his present recollection of past events. Pa.R.E. 612; *Commonwealth v. Payne*, 455 Pa. 503, 317 A.2d 208 (1974); *Dean Witter Reynolds, Inc. v. Genteel*, 346 Pa. Super. 336, 499 A.2d 637 (1985).

To use a writing to refresh memory, the following foundation must first be established: (1) that the witness' present memory is inadequate; (2) that the writing could refresh the witness' present memory; and (3) that reference to the writing actually does refresh the witness' present memory. *Commonwealth v. Montgomery*, 455 Pa. Super. 202, 687 A.2d 1131 (1996); *Commonwealth v. Sal-Mar Amusements, Inc.*, 428 Pa. Super. 321, 630 A.2d 1269 (1993); *Commonwealth v. Carr*, 370 Pa. Super. 1, 535 A.2d 1120 (1987); *Commonwealth v. Lamb*, 309 Pa. Super. 415, 455 A.2d 678 (1983); *Commonwealth v. Proctor*, 253 Pa. Super. 369, 385 A.2d 383 (1978).

The proper procedure for a party to refresh his own witness' recollection is to show the writing, or other evidence, to the witness; after the witness' recollection is refreshed, the direct examination may proceed with the witness testifying from present recollection. *Commonwealth v. Payne*, 455 Pa. 503, 317 A.2d 208 (1974); *Commonwealth v. Lamb*, 309 Pa. Super. 415, 455 A.2d 678 (1983).

While the rule permits a witness to use a prior writing to refresh his present memory of past events, the witness must testify from present, albeit refreshed, memory and not from the writing itself. *Commonwealth v. Canales*, 454 Pa. 422, 311 A.2d 572 (1973). Once the writing has refreshed the witness' present memory, it has served its purpose and may not be introduced into evidence. Therefore, a witness may use a memorandum or other aid for the purpose of refreshing memory even though the writing itself may not be competent evidence. *Commonwealth v. Weeden*, 457 Pa. 436, 322 A.2d 343 (1974). In commenting upon prior writings used to refresh the memory of a witness, Professor Wigmore has said that "[i]t follows from the nature of the purpose for which the paper is used that it is in no strict sense evidence" and "that the offering party has not the right to treat it as evidence by reading it or showing it or handing it to the jury, is well established." 3 J. Wigmore, Evidence § 763

(Chadbourn rev. 1972). The reason such writings are not admissible into evidence is that they are only a repetition of the witness' testimonial utterances in the courtroom. *Commonwealth v. Canales*, 454 Pa. 422, 311 A.2d 572 (1973). However, the opposing party may introduce into evidence those portions of the writing which relate to the testimony of the witness. Pa.R.E. 612(a).

Once a witness has resorted to a writing or other object to refresh recollection, the adverse party is entitled to inspect the writing and to have it available for reference in cross-examining the witness. *Commonwealth v. Proctor*, 253 Pa. Super. 369, 385 A.2d 383 (1978).

Compare: Fed. R. Evid. 612.

Research References

Packel & Poulin, Pennsylvania Evidence § 612-1 (4th ed. 2013)

McCormick, Evidence § 9 (7th ed. 2013)

RELEVANCE

See: Pa.R.E. 401.

Objection

- *[To a question]* Objection. The information sought by the question is irrelevant to any issue in this case.

- *[To an* answer] Objection, irrelevant. I move the answer be stricken and the jury be instructed not to consider it for any purpose.

Response

- The evidence sought by the question has a logical bearing on an issue in this case because *[explain]*.

- The testimony goes to the weight or credibility of the evidence.

Pennsylvania Law

Evidence is relevant if it logically tends to establish a material fact in the case, tends to make a fact at issue more or less probable or supports a reasonable inference or presumption regarding a material fact. Rule 401; *Commonwealth v. Lesko*, 15 A.3d 345 (Pa. 2011); *Commonwealth v. Kennedy*, 959 A.2d 916 (Pa. 2008); *Commonwealth v. Dillon*, 925 A.2d 131 (Pa. 2007); *Commonwealth v. Cousar*, 928 A.2d 1025 (Pa. 2007); *Commonwealth v. Edwards*, 588 Pa. 151, 903 A.2d 1139 (2006); *Commonwealth v. Collins*, 888 A.2d 564 (Pa. 2005); *Commonwealth v. Semenza*, 127 A.3d 1 (Pa. Super. 2015); *Commonwealth v. Fransen*, 42 A.3d 1100 (Pa. Super. 2012); *Joseph v. North Whitehall Tp. Bd. of Sup'rs.*, 16 A.3d 1209 (Pa. Cmwlth. 2011). To be relevant and admissible, evidence need not be conclusive. *Commonwealth v. Foley*, 38 A.3d 882 (Pa. Super. 2012). Although the rule makes no reference to credibility, evidence relating to credibility falls under the definition of "relevant evidence" because the outcome of an action is often determined by the jurors' assessment of the credibility of the witness.

In *Commonwealth v. McNeely*, 368 Pa. Super. 517, 520, 534 A.2d 778, 779 (1987), the court said:

> **Relevance** is comprised of two fundamental components: **materiality** and **probative value**. **Materiality** looks to the relation between the propositions for which the evidence is offered and the issues in the case. If the evidence is offered to help prove a proposition which is not a matter in issue, the evidence is immaterial. **Probative value**, on the other hand, deals with the tendency of the evidence to establish the proposition that it is offered to prove. McCormick, Evidence, § 185 at 541 (Cleary 3d ed. 1984).

Evidence which is offered for one purpose need not be excluded merely because it is inadmissible for another. *Orlando v. Herco, Inc.*, 351 Pa. Super. 144, 505 A.2d 308 (1986).

However, relevant evidence may be excluded if its probative value is outweighed by the danger of unfair prejudice, confusion of the issues, misleading the jury, waste of time or needless presentation of cumulative evidence. Pa.R.E. 403; *Commonwealth v. Hitchko*, 123 A.3d 731 (Pa. 2015); *Commonwealth v. Hicks*, 91 A.3d 47 (Pa. 2014) (to determine whether otherwise relevant evidence should be excluded based on its prejudicial effect requires a fact-intensive, context specific inquiry); *Commonwealth v. Sanchez*, 36 A.3d 24 (Pa. 2011); *Conroy v. Rosenwald*, 940 A.2d 409 (Pa. Super. 2007); *Henery v. Shadle*, 443 Pa. Super. 331, 661 A.2d 439 (1995). Because virtually all evidence is prejudicial to one party or another, the prejudice must be *unfair* to justify exclusion under Pa.R.E. 403. *Commonwealth v. Treiber*, 582 Pa. 646, 874 A.2d 26 (2005). Unfair prejudice includes the possibility that the evidence will enflame the jury to make a decision on the basis of a factor unrelated to the issues properly before it. In the context of criminal cases, unfair prejudice speaks to the capacity of some relevant evidence to lure the fact-finder into declaring guilt on a ground different from the proof specific to the offense charged. *Commonwealth v. Flamer*, 53 A.3d 82 (Pa. Super. 2012); *Commonwealth v. Owens*, 929 A.2d 1187 (Pa. Super. 2007).

The question of **remoteness** *is basically one of relevance. Hooker v. State Farm Fire and Cas. Co.*, 880 A.2d 70 (Pa.Cmwlth. 2005); *Tolentino v. Bailey*, 230 Pa. Super. 8, 326 A.2d 920 (1974). Remoteness relates not merely to the passage of time, but to the undermining of reasonable inferences due to the likelihood of supervening factors. *See, e.g., Commonwealth v. Reed*, 990 A.2d 1158 (Pa. 2010) (prior PFAs relevant to pattern of abuse which culminated in murder); *Commonwealth v. Drumheller*, 570 Pa. 117, 808 A.2d 893 (2002) (rejecting argument that abuse resulting in PFAs over three-year period was too remote to be admissible; evidence was relevant to events that formed history of case and defendant's motive, malice and intent re victim's murder); *Commonwealth v. Tyson*, 119 A.3d 353 (Pa. Super. 2015) (prior rape conviction with five year look-back period not too remote or unduly prejudicial to preclude admission under common plan or scheme exceptions to Rule 404(b)); *Commonwealth v. Smith*, 808 A.2d 215 (Pa. Super. 2002) (because issue of intoxication was hotly contested, evidence that defendant was drinking eight hours before fatal accident was relevant; jury could assign weight, if any, due to remoteness).

The following cases are instructive: **Admitted**, *Commonwealth v. U.S. Mineral Products*, 956 A.2d 967 (Pa. 2008) (lack of fire safety features relevant to market value of building prior to severe fire); *Quinby v. Plumsteadville Family Practice*, 907 A.2d 1061 (Pa. 2006) (error to exclude both audio portion of videotape made twenty-two months prior to incident to show strength of decedent's voice and videotape deposition taken one day prior to his death; both were relevant to pace and extent of decedent's physical decline); *Commonwealth v. DeJesus*, 880 A.2d 608 (Pa. 2005) (testimony that subsequent to crime, defendant had a sawed-off shotgun (which was not the murder weapon) and said "fuck them" in response to request to surrender was relevant in aggregate context; evidence made clear defendant knew of his fugitive status and had intent and means to repel police custody, all of which suggested consciousness of guilt); *Commonwealth v. Johnson*, 556 Pa. 216, 727 A.2d 1089 (1999) (no error to admit defendant's statements that he would have shot victims earlier; premeditation was in issue and statement made it more probable that defendant intended to kill when he shot victims later that day); *Commonwealth v. Williams*, 537 Pa. 1, 640 A.2d 1251 (1994) (weapon in defendant's possession properly admitted even though it could not positively be identified as weapon used in crime since it tended to prove defendant had weapon similar to gun used in perpetration of crime); *Commonwealth v. Talbert*, 129 A.3d 536 (Pa. Super. 2015) (defendant-authored rap lyrics, describing a scenario matching facts and circumstances of murders); *Commonwealth v. Kubis*, 978 A.2d 391 (Pa. Super. 2009) (gloves found in defendant's vehicle became relevant when defense counsel opened the door by asking detective if defendant's fingerprints were found at crime scene); *Buchhalter v. Buchhalter*, 959 A.2d 1260 (Pa. Super. 2008) (facts surrounding prior PFA consent order relevant to understanding reasonableness of ex-wife's fear relative to present petition); *Commonwealth v. Sasse*, 921 A.2d 1229 (Pa. Super. 2007) (evidence of character and conduct of a witness relevant only as it relates to character for truthfulness or untruthfulness of the witness, citing Rules 608 and 609); *Commonwealth v. Maloney*, 876 A.2d 1002 (Pa. Super. 2005) (in prosecution for furnishing alcohol to minor, college student's public drunkenness relevant to timeline of events); *Raker v. Raker*, 847 A.2d 720 (Pa. Super. 2004) (in protection from abuse cases, some flexibility must be allowed in admitting evidence relating to past acts of abuse); *Commonwealth v. Seibert*, 799 A.2d 54 (Pa. Super. 2002) (in prosecution for homicide by vehicle and DUI, defendant properly permitted to present evidence of other accidents to show dangerous condition of roadway caused accident and death); *Commonwealth v. DiStefano*, 782 A.2d 574 (Pa. Super. 2001) (where issue was whether defendant killed woman murdered by ligature strangulation, evidence in diary and journal of his proclivity for oxygen-deprivation sexual techniques relevant to support reasonable inferences regarding a fact at issue); *Hutchison ex rel. Hutchison ex rel Hutchison v. Luddy*, 763 A.2d 826 (Pa. Super. 2000) (evidence of other pedophilic activity by defendant and other priests relevant to issue of diocesean liability under Restatement (Second) Torts § 317 (duty of master to control conduct of servant)); *In re N.C.*, 763 A.2d 913 (Pa. Super. 2000) (evidence of recent squalid living conditions relevant to issue of whether parents were unable to care for children); *Commonwealth v. Wax*, 391 Pa. Super. 314, 571 A.2d 386 (1990) (evidence of affluent lifestyle and financial difficulties relevant to motive for committing crime of arson for monetary gain); *Meter v. Com., Dep't of Transp.*, 41 A.3d 901 (Pa. Cmwlth. 2012) (driving records can be relevant where medical condition involves drug or alcohol abuse); **Excluded**, *Commonwealth v. Briggs*, 12 A.3d 291, 340 (Pa. 2011) (excluding evidence of defendant's behavior on the day before the shooting; "[t]o hold otherwise would contravene the well-recognized evidentiary principle of *res inter alios acta*, which provides that 'a thing or event which occurs at a time different from the time in issue is generally not admissible to prove what occurred at the time in issue' " (citations omitted)); *Commonwealth v. Montalvo*, 986 A.2d 84 (Pa. 2009) (criminal record of accomplice not relevant to defendant's guilt or innocence); *Commonwealth v. Laich*, 566 Pa. 19,

777 A.2d 1057 (2001) (error admitting deceased victim's hearsay statement about nature of her relationship with defendant; victim's state of mind about relationship irrelevant where defense admitted killing but claimed it was in heat of passion); *Commonwealth v. Young*, 561 Pa. 34, 748 A.2d 166 (1999) (*Young I*) (no error to exclude warden's testimony as to defendant's reputation for nonviolence in jail; not relevant to defendant's reputation in community at time of murder); *Commonwealth v. Holloway*, 559 Pa. 258, 739 A.2d 1039 (1999) (accomplice's acquittal cannot be offered into evidence to create impression defendant is equally innocent); *Commonwealth v. Eubanks*, 511 Pa. 201, 512 A.2d 619 (1986) (questions concerning defendant's religious beliefs irrelevant to any issue in rape case); *Commonwealth v. Story*, 476 Pa. 391, 383 A.2d 155 (1978) (evidence of victim's family life irrelevant and prejudicial, and its admission in first degree murder prosecution was reversible error); *Commonwealth v. Tyack*, 128 A.3d 254 (Pa. Super. 2015) (where statute forbade possession of an electronic incapacitation device, evidence that it was missing batteries was irrelevant); *Czimmer v. Janssen Pharmaceuticals, Inc.*, 122 A.3d 1043 (Pa. Super. 2015) (evidence that plaintiff had been on antidepressant irrelevant to whether manufactured failed to warn of potential birth defect risks associated with migraine-prevention drug if used during pregnancy); *Parr v. Ford Motor Co.*, 109 A.3d 682 (Pa. Super. 2014) (safety standards promulgated after the sale of the product are irrelevant and inadmissible to show the product was defectively designed or contained inadequate warnings when manufactured); *Buckman v. Verazin*, 54 A.3d 956 (Pa. Super. 2012) (doctor's actions when operating on other patients not probative of what his actions were in caring for plaintiff; medical records of others irrelevant); *Knowles v. Levan*, 15 A.3d 504 (Pa. Super. 2011) (where only issue was damages, improper to admit

evidence concerning cause of accident such as use of drugs and alcohol; admission of liability makes all such evidence irrelevant); *In re R.M.G.*, 997 A.2d 339 (Pa. Super. 2010) (mother's success in babysitting older children for limited time irrelevant as to whether she is capable of custody of two-year-old child); *Hawkey v. Peirsel*, 869 A.2d 983 (Pa. Super. 2005) (whether physician was board certified was irrelevant in malpractice action; board certification is not a legal requirement to practice medicine in Pennsylvania and the real issue was whether treatment met standard of care); *Commonwealth v. Walter*, 849 A.2d 265 (Pa. Super. 2004) (in murder case for death of infant, evidence of prior injury to child irrelevant because nothing connected defendant to that injury); *Commonwealth v. Farmer*, 758 A.2d 173 (Pa. Super. 2000) (because defendant could not show victim was on medication at time of rape, evidence of previous drug treatment for depression was irrelevant to her credibility); *Commonwealth v. Day*, 399 Pa. Super. 399, 582 A.2d 655 (1990) (evidence of prior acquittal irrelevant to charge of terrorizing prosecution witness); *Kearns by Kearns v. DeHaas*, 377 Pa. Super. 200, 546 A.2d 1226 (1988) (university study on average automobile stopping distances irrelevant where witness could not apply it to facts of case); *Burns v. Pepsi-Cola Metro. Bottling Co.*, 353 Pa. Super. 571, 510 A.2d 810 (1986) (where wife was claiming loss of consortium, her alleged extra-marital affair three years before accident properly excluded as too remote to be relevant); *Commonwealth v. Barkelbaugh*, 526 Pa. 133, 584 A.2d 927 (1990) and *Commonwealth v. Haight*, 332 Pa. Super. 269, 481 A.2d 357 (1984), *affirmed* 514 Pa. 438, 525 A.2d 1199 (1987) (evidence of defendant's poverty as motive to commit crime irrelevant and reversible error); *but see Commonwealth v. Brown*, 911 A.2d 576 (Pa. Super. 2006) (no absolute bar to all evidence of financial difficulties; here relevance was that defendant blamed victim for his financial dif-

ficulties and now had money after robbery/
homicide); *Ariondo v. Munsey*, 122 Pa.Cmwlth. 475,
553 A.2d 94 (1989) (state budgetary limitations irrelevant to PennDOT's duty to protect against
dangerous highway condition).

Occurrence or Absence of Other Accidents

Evidence of similar accidents involving the
same product is admissible in negligence or product liability actions to establish notice, the existence of a defect, or to refute testimony by the
defense that a given product was designed without
safety hazards. *Hutchinson v. Penske Truck Leasing
Co.*, 876 A.2d 978 (Pa. Super. 2005) (reversible error to admit studies of heavy truck accidents where
there was no substantial similarity to this truck,
accident or circumstances of this case); *DiFran-
cesco v. Excam, Inc.*, 642 A.2d 529 (Pa. Super. 1994);
Cornell Drilling Co. v. Ford Motor Co., 241 Pa.
Super. 129, 359 A.2d 822 (1976); *Smith v. Ingersoll-
Rand Co.*, 214 F.3d 1235 (10th Cir. 2000); *Ponder
v. Warren Tool Corp.*, 834 F.2d 1553 (10th Cir. 1987)
(collecting cases). Admission of other accidents or
complaints is predicated on a showing that the circumstances surrounding them were substantially
similar to those involved in the present case. *Blumer
v. Ford Motor Co.*, 20 A.3d 1222 (Pa. Super. 2011)
(in all prior incidents, Ford trucks had unexplained
parking brake failure while parked on incline);
Hutchinson, 876 A.2d 978 (Pa. Super. 2005); *Majdic
v. Cincinnati Mach. Co.*, 537 A.2d 334 (Pa. Super.
1988); *Valentine v. Acme Markets, Inc.*, 687 A.2d
1157 (Pa. Super. 1997) (proponent of evidence bears
burden of establishing similarity between other accidents and the accident at issue *before* the evidence is admitted); *Eiland v. Westinghouse Elec.
Corp.*, 58 F.3d 176 (5th Cir. 1995). The rationale
for this rule is simple. In such cases, the jury is
invited to infer from the presence of other accidents:
(1) that a dangerous condition existed, (2) which

caused the accident. As the circumstances and conditions of the other accidents become less similar to the accident under consideration, the probative force of such evidence decreases. But the danger that the evidence will be unfairly prejudicial remains. "[T]he jury might infer from evidence of the prior accident alone that ultra-hazardous conditions existed . . . and were the cause of the later accident without those issues ever having been proved." *Gardner v. Southern Ry. Sys.*, 675 F.2d 949 (7th Cir. 1982).

Whether accidents are substantially similar depends largely on the theory of the case. *Four Corners Helicopters, Inc. v. Turbomeca, S.A.*, 979 F.2d 1434 (10th Cir. 1992). "Differences in the nature of the defect alleged may affect a determination whether the accidents are substantially similar . . . . How substantial the similarity must be is in part a function of the proponent's theory of proof." *Ponder*, 834 F.2d at 1560. To show the existence of a dangerous condition requires a high degree of similarity. *Smith v. Ingersoll-Rand Co.*, 214 F.3d 1235 (10th Cir. 2000); *Nachtsheim v. Beech Aircraft Corp.*, 847 F.2d 1261 (7th Cir. 1988). The requirement is relaxed, however, when the evidence of other accidents is offered to prove notice or awareness of the potential defect. *Houdeshell Ex. Rel. Bordas v. Rice*, 939 A.2d 981 (Pa. Super. 2007); *Wheeler v. John Deere Co.*, 862 F.2d 1404 (10th Cir. 1988); *Exum v. General Elec. Co.*, 819 F.2d 1158 (D.C. Cir. 1987). Any differences in the accidents not affecting a finding of substantial similarity go to the weight of the evidence. *Jackson v. Firestone Tire & Rubber Co.*, 788 F.2d 1070 (5th Cir. 1986).

Relevant evidence encompasses evidence tending to establish negative as well as positive facts. *Spino v. John S. Tilley Ladder Co.*, 671 A.2d 726 (Pa. Super. 1996); *Orlando v. Herco, Inc.*, 351 Pa. Super. 144, 505 A.2d 308 (1986); *Michetti v. Linde Baker Material Handling Corp.*, 969 F.Supp. 286

(E.D. Pa. 1997).

In general, courts have recognized that the absence of prior accidents may be admissible to show: (1) absence of defect or other condition alleged; (2) lack of causal connection between the injury and the alleged defect or condition; and (3) the nonexistence of an unduly dangerous situation. *Spino*, 671 A.2d 726 (Pa. Super. 1996) (proper to admit fact that company had manufactured 100,000 wooden ladders without similar mishap); *Orlando*, 351 Pa. Super. 144, 505 A.2d 308 (1986) (evidence that other guests ate same food on same night without illness was admissible); *Espeaignnette v. Gene Tierney Co., Inc.*, 43 F.3d 1 (1st Cir. 1994) (fact that company received no reports of similar accidents tends to disprove causation); *DeMarines v. KLM Royal Dutch Airlines*, 580 F.2d 1193 (3d Cir. 1978) (in personal injury action where plaintiff claimed injury caused by pressurization of aircraft, error to exclude evidence of absence of any other claims arising from that flight; proof of absence of claims makes existence of alleged defect less probable than it would be without evidence).

Evidence of the absence of prior accidents may not be admitted unless the offering party first establishes that the lack of accidents was with regard to a product substantially identical to the one at issue and used in settings and circumstances sufficiently similar to those surrounding the product at issue at the time of the accident. *Klonowski v. International Armament Corp.*, 17 F.3d 992 (7th Cir. 1994).

Admissibility of Weapons Evidence

The general rule is that where a weapon cannot be specifically linked to a crime, the weapon is not admissible as evidence. *Commonwealth v. Robinson*, 554 Pa. 293, 721 A.2d 344 (1998). The exception to this general rule is where the accused had a weapon or implement suitable to the commission of the crime charged. This weapon is always a proper ingredient of the case for prosecution. 554 Pa. at 306, 721 A.2d at 351.

The prosecution need not establish that a particular weapon was actually used in the commission of a crime in order for it to be admissible at trial. *Commonwealth v Edwards*, 903 A.2d 1139 (Pa. 2006) (collecting cases). The Commonwealth need only lay a foundation that would justify an inference by the fact finder of the likelihood that the weapon was used in the commission of the crime. *Commonwealth v Edwards*, 903 A.2d 1139 (Pa. 2006). *See, e.g., Commonwealth v. Owens*, 929 A.2d 1187 (Pa. Super. 2007) (handgun parts and ammunition relevant as tending to prove defendants had weapons similar to the ones used in the crime whereas rifle scopes and ammunition were not relevant to any of the events in question); *Commonwealth v. Miller*, 897 A.2d 1281 (Pa. Super. 2006) (knife set minus the one found in defendant's car relevant to show he had possession of a knife that could have been one of the murder weapons). The cited cases deal with weapons that might have been used. Possession of a handgun may be relevant even if the particular gun possessed cannot be proven to be the one used in the crime. That it was possessed may allow the inference that it could have been used. *Commonwealth v. Christine*, 125 A.3d 394 (Pa. 2015) (unfortunately, some appellate decisions have omitted language referring to the need for a foundation justifying an inference the weapon was used in the crime).

Intoxication

Proof of intoxication is relevant where careless or reckless behavior, such as driving a car is the matter at issue. *Fisher v. Dye*, 386 Pa. 141, 125 A.2d 472 (1956). However, the mere fact of drinking intoxicating liquor is not admissible, being unfairly prejudicial, unless it establishes a degree of intoxication which proves unfitness to drive. *Fisher v. Dye*, 386 Pa. 141, 125 A.2d 472 (1956). See also *Commonwealth v. Williams*, 91 A.3d 240 (Pa. Super. 2014) (Evidence of a witness' intoxication is admissible impeachment evidence where the witness was intoxicated during the event to which he or she testifies; here victim's BAC evidence would have allowed jury to assess credibility and weight of testimony); *Braun v. Target Corp.*, 983 A.2d 752 (Pa. Super. 2009) (alcohol consumption relevant to prove unfitness of iron worker to perform work from a lift platform eighteen feet above ground); *Locke v. Claypool*, 426 Pa. Super. 528, 627 A.2d 801 (1993) (applying unfitness standard to evidence of bicyclist's intoxication); *Ackerman v. Delcomico*, 336 Pa. Super. 569, 486 A.2d 410 (1984) (applying unfitness standard to evidence of pedestrian's intoxication).

Compare: Fed. R. Evid. 401.

Research References

Packel & Poulin, Pennsylvania Evidence §§ 401-1–402-1 (4th ed. 2013)

McCormick, Evidence Chapter 16 (7th ed. 2013)

RELIGIOUS BELIEF

See: Pa.R.E. 610.

Objection

- Objection. The question is irrelevant and prejudicial and directly violates Rule 610 with respect to religious belief.

Response

- Religious beliefs are relevant to the merits of the case because (*explain*).

Pennsylvania Law

Pa.R.E. 610 bars evidence of a witness' religious beliefs for the purpose of showing that his credibility is impaired or enhanced as a result of those beliefs. The purpose of the rule is to guard against any prejudice which may result from the disclosure of a witness' faith.

Statutory law also restricts evidentiary use of religious belief. 42 Pa. C.S.A. § 5902 provides:

(b) Religious belief may not be shown. No witness shall be questioned, in any judicial proceeding, concerning his religious belief; nor shall any evidence be heard upon the subject, for the purpose of affecting either his competency or credibility.

Evidence of religious belief is both irrelevant and prejudicial, *Commonwealth v. Eubanks*, 511 Pa. 201, 512 A.2d 619 (1986); *Commonwealth v. Greenwood*, 488 Pa. 618, 413 A.2d 655 (1980); *Commonwealth v. Mimms*, 477 Pa. 553, 385 A.2d 334 (1978), and cannot be used either to impeach or to bolster the credibility of a witness. *Commonwealth v. Myer*, 340 Pa. Super. 176, 489 A.2d 900 (1985).

However, the prohibition of the statute is not a per se rule of exclusion under all circumstances, *Commonwealth v. Eubanks*, 511 Pa. 201, 512 A.2d

619 (1986), (concurring opinion), and occasionally such evidence has been deemed relevant to other issues in a case. *See, e.g., Jacobs v. Chatwani*, 922 A.2d 950 (Pa. Super. 2007) (evidence that plaintiff was a Jehovah's Witness who refused blood transfusions for religious reasons was admissible because relevant to doctor's decision-making process re treatment); *Commonwealth v. Riggins*, 374 Pa. Super. 243, 542 A.2d 1004 (1988); *Commonwealth v. Rainey*, 271 Pa. Super. 240, 412 A.2d 1106 (1979); *Commonwealth v. Griffin*, 271 Pa. Super. 228, 412 A.2d 897 (1979) (identification of sect was part of witness identification); *Commonwealth v. Covil*, 474 Pa. 375, 378 A.2d 841 (1977) (statement about Muslims admitted to show motive for killing).

Compare: Fed. R. Evid. 610.

Research References

Packel & Poulin, Pennsylvania Evidence § 610-1 (4th ed. 2013)

McCormick, Evidence § 46 (7th ed. 2013)

REOPENING THE CASE—MOTION

See: Pa.R.E. 611(a).

Form

- I respectfully request leave of court to reopen [*plaintiff's*] [*defendant's*] case for the purpose of introducing evidence on the issue of [*state specifically*].

- I respectfully request leave of court to reopen [*plaintiff's*] [*defendant's*] case for the purpose of allowing the witness to correct her testimony with respect to [*state specifically*].

- Objection. To reopen the case at this point will cause unfair prejudice [*explain*]; this is a belated attempt to reverse an earlier tactical decision [*specify*]; the "new" evidence has no/little probative value because [*specify*].

Pennsylvania Law

Pa.R.E. 611(a) provides that the court shall exercise reasonable control over the order of interrogating witnesses. The general rule is that the court may, in its discretion, permit either party to reopen its case at any time prior to the verdict in order to prevent a failure or miscarriage of justice. A case may be reopened sua sponte when it is desirable that further testimony be taken in the interest of a more accurate adjudication and where an honest purpose would be served without unfair disadvantage. *Commonwealth v. Safka*, 141 A.3d 1239 (Pa. 2016); *Commonwealth v. Best*, 120 A.3d 329 (Pa. Super. 2015); *Commonwealth v. Baldwin*, 58 A.3d 754 (Pa. 2012); *Commonwealth v. Smith*, 548 Pa. 65, 694 A.2d 1086 (1997); *Commonwealth v. Tharp*, 525 Pa. 94, 575 A.2d 557 (1990); *Commonwealth v. Beck*, 522 Pa. 194, 560 A.2d 1370 (1989); *Commonwealth v. Deitch Co.*, 449 Pa. 88, 295 A.2d 834 (1972); *Bretz v. Central Bucks School Dist.*, 86 A.3d 306 (Pa.Cmwlth 2014); *Commonwealth v. Safka*, 95 A.3d 304 (Pa. Super.

2014); *Beaumont v. ETL Servs., Inc.*, 761 A.2d 166 (Pa. Super. 2000); *In Re Millcreek Tp. School Dist*, 143 A.3d 1037 (Pa.Cmwlth. 2016). The matter of reopening is not limited in its application to any particular stage of the trial, *Van Buren v. Eberhard*, 377 Pa. 22, 104 A.2d 98 (1954); *Commonwealth v. Best*, 120 A.3d 329 (Pa. Super. 2015), and will not be reversed unless there has been a clear abuse of discretion. *In re J.E.F.*, 487 Pa. 455, 409 A.2d 1165 (1979).

Reopening a case has been allowed where the evidence had been omitted by accident, inadvertence, or even because of mistake as to its necessity. *Commonwealth v. Tharp*, 525 Pa. 94, 575 A.2d 557 (1990); *Commonwealth v. Evans*, 488 Pa. 38, 410 A.2d 1213 (1979); *Seaboard Container Corp. v. Rothschild*, 359 Pa. 51, 58 A.2d 800 (1948); *Commonwealth v. Beloff*, 166 Pa. Super. 286, 70 A.2d 689 (1950). Courts have stated that a case may be reopened where it is desirable that further testimony be taken in the interest of a more accurate adjudication, *Thomas v. Waters*, 350 Pa. 214, 38 A.2d 237 (1944), and where an honest purpose would be justly served without unfair disadvantage, *Van Buren v. Eberhard*, 377 Pa. 22, 104 A.2d 98 (1954); *Crystal Forest Associates, LP v. Buckingham Tp. Sup'rs.*, 872 A.2d 206 (Pa. Cmwlth. 2005) (proper to reopen record in zoning appeal hearing where township counsel by harassing tactics prevented landowner from offering complete testimony).

Although the cases take a liberal and flexible approach, reopening arguably does afford the opportunity to color or manufacture testimony to remedy deficiencies. Therefore, any such request will be carefully considered by the court and counsel should be prepared to explain fully the necessity for reopening.

Permission to reopen was properly denied where the potential for disruption or prejudice in the proceedings was significant, *Commonwealth v. Baldwin*, 8 A.3d 901 (Pa. Super. 2010); where the omission of evidence was intentional, *Ebersole v. Beistline*, 368 Pa. 12, 82 A.2d 11 (1951), or was cumulative of earlier testimony, *Commonwealth v. Smith*, 548 Pa. 65, 694 A.2d 1086 (1997). *See, Silver v. Miller*, 204 Pa. Super. 16, 201 A.2d 308 (1964). A trial judge cannot, during a post-sentence hearing, reopen the trial and admit additional evidence for the defense. *Commonwealth v. Nock*, 414 Pa. Super. 326, 606 A.2d 1380 (1992).

Compare: Fed. R. Evid. 611(a).

Research Reference

Packel & Poulin, Pennsylvania Evidence § 611-2 (4th ed. 2013)

REPETITION

See: Pa.R.E. 611(a).

Objection

- Objection. The question is repetitive.
- Objection. The question has been asked and answered.

Response

- The witness has not answered this question.
- I have not asked this question previously.

Pennsylvania Law

Pa.R.E. 611 (a) provides that the court shall exercise reasonable control over the mode of interrogating witnesses. If a question has been asked and answered, the trial court has broad discretion to limit or exclude repetitive questions. *Commonwealth v. Simmons*, 482 Pa. 496, 394 A.2d 431 (1978); *Commonwealth v. Conde*, 822 A.2d 45 (Pa. Super. 2003) (trial court entitled to limit scope of cross-examination to prevent repetitive inquiries); *Commonwealth v. Delligatti*, 371 Pa. Super. 315, 538 A.2d 34 (1988); *Commonwealth v. Stoner*, 284 Pa. Super. 364, 425 A.2d 1145 (1981); *Cockcroft v. Metropolitan Life Ins. Co.*, 133 Pa. Super. 598, 3 A.2d 184 (1938). Repetition also occurs when several witnesses provide the very same evidence. *Whitaker v. Frankford Hosp.*, 984 A.2d 512 (Pa. Super. 2009) (testimony of two experts repetitive to the extent that standard-of-care expert addressed issue of causation and causation expert addressed deviation from standard of care). Repetition wastes time and places undue emphasis on evidence through cumulative testimony. The form of the question does not have to be absolutely identical in order to raise this objection. If a new question calls for an answer previously given on cross-examination, the question is objectionable as repetitious. The objection applies not only when an answer has already been given but also when a witness testifies that he does not know or remember a matter.

Compare: Fed. R. Evid. 611(a).

Research Reference

McCormick, Evidence Chapter 2 (7th ed. 2013)

RES GESTAE

See: Pa.R.E. 803(1), (2) and (3).

"Res gestae" is a generic term encompassing four discrete exceptions to the hearsay rule:

(1) declarations as to present bodily conditions;
(2) declarations of present mental states and emotions;
(3) excited utterances; and
(4) declarations of present sense impressions.

Commonwealth v. Chamberlain, 557 Pa. 34, 731 A.2d 593 (1999). The feature common to all cases in which evidence has been said to have been received as part of the res gestae is relevance via contemporaneity. A statement is received because it was made contemporaneously with the event to which it relates. *See* Hearsay Exceptions.

Research Reference

McCormick, Evidence § 268 (7th ed. 2013)

RULE OF COMPLETENESS (REMAINDER OF OR RELATED WRITINGS OR RECORDED STATEMENTS)

See: Pa.R.E. 106.

Form

- Your Honor, for the witness to read only the first paragraph of the document leaves the jury with a very misleading impression because [*specify*]. Pursuant to Pa.R.E. 106, I ask that the witness be directed to read the second and third paragraphs also.

- Your Honor, my opponent has indicated she intends at this time to read into the record the deposition of John Doe at page 20, lines 13–17. I would ask under the rule of completeness, set forth in Pa.R.E. 106 and Pa.R.Civ.P. 4020(a)(4), that she also be required to read lines 5–12 and 18–25 since they are relevant to the issue and place the portion being offered in proper context.

Commentary

Whenever fragmentary statements are introduced or other written matters are taken out of context, misleading impressions can be created. Pa.R.E. 106 provides:

> When a writing or recorded statement or part thereof is introduced by a party, an adverse party may require the introduction at that time of any other part or any other writing or recorded statement which ought in fairness to be considered contemporaneously with it.

The rule is based on two considerations. The first is the misleading impression created by taking matters out of context. *Commonwealth v. Passmore*, 857 A.2d 697 (Pa. Super. 2004) (rule permits adverse party to introduce related writings so that the documents originally introduced are not read out of context); accord, *Commonwealth v. Bryant*, 57 A.3d 191 (Pa. Super. 2012). The second is the inadequacy of repair work when delayed to a point later in the trial. *See Beech Aircraft Corp. v. Rainey*, 488 U.S. 153, 172, 109 S.Ct. 439, 451, 102 L.Ed.2d 445 (1988) ("[W]hen one party has made use of a portion of a document, such that misunderstanding or distortion can be averted only through presentation of another portion, the material required for completeness is *ipso facto* relevant and therefore admissible . . . ."); *Pedretti v. Pittsburgh Rys. Co.*, 417 Pa. 581, 209 A.2d 289 (1965) (trial court erred in admitting deposition exhibit without accompanying testimony).

Where there is no attempt to admit the writing into evidence but a party uses the document in such a way that it is "tantamount" to introduction of the document itself, Pa.R.E. 106 should apply because the same concerns about fairness and completeness are present.

To determine whether an omitted portion is necessary, the trial court considers whether it: (1) is relevant to the issue and explains the admitted evidence; (2) places the admitted evidence in context; (3) avoids misleading the jury; and (4) ensures fair and impartial understanding of the evidence.

In criminal cases where multiple defendants are involved and statements have been redacted to avoid *Bruton*[1] problems, the rule of completeness is violated only when the statement in its edited form effectively distorts the meaning of the statement or excludes information substantially exculpatory of the non-testifying defendant. When it appears that literal compliance with *Bruton* may abridge the

---

[1] In *Bruton v. United States*, 391 U.S. 123, 88 S.Ct. 1620, 20 L.Ed.2d 476 (1968), the United States Supreme Court held that, when the prosecution seeks to admit the statement of a non-testifying defendant and portions of the statement incriminate a co-defendant, then those portions must be omitted to protect the co-defendant's right of confrontation.

rule of completeness, a district court must decide whether a severance for separate trials is necessary. That determination must be based on whether admission of the edited statement would distort the meaning of the original in a way that gives rise to a serious risk that a joint trial would compromise a specific trial right of one of the defendants, or prevent the jury from making a reliable judgment about guilt or innocence. *Zafiro v. United States*, 506 U.S. 534, 113 S.Ct. 933, 122 L.Ed.2d 317 (1993).

The rule codified by Pa.R.E. 106 does not render admissible portions of testimony which are otherwise inadmissible. *Majczyk v. Oesch*, 789 A.2d 717 (Pa. Super. 2001) (no error by excluding irrelevant portions of expert's deposition). Where, however, the court allows the offering party to read deposition testimony, which is inadmissible under some rule of evidence, the proponent has opened the door and the doctrine of curative admissibility should be invoked (*see*, Opening the Door).

Pa.R.E. 106 is limited to writings and recorded statements and does not apply to oral statements such as conversations. Ohlbaum on The Pennsylvania Rules of Evidence § 106.06 (2002–2003 ed).

Note: Pa.R.Civ.P. 4020(a)(4) which applies to deposition testimony also incorporates a form of the "rule of completeness" and substantially restates the evidentiary rule:

> If only part of a deposition is offered in evidence by a party, any other party may require him to introduce all of it which is relevant to the part introduced . . . .

Compare: Fed. R. Evid. 106; Fed. R. Civ. Pro. 32(a)(4).

Research References

Packel & Poulin, Pennsylvania Evidence § 106-1 (4th ed. 2013)

McCormick, Evidence § 56 (7th ed. 2013)

SEQUESTER WITNESSES—MOTION

See: Pa.R.E. 615.

Form

- I respectfully request the Court pursuant to Pa.R.E. 615 to order that all witnesses for [*plaintiff*] [*defendant*] be excluded from the courtroom until they are actually called to the witness stand; and that the witnesses be ordered not to discuss the case with one another and not to talk with any witness who has already testified. I would further ask that once a witness has testified, he be ordered not to relate his testimony or to discuss what occurred in the courtroom. I also ask that opposing counsel be instructed to advise his witnesses as to the purpose and effect of the Court's sequestration order.

Pennsylvania Law

In some cases, counsel may wish to request that witnesses be sequestered: that is, that they not be present in the courtroom while other witnesses testify. The purpose of sequestration is to prevent witnesses from altering their testimony in light of what they have heard from other witnesses or observed from counsel's cross-examination or trial tactics. *Geders v. United States*, 425 U.S. 80, 96 S.Ct. 1330, 47 L.Ed.2d 592 (1976); *Commonwealth v. Counterman*, 553 Pa. 370, 719 A.2d 284 (1998); *Commonwealth v. Henry*, 550 Pa. 346, 706 A.2d 313 (1997).

Pa.R.E. 615 makes witness exclusion a matter within the discretion of the court, except that the court may not exclude: (1) a party who is a natural person; (2) the designated representative of a corporate party; or (3) a person whose presence is shown by a party to be essential to the presentation of the party's case (typically, but not always, an expert witness). See, e.g., *Roller Concrete, Inc. v. Tube City IMS, LLC*, 115 A.3d 312 (Pa. Super. 2015) (sequestration order lifted to allow key employee to be present). In criminal cases these exceptions are applied to allow the Commonwealth's case agent to remain at counsel table with the prosecutor, hear the other witnesses testify, and nevertheless testify on behalf of the prosecution. *Commonwealth v. Stevenson*, 894 A.2d 759 (Pa. Super. 2006); Pa.R.E. 615(2).

Requests for sequestration "should be as specific as possible and supported by reasons aimed at the interests of justice." *Commonwealth v. Holland*, 480 Pa. 202, 213, 389 A.2d 1026, 1031 (1978); *Commonwealth v. Atwell*, 785 A.2d 123 (Pa. Super. 2001).

Despite the narrowness of the text of Pa.R.E. 615, trial courts are free to broaden the scope of their orders beyond courtroom exclusion. In addition to exclusion, the court may take further measures of separation designed to prevent communication between witnesses, such as ordering them to remain physically apart, ordering them not to discuss the case with one another or with any other person and ordering them not to read a transcript of the trial testimony of other witnesses. To avoid any misunderstandings about the scope of a Pa.R.E. 615 order, these additional measures should be clearly set forth in the court's order.

Sequestration orders prohibiting discussions between witnesses do permit witnesses to discuss the case with counsel for either party. *United States v. Rhynes*, 218 F.3d 310, 317 (4th Cir. 2000) (collecting cases and authorities). However, occasionally during trial, counsel may wish to request a limited sequestration order applicable to a particular witness to cover recess or lunch periods. *See Perry v. Leeke*, 488 U.S. 272, 109 S.Ct. 594, 102 L.Ed.2d 624 (1989) (court order directing accused not to consult with his attorney during brief recess, called while accused was on witness stand, did not violate 6th Amendment right to counsel). In *Perry*, the United States Supreme Court held only that witnesses may be prohibited from speaking with lawyers between direct and cross-examination to prevent unethical coaching; it did not generally prohibit lawyer-witness contact as a part of a sequestration order. *Rhynes*, 218 F.3d at 317 n.7.

Ideally, the sequestration motion should be made *in limine* or at the start of trial, but no rule precludes a party from making such motion at any other time. Since not all witnesses may be present when a sequestration order is entered, it is good practice to request that counsel be ordered to advise all of their witnesses of the sequestration order and its effect.

Jury sequestration is a matter within the trial court's discretion and may be utilized at any time during the course of trial when the interest of justice so requires. *Commonwealth v. Wright*, 961 A.2d 119 (Pa. 2008).

Compare: Fed. R. Evid. 615 (witness exclusion mandatory upon request).

Research References

Packel & Poulin, Pennsylvania Evidence § 615-1 (4th ed. 2013)

McCormick, Evidence § 50 (7th ed. 2013)

SEQUESTRATION—VIOLATION OF ORDER

See: Pa.R.E. 615.

Objection

- Objection. The Court previously granted my motion to have all witnesses sequestered. This witness intentionally disobeyed that order and has learned what other witnesses have testified to for purposes of tailoring her own testimony. I respectfully request that the Court preclude this witness from testifying.

Response

- The sequestration order was unintentionally violated; the violation was not serious and will have no impact on the testimony of the witness.

Pennsylvania Law

Sequestration of prospective witnesses is a matter within the discretion of the trial court. Pa.R.E. 615; *Commonwealth v. Yount*, 455 Pa. 303, 314 A.2d 242 (1974). The Rule, a codification of common law, seeks to prevent the tailoring of a witness's testimony to evidence given earlier in the trial and is designed to discourage and expose fabrication, inaccuracy and collusion. *Geders v. United States*, 425 U.S. 80, 96 S.Ct. 1330, 47 L.Ed.2d 592 (1976). Except for the three categories of witnesses exempted by the Rule (*see* "Sequester Witnesses-Motion") the court, on request, has discretion to exclude all witnesses from the courtroom.

Once a sequestration order is in effect and a possible violation is brought to the court's attention, the trial court must determine, as a question of fact, whether there has been a violation and, if so, the remedy required. *Commonwealth v. Smith*, 464 Pa. 314, 346 A.2d 757 (1975); *Commonwealth v. Martin*, 440 Pa. 150, 269 A.2d 722 (1970); *Commonwealth v. Turner*, 389 Pa. 239, 133 A.2d

187 (1957); *Commonwealth v. Schwartz*, 419 Pa. Super. 251, 615 A.2d 350 (1992). The court may preclude a witness from testifying; strike testimony already given; instruct the jury it can consider the violation in evaluating the credibility of a witness; or, if the violation is unintentional, without impact or prejudice, simply allow the witness to testify. See *Commonwealth v. Snowdy*, 412 Pa. Super. 493, 603 A.2d 1044 (1992).

In determining a sanction, if any, the trial court will consider (1) the seriousness of the violation; (2) its impact on the testimony of the witness; and (3) its probable impact on the outcome of the trial. *Commonwealth v. Smith*, 464 Pa. 314, 346 A.2d 757 (1975).

The trial court will also consider whether the witness intentionally disobeyed the order of sequestration so that he could determine what other witnesses were testifying to, and whether the party calling the witness procured his disobedience. *Commonwealth v. Mokluk*, 298 Pa. Super. 360, 444 A.2d 1214 (1982); *Commonwealth v. Floyd*, 259 Pa. Super. 552, 393 A.2d 963 (1978). In *Commonwealth v. Scott*, 496 Pa. 78, 436 A.2d 161 (1981), the Pennsylvania Supreme Court held that barring the testimony of a defense witness in a criminal case constitutes a denial of the defendant's rights to due process and compulsory process unless defendant or his counsel cooperated in the violation of the sequestration order; *Commonwealth v. Robertson*, 874 A.2d 1200 (Pa. Super. 2005) (same).

Compare: Fed. R. Evid. 615.

Research References

Packel & Poulin, Pennsylvania Evidence § 615-1 (4th ed. 2013)

McCormick, Evidence § 50 (7th ed. 2013)

SETTLEMENT: OFFERS TO COMPROMISE

See: Pa.R.E. 408.

Objection

- Objection. [*Request sidebar*] The question is improper under Rule 408 because it relates to an offer to settle or compromise a disputed claim.

Response

- The "other purpose" exception set forth in Rule 408 applies here because [*specify why exclusion is not required*].

Pennsylvania Law

Pa.R.E. 408 excludes any evidence of settlement or settlement offers when offered to prove liability for or invalidity of a claim or its amount. Evidence of conduct or statements made in settlement negotiations is also inadmissible under the rules of evidence and by state statute. *Dept. of Public Welfare v. Gant*, 142 A.3d 964 (Pa.Cmwlth. 2016); *Reading Radio, Inc. v. Fink*, 833 A.2d 199 (Pa. Super. 2003) (citing 42 Pa.C.S.A. § 6141(c)). The exclusion applies regardless of which party attempts to offer the evidence.

The purpose of the rule is to promote the public policy favoring compromise and settlement of disputes and to encourage honesty and candor in settlement negotiations.

If an offer to settle a dispute could be used as evidence of the weakness of a claim or defense, parties would seldom come to the negotiating table. The rule, therefore, provides wide protection to both an actual settlement and offer to settle and to negotiations and conduct associated with the settlement or offer to settle.

Other Purposes Exception

Pa.R.E. 408 does not exclude use of compromise evidence when it is offered to prove something other than liability for, or invalidity of, a claim or its amount. For example, compromise evidence can be admitted to prove the bias or prejudice of a witness, to negate a contention of undue delay in pursuing a claim, to prove agency, ownership or control, or to support a claim that an illegal act occurred during the course of settlement negotiations.

Where a plaintiff has allied himself with a settling defendant via a "Mary Carter" or similar "settlement" agreement, those terms which serve to reveal the existence of a potential bias must be presented to the jury. *Commonwealth v. United States Mineral Prods. Co.*, 809 A.2d 1000 (Pa.Cmwlth. 2002), order rev'd, 587 Pa. 236, 898 A.2d 590 (2006) (in multi-defendant products liability action, jury entitled to know terms of settlement agreement between Commonwealth and U.S. Mineral providing that U.S. Mineral would continue its defense but would make its expert witness available to testify and would make cash payment with cap on liability).

Compare: Fed.R.Evid. 408.

Research References

Packel & Poulin, Pennsylvania Evidence § 408-1 (4th ed. 2013)

McCormick, Evidence § 266 (7th ed. 2013)

SPECULATION

See: Pa.R.E. 602.

Objection

- Objection. The question calls for speculation by the witness.

Response

- The question is based on facts of record and this witness has the ability to respond based upon personal knowledge.

Pennsylvania Law

No witness is permitted to guess or to state an opinion based on mere conjecture. Pa.R.E. 602; *Collins v. Hand*, 431 Pa. 378, 246 A.2d 398 (1968); *Winschel v. Jain*, 925 A.2d 782 (Pa. Super. 2007) (mere speculation does not constitute evidence and is properly excluded). Any question that asks the witness to guess or engage in conjecture is objectionable since speculation as to what could have happened is usually of little probative value. Technically this objection falls within the realm of competency since the rule is simply an application of the general principle that a witness's testimony must be based on personal knowledge. Pa.R.E. 602; 7 Wigmore, Evidence § 1917 (Chadbourn rev. 1978); *see Smith v. Clark*, 411 Pa. 142, 190 A.2d 441 (1963); *Johnson v. Peoples Cab Co.*, 386 Pa. 513, 126 A.2d 720 (1956); *Eichman v. McKeon*, 824 A.2d 305, 320 n.8 (2003) (because detective testified he could not determine cause of fire, no error in sustaining objection to questions designed to invite speculation on cause); *Kearns by Kearns v. DeHaas*, 377 Pa. Super. 200, 546 A.2d 1226 (1988) (opinion as to cause of accident speculative and inadmissible where police officer did not witness accident); *Marks v. Lumbermen's Ins. Co.*, 160 Pa. Super. 66, 49 A.2d 855 (1946) (opinion as to behavior of a hurricane is pure guesswork); *Butler v. City of Pittsburgh*, 113 Pa.Cmwlth. 406, 537 A.2d 112 (1988) (opinion testimony properly excluded as guesswork when based on photographs and observation several years after the accident).

A verdict based upon testimony which is speculative or conjectural is impermissible. *Commonwealth v. Pronkoskie*, 477 Pa. 132, 383 A.2d 858 (1978); *Commonwealth v. Farquharson*, 467 Pa. 50, 354 A.2d 545 (1976); *Van Zandt v. Holy Redeemer Hosp.*, 806 A.2d 879 (Pa. Super. 2002); *Rohm & Haas Co. v. Continental Cas. Co.*, 732 A.2d 1236 (Pa. Super. 1999).

Expert Witness:

The Pennsylvania Supreme Court has held that "[n]o matter how skilled or experienced the witness may be, he will not be permitted to guess or to state a judgment based on mere conjecture." *Collins v. Hand*, 431 Pa. 378, 389, 246 A.2d 398, 404 (1968). "When a party must prove causation through expert testimony, the expert must testify with 'reasonable certainty' that 'in his professional opinion' the result in question did come from the cause alleged." *Cohen v. Albert Einstein Med. Ctr.*, 405 Pa. Super. 392, 399, 592 A.2d 720, 723 (1991) (citations omitted). "An expert fails this standard of certainty if he testifies that the alleged cause 'possibly' or 'could have' led to the result, that it 'could very properly account' for the result, or even that it was 'very highly probable' that it caused the result." *Kravinsky v. Glover*, 263 Pa. Super. 8, 21–22, 396 A.2d 1349, 1356 (1979) (citations omitted); *accord*, *Hoffman v. Brandywine Hosp.*, 443 Pa. Super. 245, 661 A.2d 397 (1995). "This issue is not merely one of semantics. There is a logical reason for the rule. If the fact finder chooses to believe it, he can find as fact what the expert gave as opinion." *Cohen*, 405 Pa. Super. at 398–399, 592 A.2d at 723 (citation omitted). "[I]t is the intent of our law that if

. . . the expert cannot form an opinion with sufficient certainty so as to make a [professional] judgment, there is nothing in the record with which a jury can make a decision with sufficient certainty so as to make a legal judgment." *McMahon v. Young*, 442 Pa. 484, 485–486, 276 A.2d 534, 535 (1971). However, an expert need not testify with absolute certainty or rule out all possible causes of a condition. *Mitzelfelt v. Kamrin*, 526 Pa. 54, 584 A.2d 888 (1990). Likewise, the testimony need not be expressed in precisely the language used to enunciate the legal standard. *In re Jones*, 432 Pa. 44, 246 A.2d 356 (1968).

Compare: Fed. R. Evid. 602.

Research References

Packel & Poulin, Pennsylvania Evidence § 602-1 (4th ed. 2013)

McCormick, Evidence § 10 (7th ed. 2013)

SUBSEQUENT REMEDIAL MEASURES

See: Pa.R.E. 407.

Objection

- Objection. The question relates to remedial measures taken after the accident and that evidence is inadmissible.

Response

- The question is proper under the circumstances because the evidence is being offered [*for the limited purpose of showing ownership, control, feasibility of precautionary measures*] [*to impeach the credibility of the witness*].

Pennsylvania Law

Pa.R.E. 407 excludes evidence of remedial actions taken after an injury or harm which, if taken previously, would have made the injury or harm less likely to occur if the evidence is offered for the purpose of proving negligence, culpable conduct, product defect, design defect, or failure to warn. The rule applies only in favor of the party who took the subsequent remedial measures. It does not apply when one other than the alleged tortfeasor took the action because the reason for the rule (to encourage remedial measures) is not implicated.

The justification for Pa.R.E. 407 is twofold. First, as an admission of fault, the probative value of subsequent remedial measures is limited. Second, exclusion is important to foster a social policy of encouraging persons to take steps in furtherance of added safety. *Duchess v. Langston*, 564 Pa. 529, 769 A.2d 1131 (2001) (holding that Pa.R.E. 407 is fully applicable in strict products liability litigation).

Exceptions

Pa.R.E. 407 is not a general rule of exclusion.

The rule explicitly provides that subsequent remedial measures may be admissible when offered for some purpose other than to prove culpable conduct such as when ownership, control or the feasibility of precautionary measures are controverted or for impeachment. Illustrative cases include: *Duchess*, 564 Pa. 529, 769 A.2d 1131 (2001); *Incollingo v. Ewing*, 444 Pa. 263, 282 A.2d 206 (1971) (feasibility of precautionary measures contested); *Leghart v. Montour R.R. Co.*, 395 Pa. 469, 150 A.2d 836 (1959) (testimony that railroad crew made repairs admissible to show accident site was under its control and not state or county highway departments); *Wenger v. West Pennsboro Twp.*, 868 A.2d 638 (Pa.Cmwlth. 2005) (defendant's engineering study of dangerous intersection authored after accident admissible for limited purpose of proving that traffic device proposed by plaintiff's expert was feasible and appropriate); *Harsh v. Petroll*, 840 A.2d 404 (Pa.Cmwlth. 2003) (new GM engineering method of documenting potential failures admissible to establish feasibility of change in assembly process and to impeach GM's assertion could not apply to 1995 model car year); *Daniel v. Wyeth Pharmaceuticals, Inc.*, 15 A.3d 909 (Pa. Super. 2011) (subsequent remedial measures can be introduced on the issue of causation if causation is in controversy); *Smalls v. Pittsburgh-Corning Corp.*, 843 A.2d 410 (Pa. Super. 2004) (evidence of warning label added after plaintiff's exposure admissible to impeach and rebut defense witness' claim that product was not prone to create dust); *Carney v. Otis Elevator Co.*, 370 Pa. Super. 394, 536 A.2d 804 (1988) (evidence of elevator company's subsequent repair of elevator after it injured passenger was admissible to impeach credibility of maintenance worker who claimed elevator doors were in working order on day doors were replaced).

By its terms, Rule 407 has no application to measures taken *prior* to the occurrence of the event. *Blumer v. Ford Motor Company*, 20 A.3d 1222 (Pa.

Super. 2011) (design changes to truck parking brake made by Ford *prior* to accident were admissible to show existence of alternative design) (collecting cases).

Impeachment

Unrestricted use of subsequent remedial measures to impeach a witness carries with it the distinct danger that the exception will undermine or nullify the Rule. In the federal system, pursuant to Fed. R. Evid. 403, trial courts generally limit the use of such evidence to situations where it is offered for impeachment by direct contradiction, or as one commentator has said: "cases in which defense witnesses have made extravagant claims of safety." Prof. Daniel J. Capra, *Case Law Divergence from the Federal Rules of Evidence*, 197 F.R.D. 531, 536 (2000); *see, e.g., Wood v. Morbark Indus., Inc.*, 70 F.3d 1201 (11th Cir.1995) (post-accident design change admissible for impeachment where defense witness testified that original design was safest possible design); *Harrison v. Sears, Roebuck & Co.*, 981 F.2d 25 (1st Cir.1992) (a desire merely to undercut an expert's credibility is not sufficient to trigger the impeachment exception to Rule 407); *Kelly v. Crown Equip. Co.*, 970 F.2d 1273 (3d Cir.1992) (where expert did not say that forklift design was the best or the only one possible but did testify it was an excellent and proper design, evidence of subsequent changes could not be offered to contradict him); *Petree v. Victor Fluid Power, Inc.*, 887 F.2d 34 (3d Cir.1989) ("*Petree II*") (where expert opined that hydraulic press posed no inherent danger and warning labels were unnecessary, error to exclude evidence that company had begun using warning labels because such evidence would have directly impeached expert); *Muzyka v. Remington Arms Co., Inc.*, 774 F.2d 1309 (5th Cir.1985) (design change should have been admitted for impeachment where defense witnesses testified that the product was the best and safest product of its kind).

The *Duchess* court also said that: "where a decision is made that the evidence [of subsequent remedial measures] should be admitted, an effective limiting instruction is appropriate." 564 Pa. at 556, 769 A.2d at 1147.

Compare: Fed. R. Evid. 407

Research References

Packel & Poulin, Pennsylvania Evidence §§ 407-1–407-2 (4th ed. 2013)

McCormick, Evidence § 267 (7th ed. 2013)

SUMMARIES

See: Pa.R.E. 1006.

Objection

- The evidence on which this summary is based is inadmissible and, therefore, the summary is inadmissible.
- The summary does not fairly and accurately represent the underlying evidence because [*explain*].
- My opponent cannot meet the foundational requirements since he/she never made the underlying evidence available.

Response

- The underlying evidence is admissible [*explain*].
- The summary is an accurate representation of the underlying evidence [*explain*].
- The underlying evidence was made available [*explain*].

Pennsylvania Law

Identical to the federal rule[1] and consistent with prior Pennsylvania law, Pa.R.E. 1006 provides:

The contents of voluminous writings, recordings, or photographs which cannot conveniently be examined in court may be presented in the form of a chart, summary or calculation. The originals, or duplicates, shall be made available for examination or copying, or both, by other parties at reasonable time and place. The court may order that they be produced in court.

Because the summaries themselves are the evidence, there is no need to introduce the underlying voluminous material into evidence. *See Department of Transp. v. Anjo Constr. Co.*, 666 A.2d 753 (Pa.

---

[1] Given the dearth of state appellate decisions since the 1998 enactment of the Pennsylvania Rules, federal cases are cited for whatever guidance they may provide.

Cmwlth.1995); *Royal Pioneer Paper Box Mfg. Co. v. Louis De Jonge & Co.*, 179 Pa. Super. 155, 115 A.2d 837 (1955); *see also United States v. Samaniego*, 187 F.3d 1222 (10th Cir.1999); *United States v. Bakker*, 925 F.2d 728 (4th Cir.1991).

Admission of summaries as substantive evidence is conditioned, however, on the requirement that the evidence upon which they are based must be admissible. *See* Goode and Wellborn, Courtroom Handbook on Federal Evidence Chapter 5, Rule 1006 (annual edition); *B.F. Goodrich v. Betkoski*, 99 F.3d 505, 525 (2d Cir.1996); *United States v. Johnson*, 594 F.2d 1253, 1255 (9th Cir.1979) ("We do not believe that Congress intended that counsel could abrogate other restrictions on . . . admissibility—like the hearsay rule-by the use of summaries . . . ."). Although proper foundation also requires that summary charts fairly represent and summarize the evidence on which they are based, *United States. v. Koskerides*, 877 F.2d 1129 (2d Cir. 1989); *Herman v. Davis Acoustical Corp.*, 21 F.Supp.2d 130 (N.D.N.Y.1998), courts have also said that the inaccuracy of a summary goes to the weight, rather than the admissibility of the evidence. *"BD" ex rel. Jean Doe v. DeBuono*, 193 F.R.D. 117 (S.D.N.Y.2000) (*citing In re Richardson-Merrell, Inc. Bendectin Prods.*, 624 F.Supp. 1212 (S.D.Ohio 1985)). The person who prepared the summary must be available for cross-examination. *Keller v. Porta*, 172 Pa. Super. 651, 94 A.2d 140 (1953).

"Made Available" Requirement

The First Circuit has said that to satisfy the "made available" requirement, a party seeking to use a summary under Rule 1006 must identify its exhibit, provide a list or description of the documents supporting the exhibit and state when and where the documents can be reviewed. *Air Safety v. Roman Catholic Archbishop of Boston*, 94 F.3d 1, 8

(1st Cir.1996). This gives the opponent the ability to check the summary's accuracy and prepare for cross-examination. The court also said Rule 1006 operates independently of the discovery rules and that failure to request or obtain the documents during discovery does not negate a party's absolute right to subsequent production of material under Rule 1006 should that material become incorporated in a chart, summary or calculation. *Air Safety v. Roman Catholic Archbishop of Boston*, 94 F.3d 1, 8 (1st Cir.1996)*; cf. Coates v. Johnson & Johnson*, 756 F.2d 524, 549–50 (7th Cir.1985) (rule requires that the underlying material, not the summary itself, be made available to adverse party before trial).

The following cases illustrate the operation of the Rule: **Pennsylvania:** *Scaife Co. v. Rockwell-Standard Corp.*, 446 Pa. 280, 285 A.2d 451 (1971) (summary of voluminous business records, some of which were now destroyed but all of which had been available to defendant who did not inspect them); *Anjo Const. Co.*, 666 A.2d 753 (Pa.Cmwlth.1995) (re-constructed bid that was a summary of volumes of documents used to calculate original bid); *Royal Pioneer Paper Box Mfg. Co.*, 179 Pa. Super. 155, 115 A.2d 837 (1955) (summary of production records as proof of damages); *Keller v. Porta*, 172 Pa. Super. 651, 94 A.2d 140 (1953) (summary of invoice charges). **Federal:** *United States v. Richardson*, 233 F.3d 1285 (11th Cir.2000) (court will permit use of summary charts [here, transactional histories of bank accounts] incorporating certain assumptions so long as supporting evidence has been presented previously to jury and court makes it clear it is jury's decision as to what weight should be given to evidence); *United States v. Leon-Reyes*, 177 F.3d 816 (9th Cir.1999) (in prosecution for perjury, summaries of testimony from prior trial offered not for truth but to show materiality of defendant's allegedly false testimony); *United States v. Samaniego*, 187 F.3d at 1224–25 (in prosecution for drug trafficking, reversible error to allow FBI agent to testify from summaries of subpoenaed telephone records without first establishing admissibility of underlying records); *Air Safety v. Roman Catholic Archbishop of Boston*, 94 F.3d at 8 (no error excluding summary exhibits where offering party failed to identify and make available underlying documents); *Consorti v. Armstrong World Indus., Inc.*, 64 F.3d 781 (2d Cir.1995) (similar); *Herman v. Davis Acoustical Corp.*, 21 F.Supp.2d at 135–36 (in wage violations case, no error to admit summary exhibit constructed from contractors' payroll records).

Compare: Fed.R.Evid. 1006

Research References

Packel & Poulin, Pennsylvania Evidence § 1006-1 (4th ed. 2013)

McCormick, Evidence § 233 (7th ed. 2013)

SURPRISE

See: Pa.R.E. 611(a), (c).

Form

- Your Honor, in light of the answers given by this witness to my questions, I must plead surprise and request leave of court to proceed by cross-examining the witness.

Pennsylvania Law

When a witness turns hostile by telling a different version on the witness stand than he told the calling party prior thereto, the calling party may plead surprise and request leave to use leading questions to cross-examine the witness and impeach him by his prior inconsistent statement. *Commonwealth v. Douglas*, 558 Pa. 412, 737 A.2d 1188 (1999) (prosecutor allowed to cross-examine witness who changed story and now denied seeing shooting to detriment of Commonwealth's case); *Commonwealth v. Bibbs*, 970 A.2d 440 (Pa. Super. 2009) (similar).

Although common law prohibited a party from impeaching his own witness Pa.R.E. 607 completely abolishes this prohibition. Pennsylvania courts hold that it is within the discretion of the trial judge to permit a party to cross-examine its own witness, when it is believed that the interest of truth and justice so require. *Commonwealth v. Dancer*, 452 Pa. 221, 305 A.2d 364 (1973), superseded by Rule as stated in *Commonwealth v. Kimball*, 563 Pa. 256, 759 A.2d 1273 (2000); *see* Pa.R.E. 611(a) (court discretion over mode of interrogation).

Where a party is surprised by a change in its own witness' testimony, the court may allow the party to cross-examine the witness if the trial testimony: (1) is unexpected; (2) contradicts the witness' earlier statements; and (3) is harmful to the party's case. *See Commonwealth v. Chambers*,

546 Pa. 370, 685 A.2d 96 (1996) (citing *Commonwealth v. Smith*, 511 Pa. 343, 353, 513 A.2d 1371, 1376 (1986)); *Tiburzio-Kelly v. Montgomery*, 452 Pa. Super. 158, 681 A.2d 757 (Pa. Super. 1996) (rejecting request; claim of surprise is diminished when counsel did not previously interview witness for a statement).

Surprise, in its legal connotation, does not include disappointment or frustration on the part of the one seeking to have a witness testify contrary to what the witness has indicated he will do. *Commonwealth v. Turner*, 389 Pa. 239, 133 A.2d 187 (1957).

Since the purpose of cross-examination and impeachment is to induce the jury to believe the testimony of the witness, there must be something in the witness' testimony, which if not disbelieved by the jury, will be hurtful or injurious to the party calling him. *Commonwealth v. Thomas*, 459 Pa. 371, 329 A.2d 277 (1974); *Commonwealth v. Quartman*, 253 Pa. Super. 460, 385 A.2d 429 (1978).

When a witness claims he does not know or cannot remember, courts generally will not allow cross-examination since the in-court declaration does not harm the calling party or aid the opposing party. *Commonwealth v. Knudsen*, 443 Pa. 412, 278 A.2d 881 (1971).

The scope of cross-examination is to allow an opportunity to dispute the unexpected adverse statements made by the witness by showing the jury that he stated otherwise on a prior occasion. Cross-examination cannot be used to introduce additional facts which the witness did not specifically controvert. *Commonwealth v. Dancer*, 452 Pa. 221, 305 A.2d 364 (1973).

The Superior Court has said that a party calling a witness as if on cross is bound by the witness' testimony unless it is contradicted by other evidence, or is inherently incredible. *Alfonsi v. Huntington Hosp., Inc.*, 798 A.2d 216 (Pa. Super.

2002).

Compare: Fed. R. Evid. 611 (a) and (c).

Research Reference

Packel & Poulin, Pennsylvania Evidence §§ 611-1–611-4 (4th ed. 2013)

UNFAIR PREJUDICE

See: Pa.R.E. 403.

Objection

- Objection. May we approach the bench to discuss my objection? [*At sidebar*] This evidence has little probative value, if any, and is unfairly prejudicial to my client for the following reasons [*specify*]. The evidence warrants a mistrial if the jury hears it, and, therefore, I ask that the evidence be excluded.

Response

- The probative value of this evidence and its importance to the case justify its admission [*explain*]. A cautionary instruction to the jury will avoid any unfair prejudice.

Commentary

Pa.R.E. 403 codifies the court's power to exclude otherwise relevant evidence whose probative value is outweighed by the danger of unfair prejudice. *Commonwealth v. Sanchez*, 36 A.3d 24 (Pa. 2011); *Stalsitz v. Allentown Hosp.*, 814 A.2d 766 (Pa. Super. 2002). Because virtually all evidence is prejudicial to one party or another, to justify exclusion under Pa.R.E. 403, the prejudice must be unfair. *Commonwealth v. Treiber*, 582 Pa. 646, 874 A.2d 26 (2005); *Commonwealth v. Antidormi*, 84 A.3d 738 (Pa. Super. 2014); *Commonwealth v. Foley*, 38 A.3d 882 (Pa. Super. 2012); *Mahan v. Am-Gard, Inc.*, 841 A.2d 1052 (Pa. Super. 2003); *Daset Mining Corp. v. Indus. Fuels Corp.*, 326 Pa. Super. 14, 473 A.2d 584 (1984) (unfair prejudice does not include damage that occurs to a party's case because of the legitimate probative force of the evidence).

A court is not required to sanitize a trial to eliminate all unpleasant facts from a jury's consideration where those facts are relevant to the issues at hand and form a part of the history and natural development of the events and offenses for which the defendant is charged. *Commonwealth v. Hairston*, 84 A.3d 657 (Pa. 2014); *Commonwealth v. Page*, 965 A.2d 1212 (Pa. Super. 2009). Thus, "unfair prejudice" means an undue tendency to suggest decision on an improper basis, which is commonly, though not necessarily, an emotional one or to divert the jury's attention away from its duty of weighing the evidence impartially. *Commonwealth v. Hitcho*, 123 A.3d 731 (Pa. 2015); *Commonwealth v. Brown*, 987 A.2d 699 (Pa. 2009); *Commonwealth v. Vandivner*, 962 A.2d 1170 (Pa. 2009); *Ely v. Susquehanna Aquacultures, Inc.*, 130 A.3d 6 (Pa. Super. 2015); *Klein v. Aronchick*, 85 A.3d 487 (Pa. Super. 2014); *Commonwealth v. Enders*, 407 Pa. Super. 201, 595 A.2d 600 (1991) (the inquiry is whether the evidence is so prejudicial that it may inflame the jury to make a decision based on something other than the legal propositions relevant to the case); *Whistler Sportswear, Inc. v. Rullo*, 289 Pa. Super. 230, 433 A.2d 40 (1981).

Unlike some other evidentiary exclusions which may bar evidence for one purpose only to have it admitted for another purpose, exclusion under Pa.R.E. 403 is absolute. Once the probative value of a piece of evidence is found to be outweighed by the danger of unfair prejudice, there is no other evidentiary rule that can operate to make that same evidence admissible.

In weighing the probative value of evidence against the dangers and considerations enumerated in the rule, Pa.R.E. 403 balancing is a quintessentially fact-sensitive enterprise. *Spring / United Management Company v. Mendelsohn*, 552 U.S. 379, 388, 128 S.Ct. 1140, 170 L.Ed. 2d 1 (2008); *Commonwealth v. Hicks*, 91 A.3d 47 (Pa. 2014) (unlike other Rules of Evidence, Rule 403 requires a trial court to weigh probative value and prejudice—the costs and benefits of relevant evidence—viewing it as a part of a whole and not an isolation);

Commonwealth v. Jordon, 65 A.3d 318 (Pa. 2013) (trial court must balance evidentiary value against potential dangers of unfairly prejudicing the accused, inflaming the passions of the jury or confusing the jury).

The following criminal cases illustrate the rule: *Commonwealth v. Rivera*, 983 A.2d 1211 (Pa. 2009) (admission of defendant's *crimin falsi* juvenile offenses more probative than prejudicial where defendant's credibility was crux of case; defendant claimed self-defense allegedly believing plain clothes officer was trying to kill him, not realizing decedent was a policeman); *Commonwealth v. Wright*, 961 A.2d 119 (Pa. 2008) (911 tapes were tantamount to victim testifying from beyond the grave, identifying shooter and what was taking place; probative value dwarfed any potential danger); *Commonwealth v. Serge*, 896 A.2d 1170 (Pa. 2006) (computer generated animation depicting prosecution's theory of how shooting took place was neither inflammatory nor unfairly prejudicial); *Commonwealth v. Boczkowski*, 577 Pa. 421, 846 A.2d 75 (2004) (probative value of evidence that both of defendant's wives died in similar fashion outweighed potential for unfair prejudice; evidence negated claim of accident); *Commonwealth v. Small*, 741 A.2d 666 (Pa. 1999), *Commonwealth v. Drew*, 459 A.2d 318 (Pa. 1983), and *Commonwealth v. Williams*, 91 A.3d 240 (Pa. Super. 2014) (evidence of intoxication during the events that are the subject of the witness' testimony is admissible impeachment evidence; evidence of a witness' intoxication at other times is not admissible); *Commonwealth v. Buehl*, 510 Pa. 363, 508 A.2d 1167 (1986) (inflammatory photographs are admissible only upon a showing that the photos are of such evidentiary value that their need clearly outweighs the potential for unfair prejudice); *Commonwealth v. Williams*, 48 A.3d 1265 (Pa. Super. 2012) (bias evidence can be excluded if there is danger of unfair prejudice); *Commonwealth v.*

Priest, 18 A.3d 1235 (Pa. Super. 2011) (trauma unit videotape of dying victim identifying the shooter established a material fact, i.e., the perpetrator; argument of prejudice was merely bald assertion); *Commonwealth v. DiStefano*, 782 A.2d 574 (Pa. Super. 2001) (where issue was whether defendant killed victim murdered by ligature strangulation, evidence of his proclivity for engaging in oxygen-deprivation techniques for sexual pleasure had highly probative value which was not outweighed by danger of unfair prejudice); *Commonwealth v. Horvath*, 781 A.2d 1243 (Pa. Super. 2001) (in prosecution for reckless endangerment, no error to prohibit Commonwealth from referring to summary convictions for reckless driving, failure to drive at safe speed and harassment arising from same incident; risk of prejudice outweighed probative value because jury might automatically equate these convictions with reckless endangerment); *Commonwealth v. Galloway*, 771 A.2d 65 (Pa. Super. 2001) (probative value of allowing widow to hold murdered husband's bloody shirt to show location of bullet wounds not outweighed by prejudicial effect; sympathy for widow and unfair prejudice are not synonymous); *Commonwealth v. Weaver*, 768 A.2d 331 (Pa. Super. 2001) (rejecting contention that videotape of defendant's field sobriety test was prejudicial and confusing; tape's primary purpose was to assist jury's understanding of nature of tests and to support police officer's observations); *Commonwealth v. Groff*, 356 Pa. Super. 477, 514 A.2d 1382 (1986) (tape of phone call recording screams of shooting victim would inflame the minds and passions of jury).

For operation of the Rule in civil cases, *see*: *Morreale v. Prince*, 436 Pa. 51, 258 A.2d 508 (1969) (admitting evidence that litigant was in bar prior to motor vehicle accident without proof of intoxication was so prejudicial as to require new trial); accord, *Cook v. Philadelphia Transp. Co.*, 414 Pa. 154, 199 A.2d 446 (1964); *see generally, Braun v. Target*

Corp., 983 A.2d 752 (Pa. Super. 2009) (fact of drinking not admissible unless it reasonably establishes a degree of intoxication which proves unfitness to perform, here, work on high lift at construction site); *Callahan v. National R.R. Passenger Corp.*, 979 A.2d 866 (Pa. Super. 2009) (history of substance abuse, while prejudicial is probative of life expectancy where permanent personal injury is alleged); *Locke v. Claypool*, 426 Pa. Super. 528, 627 A.2d 801 (1993) (applying unfitness standard to evidence of bicyclist's intoxication); *Nigra v. Walsh*, 797 A.2d 353 (Pa. Super. 2002) (no error to exclude testimony that doctor performed 90% of his independent medical examinations on behalf of defendants; prejudicial effect outweighed probative value); *Hutchison ex rel Hutchison v. Luddy*, 763 A.2d 826 (Pa. Super. 2000) (probative value of other incidents of priests' pedophilic activity went to issue of diocesan notice, knowledge and ability to control and was not outweighed by unfair prejudice); *Brinich v. Jencka*, 757 A.2d 388 (Pa. Super. 2000) (in contractor's action for breach of contract against homeowners, evidence of contractor's alleged prior conduct with business partners amounted to collateral attack on his credibility with potential for prejudice outweighing any probative value); *Leahy v. McClain*, 732 A.2d 619 (Pa. Super. 1999) (where accident happened on dark, snowy night, photos of scene taken on sunny day were inadmissible because of danger of unfair prejudice or confusion).

Compare: Fed. R. Evid. 403.

Research References

Packel & Poulin, Pennsylvania Evidence § 403-1 (4th ed. 2013)

McCormick, Evidence § 185 (7th ed. 2013)

VAGUE AND AMBIGUOUS QUESTION

See: Pa.R.E. 611(a).

Objection

- Objection. The question is vague and ambiguous because [*specify*].

Response

[*Unless the question is clear and the objection merely a stalling tactic, it is better to rephrase the question*].

Pennsylvania Law

Pa.R.E. 611(a) provides that the court shall exercise reasonable control over the mode of interrogating witnesses. A question should be posed in a reasonably clear and specific manner so that the witness can understand what is being asked. A vague and ambiguous question is one which is indefinite and uncertain as to its meaning or susceptible to several different interpretations. A witness is not required to answer questions which are uncertain in meaning, Commonwealth v. Sultzaberger, 62 Dauph. Co. Rpt. 27 (1951), since such questions are clearly improper. *MacBrine-McAdams Realty Co. v. Morris*, 129 Pa. Super. 604, 196 A. 511 (1938).

Compare: Fed. R. Evid. 611(a).

Research References

McCormick, Evidence § 7 (7th ed. 2013)

Haydock and Sonsteng Trial: Advocacy Before Judges, Jurors And Arbitrators Chapter 5, § 5.6 pp. 186–187 (4th ed. 2011)

VOIR DIRE OF A WITNESS

See: Pa.R.E. 104(a), 611(a).

Form

- Objection, this witness is incompetent to give testimony because [*specify*]. I respectfully ask the court's permission to conduct voir dire of the witness. I believe I will be able to show that her testimony is not admissible.
- I object to the testimony of plaintiff's expert and request the right to conduct voir dire. I will be able to show that he lacks the knowledge, skill, training or experience to render an opinion in this case.
- I object to the admissibility of Exhibit 5 and request permission to conduct voir dire. I will be able to show that the witness cannot properly authenticate the document.

Commentary

As a preliminary question under Pa.R.E. 104(a), the trial court has discretion to allow opposing counsel to challenge the competency of an expert or other person by voir dire of the witness. This is done by interrupting direct examination and allowing opposing counsel to examine the witness by leading questions for the purpose of establishing grounds for an objection.

Courts also will permit voir dire questioning if the attorney appears able to establish the inadmissibility of the evidence. Usually, the opposing attorney can ask a reasonable number of questions to establish lack of admissibility. The interrogation may not develop into questions that should be asked on cross-examination. Questioning that extends beyond proper voir dire and into cross-examination should be objected to as improper. *See* Pa.R.E. 611(a).

The request for voir dire is often preceded by an objection that there is no foundation for the evidence sought to be admitted. "Lack of foundation" is a shorthand way of asserting that the party offering the testimony has not met certain requirements of the rules of evidence. This objection may be employed with respect to at least each of the following:

1. Competency of a lay witness, Pa.R.E. 601.
2. Qualifications of an expert witness, Pa.R.E. 702.
3. Introduction of opinion testimony including a determination of scientific reliability and validity, Pa.R.E. 701–705.
4. Personal knowledge, Pa.R.E. 602.
5. Unavailability in connection with a hearsay exception, Pa.R.E. 804(a).
6. Satisfaction of the requirements of a hearsay exception, Pa.R.E. 803, 803.1 and 804(b).
7. Authentication or identification, Pa.R.E. 901.
8. Admissibility of evidence other than the original writing, Pa.R.E. 1004.
9. The existence or waiver of a privilege, Pa.R.E. 501.
10. Relevancy, Pa.R.E. 401.

In a voir dire proceeding to determine the competency of a witness, the relevant inquiries involve: (1) the capacity to perceive an event with accuracy; (2) the ability to remember; (3) the ability to understand questions and communicate a response; and (4) a consciousness of the duty to tell the truth. *Commonwealth v. Goldblum*, 498 Pa. 455, 447 A.2d 234 (1982); *Commonwealth v. Trudell*, 371 Pa. Super. 353, 538 A.2d 53 (1988).

When expert testimony is challenged, voir dire must demonstrate that the witness lacks knowledge, skill, training or experience in the area upon which he is to give an opinion. *See, Steele v. Shepperd*, 411 Pa. 481, 192 A.2d 397 (1963); *Dierolf v. Slade*, 399 Pa. Super. 9, 581 A.2d 649 (1990); *Palmer v. Lapp*, 392 Pa. Super. 21, 572 A.2d 12 (1990). See also *McEwing v. Lititz Mut. Ins. Co.*, 77 A.3d 639, 649 (Pa. Super. 2013) (failure to object to qualifications of expert witness waives the issue on appeal).

In *Commonwealth v. Washington*, 554 Pa. 559, 722 A.2d 643 (1998), the Pennsylvania Supreme Court created a *per se* rule requiring the trial judge to conduct child witness competency hearings outside the presence of the jury. Whether to conduct voir dire examination of other witnesses in the presence of the jury is left to the discretion of the trial court.

With the court's permission, voir dire also can be used to show that certain demonstrative evidence is inadmissible. For example, a witness may identify a document which the proponent offers. By interposing an objection and requesting voir dire, the opposing attorney may question the witness in an attempt to show that the witness cannot sufficiently authenticate the document.

Compare: Fed.R.Evid. 104(a), 611(a).

Research Reference

McCormick, Evidence § 52 (7th ed. 2013)

Pennsylvania Rules of Evidence

Rule 101. Scope; Adoption and Citation

(a) Scope. These rules of evidence govern proceedings in all courts of the Commonwealth of Pennsylvania's unified judicial system, except as otherwise provided by law.

(b) Adoption and Citation. These rules of evidence are adopted by the Supreme Court of Pennsylvania under the authority of Article V § 10(c) of the Constitution of Pennsylvania, adopted April 23, 1968. They shall be known as the Pennsylvania Rules of Evidence and shall be cited as "Pa.R.E."

Adopted May 8, 1998, effective Oct. 1, 1998; Comment revised Dec. 30, 2005, effective Feb. 1, 2006; rescinded and replaced January 17, 2013, effective March 18, 2013.

Rule 102. Purpose

These rules should be construed so as to administer every proceeding fairly, eliminate unjustifiable expense and delay, and promote the development of evidence law, to the end of ascertaining the truth and securing a just determination.

Adopted May 8, 1998, effective Oct. 1, 1998; rescinded and replaced January 17, 2013, effective March 18, 2013.

Rule 103. Rulings on Evidence

(a) Preserving a Claim of Error. A party may claim error in a ruling to admit or exclude evidence only:

(1)   if the ruling admits evidence, a party, on the record:

(A)   makes a timely objection, motion to strike, or motion *in limine*; and

(B)   states the specific ground, unless it was apparent from the context; or

(2)   if the ruling excludes evidence, a party informs the court of its substance by an offer of proof, unless the substance was apparent from the context.

(b) Not Needing to Renew an Objection or Offer of Proof. Once the court rules definitively on the record—either before or at trial—a party need not renew an objection or offer of proof to preserve a claim of error for appeal.

(c) Court's Statement About the Ruling; Directing an Offer of Proof. The court may make any statement about the character or form of the evidence, the objection made, and the ruling. The court may direct that an offer of proof be made in question-and-answer form.

(d) Preventing the Jury from Hearing Inadmissible Evidence. To the extent practicable, the court must conduct a jury trial so that inadmissible evidence is not suggested to the jury by any means.

Adopted May 8, 1998, effective October 1, 1998; amended November 2, 2001, effective January 1, 2002; rescinded and replaced January 17, 2013, effective March 18, 2013.

Rule 104. Preliminary Questions

(a) In General. The court must decide any preliminary question about whether a witness is qualified, a privilege exists, or evidence is admissible. In so deciding, the court is not bound by evidence rules, except those on privilege.

(b) Relevance That Depends on a Fact. When the relevance of evidence depends on whether a fact exists, proof must be introduced sufficient to support a finding that the fact does exist. The court may admit the proposed evidence on the condition that the proof be introduced later.

(c) Conducting a Hearing So That the Jury Cannot Hear it. The court must conduct any hearing on a preliminary question so that the jury cannot hear it if:

(1) the hearing involves evidence alleged to have been obtained in violation of the defendant's rights;

(2) a defendant in a criminal case is a witness and so requests; or

(3) justice so requires.

(d) Cross-Examining a Defendant in a Criminal Case. By testifying on a preliminary question, a defendant in a criminal case does not become subject to cross-examination on other issues in the case.

(e) Weight and Credibility. Even though the court rules that evidence is admissible, this does not preclude a party from offering other evidence relevant to the weight or credibility of that evidence.

Adopted May 8, 1998, effective October 1, 1998; Comment revised March 29, 2001, effective April 1, 2001; March 29, 2005, effective May 2, 2005; Comment revised May 15, 2007, effective June 15, 2007; Comment revised Jan. 9, 2009, imd. effective; rescinded and replaced January 17, 2013, effective March 18, 2013.

Rule 105. Limiting Evidence that is not Admissible Against Other Parties or for Other Purposes

If the court admits evidence that is admissible against a party or for a purpose—but not against another party or for another purpose—the court, on timely request, must restrict the evidence to its proper scope and instruct the jury accordingly. The court may also do so on its own initiative.

Adopted May 8, 1998, effective October 1, 1998; Comment revised March 10, 2000, effective immediately; rescinded and replaced January 17, 2013, effective March 18, 2013.

Rule 106. Remainder of or Related Writings or Recorded Statements

If a party introduces all or part of a writing or recorded statement, an adverse party may require the introduction, at that time, of any other part—or any other writing or recorded statement—that in fairness ought to be considered at the same time.

Adopted May 8, 1998, effective Oct. 1, 1998; rescinded and replaced January 17, 2013, effective March 18, 2013.

Rule 201. Judicial Notice of Adjudicative Facts

(a) Scope. This rule governs judicial notice of an adjudicative fact only, not a legislative fact.

(b) Kinds of Facts That May Be Judicially Noticed. The court may judicially notice a fact that is not subject to reasonable dispute because it:

(1) is generally known within the trial court's territorial jurisdiction; or

(2) can be accurately and readily determined from sources whose accuracy cannot reasonably be questioned.

(c) Taking Notice. The court:

(1) may take judicial notice on its own; or

(2) must take judicial notice if a party requests it and the court is supplied with the necessary information.

(d) Timing. The court may take judicial notice at any stage of the proceeding.

(e) Opportunity to Be Heard. On timely request, a party is entitled to be heard on the propriety of taking judicial notice and the nature of the fact to be noticed. If the court takes judicial notice before notifying a party, the party, on request, is still entitled to be heard.

(f) Instructing the Jury. The court must instruct the jury that it may, but is not required to, accept as conclusive any fact judicially noticed.
Adopted May 8, 1998, effective Oct. 1, 1998; rescinded and replaced January 17, 2013, effective March 18, 2013.

Rule 301. Presumptions

Presumptions as they now exist or may be modified by law shall be unaffected by the adoption of these rules.
Adopted May 8, 1998, effective Oct. 1, 1998; rescinded and replaced January 17, 2013, effective March 18, 2013.

Rule 401. Test for Relevant Evidence

Evidence is relevant if:

(a) it has any tendency to make a fact more or less probable than it would be without the evidence; and

(b) the fact is of consequence in determining the action.
Adopted May 8, 1998, effective Oct. 1, 1998; rescinded and replaced January 17, 2013, effective March 18, 2013.

Rule 402. General Admissibility of Relevant Evidence

All relevant evidence is admissible, except as otherwise provided by law. Evidence that is not relevant is not admissible.
Adopted May 8, 1998, effective Oct. 1, 1998; rescinded and replaced January 17, 2013, effective March 18, 2013.

Rule 403. Excluding Relevant Evidence for Prejudice, Confusion, Waste of Time, or Other Reasons

The court may exclude relevant evidence if its

probative value is outweighed by a danger of one or more of the following: unfair prejudice, confusing the issues, misleading the jury, undue delay, wasting time, or needlessly presenting cumulative evidence.

Comment: Pa.R.E. 403 differs from F.R.E. 403. The Federal Rule provides that relevant evidence may be excluded if its probative value is "substantially outweighed." Pa.R.E. 403 eliminates the word "substantially" to conform the text of the rule more closely to Pennsylvania law. *See Commonwealth v. Boyle*, 498 Pa. 486, 447 A.2d 250 (1982).

"Unfair prejudice" means a tendency to suggest decision on an improper basis or to divert the jury's attention away from its duty of weighing the evidence impartially.

Adopted May 8, 1998, effective Oct. 1, 1998; rescinded and replaced January 17, 2013, effective March 18, 2013.

Rule 404. Character Evidence; Crimes or Other Acts

(a) Character Evidence.

(1) Prohibited Uses. Evidence of a person's character or character trait is not admissible to prove that on a particular occasion the person acted in accordance with the character or trait.

(2) Exceptions for a Defendant or Victim in a Criminal Case. The following exceptions apply in a criminal case:

(A) a defendant may offer evidence of the defendant's pertinent trait, and if the evidence is admitted, the prosecutor may offer evidence to rebut it;

(B) subject to limitations imposed by statute a defendant may offer evidence of an alleged victim's pertinent trait, and if the evidence is admitted the prosecutor may:

(i)   offer evidence to rebut it; and

(ii)   offer evidence of the defendant's same trait; and

(C)   in a homicide case, the prosecutor may offer evidence of the alleged victim's trait of peacefulness to rebut evidence that the victim was the first aggressor.

(3) Exceptions for a Witness. Evidence of a witness's character may be admitted under Rules 607, 608, and 609.

(4) Exception in a Civil Action for Assault and Battery. In a civil action for assault and battery, evidence of the plaintiff's character trait for violence may be admitted when offered by the defendant to rebut evidence that the defendant was the first aggressor.

(b) Crimes, Wrongs or Other Acts.

(1) Prohibited Uses. Evidence of a crime, wrong, or other act is not admissible to prove a person's character in order to show that on a particular occasion the person acted in accordance with the character.

(2) Permitted Uses. This evidence may be admissible for another purpose, such as proving motive, opportunity, intent, preparation, plan, knowledge, identity, absence of mistake, or lack of accident. In a criminal case this evidence is admissible only if the probative value of the evidence outweighs its potential for unfair prejudice.

(3) Notice in a Criminal Case. In a criminal case the prosecutor must provide reasonable notice in advance of trial, or during trial if the court excuses pretrial notice on good cause shown, of the general nature of any such evidence the prosecutor intends to introduce at trial.

Adopted May 8, 1998, effective October 1, 1998; Comment revised November 2, 2001, effective January 1,

2002; amended Feb. 28, 2006, effective March 31, 2006; rescinded and replaced January 17, 2013, effective March 18, 2013.

Rule 405. Methods of Proving Character

(a) By Reputation. When evidence of a person's character or character trait is admissible, it may be proved by testimony about the person's reputation. Testimony about the witness's opinion as to the character or character trait of the person is not admissible.

(1) On cross-examination of the character witness, the court may allow an inquiry into relevant specific instances of the person's conduct probative of the character trait in question.

(2) In a criminal case, on cross-examination of a character witness, inquiry into allegations of other criminal conduct by the defendant, not resulting in conviction, is not permissible.

(b) By Specific Instances of Conduct. Specific instances of conduct are not admissible to prove character or a trait of character, except:

(1) In a civil case, when a person's character or a character trait is an essential element of a claim or defense, character may be proved by specific instances of conduct.

(2) In a criminal case, when character or a character trait of an alleged victim is admissible under Pa.R.E. 404(a)(2)(B) the defendant may prove the character or character trait by specific instances of conduct.

Adopted May 8, 1998, effective Oct. 1, 1998; amended July 20, 2000, effective Oct. 1, 2000; rescinded and replaced January 17, 2013, effective March 18, 2013.

Rule 406. Habit; Routine Practice

Evidence of a person's habit or an organization's routine practice may be admitted to prove that on a particular occasion the person or organization acted in accordance with the habit or routine practice. The court may admit this evidence regardless of whether it is corroborated or there was an eyewitness.

Adopted May 8, 1998, effective Oct. 1, 1998; rescinded and replaced January 17, 2013, effective March 18, 2013.

Rule 407. Subsequent Remedial Measures

When measures are taken by a party that would have made an earlier injury or harm less likely to occur, evidence of the subsequent measures is not admissible against that party to prove:

- negligence;
- culpable conduct;
- a defect in a product or its design; or
- a need for a warning or instruction.

But the court may admit this evidence for another purpose such as impeachment or—if disputed—proving ownership, control, or the feasibility of precautionary measures.

Adopted May 8, 1998, effective Oct. 1, 1998; amended June 12, 2003, effective July 1, 2003; rescinded and replaced January 17, 2013, effective March 18, 2013.

Rule 408. Compromise Offers and Negotiations

(a) Prohibited Uses. Evidence of the following is not admissible—on behalf of any party—either to prove or disprove the validity or amount of a disputed claim or to impeach by a prior inconsistent statement or a contradiction:

(1) furnishing, promising, or offering—or accepting, promising to accept, or offering to accept—a valuable consideration in compromising or attempting to compromise the claim; and

(2) conduct or a statement made during compromise negotiations about the claim.

(b) Exceptions. The court may admit this evidence for another purpose, such as proving a witness's bias or prejudice, negating a contention of undue delay, or proving an effort to obstruct a criminal investigation or prosecution.

Adopted May 8, 1998, effective October 1, 1998; amended March 10, 2000, effective July 1, 2000; Comment revised March 29, 2001, effective April 1, 2001; amended Sept. 18, 2008, effective Oct. 30, 2008; rescinded and replaced January 17, 2013, effective March 18, 2013.

Rule 409. Offers to Pay Medical and Similar Expenses

Evidence of furnishing, promising to pay, or offering to pay medical, hospital, or similar expenses resulting from an injury is not admissible to prove liability for the injury.

Adopted May 8, 1998, effective Oct. 1, 1998; Comment revised Dec. 30, 2005, effective Feb. 1, 2006; rescinded and replaced Jan. 17, 2013, effective March 18, 2013; Comment revised July 30, 2015, effective October 1, 2015.

Rule 410. Pleas, Plea Discussions, and Related Statements

(a) Prohibited Uses. In a civil or criminal case, evidence of the following is not admissible against the defendant who made the plea or participated in the plea discussions:

(1) a guilty plea that was later withdrawn;

(2) a *nolo contendere* plea;

(3) a statement made in the course of any proceedings under Rules 311, 313, 409, 414, 424, 550 or 590 of the Pennsylvania Rules of Criminal Procedure, Rule 11 of the Federal Rules of Criminal Procedure, or a comparable rule or procedure of another state; or

(4) a statement made during plea discussions with an attorney for the prosecuting authority if the discussions did not result in a

guilty plea or they resulted in a later with-drawn guilty plea.

(b) Exceptions. The court may admit a statement described in Rule 410(a)(3) or (4):

(1) in any proceeding in which another statement made during the same plea or plea discussions has been introduced, if in fairness the statements ought to be considered together; or

(2) in a criminal proceeding for perjury, false swearing or unsworn falsification to authorities, if the defendant made the statement under oath, on the record, and with counsel present.

Adopted May 8, 1998, effective Oct. 1, 1998; Comment revised March 23, 1999, effective immediately; amended March 10, 2000, effective immediately; amended March 29, 2001, effective April 1, 2001; rescinded and replaced January 17, 2013, effective March 18, 2013.

Rule 411. Liability Insurance

Evidence that a person was or was not insured against liability is not admissible to prove whether the person acted negligently or otherwise wrongfully. But the court may admit this evidence for another purpose, such as proving a witness's bias or prejudice or proving agency, ownership, or control.

Adopted May 8, 1998, effective Oct. 1, 1998; rescinded and replaced January 17, 2013, effective March 18, 2013.

Rule 412. Sex Offense Cases: The Victim's Sexual Behavior or Predisposition (Not Adopted)

Comment rescinded and replaced January 17, 2013, effective March 18, 2013.

Rule 501. Privileges

Privileges as they now exist or may be modified by law shall be unaffected by the adoption of these rules.

Adopted May 8, 1998, effective Oct. 1, 1998; rescinded and replaced January 17, 2013, effective March 18, 2013.

Rule 502. Attorney-Client Privilege and Work Product; Limitations on Waiver (Not Adopted)

Rule 601. Competency

(a) General Rule. Every person is competent to be a witness except as otherwise provided by statute or in these rules.

(b) Disqualification for Specific Defects. A person is incompetent to testify if the court finds that because of a mental condition or immaturity the person:

(1) is, or was, at any relevant time, incapable of perceiving accurately;

(2) is unable to express himself or herself so as to be understood either directly or through an interpreter;

(3) has an impaired memory; or

(4) does not sufficiently understand the duty to tell the truth.

Adopted May 8, 1998, effective Oct. 1, 1998. Amended Nov. 2, 2007, effective Dec. 14, 2007; rescinded and replaced January 17, 2013, effective March 18, 2013.

Rule 602. Need for Personal Knowledge

A witness may testify to a matter only if evidence is introduced sufficient to support a finding that the witness has personal knowledge of the matter. Evidence to prove personal knowledge may consist of the witness's own testimony. This rule does not apply to a witness's expert testimony under Rule 703.

Adopted May 8, 1998, effective Oct. 1, 1998; rescinded and replaced January 17, 2013, effective March 18, 2013.

Rule 603. Oath or Affirmation to Testify Truthfully

Before testifying, a witness must give an oath or affirmation to testify truthfully. It must be in a form designed to impress that duty on the witness's conscience.

Adopted May 8, 1998, effective Oct. 1, 1998; rescinded and replaced January 17, 2013, effective March 18, 2013.

Rule 604. Interpreter

An interpreter must be qualified and must give an oath or affirmation to make a true translation.

Adopted May 8, 1998, effective Oct. 1, 1998; Comment revised March 29, 2001, effective April 1, 2001; amended and Comment revised March 21, 2012, effective in 30 days [April 20, 2012]; rescinded and replaced January 17, 2013, effective March 18, 2013.

Rule 605. Judge's Competency as a Witness

The presiding judge may not testify as a witness at the trial or other proceeding.

Adopted May 8, 1998, effective Oct. 1, 1998; rescinded and replaced Jan. 17, 2013, effective March 18, 2013; amended April 29, 2016, effective immediately.

Rule 606. Juror's Competency as a Witness

(a) At the Trial. A juror may not testify as a witness before the other jurors at the trial. If a juror is called to testify, the court must give a party an opportunity to object outside the jury's presence.

(b) During an Inquiry into the Validity of a Verdict

(1) Prohibited Testimony or Other Evidence. During an inquiry into the validity of a verdict, a juror may not testify about any statement made or incident that occurred during the jury's deliberations; the effect of anything on that juror's or another juror's vote; or any juror's mental processes concerning the verdict. The court may not receive a juror's affidavit or evidence of a juror's statement on these matters.

(2) Exceptions. A juror may testify about whether:

(A)   prejudicial information not of record and beyond common knowledge and experience was improperly brought to the jury's attention; or

(B)   an outside influence was improperly brought to bear on any juror.

Adopted May 8, 1998, effective Oct. 1, 1998. Amended Sept. 17, 2007, effective Oct. 17, 2007; rescinded and replaced January 17, 2013, effective March 18, 2013.

Rule 607. Who May Impeach a Witness, Evidence to Impeach a Witness

(a) Who May Impeach a Witness. Any party, including the party that called the witness, may attack the witness's credibility.

(b) Evidence to Impeach a Witness. The credibility of a witness may be impeached by any evidence relevant to that issue, except as otherwise provided by statute or these rules.

Adopted May 8, 1998, effective Oct. 1, 1998; rescinded and replaced January 17, 2013, effective March 18, 2013.

Rule 608. A Witness's Character for Truthfulness or Untruthfulness

(a) Reputation Evidence. A witness's credibility may be attacked or supported by testimony about the witness's reputation for having a character for truthfulness or untruthfulness. But evidence of truthful character is admissible only after the witness's character for truthfulness has been attacked. Opinion testimony about the witness's character for truthfulness or untruthfulness is not admissible.

(b) Specific Instances of Conduct. Except

as provided in Rule 609 (relating to evidence of conviction of crime),

    (1)   the character of a witness for truthfulness may not be attacked or supported by cross-examination or extrinsic evidence concerning specific instances of the witness' conduct; however,

    (2)   in the discretion of the court, the credibility of a witness who testifies as to the reputation of another witness for truthfulness or untruthfulness may be attacked by cross-examination concerning specific instances of conduct (not including arrests) of the other witness, if they are probative of truthfulness or untruthfulness; but extrinsic evidence thereof is not admissible.

Adopted May 8, 1998, effective Oct. 1, 1998; rescinded and replaced January 17, 2013, effective March 18, 2013.

Rule 609. Impeachment by Evidence of a Criminal Conviction

(a) In General. For the purpose of attacking the credibility of any witness, evidence that the witness has been convicted of a crime, whether by verdict or by plea of guilty or *nolo contendere*, must be admitted if it involved dishonesty or false statement.

(b) Limit on Using the Evidence After 10 Years. This subdivision (b) applies if more than 10 years have passed since the witness's conviction or release from confinement for it, whichever is later. Evidence of the conviction is admissible only if:

    (1)   its probative value substantially outweighs its prejudicial effect; and

    (2)   the proponent gives an adverse party reasonable written notice of the intent to use it so that the party has a fair opportunity to contest its use.

(c) Effect of Pardon or Other Equivalent

Procedure. Evidence of a conviction is not admissible under this rule if the conviction has been the subject of one of the following:

(1)   a pardon or other equivalent procedure based on a specific finding of innocence; or

(2)   a pardon or other equivalent procedure based on a specific finding of rehabilitation of the person convicted, and that person has not been convicted of any subsequent crime.

(d) Juvenile Adjudications. In a criminal case only, evidence of the adjudication of delinquency for an offense under the Juvenile Act, 42 Pa.C.S. §§ 6301 *et seq.*, may be used to impeach the credibility of a witness if conviction of the offense would be admissible to attack the credibility of an adult.

(e) Pendency of an Appeal. A conviction that satisfies this rule is admissible even if an appeal is pending. Evidence of the pendency is also admissible.

Adopted May 8, 1998, effective Oct. 1, 1998; Comment revised March 29, 2001, effective April 1, 2001; rescinded and replaced January 17, 2013, effective March 18, 2013.

Rule 610. Religious Beliefs or Opinions

Evidence of a witness's religious beliefs or opinions is not admissible to attack or support the witness's credibility.

Adopted May 8, 1998, effective Oct. 1, 1998; rescinded and replaced January 17, 2013, effective March 18, 2013.

Rule 611. Mode and Order of Examining Witnesses and Presenting Evidence

(a) Control by the Court; Purposes. The court should exercise reasonable control over the mode and order of examining witnesses and presenting evidence so as to:

(1)   make those procedures effective for determining the truth;

(2)   avoid wasting time; and

(3)   protect witnesses from harassment or undue embarrassment.

(b) Scope of Cross-Examination. Cross-examination of a witness other than a party in a civil case should be limited to the subject matter of the direct examination and matters affecting credibility, however, the court may, in the exercise of discretion, permit inquiry into additional matters as if on direct examination. A party witness in a civil case may be cross-examined by an adverse party on any matter relevant to any issue in the case, including credibility, unless the court, in the interests of justice, limits the cross-examination with respect to matters not testified to on direct examination.

(c) Leading Questions. Leading questions should not be used on direct or redirect examination except as necessary to develop the witness's testimony. Ordinarily, the court should allow leading questions:

(1)   on cross-examination; and

(2)   when a party calls a hostile witness, an adverse party, or a witness identified with an adverse party. A witness so examined should usually be interrogated by all other parties as to whom the witness is not hostile or adverse as if under redirect examination.

Adopted May 8, 1998, effective Oct. 1, 1998; rescinded and replaced Jan. 17, 2013, effective March 18, 2013; amended Sept. 18, 2014, effective immediately.

Rule 612. Writing or Other Item Used to Refresh a Witness's Memory

(a) Right to Refresh Memory. A witness may use a writing or other item to refresh memory for the purpose of testifying while testifying, or before testifying.

(b) Rights of Adverse Party.

(1)   If a witness uses a writing or other item

to refresh memory while testifying, an adverse party is entitled to have it produced at the hearing, trial or deposition, to inspect it, to cross-examine the witness about it, and to introduce in evidence any portion that relates to the witness's testimony.

(2) If a witness uses a writing or other item to refresh memory before testifying, and the court in its discretion determines it is necessary in the interests of justice, an adverse party is entitled to have it produced at the hearing, trial or deposition, to inspect it, to cross-examine the witness about it, and to introduce in evidence any portion that relates to the witness's testimony.

(c) Rights of Producing Party. If the producing party claims that the writing or other item includes unrelated matter, the court must examine it in camera, delete any unrelated portion, and order that the rest be delivered to the adverse party. Any portion deleted over objection must be preserved for the record.

(d) Failure to Produce or Deliver. If the writing or other item is not produced or is not delivered as ordered, the court may issue any appropriate order. But if the prosecution does not comply in a criminal case, the court must strike the witness's testimony or—if justice so requires—declare a mistrial, or the court may use contempt procedures.

Adopted May 8, 1998, effective Oct. 1, 1998; amended March 23, 1999, effective immediately; rescinded and replaced January 17, 2013, effective March 18, 2013.

Rule 613. Witness's Prior Inconsistent Statement to Impeach; Witness's Prior Consistent Statement to Rehabilitate

(a) Witness's Prior Inconsistent Statement to Impeach. A witness may be examined concerning a prior inconsistent statement made by the witness to impeach the witness's credibility. The statement need not be shown or its contents disclosed to the witness at that time, but on request the statement or contents must be shown or disclosed to an adverse party's attorney.

(b) Extrinsic Evidence of a Witness's Prior Inconsistent Statement. Unless the interests of justice otherwise require, extrinsic evidence of a witness's prior inconsistent statement is admissible only if, during the examination of the witness,

(1) the statement, if written, is shown to, or if not written, its contents are disclosed to, the witness;

(2) the witness is given an opportunity to explain or deny the making of the statement; and

(3) an adverse party is given an opportunity to question the witness.

This paragraph does not apply to an opposing party's statement as defined in Rule 803(25).

(c) Witness's Prior Consistent Statement to Rehabilitate. Evidence of a witness's prior consistent statement is admissible to rehabilitate the witness's credibility if the opposing party is given an opportunity to cross-examine the witness about the statement and the statement is offered to rebut an express or implied charge of:

(1) fabrication, bias, improper influence or motive, or faulty memory and the statement was made before that which has been charged existed or arose; or

(2) having made a prior inconsistent statement, which the witness has denied or explained, and the consistent statement supports the witness's denial or explanation.

Adopted May 8, 1998, effective Oct. 1, 1998; amended March 23, 1999, effective immediately; amended March 10, 2000, effective July 1, 2000; rescinded and replaced January 17, 2013, effective March 18, 2013.

Rule 614. Court's Calling or Examining a Witness

(a) Calling. Consistent with its function as an impartial arbiter, the court, with notice to the parties, may call a witness on its own or at a party's request. Each party is entitled to cross-examine the witness.

(b) Examining. Where the interest of justice so requires, the court may examine a witness regardless of who calls the witness.

(c) Objections. A party may object to the court's calling or examining a witness when given notice that the witness will be called or when the witness is examined. When requested to do so, the court must give the objecting party an opportunity to make objections out of the presence of the jury.

Adopted May 8, 1998, effective Oct. 1, 1998; rescinded and replaced January 17, 2013, effective March 18, 2013.

Rule 615. Sequestering Witnesses

At a party's request the court may order witnesses sequestered so that they cannot learn of other witnesses' testimony. Or the court may do so on its own. But this rule does not authorize sequestering:

    (a) a party who is a natural person;

    (b) an officer or employee of a party that is not a natural person (including the Commonwealth) after being designated as the party's representative by its attorney;

    (c) a person whose presence a party shows to be essential to presenting the party's claim or defense; or

    (d) a person authorized by statute or rule to be present.

Adopted May 8, 1998, effective Oct. 1, 1998; rescinded and replaced January 17, 2013, effective March 18, 2013.

Rule 701. Opinion Testimony by Lay Witnesses

If a witness is not testifying as an expert, testimony in the form of an opinion is limited to one that is:

    (a)   rationally based on the witness's perception;

    (b)   helpful to clearly understanding the witness's testimony or to determining a fact in issue; and

    (c)   not based on scientific, technical, or other specialized knowledge within the scope of Rule 702.

Adopted May 8, 1998, effective October 1, 1998; amended Nov. 2, 2001, effective Jan. 1, 2002; rescinded and replaced January 17, 2013, effective March 18, 2013.

Rule 702. Testimony by Expert Witnesses

A witness who is qualified as an expert by knowledge, skill, experience, training, or education may testify in the form of an opinion or otherwise if:

    (a)   the expert's scientific, technical, or other specialized knowledge is beyond that possessed by the average layperson;

    (b)   the expert's scientific, technical, or other specialized knowledge will help the trier of fact to understand the evidence or to determine a fact in issue; and

    (c)   the expert's methodology is generally accepted in the relevant field.

Adopted May 8, 1998, effective Oct. 1, 1998; Comment revised April 1, 2004, effective May 10, 2004; rescinded and replaced January 17, 2013, effective March 18, 2013.

Rule 703. Bases of an Expert's Opinion Testimony

An expert may base an opinion on facts or data

in the case that the expert has been made aware of or personally observed. If experts in the particular field would reasonably rely on those kinds of facts or data in forming an opinion on the subject, they need not be admissible for the opinion to be admitted.

Adopted May 8, 1998, effective Oct. 1, 1998; Comment revised Sept. 11, 2003, effective Sept. 30, 2003; rescinded and replaced January 17, 2013, effective March 18, 2013.

Rule 704. Opinion on an Ultimate Issue

An opinion is not objectionable just because it embraces an ultimate issue.

Adopted May 8, 1998, effective Oct. 1, 1998; rescinded and replaced January 17, 2013, effective March 18, 2013.

Rule 705. Disclosing the Facts or Data Underlying an Expert's Opinion

If an expert states an opinion the expert must state the facts or data on which the opinion is based.

Adopted May 8, 1998, effective Oct. 1, 1998; rescinded and replaced January 17, 2013, effective March 18, 2013.

Rule 706. Court-Appointed Expert Witnesses

Where the court has appointed an expert witness, the witness appointed must advise the parties of the witness's findings, if any. The witness may be called to testify by the court or any party. The witness shall be subject to cross-examination by any party, including a party calling the witness. In civil cases, the witness's deposition may be taken by any party.

Adopted May 8, 1998, effective Oct. 1, 1998; rescinded and replaced January 17, 2013, effective March 18, 2013.

Rule 801. Definitions that Apply to this Article

(a) Statement. "Statement" means a person's oral assertion, written assertion, or nonverbal conduct, if the person intended it as an assertion.

(b) Declarant. "Declarant" means the person who made the statement.

(c) Hearsay. "Hearsay" means a statement that

(1) the declarant does not make while testifying at the current trial or hearing; and

(2) a party offers in evidence to prove the truth of the matter asserted in the statement.

Adopted May 8, 1998, effective Oct. 1, 1998; Comment revised March 29, 2001, effective April 1, 2001; rescinded and replaced January 17, 2013, effective March 18, 2013.

Rule 802. The Rule Against Hearsay

Hearsay is not admissible except as provided by these rules, by other rules prescribed by the Pennsylvania Supreme Court, or by statute.

Adopted May 8, 1998, effective Oct. 1998; Comment revised March 23, 1999, effective immediately; Comment revised March 10, 2000, effective immediately; Comment revised March 29, 2001, effective April 1, 2001; rescinded and replaced Jan. 17, 2013, effective March 18, 2013; Comment revised February 19, 2014, effective April 1, 2014; Comment revised November 9, 2016, effective January 1, 2017.

Rule 803. Exceptions to the Rule Against Hearsay—Regardless of Whether the Declarant Is Available as a Witness

The following are not excluded by the rule against hearsay, regardless of whether the declarant is available as a witness:

(1) Present Sense Impression. A statement describing or explaining an event or condition, made while or immediately after the declarant perceived it.

(2) Excited Utterance. A statement relating to a startling event or condition, made while the declarant was under the stress of excitement that it caused.

(3) Then-Existing Mental, Emotional, or Physical Condition. A statement of the declarant's then-existing state of mind (such as motive, intent or plan) or emotional, sensory, or physical condition (such as mental feeling, pain, or bodily health), but not including a statement of memory or belief to prove the fact remembered or believed unless it relates to the validity or terms of the declarant's will.

(4) Statement Made for Medical Diagnosis or Treatment. A statement that:

(A) is made for—and is reasonably pertinent to—medical treatment or diagnosis in contemplation of treatment; and

(B) describes medical history, past or present symptoms, pain, or sensations, or the inception or general character of the cause or external source thereof, insofar as reasonably pertinent to treatment, or diagnosis in contemplation of treatment.

(5) Recorded Recollection (Not Adopted)

(6) Records of a Regularly Conducted Activity. A record (which includes a memorandum, report, or data compilation in any form) of an act, event or condition if,

(A) the record was made at or near the time by—or from information transmitted by—someone with knowledge;

(B) the record was kept in the course of a regularly conducted activity of a "business", which term includes business, institution, association, profession, occupation, and calling of every kind, whether or not conducted for profit;

(C) making the record was a regular practice of that activity;

(D) all these conditions are shown by the testimony of the custodian or another qualified witness, or by a certification that complies with Rule 902(11) or (12) or with a statute permitting certification; and

(E) the opponent does not show that the source of information or other circumstances indicate a lack of trustworthiness.

(7) Absence of a Record of a Regularly Conducted Activity (Not Adopted)

(8) Public Records. A record of a public office if:

(A) the record describes the facts of the action taken or matter observed;

(B) the recording of this action or matter observed was an official public duty; and

(C) the opponent does not show that the source of the information or other circumstances indicate a lack of trustworthiness.

(9) Public Records of Vital Statistics (Not Adopted)

(10) Non–Existence of a Public Record. Testimony—or a certification—that a diligent search failed to disclose a public record if:

(A) the testimony or certification is admitted to prove that

(i) the record does not exist; or

(ii) a matter did not occur or exist, if a public office regularly kept a record for a matter of that kind.

(B) in a criminal case:

(i) the attorney for the Commonwealth who intends to offer a certification files and serves written notice of that intent upon the defendant's attorney or, if unrepresented, the defendant, at least 20 days before trial; and

(ii) defendant's attorney or, if unrepresented, the defendant, does not file and serve a written demand for testimony in lieu of the certification within 10 days of service of the notice.

(11) Records of Religious Organizations Concerning Personal or Family History. A statement of birth, legitimacy, ancestry, marriage, divorce, death, relationship by blood or marriage, or similar facts of personal or family history, contained in a regularly kept record of a religious organization.

(12) Certificates of Marriage, Baptism, and Similar Ceremonies. A statement of fact contained in a certificate:

(13) Family Records. A statement of fact about personal or family history contained in a family record, such as a Bible, genealogy, chart, engraving on a ring, inscription on a portrait, or engraving on an urn or burial marker.

(14) Records of Documents That Affect an Interest in Property. The record of a document that purports to establish or affect an interest in property if:

(A)   the record is admitted to prove the content of the original recorded document, along with its signing and its delivery by each person who purports to have signed it;

(B)   the record is kept in a public office; and

(C)   a statute authorizes recording documents of that kind in that office.

(15) Statements in Documents That Affect an Interest in Property. A statement contained in a document, other than a will, that purports to establish or affect an interest in property if the matter stated was relevant to the document's purpose—unless later dealings with the property are inconsistent with the truth of the statement or the purport of the document.

(16) Statements in Ancient Documents. A statement in a document that is at least 30 years old and whose authenticity is established.

(17) Market Reports and Similar Commercial Publications. Market quotations, lists, directories, or other compilations that are generally relied on by the public or by persons in particular occupations.

(18) Statements in Learned Treatises, Periodicals, or Pamphlets (Not Adopted)

(19) Reputation Concerning Personal or Family History. A reputation among a person's family by blood, adoption, or marriage—or among a person's associates or in the community—concerning the person's birth, adoption, legitimacy, ancestry, marriage, divorce, death, relationship by blood, adoption, or marriage, or similar facts of personal or family history.

(20) Reputation Concerning Boundaries or General History. A reputation in a community—arising before the controversy—concerning boundaries of land in the community or customs that affect the land, or concerning general historical events important to that community, state or nation.

(21) Reputation Concerning Character. A reputation among a person's associates or in the community concerning the person's character.

(22) Judgment of a Previous Conviction (Not Adopted)

(23) Judgments Involving Personal, Family, or General History or a Boundary (Not Adopted)

(24) Other Exceptions (Not Adopted)

(25) An Opposing Party's Statement. The statement is offered against an opposing party and:

(A) was made by the party in an individual or representative capacity;

(B) is one the party manifested that it adopted or believed to be true;

(C) was made by a person whom the party authorized to make a statement on the subject;

(D) was made by the party's agent or employee on a matter within the scope of that relationship and while it existed; or

(E) was made by the party's coconspirator during and in furtherance of the conspiracy.

The statement may be considered but does not by itself establish the declarant's authority under (C); the existence or scope of the relationship under (D); or the existence of the conspiracy or participation in it under (E).

Adopted May 8, 1998, effective Oct. 1, 1998; Comment revised March 23, 1999, effective immediately; Comment revised March 10, 2000, effective immediately; Comment revised May 16, 2001, effective July 1, 2001; amended Nov. 2, 2001, effective Jan. 1, 2002; rescinded and replaced Jan. 17, 2013, effective March 18, 2013; amended November 9, 2016, effective January 1, 2017.

Rule 803.1. Exceptions to the Rule Against Hearsay—Testimony of Declarant Necessary

The following statements are not excluded by the rule against hearsay if the declarant testifies and is subject to cross-examination about the prior statement:

(1) Prior Inconsistent Statement of Declarant-Witness. A prior statement by a declarant-witness that is inconsistent with the declarant-witness's testimony and:

(A) was given under oath subject to the penalty of perjury at a trial, hearing, or other proceeding, or in a deposition;

(B) is a writing signed and adopted by the declarant; or

(C) is a verbatim contemporaneous electronic, audiotaped, or videotaped recording of an oral statement.

(2) Prior Statement of Identification by Declarant-Witness. A prior statement by a declarant-witness identifying a person or thing, made after perceiving the person or thing, provided that the declarant-witness testifies to the making of the prior statement.

(3) Recorded Recollection of Declarant-Witness. A memorandum or record made or adopted by a declarant-witness that:

(A) is on a matter the declarant-witness once knew about but now cannot recall well enough to testify fully and accurately;

(B) was made or adopted by the declarant-witness when the matter was fresh in his or her memory; and

(C) the declarant-witness testifies accurately reflects his or her knowledge at the time when made.

If admitted, the memorandum or record may be read into evidence and received as an exhibit, but may be shown to the jury only in exceptional circumstances or when offered by an adverse party.

Adopted May 8, 1998, effective Oct. 1, 1998; amended March 10, 2000, effective July 1, 2000; rescinded and replaced January 17, 2013, effective March 18, 2013.

Rule 804. Exceptions to the Rule Against Hearsay—When the Declarant is Unavailable as a Witness

(a) Criteria for Being Unavailable. A declarant is considered to be unavailable as a witness if the declarant:

(1) is exempted from testifying about the subject matter of the declarant's statement because the court rules that a privilege applies;

(2)   refuses to testify about the subject matter despite a court order to do so;

(3)   testifies to not remembering the subject matter;

(4)   cannot be present or testify at the trial or hearing because of death or a then-existing infirmity, physical illness, or mental illness; or

(5)   is absent from the trial or hearing and the statement's proponent has not been able, by process or other reasonable means, to procure:

(A)   the declarant's attendance, in the case of a hearsay exception under Rule 804(b)(1) or (6); or

(B)   the declarant's attendance or testimony, in the case of a hearsay exception under Rule 804(b)(2), (3), or (4).

But this subdivision (a) does not apply if the statement's proponent procured or wrongfully caused the declarant's unavailability as a witness in order to prevent the declarant from attending or testifying.

(b) The Exceptions. The following are not excluded by the rule against hearsay if the declarant is unavailable as a witness:

(1) Former Testimony. Testimony that:

(A)   was given as a witness at a trial, hearing, or lawful deposition, whether given during the current proceeding or a different one; and

(B)   is now offered against a party who had—or, in a civil case, whose predecessor in interest had—an opportunity and similar motive to develop it by direct, cross-, or redirect examination.

(2) Statement Under Belief of Imminent Death. A statement that the declarant, while believing the declarant's death to be imminent, made about its cause or circumstances.

Comment: Pa.R.E. 804(b)(2) differs from F.R.E. 804(b)(2) in that the Federal Rule is applicable in criminal cases only if the defendant is charged with homicide. The Pennsylvania Rule is applicable in all civil and criminal cases, subject to the defendant's right to confrontation in criminal cases.

In *Crawford v. Washington*, 541 U.S. 36 (2004), the Supreme Court interpreted the Confrontation Cause in the Sixth Amendment of the United States Constitution to prohibit the introduction of "testimonial" hearsay from an unavailable witness against a defendant in a criminal case unless the defendant had an opportunity to confront and cross-examine the declarant, regardless of its exception from the hearsay rule. However, in footnote 6, the Supreme Court said that there may be an exception, *sui generis*, for those dying declarations that are testimonial.

(3) Statement Against Interest. A statement that:

(A) a reasonable person in the declarant's position would have made only if the person believed it to be true because, when made, it was so contrary to the declarant's proprietary or pecuniary interest or had so great a tendency to invalidate the declarant's claim against someone else or to expose the declarant to civil or criminal liability; and

(B) is supported by corroborating circumstances that clearly indicate its trustworthiness, if it is offered in a criminal case as one that tends to expose the declarant to criminal liability.

(4) Statement of Personal or Family History. A statement made before the controversy arose about:

(A) the declarant's own birth, adoption,

legitimacy, ancestry, marriage, divorce, relationship by blood, adoption or marriage, or similar facts of personal or family history, even though the declarant had no way of acquiring personal knowledge about that fact; or

(B) another person concerning any of these facts, as well as death, if the declarant was related to the person by blood, adoption, or marriage or was so intimately associated with the person's family that the declarant's information is likely to be accurate.

(5) Other exceptions (Not Adopted)

(6) Statement Offered Against a Party That Wrongfully Caused the Declarant's Unavailability. A statement offered against a party that wrongfully caused—or acquiesced in wrongfully causing—the declarant's unavailability as a witness, and did so intending that result.

Adopted May 8, 1998, effective Oct. 1, 1998. Comment revised March 10, 2000, effective immediately; Comment revised Dec. 17, 2004, effective Jan. 31, 2005; rescinded and replaced January 17, 2013, effective March 18, 2013.

Rule 805. Hearsay Within Hearsay

Hearsay within hearsay is not excluded by the rule against hearsay if each part of the combined statements conforms with an exception to the rule.

Adopted May 8, 1998, effective Oct. 1, 1998; rescinded and replaced January 17, 2013, effective March 18, 2013.

Rule 806. Attacking and Supporting the Declarant's Credibility

When a hearsay statement has been admitted in evidence, the declarant's credibility may be attacked, and then supported, by any evidence that would be admissible for those purposes if the declarant had testified as a witness. The court may admit evidence of the declarant's inconsistent statement or conduct, regardless of when it occurred or whether the declarant had an opportunity to explain or deny it. If the party against whom the statement was admitted calls the declarant as a witness, the party may examine the declarant on the statement as if on cross-examination.

Adopted May 8, 1998, effective Oct. 1, 1998; rescinded and replaced January 17, 2013, effective March 18, 2013.

Rule 807. Residual Exception (Not Adopted)

Comment rescinded and replaced January 17, 2013, effective March 18, 2013.

Rule 901. Authenticating or Identifying Evidence

(a) In General. To satisfy the requirement of authenticating or identifying an item of evidence, the proponent must produce evidence sufficient to support a finding that the item is what the proponent claims it is.

(b) Examples. The following are examples only—not a complete list—of evidence that satisfies the requirement:

(1) *Testimony of a Witness with Knowledge.* Testimony that an item is what it is claimed to be.

(2) *Nonexpert Opinion about Handwriting.* A nonexpert's opinion that handwriting is genuine, based on a familiarity with it that was not acquired for the current litigation.

(3) *Comparison by an Expert Witness or the Trier of Fact.* A comparison with an authenticated specimen by an expert witness or the trier of fact.

(4) *Distinctive Characteristics and the Like.*

The appearance, contents, substance, internal patterns, or other distinctive characteristics of the item, taken together with all the circumstances.

(5) *Opinion About a Voice.* An opinion identifying a person's voice—whether heard firsthand or through mechanical or electronic transmission or recording—based on hearing the voice at any time under circumstances that connect it with the alleged speaker.

(6) *Evidence About a Telephone Conversation.* For a telephone conversation, evidence that a call was made to the number assigned at the time to:

(A) a particular person, if circumstances, including self-identification, show that the person answering was the one called; or

(B) a particular business, if the call was made to a business and the call related to business reasonably transacted over the telephone.

(7) *Evidence About Public Records.* Evidence that:

(A) a document was recorded or filed in a public office as authorized by law; or

(B) a purported public record or statement is from the office where items of this kind are kept.

(8) *Evidence About Ancient Documents or Data Compilations.* For a document or data compilation, evidence that it:

(A) is in a condition that creates no suspicion about its authenticity;

(B) was in a place where, if authentic, it would likely be; and

(C) is at least 30 years old when offered.

(9) *Evidence About a Process or System.* Evidence describing a process or system and showing that it produces an accurate result.

(10) *Methods Provided by a Statute or a Rule.* Any method of authentication or identification allowed by a statute or a rule prescribed by the Supreme Court.

Adopted May 8, 1998, effective Oct. 1, 1998; rescinded and replaced January 17, 2013, effective March 18, 2013.

Rule 902. Evidence That is Self-Authenticating

The following items of evidence are self-authenticating; they require no extrinsic evidence of authenticity in order to be admitted:

(1) Domestic Public Documents That Are Sealed and Signed. A document that bears:

(A) a seal purporting to be that of the United States; any state, district, commonwealth, territory, or insular possession of the United States; the former Panama Canal Zone; the Trust Territory of the Pacific Islands; a political subdivision of any of these entities; or a department, agency, or officer of any entity named above; and

(B) a signature purporting to be an execution or attestation.

(2) Domestic Public Documents That Are Not Sealed But Are Signed and Certified. A document that bears no seal if:

(A) it bears the signature of an officer or employee of an entity named in Rule 902(1)(A); and

(B) another public officer who has a seal and official duties within that same entity certifies under seal—or its equivalent—that the signer has the official capacity and that the signature is genuine.

(3) Foreign Public Documents. A document that purports to be signed or attested by a person who is authorized by a foreign country's law to do so. The document must be accompanied by a final certification that certifies the genuineness of the signature and official position of the signer or attester—or of any foreign official whose certificate of genuineness relates to the signature or attestation or is in a chain of certificates of genuineness relating to the signature or attestation. The certification may be made by a secretary of a United States embassy or legation; by a consul general, vice consul, or consular agent of the United States; or by a diplomatic or consular official of the foreign country assigned or accredited to the United States. If all parties have been given a reasonable opportunity to investigate the document's authenticity and accuracy, the court may for good cause, either:

(A)   order that it be treated as presumptively authentic without final certification; or

(B)   allow it to be evidenced by an attested summary with or without final certification.

(4) Certified Copies of Public Records. A copy of an official record—or a copy of a document that was recorded or filed in a public office as authorized by law- if the copy is certified as correct by:

(A)   the custodian or another person authorized to make the certification; or

(B)   a certificate that complies with Rule 902(1), (2), or (3), a statute or a rule prescribed by the Supreme Court.

(5) Official Publications. A book, pamphlet, or other publication purporting to be issued by a public authority.

(6) Newspapers and Periodicals. Printed material purporting to be a newspaper or periodical.

(7) Trade Inscriptions and the Like. An inscription, sign, tag, or label purporting to have been affixed in the course of business and indicating origin, ownership, or control.

(8) Acknowledged Documents. A document accompanied by a certificate of acknowledgment that is lawfully executed by a notary public or another officer who is authorized to take acknowledgments.

(9) Commercial Paper and Related Documents. Commercial paper, a signature on it, and related documents, to the extent allowed by general commercial law.

(10) Presumptions Authorized by Statute. A signature, document, or anything else that a statute declares to be presumptively or prima facie genuine or authentic.

(11) Certified Domestic Records of a Regularly Conducted Activity. The original or a copy of a domestic record that meets the requirements of Rule 803(6)(A)-(C), as shown by a certification of the custodian or another qualified person that complies with Pa.R.C.P. No. 76. Before the trial or hearing, the proponent must give an adverse party reasonable written notice of the intent to offer the record—and must make the record and certification available for inspection—so that the party has a fair opportunity to challenge them.

(12) Certified Foreign Records of a Regularly Conducted Activity. In a civil case, the original or a copy of a foreign record that meets the requirements of Rule 902(11), modified as follows: the certification rather than complying with a statute or Supreme Court rule, must be signed in a manner that, if falsely made, would subject the maker to a criminal penalty in the country where the certification is signed. The proponent must also meet the notice requirements of Rule 902(11).

(13) Certificate of Non–Existence of a Public Record. A certificate that a document was not recorded or filed in a public office as authorized by law if certified by the custodian or another person authorized to make the certificate.

Adopted May 8, 1998, effective Oct. 1, 1998; amended Nov. 2, 2001, effective Jan. 1, 2002; amended Feb. 23, 2004, effective May 1, 2004; rescinded and replaced Jan. 17, 2013, effective March 18, 2013; amended November 9, 2016, effective January 1, 2017.

Rule 903. Subscribing Witness's Testimony

A subscribing witness's testimony is necessary to authenticate a writing only if required by the laws of the jurisdiction that governs its validity.

Adopted May 8, 1998, effective Oct. 1, 1998; rescinded and replaced January 17, 2013, effective March 18, 2013.

Rule 1001. Definitions that Apply to this Article

In this article:

(a) A "writing" consists of letters, words, numbers, or their equivalent set down in any form.

(b) A "recording" consists of letters, words, numbers, or their equivalent recorded in any manner.

(c) A "photograph" means a photographic image or its equivalent stored in any form.

(d) An "original" of a writing or recording means the writing or recording itself or any counterpart intended to have the same effect by the person who executed or issued it. For electronically stored information, "original" means any printout—or other output readable by sight—if it accurately reflects the information. An "original" of a photograph includes the negative or a print from it.

(e) A "duplicate" means a copy produced by a mechanical, photographic, chemical, electronic, or other equivalent process or technique that accurately reproduces the original.

Adopted May 8, 1998, effective Oct. 1, 1998; rescinded and replaced January 17, 2013, effective March 18, 2013.

Rule 1002. Requirement of the Original

An original writing, recording, or photograph is required in order to prove its content unless these rules, other rules prescribed by the Supreme Court, or a statute provides otherwise.

Adopted May 8, 1998, effective Oct. 1, 1998; rescinded and replaced January 17, 2013, effective March 18, 2013.

Rule 1003. Admissibility of Duplicates

A duplicate is admissible to the same extent as the original unless a genuine question is raised about the original's authenticity or the circumstances make it unfair to admit the duplicate.

Adopted May 8, 1998, effective Oct. 1, 1998; Comment revised March 29, 2001, effective April 1, 2001; rescinded and replaced January 17, 2013, effective March 18, 2013.

Rule 1004. Admissibility of Other Evidence of Content

An original is not required and other evidence of the content of a writing, recording, or photograph is admissible if:

(a) all the originals are lost or destroyed, and not by the proponent acting in bad faith;

(b) an original cannot be obtained by any available judicial process;

(c) the party against whom the original would be offered had control of the original; was at that time put on notice, by pleadings or otherwise, that the original would be a subject of proof at the trial or hearing; and fails to produce it at the trial or hearing; or

(d) the writing, recording, or photograph is not closely related to a controlling issue.

Adopted May 8, 1998, effective Oct. 1, 1998; rescinded and replaced January 17, 2013, effective March 18, 2013.

Rule 1005. Copies of Public Records to Prove Content

The proponent may use a copy to prove the content of an official record—or of a document that was recorded or filed in a public office as authorized by law—if these conditions are met: the record or document is otherwise admissible; and the copy is certified as correct in accordance with Rule 902(4) or is testified to be correct by a witness who has compared it with the original. If no such copy can be obtained by reasonable diligence, then the proponent may use other evidence to prove the content.

Adopted May 8, 1998, effective Oct. 1, 1998; rescinded and replaced January 17, 2013, effective March 18, 2013.

Rule 1006. Summaries to Prove Content

The proponent may use a summary, chart, or calculation to prove the content of voluminous writings, recordings, or photographs that cannot be conveniently examined in court. The proponent must make the originals or duplicates available for examination or copying, or both, by other parties at a reasonable time and place. And the court may order the proponent to produce them in court.

Adopted May 8, 1998, effective Oct. 1, 1998; rescinded and replaced January 17, 2013, effective March 18, 2013.

Rule 1007. Testimony or Statement of a Party to Prove Content

The proponent may prove the content of a writing, recording, or photograph by the testimony, deposition, or written statement of the party against whom the evidence is offered. The proponent need not account for the original.

Adopted May 8, 1998, effective Oct. 1, 1998; rescinded and replaced January 17, 2013, effective March 18, 2013.

Rule 1008. Functions of the Court and Jury

Ordinarily, the court determines whether the proponent has fulfilled the factual conditions for admitting other evidence of the content of a writing, recording, or photograph under Rule 1004 or 1005. But in a jury trial, the jury determines—in accordance with Rule 104(b)—any issue about whether:

    (a)   an asserted writing, recording, or photograph ever existed;

    (b)   another one produced at the trial or hearing is the original; or

    (c)   other evidence of content accurately reflects the content.

Adopted May 8, 1998, effective Oct. 1, 1998; rescinded and replaced January 17, 2013, effective March 18, 2013.